JEWISH WOMEN IN ENLIGHTENMENT BERLIN

THE LITTMAN LIBRARY OF
JEWISH CIVILIZATION

Dedicated to the memory of
LOUIS THOMAS SIDNEY LITTMAN
*who founded the Littman Library for the love of God
and as an act of charity in memory of his father*
JOSEPH AARON LITTMAN
and to the memory of
ROBERT JOSEPH LITTMAN
who continued what his father Louis had begun
יהא זכרם ברוך

*'Get wisdom, get understanding:
Forsake her not and she shall preserve thee'*

PROV. 4: 5

The Littman Library of Jewish Civilization is a registered UK charity
Registered charity no. 1000784

JEWISH WOMEN IN ENLIGHTENMENT BERLIN

◆

NATALIE NAIMARK-GOLDBERG

London
The Littman Library of Jewish Civilization
in association with Liverpool University Press

The Littman Library of Jewish Civilization
Registered office: 4th floor, 7–10 Chandos Street, London W1G 9DQ

in association with Liverpool University Press
4 Cambridge Street, Liverpool L69 7ZU, UK
www.liverpooluniversitypress.co.uk/littman
Managing Editor: Connie Webber

Distributed in North America by
Oxford University Press Inc., 198 Madison Avenue,
New York, NY 10016, USA

First published in hardback 2013
First issued in paperback 2016

© *Natalie Naimark-Goldberg 2013*

All rights reserved.
No part of this publication may be reproduced,
stored in a retrieval system, or transmitted, in any form or by
any means, without the prior permission in writing of
The Littman Library of Jewish Civilization

This book is sold subject to the condition that it shall not,
by way of trade or otherwise, be lent, re-sold, hired out or
otherwise circulated without the publisher's prior consent in any
form of binding or cover other than that in which it is published
and without a similar condition including this condition
being imposed on the subsequent purchase

Catalogue records for this book are available from the
British Library and the Library of Congress
ISBN 978-1-906764-93-7

Publishing co-ordinator: Janet Moth
Copy-editing: Gillian Somerscales and Philippa Claiden
Indexing: Natalie Naimark-Goldberg
Designed by Pete Russell, Faringdon, Oxon.
Typeset by Hope Services (Abingdon) Ltd

Printed and bound in Great Britain by
CPI Group (UK) Ltd., Croydon, CR0 4YY

*In loving memory of
my great-grandmother*
NESZA YIDDES (JUDITH) SZTURM
נעשע יהודית שטורם ז״ל

*a brave woman from Kryłów, Poland
lost without trace during the Holocaust*

Acknowledgements

It is a great pleasure to express my gratitude and appreciation for the kind assistance and support I have received from individuals and institutions while writing this book.

The book is based on a doctoral dissertation written at Bar-Ilan University's department of Hermeneutics and Cultural Studies with the help of a generous scholarship in the form of a Doctoral Fellowship of Excellence from this institution. In the course of my studies I also benefited from grants by the Fanya Gottesfeld Heller Center for the Study of Women in Judaism at Bar-Ilan University and the Leo Baeck Institute in Jerusalem, which helped me make necessary research trips to Germany. During the final years of the work I enjoyed the support of the German–Israeli Foundation (GIF) and the Israel Science Foundation (ISF) as part of a research team working on projects on the Haskalah and the emergence of the modern Jewish book market.

My deepest gratitude goes to Shmuel Feiner, a distinguished scholar of modern Jewish history and a pioneer in the historical study of Jewish women and Enlightenment. I could not have wished for a more expert, encouraging, and supportive supervisor when writing my thesis, nor for a more generous and valuable collaborator in successive projects.

The years spent with the GIF and ISF research projects were of immense benefit. I owe special thanks to Zohar Shavit, who also read an early version of this book and made important comments. Tal Kogman, who over the course of the work has become not only a colleague but also a close friend, read and commented on parts of this book. Meetings with Israeli partners in these projects, including Shmuel Feiner, Stefan Litt, and Hagit Cohen (in addition to Shavit and Kogman), and with the German partners, Christoph Schulte, Andreas Kennecke, and William Hiscott, offered opportunities for wide-ranging and fruitful discussions, which helped me place the subject of my book in a wider perspective and sharpened important insights about the German and Jewish Enlightenment.

Different versions of the manuscript were read by Moshe Rosman, Tova Cohen, and Galili Shahar. It is a great honour to have benefited from the constructive criticism and helpful comments of these distinguished scholars. Elisheva Baumgarten suggested directions for research in the very first stages of the project. Robert Liberles made important recommendations concerning the chapter on visits to the spas. I also want to thank Pascale Mermelstein-Matisse for our productive discussions of the historical sources, and Barbara Ann Schmutzler for revising my translations of the sources from German into English. Special thanks go to the librarians and staff at the Jerusalem National Library, and especially to Shlomo Goldberg for facilitating my work. I am also grateful for the support of the staff at the Littman Library throughout the preparation of this book.

Personal support is at least as important as academic support. My brother Natan Naimark combined both, sharing his erudition with me and unsparingly giving me any help he could provide. My sister Debbie Friedman and her family in Frankfurt offered me their hospitality during my study visits to Germany. My parents, Jacobo and Sara Naimark, and my sister Lotty Harari have accompanied me with enthusiasm and expectation on the road towards the 'birth' of this book.

It is my closest family on whom I relied during the long years of the book's gestation. Aviva and Tamar, my eldest daughters, were adult enough to take an active interest in the project; Sharon and Alon looked on with curiosity at their mother, respecting the long hours spent immersed in academic work. But it is to the man by my side, Nir, that I owe the possibility of having been able to devote myself to writing this book. His immense pride, his loving support, and his practical assistance were a constant source of encouragement, for which I remain for ever in his debt.

*

Earlier versions of Chapters 2 and 4 were published previously as, respectively, 'Reading and Modernization: The Experience of Jewish Women in Berlin around 1800', *Nashim*, 15 (Spring 2008), 58–87, and 'Health, Leisure and Sociability at the Turn of the Nineteenth Century: Jewish Women in German Spas', *Leo Baeck Institute Yearbook*, 55 (2010), 63–91.

Contents

List of Illustrations — x
Note on the Translation of Sources and the Use of Names — xi
Note on Transliteration — xiii

Introduction — 1

1. Private Letters: An Alternative Sphere for Cultural Discourse — 31
2. Jewish Women and the Reading Public — 64
3. Going Public: Jewish Women in the Field of Literature and Publishing — 102
4. Sociability and Acculturation in German Spas — 146
5. Social Gatherings in Private Homes — 180
6. Female Emancipation — 216
7. Between Acculturation and Conversion — 257
8. Conclusion — 294

Bibliography — 303
Index — 333

Illustrations

1. Rahel Levin and her brother Markus Levin — 3
2. Manuscript of a letter sent by Marianne Meyer to Goethe — 53
3. Fromet Mendelssohn, née Gugenheim — 77
4. Title page of the second edition of Esther Gad's travelogue — 117
5. Dorothea Mendelssohn, later Veit, later Schlegel — 123
6. Germaine de Staël — 143
7. View of the promenade at Pyrmont, *c.*1780 — 159
8. Rahel Levin, later Varnhagen von Ense — 187
9. Recha Meyer, née Mendelssohn — 249
10. Friederike Unzelmann-Bethmann — 255
11. Henriette Mendelssohn, née Meyer — 266
12. Amalie Beer — 277
13. Lea Mendelssohn-Bartholdy, née Salomon — 283

Note on the Translation of Sources and the Use of Names

MOST of the sources used in this study are German, and in most cases the English translations are mine. The original texts are for the most part personal letters written in the late eighteenth and early nineteenth centuries; they do not always abide by today's rules of grammar and syntax, and this may be reflected in the translations. Punctuation has been slightly changed in some places and adapted to modern standards for purposes of clarity. In the few instances where printed translations of the texts were available I have used them, unless they were problematic for some reason. German spelling, especially in names of literary sources, may differ from today's spelling but has been left unchanged.

The problem of how to name historical subjects is familiar to all those who study women from the past, and is especially complex in the case of the women in this study. First, some of them married more than once, and their surnames changed accordingly. In addition, because they were modernizing Jews they often changed their forenames as well as their family names. When considering which name might be most appropriate to use for each of these women, the historian is thus faced with many decisions: whether to use her original Jewish forename or her Germanized forename, her maiden surname or her married surname—and if the latter, the first husband's surname or that of a second or later husband, and in either case his Jewish family name or his Germanized family name, if he was a modernizing Jew. The option of using the name most relevant to the specific point in time being discussed, a solution adopted by some historians of women, seemed to me inappropriate, since it would make it extremely difficult to track each individual's story. Also, presenting the different names of each person every time that individual was mentioned seemed inconvenient.

Since no solution seemed to be completely satisfactory, I decided not to try to be consistent by applying one rule to all cases. In most cases I have used the woman's original Jewish forename and her maiden family name—even when referring to her after marriage and/or conversion. For better-known individuals I have used the name with which each was most closely identified—the name under which she has entered posterity (as, for instance, in the case of Henriette Herz). However, in cases where a woman had more than one husband, and therefore more than one married name under which she entered public awareness, I have used her maiden name. An example is Dorothea Mendelssohn. Named Brendel at the time of her birth, and sometimes called Veit or Schlegel, the surnames of her two husbands, she is here referred to using the forename she adopted in the 1790s and by which she became known, and her maiden surname, which she never entirely dropped.

Note on Transliteration

THE transliteration of Hebrew in this book reflects consideration of the type of book it is, in terms of its content, purpose, and readership. The system adopted therefore reflects a broad approach to transcription, rather than the narrower approaches found in the *Encyclopaedia Judaica* or other systems developed for text-based or linguistic studies. The aim has been to reflect the pronunciation prescribed for modern Hebrew, rather than the spelling or Hebrew word structure, and to do so using conventions that are generally familiar to the English-speaking reader.

In accordance with this approach, no attempt is made to indicate the distinctions between *alef* and *ayin*, *tet* and *taf*, *kaf* and *kuf*, *sin* and *samekh*, since these are not relevant to pronunciation; likewise, the *dagesh* is not indicated except where it affects pronunciation. Following the principle of using conventions familiar to the majority of readers, however, transcriptions that are well established have been retained even when they are not fully consistent with the transliteration system adopted. On similar grounds, the *tsadi* is rendered by 'tz' in such familiar words as barmitzvah. Likewise, the distinction between *ḥet* and *khaf* has been retained, using *ḥ* for the former and *kh* for the latter; the associated forms are generally familiar to readers, even if the distinction is not actually borne out in pronunciation, and for the same reason the final *heh* is indicated too. As in Hebrew, no capital letters are used, except that an initial capital has been retained in transliterating titles of published works (for example, *Shulḥan arukh*).

Since no distinction is made between *alef* and *ayin*, they are indicated by an apostrophe only in intervocalic positions where a failure to do so could lead an English-speaking reader to pronounce the vowel-cluster as a diphthong—as, for example, in *ha'ir*—or otherwise mispronounce the word.

The *sheva na* is indicated by an *e*—*perikat ol*, *reshut*—except, again, when established convention dictates otherwise.

The *yod* is represented by *i* when it occurs as a vowel (*bereshit*), by *y* when it occurs as a consonant (*yesodot*), and by *yi* when it occurs as both (*yisra'el*).

Names have generally been left in their familiar forms, even when this is inconsistent with the overall system.

INTRODUCTION

THIS STUDY explores the activities of a fascinating group of Jewish women who lived in Berlin at the end of the eighteenth century and the beginning of the nineteenth. They were among the first in Ashkenazi society to undergo an accelerated process of modernization, take an active part in European culture, and adopt early feminist positions on the role of women in society and culture. Based on the numerous sources they left behind—mainly personal letters, but also publications and other writings—this book describes various aspects of their involvement in the intellectual, cultural, and social scene of the time and discusses their thought, which, I shall argue, was nurtured in a crucial way by the Enlightenment.

The women portrayed in this book were all born in what were then German lands, most of them in Berlin, in the 1760s and 1770s. A few, such as Rahel Levin, Dorothea Mendelssohn, and Henriette Herz, are familiar figures in Jewish history, primarily as leaders of the Jewish salons in Berlin; others, including Fradchen Liebmann, Sara and Marianne Meyer, Henriette Mendelssohn, and Esther Gad, are less well known, even though they belonged to the same social circles. Though never formally associated as a group, they were united by ties of friendship, a common background, and similar patterns of acculturation—namely, radical assimilation, eventually to the point of conversion and, for some, marriage to non-Jews. Raised in families belonging to the Jewish economic and intellectual elite that came to prominence in Berlin in the last third of the eighteenth century, although it had been visible in this and other European cities for some time, these young women were exposed to non-Jewish culture and society from their earliest years.[1] Their families were influenced by secularizing trends in their

---

[1] On the Berlin Jewish elite see Lowenstein, *The Berlin Jewish Community*; id., 'Jewish Upper Crust'; Michaelis, 'The Ephraim Family'; id., 'The Ephraim Family and their Descendants'. On the Jewish economic and social elite that emerged in German lands in earlier decades, and their luxurious and acculturated way of life, see Stern, *The Court Jew*. Selma Stern's study focuses mainly on the

surroundings and led an acculturated lifestyle, expressed variously in the abandonment of a distinctively Jewish external appearance, a gradual transition in both spoken and written language use from Yiddish to High German, regular visits to concerts and the theatre, and increased laxity in religious observance.[2] Children of both sexes in these wealthy families were given a largely private education, not only in Jewish matters—in which boys typically received a more thorough grounding, girls a rather superficial introduction—but also in secular fields. The latter encompassed not only the knowledge considered necessary to prepare daughters for their future as housewives and sons for their future professional lives, but also general education focused on European culture.[3] Thus equipped, and living in an atmosphere that nurtured enlightened values such as tolerance and sociability, the German Jewish women discussed in this study (like other Jews of the time) enjoyed a considerable degree of social and cultural interaction with non-Jews.[4]

By examining in detail practices that occupied a prominent place in their lives, their attitudes, and the crucial decisions they took, this study aims to offer the reader a close acquaintance with this specific group of women, providing a picture of them that departs in significant respects from their familiar image. It also aims at contributing more generally to the study of Jewish modernization, and more specifically to the study of Jewish women's lives and outlooks at the onset of modernity.[5] It is true that since this group of

second half of the 17th century and the first half of the 18th, but touches also on the Jewish elite at the end of the 18th century. See also Ries and Battenberg (eds.), *Hofjuden—Ökonomie und Interkulturalität*. The lifestyle of the Anglo-Jewish elite is described in Endelman, *The Jews of Georgian England*, 118–65.

[2] The modernizing trends affecting the Jewish community in Berlin in the last decades of the 18th century are discussed in Lowenstein, *The Berlin Jewish Community*, 43–54. For a thorough study of these and many other phenomena of acculturation and secularization among Jews in the cities of western and central Europe, see Feiner, *The Origins of Jewish Secularization*.

[3] As Mordechai Eliav indicates, throughout the 18th century many Jewish families, especially those in the economic elite, employed private tutors to expand the general education of their children far beyond traditional learning (Eliav, *Jewish Education in Germany* (Heb.), 15 ff.).

[4] Michael Meyer, quoting a study by Jacob Toury, affirms that during the 18th century the wealthiest Jews (interestingly, along with the poorest classes—'destitute Jewish vagrants') 'mingled freely with their gentile counterparts and adopted some of their values', while 'the bulk of German Jews still retained their traditional norms' (Meyer, 'Where Does the Modern Period of Jewish History Begin?', 335–6). Speaking of English Jewry in the 18th century, Todd Endelman similarly claimed that 'the weakening of traditional practice and knowledge was most pronounced among the very rich and the very poor' (Endelman, *The Jews of Britain*, 54).

[5] For a survey of various perceptions of Jewish modernity as reflected in the different periodizations proposed by leading historians since the 19th century for the beginning of the modern period in Jewish history, see Meyer's classical essay, 'Where Does the Modern Period of Jewish History Begin?', and Moshe Rosman's more recent reassessment in *How Jewish Is Jewish History?*, 56–81.

PLATE 1. Rahel Levin (1771–1833) and her brother Markus Levin (1772–1826) Oil painting by Johann Christoph Frisch (*c.*1783)
© bpk / SBB / Dietmar Katz

women 'deserted the faith' it is legitimate to ask whether their experience has any contribution to make to our understanding of the modernization of the Jews.[6] To this it may be responded that not only do the majority of the sources discussed in this study refer to the years when these women still were Jews, most of them having converted only in their thirties or even as late as their forties or fifties, but their extensive involvement in non-Jewish culture and society, and the fact that their modernization did not lead to a 'Jewish' response, was in fact a pattern followed by numerous Jews, and as such is of interest to Jewish historians.[7] Furthermore, these women's deeds and aspirations, while distinctive in significant ways, also bear striking similarities to those of other modern Jewish women who remained affiliated to Judaism, suggesting that a study of these individuals can illuminate acculturation and secularization trends affecting modernizing Jewish women in a wider historical context.

WOMEN AND ENLIGHTENMENT

Enquiring into the modernization of a specific group of women, as I do in this study, is part of a relatively new trend in Jewish historiography. Once occupied with presenting overarching descriptions of the transformation of Jewish life in modern times, in recent decades historians have turned to examining the particular experiences of different groups in different areas, coming to understand that, contrary to previous supposition, the transition from a traditional to a modern world may not be reducible to a single paradigm valid for all Jews.[8] One line of revision that historians have followed in this respect focuses on geographical distinctions, insisting on the existence of important differences between the dynamics of modernization in various

---

[6] 'Jewish modernization', like 'modernization' itself but to an even greater extent, is a complex term, encompassing political, economic, demographic, cultural, and social processes. The emphasis in this study will be on the cultural and social aspects. For a discussion on the meanings of Jewish modernization, with an emphasis on the modernization of German Jewry, see Meyer, 'Reflections on Jewish Modernization'; Lowenstein, 'The Pace of Modernisation of German Jewry'. See also Todd Endelman's reflections on the use of terms borrowed from modernization theory by Jewish historians in his preface to the second edition of *The Jews of Georgian England*, pp. xvii–xviii.

[7] On the inclusion of radically assimilated Jews and apostates in the domain of Jewish history, see Endelman, *Radical Assimilation in English Jewish History*, and Mendelsohn, 'Should We Take Notice of Berthe Weill?'. The problem of defining the subject of Jewish history is discussed in Rosman, *How Jewish Is Jewish History?*, 20–34.

[8] Birnbaum and Katznelson, 'Emancipation and the Liberal Offer'; Frankel, 'Assimilation and the Jews in Nineteenth-Century Europe'. Writing in 1992 about the 'new historiography' in modern Jewish history, Frankel affirmed: 'If the classic historians sought the underlying laws of development, the grand generalizations, then the newer history rests more on differentiation' (ibid. 18). Cf. Rosman, *How Jewish Is Jewish History?*, 16–18.

Jewish communities.⁹ Another fruitful line of revision has come from a gender perspective. As feminist historians began to question the omission of women's experience from the writing of Jewish history as it had been taking place for generations and called for 'the study of Jewish women' to be integrated into 'the study of "the Jews"',[10] scholars of the modern age asserted that not only geographical diversity but also differences related to gender must be taken into account when describing the transition of Jews from a traditional to a modern society. Challenging the 'sex-blindness' of traditional historiography,[11] they insisted on the need to emphasize the differences between the experiences of men and women in the modern world. Moreover, drawing on the understanding of gender that began to become widespread in the 1960s and 1970s, according to which the differences that exist in every society between men and women do not emanate necessarily and naturally from innate biological differences between male and female, but rather depend on culture and change with time and place, these scholars insisted on the importance of paying attention to the changing perceptions of gender in different periods and societies. The introduction of the concept of gender to the study of history offers the possibility of examining the past from a genuinely new perspective.[12] Among other things, it invites an emphasis on the distinctive experiences of Jewish women at the beginning of modernity and the concomitant reconfiguration of the gender order.

This focus on gender has yielded new insights, altering the way we conceive of Jewish modernization. Referring specifically to the German context,

---

[9] The collection of essays edited by Jacob Katz, *Toward Modernity*, was a first attempt to present comparative descriptions of Jewish modernization in various regions. Many have claimed that these essays are in tension with Katz's own tendency to depict a unified 'European Jewish model' (the book's subtitle) of Jewish modernization based on the German experience. See Birnbaum and Katznelson, 'Emancipation and the Liberal Offer', esp. pp. 21–2. Todd Endelman revised Katz's germanocentric thesis by contrasting it with the case of English Jewry; Yosef Kaplan did so through a study of the Sephardi diaspora in western Europe: Endelman, *The Jews of Georgian England*; Kaplan, *An Alternative Path to Modernity*. See also Elisheva Carlebach's revision of Katz's model from the perspective of the early modern period in Ashkenaz (Carlebach, 'Early Modern Ashkenaz'). (Originally used of the area of Jewish settlement in northern France and Germany on the banks of the Rhine, the term 'Ashkenaz' later became identified with German Jews, 'Ashkenazim'; it then evolved to include Poland, Lithuania, and other areas settled by Ashkenazim.)   [10] Magnus, '"Out of the Ghetto"'.

[11] This expression was used by historian Gisela Bock, referring to historiography in general: Bock, 'Women's History and Gender History', 11.

[12] There is an extensive literature on theoretical approaches to gender and history. In addition to Joan W. Scott's (by now classic) programmatic essay 'Gender: A Useful Category of Historical Analysis' (first pub. in 1986 in *The American Historical Review*), these studies include, among many others, Bock, 'Women's History and Gender History'; Offen et al. (eds.), *Writing Women's History*; 'AHR Forum: Revisiting "Gender: A Useful Category of Historical Analysis"'; Wiesner-Hanks, *Gender in History*, 1–23; Rose et al., 'Gender History/Women's History'.

historian Marion Kaplan insisted on the central role of women in the consolidation of a modern way of life among German Jews in the last decades of the nineteenth century and the early years of the twentieth. Objecting to the neglect of women in historical accounts of the modernization of the Jews, Kaplan placed them at centre stage and focused on their experiences to construct a different account of this process. Whereas historians had hitherto devoted their attention to the public activities of (mostly male) Jews and had concluded that modern German Jewry had largely assimilated, Kaplan contended that a focus on women and the private sphere yielded a more complex picture, revealing 'both the Jewish attempt to become like other Germans and Jewish resistance to homogenization'.[13] Kaplan also showed that, despite the constricting bourgeois ideology of 'separate spheres', according to which the public realm was men's domain while women were properly confined to the domestic arena, Jewish women in Imperial Germany were able to 'exert considerable influence on their community', artfully using the cult of domesticity to enhance their status and expand their activities beyond their households.[14]

Paula Hyman, too, placed women and gender at the centre of her research on the assimilation of the Jews, reconstructing the experiences of Jewish women facing the challenges of modernity and examining the role of ideas about gender in the shaping of a modern Jewish identity. An emphasis on the historical context in which the encounter of women with modernity took place allowed Hyman to discern important differences between eastern Europe on the one hand and central and western Europe and the United States on the other, and to outline two models of gender and assimilation among Ashkenazi Jewry.[15] More recently, Benjamin Maria Baader examined the changes in gender roles that accompanied the process of embourgeoisement of Jewish society in Germany from the last decades of the eighteenth century, noting the important implications of these transformations for women's place in the community. As Baader showed, with the decline in the modern period of male religious ideals such as rabbinic study and communal Hebrew prayer, bourgeois values emerged which allowed women to organize themselves around voluntary associations with philanthropic and patriotic goals, and to take a more active part in religious and communal life.[16] As Kaplan, Hyman, Baader, and other scholars clearly show, the history of Jewish modernization may look radically different when examined from a gender perspective.

[13] Kaplan, 'Women and the Shaping of Modern Jewish Identity', 57. Cf. Richarz, 'Der jüdische Weihnachtsbaum', esp. p. 65.   [14] Kaplan, *The Making of the Jewish Middle Class* (here p. 17).
[15] Hyman, *Gender and Assimilation*; ead., 'Two Models of Modernization'.
[16] Baader, *Gender, Judaism, and Bourgeois Culture in Germany*; id., 'When Judaism Turned Bourgeois'.

The present study of a group of Jewish women living in Berlin around 1800 follows the trend of examining the experience of modern Jews with eyes sensitive to gender, and, like the studies mentioned above, it illuminates certain aspects of that experience that passed unnoticed or were misinterpreted when viewed from a perspective uninformed by gender. What emerges most clearly is a different picture of the cultural life of the Jews at this time, revealing the surprising extent of Jewish women's participation in the intellectual, cultural, and social scene in German-speaking lands during the late eighteenth and early nineteenth centuries. At the same time as it challenges assumptions regarding the alleged gender divisions of the time and questions the actual power of gender norms to determine the reality of women's lives, this study sets out to trace the rise of a feminist awareness among these women, which (as will become clear) was coupled with an impressive effort to increase their active participation in contemporary culture.[17] Questioning the prevailing gender order—first and foremost, the persistent attempts to exclude women from cultural activity—these women demanded the right to join current discourse and public debate in the capacity of rational beings. They tried to improve their hitherto marginal place in culture and society, using various means and asserting their mental capacity as women, adopting an attitude which I claim was informed to a great extent by the ethos of the Enlightenment.

Indeed, as I shall show in the chapters that follow, close study of the words and deeds of these Jewish women reveals that they embodied the spirit of Enlightenment, as captured by the German philosopher Immanuel Kant in 1784. In his short but very influential essay 'An Answer to the Question: "What Is Enlightenment?"', published in the *Berlinische Monatsschrift* ('Berlin Monthly'), Kant defined what he perceived as the essence of the Enlightenment as 'man's emergence from his self-incurred immaturity', glossing immaturity as 'the inability to use one's own understanding without the guidance of another'.[18] An individual who willingly and submissively accepts the authority of another, instead of using his own reason, is in Kant's opinion responsible for his dependent state. This person may work himself

---

[17] Even though the words 'feminism' and 'feminist' originated in late 19th-century French political discourse and are strongly associated with the organized movements for women's emancipation of the 19th and 20th centuries, they apply to the challenges to male hegemony and the subordination of women advanced in theory and practice in the last three centuries by women and sympathetic male allies, in an effort to obtain justice for women and empower them to realize their full potential. See Offen, *European Feminisms*, esp. pp. 1–30.

[18] Kant, 'An Answer to the Question: "What Is Enlightenment?"', 54. For a philosophical discussion of Kant's essay, see Foucault, 'What Is Enlightenment?'.

out of his condition of tutelage by making a change in himself, if only he demonstrates the determination and the courage necessary to do so. Although in the same essay Kant imposed limits on the autonomy of the individual in order to safeguard social order and the state, his famous motto '*Sapere aude!* [Dare to know!] Have courage to use your own understanding!' represents the battle cry of the Enlightenment and is seen today as one of its most prominent features.[19]

Kant had little regard for women as rational beings and did not intend his words to be applied to them. Nevertheless, his approach encapsulated the attitude of many contemporary members of the female sex, among them the Jewish women discussed here. As we shall see, these women consciously cultivated their minds and attempted to exercise their own judgement, in order to analyse not only cultural products such as books and plays, sweeping political events such as the French Revolution or the Napoleonic wars, or trends in contemporary thought such as voguish pedagogical theories, but also the prevailing gender norms that were intended to shape the world in which they lived. Aware of their inferior place in society as women, they criticized the institutions that confined them and subjected them to masculine authority and—borrowing Kant's formulation—'dared' to think and act according to their own understanding, striving to change their lives. Their endeavours to escape blind obedience to tradition and/or social conventions, and to exchange a condition of tutelage and dependence for one of maturity and personal autonomy (echoing Kant again), involved adopting a secular outlook that granted great power to the critical ability of the individual and significantly weakened the power of tradition and religion.[20]

Presenting these Jewish women as part of the Enlightenment, in fact as 'enlightened women', a phrase that will frequently be used to describe them throughout this study, postulates a connection between two concepts that

---

[19] Kant, 'An Answer to the Question: "What Is Enlightenment?"', 54. Historian Roy Porter, even though he regarded the optimistic tone of Kant's essay (shared by many other thinkers of Kant's time) with scepticism, judged the critical attitude to be the most prominent feature of the Enlightenment. In Porter's words, the thinkers of the Enlightenment 'were, above all, *critics*' (Porter, *The Enlightenment*, 3). Carla Hesse, like Kant, saw 'critical reason, rather than universal laws of nature, as the defining feature of the Enlightenment' and used this strain of Enlightenment thought to trace the case of French women's participation in public reasoning and their becoming modern selves (Hesse, *The Other Enlightenment*; quote from p. xii). These and many other recent studies define the Enlightenment 'as an attitude of mind, rather than a coherent system of beliefs' (Munck, *The Enlightenment*, 7).

[20] This is not to claim that a secular outlook necessarily implied rejecting religion as a whole, but rather that religion was perceived as having less control over one's life or was thought of as less relevant to certain aspects of life. On the connection between Enlightenment and religion, see Porter's evaluation in *The Enlightenment*, esp. pp. 64–9, and Outram, *The Enlightenment*, 31–46.

was far from obvious to earlier scholars. For a long time, the Enlightenment was perceived by historians as a male movement, in which women played no significant role. Only in recent years have scholars from the fields of women's and gender history started to investigate seriously the connection between women and the Enlightenment.[21] Going far beyond the well-established theme of 'women in Enlightenment thought', which is essentially the examination of women as an aspect of the thought of enlightened men,[22] they turned their attention to uncharted areas in the history of the movement as well as to various activities which had previously not received appropriate attention. They were thus able to emphasize the involvement of women in the Enlightenment and their active contribution to the cultural production of their time.[23] While the first way of connecting women and the Enlightenment—by studying the attitude of the Enlightenment towards women and gender—treated women as passive objects for the contemplation of mainly male thinkers, the second path considers women as active agents in history, who take part in the production and dissemination of ideas and opinions.

Recent developments in the study of the Enlightenment, closely related to wider historiographical trends, contribute to the inclusion of women in the narrative, and are highly relevant to the present case. Among these is the growing interest among scholars in questions related to the diffusion of enlightened ideas, their carriers and consumers, which has been accompanied by a conscious distancing from the methods of the earlier history of ideas which long dominated Enlightenment research.[24] Since the 1970s especially, voices have been raised against the presentation of the Enlightenment in isolation from its wider historical context.[25] Building upon the influential

---

[21] Works on this subject include: Goodman, *The Republic of Letters*; Opitz, Weckel, and Kleinau (eds.), *Tugend, Vernunft und Gefühl*; Hesse, *The Other Enlightenment*; Knott and Taylor (eds.), *Women, Gender and Enlightenment*. A book that deals with the Enlightenment in general but combines an extensive discussion on women and gender is Outram, *Panorama of the Enlightenment*.

[22] One prominent example of this type of study is Hoffmann, *La Femme dans la pensée des Lumières*.

[23] Opitz and Weckel, 'Einleitung', in Opitz, Weckel, et al. (eds.), *Ordnung, Politik und Gesellschaft der Geschlechter*, 7–21; Opitz, Weckel, and Kleinau (eds.), *Tugend, Vernunft und Gefühl*; Hesse, *The Other Enlightenment*; Knott and Taylor (eds.), *Women, Gender and Enlightenment*; Goodman, *The Republic of Letters*; Goodman, 'Public Sphere and Private Life'; Weckel, *Zwischen Häuslichkeit und Öffentlichkeit*; Albrecht et al. (eds.), *Formen der Geselligkeit in Nordwestdeutschland*. Cf. Landes, *Women and the Public Sphere*, and Eley, 'Nations, Publics, and Political Cultures', esp. pp. 307–19, who emphasize the masculine character of the new cultural institutions of the 18th century.

[24] For an overview of scholarship on the Enlightenment, see Outram, *The Enlightenment*, 1–13; Porter, *The Enlightenment*. In the Jewish context, see Feiner, *The Jewish Enlightenment*, 1–17.

[25] This type of criticism was made in particular of Ernst Cassirer's classic 1932 study *Die Philosophie der Aufklärung*, which saw the Enlightenment 'as an intellectual movement . . . and displayed little interest in its social or political context, or in the impact of these ideas' (Outram, *The*

study by Jürgen Habermas discussing the flourishing of the public sphere in the eighteenth and early nineteenth centuries, first published in Germany in 1962 and translated into English many years later under the title *The Structural Transformation of the Public Sphere*, research increasingly shifted away from the protracted (and frustrating) attempt to grasp an unchanging ideological essence at the heart of the Enlightenment and towards the elucidation of its social basis and the ways in which knowledge, ideas, and opinions were transmitted.[26] Attention ceased to be directed uniquely at the great thinkers and turned instead to a wider spectrum of society as scholars sought to understand how new ways of thinking became more and more widely disseminated and more and more deeply entrenched among different groups of the population. The Enlightenment was now conceived of by many as a 'process',[27] and study of it centred on the diffusion of ideas through various means of communication, including printed material such as books, newspapers, journals, and pamphlets; institutions of sociability typical of the eighteenth century, such as coffee-houses and societies of various kinds; and informal social contacts in the streets, at the markets, at holiday resorts, and in other contexts.

A gender approach is well served by this focus on the 'vantage point of more ordinary people—those who read newspapers, frequented coffee-houses or societies, shared in popular entertainment, became interested in current social issues, or simply walked round town with an open mind'.[28] While women's part in the Enlightenment was naturally played down as long as scholarly attention was directed towards the pantheon of *philosophes* (since women did not belong to their ranks), the new historiographical approach is helping to reconstruct the place of women in the Enlightenment and the place of the Enlightenment in the lives of women in the eighteenth

---

Enlightenment, 3–4). Peter Gay's two-volume *The Enlightenment: An Interpretation*, published in the 1960s, has also been the target of criticism in recent decades. Although Gay 'advocated what he called the "social history of ideas"', it is claimed against him that he actually focused on a small group of thinkers, and that his 'interest in the social context of ideas' was 'minimal at best' (Porter, *The Enlightenment*, 40; Outram, *The Enlightenment*, 4).

[26] The dissemination of the Enlightenment among a wide public in European countries in the 18th century is surveyed by Munck, *The Enlightenment*, and Melton, *The Rise of the Public*.

[27] Kant spoke clearly of the Enlightenment as a dynamic process (rather than as a given situation): 'If it is now asked whether we at present live in an *enlightened* age [i.e. in a state of enlightenment], the answer is: no, but we do live in an age of *enlightenment* [i.e. in the midst of a process]' (Kant, 'An Answer to the Question: "What Is Enlightenment?"', 58). For a discussion on the Enlightenment as a process, see Vierhaus, 'Aufklärung als Prozeß—*der Prozeß der Aufklärung*'; Bödeker, 'Aufklärung als Kommunikationsprozeß'.   [28] Munck, *The Enlightenment*, p. vii.

century.²⁹ Contrary to the received wisdom that women had nothing to do with the world of Enlightenment, recent studies show that although women of that period did not usually belong to the institutionalized circles established by the 'movement of the Enlightenment',³⁰ they definitely made up an important and fundamental component of the enlightened public that became established over the course of the eighteenth century.³¹ Rather than being portrayed automatically as passive, silent, or hidden figures in a male world, women are now depicted as carriers and mediators of ideas who penetrated the public sphere as readers, spectators, and writers and left their own mark on the culture of the time. Using means of communication that until recently were accorded little attention in historical accounts because they were hardly considered appropriate objects of academic interest—a conversation about a play or a book, a private letter expressing one's impression of a new place visited, or one's personal opinion about a social, political, or cultural phenomenon—women in the eighteenth century, especially bourgeois women, joined the branched network of communication that spread throughout European cities, and thus participated in Enlightenment culture.³² Among them were the women studied here.

ENLIGHTENED JEWISH WOMEN AND THE HASKALAH

If, as I have claimed above, the connection between women and Enlightenment in the European historical context has been made only recently, the same is true to an even greater extent in Jewish historiography. Relatively little has been written about the relationship between Jewish women and the Enlightenment—despite the fact that the Enlightenment was the most significant cultural current in eighteenth-century Europe. This omission may be largely explained by the fact that for many years Jewish engagement with the Enlightenment was identified with the Haskalah, one of the central Jewish intellectual and social movements of modern times, and the study of Jewish participation in Enlightenment culture was largely

---

²⁹ For a well-formulated critique of the widespread perception of the Enlightenment as a male movement, see Opitz and Weckel, 'Einleitung', in Opitz, Weckel, et al. (eds.), *Ordnung, Politik und Geselligkeit der Geschlechter*, 7–21. See also Outram, *The Enlightenment*.

³⁰ On the Enlightenment as a (male and elitist) movement, see Darnton, 'George Washington's False Teeth', esp. p. 34.

³¹ The coming into being during the Enlightenment of a modern public, which gathered 'private individuals rendering judgment on what they read, observed, or otherwise experienced', is the subject of James van Horn Melton's *The Rise of the Public* (quotation from p. 1).

³² As Gisella Bock emphasized, overturning 'the hierarchies between the historically important and unimportant' was and is a necessary condition for exploring the history of women (Bock, 'Women's History and Gender History', 7).

confined to this movement. The Haskalah, however, was mainly a male movement, especially in its eighteenth-century central European version. Its proponents, the maskilim, who proclaimed the goal of intellectual renewal and social transformation among the Jewish people, saw themselves as members of a male intellectual elite, whose writings and institutions were created primarily by and for men. They established a public sphere, with a Hebrew periodical (*Hame'asef*, established in 1783) whose editors, contributors, and readers were all male; printing presses—most notably the Orientalische Buchdruckerei (the Oriental Printing Press), established in Berlin in 1784— which published texts by male authors intended for a male readership;[33] and exclusively male associations, such as the Society of Friends of the Hebrew Language (Hevrat Doreshei Leshon Ever, founded in 1782), and later the Society for the Promotion of Goodness and Justice (Hevrat Shoharei Hatov Vehatushiyah, founded in 1787). Similarly, the first modern Jewish school, the Freischule (Free School), which was established in Berlin in 1778 and served as a model for similar institutions in other Jewish communities, was intended for boys only.[34] With a movement that excluded women so comprehensively taken to represent the incarnation of the Enlightenment among European Jews, it comes as no surprise that women were left out of the debate on the Enlightenment among the Jews, and were presumed to be absent from Enlightenment culture (at least in the eighteenth century).[35]

This perception that the Jewish Enlightenment was a purely male phenomenon is now changing, as the study of the Haskalah goes through important transformations. Just as in the case of Jewish modernization, of which it is part, the study of the Haskalah now includes the examination of more specific cases, leading to fewer generalized assertions and to a more varied perception of the Jewish Enlightenment. Here, too, new emphasis has been placed on the varying geographical and cultural context, which is now claimed to have had a decisive influence on the nature of the Enlightenment as manifested among Jews in different places.[36] David Ruderman portrayed the particular expressions of Enlightenment typical of Jews active in the

---

[33] On the history of this institution, see Lohmann, '"Sustenance for the Learned Soul"'.

[34] Maskilic schools started to accept female pupils only from 1798. Efforts to integrate Jewish girls into maskilic schools and the 'new approach' to female education among the maskilim are discussed in the chapter 'Girls' Education' in Eliav, *Jewish Education in Germany* (Heb.), 271–9.

[35] One of the rare examples of a study that states a connection between an 18th-century Jewish woman and the Enlightenment is Spiel, *Fanny von Arnstein*, the English subtitle of which is *Daughter of the Enlightenment*.

[36] This emphasis on different variations of the Enlightenment among the Jews is parallel to the insistence on regional strands of Enlightenment in general historiography. See Porter and Teich (eds.), *The Enlightenment in National Context*; Munck, *The Enlightenment*, 3–7.

English cultural milieu;³⁷ Lois Dubin stressed the independent attitude of the community in Trieste towards the Haskalah and modernization, which differed significantly from the position of the maskilim in Berlin, despite some points of contact and similarity;³⁸ Nancy Sinkoff described the moderate and even conservative outlook of an east European maskil, Mendel Lefin of Satanow, developed in the pre-absolutist context of the Polish–Lithuanian Commonwealth where he lived, in very different conditions from those prevailing in central Europe;³⁹ David Fishman depicted the encounter of a circle of maskilim in the Byelorussian town of Shklov with the ideas of the Enlightenment as early as the 1770s, long before the purported beginnings of the Haskalah in eastern Europe.⁴⁰ By turning their attention to other places in this way, scholars are questioning the extent to which the Berlin Haskalah, previously perceived in almost paradigmatic terms, actually represented the interaction of Jews with the Enlightenment. At the same time, scholars such as Shmuel Feiner and David Sorkin have offered a historical portrait of this movement, presenting it as a concrete and discrete phenomenon, limited in temporal and geographical reach and distinguishable from other contemporary secularization trends in Jewish culture.⁴¹ The Haskalah is now recognized as a multifaceted movement, articulated in many different ways in the many different settings where Jews lived.

Here again, as in the case of Jewish modernization, the gender perspective has much to contribute in enriching our picture of the history of Jews and the Enlightenment. Devoted as it is to challenging cohesive depictions of the past as valid for an entire people, social group, or nation, gendered historical criticism helps us to understand that (as is true in innumerable other cases) the study of Jews' encounter with the European Enlightenment has hitherto focused mainly on the experiences of men—and a restricted group of men at that—while ignoring or misinterpreting manifestations of enlightened traits among Jewish women. The gender approach prompts the historian to search in other places and look for different kinds of traces, perhaps peculiar to women, to reconsider the available data and re-evaluate past assertions.

---

³⁷ Ruderman, *Jewish Enlightenment in an English Key*; id., 'Was there a "Haskalah" in England?'.
³⁸ Dubin, *The Port Jews of Habsburg Trieste*.   ³⁹ Sinkoff, *Out of the Shtetl*.
⁴⁰ Fishman, *Russia's First Modern Jews*.
⁴¹ Feiner and Sorkin, 'Introduction', in eid. (eds.), *New Perspectives on the Haskalah*, 1–7. See also Sorkin, 'The Berlin Haskalah' (Heb.); Feiner, *The Jewish Enlightenment*; and especially Feiner's recent publication, *The Origins of Jewish Secularization*, in which he clearly distinguishes between the Haskalah as a movement of cultural and social revival and other processes of acculturation in 18th-century Ashkenazi Jewish society, involving religious criticism and laxity in religious observance, which existed outside the maskilic revolution.

One such assertion worth revising is an idea that was disseminated by maskilic discourse and bequeathed to later generations, namely that for the Jews there was one normative path to joining the Enlightenment: the path proposed by the maskilim. Leading late eighteenth-century exponents of the Haskalah emphasized in their writings a distinction between, on the one hand, 'true' maskilim, who promoted moderate and well-thought-out changes in Jewish society, based on a clear and soundly based ideology, and, on the other hand, 'false' maskilim, who tended to espouse a radical acculturation lacking a proper theoretical base.[42] The self-styled 'true maskilim' frowned on men who set themselves free from the reins of tradition and exhibited radical acculturation in their behaviour and their appearance,[43] as they did on women whose 'pseudo-enlightenment' expressed itself in the reading of novels, knowledge of European languages, visits to the theatre, and in general a close relationship with non-Jewish society.[44] Both, they claimed, were acting superficially and without serious thought, contrary to the guidance of the maskilim, who had studied in depth the ideas of the most prominent European thinkers, analysed the situation of the Jewish people, and, after reaching conclusions about the steps that in their opinion would better serve Jewish interests, were trying with all their might to disseminate their message among their co-religionists.

The patronizing attitude of the maskilim towards those they defined as 'false enlighteners' derived from a value judgement, rooted in their time and essentially subjective, which itself grew out of the sense of crisis prevailing at that period.[45] Genuinely concerned for the fate of the Jewish people, they viewed askance what they saw as a promiscuous way of life that endangered the Jewish family, one of the pillars of Jewish society, harmed the image of the Jews in the eyes of surrounding society, and stood in the way of the realization of the maskilic vision.[46] However, the distinction made by the maskilim

---

[42] Feiner, 'The Pseudo-Enlightenment'. [43] Ibid. 62–72.

[44] Feiner, 'The Modern Jewish Woman' (Heb.), 259. Feiner's analysis here is based on the play by Isaac Euchel, *Reb henoch oder woss tut me' damit*, from 1792. See the new annotated edition of this maskilic play, published by Marion Aptroot and Roland Gruschka: Euchel, *Reb henoch, oder: woß tut me damit*. See also Naimark-Goldberg, 'The (Questionable) Appraisal of Women in Euchel's *Haskala*'.

[45] In the chapter of his book *The Jewish Enlightenment* entitled 'Crisis at the Turn of the Century', Shmuel Feiner notes the anxiety that took hold of modern Jewish intellectuals 'in the face of the secularization gaining in momentum among the Jewish bourgeoisie in urban communities—a process neither intended by the maskilim nor controlled by them' (p. 293).

[46] A typical formulation of the patronizing attitude was expressed by Lazarus Bendavid, who saw himself as a true maskil and as a lay intellectual qualified to propose reforms in Jewish society. In a pamphlet of 1793, published as part of his efforts to promote Jewish emancipation and reform, Bendavid analysed contemporary Jewish society and discerned four classes of Jews, one of them com-

between 'true' and 'false' Enlightenment should not be accepted unchallenged, and certainly the dichotomy between those who claimed to act out of intellectual considerations and those who, they alleged, acted solely out of personal interest and thoughtlessness should not be accepted as a historical fact. Above all, it should not be assumed that—even in Berlin, the centre of the Haskalah—the maskilim were the only Jews who responded seriously and in depth to the stimulus provided by the European Enlightenment.

A critical attitude towards the claims of the maskilim is in tune with current trends in historical research, which deprive the intellectuals of the past—in this case the maskilim—of the role formerly accorded them as sole carriers of ideas and values. In the last four decades, the intellectual history of the Enlightenment has ceased to restrict itself to examining the works of great intellectuals and now looks for the deposition of ideas and values among a broader cross-section of the population and in simpler, more commonplace products. This approach enables the distinctions bequeathed to future generations by the maskilim to be subjected to critical scrutiny. The Jewish women and men labelled as 'false enlighteners', unlike the maskilim, did not establish a movement and did not necessarily act on the basis of ideology, with a clear-cut world-view and thought-out ideals which they sought to put into practice. Nevertheless, even though many of them did not leave behind outstanding works of literature and were not 'thinkers' in the traditional sense (though they certainly belonged to the social layer described as 'people of culture'),[47] it is appropriate to examine how at least some of them relied on the discourse of their time, on enlightened ideas, values, and perspectives that they absorbed from the surrounding culture, in order to explain, to themselves and to others, the way in which they led and experienced their lives.

To be sure, this study is not the first attempt to establish a connection between Jewish women and Enlightenment. This link has been acknowledged in studies on Jewish history and literature since the late 1990s that have challenged previous assumptions concerning Jewish women and the

prising a 'dissolute mob who have abandoned the ceremonial laws because they were too much of a burden and because they prevented them from following unhindered their unbridled passions'. Coming mostly from rich families, these Jews 'were raised without a proper education and were led astray by love and wine. They consider themselves to be enlightened, but they merely arouse contempt . . . They simulate enlightenment, but are incorrigible, uninformed vagabonds. These are the ones who, for the most part, are responsible for the bad opinion the Christians have of the Jews' (Bendavid, *Etwas zur Chrarackteristick der Juden*, 48–9; Eng. trans. from Mendes-Flohr and Reinharz (eds.), *The Jew in the Modern World*, 103–4).

[47] The concept of *gens de culture* is quoted by Porter (*The Enlightenment*, 6) from Daniel Roche, *Les Républicains des lettres: Gens de culture et Lumières au XVIII siècle* (Paris, 1988).

Haskalah. Such efforts, most of them by Israeli scholars,[48] have focused on the representation of Jewish women in the works of the maskilim, but also on nineteenth-century east European maskilot (women active in the Haskalah). Having already devoted a book to analysing the image of the Jewish woman in the eyes of the maskilim, Tova Cohen focused subsequent studies on women who themselves joined the Haskalah as active partners, as in her essay 'From the Private Sphere to the Public Sphere: The Writings of Hebrew Maskilot in the Nineteenth Century' and in *Voice of a Hebrew Maiden: Women's Writings of the Nineteenth-Century Haskalah Movement*, a collection of published and unpublished texts in various genres written by Jewish women in the second half of the nineteenth century as a contribution to the Haskalah.[49] This anthology was published in co-operation with Shmuel Feiner, who had examined the attitude of the maskilim towards women and the case of nineteenth-century maskilot in a previous, groundbreaking essay of 1998.[50] Shmuel Werses published a collection of letters sent by Miriam Markel-Mosessohn, a maskilah born in Lithuania, to the famous east European maskil Judah Leib Gordon, with an introduction discussing the life and literary activity of this enlightened Jewish woman.[51] Iris Parush, in her various studies on women, literacy, and the Jewish Enlightenment, discussed the role of Jewish women in disseminating new cultural trends in nineteenth-century eastern Europe, precisely from their allegedly marginal status in Jewish society—a status that, she claims, allowed them to expand their relatively unsupervised reading and thus enter the maskilic literary world and absorb its values.[52]

The present study complements the efforts of these fine scholars, directing its attention to a different period and a different milieu. Turning away from the second half of the nineteenth century to the years around 1800, it deals with women whose sphere of activity was not confined to the Jewish world but was rather located in the non-Jewish domain. My central goal is

---

[48] One notable contribution by a non-Israeli scholar is Carole B. Balin's *To Reveal Our Hearts*, esp. the book's first chapter, 'The Makings of a *Maskilah*: Miriam Markel-Mosessohn (1839–1920)', 13–50.

[49] Cohen, *One Beloved, the Other Hated* (Heb.); ead., 'From the Private Sphere to the Public Sphere' (Heb.); Cohen and Feiner (eds.), *Voice of a Hebrew Maiden* (Heb.). See also Cohen, 'Portrait of the *Maskilah* as a Young Woman'. Cohen is now studying the Hebrew writings of a Jewish woman from a different cultural context: Rahel Morpurgo, a nineteenth-century Italian maskilah. See Ch. 1 n. 46 below.   [50] Feiner, 'The Modern Jewish Woman' (Heb.).

[51] *The Poet's Friend* (Heb.), ed. Werses. See also Werses, 'Women's Voices in the Yiddish Weekly *Kol-mevaser*' (Heb.); and Tamar Shechter's MA thesis, 'The Portrait of a Maskilic Woman' (Heb.), which studies the letters written by Sheindel Pineles, née Perl—the daughter of the famous Galician maskil Joseph Perl—to a maskilic friend between 1821 and 1825.

[52] Parush, *Reading Jewish Women*; ead., 'Readers in Cameo'.

not to analyse how enlightened Jewish men conceived of the nature of the female sex and the role of women in the new, modern world that was coming about in front of their eyes, as many studies have done—though that endeavour has its own worth;[53] it is to focus on the discourse of women themselves and their participation in the transformation and diffusion of ideas, rather than on their appearance in the discourse of men. Given the lack of direct sources (especially compared to the sources available for studying Jewish men's encounter with the Enlightenment) and, even more crucially, the absence of such a perspective in previous research, it is impossible to present within the scope of this study a comprehensive picture of the interaction of Jewish women with the Enlightenment, and I do not set out to do this. Rather, an attempt will be made to illuminate the specific case of a group of Jewish women who experienced the Enlightenment and responded to its ideas, and thereby to contribute to the development of this field.

RE-EXAMINING THE CONNECTION WITH ROMANTICISM

Presenting these Jewish women as part of the Enlightenment may seem odd to those familiar with the widely established view that links them strongly with Romanticism—a movement perceived as running counter to the intellectual current of the Enlightenment. Generations of scholars nurtured and strengthened this association, implicitly or explicitly rejecting these women's connection to the Enlightenment, until eventually their affiliation to Romanticism came to be accepted as natural and self-evident, and was hardly ever questioned.[54]

A closer examination of the claims of scholars who assert a strong connection between these women and Romanticism, however, reveals that their contentions are often based on problematic inferences reflecting dubious assumptions about gender roles. At the root of many of these claims are two linked factors: the personal relationships formed by some of the most

---

[53] I myself implemented this approach when examining the perception of women and gender by the maskil Isaac Euchel: Naimark-Goldberg, 'The (Questionable) Appraisal of Women in Euchel's *Haskala*'.

[54] A sample of the titles of books published between the beginning of the 20th century and the present day on two outstanding women in this group, Rahel Levin and Dorothea Mendelssohn, emphasizes the enduring connection with Romanticism: Franz Deibel's *Dorothea Schlegel als Schriftstellerin im Zusammenhang mit der romantischen Schule* (1905); Margarete Susman's *Frauen der Romantik* (1929); Herbert Scurla's *Rahel Varnhagen. Die große Frauengestalt der deutschen Romantik* (1980); Barbara Becker-Cantarino's *Schriftstellerinnen der Romantik. Epoche—Werke—Wirkung* (2000); and the German title of Hannah Arendt's biography of Rahel Levin, *Rahel Varnhagen: Lebensgeschichte einer deutschen Jüdin aus der Romantik*.

prominent of these women with men associated with the nascent Romantic movement; and the assumption that women are inevitably subjugated to the influence of men, especially if the men in question are leading intellectuals.[55] The effect of this assumption is clear in Jewish historiography in this area, which from the outset has asserted the decisive influence of men, mainly the Protestant theologian Friedrich Schleiermacher, the poet and literary critic Friedrich Schlegel, the renowned writer Johann Wolfgang von Goethe (who was not actually associated with Romanticism but is seen as one of its sources of inspiration), and the philosopher Johann Gottlieb Fichte, on their female Jewish friends and readers—notably Henriette Herz, Dorothea Mendelssohn, and Rahel Levin. This type of influence was taken for granted by the nineteenth-century Jewish historian Heinrich Graetz, who valued the education of the 'salon women' and praised their knowledge,[56] but lamented that these fine Jewish women had been blinded by 'Christians of the corrupt higher ranks', whom he accuses of 'infecting' them with 'moral depravity' and thereby violating the sanctity of matrimony in Judaism and the well-known chastity of Jewish women, which had been the pride of Israel for many generations.[57] Similarly, Simon Dubnow, writing in the 1920s, despised the superficial minds of the *salonnières* and claimed that they could not resist the attraction of Romanticism. Even a 'highly gifted woman' such as Rahel Levin, Dubnow claimed, absorbed from the literary giants of her generation, including Goethe and Fichte, a poisonous contempt for her own people.[58]

Defining these women as subdued by the ideas of Romanticism, on the basis of their proximity to Romantic circles, not only fails to acknowledge that even after their acquaintance with Romantic thinkers they continued to exercise their own judgement and did not necessarily accept blindly the ideas of others; it also ignores all they did, felt, and wrote before their encounters with these men. A typical example is the case of Dorothea Mendelssohn,

---

[55] Ascribing this kind of subordination of women to men is of course a widespread phenomenon. For example, the name of the famous French writer Madame d'Épinay is often coupled with that of Jean-Jacques Rousseau (whose friend and benefactor she was): her ideas are presented as a reflection of his, and her independence and originality as a thinker hardly ever recognized (Weinreb, 'Emilie or *Emile*?').

[56] Graetz, *History of the Jews*, v. 413.

[57] Ibid. 422. It is interesting to note that Graetz's tongue-lashing of these women was so harsh that the Hebrew translator added a remark condemning his deviation from the 'objectivity' appropriate to the task of the historian: Graetz, *History of the Jews* (Heb.), ix. 130.

[58] Dubnow, *History of the Jews*, iv. 641–3 (quotation from p. 642). See also the harsh words of Adolph Kohut, a Hungarian-born Jewish historian and journalist, concerning Dorothea Mendelssohn. According to Kohut, Dorothea 'followed her romantic seducer [i.e. Friedrich Schlegel] with near total submissiveness from folly to folly' and 'did everything her man wished': Kohut, *Moses Mendelssohn und seine Familie*, 82–95 (quotations from pp. 87, 92).

which will be discussed in greater detail in the following chapters: sources dating from the third decade of her life, before her encounter with Friedrich Schlegel in 1797, when she was 33, reveal the image of a woman independent in thought and deed who reflected critically on society and culture, including the gender order in which she lived. Although there is no point in denying the fateful implications of her encounter with Schlegel, it would be wrong to interpret every act and every utterance of hers as a result of the direct influence of the opinions of this young Romantic.

Criticism on the grounds of gender stereotyping may justly be directed not only towards historians (such as Graetz and Dubnow) who failed to appreciate the value of these women's utterances and indeed even to use the texts they left as historical sources, but also towards some who did pay serious attention to their words. For example, in the light of today's gender criticism the assertions made in 1967 by Michael Meyer, who closely examined the written legacy of the most famous among these women, are debatable in their reliance on a presumed dichotomy between the maleness of reason and knowledge on the one hand, and the femaleness of emotions and passions on the other.[59] In discussing the generation of German Jewry after Mendelssohn, Meyer postulates a clear division between rational men and emotional women; between Jewish men's persistent commitment to the universalistic values of the Enlightenment and Jewish women's attraction to the individuality and sentimentalism of the new Romantic movement propagated by young German intellectuals—again identifying Schleiermacher, Schlegel, Goethe, and Fichte.[60] The strong connection between women and Romanticism posited by Meyer will be reassessed in subsequent chapters when I come to interpret some of the texts on which he based his claims, as well as other sources not included in his discussion.

Not all who supported the association of these women with Romanticism based their claims on problematic gender assumptions, however. For example, one scholar who endorsed this connection was Margarete Susman, who saw in Romanticism a promise more than a threat, and who perceived in it more potential for female empowerment than for women's subordination to men.[61] While for Graetz Romanticism was a libertine and therefore unwelcome movement, and for Dubnow it was responsible for the revival of antisemitism in European culture, Susman discovered in it a significant message especially relevant to the women involved with this movement.[62]

---

[59] Lloyd, 'The Man of Reason'.
[60] Meyer, *The Origins of the Modern Jew*, 85–114.
[61] On the connection between Romanticism and feminism, see Johnson, 'The Quest for the Self'.
[62] On the life of this prolific Jewish writer, see Ueckert, 'Über Margarete Susman'.

Susman valued Romanticism as an exceptional period in which intellectual women developed a rare, though short-lived, self-consciousness. In her 1929 book dedicated to the 'women of Romanticism',[63] women occupy centre stage and indeed are presented as the ultimate incarnation of Romanticism— or rather, of early Romanticism, which she clearly distinguished from its later versions:[64] their life perfectly epitomizes the spirit of the time, and represents the highest achievement of this movement, of greater value than the words written by any contemporary thinker. In fact, Susman sees no better way to describe Romanticism than by discussing the lives of five representative women, two of them Jewish: Dorothea Mendelssohn and Rahel Levin.[65]

But even when, as in Susman's case, the connection of women with Romanticism is based on thorough study, it may still be questioned and revised, and certainly challenged as the sole context of reference for discussing the life and thought of the Jewish women with whom I am concerned here. Notwithstanding the assertion by so many scholars, including modern students of German literature, of their affiliation with Romanticism, a reading of the sources corroborates the counter-claim that, even though it is possible to find Romantic traces in their texts, numerous other features connect them to the cultural and social world of the Enlightenment, justifying their description as 'enlightened women'.[66] Despite the ambivalent attitude

---

[63] Susman's book, *Frauen der Romantik*, was first published in 1929, then again in 1931, 1960, and more recently in 1996. According to Barbara Hahn's afterword to the last edition, at the time of its first publication the book made a deep impression on many female (especially Jewish female) readers, as attested by the numerous reviews published at the time, most of which were written by Jewish women (Susman, *Frauen der Romantik*, 224–5).

[64] In the first edition of the book to be published after the Second World War, Susman was careful to emphasize that she was referring to the early, moderate Romanticism, not to its later version which called for a return to the pagan world of Germanic tribes and triggered a fierce nationalism. See her short preface to the 1960 edition (as printed in the 1996 edition), 12–14.

[65] Hannah Arendt, in the 1956 preface to her famous biography of Rahel Levin, also characterizes Levin as a 'typically "Romantic" personality', who strove 'to live life as if it were a work of art' (Arendt, *Rahel Varnhagen*, 83, 81). However, although Arendt stressed that for a Jewish woman at the turn of the 18th and 19th centuries, whose aspiration was to 'escape from Judaism' and assimilate, 'appealing to the spirit of the Enlightenment was no longer of any use' (*Rahel Varnhagen*, 103, 105), she also detected in Levin traits identified with the Enlightenment, such as her hatred for the bigotry that characterized the '"new-fashioned" religiosity' of her time (p. 145). Arendt's biography, written in Germany in the 1930s, was published only in the late 1950s, first in English and then in the original German as *Rahel Varnhagen: Lebensgeschichte einer deutschen Jüdin aus der Romantik*. The English version, which has gone through three editions, makes no mention of the connection to Romanticism in its title. The book has also been published in other languages, including French, Spanish, and Italian. Quotes here are taken from the 1997 English edition by Liliane Weissberg.

[66] An exceptional study that unequivocally connects one of the women discussed here, Rahel Levin, with the Enlightenment, is the biography written by Heidi Thomann Tewarson, *Rahel Levin Varnhagen*.

towards women prevalent in the Enlightenment, and the complex attitude of these women themselves towards enlightened ideas and values—both of which will receive attention in this study, especially in the context of women's entry into the world of publishing—this movement provided them with a space in which they could actively develop their place in society and culture, and supplied them with the tools necessary to reflect on their situation as women, thereby eventually serving as a source of female empowerment.[67]

Chronologically, this book focuses on the end of the eighteenth century and the beginning of the nineteenth, a period of transition from Enlightenment to Romanticism. Referring to people who lived then as 'enlightened' requires clarification and qualification, for these years are not an obvious part of what is commonly known as the age of Enlightenment in Germany. Opinions vary as to when that period came to an end. While some accounts characterize the years around 1780 as the 'high point' of the 'social prestige' associated with the Enlightenment,[68] there are scholars who identify a 'severe crisis' in the German *Aufklärung* as early as the mid-1770s,[69] or who find in the last third of the eighteenth century in Germany the 'roots of romanticism'.[70] Both historical and literary periodizations vary in how they classify the years immediately preceding 1800,[71] and the last decade of the eighteenth century may appear under the heading of the *Spätaufklärung* (late Enlightenment), the classical period in literature, or the *Frühromantik* (early Romanticism), certainly in the German context. Given these overlapping definitions, it seems reasonable to suggest that in the 1790s the Enlightenment began to lose its dominance[72]—especially when, following the French Revolution, conservative

---

[67] I addressed this contradiction in Naimark-Goldberg, '"The Mind Has No Sex"' (Heb.). See also the Conclusion to this volume.

[68] Müller, *Die Aufklärung*, 11, quoting H. Möller, *Vernunft und Kritik. Deutsche Aufklärung im 17. und 18. Jahrhundert* (Frankfurt am Main, 1986), 25.

[69] Schneiders (ed.), *Lexikon der Aufklärung*, 19.   [70] Berlin, *The Roots of Romanticism*.

[71] Different time frames have been suggested for the European Enlightenment. Dates that have been proposed for its origins include the 1680s, when Newton published his *Principia Mathematica* and Locke his *Letter Concerning Toleration*, and the 1720s, when the Enlightenment began to consolidate as a movement. Its demise has also been variously dated to 1789 (the French Revolution), 1794 (end of the Reign of Terror in France), and around 1800, with the emergence of nationalism in Europe as a result of the Napoleonic wars. A different periodization—1650–1750—was proposed by Jonathan Israel for what he referred to as the 'radical enlightenment' (see Israel, *Radical Enlightenment*). As to the Jewish Enlightenment, even though the end of the 18th century marks the end of the Berlin Haskalah, in eastern Europe the movement flourished throughout the 19th century. On the process that saw the centre of the Haskalah shift from Berlin to the east, see Feiner, 'Out of Berlin' (Heb.).

[72] Dominance and not absolute control, since parallel to the Enlightenment there always existed currents that opposed it. As Isaiah Berlin pointed out, opposition to its central ideas is 'as old as the movement itself' (Berlin, 'The Counter-Enlightenment', 1).

and anti-Enlightenment forces emerged that held it responsible for overthrowing the monarchy and the church—but that it would nevertheless be a mistake to speak of the end of the Enlightenment as early as this.[73]

The gradual transition from one period to another is clearly reflected in the close connection between the late Enlightenment and early Romanticism, emphasized in recent scholarship. For a long time, it was common to view the birth of German Romanticism as marking the death of the Enlightenment. Romanticism was perceived as the antithesis of the Enlightenment, in fact as a reaction against it. While Enlightenment was defined by reason, Romanticism was defined by emotion, passion, irrationalism. The cosmopolitanism ascribed to the former was set against the nationalism of the latter; Enlightenment's universalism against Romanticism's relativism, cultural particularity, and individualism.

But in recent decades these dichotomies have been challenged, and they are now partly explained as a product of the nineteenth century (reflecting the biases of that period), and of Romanticism itself, that persisted well into the twentieth. It is claimed that Romanticism (in particular its later variants) saw a need to present a monolithic definition of the Enlightenment in order to pose as its opposite, hoping to blur any possible similarity with the earlier movement.[74] On the contrary, scholars now point to the presence, at the heart of Enlightenment, of features earlier perceived to be attributes unique to Romanticism.[75] Moreover, as Frederick Beiser, a scholar who has devoted considerable effort to clarifying the 'ambivalent and complex' relationship between early Romanticism and *Aufklärung*, has affirmed, although 'in some crucial respects, the early romantics did react against the legacy of the Enlightenment . . . in other important respects, the early romantics continued with, and indeed radicalized, the legacy of the Enlightenment'.[76] Ernst

---

[73] Müller, *Die Aufklärung*, 11.

[74] Lawrence Klein claims that postmodernism has taken a similar step. Despite its rejection of meta-narratives, it has tended to foster its own grand narrative, as is obvious in the uniform and simplistic way in which it presents the Enlightenment, in order to position itself as its opposite. Contrary to this approach, Klein calls for the adoption of a position more in accord with the postmodernist spirit, emphasizing precisely the *variety* that existed within the Enlightenment (Klein, 'Enlightenment as Conversation'). Postmodernism's most eloquent argument against meta-narratives may be found in Lyotard, *The Post-Modern Condition*.

[75] A good example is provided by Fania Oz-Salzberger in the concept of 'sentiment', which, as she shows, coexisted well with that of 'reason' in 18th-century culture: Oz-Salzberger, 'From Desperate Lover to Political Economist' (Heb.).

[76] Beiser, *The Romantic Imperative*, 45, 4. According to Beiser, the early Romantics 'never lost their beliefs in the need for and value of self-restraint, criticism, and systematicity. They continued to believe in the desirability of *Bildung*, the possibility of progress, the perfectibility of the human race, and even the creation of the Kingdom of God on earth' (ibid. 4).

Behler, another leading scholar in the field, has shown that in their early works (from around 1800) intellectuals such as the brothers Friedrich and August Schlegel, Novalis, and others, considered the founders of German Romanticism, developed and expanded themes that occupied the Enlightenment, and that a real rupture with and clear opposition to the Enlightenment emerged only later.[77]

In fact, when discussing the continuity and overlap between Romanticism and Enlightenment, as well as Romanticism's own position towards the Enlightenment, it is crucial to distinguish between different phases of Romanticism.[78] It then becomes clear that Romanticism as a whole did not reject the Enlightenment as a whole, but rather went through different periods and significant transformations throughout its course, changing its stance towards the Enlightenment in the process. Initially ambivalent, Romanticism later became more hostile towards the earlier movement; however, to project that latter position, embraced by some of the exponents of late Romanticism, on to early Romantics is to commit an error of anachronism in judging all of Romanticism on the basis of its later, more conservative, phase.[79]

If continuity and overlap between the two movements may be found among the most prominent representatives of early Romanticism, the same is true to an even greater extent of the world-view and values of other contemporaries. This recognition is relevant to the case of the Jewish women discussed in this book. Living at a time when Enlightenment was losing its dominance in contemporary culture, and imbued as they were with the latest cultural developments, they undoubtedly engaged with Romanticism, embracing some aspects of its earlier world-view and rejecting others. They also associated with some of the foremost representatives of this movement in its early stages. Yet enlightened ideas remained central to them—which is not surprising, since the Enlightenment 'was still the reigning ideology in late eighteenth-century Berlin'.[80] It is their proximity to the cultural world of the Enlightenment which will be emphasized in this study, as a counterweight to the more common insistence on their affiliation with Romanticism.

---

[77] Behler, 'Le Premier Romantisme'.

[78] Another study that emphasizes the need to differentiate between the various phases of Romanticism, besides those by Beiser and Behler mentioned above, is Schmidt, 'From Early to Late Romanticism'.   [79] Beiser, *The Romantic Imperative*, 43–55.

[80] Ibid. 45. Ursula Isselstein characterizes Rahel Levin as a 'humanist Enlightenment thinker in a Romantic age' (Isselstein, *Der Text aus meinem beleidigten Herzen*, 9).

BEYOND THE CONFINES OF THE SALONS

Just as I suggest reconsidering the relationship of these Jewish women to Romanticism, I also propose to uncouple their names from another context with which they have been traditionally tied: the salons. From the nineteenth century up to the present day, the names of women such as Rahel Levin and Henriette Herz have been invariably linked with the social-cultural gatherings held at Jewish homes in Berlin in the last decades of the eighteenth century and the first years of the nineteenth, and they have been discussed almost exclusively in this context—again, in close connection with Romanticism, which was perceived as favourable to the emergence of this semi-formal, female-led institution. The reason for reviewing this connection is not to suggest that the description of these women as *salonnières* is false, or that they were not engaged in the sort of activity implied by the term 'salon' (although the precise nature of these events also needs to be reviewed, as I shall show in Chapter 5). Rather, the main thrust here is against the use of the salon as the sole framework within which to understand the lives and experiences of these women. Releasing the women from their exclusive role as *salonnières* opens up new avenues for interpreting the sources they left and offers the possibility of focusing on important aspects of their lives and activities that have hitherto been accorded less attention.

Reliance on the salons as the framework for discussion of the women considered here is conspicuous in Jewish historiography. Discussion of their assimilation and marriage outside Judaism—the themes of their lives that most concerned Jewish historians from the nineteenth century onwards—has often accorded the salons a central role in these processes.[81] The attitude of Jewish scholars towards the institution of the salon has been ambivalent. On the one hand, many historians have seen the prominence of Jewish women as hostesses who received non-Jewish aristocrats and diplomats, intellectuals and artists in their homes as a significant aspect of a pro-emancipatory historical narrative, showing that the Jews were able to integrate into German society. On the other hand, Jewish historians concerned about the fate of the Jewish people in the light of the assimilatory process under way during

---

[81] Besides Graetz and Dubnow, mentioned above, see e.g. Katz, *Tradition and Crisis*, 222–3; Graupe, *The Rise of Modern Judaism*, 123–36, esp. p. 134 ff.; Hertz, *Jewish High Society*; Lowenstein, *The Berlin Jewish Community*. Lowenstein emphasizes, however, that 'cross-religious love affairs' were by no means rare in the Berlin Jewish community at the time, and that these occurred outside the salons as well: p. 104. The most famous figures among this female group were discussed by Kayserling in his book on Jewish women throughout history, *Die jüdischen Frauen in der Geschichte, Literatur und Kunst*, under the topic 'Die Berliner Salons' ('The Berlin Salons', pp. 182–219).

the nineteenth century looked askance at the salons for bringing Jewish women and non-Jewish men together. Seeing the activity of Jewish women in the salons as the source of their assimilation, conversion, and marriage to non-Jews, they described these institutions pejoratively as places of 'social amusement for its own sake' that served as an 'assimilatory social framework' and 'a way station in the transition to Christianity',[82] perceived by the visitors—if not by the hostesses—as offering no more than an occasional and marginal adventure beyond the fixed borders of society.[83]

The salon remains central to explanations of the lives of this group of Jewish women to this day. For example, it provides the focus in one of the most influential books of our times on the topic, *Jewish High Society in Old Regime Berlin*, first published more than two decades ago and reprinted in 2005. In her remarkable account, historian Deborah Hertz examines the circumstances that led a group of about twenty Jewish women within the economic elite of Berlin at the end of the eighteenth century to deviate from the traditional image of the Jewish woman, ideally devoted to the values of the Jewish religion, the home, and the family, so far as to opt instead for a life of extreme assimilation, in many cases in a new marital relationship with a non-Jewish partner. To explain these choices, Hertz returns to their activities at the salons, which she perceives to a large extent as 'a courtship arena for misalliances' and a 'marketplace' for meeting new partners.[84] With the temptations of conversion and marriage to German aristocrats inherent in them, Hertz suggests, the mixed salons offered women the possibility of rebelling against the traditional system of arranged marriage and setting themselves free from relationships forced upon them in their youth by their parents, often contrary to their own wishes. In addition, the advantageous matrimonial opportunities on offer at the mixed salons held out to these women the chance of rising on the social ladder, which according to Hertz was their greatest hope.[85] In her eyes, marriage was the only route to social advancement open to women in the

---

[82] Katz, *Tradition and Crisis*, 223.   [83] Katz, *Out of the Ghetto*, 56.

[84] Hertz, *Jewish High Society*, 207. In addition to this book, see Hertz's numerous essays on the subject, including 'Intermarriage in the Berlin Salons', 'Seductive Conversion in Berlin', and 'Emancipation through Intermarriage?'. See also her latest book, *How Jews Became Germans*.

[85] The claim that women established salons mainly in order to achieve social prominence has been strongly criticized by the scholar of the Enlightenment Dena Goodman. Referring to the French salons in the 18th century, Goodman wrote: 'Why did women form salons? Not, I think, because they sought fame and power through their association with brilliant and powerful men. This is the sort of explanation that assumes the centrality of men in understanding the actions of women . . . Rather than social climbers, the salonnières of the Enlightenment must be viewed as intelligent, self-educated, and educating women who reshaped the social forms of their day to their own social, intellectual, and educational needs' (Goodman, 'Enlightenment Salons', 332–3). See also ead., *The Republic of Letters*.

eighteenth century,[86] and accordingly many Jewish women made the most of the opportunities offered by contacts established at the salons.

Hertz's depiction refines the image proposed by previous scholars, who presented the *salonnières* as 'talented but sinful Jewish women', 'misled by [the] seductive influences' of Christians of rank who gathered around them, and the salon itself as a 'Midianite tent'.[87] But at the same time it maintains the bond established by the first modern Jewish historians, linking every discussion of these women with the salons and with the romantic relations said to have been developed under the cover of this institution. The present study proposes to sever this bond and turn the spotlight away from the salons as the single central practice in which these Jewish women were involved (without, however, totally disregarding them or rejecting their significance), directing it instead towards various other cultural and social activities that played key roles in their lives and in their modernization, in particular letter-writing, reading, publishing, and visiting the spas (the subjects, respectively, of Chapters 1–4).[88] These practices have hitherto been given hardly any emphasis in Jewish historiography on this group of women, despite the remarkable fact that they figure prominently in their own writings. Also, themes such as marriage, divorce, and conversion are discussed here without relying on the salons as the sole or central explanation for these processes. The women's controversial decisions concerning marriage and divorce are examined in the light of ideas and values prevalent at the end of the eighteenth century, such as liberty, equality, independence, natural rights, and the pursuit of happiness (a topic considered in more detail in Chapter 6). Their conversion to Christianity is depicted as part of a protracted process of acculturation that spanned years, even decades. The act of conversion is seen not as a moment of crisis, a leap that divided the individual's life into two distinct periods, but as a step in a gradual process of assimilation which began long before the formal rite of baptism, and in which the salons and the social encounters constituted only one among its many elements. (For more on this see Chapter 7.)

A point that must be stressed in this context concerns the place of these women in Jewish historiography as a result of the change suggested. The persistent focus on salons encloses the story of these women as that of an exceptional (though prominent and significant) chapter in Jewish history, an anomalous case that barely contributes to the understanding of the history of most Jews, and of Jewish women in particular—the phenomenon

---

[86] Hertz, *Jewish High Society*, 211.   [87] Graetz, *History of the Jews*, v. 425, 413, 422.
[88] Socializing in private homes will also be considered, although it will be presented in a different light from that usual in discussions of the salons. See Ch. 5.

of the salons being considered alien to most Jews, certainly at the time. Relinquishing the use of this institution as the overall explanation for all the phenomena in which these women were involved, as proposed here, helps integrate these women into the history of the Jews, and more specifically into the history of Jewish women. As this study shows, a discussion of various aspects of these women's lives formerly disregarded because of the intensive and almost exclusive focus on the salon helps shed light on wider acculturation and secularization trends affecting both them and other modernizing Jewish women in different historical settings. As we shall see, these activities have a great deal to tell us about the deeds and aspirations not only of these but also of other Jewish women in the modern period; about their encounter with modernity, and more specifically about the various ways in which they could participate actively and consciously as cultivated members of the emerging public.

LISTENING TO WOMEN'S VOICES

This shift in perspective is closely connected with an important choice concerning the historical sources used for this study. Special attention is paid to the voices of women, emphasizing a close reading of the women's own writings. First and foremost among the latter are the numerous epistolary relationships these women maintained, parts of which have survived to the present, constituting an extraordinary treasure trove in the history of Jewish women, where personal sources are hard to find. The literary texts they created, such as memoirs, books, essays, and even poems, also contain fascinating information. This study takes advantage of the rare opportunity to listen to women's voices from the past, as preserved in the numerous sources they left behind. It places these sources at the centre of its research, approaching them from a new perspective, with a new set of questions. As a result, a picture of these women is revealed that differs significantly from the image of them that has become widely established.

The importance accorded here to a direct reading of these texts is worth emphasizing, as it makes this study very different from that of Deborah Hertz on the salons, which asks a different type of question and has recourse for the most part to a different kind of documentation. Seeking to discover the reasons for the rise and fall of the Berlin Jewish salons and to understand the role of this institution in the lives of the Jewish hostesses through the prism of social history, Deborah Hertz favoured mainly official records and secondary sources to help her chart salon society and draw patterns of social mobility based on statistical information and a demographic analysis of the Berlin intelligentsia at that time,[89] while giving very little emphasis to the voices of the women themselves (although it must be stressed that Hertz made an important contribution to the dissemination of exactly those personal sources by publishing the correspondence between Rahel Levin and her Jewish friend Rebecca Salomon).[90]

The present study, by listening closely to the words of these women as set down in the texts they left behind, joins a salient trend among scholars in the field of German studies. In books and essays published in Europe and the United States from the 1980s onwards scholars have investigated the lives and activities of some of the most prominent figures discussed in this study, paying particular attention to their own writings. By this means, and in particular through close examination of the numerous manuscripts deposited in various European archives, notably the 'Varnhagen collection' rediscovered in Kraków (on this archive see Chapter 1 below), they have made new discoveries about the social and cultural activity of these women and the context in which their lives evolved. Examples of this work are the illuminating publications by Barbara Hahn and Ursula Isselstein, many of which deal with Rahel Levin,[91] and the updated and balanced intellectual biography of the same Rahel Levin written by Heidi Thomann Tewarson, based on a meticulous study of her letters.[92] These and other studies of Levin and similar historical figures all embody the penetrating insights and new assessments of more or less well-known historical figures that derive from a close reading of the personal sources, coupled with the use of tools from cultural and gender studies.

There remain, however, important differences between the work of these scholars and the present study. These include the attention paid by the

[89] It is worth noting her use of the *Judenkartei*, a record of Jewish conversions to Protestantism in Berlin collected in the Nazi era, to examine patterns of conversion in this city emerging from the statistical data derived from this unique source. On the other hand, however, her chapter on conversion and intermarriage significantly makes no use of the women's personal sources to examine these phenomena—except for a cursory mention of Henriette Herz's memoirs as edited and amended by Julius Fürst in one of the footnotes (Hertz, *Jewish High Society*, 208 n. 5).

[90] *Briefe an eine Freundin*, ed. Hertz.

[91] Isselstein has published extensively on Rahel Levin and her family: *Der Text aus meinem beleidigten Herzen. Studien zu Rahel Levin Varnhagen*; 'Emanzipation wovon und wofür?'; and 'Die Titel der Dinge sind das Fürchterlichste! Rahel Levins "Erster Salon"'. Hahn's bibliography is extensive and covers other Jewish women as well. Her studies include *'Antworten Sie mir!' Rahel Levin Varnhagens Briefwechsel*; *Unter falschem Namen*; '"Geliebtester Schriftsteller". Esther Gads Korrespondenz mit Jean Paul'; and *The Jewess Pallas Athena*. See also the collection of essays co-edited by Hahn and Isselstein, *Rahel Levin Varnhagen. Die Wiederentdeckung einer Schriftstellerin*.

[92] Thomann Tewarson, *Rahel Levin Varnhagen*. See also ead., 'German-Jewish Identity'; and 'Jüdinsein um 1800', focused on 'the four best known Jewish women—Dorothea Schlegel [i.e. Mendelssohn], Henriette Herz, Rahel Levin and Henriette Mendelssohn' (p. 47).

present book to a considerable number of women and not to just one or a few individuals—so that, rather than being dominated (as most such studies have been) by an imposing figure (usually that of Rahel Levin), it presents the reader with a collective picture of a group of modernizing Jewish women rather than with the personal biography of one significant woman. Another difference is that this study makes a point of placing the lives of enlightened Jewish women in the context of Jewish modernization and, more specifically, the modernization and secularization of Jewish women. To this end, it draws comparisons with Jewish women living in other periods and/or places and with contemporary Jewish men—maskilim as well as other Jewish intellectuals—using sources and secondary literature absent from the works of German scholars.

The focus within *Germanistik* on one or a few particular figures has not been without its advantages. On the contrary, in addition to offering a revised picture of some of the women studied here, it has yielded a most valuable contribution to research—the scholarly publication of new archival sources. A great deal of research has taken the form of exploring archives and collecting and publishing documents by or related to the particular historical figure under scrutiny that had not previously seen the light of day. Thus, for instance, Consolina Vigliero worked on the correspondence between Rahel Levin and her brother Ludwig Robert (who was born Liepmann Levin but became known as an author by this name); Birgit Anna Bosold deciphered and analysed the correspondence of Fradchen Liebmann;[93] and Silke Schlichtmann is currently collecting and copying the correspondence of Sara and Marianne Meyer and preparing a scholarly edition of their writings.[94] This collective effort has enriched and continues to enrich the reservoir of sources available to scholars today, and enables more comprehensive studies of larger groups of individuals, such as the present work.

The documents published in recent years join a large corpus of printed sources, mainly personal correspondence published since the nineteenth century, many of which have thereby been saved from loss, large numbers of the original letters having by now disappeared. These early publications have shortcomings that must be taken into account when using them as historical

---

[93] Levin Varnhagen, *Briefwechsel mit Ludwig Robert*; Bosold, 'Friederike Liman'. The edition of Rahel Levin's correspondence with her brother is part of a wider editiorial project headed by Barbara Hahn and Ursula Isselstein, which is bringing to light unpublished correspondence from the Varnhagen collection.

[94] The tentative title of the edition in progress, prepared in co-operation with Barbara Hahn, is *Schreibwechsel/Briefwechsel. Marianne von Eybenberg und Sara von Grotthuß: Texte und Korrespondenzen mit Johann Wolfgang von Goethe und anderen Freunden* (Göttingen, forthcoming).

sources. The difficulties derive mainly from the intervention of editors or publishers, who at times 'corrected' the language used by these women, deleted fragments from the original letters which seemed to them too private or trivial and therefore unsuitable for publication, or offered the reader a tendentious presentation of the letters.[95] Such caveats notwithstanding, these printed texts—used with care, as indeed all sources should be—constitute valuable historical resources.

A critical reading of both these and recently published sources, using a gender perspective and applying tools from cultural history, contributes to the examination of my central theme, namely the conflicts, the challenges, and the transformations experienced by the Jews, and more precisely by Jewish women, at the beginning of modernity. The comparisons made throughout this study between the women on whom it focuses and other groups, such as contemporary Jewish men (mainly maskilim), Jewish women living in other historical contexts, and contemporary non-Jewish women, will highlight both the unique characteristics in their modernization and the traits shared with these various groups, as well as the changes that took place in their lives and their ways of thinking. This comparative approach deliberately situates the subject in the context of today's discourse on women and gender in Jewish historiography, which is developing vigorously, and makes it possible to present the story of these women in a new light: not as a marginal and exceptional phenomenon in Jewish history, of little relevance to most Jewish women and the Jewish people at large, but as a part of processes that affected and transformed Jewish society at the beginning of modern times.

---

[95] One telling example is the presentation of part of Henriette Herz's correspondence, as illuminating the love life of Friedrich Schleiermacher, in Boenigk (ed.), *Schleiermacher und seine Lieben*: see Ch. 1 below, around n. 30. Some editions of the Jewish women's correspondence left out fragments of their letters. One such case is Ludwig Geiger's edition of Marianne and Sara Meyer's correspondence with Goethe. For example, in his note to an 1804 letter from Marianne, Geiger indicates that he has left out a fragment that contained news concerning the theatre and personal information (Geiger, 'Einundzwanzig Briefe', 114). In some cases, Geiger gives the content of omitted fragments or letters in his notes, in condensed form. Similarly, the editor of Henriette Herz's letters to August Twesten, one of her German friends, specifically indicates that he has omitted fragments of her letters, containing for instance 'a passage about Betty Meyer and her mother', i.e. Recha Mendelssohn, or 'outspoken notes on prominent personages': Heinrici (ed.), 'Briefe von Henriette Herz an August Twesten', 314, 310.

ONE

PRIVATE LETTERS
An Alternative Sphere for Cultural Discourse

IN MARCH 1793 Rahel Levin received an excited letter from her friend David Veit in the city of Gotha. The reason he was so thrilled was clear: carrying a letter of recommendation from the writer Karl Philipp Moritz,[1] and accompanied by his uncle, the Berlin banker Simon Veit, the Jewish medical student had been received very politely by the celebrated poet, writer, and playwright Johann Wolfgang von Goethe at his residence in Weimar. As the young Veit indicated in his letter to Levin, with whom he had established a close friendship in the years he had spent in the Prussian capital Berlin,[2] in the course of his journey he had also had audiences with other famous men of letters: 'I really saw them all, and engaged in quite extensive conversations with each one of them—Goethe, Wieland, Herder.'[3] Veit described in meticulous detail the short visits he had paid to these distinguished intellectuals and his impressions of each of them.[4] His correspondent—the eldest child of Levin Marcus, a wealthy banker and jewellery dealer, and his third wife, Chaie[5]—had no difficulty in recognizing the individuals he described, even

---

[1] Moritz, a German author, educator, and editor who lived in Berlin, had close friendships with leading Jewish maskilim, most notably Salomon Maimon. See also below, Ch. 2 n. 72.

[2] David Veit was born in Breslau, the city where his mother Bella Heymann's family lived, but in 1788 he moved to Berlin, the home town of his father Joseph Veit, a scion of one of the oldest Jewish families in the city (Zondek, 'Dr. Med. David Veit', 50).

[3] *Briefwechsel zwischen Rahel und David Veit*, i. 1. The writer and publisher Christoph Martin Wieland was one of the most influential figures of the German Enlightenment. Johann Gottfried von Herder, critic, philosopher, and theologian, had a profound influence on German thought.

[4] He accords the most thorough descriptions to Goethe and, to a lesser extent, Wieland. In contrast, his reticence concerning Herder is worth noting: 'If you know Herder from his writings, I must not tell you anything, and if you do not know him, I certainly must not tell you anything. Never before has a person complimented my prejudices as Herder did' (*Briefwechsel zwischen Rahel und David Veit*, i. 9).

[5] According to the records in the possession of Jacob Jacobson, the historian and archivist of the Berlin Jewish community, Levin Marcus had apparently divorced twice before marrying Rahel's mother (Jacobson, *Jüdische Trauungen in Berlin*, 113, 151).

though she had never met them face to face. Still only in her early twenties, she already displayed an impressive familiarity with the writings of these authors, to the point of being able to analyse their individual attributes.[6] Sharing the contents of the letter with members of her family and friends, including 'Mrs Veit'—Dorothea Mendelssohn, who was married to David Veit's uncle Simon, mentioned above—Rahel avidly read every word written by her friend about these luminaries of German culture, from his descriptions of their physique and dress to their utterances and their attitude towards their guests. Bitterly regretting that her woman's eyes were forbidden to enjoy these exciting sights and were expected to find satisfaction in 'Berlin's pavement' only, she asked him to go on sharing with her the experiences of his journey.[7]

Even in that first letter (of those preserved) from the many exchanged between Rahel Levin and David Veit, it is apparent that the initial impression of a man who sees, learns, knows, and transmits his knowledge to a woman who listens passively and receptively is an illusion. The rules of the game are clear from the beginning and indicate that there was no gender-based hierarchical relationship between the correspondents but rather a reciprocal connection, of which the actors themselves were well aware. Veit, who saw himself as a student of the art of writing and whose literary inclinations would in the course of time be reflected in the original texts and translations on literary and medical subjects that he eventually published,[8] put himself in the hands of his wise female friend, inviting her to evaluate his literary skills as deployed in his letter. Relying fully on her critical insight, he enquired: 'To what extent were you able to make sense of my description? How much of it do you believe? Should I continue in this way?'[9] For all David Veit's wanderings between German universities—his studies in Göttingen, Jena, and Halle, his contact with lecturers and writers, his close acquaintance with German culture—he was not the dominant partner in this epistolary relationship with his friend back in Berlin. Not only did Rahel Levin gain from her friend's knowledge, she nurtured him with her insights, her understanding, and her wisdom. As she wrote in her reply to this first surviving letter: 'I

---

[6] For example, Rahel wrote about Wieland, whom she had never met: 'I also like his patience to observe everything, it is so typical of him [*recht Wieland'sch*]'. *Briefwechsel zwischen Rahel und David Veit*, i. 13.   [7] Ibid. 13–14, 12.   [8] Zondek, 'Dr. Med. David Veit', 56 ff.

[9] *Briefwechsel zwischen Rahel und David Veit*, i. 7. Two months later, in October 1793, David Veit wrote a poem and sent it to Rahel Levin hoping to obtain her reaction. 'I really do not know its value myself', he confessed, asking for her evaluation (ibid. i. 24). In reply, Levin opened up a fruitful and critical discussion with him about the quality of the poem, its intentions, and the use of language, which spread over several letters.

certainly know something you would like to know. I *can* describe it *well* and will do so, I will gladly sacrifice the time to you.'[10]

The exchange of letters between these two young Jews, along with the hundreds of other missives written and received by Rahel Levin and women of her generation, keep alive for us the reciprocal relationships between these Jewish women and their correspondents of both sexes. As we shall see, the network of correspondence they sustained with many people in many cities in the German lands and even further afield constituted from their point of view a crucial means of participating in cultural discourse. Letters were an important channel through which these women could not only expand their horizons and acquire knowledge, but also demonstrate their intellectual abilities and participate in public discourse on literature, theatre, politics, and religion, among many other subjects. A study of their correspondence enables us to examine the involvement of these Jewish women in the contemporary world of culture—an involvement at times hidden from the public gaze and partly revealed in their epistles.

ON THE PRESERVATION OF LETTERS

Before analysing the role of personal correspondence as a vehicle for circulating ideas and opinions, something should be said about the collection and preservation of the letters that serve as the main source for this study. The correspondence between David Veit and Rahel Levin is just a fragment of the thousands of letters written and received by Levin which have survived to the present. The preservation of her voluminous correspondence, and that of other Jewish women, is an extraordinary phenomenon that deserves some comment. In pre-modern times, private letters, diaries, and similar documents were not usually preserved. The historian Cecil Roth seems to have been correct in assuming that people did not imagine the world would be interested in the content of letters and certainly did not believe that 'such trivialities were worth transmitting to posterity'.[11] Therefore, in most cases we have accident to thank for the survival of letters from these long-distant periods.[12]

---

[10] Ibid. i. 10.

[11] Roth (ed.), *Anglo-Jewish Letters*, p. xii. Before the modern period, isolated letters were sometimes preserved, not necessarily for their intrinsic value but in order to serve as models for letter-writing. See e.g. the 15th-century Spanish letter-writing manual, which includes letters written by Jews between 1303 and 1451, published in Beinart, 'A Fifteenth-Century Hebrew Formulary from Spain' (Heb.).

[12] Two cases exemplify rare episodes in which coincidental circumstances led to the preservation of private letters written by Jews in pre-modern times. One is the case of the Cairo Genizah—a

From the beginning of modern times, however, a new factor intervened. To be sure, chance still played a role in preserving letters; but it ceased to be the main factor responsible for saving these cultural treasures from loss. The act of preservation became less fortuitous and more often attributable to the concerns of the preserving society, with a decisive gender element which privileged the preservation of men's letters—especially famous men's letters—over women's. Those of the latter that were saved were for the most part related in some way to the lives of male intellectuals and statesmen and deemed to contribute to knowledge about these men's deeds and personalities. This explains, for instance, the preservation of letters sent by Maria Celeste to her father, Galileo Galilei; or those written by Abigail Adams, wife of the second US president and mother of the sixth.[13] Similar factors led to the survival of letters by some Jewish women: for example, those sent in the seventeenth century by Bella Perlhefter to the (Christian) German Hebraist Johann Christoph Wagenseil were found in his possession after his death;[14] and the correspondence of Adelheid Zunz, wife of the nineteenth-century German scholar of Judaism Leopold Zunz, was kept among his papers and her letters were published along with those of her husband—albeit partially, 'only insofar as they concern[ed] Zunz'.[15]

The preservation of Rahel Levin's letters as a self-contained collection was no accident, but it was certainly exceptional. Levin herself took care to

chamber in a synagogue in Fustat, Old Cairo, where writings that are beyond use (mainly in Hebrew script) were deposited between the 10th and 19th centuries: numerous letters were found here when scholarly study of the contents began at the end of the 19th century, including some written by traders and Jewish women. See Goitein (ed.), *Letters of Medieval Jewish Traders*; Kraemer, 'Women's Letters from the Cairo Genizah' (Heb.); Turniansky, 'A Correspondence in Yiddish from Jerusalem' (Heb.). Another unusual case is that of a packet of letters sent by Jews in Prague—men, women, and children—in 1619 to friends and relatives in Vienna. The letters, written hastily in a time of war, all on the same day and in the same place, were intercepted, never reaching their addressees: they ended up in the royal archives, where they were kept until their publication in 1911 (Landau and Wachstein, *Jüdische Privatbriefe aus dem Jahre 1619*).

[13] On Maria Celeste's correspondence, see Sobel, *Galileo's Daughter*. For that of Abigail Adams, see Gelles, *First Thoughts: Life and Letters of Abigail Adams*.

[14] In addition to two letters written by Bella Perlhefter to Wagenseil between 1674 and 1675—in Hebrew, an exceptional accomplishment by a Jewish woman at the time—two other letters that she sent to her husband, Issachar Behr Eybeschütz (Perlhefter), while serving as Hebrew instructor at Wagenseil's home were found in the estate of the Christian scholar. See Weinryb, 'Historisches und Kulturhistorisches aus Wagenseils hebräischem Briefwechsel', which also includes an additional letter to Wagenseil by another Jewish woman.

[15] *Leopold and Adelheid Zunz*, ed. Glatzer, p. viii. Some of the letters that Sheindel Pineles, daughter of the Galician maskil Joseph Perl, sent from Tarnopol to her maskilic friend Moses Inlander in Brody were also preserved, but this fact was unrelated to her family connections. See Shechter, *The Portrait of a Maskilic Woman* (Heb.), esp. p. 18.

store them diligently from an early stage in her epistolary career—an uncommon step at the time—frequently asking her correspondents to return her letters once read in order to preserve both sides of the exchange.[16] When she met the man who would eventually become her husband, Karl August Varnhagen, Levin recruited his help in organizing the great amount of material she had accumulated. In this way, the couple laid the foundations of the voluminous archive known as the 'Varnhagen collection'. Over the course of their married life Rahel even co-operated with Varnhagen in the preparations for the (partial) publication of her letters, so that he was able to release the first compilations immediately after her death.[17] Additional volumes prepared for publication by him were eventually seen into print by his niece Ludmilla Assing after his death;[18] they were followed by many other editions of her letters, which have continued to appear right up to the present.

Although the Varnhagen archive is based on the letters received and sent by Rahel Levin, it includes much more than these. The collection expanded after Rahel's death as it had during her married life, and the archive succeeded in gathering the literary legacy of a whole generation of women which otherwise would have certainly disappeared.[19] As not only a 'chronicler and archivist of his time',[20] but in equal measure as Rahel's admirer, Varnhagen collected for years, in an almost compulsive way, everything that had to do with his wife and her era, in order to preserve it for future generations. The thousands of letters and documents contained in this collection today constitute an inexhaustible source for learning about figures from the past, including many individuals who would otherwise remain anonymous.[21] Since the archive's rediscovery in the late 1970s at the Jagiellonian Library in Kraków,

---

[16] 'Rahel was the only one who already during her lifetime took care that her letters and those of her correspondents were gathered and saved carefully. It may be said that the idea of the Varnhagen collection came from her' (Hahn, 'Rahels Schriften II', 37). In her study of German women's epistolary writing, Lorely French found a German female author from the same period as Rahel Levin who took a similar approach to her correspondence, Helmina von Chézy, who was also 'very intrigued by the collection process' (French, *German Women as Letter Writers*, 98).

[17] In the year of her death, 1833, Varnhagen published in Berlin the first collection of letters under the title *Rahel. Ein Buch des Andenkens für ihre Freunde*. A year later he released yet another anthology, *Angelus Silesius und Saint-Martin, Auszüge (von Rahel)*, and in 1836 he saw into print the further collection *Galerie von Bildnissen aus Rahel's Umgang und Briefwechsel*.

[18] These included *Rahel und David Veit*, 2 vols. (Leipzig, 1861); *Briefwechsel zwischen Varnhagen und Rahel*, 6 vols. (Leipzig, 1874/5); *Aus Rahels Herzensleben. Briefe und Tagebuchblätter* (Leipzig, 1877).

[19] Hahn, '"Weiber verstehen alles à la lettre"', 22. [20] Isselstein, 'Rahels Schriften I', 18.

[21] As Barbara Hahn points out, another important archive which still needs to be investigated is the Brinckmann collection, legacy of the Swedish diplomat Karl Gustav von Brinckmann, who was a close friend of many of the enlightened Jewish women and also a compulsive collector of contemporary letters and documents (Hahn, *The Jewess Pallas Athena*, 43–4).

after being evacuated from the Prussian State Library in Berlin during the Second World War and believed lost,[22] its renewed study has brought to light new correspondences, significantly those of previously unknown Jewish women. One interesting exchange (albeit from a somewhat later period) found in the Varnhagen collection is that between Rahel de Castro, a Jewish woman from a Portuguese family who lived in Altona near Hamburg, and Varnhagen's two nieces—Ludmilla, mentioned above, and her sister Ottilie —whose father, also a Portuguese Jew, had converted to Christianity.[23] Another body of correspondence from the same archive, this time from the period discussed in the present study, consists of the letters of Fradchen Liebmann, a close friend and relative of Rahel Levin; these were transcribed and published several years ago,[24] significantly contributing to our understanding of the way of life of assimilating Jews in Berlin from a female perspective, as we shall see later.

Personal considerations also played a central role in determining the fate of some of their letters in quite a different way. While Rahel Levin consciously chose to keep and organize her letters, and her husband to work towards their preservation and publication, some of her friends equally deliberately decided to ensure their letters would not survive. Some destroyed an entire correspondence, usually out of fear that the letters might reach the wrong hands or become public knowledge. Thus Henriette Herz burned most of the letters in her possession.[25] Dorothea Mendelssohn destroyed considerable portions of her correspondence with Friedrich Schlegel and others, and in 1833, when Karl August Varnhagen wrote to her after Rahel's death to request the letters that his late wife had sent to her and to Schlegel, her second husband, Dorothea explained why she could not oblige:

It pains me not to be able to fulfil your request regarding the early letters of the dear deceased. Long ago, we [Dorothea and Friedrich Schlegel] made it our habit to destroy every letter that had been answered; this was an inevitable step, in light of our frequent change of whereabouts and domicile. Friedrich, of blessed memory, was bothered by the increasingly rampant piling up of older papers and correspondence; moreover, he quite detested the misuse rampant in our time of printed let-

---

[22] Hertz, 'The Varnhagen Collection is in Krakow'.

[23] The sisters Ottilie and Ludmilla Assing from Hamburg were the daughters of Rosa Maria, Varnhagen's sister, and David Assur (later Assing), a Portuguese Jew who converted at the time of marriage but remained connected with the Jewish community and with Judaism, as his daughters also seem to have done (Dick, 'Freundinnen. Rahel de Castro, Ludmilla Assing, Ottilie Assing'; ead., '"Wie Sie sicher durch Fräulein Rahel de Castro wissen . . ."').

[24] Bosold, 'Friederike Liman'. These letters were transcribed and analysed by Birgit Anna Bosold as part of her dissertation, and they are available online.

[25] Boenigk (ed.), *Schleiermacher und seine Lieben*, 1.

ters of people who had just passed away—(a feeling which I entirely shared with him). Therefore we decided not to expose all the letters, especially those from beloved persons, to the danger of being read by strangers for whose eyes they were not meant. Thus I witnessed the burning of a package with all of Rahel's epistles.[26]

Rahel's conscious efforts to save her correspondence were thus not the norm; but even those women who did decide to keep their letters could not be certain that later generations would be able to read them. The preservation of many of these letters was determined mainly by factors other than the writer's will, first and foremost—as already noted—whether she had any connection with famous men; and so was their publication, on which awareness of her very existence among later generations would largely depend.[27] Thus, for instance, the majority of Sara and Marianne Meyer's surviving letters—representing only a small fraction of their copious correspondence—were kept in the Goethe archive, along with those of a list of other women who gained immortality thanks to their relationship and correspondence with Goethe.[28] Even today the Meyer sisters are known almost exclusively through fragments of their epistolary exchange with Goethe, published more than a hundred years ago in the *Goethe Jahrbuch* ('Goethe Yearbook') and in the collection of letters *Goethe und Österreich* ('Goethe and Austria', which contains only Marianne's epistles), emphasizing in both cases their position in relation to this famous author and to German culture.[29] In a similar way, the proximity of Henriette Herz to prominent male figures ensured the preservation and publication of at least a small part of her correspondence. Her letters to the Jewish (turned Christian) publicist Ludwig Börne and to the German philologist Immanuel Bekker were deposited in their personal archives and printed in 1905 and 1972

---

[26] *Briefe von und an Friedrich und Dorothea Schlegel*, ed. Behler, vol. xxiii, pp. xxvii–xxviii. As Bosold points out, acts of 'auto da fé' (i.e. burning) of old letters were not at all exceptional at the time. There are testimonies to Goethe, for example, destroying whole batches of correspondence, especially from his early years (Bosold, 'Friederike Liman', 251).

[27] As Lorely French notes, 'women's letters have most often been published because they allow the scholar to disseminate views of the predominant male figures of the day ... women's letters are often published because of their contacts with renowned men. Rare, however, is the edition of a man's letters published because of his relationship to a famous woman' (French, *German Women as Letter Writers*, 31–2).

[28] Goethe and his time serve as the focus for many published works on the epistolary and literary activity of women writing between 1790 and 1830. See e.g. Helga Haberland and Wolfgang Pehnt (eds.), *Frauen der Goethezeit in Briefen, Dokumenten und Bildern. Von der Gottschedin bis zu Bettina von Arnim* (Stuttgart, 1960); Günter Jäcke (ed.), *Frauen der Goethezeit in ihren Briefen* (Berlin, 1964); Marie-Claire Hoock-Demarle, *La Femme au temps de Goethe* (Paris, 1987); Margaret C. Ives (ed.), *Women Writers of the Age of Goethe*, vols. i–ix (Lancaster, 1989–98). On this phenomenon, see French, *German Women as Letter Writers*, 32.

[29] Geiger (ed.), 'Einundzwanzig Briefe'; Sauer (ed.), *Goethe und Österreich*.

respectively. Another collection of her personal letters appeared in a book purportedly dealing—as stated in its title—with the intimate life of a close friend of hers, the famous Protestant theologian and philosopher Friedrich Daniel Ernst Schleiermacher.[30] The letters of Dorothea Mendelssohn, published in various editions since 1881, appeared in the 1980s within a critical edition of the writings of her second husband, Friedrich Schlegel, implicitly subordinating her presence to his.[31] And if a few of the letters written by her mother, Fromet Mendelssohn (née Gugenheim), and some of Fromet's female acquaintances (such as Rösel Meyer, Sara and Marianne's mother, and Sara Götting) were also preserved and made available to the public, it was on account of their connection with the outstanding figure of modern German Jewry, Moses Mendelssohn, and as an appendix illuminating the story of his life.[32] The value accorded to letters written by women connected with famous men was a mixed blessing: while such an association ensured the survival of certain female voices, the lack of it doomed many others to silence and oblivion.[33]

The personal letters that survived despite everything will help us acquaint ourselves with the enlightened Jewish women of the late eighteenth and early nineteenth centuries. These letters, as well as other sources they left, make it possible to approach them as 'active agent[s] of history',[34] one of the most pressing calls in gender historiography. By reading the sources from the point of view of the women's own experiences and not as chapters appended to the life stories of prominent men—by turning women into the subject of the story and placing them centre stage—it becomes possible to illuminate their image in such a way that it appears quite different from its usual representation.

---

[30] Boenigk (ed.), *Schleiermacher und seine Lieben*. The comments added by the editor in among the various letters, in order to complete the picture of the 'loves of Schleiermacher', reinforce the place of the letters in a clear male context.

[31] *Briefe von und an Friedrich und Dorothea Schlegel*, ed. Behler. Many of Dorothea Mendelssohn's letters were compiled and published in a previous collection from 1881: *Dorothea v. Schlegel und deren Söhne, Briefwechsel*, ed. Raich.

[32] Fromet Gugenheim, who lived in Hamburg before her marriage, maintained an intense correspondence with her fiancé Moses Mendelssohn in Berlin; but whereas a considerable number of letters by Moses Mendelssohn survived, only few of Fromet's did. See Mendelssohn, *Brautbriefe*. Letters written by Fromet, Rösel Meyer, and Sara Götting were printed in Mendelssohn, *Gesammelte Schriften. Jubiläumsausgabe*, vol. xix.

[33] It is obvious that the vast majority of letters written in the past—not only those of women—were doomed to oblivion. The purpose here is to criticize the androcentrism which until recently dominated all aspects of the preservation and publication of letters.

[34] Scott, 'Women's History', 18.

THE ERA OF LETTER-WRITING: PARTICIPATION IN EPISTOLARY CULTURE

It is a commonplace that personal letters constitute a valuable historical resource. They disclose a whole world of values, outlooks, concerns, feelings, fears, hesitations, events, interpersonal relations, and much more. Despite the difficulty inherent in trying to reconstruct the past on the basis of such intimate documents, by paying special attention to their particular nature and to the editorial intervention in their publication, and by using additional sources to help place them in the appropriate context, the historian may derive great scholarly benefit from them. The letters at issue here, however, have a significance that goes well beyond their usefulness as a source of information. As well as valuing them for their documentary function, it is imperative to examine attentively the act of corresponding itself, as an activity to which these women dedicated considerable time and effort.

In adopting letter-writing as a central practice in their lives, these women were joining a prevalent tendency among the educated classes in European countries, including the German lands. The exchange of letters in previous times is dwarfed in comparison to its dimensions and contents in the eighteenth century. Not for nothing was this called, among its many appellations, 'the century of the letter'.[35] The phenomenon of intensive letter-writing owed its expansion in part to the development and institutionalization of postal services, but no less crucial was the cultural context in which this practice evolved, which pertains also to the women discussed here.

The epistolary form was extremely widespread in eighteenth-century European literature, enabling writers of letters to draw inspiration from its use in various cultural products in formulating their own missives. The genre of the epistolary novel, for instance, educated generations of letter-writers. From Samuel Richardson in England through Jean-Jacques Rousseau in France to Goethe in Germany, renowned writers, through their fictive letters, provided inspiration to their devoted readers, many of whom eagerly appropriated this personal form of expression.[36] Collections of the private letters of famous personalities were published as popular books and further

---

[35] The cultural historian Georg Steinhausen made this assertion in *Geschichte des deutschen Briefes*, quoted in French, *German Women as Letter Writers*, 37. See also Schneiders (ed.), *Lexikon der Aufklärung*, 69; Wittmann, 'Das Jahrhundert des Briefes'.

[36] Another famous 18th-century author who favoured the epistolary genre was Montesquieu, whose renowned *Persian Letters* were published in 1721.

contributed to shaping the writing style of educated correspondents.[37] Exemplary letters published in moral weeklies (in most cases ethical texts presented in epistolary form), and readers' letters published in periodicals, also exposed readers of the eighteenth century to the epistolary form and both enabled and encouraged them to employ it. Commentators and intellectuals also favoured the personal epistle as a vehicle for the wider expression of their opinions and criticism, frequently preferring this lighter form of expression to that of the erudite essay in addressing the reading public.[38] In addition, from the mid-eighteenth century the German-speaking readership had at its disposal new manuals for letter-writing (*Briefsteller*)—notably Christian Fürchtegott Gellert's popular 1751 volume of model letters entitled *Briefe, nebst einer Praktischen Abhandlung von dem guten Geschmacke in Briefen* ('Letters, along with a Practical Treatise on Good Taste in Letters'), which was very influential in eradicating the ceremonial style and promoting a more natural epistolary form.

The widespread use of the epistolary medium penetrated the intellectual activity of modern Jews. From the second half of the eighteenth century Jewish maskilim used the form of the letter to transmit their innovative messages. This is clearly seen as early as the 1750s, in the first attempt to establish a Hebrew weekly—*Kohelet musar* ('The Preacher of Morals'). This short-lived publication was presented partly as an exchange of letters, emulating the moralistic weeklies then popular in Germany and across Europe, by which it was inspired.[39] In *Hame'asef* ('The Gatherer')—the first fully fledged modern Hebrew periodical, established by maskilim from Königsberg and Berlin in 1783 and one of the leading projects of the Berlin Haskalah[40]—readers from maskilic circles in different places in Europe contributed to public debate through their letters to the editor, thus joining the nascent Jewish public sphere.[41] The maskilim also used the epistolary form in their

---

[37] From the first half of the 18th century collections of letters had been translated from English and French into German: among them were those of several renowned French women, notably Madame de Sévigné.

[38] Nörtemann, 'Brieftheoretische Konzepte im 18. Jahrhundert', 220–1; Schwarz, '"Brieftheorie" in der Romantik', 225–6.   [39] Gilon, *Mendelssohn's 'Kohelet musar'* (Heb.).

[40] On *Hame'asef*, see Feiner, *The Jewish Enlightenment*; Tsamriyon, *Hame'asef* (Heb.); Pelli, *The Gate to Haskalah* (Heb.). Pelli claims that even though *Kohelet musar* preceded the publication of *Hame'asef* by some thirty years, the latter still deserves to be called 'the first modern Hebrew periodical', for *Kohelet musar* was a short-lived enterprise (only two issues were printed), and thus to be seen as a pioneering but ephemeral phenomenon, as opposed to the regular and sustained publication of *Hame'asef* (ibid. 17).

[41] The seven volumes of *Hame'asef* were published in Königsberg, Berlin, and Breslau consecutively between 1783 and 1797.

critical prose. In the fictional *Igerot meshulam ben uriyah ha'eshtemo'i* ('Letters of Meshulam the Son of Uriah the Eshtemoi') published in 1789–90, Isaac Euchel imitated the epistolary style common in European literature when setting out to impart moral precepts to a Jewish readership;[42] and the German epistles written years earlier by Moses Mendelssohn on issues of European culture, as part of a common literary project with his friends Gotthold Ephraim Lessing and Friedrich Nicolai called *Briefe, die neueste Litteratur betreffend* ('Letters Concerning the Newest Literature'), were simply essays formulated in an ostensibly personal form, addressed to an unknown recipient.[43]

Women also employed the epistolary form in order to participate in the intellectual activity of the Haskalah, but this happened only in a later period. In the nineteenth century, especially in the latter half, Jewish women actively sought to join the Haskalah movement by various means, including writing letters in Hebrew to editors of Hebrew journals and to maskilic thinkers and writers, discussing, along with private matters, issues of public and cultural concern for the Jews.[44] In addition to the letters from women that were occasionally published in journals of the Haskalah, numerous others were preserved in manuscript form in the archives of the addressees, and some of these are now being published.[45] The medium of the letter served Jewish women, mainly in eastern Europe and especially from the 1870s onwards, as an ideal instrument with which to penetrate the Hebrew Haskalah.[46] In the words of the literary scholar Tova Cohen, the epistolary genre constituted 'the entrance gate of the Hebrew maskilot to the male club of the Haskalah', and the letters sent by women to contemporary maskilim were 'a conscious

---

[42] See Yehuda Friedlander's discussion of this text and its use of the epistolary structure: Friedlander, *Studies in Hebrew Satire* (Heb.), i. 19–39. Cf. Pelli, 'The Beginning of the Epistolary Genre'.

[43] The *Briefe* were published weekly (though not continuously) and anonymously between 1759 and 1765. Mendelssohn's letters now appear in the new edition of his writings: Mendelssohn, *Gesammelte Schriften. Jubiläumsausgabe*, vol. v, pt. 1. On these letters as a critical enterprise and on Mendelssohn's contribution to this project, see the introduction by Eva J. Engel: ibid., pp. ix–lxxxiii.

[44] Cohen, 'From the Private Sphere to the Public Sphere' (Heb.); Cohen and Feiner (eds.), *Voice of a Hebrew Maiden* (Heb.), 47–61. In English, see Cohen, 'Maskilot, Nineteenth Century'.

[45] See e.g. *The Poet's Friend* (Heb.), ed. Werses; Cohen and Feiner (eds.), *Voice of a Hebrew Maiden* (Heb.).

[46] An exceptional case of a maskilah (a Jewish woman committed to the Haskalah) who lived not in eastern Europe but in Italy and was involved in literary work somewhat earlier is that of Rahel Morpurgo, née Luzzatto, a poet from Trieste who impressed the reading public with her Hebrew poems. Her letters to her cousin, the scholar and poet Samuel David Luzzatto (Shadal), and to Mendel Stern, the editor of the Hebrew journal *Kokhevei yitshak*, were printed in that periodical in the middle of the 19th century.

effort to be included in the maskilic "network" and the maskilic cultural world'.[47] Letters written by women in Yiddish also served as a means of intervening in maskilic discourse and contributing to public debate, as demonstrated by the missives they sent to the editorial of *Kol mevaser*, a Yiddish periodical with clear maskilic tendencies, which first appeared in Odessa in 1862.[48]

Decades before these letters were sent, and prior to the appearance of the 'Hebrew maskilot'[49]—the phenomenon of letter-writing reached an extraordinary level among enlightened Jewish women—though, significantly, not as part of an effort to join a specifically Jewish discourse. Letter-writing was one of the main and most valued occupations of intellectual Jewish women in late eighteenth-century Berlin—as witnessed most tangibly by the enormous numbers of letters some of them wrote. Those that survived, of course, are only a portion of the number written; and, extrapolating from the considerable quantities of those that have survived, and on the basis of contemporary testimony, it may be inferred that very many other letters disappeared. Besides the quantitative evidence, the importance of this activity for the letter-writers emerges from the content of the letters themselves: specific comments refer to the great amount of time devoted to it (certainly at particular periods of their lives); reflections on the act of letter-writing indicate that this was not seen simply as a neutral and obvious means of communication, but was considered by many of the correspondents, women and men, as an event of considerable significance. However, while this constant correspondence was for some a source of pleasure, it should not be assumed that all the women actually enjoyed writing letters: Henriette Mendelssohn, for example, the youngest of Moses Mendelssohn's daughters, expressed her 'insuperable aversion' to this pursuit.[50] Nevertheless, even for her and certainly for other women, writing letters constituted a legitimate and important, indeed central, practice in their lives.

As letter-writers, these Jewish women belonged to a select group of educated females, a group that during the eighteenth century was expanding both within Germany and across Europe and becoming conspicuous in the

---

[47] Cohen, 'From the Private Sphere to the Public Sphere' (Heb.), 254, 253.

[48] Werses, 'Women's Voices in the Yiddish Weekly *Kol-mevaser*' (Heb.).

[49] The phrase is Tova Cohen's, used to describe those Jewish women in the second half of the 19th century who 'knew Hebrew well, read maskilic literature, wrote in Hebrew and tried to enter the Haskalah movement', as opposed to those who received a European education: Cohen, 'From the Private Sphere to the Public Sphere' (Heb.), 239.

[50] *Bankiers, Künstler und Gelehrte*, ed. Gilbert, 5. See also Henriette Mendelssohn's letter to Rahel Levin from 1800 in Varnhagen von Ense (ed.), *Galerie von Bildnissen*, i. 67–72.

culture of the period, despite its small size in relation to the general population.[51] Only women who were educated enough to write well, and affluent enough to enjoy the leisure to compose their letters and the economic means necessary to cover the substantial postage expenses, could conduct an intensive correspondence.[52] The Jewish women discussed here were both, belonging to a class for which neither material restrictions (money to pay for paper, ink, and postal services, and to fund their leisure time) nor cultural limitations (literacy, education, and verbal capacity) constituted a serious obstacle.

But these were simply the objective preconditions for engagement in an activity whose significance went far beyond its prevalence alone. What made the enlightened Jewish women of Berlin dedicate so much time to writing letters? What significance did the exchange of letters have for the correspondents? And what kind of content did they seek to pour into their missives? Two prominent threads in the answers to these questions that are central to how the letter was used in the eighteenth century will not be discussed separately in this study: these are, first, the use of the letter as a means to cultivate female friendship (which constituted a central component in the life of women, and most notably in the life of intellectual women) and, second, the function of the letter as an instrument for self-examination and for expressing the new bourgeois subjectivity.[53] Here I shall concentrate on another important role that the letter fulfilled in the lives of enlightened Jewish women: as a medium that decisively contributed to their integration into the educated public both in Germany and in Europe at large.

---

[51] Reinhard Nickisch, who studied the culture of letter-writing in Germany, indicates that in the 18th century this phenomenon was restricted to the narrow stratum of women from the educated middle class and from the aristocracy (Nickisch, 'Briefkultur', 390–1).

[52] According to Barbara Becker-Cantarino, in German lands at the end of the 18th century postal expenses were still high. A sender would frequently gather several letters, addressed to different family members and friends, and dispatch them in one delivery in order to reduce the expense. One piece of data provided by Becker-Cantarino indicates that the cost of sending a letter from Magdeburg to Berlin at the end of the century amounted to 2.5 *groschen*, the price of 3kg of bread or 1lb of meat (Becker-Cantarino, *Schriftstellerinnen der Romantik*, 162–3).

[53] The first aspect is discussed widely in French, *German Women as Letter Writers*, esp. pp. 75–111. The second aspect of the letter is discussed in Habermas, *The Structural Transformation of the Public Sphere*, 48–9; Wittmann, 'Das Jahrhundert des Briefes'. As Joan B. Landes points out, 'In letters, men and women explored their unique subjectivity and shared it intimately with a sympathetic Other' (Landes, *Women and the Public Sphere*, 62). A clear example of this aspect emerges in the discussion of the correspondence the enlightened Jewish women maintained with co-members of the Tugendbund (League of Virtue), a society they established in 1787. See Seibert, 'Der "Tugendbund"'. On the society itself, see Ch. 5 below.

THE LETTER AS A CULTURAL AGENT: THE PUBLICNESS OF THE PRIVATE LETTER

As noted at the outset of this chapter, the epistolary exchange between Rahel Levin and David Veit, like the correspondence of other enlightened Jewish women at this period, illustrates how letters enabled women to participate in contemporary culture as active agents and not merely as passive recipients of men's words. Indeed, as historians and literary critics alike have noted in recent years, the private letter served as a means by which women could take an active role not only in their personal relationships but in the public sphere. This approach to private letters, though, is not self-evident. If the letter was 'private', how could it be an instrument for entry into the public sphere? Moreover, it is widely assumed that the dominant ideology in Europe at this time deemed women unsuited to public discourse, and that as a result their sphere of activity was confined to the private and domestic, in accordance with the precepts of many contemporary bourgeois theoreticians. If this is so, how can we speak of women participating in the public sphere during this time at all—through their correspondence or in any other way?

As will become clear below, it makes sense to begin with the latter question. In former times scholars tended to assume more readily than today that women's lives conformed to the prevailing gender ideology. These days, scholars in the fields of history, literature, and culture compare the gender ideology prevalent in a certain period with the reality that emerges from historical sources, and find in many cases a marked disparity between the two. In order to write about the reality of women's lives, it is claimed, it is essential to 'take a fresh look at the sources',[54] letting go of a certain vision of the past—a vision usually determined by the normative discourse on women in the period under research, but also by gender perceptions considered universal by the investigator. In a now classic essay in gender historical research, Gisela Bock contributed to challenging a number of dichotomies that had guided historiography for a long time, based on traditional assumptions regarding the relations between the sexes.[55] One of the dichotomies that has been (and is still being) revised is the division between the public sphere (covering the political, economic, social, and cultural areas of activity) and the private sphere (the world of home, the family, and personal relations). According to the conventional view the private sphere, identified with women, and the public sphere, identified with men, were always two different and clearly separated areas of activity. In recent decades, however, women's studies have

---

[54] Davis and Farge, 'Women as Historical Actors', 2.   [55] Bock, 'Challenging Dichotomies'.

demonstrated that the relations between the two spheres were—and still are—complex and flexible, and cannot be reduced to a formula that presents them as binary opposites.[56] Rather, these relations vary across cultures, and need to be studied separately in context in order to find out the specific character of the gender division at a particular time and place, and to understand how women succeeded in taking part in social and cultural life in each period—at times despite ideals opposed to any such participation.[57]

One of the numerous studies inspired by these insights is a book by Ulrike Weckel that sheds new light on the gender division of bourgeois society in Germany in the late eighteenth century.[58] On the basis of a comprehensive examination of German periodicals edited and read by women, Weckel questioned the traditional premise of the sharp division between public and private spheres and the total exclusion of women from the public realm. While acknowledging the undeniable consequences for historical reality of contemporary gender discourse—a discourse which decried the 'public woman' and sought to establish a scientific basis for relegating women to the domestic sphere—she showed that women participated, as readers, writers, and even editors, in one of the central organs of the eighteenth-century public sphere: the periodical. Weckel attributes the failure of previous historical texts on this period to recognize this participation of women in the German public sphere to the negligence of scholars in failing to look for it, having taken the prescriptive words of eighteenth-century thinkers as an unquestionable truth. Thus, she explains, just three or four decades ago even feminist scholars accepted the 'separation of spheres' as a fact and adopted it as the key to explaining the evident asymmetry in the relations between the sexes and the male dominance which they saw throughout history, or as a

---

[56] The critical attitude towards the dichotomous view of two gendered spheres of activity has influenced the study of different periods in Jewish historiography. See e.g. Tal Ilan's findings regarding the participation of Jewish women from certain social ranks in some aspects of public life during the Second Temple period, despite rabbinic rulings intended to keep women away from the public domain (Ilan, 'A Window onto the Public Realm' (Heb.)). Shulamit Valler also dedicated her book *Women in Jewish Society in the Talmudic Period* (Heb.) to studying women's participation 'in social life, in the business and legal fields', i.e. in the public sphere of the time. Drawing on talmudic sources and paraphrasing the famous hymn 'Eshet ḥayil' ('Woman of Valour', Prov. 31, sung or recited in many Jewish homes on Friday evenings before the sabbath meal), she concludes that along with women who lived according to the accepted rule that 'the entire glory of the princess lies on the inside' (Ps. 45: 14), there were also 'women of valour' of a different type: those who 'plan for a field and buy it', those who 'plant a vineyard with the fruit of their hands', and also those who 'open their mouth in wisdom and the lesson of kindness is on their tongue' (Valler, *Women in Jewish Society in the Talmudic Period* (Heb.); quotations from pp. 11, 9).

[57] Klein, 'Gender and the Public/Private Distinction in the Eighteenth Century'; Vickery, 'Golden Age to Separate Spheres?'   [58] Weckel, *Zwischen Häuslichkeit und Öffentlichkeit*.

model that enabled them to investigate women in their typical environment (home and the family). Today, on the contrary, many are sceptical about the validity of this differentiation, seeing it as an artificial construct that did not exist in reality (or not, at least, in absolute form), and focus on the overlap between male and female participation in both spheres of activity.[59]

As part of this trend of questioning both the clear-cut division between the two spheres and women's confinement to the private sphere in Germany around 1800, the subject of letter-writing has received particular attention. Literary critics now posit the epistolary form as a 'serious' genre in the literary canon, claiming that academic study neglected it in the past, among other things because it was conceived as a typically female genre, and therefore a marginal one. They see the eighteenth-century transformation of the personal letter into a literary product, which could potentially enter the public domain through publication, as a sign of the blurred border between the public and the private spheres.[60] But it is not only its literary character that draws the letter closer to the public sphere: as a typical means of communication, the letter—even if it remained unpublished, as was commonly the case—fulfilled an important role in spreading representations and interpretations of the world, and in the transmission of news, ideas, and information.[61]

In the eighteenth century, the personal letter was not usually conceived of as an element of the public sphere. On the contrary, it was seen (as, indeed, it commonly is today) as embodying the intimacy of the private sphere, especially when written by a woman. It was precisely because of the allegedly private nature of the letter, as opposed to the public character of other writing genres, that pedagogues and ideologues in the second half of the eighteenth century encouraged women to write letters: they believed that in this way women could be provided with an outlet for personal expression without having to step into the public domain and without endangering the position of male authors through unwelcome and unnecessary competition.[62]

However, as the case of the enlightened Jewish women makes clear, personal letters cannot unequivocally be classified as belonging *exclusively* to the private sphere. First of all, an examination of the letters written and received by these women shows that this medium constituted a vehicle (an alternative

---

[59] Weckel, *Zwischen Häuslichkeit und Öffentlichkeit*, 8 ff.

[60] Nörtemann, 'Brieftheoretische Konzepte im 18. Jahrhundert'; see also introd. to Runge and Steinbrügge (eds.), *Die Frau im Dialog*, 7–11.

[61] On the central role of epistolary writing in the Republic of Letters that functioned through the French salons of the 18th century, see Goodman, *The Republic of Letters*, 136 ff.

[62] Nickisch, 'Briefkultur'. Epistolary writing is characterized by Nickisch as a '"private" literary genre' (p. 391).

one, if the institutions of the 'male' public sphere such as coffee-houses and learned societies are seen as 'normative') for the exchange of information and opinions on issues of public interest such as literature, theatre, art, society, religion, and even politics. Moreover, the exchanges that took place through these letters were not restricted to their writers and addressees, for in those days it was common to share with others the contents of letters that one sent and received. Thus the enlightened Jewish women passed entire letters or extracts from them to family members and friends, read them aloud in their homes or in broader social and intellectual circles, and sent copies to others who lived out of town. The 'private' character of the personal letter was thus considerably blurred. Finally, as noted above, certain letters 'officially' became part of the public sphere in print. In short, letters enabled enlightened women to participate in public discourse, express their own views and learn about the opinions of others, transmit and receive information about a variety of cultural products, and send and receive new reading materials—thus performing functions similar in principle to the interaction that took place in coffee-houses, literary societies, and other social frameworks from which women were frequently excluded because of their sex.

In view of these roles, the letter had a particular importance for educated women. It is true that men also wrote and read letters with similar ends in view, especially keeping in touch with distant interlocutors. In this respect, it seems that in the eighteenth century the personal letters written by men as well as women still fulfilled to a great extent the function of the 'erudite letter', a central component of the 'republic of letters' in seventeenth-century Europe. Before the existence of journals, the erudite letter served as a principal channel for transmitting information and discussing ideas, providing at times the only form of communication between intellectuals throughout Europe, many of whom never met one another in person, and this role continued also in the eighteenth century and beyond.[63] Nevertheless, there are substantial gender differences in the use and significance of letters in the period with which we are concerned here. In the first instance, the letter was of greater relative importance to women because they had so many fewer options than men for gaining access to institutionalized knowledge. Excluded from universities and learned societies, literate eighteenth-century women turned to the letter as a preferred medium of expression that opened doors on

---

[63] Kronick, 'The Commerce of Letters'. This was also true in the Jewish world: thus, for instance, 'the most important element in the development of the Galician Haskalah into a cohesive movement [at the beginning of the 19th century] was the extensive network of personal correspondence between its members' (Feiner, *Haskalah and History*, 76–7).

the world of culture and knowledge, becoming, among other things, a learning tool for those who aspired to expand their education.[64]

The letter was also important in relieving the isolation of many women. Very frequently—and especially within well-to-do families in the eighteenth and nineteenth centuries—women found themselves confined in the home or its immediate environs; and for these women the letter served to establish social and intellectual contact not only with distant friends and acquaintances but even with individuals they had never met in person. Through correspondence they could not only expand their contacts beyond the restricted geographical area in which they spent their lives but also bypass the gender limitations which made it difficult for them to step out of the domestic sphere.[65]

However, this factor is of only limited relevance to the case of enlightened Jewish women in Berlin around 1800. Most of these women were not confined in their homes for large parts of their lives. They had busy lives, including opportunities to receive guests at home, make reciprocal visits, and meet a variety of people on outings.[66] Also, they used to travel out of town (although not as freely or as frequently as men). Thus in their case we cannot speak of a complete isolation that could be relieved only with the help of letters, even though there were certainly moments of this kind.[67] For these women, the letter did not constitute the sole path to communication with the world and participation in cultural discourse: in the following chapters we shall see how they made use of other practices (such as visits to spas and social meetings). In fact, for them the letter performed a central but not an exclu-

---

[64] On this feature of the letter, see Niemeyer, 'Der Brief als weibliches Bildungsmedium'. Niemeyer claims that the exclusion of women from higher learning became more pronounced in the 18th century.

[65] Gender limitations placed obstacles even in the way of friendships between women, and the letter made it possible to overcome these obstacles and foster strong relationships with other women—relationships which played an important role in their lives. See French, *German Women as Letter Writers*, 78.

[66] It is interesting to compare the case of Rahel de Castro, who lived in Hamburg-Altona in the 19th century (see above, around n. 23). De Castro had close relations with distinguished women and men in the Jewish community—including Leopold and Adelheid Zunz, Gabriel Riesser, and Salomon and Johanna Steinheim; the house of her parents and brothers, where she lived as a spinster, was open to visitors and offered musical soirées attended by numerous guests as well as family members; and during occasional trips she made new acquaintances. However, she lived in a social environment significantly less open than the one in which the enlightened Jewish women lived (Dick, '"Wie Sie sicher durch Fräulein Rahel de Castro wissen..."').

[67] For example, after her marriage to Schlegel, Dorothea Mendelssohn often remained alone at home while her husband travelled throughout Europe, and her correspondence with her friends somewhat relieved her solitude (Becker-Cantarino, *Schriftstellerinnen der Romantik*, 164).

sive role, surrounded by other practices that mutually complemented and supported each other to expand and maintain their branched network of relationships.

EPISTOLARY DIALOGUES

One of the women who nurtured a web of relationships through (among other things) the exchange of letters was Marianne Meyer, also known as Frau von Eybenberg. Of all the correspondences she kept up with relatives and friends, male and female, Jews and non-Jews, the best-preserved is unsurprisingly that with Goethe. Goethe corresponded with many people, writers, relatives, and learned women among them. Thanks to a policy of preservation which accorded great value to the biographical documentation of authors who entered the literary canon, his epistolary exchanges nowadays fill numerous printed volumes, as well as the archives where manuscript collections of his letters are kept. The fate of Marianne's personal letters was quite different: she no doubt corresponded with other people besides Goethe, but most of her letters to them have disappeared. Despite the fact that Meyer's literary remnants, especially those so far published, were preserved in the context of this most illustrious author and therefore include mainly the things she wrote to and about him, it is possible to read them in such a way that not the man of letters but the enlightened woman stands in the spotlight. By diverting the focus from Goethe to Meyer, her experiences and her actions, it becomes possible to glean from their correspondence details about Marianne's world-view and self-perception, and about her active involvement in various aspects of contemporary culture. Even in her correspondence with so authoritative and prominent a figure in German culture as Goethe, her image emerges as that of an independent, active individual.[68]

As the daughter of Aaron and Rösel Meyer, but mainly as the granddaughter of Veitel Heine Ephraim, a wealthy Prussian businessman who, through the concession to mint Prussian coins, amassed a fortune and gained an influential position during the Seven Years War (1756–63),[69] Marianne Meyer belonged to the legendary elite of Berlin Jewry. Her family was exempted from

---

[68] This theme will be discussed here specifically but also appears in later chapters.

[69] *Münzjuden* or Jewish mint entrepreneurs played a vital role in Prussia in the 1750s and 1760s. See Stern, *The Court Jew*, 162–76. On the rapid rise of three Jewish families—Itzig, Ephraim, and Isaac-Fliess—in Berlin during the Seven Years War, see Lowenstein, *The Berlin Jewish Community*, 25–32; id., 'Jewish Upper Crust'. On the Ephraims, see Michaelis, 'The Ephraim Family'; id., 'The Ephraim Family and their Descendants' (on Marianne Meyer and her sister Sara, pp. 226–32).

most discriminatory laws against the Jews by virtue of the 'General Privilege' granted by the Prussian king Frederick the Great during the war to a handful of Jewish families who contributed to the state's economy and to the Prussian military effort.[70] The sudden conversion to Christianity of Marianne and her sister Sara in 1788, at the ages of 18 and 25 respectively, caused commotion within their family; under pressure from their parents, both sisters soon reverted to the Jewish religion. Their change of faith even attracted the intervention of Frederick William II, the new Prussian king, who turned to the heads of the Protestant Church in Berlin demanding an explanation for the quick baptism of the Meyer sisters without their adequate preparation—a patently irregular procedure. Their subsequent return to Christianity—it is hard to talk about a 'new conversion', since there was no second baptism[71]—took place at the end of the 1790s, when both sisters married Christian noblemen. Sara married the Livonian Baron Ferdinand Dietrich von Grotthuß, a Prussian officer, who after his retirement and impoverishment became postmaster in the city of Oranienburg, and took the name of Sophie von Grotthuß; Marianne, Prince Heinrich XIV von Reuss, the Austrian envoy in Berlin. However, since the latter alliance remained secret owing to the prince's rank—the couple even kept separate residences—Marianne retained her maiden name; only after his early death in 1799 was she granted, as a compromise, a title of nobility, being known from then on as Madame von Eybenberg.[72]

It was shortly before returning to Christianity, while officially Jewish, that Marianne (and Sara) Meyer met Goethe for the first time. The acquaintance began in the summer of 1795 during a visit to Carlsbad, a fashionable Bohemian spa. Here Marianne Meyer and Goethe spent happy hours in conversation, and after their return home—Goethe to Weimar and Meyer to Berlin—they began a long exchange of letters which strengthened their friendship and lasted until Marianne's premature death, nearly two decades

---

[70] The Ephraims were the second family to receive the 'General Privilege', which until 1790 was granted only to a few dozen Jews. See Lowenstein, 'Jewish Upper Crust', 185.

[71] Protocols found in the state archives in Berlin before the Second World War testified that their return to Christianity was not a simple issue at all. A dispute between the king (who required them to be baptized a second time) and the Church (which saw the repetition of this sacrament as illicit) was eventually resolved in favour of the Church. This case is discussed in Geiger, 'Vor hundert Jahren', 225–6, and more recently in Hahn, *The Jewess Pallas Athena*, 20–3.

[72] See the editor's notes in Geiger (ed.), 'Einundzwanzig Briefe', 96–7. Friedrich Schlegel, who frequented the circle of enlightened Jewish women in Berlin, wrote to his sister-in-law Caroline Schlegel in a letter of February 1799 concerning Marianne's secret wedding and her situation following her husband's death: 'Prince von Reuss passed away, prior to which he declared that he was (secretly) married to Marianne. I have not seen her yet, she is not well and almost sick. It is to be hoped that everything was done according to the law and thoroughly, and that she will be able to live comfortably': *Briefe von und an Friedrich und Dorothea Schlegel*, ed. Behler, xxiv. 231.

later, at the age of 42. From the very beginning of this correspondence—in Marianne's first missive to Goethe, dated 22 September 1795—there was an expectation that they would meet again, and indeed they did, both while on vacation at various watering places and in Goethe's home town of Weimar.[73] But the persistence of the relationship for so many years is mainly attributable to the letters they sent each other—from Berlin and Weimar, and also from Teplitz, Vienna, and the many other places each of them visited.[74]

Marianne Meyer seems to have had no hesitation in sharing the most personal affairs with Goethe in her letters to him. She described, among other things, her complex relationship with her mother—who, she said, 'had the best intention' of making her life miserable;[75] the emotional state of her sister Sara, who she feared was 'close to madness';[76] her dissatisfaction with her life in Berlin, despite the friendly company that surrounded her;[77] and her grief at the early death of her husband.[78] Like other contemporary admirers, Marianne undoubtedly believed that nobody understood the human soul better than Goethe and saw him as someone who could sympathize with her personal problems. Their friendship was also expressed through material tokens: the presents that made their way from Berlin to Weimar included delicacies such as chocolates and caviar as well as more practical items such as cups and scarves;[79] Goethe reciprocated with books, a ring, and other presents;[80] and they both sent each other locks of their own hair.[81] However,

---

[73] Their last encounter took place in Carlsbad in 1810.

[74] Part of this correspondence was published in 1893 by Ludwig Geiger in the journal he edited, the *Goethe Jahrbuch*: Geiger (ed.), 'Einundzwanzig Briefe'. Besides Marianne's twenty-one letters to Goethe and Goethe's two letters to Marianne in the main text, additional letters were quoted in the long notes that Geiger appended. Another part of this correspondence was published in Sauer (ed.), *Goethe und Österreich*. The complete list of the letters between Marianne Meyer and Goethe kept today at the Goethe archive in Weimar appears in the catalogued edition of Goethe's correspondence, available on the Internet: see *Briefe an Goethe*, ed. Hahn and Koltes <http://ora-web.weimar-klassik.de/swk-db/goeregest/index.html>. Although this edition presents only a summary of the content of the letters along with partial quotations from them, it is a reliable source and enables gaps in previous editions to be filled. A forthcoming new edition (see above, Introd. n. 94) will include the content of all known letters written by Marianne Meyer to Goethe and other correspondents—an important contribution to historical research.

[75] Geiger (ed.), 'Einundzwanzig Briefe', 28.

[76] Ibid. 29.

[77] Letter of 20 Mar. 1798, *Briefe an Goethe*, ed. Hahn and Koltes.

[78] Letter of 12 Apr. 1799, ibid.

[79] Geiger (ed.), 'Einundzwanzig Briefe', 110, 28. On 4 April 1803, for instance, Goethe wrote to Marianne: 'For several weeks now I have partaken of a desirable breakfast with your good chocolate, and I feel obliged to thank you' (Goethe, *Goethes Briefe*, ii. 447).

[80] Geiger (ed.), 'Einundzwanzig Briefe', 106, 110.

[81] See e.g. letter of 12 Oct. 1795, in *Briefe an Goethe*, ed. Hahn and Koltes; also Geiger (ed.), 'Einundzwanzig Briefe', 106.

parallel to all this runs a different kind of reciprocity—an intensive cultural exchange.

It is important to state clearly at the outset that there is no intention here to claim that there existed a 'symmetrical' relationship between these two correspondents, or that an intellectual dialogue took place between them of the kind that went on between Goethe and other men of letters, such as Friedrich Schiller, his friend and partner in several cultural enterprises. Marianne admired Goethe very much and was proud of her relationship with him; their correspondence was probably more significant to her than it was to him. It is clear who was the admired writer and who the admiring reader, and these roles are reflected in their correspondence.[82] Nevertheless, it is also clear from an examination of the letters emphasizing Marianne Meyer's point of view that the flow of knowledge and information was not all one way, and that there was a mutual nourishment from which the famous poet profited no less than the learned woman.[83]

One of the central and recurring subjects discussed in the letters between Marianne Meyer and Goethe was theatre. Marianne, like many other enlightened Jewish women, was particularly fond of this art form, on which she expressed well-informed opinions with confidence. Her letters deal extensively with the performing arts, with constant encouragement from Goethe, himself director of the Weimar Court Theatre, to share with him her insights as a critical spectator of the productions staged in her home town. Thus, for instance, she willingly agreed to formulate detailed evaluations of the performances given in Berlin by one of the most prominent figures in German theatre at the end of the eighteenth century and the beginning of the nineteenth, August Wilhelm Iffland.[84] Later, when she moved to Vienna upon the death of her husband—apparently as a precondition of receiving the allowance promised her as the widow of an Austrian prince—Marianne continued to send reports on theatrical topics, now focusing on the state of the theatre in the Habsburg capital, lamenting what she saw as the

---

[82] The position of the admiring reader was by no means exclusively reserved to women. As Silke Schlichtmann argues, letters showing veneration for an admired author were also penned by male readers—a point she exemplifies by analysing male letters to Goethe along with those by women. See Schlichtmann, 'Did Women Really Read Differently?', 205–6.

[83] More than a century ago, Ludwig Geiger wrote of the poet's letters to Sara and Marianne Meyer, perhaps somewhat overstating the case: 'In his letters, there is no trace of religious antagonism, nor arrogance anywhere from the side of the poet and man towards dabbling women; the great man posits himself as equal to the women and talks to them as he feels, like a friend' (Geiger, 'Die Juden und die deutsche Literatur', 327).

[84] Letter of 11 Mar. 1797, *Briefe an Goethe*, ed. Hahn and Koltes. Iffland, an actor, theatre director, and playwright, arrived at the national theatre of Berlin in 1796.

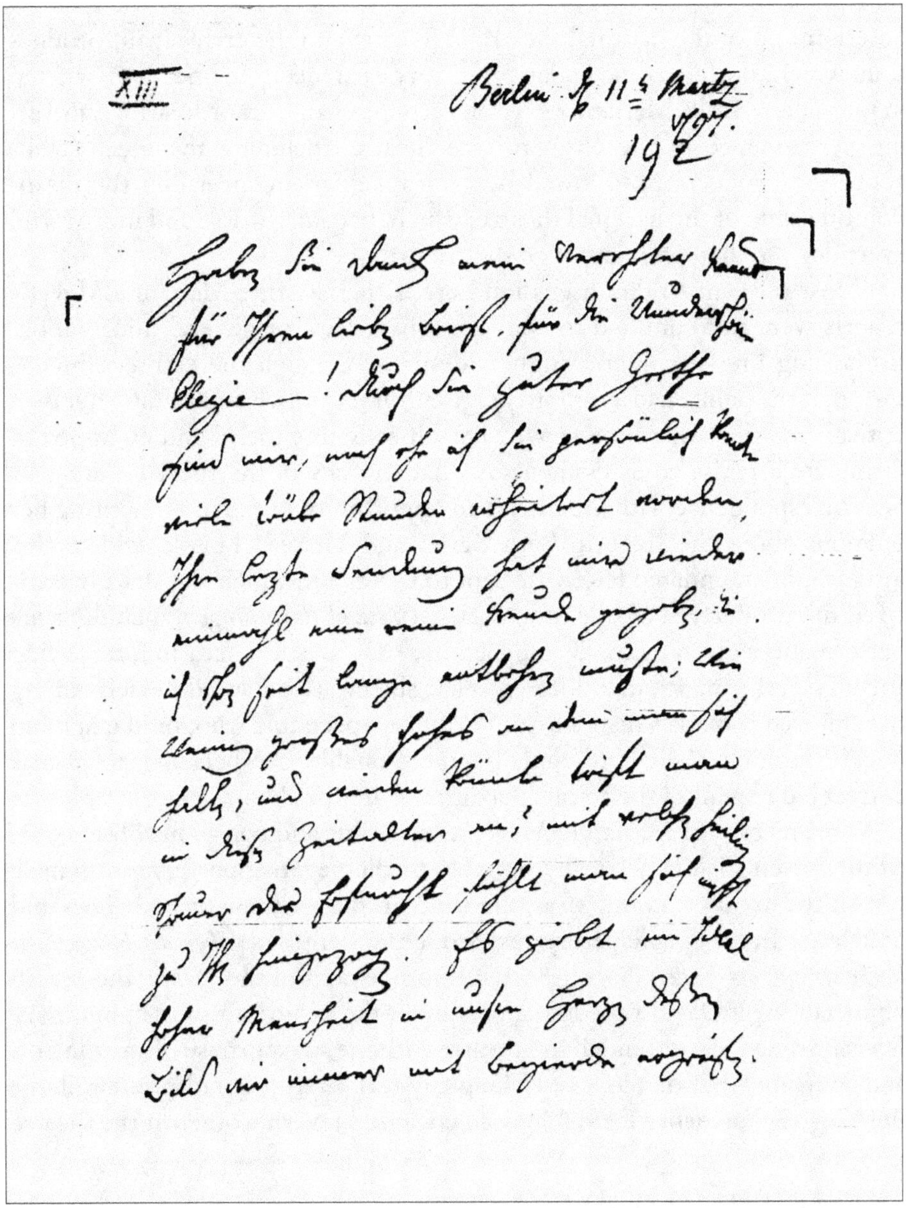
XIII

Berlin d. 11. Martz 1797.

19

PLATE 2. Manuscript of a letter sent by Marianne Meyer (1770–1812) to Goethe from Berlin, dated 11 March 1797

From the Goethe- und Schiller-Archiv, Weimar; photo: Klassik Stiftung Weimar

deterioration of the national theatre in Vienna and the extravagant productions which, she felt, could endanger its very existence.[85] In one letter, written in journalistic style, Marianne gave an account of an extraordinarily captivating performance in the city's private theatre, including technical details about the production, followed by critical remarks concerning the disappointing state of the national theatre, which 'becomes worse and more awful every day', so that 'one cannot go there any more'.[86]

Most relevant to the discussion here is the fact that Marianne Meyer's reports were not confined to conveying bare facts or general information. Embracing the view, increasingly widespread through the eighteenth century, that the public had a right to judge cultural works,[87] and valuing her own critical faculties, Marianne viewed herself as both entitled and equipped to formulate a reasoned assessment of what she saw in the theatres, and saw her correspondence with Goethe as an opportunity to express in writing her opinions about the stage in both Berlin and Vienna. This is evident, for instance, in an undated letter she sent to Goethe in which she sharply criticized the production of one of his plays, *Goetz of Berlichingen*, including the performances given by the leading actors.[88] On another occasion, reviewing Iffland's performance in a different play, she clearly counted herself among the cultured classes as distinct from ordinary spectators who, unlike her and notwithstanding their loud applause, were unable, she believed, to form a correct judgement of the actor's performing abilities.[89]

This picture of Marianne Meyer as a serious and conscious observer of cultural events is diametrically opposed to the negative portrayal of female Jewish theatregoers common at the time, in the writings of both Jews and non-Jews. In an emancipatory text from 1798 entitled *Über die bürgerliche Verbesserung der Juden* ('On the Civil Improvement of the Jews'), the Jewish physician Wolf Davidson complained about the behaviour of contemporary Jewish women who attended the theatre with the sole purpose of showing off and courting Christian lovers, lacking any real interest in culture. Similarly, the Christian preacher Daniel Jenisch criticized Jewish women at the theatre

---

[85] Geiger (ed.), 'Einundzwanzig Briefe', 38–43.   [86] Ibid. 42.

[87] Habermas discusses the process by which, beginning in the 18th century, works of art became products accessible in principle to everyone, leading to the formation of the public as a critical authority entitled to judge these cultural products and determine their significance (Habermas, *The Structural Transformation of the Public Sphere*, 36–43). Habermas cites the following statement from the mid-18th century to illuminate his point: 'A painting on exhibition is like a printed book seeing the day, a play performed on the stage—anyone has the right to judge it' (ibid. 40).

[88] Geiger (ed.), 'Einundzwanzig Briefe', 45–6.

[89] Letter of 29 Oct. 1796, *Briefe an Goethe*, ed. Hahn and Koltes.

who tried to make an impression by pretending to dominate contemporary cultural discourse while in fact merely making themselves ridiculous and exhibiting their ignorance.[90] As Marianne Meyer's letters and those of many of her Jewish friends show, this biased opinion did not correspond to reality—or at least, there was a significant number of cases in which such criticism was unfounded.

Goethe valued Marianne Meyer's judgements about literature as well as theatre, and urged her to share with him her impressions of what she had read. He was interested in the impact of his own works on his wider readership as well as in the reactions of his colleagues; and, like many of his contemporaries, he used his correspondence with women to gain insight into the responses of the reading public at large.[91] His friend and secretary Friedrich Wilhelm Riemer testified to Goethe's special esteem for the Jewish women among his female readership.[92] According to Riemer, since these women were a sensitive audience with a 'penetrating intellect' and 'peculiar wit',

Goethe was willing to present his recent poetical productions to them, either individually or in groups—for instance in Carlsbad ... for he could always be assured of a certain response, as I am able to testify from my own observation with regard to Frau von Eibenberg [sic], Frau von Gotthaus [sic], Frau von Eskeles and Fliess, and others.[93]

There is ample evidence that Goethe believed he had good reason occasionally to send some of his manuscripts to Marianne and Sara Meyer and

---

[90] Davidson, *Ueber die bürgerliche Verbesserung der Juden*, 82; Jenisch's criticism was voiced in *Berlin. Eine Satyre*, published in 1795 under the pen-name Gottschalk Necker. A fictive dialogue between two Jewish women at the theatre, with absurd distortions and incorrect use of Kantian terminology (e.g. 'cacagorische Ambaradif' instead of 'categorische Imperativ', i.e. categorical imperative), is quoted from Jenisch's text in Paul, 'Die Formierung des jüdischen Theaterpublikums', 74–5.

[91] Barbara Hahn has insisted on the centrality of the correspondence between male writers and female readers in the emergence of the image of the modern author. See Hahn, '"Weiber verstehen alles à la lettre"'. For an interesting debate on the consequences when a female correspondent tried to step out of her role as admiring reader and become a writer herself, see the discussion of Marianne's sister Sara Meyer and Goethe, in Anderson, 'Franco-German Conversations', esp. pp. 559–68.

[92] Riemer, a philologist, was Goethe's personal secretary and worked closely alongside him for many years.

[93] Friedrich Wilhelm Riemer, *Mittheilungen über Goethe aus mündlichen und schriftlichen, gedruckten und ungedruckten Quellen* (Berlin, 1841), 428–9, as quoted in Katz, 'German Culture and the Jews', 87. Concerning the names mentioned here: 'Frau von Gotthaus' (actually Grotthuss) is Sara Meyer, Marianne's sister. By 'Frau von Eskeles and Fliess' he without doubt meant Cäcilie (Zipora) Itzig, who, following her divorce from Benjamin Isaac Wulff and her marriage to Bernhard von Eskeles, moved from Berlin to Vienna, and her sister-in-law Eleonore (Lea) Eskeles, who at a young age had married a Berlin Jew by the name of Fließ but at this point lived in her native Vienna separated from her husband. Both women corresponded for some time with Goethe, after meeting him at the spa in Franzensbad. This correspondence was partly published in Sauer (ed.), *Goethe und Österreich*, 252–89.

that he valued their opinions. For instance, among the fragments of unfinished works he sent with letters to both sisters were the portions from his famous autobiography *Dichtung und Wahrheit* ('Poetry and Truth') that he sent to Sara: he later wrote thanking her for her views on the text.[94]

If Goethe used his correspondence with Marianne Meyer to enhance his performance as a writer and theatre director, she, for her part, likewise took advantage of her correspondence with Goethe for her own needs, using it not only to give expression to her reasoned judgements but also to further her own education and to stay abreast of the latest developments in the cultural field. More than once she turned to him asking for explanation of a phrase or an expression that appeared in one of his works and was not clear to her.[95] Beyond that, their correspondence furnished her with up-to-date news about his work, including pieces he was about to publish and sometimes even copies of texts that were only just going into print or had very recently been published. 'Your lovely letter and the *wonderful* Idyll very pleasantly surprised me', she wrote in thanking him for one such attachment to a letter.[96] At times he also confided to her the motives that had prompted him to shape a story or a character in a certain way. When referring to a new play that had just been staged, *Die natürliche Tochter* ('The Natural Daughter'), he described in detail in a letter to Marianne the characteristics he had tried to invest in its female character, and added: 'If you, dear friend, read the play some day, you should judge whether this "natural daughter" may stand alongside her other female siblings.'[97]

It would be unrealistic to expect this long epistolary dialogue to be uniformly regular and harmonious, and indeed it clearly had its ups and downs. Long periods of silence, initiated at different times by either side, troubled the relationship from time to time. Now and again Meyer complained about the length of time she had to wait for replies to her letters; some of them, in fact, remained unanswered. On the other hand, on at least two occasions she herself apologized for having let so much time pass before answering a letter from him; on one of these she explained that health problems had prevented

---

[94] See Goethe's letter to Sara Meyer of 9 May 1814 and Ludwig Geiger's note on it in Geiger et al., 'Zweiunddreissig Briefe Goethes', 184–5.

[95] In a letter of 2 Feb. 1796 (*Briefe an Goethe*, ed. Hahn and Koltes), for example, Marianne asks the meaning of a certain expression in one of Goethe's poems.

[96] Geiger (ed.), 'Einundzwanzig Briefe', 31. According to Ludwig Geiger, 'Idyll' is the nickname given by Goethe to his 'Alexis und Dora', printed in the *Musenalmanach* of 1797. If so, a copy of the text reached Marianne's hands before publication, for the letter in which she thanks him for the text is dated September 1796. [97] Goethe, *Goethes Briefe*, ii. 448.

her from responding earlier.[98] None of this, however, detracts from the significance of letter-writing as a vehicle for social and cultural communication in the life of a woman such as Marianne Meyer. The medium clearly enabled her to involve herself deeply and actively in the German and wider European intellectual scene and to consolidate her position as a member of the educated public.

The brief reading of Marianne Meyer's letters offered here represents an attempt to move her image away from the position it has historically occupied as a secondary character in Goethe's life, emphasizing instead her own experiences and presenting her as a woman who valued her own capabilities, saw herself as a member of the educated public, and took an active part in literary and cultural discourse, employing the informal but effective means of the letter. Such a feminist reading—resisting the hegemonic reading that assumes the centrality of men and striving instead to reconstruct women's subjectivity—is useful also in the case of other correspondences between Jewish women and contemporary men of letters less famous than Goethe. The epistolary exchange between Lea Salomon and Garlieb Merkel, a publicist, journal editor, and writer born in Latvia who was 'intimately acquainted' with her family,[99] serves to exemplify both the place of cultural issues and debates in the personal correspondence of enlightened Jewish women, and the position of these women in cultural discourse.

Lea was born in Berlin, the daughter of Levin Jakob Salomon and Bella Salomon, née Itzig, whose own father, Daniel Itzig, was one of the wealthiest Jews in the city. The Salomon family owned an impressive garden that had once belonged to a Prussian official named Bartholdy; this name would be adopted by Lea's brothers and eventually also her mother, who chose it as her official surname in 1812, at the time of the Edict of Emancipation. Some time after Lea herself married Abraham Mendelssohn, Moses Mendelssohn's son, he too adopted the name, which was thus transmitted to their children, including the famous composer Felix Mendelssohn-Bartholdy.[100] Two long letters that Lea Salomon sent to Merkel in 1799, before her marriage to Abraham in 1804, constitute excellent testimony to the kind of cultural intercourse that went on in this type of correspondence.[101] Not only did the letters serve Salomon as a showcase for her abilities as a writer; they also allowed her

---

[98] Letter of 10 Dec. 1800, *Briefe an Goethe*, ed. Hahn and Koltes.

[99] Hensel, *The Mendelssohn Family*, i. 61.

[100] Jacobson, 'Von Mendelssohn zu Mendelssohn-Bartholdy'. On Lea Salomon, see Bartsch, '"In voller geistiger Lebendigkeit"'.

[101] The letters, kept by Merkel, were returned by him to the Mendelssohn family after Lea's death in 1842, and were published by her grandson Sebastian Hensel in his biography of the Mendelssohn

to launch and conduct a lively discussion on literature, music, and theatre with this man of letters, who lived in Weimar at the time and was well acquainted with many leading figures in German cultural life. In her first preserved letter, for instance, she initiated a discussion focused on Schiller's drama *Wallenstein's Death*, asking Merkel for his opinion on the play and offering her own evaluation: 'According to my imperfect notions, it is a masterpiece. The abundance of thought, the charm of expression, the noble simplicity and poetical beauty, added to the interesting subject, will not be equalled nor even imitated for a long time.' Merkel evidently complied with Lea's request in his response (which is lost), for in her second letter we read:

Pray do not give me the *public* as an authority against the merits of 'Wallenstein'. Real art is certainly felt and understood only by the few refined minds; and the circumstance that a commonplace, tragic-comic family quarrel by the natural pen of Iffland is more likely to attract the multitude than the grand heroes of Schiller, surely does not prove the superiority of Iffland's genius. Your fine sense of the beauties of art could not draw this conclusion![102]

Thus, rather than accepting submissively and passively the opinion of this man of letters, Lea Salomon expressed her disagreement with surprising self-assurance. Interestingly, like Marianne Meyer, Salomon too drew a line between the common taste of 'the multitude', or the public at large, and the refined taste of a connoisseur like herself or her interlocutor. Dividing the public according to cultural criteria rather than according to gender or religion, she implicitly placed herself on the side of the cultivated public, of the 'few refined minds' who unlike the masses could feel and understand 'real art'.

Besides literary discussions of this kind and discussions about music—a field that attracted her passionate interest, as would become clear in the education she gave her children, above all the two eldest, Fanny and Felix, both of whom became accomplished musicians[103]—another interesting issue that Lea Salomon invited Merkel to debate with her in their correspondence was the wave of conversion occurring at the time among modernizing Jews. On a previous occasion, Merkel had apparently expressed a wish to write a book about the Jews—a notion Salomon trenchantly dismissed as a 'dreadful idea'

---

family, which includes numerous fragments of letters and journals. Quotations here are taken from the English translation of the book: Hensel, *The Mendelssohn Family*.

[102] Hensel, *The Mendelssohn Family*, i. 69.

[103] They received their first lessons in music from her, to be followed later by private tutoring by the most influential musicians of the time (Reich, 'The Power of Class'; Bartsch, '"In voller geistiger Lebendigkeit"').

in her first preserved letter.[104] After mentioning in her following letter the case of one of her cousins who had recently converted to Christianity, and voicing her opinion on conversions prompted more by professional interests than by religious conviction, as she thought her cousin's was, she turned to Merkel with a plea: 'I believe I never heard your opinion on this subject, and it is very interesting and important to me. Write to me about it, and tell me how you are going to treat the matter in your book.'[105]

Unfortunately no more letters are available to show us how this dialogue on the conversion of Jews between the young Jewish woman and the Christian intellectual developed. The main point remains, however, that the letter served as an ideal medium through which to conduct a learned dialogue on a variety of subjects, including the delicate theme of religious convictions and practices. Lea Salomon's letters reveal the assumption by this young Jewish woman of a position that could hardly be perceived as typically feminine by contemporary standards, as she initiated literary dialogues and steered the discussion according to her own interests, expressing her views openly and with self-confidence, and even at times amiably reprimanding her male correspondent when his opinions deviated from what she expected to hear from an educated and enlightened man such as him. Her readiness to take the initiative in this way belies the hierarchy that might be expected to exist in the correspondence between a man of letters and a woman who could easily be considered no more than a dilettante in cultural matters.

The epistolary dialogues between Marianne Meyer and Goethe and between Lea Salomon and Garlieb Merkel illustrate both the involvement of two enlightened Jewish women in contemporary German culture and the letter's significance as a means of participating in current debates. No less important than their correspondence with male intellectuals was the exchange of letters between the women themselves—not only because these letters helped maintain their deep friendships and provided them with emotional support, important though these aspects of their correspondence are, but also because, as noted above, their letters formed part of a network for transferring information and opinions and a platform for the discussion of subjects of general interest. The letters sent by Dorothea Mendelssohn to her friend Rahel Levin will serve to illuminate this point.

Dorothea and Rahel were passionately interested in, and exceptionally well informed about, a wide range of areas of contemporary culture, and this is reflected in the letters they wrote. Dorothea's profound regard for Rahel's

---

[104] Hensel, *The Mendelssohn Family*, i. 66.
[105] Ibid. 67–8 (quotation from p. 68). See also Ch. 7 below.

opinions, and the satisfaction she derived from discussing with her friend new publications, theatrical productions, and operatic performances, were without doubt the fruit of long years of friendship and personal contact. In fact, her letters may be read at times as a substitute for the experiences they shared and the conversations they held during the time when they both lived in Berlin. 'I must tell you about the French opera in Rheinsberg. Ah! Never have I wanted so heartily to have you at my side as that evening', wrote Dorothea to Rahel in 1792, during a holiday in Strelitz.[106] In Rahel's physical absence, Dorothea shared with her friend in writing her impressions of the performance she had attended when visiting the town of Rheinsberg. Her detailed report included a depiction of the atmosphere at the theatre, encompassing the facilities and the audience—including the class distinctions as reflected in the distribution of seats—as well as a long discussion of the production itself, with meticulous criticism of the singers and their performances, their movements on stage, and their attire. Ruthlessly, she summarized: 'Lots of silk, lots of fur, lots of rich belts and powdered curls, lots of grimaces, but not even a spark of singing, or style, or real acting.'[107] Written in a journalistic-polemical tone, her letter moved into a broader sociopolitical critique fuelled by an event that was shaking the whole Western world—the French Revolution:

About Rheinsberg itself you must already know a lot; people live by and through the prince here.[108] This is well calculated, so that they will pray for his long life! But this senseless power and wealth are disgusting. *His house*, *his* garden and all he can overlook from *his* window is lush and magnificent. But if you go just one house further, just around the corner, you will find no roof intact, no clean street, no completely dressed child. Scantiness and misery everywhere; and even this miserable existence is very precarious; with his life, theirs end too, they subsist only on the overflow of his excess, and through the thousand superfluous things they have to provide for him, without having the bare necessities or the prospect of owning them in the future through their own diligence. The land on which *he* was capricious enough to build his palace is poor, nothing but deep sand all around, and only the paths on which *he* treads were made to blossom through an effort. Damned aristocrat, I could not resist exclaiming. It came alive inside me, how an entire people can all at once revolt against the revelling tyrants, who have eternal symphonies played for themselves and thus do not hear the screams of misery which would otherwise reach their ears. Such an opera costs more than it would cost to have a collapsed little house rebuilt in which peace and welfare could dwell. I imag-

---

[106] *Briefe von und an Friedrich und Dorothea Schlegel*, ed. Behler, xxiii. 62.   [107] Ibid. 64.
[108] Rheinsberg was the home of Prince Heinrich of Prussia, a brother of the Prussian king Frederick II (the Great), from whom he received the palace in Rheinsberg as a present.

ined all of France to be like this, and now I understood the French. Forgive me for my zeal, my dear lady *aristocrat*! You should only see Rheinsberg.[109]

The revolutionary events in France clearly influenced Dorothea's analysis of what she saw for herself during her vacation. Her sense of frustration, and the harshness of her criticism of egotistical despots who ignore the suffering of those around them and busy themselves exclusively with their own well-being, all poured out in this letter to a female Jewish friend, testify to the deep impression left by the dramatic events of the French Revolution on so many people at this time throughout Europe. Her arguments in favour of a more reasonable allocation of resources would be further developed in the novel she published almost a decade later, *Florentin*.[110]

After Dorothea left Berlin in 1799, having divorced her Jewish husband Simon Veit and moved with her beloved Friedrich Schlegel first to Jena and later to Paris and other European cities, she and Rahel Levin sought to overcome the geographical distance that separated them through their correspondence. The letters they exchanged enabled them to continue nurturing their relationship and each other, communicating experiences, news, and ideas they absorbed in the different places where they lived. A recurrent topic of their correspondence was the discussion of recent literary works by women and on women, which offered them the opportunity to shape and share their critical opinions on female models not only in literature but also in real life. From Jena, Dorothea asked Rahel to comment on a new book by Madame de Genlis, a prolific French writer, and on the translation made of it by their mutual friend Madame Bernard—Esther Gad, an enlightened Jewish woman from Breslau who lived in Berlin in the closing years of the eighteenth century—perhaps even before having read it herself.[111] The work in question was Genlis' *Les Mères rivals ou la calomnie* ('The Rival Mothers; or Calumny'), first published in 1800; Esther Gad's German translation appeared in three volumes between 1800 and 1802 under the title *Die beiden Mütter oder die Folgen der Verläumdung*. Later Dorothea asked Rahel's opinion on a book written by Madame de Staël, another prominent and very influential French writer in whom both Jewish

---

[109] *Briefe von und an Friedrich und Dorothea Schlegel*, ed. Behler, xxiii. 64.

[110] See discussion in Ch. 3 below.

[111] *Dorothea v. Schlegel und deren Söhne, Briefwechsel*, ed. Raich, i. [12]. Gad had established close contact with Stéphanie-Félicité de Genlis while both were living in Berlin. Because of her involvement in revolutionary politics, Genlis had to leave France in 1789, and she spent several years in the Prussian capital before returning to Paris in 1800. While in Berlin she became also acquainted with other enlightened Jewish women discussed in this study. Lea Salomon, for instance, wrote in August 1799 that Madame de Genlis lived 'near our garden [the house of the Salomon family in Berlin], and we see her daily' (Hensel, *The Mendelssohn Family*, i. 71).

women were keenly interested, as they were in Genlis.[112] 'If you have by any chance already read *Pauline*, write me something about it', she begged, before broadening the discussion about this short story to encompass issues that interested her by adding her own interpretation of the main character.[113] Mendelssohn's special interest in the work of these writers and on the gender issues that arose from them would, again, find its way into the public sphere, as attested by a review of contemporary French literature written by women, 'Gespräch über die neuesten Romane der Französinnen', that she published in 1803 in *Europa*, a journal edited by Friedrich Schlegel.

As part of the early Romantic circle in Jena around 1800, Dorothea also used her letters to keep Rahel Levin up to date on what its active members were doing. She told her friend, for instance, about the positive reactions to the new issue of *Athenaeum*, the literary magazine established by the brothers August and Friedrich Schlegel in 1798 and published until 1800: 'Do you already have the *Athenaeum*? What do you think about the criticism of Schmidt, Mathisson, and Voss, and about the antiphony [*Wechselgesang*] in which these kindred minds merge? Is it not so thorough as amusing, so dignified as witty? Papa Goethe was mighty pleased with it. Schlegel had to read it three times to him without interruption.'[114] Later in her letter she encouraged Rahel to write to Friedrich and praise him for the poem he had published in the magazine. In addition, Dorothea gave Rahel advance news of imminent literary events, as when she told her that August Schlegel's poems were to be published in the forthcoming book fair—news she accompanied with a personal assessment that was both glowing—'You will find wonderful things in them, especially among the later ones, where again the sonnets feature superbly as a form which he was the first among Germans to bring to such perfection'—and more critical: 'The poems from his earlier artistic period I find somewhat weak; especially those that speak about love. The latter seems to be his weakness rather than his strength', she noted.[115]

Even so small a sample of the numerous letters written by the enlightened Jewish women at the end of the eighteenth century and the beginning of

---

[112] According to Carla Hesse, 'Staël and Genlis attempted to recover the right to literary achievement for women in light of what appeared to them both as efforts by modern science to reduce women to their objective corporeal essence—to render them seen, but not heard' (Hesse, *The Other Enlightenment*, 136).

[113] *Dorothea v. Schlegel und deren Söhne, Briefwechsel*, ed. Raich, i. [14]. Dorothea Mendelssohn is referring here to Staël's 'Histoire de Pauline' ('The Story of Pauline'), published in 1795.

[114] *Dorothea v. Schlegel und deren Söhne, Briefwechsel*, ed. Raich, i. [11]. The word used here by Dorothea, *Wechselgesang*, refers to a piece named 'Wettgesang dreier Poeten', a parodical poetic competition published by August Schlegel in the third volume of the *Aethenäum*, emulating and mocking the three authors mentioned above.   [115] Ibid. [11]–[12].

the nineteenth as that given here enables us to reconstruct at least to a certain extent the important cultural role in their lives played by the act of letter-writing. Taken singly, the utterances and verbal exchanges presented above may seem to lack historical significance, and even to be rather trivial. Only when seen as elements of a larger picture do these pieces of information, taken from just a small number of the many letters they wrote, acquire their true significance.

TWO

JEWISH WOMEN AND THE READING PUBLIC

A SALIENT FEATURE emerging from the personal testimonies left by the enlightened Jewish women discussed in this study is the prominent place of reading in their lives. These women had at their disposal not only the indispensable skill of literacy, shared by the ever-growing reading public across Europe, but also—thanks to the relative financial comfort which allowed most of these women to delegate housework to others—the necessary spare time to use it, and in most cases no children of their own to make additional demands on their time and attention. Thus they were able to make reading a primary activity to which they dedicated a significant amount of time and effort.

An illustrative account of real craving for books—unthinkable in earlier centuries, especially among women—may be found in Henriette Herz's memoirs. Reading figures as one of the central motives she chose to emphasize when recounting the events of her life, from her childhood until well into adulthood. In the autobiographical text which she started to compose in 1823 and never completed, Henriette typically depicted herself as a compulsive reader. 'I stopped playing at a very early age, and earlier than might have been good for me, I turned to reading.'[1] Whenever other activities kept her away

---

[1] Landsberg (ed.), *Henriette Herz*, 118 (Eng. trans. in Blackwell and Zantop (eds.), *Bitter Healing*, 312–13). Herz wrote the main part of her memoirs in 1823. She continued in 1829 but then suddenly stopped. A transcription of her manuscript was first printed in *Mittheilungen aus dem Literaturarchive in Berlin* in 1896 in a limited edition of 100 copies. Almost half a century earlier—two years after Herz's death—Julius Fürst had published *Henriette Herz. Ihr Leben und ihre Erinnerungen* (Berlin, 1850), usually identified as Henriette Herz's autobiography. In fact, as some critics have noted, this is an arbitrary adaptation of Herz's original material combined with testimonies that according to Fürst were transmitted to him in personal conversations between himself and his friend Henriette Herz in the later years of her life (Geiger (ed.) *Briefwechsel des jungen Börne und der Henriette Herz*, 11). A comparison of Herz's original text—as published in the *Mittheilungen* and later by Hans Landsberg in his edition of her memoirs (Landsberg (ed.), *Henriette Herz*, 101–54)—with Fürst's version reveals fun-

from books during the weekdays, she would make up for it on Saturdays and Sundays, and 'with such speed and assiduity that in one day I could read through several parts of a novel and would constantly run to the lending library not far from our house to pick up more books'.²

This urge to read did not wane as the years went by; reading continued to play a central role in her adult life, as it did in the lives of other enlightened Jewish women. It served as a source of knowledge no less than as a means of entertainment, and simultaneously fulfilled an important social function, being a prerequisite for social interaction in the modern world, the basis for cultured conversation, and a recurrent theme in learned correspondence.

JEWISH WOMEN IN THE READING PUBLIC—A REVOLUTION?

Henriette Herz's depiction of her intensive engagement with reading raises questions regarding the singularity of this phenomenon in the history of Jewish women. Was the passion for reading—especially for reading texts from European literature—expressed by Herz and her female contemporaries a new enthusiasm among Jewish women of this generation, or was it the continuation of a process which had begun within Jewish society in earlier times and had already been going on for generations? How widespread was this trend among Jewish women in Berlin, in the German lands, and in the Ashkenazi world in general? Can it be characterized as a 'revolution' in the cultural world of Jewish women—applying a term that has been used to describe the significant transformations in the history of the book and in the history of reading in the German lands in the eighteenth century?

These questions seem all the more acute and relevant in view of the fact that the reading patterns they refer to began to form during childhood, at a time when these girls were still integrated within the Jewish community. A comprehensive discussion of these and many other issues concerning Jewish women's reading practices in the early modern period and the beginning of

---

damental changes, in style and language as well as in content. In a review of two books published in 1984 purportedly reproducing Herz's memoirs—one by Ulrich Janetzki in Berlin and the other by Rainer Schmitz in Frankfurt am Main—Renate Heuer criticizes the decision of both editors from East and West Germany to rely on Fürst's version rather than on Herz's original text. In view of this, even though the authentic material is much more limited than Fürst's expanded text and includes considerably less information, it will be preferred in the present study, being a more reliable historical source. I therefore use Landsberg's edition and, when available, the English translation of the text in Blackwell and Zantop (eds.), *Bitter Healing*, 303–31. See Heuer, 'Bücherschau', 156–66.

² Landsberg (ed.), *Henriette Herz*, 121 (Eng. trans.: Blackwell and Zantop (eds.), *Bitter Healing*, 314).

the modern period could undoubtedly contribute to an understanding of Jewish modernization from a gender perspective; however, it lies beyond the scope of this study.[3] Here effort will be focused on providing sufficient context to understand the degree to which the reading habits of enlightened Jewish women in Berlin around 1800 represented an innovation.

In the context of German history, the participation of women in the reading public may be seen as part of an important cultural transformation affecting German and wider European society from the Reformation onwards: namely, the centuries-long process by which literacy spread to encompass ever greater parts of the population. Although a 'truly numerical or quantitative democratization of reading' did not occur until the nineteenth century,[4] there were many literate women in Germany long before that, and their number significantly increased throughout the eighteenth century, mostly in urban centres and notably among families of the bourgeoisie.[5] Considered in the cultural context of *Jewish* women at the beginning of modern times, the engagement with reading is even less anomalous. Not only was literacy within Jewish society in general much more widespread at this time than in non-Jewish society, where the reading public remained small until the nineteenth century;[6] numerous sources—ranging from personal testimonies to indirect evidence—clearly indicate that long before the appearance of the enlightened Jewish women in Prussia, reading was a widespread practice among Jewish women, certainly in the Ashkenazi world.[7]

---

[3] Following the lead of historians including Jacob Katz and Jonathan Israel, among others, the 'early modern period' is now considered a specific era in Jewish history, as it is in general European history, distinct from the medieval and the modern periods. Its periodization, like that of the modern period, is contested; it extends roughly from the late 15th or the 16th century until the early, middle, or late 18th century. A recent study that draws on the work done by Jewish historians on this period in specific regions to present a comprehensive description of early modern Jewish culture is David Ruderman's *Early Modern Jewry*.

[4] Wittmann, 'Was There a Reading Revolution?', 289. As Wittmann notes, the number of potential readers in Germany remained relatively low throughout the 18th century. Nevertheless, when considering certain large and influential groups of the population it may be claimed that 'alphabetization was in considerable part an achievement of the early modern period' (Hinrichs, *Einführung in die Geschichte der Frühen Neuzeit*, 103).

[5] See Brandes, 'Die Entstehung eines weiblichen Lesepublikums'.

[6] According to Wittmann, in the late 18th century the 'regularly reading public in Germany . . . numbered approximately 300,000 people, or 1,5 per cent of the adult population' (Wittmann, 'Was There a Reading Revolution?', 289). As Merry E. Wiesner affirms, 'even basic literacy was never achieved by the vast majority of women in Europe during the early modern period' (Wiesner, *Women and Gender in Early Modern Europe*, 145).

[7] In the early modern age, reading was considered part of elementary education for girls as well as boys in Ashkenazi society. The proportion of Jewish women who could read was significantly higher than in Christian society, certainly in rural areas (Chovav, *Maidens Love Thee* (Heb.), 411, esp. n. 23).

The most direct and personal evidence known to us today of the reading habits of a Jewish woman in the German cultural context[8] at the end of the seventeenth century and the beginning of the eighteenth is found in a rare, though much quoted, source: the memoirs of Glikl Hameln.[9] Glikl, a Jewish woman from Hamburg, mother of fourteen children and successful businesswoman, is known to modern readers through the autobiography she began to write after the death of her first husband in 1691. The image of Glikl which emerges from this personal account—the earliest extant autobiography written by a Jewish woman and one of the first Jewish autobiographies ever—is that of a cultivated woman who had become acquainted with Jewish and non-Jewish literature through the intensive reading of a variety of books and booklets in Yiddish.[10] On the basis of this reading, as well as of knowledge acquired by word of mouth, Glikl was able to intersperse her memoirs with stories and legends which made the events she described more tangible and helped her convey moral lessons to her audience.[11]

Even though Glikl does not seem to have been exceptional as a reader in her Jewish environment, the activities of a single wealthy, urban Jewish

---

Of course, this is not to say that all Jewish women were literate. In the early modern period, many 'could neither write nor read at all in any language' (Von Rohden, 'Introduction', in Tiktiner, *Meneket Rivkah*, 1).

[8] Beyond the German context, there exists a very interesting (and rare) personal source which offers a detailed testimony of the reading practices of yet another Ashkenazi Jewish woman in the early modern age: the letters of Abigaill Levy Franks. The correspondence of this Jewish woman, who lived in New York in the first half of the eighteenth century, with her son in London, contains fascinating information concerning her modern reading habits. For a new edition of these letters see Franks, *The Letters of Abigaill Levy Franks*.

[9] On the different names used for Glikl (also known as Glückel of Hameln; she signed herself as 'Glikl bas [daughter of] Judah Leib'), see Chava Turniansky's introduction to her annotated edition and translation of Glikl's memoirs into Hebrew: Glikl, *Memoirs* (Yid.), tet [9]; also: Davis, *Women on the Margins*, 8–9.

[10] According to Chava Turniansky it is reasonable to assume that Glikl did not read in any language other than Yiddish. There is no indication in her memoirs that she read in German. She undoubtedly possessed the technical ability to read Hebrew, but it seems she was not able to understand written texts in this language. 'Yiddish was Glikl's only language for speaking, writing and reading' (Turniansky, 'The Stories in Glikl Hamel's Work' (Heb.), 61). Cf. Davis, *Women on the Margins*, 23–30. Davis's own analysis leads her to conclude not only that Glikl might have read some Hebrew texts, but that 'it is very likely that Glikl read some High-German publications in their own Gothic print' (ibid. 25).

[11] Beyond reading, Turniansky stresses the prominent role of oral culture: 'There is no doubt that a great part of her "literary" knowledge, rooted in Jewish sources, was not acquired directly through Hebrew books, but orally, through a mediator, and of course in Yiddish, her spoken language' (Turniansky, 'The Stories in Glikl Hamel's Work' (Heb.), 53). Glikl lived in 'a society still governed by an intensive and active oral culture, which fulfilled the role of mediator between the canonical culture and an audience unable to reach this culture directly' (ibid. 62).

woman would certainly not be sufficient foundation for far-reaching generalizations on the reading habits of Jewish women in general—not even in the German lands, where the majority of Jews still lived in rural areas, let alone across the whole of Ashkenaz, which included east European Jews living under very different conditions. However, additional sources support the claim that literacy was relatively widespread among a significant proportion of Ashkenazi Jewish women in the early modern period. Literary evidence confirms the existence of a significant public of reading women well before the eighteenth century, and certainly throughout it. Not long after the invention of printing in the fifteenth century a prolific popular Yiddish literature started to develop in the Ashkenazi world, much of it addressed to women. The Yiddish library of the early modern age contained popular ethical works such as the *Brantshpigl*;[12] story books such as the *Mayse-bukh*, based largely on talmudic and midrashic tales;[13] books which combined ethics and *agadah* (rabbinic legends; in Yiddish, *agode*), such as the *Tsenerene*—a free translation of the Pentateuch written by Jacob ben Isaac Ashkenazi around 1600, which soon became the 'women's Torah', perhaps the most popular book in Yiddish literature;[14] and Yiddish translations of other books from the Bible. Besides these texts, intended for both 'women and men who are like women and cannot learn much' (a phrase commonly found on the title pages of Yiddish books), other original books were written mainly for women: collections of *tkhines* (women's supplicatory prayers),[15] and books such as *Seder mitzvot hanashim* or *Azharat nashim*, the purpose of which, according to the latter's title page, was to guide Jewish women on 'how to behave properly according to the commandments'. Although these books could have been read *to* women who were illiterate, they were also certainly read *by* many women themselves.

The conspicuous presence of women among the reading public attracted the attention of early Yiddishists and led them to far-reaching conclusions. In a pioneering piece of research on the connection between Yiddish literature and reading women, published in the second decade of the twentieth century,

---

[12] *Brantshpigl*, a morality book by Moses b. Henoch Altschuler first printed at the end of the 16th century, contains numerous chapters dealing with the duties of Jewish women, to whom it was primarily addressed (Zinberg, *Old Yiddish Literature*, 157–9; Weissler, *Voices of the Matriarchs*, 37).

[13] On the *Mayse-bukh* see Zfatman, 'The *Mayse-bukh*' (Heb.).

[14] As stated by Chone Shmeruk in 'The East European Versions of the *Tsenerene*' (Yid.), 336. According to Chava Turniansky, more than 230 editions of the *Tsenerene* have been printed since it was first published more than four centuries ago, including some recent editions. Turniansky, 'The Maskilic Versions of *Tsene-Rene*' (Heb.), 313.

[15] On women's Yiddish prayers, see Weissler, *Voices of the Matriarchs*.

Shmuel Niger highlighted the distinctively 'feminine style' of old Yiddish literature. As evidence for the close connection between literary production and female readership, he noted the explicit appeal to women on the title pages and in the prefaces to most early Yiddish publications, as well as the name given to the special typeface in which these books were printed—*vayber taytsh*, that is, 'women's script'. Although Niger rejects the assertion that old Yiddish literature (that created between the sixteenth and eighteenth centuries) was exclusively intended for women and 'simple men'—it was certainly directed to a broader, more educated audience as well—he does maintain that they were the main addressees.[16] Another scholar, Israel Zinberg, went so far as to argue that, with the invention of print and the rise of popular literature in Yiddish, 'the great revolution in the life of the Jewish woman took place'.[17] Even though these conclusions are now undergoing reassessment, as the dichotomies common in earlier studies of Yiddish literature are challenged,[18] there can be no doubt that an appreciable number of Ashkenazi Jewish women were intensely engaged in reading well before the period under study in this book.

No less remarkable than Jewish women's reading ability is the range of reading materials that were available to them. It is true that a considerable proportion of early Yiddish literature was composed of devotional texts, created for purely functionalist purposes. As Chone Shmeruk pointed out, the fact that Hebrew—the 'holy tongue'—was incomprehensible to Jewish women in Ashkenaz (and even to a considerable number of Jewish men), meant that there was no alternative to using the spoken language to enable this part of the public to continue with their traditional way of life.[19] The development of a religious corpus in Yiddish in the early modern period—comprised of original works as well as translations from Hebrew—was, according to Moshe Rosman, part of an increasing tendency in Ashkenazi

---

[16] Niger, 'Yiddish Literature and the Female Reader'.

[17] Zinberg, *Old Yiddish Literature*, 125–6. On the transformations that occurred in the Western world with the advent of printing and the shift from manuscript to printed books, see Eisenstein, *The Printing Press as an Agent of Change*. Against the insistence on the invention of printing as a decisive turning point in literary culture, Guglielmo Cavallo and Roger Chartier claim that although this certainly represented a technological transformation in book *production*, no concomitant revolution in *reading* took place. In fact, they stress the continuity from 'scribal culture' to 'print culture' (Cavallo and Chartier, introd. to *A History of Reading in the West*, 22–4).

[18] Thus Jerold Frakes claims that the conventional conception according to which Hebrew literature was written for men while early Yiddish literature was written for women and the ignorant is 'skewed' (Frakes (ed.), *Early Yiddish Texts*, p. xliii). For a critical discussion of this dichotomy, see Rosman, 'The History of Jewish Women in Early Modern Poland', 42–6.

[19] Shmeruk, *Chapters in the History of Yiddish Literature* (Heb.), 13.

Jewry 'to pay more attention to women's needs and to offer an additional place for their participation' in the religious and cultural domains.[20] For the rabbinic elite, 'it was clear that in order for them to contribute to the foundations of the community, women had to possess certain knowledge and even means for religious expression and participation'. With this purpose a new library was developed, through which 'women could obtain knowledge parallel to that in the sources of learned men; they could acquire basic Jewish knowledge and values'.[21]

Nevertheless, as Max Weinreich stressed, it is 'a serious error to imagine that Jewish intellectual needs of that time were satisfied by *teitsch ḥumash* [biblical paraphrase] and *muser sforim* [ethical treatises]', and that Jews 'thought of nothing but Torah and the commandments'.[22] Parallel to Ashkenazi religious literature, consisting mainly of books on women's commandments, *muser* books, and Yiddish translations of the Bible, a secular literature developed as well. Transcriptions,[23] translations, and adaptations of German and European works all became accessible to both female and male Yiddish-readers. This absorption of general literature into Jewish cultural production seems to have gathered pace in the eighteenth century.[24] The list of books published then includes, alongside stories of Jewish origin or on Jewish subjects, stories taken from general literature, such as adaptations from Boccaccio's *Decameron*, selections from the tales of Sinbad, stories from Cervantes, tales from *A Thousand and One Nights*, and *Robinson Crusoe*. Publishers were prompted among other things by a desire to bring fiction and

---

[20] Rosman, 'Being a Jewish Woman in Poland–Lithuania' (Heb.), 426. See also Rosman, 'The History of Jewish Women in Early Modern Poland'.

[21] Rosman, 'Being a Jewish Woman in Poland–Lithuania' (Heb.), 434, 424. See also Chovav, *Maidens Love Thee* (Heb.), 406–45, esp. pp. 417–21.

[22] Max Weinreich, *Shtaplen: Fir etyudn tsu der yidisher shprakhvisnshaft un literaturgeshikhte* (Berlin, 1923), as quoted and translated in Frakes' introduction to id. (ed.), *Early Yiddish Texts*, p. xlv. It is interesting to note that even edifying literature had to be enjoyable and entertaining to read in order to attract an audience. As Edward Fram claims in his study on *Seder mitzvot hanashim*, concerning Yiddish literature in the 16th century, a book on women's commandments such as this had to add stories and tales to the legal information it provided, just as Yiddish translations of the Bible had to be non-literal and include numerous stories, parables, and explanations so as to cater to the taste of its audience and achieve commercial success. Fram, *My Dear Daughter*, 87–90.

[23] In the mid-17th century, for instance, young Jewish men and women bought books in non-Jewish languages which they were unable to read and ordered transcriptions in Hebrew characters. Jews were thus exposed, through the numerous transcriptions that existed, to German popular literature such as folk tales and epic poems. On the extent of this phenomenon and its implications, see Shmeruk, *Chapters in the History of Yiddish Literature* (Heb.), 24–39.

[24] According to Zeev Gries, in the 18th century the printing of story books in Yiddish tripled in comparison to the 17th century (Gries, *The Book in the Jewish World*, 95).

knowledge from the world at large to a Jewish audience.[25] Thus, it may be deduced that at least some Ashkenazi Jewish women were familiar with world literature and with various literary genres, even if this was mainly through the cultural and linguistic mediation of Yiddish, and in a 'judaized' form.[26]

On the basis of this type of evidence, Zinberg perceived the flourishing of popular Yiddish literature from the sixteenth century onwards as the beginning of a culture war between 'secular' literature, imported from the surrounding culture, and popular rabbinic literature, whose aim was to guide Jewish readers in the paths of ethics and Jewish law. Using milder terms, Shmeruk stressed that 'there is no doubt that the mere penetration [of foreign literature] into the Jewish realm propelled the writing of books whose specific tendency was to serve as impetus for removing the foreign penetration, considered improper from a religious and traditional point of view'. The tension between religious literature founded on traditional Hebrew sources and external influences, he claimed, seems to have existed since the beginning of Yiddish literature.[27] It is clear, in any case, that Jewish readers of both sexes had at their disposal secular works of different kinds—adventure books, amusing tales, poems, and folk songs—which expanded their cultural horizons beyond the confined Jewish world.

In addition to the mere existence of a diversified Jewish literature for women, evidence for Jewish women's literacy emerges also from works written by men unhappy with contemporary developments in Jewish society. These sources point at the spread of new trends and add to what we know about the reading habits of Jewish women. One such work is the *Libes briv* by Isaac Wetzlar, a rich merchant from Celle. Writing in 1749 in Yiddish, Wetzlar, an early maskil, described the flaws that in his opinion afflicted contemporary Jewish society, including among other things the reading habits of Jewish women.[28] Wetzlar had no objection to the fact that women counted among the reading public. In fact, he opened his text with an appeal to 'my

---

[25] Ibid. 98–9.

[26] Shlomo Berger has recently emphasized the significant role of Yiddish literature in Jewish modernization. Yiddish, the language of the Jews par excellence, served as an important vehicle for the transfer of modern ideas from the surrounding culture to a Jewish audience (Berger, *Yiddish and Jewish Modernization* (Heb.)). On the 'Judaization' of non-Jewish texts, see Zinberg, *Old Yiddish Literature*; Aptroot, '"I know this book of mine will cause offence . . . "'; Rosman, 'The History of Jewish Women in Early Modern Poland', 48.

[27] Shmeruk stresses the positive effects of this tension, in that it encouraged the creation of original and diverse texts in Yiddish (Shmeruk, *Chapters in the History of Yiddish Literature* (Heb.), 37).

[28] On Wetzlar and his book see the introduction by Faierstein in Wetzlar, *The 'Libes briv'*, 1–42. On Wetzlar as an early maskil, see Feiner, *The Jewish Enlightenment*, 23–4.

dear brothers and sisters in this exile', thus specifically including women as an important component of his intended audience and as an integral part of the Jewish reading public.[29] What he deplored was the kind of texts published for a female readership, first and foremost the *Tsenerene*, a book which, he argued, did not cultivate a genuine acquaintance with the Bible but, on the contrary, was conducive to ignorance or deficient knowledge among its numerous female readers and even to the desecration of God's name. Far from being a reliable translation of the Bible into Yiddish, this book contained much midrashic and aggadic material (based on rabbinic legends) and included many errors. 'The women of other nations', explained Wetzlar with grief, 'know our holy written Torah [the Pentateuch] better than do our own women.'[30] In view of this situation, he insisted on the necessity of teaching women Hebrew, as a tool to understand the prayers and the Bible and to observe the commandments properly. As a practical concession to women who did not know Hebrew—the great majority—he recommended, though with resignation, another Yiddish translation of the Bible, 'printed in Amsterdam, 1670',[31] as preferable to the *Tsenerene*. Not only did Wetzlar lament the disregard of Hebrew literacy, but he was also concerned by what he perceived as a common phenomenon in contemporary Jewish society: the acquisition of European languages by young girls. He complained against 'evil scholars' who 'do not allow daughters of Israel to study the written Torah and through this learn their holy mother language, Hebrew', but showed no opposition to their learning foreign languages such as French and Italian—which should have aroused much more concern because it led to a dangerous social closeness with non-Jewish teachers.[32]

Wetzlar's disapproving comments did not have much effect on what, or how, women and girls were taught. Whereas his criticism, and that of other early maskilim, of the defective education and reading practices of Jewish boys eventually generated, among other things, the creation of a wide maskilic library in Hebrew,[33] relatively little attention was granted to the reading

---

[29] Wetzlar, *The 'Libes briv'*, 43.   [30] Ibid. 95.

[31] Ibid. 50. It may be surmised that Wetzlar was referring to the translation of the Bible into Yiddish by Yekutiel Blitz. As opposed to the two types of translation common then—the mechanical, styleless word-by-word rendition of the Hebrew text into Yiddish, and translations containing mainly *midrashim* and *agadot* (rabbinic legends from the Talmud and Midrash), such as the *Tsenerene*—Yekutiel Blitz intended to provide the reader with an accurate translation of the Bible. However, as Zinberg indicates, 'the attempt to displace *Tze'enah U-Re'enah* [*Tsenerene*] and other homiletical translations was unsuccessful' (Zinberg, *Old Yiddish Literature*, 139).

[32] Wetzlar, *The 'Libes briv'*, 94.

[33] An impressive maskilic corpus of children's literature developed at the end of the 18th century and the beginning of the 19th. Zohar Shavit has remarked on 'the incredible discrepancy between the

needs of girls or women by the maskilim in German lands[34] until this issue was urgently raised at the beginning of the nineteenth century.[35] Wetzlar's testimony, though, serves to emphasize an important feature of women's literacy, beyond the reading of Yiddish texts: their continuing ignorance of Hebrew, at a time when this language was experiencing a revival thanks to the labours of the maskilim, and their simultaneously growing familiarity with non-Jewish tongues.

As may be deduced from the various sources surveyed above, the practice of reading was widespread among Ashkenazi Jewish women in the early modern period.[36] Jewish women not only represented an important segment in the reading public; thanks to the reading materials available to them, especially in Yiddish, they could also come into contact with non-Jewish literature and culture. It would therefore be mistaken to claim that there was a dramatic change at the end of the eighteenth century regarding the act of reading itself. Unlike non-Jewish society, in which most of the population (including men) was still illiterate, among Jewish women there was no need for a large-scale literacy campaign: a significant proportion of them had been reading for a long time already, at least in Yiddish, and the important change that took place throughout the eighteenth century had to do with acquiring literacy in non-Jewish languages. Such debate on literacy as took place among the Jewish intellectual elite pertained to the language and content of reading matter, not to the activity itself, whereas in non-Jewish society opposition to reading in general, and in particular to what was known as *Vielleserei*,

---

number of books [written for children in Hebrew] and the number of their readers': indeed, she says, 'there were almost as many books as children who could read them' (Shavit, 'From Friedländer's Lesebuch to the Jewish Campe', 388). The quantity of maskilic literature for women in the 18th century did not come close.

[34] As claimed by Shmuel Feiner: 'From the outset, women were absent from the program of improvement of Jewish society proposed by the maskilim in Germany in the 1780s. The new education, the criticism against rabbinic leadership, the ideal of the new Jew, the literary activity—all these had to do exclusively with men.' Out of the extensive library produced by the maskilim, only few books were addressed to women, and even these were not typical maskilic texts: two translations into German of the Jewish prayer book by David Friedländer and Isaac Euchel were published in 1786; another maskil, Joel Loewe-Brill, dedicated his 1785 translation of the Pesach Haggadah into German to a female reader (Feiner, 'The Modern Jewish Woman' (Heb.), 256–7).

[35] In the German Jewish context, texts with a modern orientation specifically addressed to Jewish girls were written from the beginning of the 19th century, with the purpose of directing their integration into the modernization of Jewish society (Kogman, *'The Temptation is Great'* (Heb.)).

[36] The situation seems to have been very different in other Jewish communities. According to Chava Weissler, 'Ashkenazic women seem to have had a higher rate of literacy than Jewish women in many other communities; there are many more books aimed at women in Yiddish than there are in the other Jewish vernaculars' (Weissler, *Voices of the Matriarchs*, 192).

'excessive reading', was not uncommon.[37] Even in traditional Jewish circles women's reading was encouraged. Thus the Vilna Gaon (Rabbi Elijah ben Solomon Zalman), when writing his famous epistle to his family some time before 1783,[38] urged his wife to guide their daughters in their reading and see to it that they engaged in this activity on a daily basis—to be sure, with a clear religious purpose in mind:

> I possess many moral books with German [versions];[39] let them read these regularly; above all on the Sabbath—the holy of holies—they should occupy themselves with these ethical books exclusively . . . Among my books is the Book of Proverbs in German; for the Lord's sake let them read it every day, as it is chief of moral works. They should also read Ecclesiastes constantly, in your presence; for this book exposes the vanity of temporal concerns.[40]

Not only did the Vilna Gaon not reject his daughters' reading, he insisted on its importance as an essential component of their ethical education, parallel to the study of Torah by his sons.

Nonetheless, even though it is hard to identify a radical turn towards reading itself in the last generation of the eighteenth century, this is not to rule out significant transformations in its characteristics and functions. Such changes were intimately related to developments occurring in the non-Jewish cultural environment at this time, pertaining to the history of the book as well as to the history of reading. In the last decades of the eighteenth century, reading was gradually becoming an increasingly prominent practice in the lives of Germans. Expressions such as *Lesekrankheit* (reading sickness), *Lesesucht* (reading addiction), and *Lesemanie* (reading mania) were used to describe the 'epidemic' of reading (another expression employed by contemporaries in a rather disapproving tone) that took hold of an expanding public. In its unprecedented eagerness to consume new printed materials, the read-

---

[37] Hostile voices were heard in Germany, disapproving of modern reading habits in general, but particularly of women's engagement in reading, and rejecting this practice as something which corrupted the values of society and the family (Wittmann, *Geschichte des deutschen Buchhandels*, 203 ff.). Such criticism came not only from conservative and repressive circles, upset by the disturbance of the good old order, but also from leftist idealistic intellectuals, who perceived the purportedly low quality of women's reading matter and their fashionable devotion to novels as a hindrance to progress towards the improved future society they were striving for (Weckel, *Zwischen Häuslichkeit und Öffentlichkeit*, 312 n. 5).

[38] The precise year is unknown. Since the epistle was addressed to his wife, who died in 1783, it may be assumed it was written before that date.

[39] The Vilna Gaon does not seem to be referring to relatively new ethical or homiletical books such as *Kav hayashar* (published in 1705) or *Shevet musar* (published in 1712), but rather to canonical ones (e.g. Proverbs and Ecclesiastes) in Yiddish translation, as suggested by the following words.

[40] *Hebrew Ethical Wills*, ii. 316, 322.

ing public was making a transition from the intensive reading of a restricted number of books, especially canonical religious texts, that was characteristic of pre-modern times (reflected, incidentally, in the Vilna Gaon's advice concerning his daughters' reading), to the extensive reading of numerous and varied materials.[41] Correlated changes in printing, such as an impressive growth in the quantity of publications and the increasing supremacy of the small, portable format, enabled a growing audience to read a broader variety of texts. Also crucial was the increase in the number of associations and institutions, such as reading societies and lending libraries, which enabled large audiences to read a great many different materials without having to buy them. These developments had repercussions for the reading practices of enlightened Jewish women, as is clear from Henriette Herz's remarks quoted above and as will emerge further in this chapter.

Beyond these external aspects of the history of the book and reading, much research attention has recently been given to the internal aspects—the experiences of the readers themselves. Cultural historians have tried to reach a better understanding of readers' worlds and their reactions to reading material: how individual readers in different periods and societies received and interpreted written texts. In doing so they have turned away from widespread socio-statistical studies, which analyse concrete data pertaining to the production and consumption of books and yield quantitative results (dealing, for instance, with the decline of illiteracy, the book market, the explosive growth of journals and newspapers, and the contents of private libraries) towards the use of a qualitative approach, focused on the study of particular readers and social groups, and of course drawing on sources of a different kind, such as diaries, letters, and legal documents, including reports from the Inquisition.[42] In this aspect of the history of reading, too, scholars have found towards the end of the eighteenth century, if not a revolution, then at least a fundamental change.

[41] Engelsing, in *Der Bürger als Leser*, described the transition from intensive to extensive reading as a 'revolution'. His thesis is controversial: the simple opposition he proposed between two types of reading as characterizing two historical periods has been criticized by leading scholars. Cavallo and Chartier cite evidence from the Renaissance to show that 'extensive' reading was common among the humanists of the time, well before the modern period (they point at the book wheel and the commonplace book, two devices typical of that period, used by 'extensive' readers), and they claim that the enthusiastic reading of Richardson, Rousseau, and Goethe in the second half of the 18th century is hard to describe as purely extensive (Cavallo and Chartier, introd. to *A History of Reading in the West*, 25). A similar claim was advanced by Darnton, 'Readers Respond to Rousseau', 250. However, although the transition may have been less pronounced than suggested, there was undoubtedly a clear shift in this direction.

[42] One of the most outstanding examples of this type of study is Ginzburg, *The Cheese and the Worms*, which examines the reading habits of Menocchio, a 'simple man' of the 16th century, based on documents from the Inquisition.

The specific reading habits of enlightened Jewish women around the turn of the eighteenth to the nineteenth century will be examined here with this approach in mind. Some of the available sources—the letters and personal texts written by these women—may be seen as 'reading accounts', which make it possible to analyse their reading habits and their reception and appropriation of texts. Aside from the memoirs of Glikl—a document that certainly lends itself to this kind of analysis—personal sources written by Jewish women in the German lands from earlier times are scarce, and any containing information on the personal reading experiences of women even more so.

Details of the reading habits of Fromet Gugenheim before her marriage to Moses Mendelssohn in 1762, for example, may be derived from his letters to her, but not from her own personal testimony. From the letters Mendelssohn sent to his fiancée during their engagement (known as *Brautbriefe*) we may clearly conclude that, in the generation before the one discussed in this book, a woman such as Fromet, born in Hamburg, could be well acquainted with European literature. Mendelssohn writes in one of his letters: 'It pleases me very much that you are reading Shaftesbury more than once. You can learn a lot from this little booklet.'[43] We also gather that Fromet hoped to read French literature in the original, and with this purpose in mind put some effort into learning the language. Mendelssohn was impressed by her determination to do so: 'Shall I really not send you Catesby's letters[44] in German? You must have your desires very well under control, if you are able to resist your desire to read these letters until you are able to do so in French.' He admits lacking her willpower: 'I envy you for this philosophical abstinence, and I confess my weakness.'[45] Reading between the lines, we may see indications of how Mendelssohn conceived of Fromet's reading: as a means of education, certainly, but also, and no less importantly, as a means of preparing her for writing letters—maybe especially for corresponding with her beloved. It may have been no accident that most—if not all—of the books he recommended to her belong to the epistolary genre. However, notwithstanding all the valuable information which may be derived from these documents, it is difficult to ascertain Fromet's response to reading and learn about her own world-view, since her letters to her fiancé were not preserved.[46]

[43] Mendelssohn, *Brautbriefe*, 37. The editor assumes that the book mentioned was *An Inquiry Concerning Virtue* by Anthony Ashley Cooper, earl of Shaftesbury, published in German translation in 1747.

[44] As indicated by the editor of the letters, Mendelssohn may be referring to a novel of 1758 by the French author Marie Jeanne Riccoboni, published in German translation in 1761.

[45] Mendelssohn, *Brautbriefe*, 33.

[46] The only letters of Fromet's that have been preserved are from a later period and do not touch on her reading experience.

PLATE 3. Fromet Mendelssohn, née Gugenheim (1737–1812)
Miniature portrait (1767): artist unknown
© bpk / SBB

Thus the absence of women's voices from the generation immediately preceding the one discussed here makes it necessary to rely on indirect evidence to learn what little we can about the reading habits of Jewish women in central Europe at this time, and very hard to undertake any thorough analysis of their personal attitude towards reading and the material they read. In respect of the women considered in this study, the situation is very different. The relatively copious sources they left contain valuable information concerning precisely this subject. An examination of their reading practices shows striking similarities with tendencies within Jewish society which, as noted above, had begun to spread in previous generations, such as the intensification of reading and the turn to non-religious material and even non-Jewish literature. In addition, however, other features may be detected that are peculiar to the historical moment in which they lived. As the following discussion will illustrate, their specific reading habits both shaped and reflected a secular outlook that had become prevalent among cultured Europeans and was spreading among growing numbers of German Jews. In their reading, these Jewish women embraced the ethos of the Enlightenment, acting as critical, autonomous readers, and as conscious members of the emerging public.

WOMEN AS AUTONOMOUS READERS

Whereas many historical accounts present the women discussed here as culturally subordinated to the men around them—to dominant thinkers and writers with whom they were in personal contact[47]—an analysis of their reading practices calls for a more nuanced assessment. In the written sources they left, reading appears as a largely autonomous activity, usually carried out independently of close supervision by any authority, religious or of any other type. Just as contemporary maskilim rejected rabbinic power—as, for example, in their typical omission of the customary rabbinical endorsements (*haskamot*) from their publications—enlightened women rejected the need to seek the approval of any authority, Jewish or non-Jewish, when choosing their reading material. Relying on their own judgement, they read, ultimately, whatever they wished. Like many of their contemporaries, they felt the need for advice and counsel, but it was up to them to determine who would fulfil the guiding role. They may therefore be considered autonomous readers, who both decided for themselves what to read and exhibited a critical attitude towards the texts they read.

[47] See Introduction (p. 17) above, 'Re-examining the Connection with Romanticism'.

Once more, Henriette Herz's case is typical, this time in showing the interplay between independence and actively sought guidance. Her memoirs, written when she was in her sixties, indicate that as a child she was able to choose the books she read, going by herself to the lending library and deciding on her own which works she would bring back home.[48] Her parents do not seem to have expressed any opposition to the books she picked—even though at this stage she devoted most of her time to reading novels, a practice much criticized in German circles and later on also by the maskilim.[49] Nor do they seem to have protested at her visits to the lending library, a new institution which developed in the eighteenth century, more particularly in the latter half, and was so conducive to the extensive reading which Henriette's habits exemplify.[50] When returning home after a day's work, her beloved father, Dr Benjamin de Lemos, occupied himself with 'sacred books', while in the children's room Henriette, his eldest child, read 'bad novels and comedies'.[51]

Her 'enlightened' family (Henriette's own description: she commonly classified Jews in her environment according to their openness to modern culture[52]), though still strongly attached to Jewish practices,[53] understandingly accepted that a young girl should wish to read secular works, and in a

---

[48] Landsberg (ed.), *Henriette Herz*, 121, 123 (Eng. trans. in Blackwell and Zantop (eds.), *Bitter Healing*, 314, 316).

[49] On the maskilic criticism of this phenomenon, see Feiner, 'The Modern Jewish Woman' (Heb.), 259. For a specific case, see Aaron Wolfsohn-Halle's play *Silliness and Sanctimony* (Yid.) from c.1794. Wolfsohn-Halle condemns the 'false enlightenment' of Yetkhen, a young modernizing Jewish woman, reflected among other things in her 'detrimental' reading practices. An English, annotated translation of this play was printed in Berkowitz and Dauber (eds.), *Landmark Yiddish Plays*.

[50] The lending library (unlike traditional libraries, which were accessible only to a restricted audience) was an innovative feature of the 18th-century book market and a central institution of the new public sphere. It helped provide the growing reading public with cheap access to a relatively wide selection of printed materials (Wittmann, 'Was There a Reading Revolution?', 306–7; Melton, *The Rise of the Public*, 104–9).

[51] Landsberg (ed.), *Henriette Herz*, 119 (Eng. trans. in Blackwell and Zantop (eds.), *Bitter Healing*, 313).

[52] Thus, for example, she says of a childhood friend that she was a 'very reasonable girl who had a good mind, but was without education or culture since her parents did not belong to the so-called enlightened class of Jews': Landsberg (ed.), *Henriette Herz*, 122 (Eng. trans. in Blackwell and Zantop (eds.), *Bitter Healing*, 315).

[53] According to Henriette, the laws and customs of Jewish tradition were strictly followed in her parents' home. See Landsberg (ed.), *Henriette Herz*, 113 (Eng. trans. in Blackwell and Zantop (eds.), *Bitter Healing*, 310). An external source indicates that in 1769 Benjamin de Lemos, Henriette's father, as the doctor of the Berlin Jewish community, received a special permit to hold religious services in his house, despite the communal regulation forbidding private *minyanim* (for economic reasons), indicating his religious devotion (Meisl, *Protocols of the Berlin Jewish Community* (Heb.), 256).

foreign language at that.⁵⁴ If they did have any reservations, these had to do with the intensity of their daughter's reading, not with its contents: for her passion for books distracted her from other occupations, such as sewing, which was considered an indispensable component of a girl's training. For this reason her parents (more precisely, her mother) did insist on some limits to the time she devoted to reading.⁵⁵ This concern apart, it seems that Henriette's parents did not merely tolerate but actually enjoyed her enthusiasm for, and ability in, reading. Henriette recalls reciting books to her mother, who suffered from a severe eye illness caused by her 'incessant crying over the death of a two-year-old son',⁵⁶ and at times to other family members. On these occasions she preferred to read plays, owing to her embarrassment at the emotion aroused in her by novels: 'On Friday evenings I read aloud to my parents; my father preferred to hear plays; I also liked to read these aloud, preferring to read novels alone to myself since they always moved me to bitter tears, and I was ashamed to cry.'⁵⁷ Given the kinds of works she was reading, and the fact that many of them were borrowed from a lending library, it is reasonable to assume that most if not all were written in German.

Henriette's engagement and marriage, and perhaps also the beginnings of maturity, marked the beginning of a change in her reading habits. One of the first things her future husband, the philosopher and medical doctor Marcus Herz—who was fifteen years her senior—did when meeting his fiancée was to conduct a sort of 'reading examination'. 'Shortly after our engagement,' wrote Henriette, 'he asked me if I was able to read.' Since the answer was positive, 'he asked me to read something out, and after the first line he said I was certainly able to read [*ablesen*], but not with understanding [*lesen*], and that he wished to teach me, and he read out to me. Only then did I

---

⁵⁴ For a depiction of Jewish women's reading in non-Jewish languages in a different setting—eastern Europe in the second half of the 19th century—and the maskilic as well as traditional reactions to this expanding phenomenon, see Parush, *Reading Jewish Women*, 172–206. Although some historians have claimed that Parush's thesis regarding women's 'marginality' and its 'benefits'—i.e. the claim that the unequal distribution of literacy between men and women and the only partial supervision of women's literacy in traditional Jewish society unintentionally permitted Jewish women to expand the scope of their knowledge—requires reassessment (cf. review articles by Stampfer, 'Jewish Women Revisited', and Zalkin, 'Iris Parush' (Heb.)), her arguments are convincing, and it remains clear that the considerable growth of women's literacy in foreign (as well as Jewish) languages played an important role not only in their own lives but also in Jewish society in general. See also Parush, 'Readers in Cameo'.

⁵⁵ Landsberg (ed.), *Henriette Herz*, 121 (Eng. trans. in Blackwell and Zantop (eds.), *Bitter Healing*, 314).

⁵⁶ Landsberg, *Henriette Herz* (ed.), 114 (Eng. trans. in Blackwell and Zantop (eds.), *Bitter Healing*, 310).

⁵⁷ Landsberg, *Henriette Herz* (ed.), 121 (Eng. trans. in Blackwell and Zantop (eds.), *Bitter Healing*, 314–15).

understand what he had meant.'⁵⁸ This was a humiliating but instructive experience for the young girl: from it, Henriette learned to take reading seriously, as an activity that required skill and dedication. Not only the way she read, but also the material she read, changed significantly. After her marriage at the age of 15, following a long engagement, her new husband—who was a friend of Kant and attracted a considerable public to the philosophical and scientific lectures he held at his, now their, home⁵⁹—offered Henriette an alternative to reading as a purely idle pleasure.

> My propensity for reading grew, and I could now [i.e. as a married woman] satisfy it undisturbed. The first book which I read completely under the direction of my husband was Euler's *Letters to a German Princess*. Even if Herz was too busy to instruct me thoroughly, he would still explain many things to me that I did not understand.⁶⁰

The book she mentions—actually a collection of letters—had been dedicated by the mathematician and astronomer Leonhard Euler to the princess of Anhalt-Dessau. Originally published in French in 1768 and since translated into several languages, it was very popular at the time. The book covered topics considered indispensable in a person's general education, including the fundamentals of natural science and philosophy, and was read by men and women alike.⁶¹

Thus Henriette's reading entered a new phase. No longer was it merely a pastime, a way to amuse and entertain herself; it became in no small measure a practical matter, aimed at fostering her education and her personal growth. She herself seems to have perceived this change as a transition to a higher level of reading. One of the constant threads running through her memoirs, written from the perspective of several decades later, is that of her evolution as a reader, which to a certain extent provides the context for the story of her life.⁶²

---

⁵⁸ Landsberg (ed.), *Henriette Herz*, 127. (This fragment does not appear in the Eng. trans. of the memoirs in Blackwell and Zantop (eds.), *Bitter Healing*.)

⁵⁹ On Marcus Herz, see Davies, *Identity or History?*

⁶⁰ Landsberg (ed.), *Henriette Herz*, 132 (Eng. trans. in Blackwell and Zantop (eds.), *Bitter Healing*, 323).

⁶¹ Leonhard Euler, *Briefe an eine deutsche Prinzessin über verschiedene Gegenstände aus der Physik und Philosophie: Aus dem Französischen übersetzt* (Leipzig, 1769), was the first German edition. This book was also popular among the maskilim. As Tal Kogman has shown, it was one of the main textual sources used by the maskil Isaac Satanow when writing Hebrew textbooks and science books for a Jewish public (Kogman, *The Creation of Images of Knowledge* (Heb.), 26–31).

⁶² Rolf Engelsing pointed out the recurrence of this thematic element in the life stories of cultured individuals in the 18th century (Engelsing, *Der Bürger als Leser*, 198). For an interesting reading of Henriette Herz's memoirs—albeit different from the one suggested here—see Weissberg, *Life as a Goddess: Henriette Herz Writes her Autobiography*.

In this sense, the account of her life as she chooses to tell it bears a certain similarity with the autobiography of Lazarus Bendavid, a maskil also born in Berlin in the 1760s.[63] In his narrative, Bendavid presented the development of his reading habits as a central component in his spiritual and intellectual growth. A compulsive reader from early childhood, by his thirteenth year Bendavid had managed to read, in parallel to his talmudic studies, the most disparate of texts from general culture, as these came by chance into his hands. As he grew older—Bendavid indicates this several times in his autobiography—he became aware of his 'unruly' reading and devoted considerable effort to bringing order to it, in such a way as to give him a grounding in particular branches of knowledge. Henriette Herz also shaped her personal story partly in terms of her growth as a reader, progressing from what she perceived to be a 'lower' type of literature to a 'higher', more serious one. However, one significant gender-related difference is that whereas Lazarus Bendavid, like other contemporary maskilim, emphasized his diminishing focus on Jewish texts and his increasing dedication to diverse fields of general culture, in the case of a Jewish woman such as Henriette Herz the transition seems to have been more vertical than horizontal, from popular literature to materials that enjoyed a higher cultural status.

As for Henriette Herz's self-reliance as a reader, her memoirs may convey the impression that after her wedding her husband assumed supervision over her reading.[64] However, Marcus Herz's intervention should be seen less as the imposition of authority than as the provision of professional advice by a learned and experienced intellectual, a man who seems to have held in high esteem the idea of a cultured woman capable of formulating her own judgements.[65] He tried to foster his wife's education and widen her knowledge—to be sure, adopting the typically patriarchal stance of the husband who takes upon himself the mission of instructing his wife, but at the same time honouring her will and her choices of the books she would read. For example, despite some disparaging comments to Henriette, he respected her decision to read Goethe's works, for which he had no regard at all. Henriette read Goethe

---

[63] Bendavid, 'Selbstbiographie'.   [64] Davies, 'Portraits of a Lady'.

[65] In a quite surprising essay published in 1771—years before his marriage to Henriette—Marcus Herz puts words into the mouths of two Jewish women conducting a fictive intellectual discussion about a play that Herz wished to review. In this imaginary dialogue, the two women are depicted as critical spectators, fully acquainted with the literary and cultural discourse of the time. They express their opinions about particular productions and theatre in general, showing familiarity with well-known plays and even theoretical literature on the cultural role of theatre. Herz's essay, 'Freymüthiges Kaffegespräch zwoer jüdischen Zuschauerinnen über den Juden Pinkus oder über den Geschmack eines gewissen Parterrs', was republished by Gunnar Och in 1988.

even though she was well aware of her husband's distaste for this kind of work. Thus Marcus Herz's early intervention in Henriette's reading is to be seen as a first prompt to a more independent choice of material: her later selections were determined by her personal taste more than by her husband's opinions. Indeed, Henriette chose other sources of inspiration for herself from among her male and female friends—certainly after Marcus's early death in 1803, before she had turned 40.[66]

Stimulation and recommendation thus were (as indeed they still are) essential elements of modern reading culture, even among autonomous readers. Along with the propagation of secular attitudes, efforts were certainly made to replace the declining religious authority and control the content of reading among different sectors of society. Enlightened intellectuals in the eighteenth century considered it one of their primary tasks to channel the reading of those who needed guiding—those simple folk, women, and children who, according to them, were not 'mature' enough to assume responsibility for their own education. But in fact, lacking any power of enforcement, the disciplinary efforts of such intellectuals had no binding validity. When the religious canon lost its dominion, it was up to the individual to decide what to read, using the most arbitrary criterion of all: personal taste.[67]

Given the growing number of new publications flooding the book market at the end of the eighteenth century,[68] a person who took reading seriously but was not affiliated to an organized 'reading society',[69] a learning institution such as a university, or an appropriate intellectual circle could easily lose his or her way. Some enlightened Jewish women felt this danger at various points in their lives, among them the young Rahel Levin, for whom it was one of the reasons why she so much appreciated her correspondence with David Veit in her early twenties: 'I thank you again for writing [to tell] me what to read, for otherwise, I would read not one syllable in German in your absence,

---

[66] We lack concrete details regarding Fromet Gugenheim's reading habits after her marriage to Moses Mendelssohn, which could illuminate her development as a reader. However, the pre-nuptial correspondence indicates that Mendelssohn understood his role in a similar way to Marcus Herz. On the one hand, he urged Fromet to read 'useful books' and constantly offered to supply her with reading material (see e.g. Mendelssohn, *Brautbriefe*, 37); on the other hand, he did not impose the reading of certain texts but expected her to tell him which were to her taste so that he could obtain them for her (ibid. 47). [67] Engelsing, *Der Bürger als Leser*, 182.

[68] At the 1800 Leipzig book fair, for instance, 5,000 new books were exhibited (Darnton, *The Kiss of Lamourette*, 159).

[69] This social and cultural institution, typical of the 18th century, contributed to shaping the literary taste of its members and served as a framework for reading and discussing enlightened ideas. On reading societies and literary circles in Germany, see Van Dülmen, *The Society of the Enlightenment*, 82–104.

for I would not trust anybody's recommendations, and in this way I might just leave the best books unread.'[70]

The literary dialogue between Levin and Veit dated back to Veit's days in Berlin. At that time he was able not only to recommend books but also to provide her with copies of them; and she in return responded with profound insights evoked by her reading.[71] Writing from Dessau in 1793, he enquired: 'Which ones among the books I lent you [while in Berlin] are still with you?' He remembered having lent her *Moritz's Journeys*,[72] a book that belonged to the Jewish philosopher Salomon Maimon. Veit urged Rahel to finish reading the book as soon as possible and return it to its owner, for 'he needs it for [writing] Moritz's biography'.[73] In her reply, Rahel mentioned two additional works procured through Veit: 'part of Kant, and Genz's [*sic*] ideas on the revolution'.[74] This list of books, impressive for a young Jewish woman at the end of the eighteenth century, attests to her interest in a wide range of subjects, from travel literature (Moritz's book), very popular in those days, to philosophy (Kant) and politics and current affairs (Gentz).

When David Veit left Berlin in 1793 to study medicine at the University of Göttingen, he continued to mediate between his friend Rahel and the world of books. He drew her attention to recent publications with which, in his opinion, she should become acquainted and even gave her some advice on how to proceed with her reading. In November that year he wrote:

Last Sunday I read through Lessing's life story, published in Berlin, by Voss, in 1793. Mr von Brinckmann (whom I send my respectful regards) *must* have the book;[75] . . . and you *must* read it. You will find some things that you will rightly want

---

[70] *Briefwechsel zwischen Rahel und David Veit*, i. 58.

[71] See e.g. Levin's analysis of two contemporary texts, to which Veit responded with deep admiration: ibid. ii. 1 ff.

[72] Karl Philipp Moritz wrote a three-volume travel book following his stay in Italy: *Reisen eines Deutschen in Italien aus den Jahren 1786 bis 1788. In Briefen* (Berlin, 1792–3). Incidentally, he also edited the *Magazin zur Erfahrungsseelenkunde* (*Journal of Empirical Psychology*, 1783–93), a pioneering journal in this field of knowledge which included a significant number of contributions by enlightened Jewish men such as Moses Mendelsohn, Marcus Herz, Aaron Wolfsohn-Halle, Lazarus Bendavid, perhaps David Veit, and, most notably, Salomon Maimon. See Wieckenberg, 'Juden als Autoren des *Magazins zur Erfahrungsseelenkunde*', esp. pp. 134–5. On Mendelssohn's participation in Moritz's project see Altmann, *Moses Mendelssohn*, 668–71.

[73] *Briefwechsel zwischen Rahel und David Veit*, i. 20. Moritz, a close friend of Maimon, had died that same year. [74] Ibid. 23.

[75] Karl Gustav von Brinckmann, the Swedish diplomat mentioned above (Ch. 1 n. 21), possessed an impressive library. See *Briefe von und an Friedrich und Dorothea Schlegel*, ed. Behler, xxiii. 388. He shared with his Jewish women friends not only his books but also his wide knowledge of classical and modern literature.

to skip, but you should not; the remarks by the publisher (Lessing's brother) are interwoven with interesting anecdotes.[76]

Several days later, Veit suggested a new list of reading material, which this time included Lessing's theory of the fable;[77] a new translation of the *Iliad* and the *Odyssey*, 'if you feel like reading heroic poems at the moment'; and, to give her the opportunity to practise her English, a work by Hume (the title is not mentioned)—or at least, 'the later parts', because 'the first ones will probably bore you as they bored me'. He assured her that she could get the book from Mrs Veit (Rahel's friend Dorothea Mendelssohn).[78] Sometimes, in case she should find it difficult to obtain a recommended text, Veit took the trouble to copy substantial fragments in his letters. For example, in 1795 he urged Levin to read an essay on the subject of synonyms, published in a philosophical journal: 'you must read it, because you have never read anything similar of German making, nor will you in the next fifty years'.[79] Wishing to give her a taste of this prized work as soon as possible, he chose a long paragraph and attached it to his letter, accompanied by suggestions on how she might read the whole thing: 'Leave the introduction for the end—it is tiresome at times—and first read at least some presentations of synonyms, so that these will prove to you that your efforts with the introduction will not be in vain.'[80]

Levin, however, was never exclusively dependent on her friend's suggestions. Even during the years of intense correspondence with Veit, her engagement with books was directed largely by her own initiative and judgement. She was constantly searching for alternative sources of information and supply, as, for instance, in an episode she described in one of her letters. While offering her condolences at a Jewish home in Berlin, she had met a doctor by the name of Bote, a 'very reasonable' man, and the two had engaged in a lively conversation about 'books, languages, English and the like'. This acquaintance immediately proved advantageous. That same evening Dr Bote, 'unbidden, of his own initiative', lent her the *Berlinische Monatsschrift*, 'because I saw it and expressed my wish to read the article by Gentz'. Levin was very pleased to have found in the doctor not only a person with whom she could engage in literary discussions, but, more than that, 'here again a person who lends me books'.[81]

---

[76] *Briefwechsel zwischen Rahel und David Veit*, i. 52.

[77] To his recommendation of the book Veit attached an offer which implies that Rahel's reading, far from being superficial, was recognized by both as a way of learning: 'If you wish to read it [Lessing's book], please let me know; I will then send you on a piece of paper in a letter the Greek and Latin passages' (ibid. 67).   [78] Ibid. 67–8.   [79] Ibid. ii. 120–1.   [80] Ibid. 121.

[81] Ibid. i. 132–3. In another case, it was the maskil Isaac Euchel who offered to lend her a German book, 'Voss's translation', when they met on a social visit at the house of Mrs de Lemos, Henriette

A sense of disorientation among the plethora of new publications was not unique to Jewish women. Rahel Levin's brother Ludwig Robert, writing to her in 1806 from Paris, spoke of his 'bitter-melancholic' mood after his friend David Koreff had decided to move from the apartment they had shared.[82] Koreff had taken with him all his books, leaving Robert facing 'empty bookshelves, once full of masterpieces which I hoped I could study'. Not only that but Robert, an aspiring Jewish writer lacking proper connections in Paris, now stood 'without any guidance' facing alone 'the whole chaos of science'. He told his sister that after coming to terms with the new situation he was again taking advantage of Koreff's encyclopaedic knowledge and using his book supply as a reading library.[83]

For readers such as Ludwig Robert, Henriette Herz, Rahel Levin, and many other enlightened Jews attracted by the modern world of books and new ideas, networks of communication and social and intellectual relations were indispensable tools: the exchange of letters, as seen in the previous chapter, as well as personal social interaction, played a decisive role in helping them find their way through the crowded literary scene.

THE DECLINE OF THE CULTURAL SUPREMACY OF RELIGIOUS LITERATURE

The rapid decline in the number of titles dealing exclusively with religious matters and the parallel expansion of secular literature in the European book market in the second half of the eighteenth century have been well documented.[84] This process, which was apparent in Jewish literary production in Germany, as shown by the expansion of the library of the Haskalah, was also reflected in the reading practices of individual Jews, among them the enlightened Jewish women under discussion here. For many years, devotional literature played only a minor role in their lives, and they preferred belles-lettres and philosophy to purely religious works. Only as they approached Christianity later in life did some of them, at least, turn more seriously to theological works. A letter written by Henriette Herz to her friend Immanuel Bekker in 1818, for instance, indicates the texts she used to read in those days, shortly

---

Herz's mother, in January 1794. Owing to a misunderstanding, he brought her instead a book by Shakespeare (*Briefwechsel zwischen Rahel und David Veit*, i. 109, 133).

[82] David Ferdinand Koreff, a native of Breslau, met the Levins during his stay in Berlin as a medical student. After graduating in Halle, he moved to Paris, where he practised medicine and engaged in writing. Upon his return to Prussia after several years, he pursued a successful scientific and political career (Sohni, 'Koreff, David Ferdinand'; Kremer, 'David Ferdinand Koreff').

[83] Levin Varnhagen, *Briefwechsel mit Ludwig Robert*, 64.

[84] Darnton, *The Kiss of Lamourette*, 160–1; Wittmann, 'Was There a Reading Revolution?', 302.

after her conversion, as distinct from the books which attracted her attention in earlier years. Emphasizing her intellectual diligence during her stay in Italy in the company of Dorothea Mendelssohn, she indicates that 'besides the Bible in the morning and letter writing', both friends 'regularly read Dante one hour every day, and very thoroughly at that'.[85]

No less significant than the content of their reading, however, was their worldly attitude towards what they read, which could prevail even when they were reading religious texts. Rahel Levin's secular approach, for instance, persisted as she read the Bible. Before her 1814 baptism and wedding to Karl August Varnhagen, she wrote to her fiancé:

I have a dreadful lack of books. Not even one. Therefore yesterday, at a late hour, I took the Bible. I read about the betrayal and death of the Lord Jesus, and I cried a lot. I can image it so vividly; how he knew that Peter would betray him; so natural: certainly true! And how Peter himself cried, when the rooster crowed for the second time. I liked it a lot! But not at all the resurrection. It is not even written in a convincing way . . .[86]

Not only does Levin pick the New Testament for lack of a better choice; she approaches Scripture no differently from any other text, seeming to read the Bible as if it were a novel. Her words to Varnhagen belong to a discussion of a literary work and its ability faithfully to depict reality, indicating a secular reading of a devotional book. Even when the evidence shows that these women turned to theological texts, then, it should not be assumed that they always did so out of religious motivation. The connotations they attached to these texts and the ways in which they internalized and interpreted them are highly significant.

Modern secular literature also replaced religious traditional literature as the associative world of these Jewish women. Glikl used to quote extensively from traditional sources. Her autobiography is interspersed with numerous verses from the Bible, quotes from the Talmud, and phrases from Jewish prayers, all of which she had apparently absorbed either from spoken Yiddish or from Yiddish written sources,[87] thus revealing a cultural store based mainly (but not solely) on Jewish tradition. Less than a century later, enlightened Jewish women, as well as many Jewish men, drew their references from a completely different repertoire—namely, secular European (not only German) literature. When Fradchen Liebmann, a Jewish woman from Berlin,[88] wrote to tell her friend Rahel Levin in the summer of 1795 about

---

[85] *Letters to Immanuel Bekker*, ed. Putzel, 20.
[86] Kobler (ed.), *Juden und Judentum in deutschen Briefen*, 180.
[87] Turniansky, 'The Stories in Glikl Hamel's Work' (Heb.), 61.
[88] On Fradchen Liebmann, see Chs. 4–7 below.

her experiences at the spa she was visiting, a phrase inspired by Shakespeare—'bin ich nicht a wretched creature' ('am I not a wretched creature')—sufficed to convey a point through a brief expression, clear to anyone who shared a similar cultural background.[89] Henriette Mendelssohn, living in Paris, wrote in 1807 to her younger brother Nathan, who unlike his two brothers was not a banker but an inventor of scientific instruments and at that time was trying to become involved in the development of a munitions factory in Provence: 'Thus it could happen that the same springs by which Petrarch chanted such harmonious, fervent, tender verses, will activate the wheels that serve to build those machines which spread death and destruction on earth.'[90] In this ironic comment Henriette drew on the Western literary heritage, playing on Petrarch's humanist views, to express her contempt for the battles that had spilled so much blood throughout the European continent—this letter being written at the time of the Napoleonic wars. As this quotation demonstrates, Henriette's knowledge was not limited to medieval Italian poetry, though her familiarity with that is itself significant; she was also well informed about the biography of the fourteenth-century writer, who had spent many years in Provence. Immersed in a similar cultural context, Ludwig Robert, writing to his sister Rahel Levin from the French capital, inserted a quotation (albeit a faulty one) from one of Goethe's works to express his opinion about his friend Koreff.[91]

Whereas there is ample evidence in these women's writing of a close acquaintance with European literature, references to the Jewish cultural world appear much more rarely; and where they do appear, it is clear that the women's familiarity with these concepts derives from daily life, not from reading or learning. Fradchen Liebmann refers to a *nekome* (a Yiddish word taken from the Hebrew and meaning vengeance);[92] Rahel Levin and David Veit talk of a young modernizing Jewish woman full of *rishes* (another Yiddish word of Hebrew origin meaning maliciousness, especially against Jews);[93] Dorothea Mendelssohn speaks of an actress dressed 'like a Jewish

---

[89] As Bosold indicates in her edition of Liebmann's letters, Cassius is described as a 'wretched creature' in Shakespeare's *Julius Caesar* (Bosold, 'Friederike Liman', 21). In another letter, Liebmann quotes again from Shakespeare, this time from *Hamlet*: 'Alas! Poor Yorick'. And on yet another occasion she recurs to German literature, as she chooses a phrase from one of Lessing's plays (ibid. 25, 107).

[90] *Bankiers, Künstler und Gelehrte*, ed. Gilbert, 5. As Ilse Rabien has pointed out, at a young age and before converting to Christianity Nathan enjoyed state support for his inventions; in 1806 he established a workshop for the development of mathematical, physical, and astronomical instruments. After the French occupation of Berlin in 1806 Nathan tried to move his activities elsewhere, to no avail. Rabien, 'Die Mendelssohns in Bad Reinerz' (here pp. 156–7).

[91] Levin Varnhagen, *Briefwechsel mit Ludwig Robert*, 64.   [92] Bosold, 'Friederike Liman', 27.

[93] *Briefwechsel zwischen Rahel und David Veit*, i. 53, 55.

bride';[94] and Esther Gad quotes 'a Hebrew saying' (in German) in a letter to the German writer Jean Paul.[95] Jewish words and concepts may, however, have been much more common in their correspondence with family members, especially in their early letters, most of which have not survived, except for part of the Levins' correspondence.

READING AND INTROSPECTION

Rahel Levin's way of reading the Bible in the example quoted above reflects a new approach. A hundred years earlier, a woman such as Glikl, who was not confined within a Jewish environment but in regular contact with the world at large, always found a way—and perceived a need—to justify her reading of non-Jewish, non-religious texts as a means of reinforcing her faith. Like Glikl, enlightened Jewish women attached great importance to reading as a source of knowledge and values, but their motivation was very different. Whereas Glikl approached books (and life) as a deeply pious and believing Jew, her successors did so from a secular perspective, interpreting texts and reality in general not 'in essentially supernatural, other-worldly terms', but 'in terms which are essentially natural and focussed on this world'.[96]

The contrast between Glikl and enlightened Jewish women emphasizes the importance of paying attention to the different ways in which individuals at various times and in various places approach a certain text.[97] Contrary to more traditional theories regarding the relationship between the reader and the text, which assumed that the written text conveyed a purportedly stable meaning to the reader, today it is commonly accepted that 'reading is not already inscribed in the text', and that a gap exists 'between the meaning assigned to it (by its author, by custom, by criticism, and so forth) and the interpretation that its readers might make of it'.[98] Scholars dealing with the study of reading throughout the ages have adopted insights from the field of

[94] *Briefe von und an Friedrich und Dorothea Schlegel*, ed. Behler, xxiii. 63.

[95] 'Ein allgemeines Mißgeschick, ist ein Trost für eigenes' ('general misfortune is a consolation for one's own'): Hahn (ed.), '"Geliebtester Schriftsteller"', 26.

[96] Burke, 'Religion and Secularisation', 294. Such a secular attitude implies not that religion had disappeared from their lives but that it had receded from the dominant place it occupied in previous times to become just one aspect of experience. As for Glikl, it should be emphasized that signs of a new subjectivity may easily be detected in her text. Although she purportedly minimizes her own importance, and despite her unease with her autobiographical undertaking, she did after all write her memoirs, thus focusing attention on the story of her life. For a discussion of Glikl's memoirs in the framework of Jewish autobiographical writing see Moseley, *Being for Myself Alone*, 155–75.

[97] For an illuminating example of how readers in different environments find (or rather 'fabricate') varying cultural meanings based on one textual source, see Griswold, 'The Fabrication of Meaning'.

[98] Chartier, *The Order of Books*, 2.

literary criticism, especially the attention paid to the changing reader's response, and examined the significance of these insights from a historical perspective.[99] Within this conceptual framework, it is possible to examine how enlightened Jewish women interpreted the material they read, internalized its content, and integrated it within their world-view. A letter written by Sara Meyer, later Sophie von Grotthuß, illuminates the modern reading experience of a Jewish woman at the end of the eighteenth century.

In a rare testimony penned in 1796, Sara Meyer shared with Goethe, with whom she had been in contact since their meeting in Carlsbad the previous year, her emotional response after reading a new volume of his influential novel *Wilhelm Meister's Apprenticeship*. Recovering from a long mental breakdown, apparently prompted by difficult relations with her mother,[100] Sara Meyer described in her letter how the reality of her life had fused with the book's fiction: 'The curses that Meister uttered against himself when he thought of the possibility of Felix's death came to fulfilment in me, my aspiration, my wish, my goal was to commit suicide, thank God forever that none of my countless attempts to take my own life succeeded!'[101] The strong physical reaction elicited in her by reading the book may strike twenty-first-century readers as somewhat extreme:

> How I shuddered while reading that paragraph . . . Goethe, dear Goethe! Had you seen me at that moment, you would have taken my behaviour for *beaux restes* of my shattered state, and yet I never had greater possession of my senses than at that moment. No, you cannot understand me until you know my story, how profoundly it all touched and shook me; how I often had to put the book down and continue reading only the next day for fear of cramps; how I dissolved into tears at Mignon's death, to which terrible memories were attached, and had to hear harangues and threats to take the book away from me from my brothers, who love me heartily, for fear that the tension would harm my now so weakened body; how I often exclaimed, oh, this is my divine Goethe!—when you illuminated with your lovely colours something that lay dark in my heart and mind. Thank you, thank you for the jewel that delights me.[102]

---

[99] Reader-response literary criticism developed in the 1960s and 1970s, notably with the work of Wolfgang Iser, Stanley Fish, and others, giving rise to a wide research literature. For a discussion of reading theories from a feminist perspective see Orly Lubin's 'Women Reading Women' (Heb.).

[100] From the content of the letter it seems that at the time of writing she had been in a mentally fragile condition for more than a year—'erased from among the living': Geiger (ed.), 'Einundzwanzig Briefe', 46. Sara attributes her emotional collapse to tense relations with her mother, prompted, she claims, by religious hatred. It is significant that Sara, whose oscillation between Judaism and Christianity at that time (see her sister Marianne's report on this point: ibid. 29) may have caused the conflict with her mother, identifies the cause of her distress not as Judaism, but rather as 'religious hatred' in general, which was seen by enlightened people as a source of misery. On Sara's (and Marianne's) change of faith, see Ch. 1 above.   [101] Ibid. 46–7.   [102] Ibid. 47.

What is most remarkable in Sara Meyer's testimony to her reading experience here is not only the intensity of her emotional involvement, to the point of weeping and shivering, and her deep identification with the work's fictional characters, but also the fact of her sharing her reaction with the author. For a reader not to restrain the emotions aroused by reading a book, and to pick up her quill to express her feelings to the author in such a personal way, may seem exceptional. In the context of the time, however, it was not. Many readers in the latter half of the eighteenth century not only 'inhabited the text, identified with its characters and applied the vicissitudes of its plot to real life',[103] as Sara Meyer's letter to Goethe shows; they also sought to share their experiences with the author. Sara's missive, reporting her reaction to the book, belongs to a phenomenon that began to spread in England, France, and Germany from the mid-eighteenth century and is especially associated with the names of Richardson, Rousseau, Klopstock, and Goethe. For instance, as Robert Darnton has shown, French readers, male and female alike, flooded the famous Jean-Jacques Rousseau with their impassioned letters, eager to communicate to the author the strong feelings that took hold of them while devouring the six sentimental volumes of *Julie, ou la nouvelle Héloïse*. Descriptions of sighs and torment, ecstasy and tears of joy filled page after page sent not only by 'simple' readers but also by barons and priests to the venerated writer.[104]

In imitating these readers, Sara Meyer was embracing the culture of sentiment that pervaded eighteenth-century Europe.[105] However, a less immediately evident aspect of her reaction should also be emphasized. Although Meyer at first seems to be overwhelmed by her feelings, it becomes clear that her reading response was not limited to the emotional level; her reason and a drive to analyse the situation were constantly present. Even as she portrays her emotions, Sara Meyer stresses her balance of mind, her self-control even

---

[103] Cavallo and Chartier, introd. to *A History of Reading in the West*, 25. These two scholars, who as stated above reject Engelsing's theory of a revolutionary transition from intensive to extensive reading at the end of the 18th century, see the phenomenon here described as the application of old reading habits, characteristic of religious reading (intensive reading that takes hold of its readers), to a new genre, the novel. See also Wittmann, 'Was There a Reading Revolution?', 295–301.

[104] Darnton, 'Readers Respond to Rousseau', 242–3. Cf. the Hebrew letters sent by female admirers of Hebrew authors in the second half of the 19th century, in Cohen and Feiner (eds.), *Voice of a Hebrew Maiden* (Heb.).

[105] Fania Oz-Salzberger emphasizes the strong presence of sentimentality precisely in the 'age of reason'. As she explains, 'It seems as though Romanticism, especially German Romanticism, took for itself a monopoly on the emotional and the private, while denying these to be aspects par excellence of the literature and the philosophy identified with the Enlightenment' (Oz-Salzberger, 'From Desperate Lover to Political Economist' (Heb.), 38).

in her delicate situation, as when she says: 'I never had greater possession of my senses than at that moment.' A remarkable feature of her reaction to Goethe's book, no less than the outburst of feeling, lies in the act of writing it down. Her reflection on the feelings stimulated by her reading, her detailed description of her response, and her analysis of it—all these are the choices of a modern, self-conscious subject, well aware of the uniqueness of his or her personal experience. Sara Meyer places herself at the centre of attention, as an object of study, and uses reading as a means to self-reflection. Conscious of the existence of a (relatively new) science that deals with the analysis of human behaviour—one of the disciplines that emerged during the Enlightenment—she sees herself as an appropriate and even fascinating object of study for that science. 'My physical and emotional state are for me and for all those who observed me a real and not all that trivial problem in the history of psychology', she adds in the same letter to Goethe.[106] In her opinion, so it seems, her personal story may contribute to the understanding of human nature.

Sara Meyer's reading response, though perhaps extreme, was not exceptional among this group of enlightened Jewish women. She was not the only one to report having experienced a book as a chapter in her life. When Henriette Herz read Goethe's autobiography, she claimed she derived great pleasure from it for a similar reason: 'Whoever reads the book will find himself in it, in many tranquil moments of his life, and whatever he has sensed in an opaque and almost unconscious way, becomes clear and certain to him.'[107] In other words, one of the things Henriette Herz found in Goethe's story of his life—or rather, one of the things she believed it was fitting to find and then articulate in the testimony of her reading experience—was herself. Among the great qualities expected of an author as talented as Goethe was the capability to express in words what the 'simple person' felt but was unable to grasp, let alone express clearly in words. Contemporary readers, for their part, were expected to be active in their appropriation of texts, to set out to capture the meaning of the text and apply it to their own lives, carefully examining the feelings and associations aroused by the book, as Henriette Herz and Sara Meyer did.[108]

---

[106] Geiger (ed.), 'Einundzwanzig Briefe', 46.

[107] Heinrici (ed.), 'Briefe von Henriette Herz an August Twesten', 303.

[108] From today's point of view, in the light of feminist reading theories, one could easily claim that by identifying themselves with the characters in texts written by men, these women were in fact surrendering to male hegemonic power. See Fetterley, *The Resisting Reader*; Lubin, 'Woman Reads Woman'. A contrasting attitude is presented in Rahel Levin's reading response to Goethe's novel *Wilhelm Meister's Apprenticeship* as reflected in a letter to Veit of June 1795, in which she evades efforts

How these Jewish readers approached a text and internalized its content was thus characteristic of the wider cultural environment in which their reading took place. Like many of their contemporary co-religionists, they not only turned to new literary products, different from those that had traditionally served Jews, but also adopted a modern, secular attitude towards them. Starting with the Renaissance and continuing with the seventeenth-century scientific revolution and the eighteenth-century Enlightenment, the focus of attention turned increasingly from the other world to this one, and the wish to understand better the surrounding natural world and humanity itself, human nature and human society, became ever stronger.[109] Sara Meyer, Henriette Herz, and other Jewish women, like so many of their generation, wanted to learn about themselves and about human nature in general, and books provided them with a means of doing so. With the help of books, they could analyse their own feelings and reactions as well as broader issues concerning society at large.

IN THE CIRCLE OF ENLIGHTENED READERS: A DIVERSITY OF READING MATERIAL

Reading fulfilled important functions in the lives of these (and many other) modernizing Jewish women: it constituted a means to education, a leisure activity, a vehicle for introspection, and, most significantly, a basis for social communication. Texts were discussed with and frequently read in the company of friends—Jews and non-Jews, male and female, in social gatherings at their places of residence or during vacations: for instance, on the women's frequent visits to European spas.[110] Books were also a recurrent theme in their wide-ranging correspondence. Reading was in fact an indispensable precondition for their stepping beyond the limited circle of Jewish society to join the educated public that had been emerging in Germany and across Europe throughout the eighteenth century and engage in the exchange of ideas on current issues in the cultural, social, and at times even the political and economic fields.

In view of these functions, it is not surprising that the enlightened women's reading encompassed a wide range of topics and genres, including

---

by her friend and correspondent to identify her with a female character in the novel (*Briefwechsel zwischen Rahel und David Veit*, ii. 131 ff.).

[109] Obviously attention was also paid to nature and humanity in previous times. The last 500 years, however, have undeniably witnessed an impressive rise of humanism and an increasing interest in nature for its own sake, not just as a manifestation of God (although also not necessarily in non-religious terms). Taylor, *A Secular Age*. [110] See Ch. 4 below.

literary forms usually considered the exclusive domain of men. This literary breadth belies a widespread view according to which women of that period—including modernizing Jewish women—read mainly fiction, especially novels. Indeed, received wisdom in historical and literary research asserts a close connection between the novel and women: both as avid readers and as authors of novels, it has been argued, women in the eighteenth century had an important role in the rise of this genre. The special link between women and the novel (and belletristic literature in general) was also invoked in descriptions of the beginnings of modernization in Jewish society towards the end of the eighteenth century. A prevalent dichotomy in Jewish historiography—one with far-reaching implications—distinguishes between the reading habits of women, who allegedly preferred emotional literature and were inclined towards *Sturm und Drang* ('storm and stress': the literary movement that flourished in Germany in the 1770s and early 1780s) and Romanticism, and those of men, believed to have been almost exclusively attracted by the highly regarded fields of philosophy and science, preferring rationalism to newer trends in German literature.[111] An example frequently cited in asserting this purported gender polarity—which distinguishes separate routes for men and women right at the beginning of modernity—is an incident mentioned in Sara Meyer's letters. 'When I was in my thirteenth year', she wrote to Goethe in 1797,

I had a tender romance with the son of a Hamburg merchant, a handsome, good and educated youngster. Once he sent me the consolation of unfortunate lovers, the divine Werther;[112] after I had devoured it, I sent it back with a thousand underlined passages and a fervent *billet*. This dispatch was intercepted by my dear father, I was confined to my room and Mendelssohn, who was my mentor, appeared and bitterly reproached me if I could forget God and religion, and even more absurd, he took the dear W., the innocent *corpus delicti*, and threw it out of the window . . . [113]

This story, repeatedly presented as proof of Mendelssohn's firm opposition to *Sturm und Drang*,[114] reinforced the sweeping claim that most maskilic Jewish men, starting with Mendelssohn, repudiated the new German litera-

---

[111] Meyer, *The Origins of the Modern Jew*, 85–114; Lowenstein, *The Berlin Jewish Community*, 162–3.

[112] Sara Meyer is speaking, of course, of Goethe's *Sorrows of Young Werther*.

[113] Geiger (ed.), 'Einundzwanzig Briefe', 51.

[114] A different explanation could be provided for Mendelssohn's enraged reaction, based on yet another letter written by Sara Meyer to Goethe almost two decades later, in 1814, recalling the same event. From the first letter one might easily deduce that Mendelssohn's rage was aroused by the book itself, but the second version implies that what really bothered the Jewish philosopher was Sara's romantic relationship with a non-Jewish youngster: 'he feared I would love the Christian'. See Kühne (ed.), 'Ein Brief von Frau von Grotthuis an Goethe', 210.

ture that was developing in the last third of the eighteenth century.[115] Also cited as evidence of this gender division are the reports of the two parallel but separate salons held at the Herzes' home: Marcus's, which served as a meeting point for rationalistic and scientifically inclined philosophers, and Henriette's, for readers of modern German literature.[116] Berlin's female Jewish Goethe enthusiasts thus became almost emblematic figures, symbolizing the attraction of Jewish women to fictional and emotional literature, in contrast to the rationalism and enlightenment of Jewish men. Women read Goethe; men read Lessing.

The image conveyed in these descriptions is consistent with the widespread assertion of women's prominence among the novel-reading public in Europe. However, this general claim needs to be reconsidered. It is true that many women, possibly more than men, read novels, and that contemporary observers as well as later historians saw the novel as particularly appropriate for women.[117] However, characterizing the novel as a typically female genre is misleading, especially when it leads to or arises out of a disregard for women's involvement with other reading materials, such as periodicals, newspapers, and theoretical literature. Ulrike Weckel's criticism of studies on German female readers could equally be applied to Jewish historiography: 'inadmissible generalizations are made based on few testimonies'.[118] The situation in both Jewish and non-Jewish society was much more complex than is suggested by the hierarchical gender distinction which allocates 'serious' reading—reading related to science, philosophy, politics, the public sphere—to men and 'less serious', even 'trivial', reading (as novels were often perceived to be) to women. Not only is the differentiation between 'serious' and 'trivial' misguided; the gendered division of reading matter as usually presented is historically incorrect.

---

[115] Jewish men's aversion to the new cultural trends is emphasized by Michael Meyer, who claims that Mendelssohn was 'a decided opponent of Sturm und Drang emotionalism... The lifelong friend of Nicolai and Lessing could only regard Goethe's *Sorrows of Young Werther* as moral and literary degeneracy... The enlightened Jews of his own generation, his disciples, and the larger portion of the next generation shared Mendelssohn's veredict' (Meyer, *The Origins of the Modern Jew*, 85).

[116] Ibid. 101. Lowenstein indicates a less strict division: 'One need not assume that the two circles were entirely separate, since several persons are known to have been part of both' (Lowenstein, *The Berlin Jewish Community*, 106). According to Martin Davies, although there was a (partial) division between Marcus's and Henriette's guests, the two salons complemented each other (Davies, *Identity or History?*, 163–195, esp. pp. 174–8).

[117] Caricatures published in 18th-century moral weeklies, depicting male readers of novels as effeminate, are a telling example of this view (Weckel, *Zwischen Häuslichkeit und Öffentlichkeit*, 316 n. 17).

[118] Ibid. 315. See Weckel's discussion of the way in which old presumptions concerning the place of women within the reading public in the 18th century penetrated important studies in recent decades (ibid. 315–18).

First and foremost, fiction and *Sturm und Drang* literature were not read exclusively by women. Explicit testimonies indicate that at least some enlightened Jewish men of the time read works of this kind, in addition to other materials. One such was Peter Beer, a Bohemian maskil,[119] who turned to belletristic literature, albeit (as stressed by the German scholar Gunnar Och) relatively late in life and after much reading in philosophy: from the texts of Christian Wolff, a leading philosopher of the *Aufklärung*, he turned to works by Mendelssohn, Lessing, Wieland, Herder, and Kant, and ultimately also to Goethe.[120] The merchant and author Leon Gomperz, a Jew who eventually converted to Christianity, described a phenomenon he observed in the Jewish community of Königsberg around the year 1765: 'One found novels in the hands of young men and on the dressing tables of the Jewish beauties: Baumgarten's *Metaphysics*. It was enough to have a German book!'[121] Notwithstanding Gomperz's insinuation that these Jewish youngsters kept books as a fashionable thing, so as to impress others, without actually reading them, it is interesting that novels were to be found in male hands, while the women chose to exhibit philosophical works. About two decades later, when Isaac Euchel, one of the founders of the Haskalah, moved from Königsberg to Berlin in 1787, his friends chose as an appropriate epigraph for a text they wrote and printed in his honour a quote from *Iphigenia in Tauris*—a play penned by none other than Goethe.[122] Also relevant in this context is David Veit's admission of his growing enthusiasm for Goethe's *Sorrows of Young Werther*. As he declared in one of his letters to Rahel Levin, he had learned to appreciate this work with time and even imagined he would 'pass away holding the book in my hands'.[123] These enlightened Jewish men, far from shunning novels and works written by *Sturm und Drang* authors—first and foremost Goethe—read them with enthusiasm.

Moreover, women's reading—certainly that of the Jewish women discussed here—was not restricted to novels. Aware of the role of reading in facilitating their education and their participation in cultural life, these women were not satisfied with the knowledge they could derive from novels but turned also to texts of many other kinds. Their writings offer unequivocal evidence that their reading was wide and comprehensive—modern in every sense. It included not only the belles-lettres of their time and classic works of Western culture, from Homer to Shakespeare, but also the best in contem-

---

[119] Beer was a Jewish educator and writer in the Habsburg empire. For an insightful intellectual biography of this Bohemian maskil, see Hecht, *Ein jüdischer Aufklärer in Böhmen*.
[120] Och, 'Jüdische Leser', 305.   [121] The quote is cited ibid. 309.
[122] *Herrn I. A. Euchel und A. F. Wolff bey Ihrer Abreise*.
[123] *Briefwechsel zwischen Rahel und David Veit*, i. 21.

porary publishing, including periodicals, almanacs, and occasionally also the daily press, along with popular scientific literature, philosophical works, and a variety of theoretical texts written by leading Enlightenment figures. Through this reading they formed and refined their world-views in general and their stances on particular key issues, including those relating to their position as women, either by accepting the writers' views or by formulating their own critiques.

Esther Gad familiarized herself with the restrictive gender views disseminated by the enlightened German pedagogue and author Joachim Heinrich Campe by reading his 1789 *Väterlicher Rath für meine Tochter* ('Fatherly Advice to my Daughter'), which for a long time was one of the most influential guides to women's education, and then published a critical essay on it.[124] Rahel Levin could be certain that her friend Henriette Mendelssohn had 'learnt by heart' the arguments advanced by the French philosopher Denis Diderot on a subject that preoccupied them both (and many of their contemporaries) on a personal level as single women: the advantages and disadvantages of marriage.[125] As we have seen, Levin also read works by Kant, and she does not seem to have been the only Jewish woman to do so. According to an anonymous (and hostile) observer from that period, 'Critical philosophy in particular is now the golden calf they [Berlin Jewish women] worship; to be a Kantian woman [*Kantianerin*] is their supreme wish and to be considered one their greatest vanity.'[126] Even if these women did not read Kant's own works, at least they may have read about his philosophy. In the light of this evidence, the story in Sara Meyer's letter should not be viewed as exemplifying the only kind of reading that occupied her and her female contemporaries throughout their lives.

Among the varied materials read by these modernizing women, their interest in a typical medium of the public sphere—the periodical—is clearly documented in their letters and other sources. As we have seen, Rahel Levin mentions reading the *Berlinische Monatsschrift*, probably the most important periodical in the late *Aufklärung*.[127] Marianne Meyer noted that she had read the most recent issue of the *Musenalmanach* ('Muses' Almanac')—a literary periodical edited by Schiller—in 1796.[128] The same issue was sent to Rahel Levin at the spa where she was staying by Count Karl von Finckenstein, with

---

[124] See the discussion in Ch. 3 below.   [125] See the discussion in Ch. 6 below.
[126] This source, quoted by Och, *Imago Judaica*, 264, is taken from *Neuestes Gemälde von Berlin, auf das Jahr 1798* (Cologne, 1798). Cf. Jenisch's critical words against 'Kantian women' in Ch. 1 n. 90 above.   [127] See above around n. 81.
[128] Geiger (ed.), 'Einundzwanzig Briefe', 31. The *Musenalmanach* was an annual collection of lyric creations by prominent German poets.

whom she had a love affair.[129] Henriette Herz apparently even subscribed to a German women's periodical, *Pomona für Teutschlands Töchter*, published in 1783–4 under the editorship of her friend Sophie von La Roche.[130] The active participation of some of these women—Dorothea Mendelssohn, Esther Gad, Rahel Levin, and Sara Meyer—in various periodicals as contributors of essays and poems will be discussed in the next chapter.

They also read the daily press, though the evidence for that is much rarer. One such testimony has reached us from the stormy times that followed the French occupation of Berlin in 1806. Henriette Mendelssohn, who by that time had been living in Paris for several years, sought news of events in her native city in the local newspapers, though she clearly found them of limited use and value. In a letter to her younger brother, Nathan, in August 1807, she writes: 'Is it true that the [Prussian] king has entirely left it [Berlin] and wants to live in Königsberg? Thus it is being reported in the local journals, and I see no one who could tell me something else or something more intelligent than what you can read for one's two *soles* per day!'[131] In the same letter, Henriette demonstrates that she was following the political and economic situation in Europe closely, probably through the press, when hinting at a possible connection between British policy and the economic difficulties on the European continent. The mere wish to keep herself up to date on world events was also an important motivation for reading.

As typical modern readers, these Jewish women took pains to keep up with new publications in various fields of interest. Esther Gad hastened to obtain a new book by the writer she admired most, Jean Paul, from none other than the author himself, with whom she corresponded: 'You would do me a favour if you were to lend me *Titan* for two or three days.' Even though she was expecting to receive her own copy—'my good brother in Breslau committed himself long ago to purchase for me whatever is published by you . . . I will therefore certainly get it [the book], but maybe only in a few weeks' time'—Gad did not have the patience to wait that long.[132] Later she asked him to lend her for a couple of days a new philosophical book by Herder:

---

[129] Bruyn (ed.), *Rahels erste Liebe*, 91.

[130] Sophie von La Roche, a writer and also the editor of this women's periodical, was a friend of Henriette Herz and of other Jewish women. On her literary activity, see Joeres, '"That girl is an entirely different character!"'; Dawson, *The Contested Quill*. On her activity as editor, see Weckel, *Zwischen Häuslichkeit und Öffentlichkeit*. Weckel indicates that although it is difficult to ascertain which of the many names that appear in the subscription lists of various periodicals edited by women belonged to Jews, regarding the *Pomona* it is possible to identify certain Jewish names, such as Itzig, Wolff, and Henriette Herz (ibid. 253).

[131] *Bankiers, Künstler und Gelehrte*, ed. Gilbert, 6.

[132] Hahn (ed.), '"Geliebtester Schriftsteller"', 28.

'Do you have Herder's latest work? I think [it is] a continuation of the Metacritique. You know how *soon*, no how *quickly* I read good books, and you could surely lend it to me.'[133]

The urge to keep abreast of recent publications and cultural affairs, as well as the difficulties sometimes involved in this undertaking, may also be detected in the letters of Fradchen Liebmann. While taking the waters at Freienwalde in 1795, she reported to her friend Rahel Levin, who was herself on vacation in Carlsbad, that she had read 'the new novel (as it is called) by Wieland[134] . . . I do not understand the actual, ultimate purpose of this book. In short, you will read it and will probably be able to tell me about it.'[135] In her letter, Liebmann was referring to a current theoretical debate about the genre of the novel, in which Wieland's work played an important role.[136] Aware that this issue was attracting great attention at the time, she attempted to read the text critically, reflecting on the hidden meanings; but, unable to grasp them, she turned to her friend for help. If Fradchen thus appears as a not particularly bright reader—aware of the difference in intellectual capacity between Levin and herself, she anticipated learning from her friend's insights—she was certainly an enthusiastic one, eager to gain the up-to-date knowledge that was basic currency among those who frequented Berlin's educated society. Even when the traditional canonical boundaries were breached in the modern age, releasing a flood of reading material and new publications, a feeling prevailed that there were certain things with which a 'cultured' person ought to be acquainted. Moses Mendelssohn hinted at this in an essay he published on Rousseau's extremely popular book *Julie, ou la nouvelle Héloïse*: 'A work that caused a sensation in Paris, that people tear from each other's hands in Germany, spoken about in every circle—could I go without reading it?'[137]

Aware of the need to keep pace with new publications, especially those that aroused fierce debate, these women tried also to cater for their acquaintances, as when Henriette Herz expressed her wish to send a recent publication to Berthold Georg Niebuhr, a Prussian diplomat in Rome and a close

---

[133] Ibid. 29. As stated there, Esther Gad herself had lent Jean Paul two publications containing references to him.

[134] On Wieland see Ch. 1 n. 3 above. Liebmann does not give the title of the book. It may have been the last novel written by the German author, *Die geheime Geschichte des Philosophen Peregrinus Proteus*, first published in instalments in 1789 in the literary journal *Die Teutsche Merkur* (edited by Wieland himself) and as a book in 1791; or the 1794 adaptation of an earlier novel, *Geschichte des Agathon*. See Bosold, 'Friederike Liman', 9 n. 26. [135] Ibid. 8–10.

[136] According to Bosold: ibid.

[137] Mendelssohn, *Gesammelte Schriften. Jubiläumsausgabe*, vol. v, pt. 1, 366.

friend.¹³⁸ In 1819 she wrote to Immanuel Bekker, a mutual friend: 'I wish I knew about someone travelling to Rome in order to send Niebuhr the issue of the Sophronizon in which Voss wrote an extremely long treatise against Stolberg under the title: how did Fritz St[olberg] become an illiberal?'¹³⁹ This text was highly controversial because of the outspoken views it contained against the aristocracy and the Catholic spirit, and in general against the Romanticism of those days. It was written by Johann Heinrich Voss, poet and lecturer at the University of Heidelberg, against the aristocrat Stolberg, who had been a close friend until he converted to Catholicism in 1800, an act Voss strongly deplored. As a reader who followed issues of interest to a cultured audience, Henriette Herz saw fit to participate in the public discussion aroused by the essay, articulating her negative opinion about its prevailing tone (as opposed to the ideas expressed): 'No, dear B[ekker], no law-abiding person should write or think like that, even against one who is not law-abiding—nobody should turn *so* bitter. And all this bitterness he carried with him for well over twenty years.' If Bekker had already read the book, she added, she would elaborate on her thoughts about it. From her words it may be deduced that this publication was the subject of discussion in her circle of friends: 'I have not yet spoken about it with Schl[eiermacher], Mrs. H[umboldt]¹⁴⁰ thinks like me.' A few lines later, after Schleiermacher had paid her a visit that same day, she could share with Bekker his opinion about the book: 'Schleiermacher is *very* happy *with part* of Voss' book, with what has to do with the aristocracy. The bitterness, the vehemence, the gossip, he rejects like I do.'¹⁴¹

As is clear from this example, keeping abreast of new publications was not a local matter. Beyond the literary developments in Berlin or other cities where they lived, enlightened Jewish women updated themselves and others regarding publications which appeared not only in German cities but also in other European countries, in no small measure with the help of the network of letters and social connections discussed in the previous chapter. They were equally wide-ranging in their linguistic skills. They were fluent speakers, readers, and writers not only in German but also in French, the language of culture in Europe in those days.¹⁴² Many of them also invested great efforts in

---

[138] During her stay in Italy in 1817–19, just before this letter was written, Henriette Herz established a close friendship with Niebuhr and his family.

[139] *Letters to Immanuel Bekker*, ed. Putzel, 40.

[140] Caroline von Humboldt, a friend of Henriette Herz and other enlightened Jewish women, was married to Wilhelm von Humboldt (on Humboldt, see n. 145 below).

[141] *Letters to Immanuel Bekker*, ed. Putzel, 40–1.

[142] Moses Mendelssohn's words to his future wife Fromet Gugenheim before she moved to Berlin indicate the importance there of fluency in French, at least one generation earlier: 'Learn this language [French], which has almost become a mother tongue here' (Mendelssohn, *Brautbriefe*, 43).

acquiring additional languages, both ancient and modern. They learned English and Italian, as well as Greek and Latin, and used them to expand their reading. On the other hand, there is no evidence they read in Yiddish, let alone Hebrew,[143] even though it is clear that most if not all of them learned the Hebrew characters in their early years: in 1785 Dorothea and Recha Mendelssohn, for instance, received a letter from their brother Joseph in Western Yiddish (in Hebrew characters) in reply to a letter they had sent him, probably using the same language;[144] Henriette Herz taught the Hebrew alphabet to her friend Wilhelm von Humboldt, and both used it as a secret code;[145] and this alphabet appears also in Rahel Levin's early letters to her relatives.

To conclude, these enlightened Jewish women constituted part of the curious, critical, and informed public that characterized the modern Western world. Long before they converted to Christianity, they devoted themselves to European literature, neglecting the Jewish texts—devotional as well as profane—written in Yiddish that were very popular among more traditional Jewish women. The evidence presented here indicates that the reading habits of enlightened Jewish women exposed them to many sources of knowledge and to different and varied ways of thinking in European culture. The women, as readers with a secular world-view, exhibited independence and initiative, and chose to expand their horizons through a variety of reading material, covering many intellectual fields. Thus they strengthened their connection with non-Jewish culture and successfully joined, as critical readers, the enlightened public.

On the key role of French in the acculturation process of German Jews, see Hahn, '"Apprenez l'européen!"'.

[143] It is, however, interesting that Henriette Herz attests that as a child she received basic instruction in Hebrew with a private teacher—'I began to translate the Bible [as part of her studies] and I even tackled some of its commentators'—although it is impossible to know how far she mastered the language (Landsberg (ed.), *Henriette Herz*, 106 (Eng. trans. in Blackwell and Zantop (eds.), *Bitter Healing*, 306)).

[144] The letter, sent from Hamburg, was published in Mendelssohn, *Gesammelte Schriften. Jubiläumsausgabe*, xix. 306–9.

[145] A letter sent by the young Wilhelm von Humboldt to Henriette Herz in 1786, for instance, was written in Hebrew characters, according to Landsberg (ed.), *Henriette Herz*, 161. Humboldt, a German thinker and statesman, eventually a minister in the Prussian government, used to visit the Herzes' home in the company of his brother Alexander. He attended Marcus Herz's lectures and was close to his wife Henriette and her circle of friends.

THREE

GOING PUBLIC
Jewish Women in the Field of Literature and Publishing

THE TWO PRECEDING CHAPTERS on letter-writing and reading have emphasized the active participation of enlightened Jewish women around 1800 in the field of literature as enthusiastic though critical readers of contemporary literary products. Their involvement with literature, however, was not confined to their consumption of written texts: it also included the process of creation, as authors of their own works. This chapter examines the literary activity of some of these women, discussing their attitudes towards authorship and what the crucial decision to publish their writings meant in the context of their time.

As female authors, these Jewish women of letters were part of a broader phenomenon in contemporary Europe. Throughout the eighteenth century and especially towards its end, a female writing culture was developing simultaneously in various lands.[1] Although the pace and nature of this literary expansion differed from place to place, depending on specific local conditions, countries including Germany, France, and England all saw a dramatic increase in the number of women active in the field of literature—parallel, to be sure, to an analogous proliferation of male authors. Writing retrospec-

---

[1] Carla Hesse, for instance, found a dramatic expansion in the number of women publishing in France in the last decade of the 18th century, following the French Revolution (Hesse, *The Other Enlightenment*). Referring to English literature, Judith Phillips Stanton noted 'the steady emergence of women writers early in the eighteenth century, followed by their explosive increase in its final three decades' (Phillips Stanton, 'Statistical Profile of Women Writing in English', 253). As for Germany, Ruth Dawson has indicated that even though gender constructions in the 18th century 'made almost no allowance' for a woman who wished to write and print her works, 'write and publish women did. Between 1770 and 1800 the numbers of women writing and the quantity of texts they produced far surpassed any previous period in German literary history' (Dawson, *The Contested Quill*, 15). See also Weckel, *Zwischen Häuslichkeit und Öffentlichkeit*.

tively, the author and feminist thinker Virginia Woolf noted and highlighted the entrance of women into the world of letters at that time, which she perceived as a momentous event of far-reaching consequences for modern human history. 'Towards the end of the eighteenth century', she wrote, 'a change came about which, if I were rewriting history, I should describe more fully and think of greater importance than the Crusades or the Wars of the Roses. The middle-class woman began to write.'[2] Although Woolf was referring to the English context, her claim regarding women's growing participation in the book market is valid for other places in Europe as well. In Germany, too, women joined the ranks of writers in ever-growing numbers with their varied products, experimenting with different cultural and literary trends and adopting new themes and techniques.[3]

For a long time this increased literary activity of women around 1800, like much of women's literary contribution in the past, remained largely hidden. Excluded from the literary canon dominated by a male hegemony, works by women authors in general were consistently forgotten by the reading public and by scholars at large.[4] It is only in recent decades that many neglected women writers have been rediscovered and their works reprinted and subjected to new interpretations. Literary critic Elaine Showalter described this change in the study of literature as resulting from the impact of the feminist critical revolution which, after a first phase focused on exposing the age-old misogyny of literary texts written by men, turned to women's writing, leading to the 'massive recovery and rereading of literature

---

[2] Woolf, *A Room of One's Own*, 66. When examining 'the possible explanations for women's rapid move from relative literary obscurity into the limelight of literary production', Josephine Donovan, in 'The Silence is Broken', points to the demise of classical control over literature, which for centuries had prevented women from writing, excluded as they were from classical education; the concomitant emergence of new genres such as the novel—which was favourable to women, as it was not ruled by traditional models and forms and emphasized individuality and personal experience as legitimate sources for literary expression; and 'the gradual replacement of literary patrons by capitalist booksellers', whose primary interest was marketing to a large audience, including a growing female readership, and who cared little about classical doctrine (quotations here from pp. 205, 212). Hesse, *The Other Enlightenment*, esp. pp. 31–55, puts special emphasis on the democratization and commercialization of cultural life in explaining the increased number of women in print in France after the French Revolution. An additional factor, especially emphasized in this chapter, is women's growing sense of self-assertion, prompted to a large extent by enlightened ideas.

[3] 'Whereas Georg Christian Lehms, in his encyclopedia *Teutschlands galante Poetinnen* (Frankfurt, 1715), had listed 111 women authors for all of German history to date, Carl Wilhelm von Schindel (*Die deutschen Schriftstellerinnen des neunzehnten Jahrhunderts*, Leipzig, 1825) mentions 550 women writers for the turn of the century alone' (Zantop, 'Trivial Pursuits?', 19).

[4] On the exclusion of women's works from the literary canon, see Naveh, 'Life Outside the Canon' (Heb.).

by women'.⁵ This development has benefited the Jewish women discussed here, whose literary activity and works—though not entirely ignored by past generations—have attracted growing interest in recent decades.

This new, close attention to women's writing and rediscovery of female authors could not have come about without a crucial change in the attitude of those studying this period regarding the correlation between past discourse and historical reality.⁶ Ideas spread in the years around 1800 by prominent thinkers emphasizing the polarity between women's and men's fields of activity led subsequent generations of scholars to assume that women hardly ever took an active part in cultural production, considered men's domain, and consequently to neglect women's participation in the public literary sphere. By choosing as the point of departure the examination of social and cultural practices rather than the tenets of gender ideology—that is, by approaching research with questions such as 'What did women do?' before asking 'What were women told to do?' or 'What were women's roles thought to be?', it has become possible to uncover women's active participation in fields once thought to be beyond their reach—including that of literary production.⁷ Indeed, scholars (especially women) who have followed this path have found that despite the discourse on women's exclusion from the public sphere, and despite the negative image of the woman who wrote and published as disruptive of the gender order—not only because her interest in literature allegedly led her to neglect her domestic duties, but also because, through her exposure in print, her husband was forced to share her with all human kind, in Friedrich Schiller's words⁸—women refused to remain silent. Declining to

---

⁵ See Showalter, 'Introduction: The Feminist Critical Revolution', 6.

⁶ See Ch. 1 above, around n. 54.

⁷ Carla Hesse insists on the disadvantages of studies based excessively on discursive analysis and claims that such an approach often distorts the historical picture. In her opinion, scholars who examined women's participation in French culture before and after the French Revolution focused almost exclusively on the analysis of gender norms and discursive representations. The history of women's silence and exclusion resulting from this approach is totally different from the picture that Hesse presents in her book (Hesse, *The Other Enlightenment*, 32–3). A similar approach was adopted by Yaffah Berlovitz when studying the literary production of women writing in Hebrew in the first half of the 20th century (Berlovitz, 'Women's Literature in the Yishuv Period' (Heb.)), by Ulrike Weckel in her book on female editors of journals for women in Germany at the end of the 18th century (Weckel, *Zwischen Häuslichkeit und Öffentlichkeit*), and by Helen Fronius in her study of German female writers in the period 1770–1820 (Fronius, 'Der reiche Mann und die arme Frau'; Fronius, *Women and Literature in the Goethe Era*).

⁸ In Schiller's 1788 poem 'Die berühmte Frau. Epistel eines Ehemanns an einen andern', the husband of a woman writer finds reason to envy the fate of a cuckolded man, who has to share his wife with only one lover. See Weckel, 'Der Fieberfrost des Freiherrn', 368; Fronius, *Women and Literature in the Goethe Era*, 57 ff.

accept that they should feel satisfied working with the needle alone, they also picked up the quill.⁹

Clearly the prevalent discourse of the time should not be ignored. Cultural norms obviously had actual implications and decisively influenced women's lives and society at large. They had a wide range of impacts on the legal, economic, social, pedagogic, and political fields. No less important, they played a central role in shaping the way in which women conceived of their place and their *Bestimmung* (designated purpose) in society. Nevertheless, for all the importance of the prevailing norms, it is evident that discourse does not necessarily indicate deeds. As the discussion in this chapter will show, the gender discourse at the end of the eighteenth century and the beginning of the nineteenth left room for interpretation and allowed for a wide range of behaviour. Contemporary women did not—at least, not all of them, by any means—submit themselves in total passivity to the dictates of society. Some, including the women discussed in this study, used the dominant discourse—the discourse of the late Enlightenment—to breach the bounds set by the established gender discourse and assert their place as active agents who participated not only in cultural and literary achievements but also in shaping the gender discourse itself.

In the context of Jewish history these women authors, who wrote only in non-Jewish languages, primarily German, fulfilled a pioneering role: to figure among the first Jewish women in modern times to take an active part in the European literary world. To be sure, they were not the first Jewish women to go into print. Many years earlier Rebecca Tiktiner, who lived in Prague in the sixteenth century, had written for publication, her most prominent work being *Meneket rivkah* ('Rebecca's Nurse'), a Yiddish book of moral conduct printed posthumously. Leah Horowitz, born in the early eighteenth century and growing up in Bolechów, Poland, was another Ashkenazi woman who wrote for publication, especially *tkhines*—prayers intended for a primarily female Jewish audience—using her Yiddish mother tongue as well as Hebrew and Aramaic. Sarah bas Tovim, who is thought also to have lived in the first half of the eighteenth century, was yet another prolific and popular writer of *tkhines*.¹⁰

---

⁹ The image of the needle and the quill, or rather the needle instead of the quill, propagated in the discourse of the time, obviously represents the opposition between women's domestic roles and their intellectual activity.

¹⁰ On Rebecca Tiktiner see the critical annotated edition of *Meneket rivkah* with an introduction and commentary by Frauke von Rohden and accompanied by an English translation of the text: Tiktiner, *Meneket Rivkah*. On Leah Horowitz and Sarah bas Tovim see Weissler, *Voices of the Matriarchs*.

Nor were the enlightened German Jewish women the first to reach beyond Jewish society and publish in a non-Jewish language, as part of the European cultural scene. They were preceded by Italian women such as Devora Ascarelli, who in the sixteenth century translated Hebrew prayers into Italian and composed her own poetry, and 'may have been one of the first Jewish women to have her work printed in Italian';[11] and the seventeenth-century Venetian poet Sarra Copia Sulam, who used this language to write sonnets and letters, as well as a pamphlet published in 1621 defending her religious beliefs against attacks by an Italian poet and priest with whom she had been on friendly terms.[12] Another earlier writer was Isabel de Correa, a Sephardi woman in the Netherlands (apparently from a family of Conversos, that is, of Iberian Jews forced to convert to Christianity), who towards the end of the seventeenth century published a Spanish translation of a famous work, *Il pastor fido* ('The Faithful Shepherd') by Giovanni Battista Guarini, to which she appended two original contributions—a dedication and an introduction—that reveal her erudition and include fascinating reflections on her literary activity as a woman.[13] Significantly, the German Jewish female writers discussed here certainly preceded by several decades the acclaimed group of Victorian Anglo-Jewish women writers, even though the literary activity of the latter may have had stronger repercussions in the Jewish world.[14]

Like other women who aspired to achieve authorial status, the enlightened Jewish women faced a considerable challenge in attempting to enter the literary marketplace and, in so doing, constantly confronting restrictive social and cultural norms. This required them either to make explicit attacks on, or to resist in less overt but still determined ways, contemporary criticism of female public activity.

This chapter will take a close look at the literary careers and the attitudes towards publishing of four of the Jewish women writers from the period, namely Esther Gad, Dorothea Mendelssohn, Rahel Levin, and Sara Meyer. Another who was active in the literary sphere is Henriette Herz. As noted

---

[11] Henry and Taitz, *Written out of History*, 127. See also Adelman, 'Finding Women's Voices in Italian Jewish Literature'.

[12] Adelman, 'The Educational and Literary Activities of Jewish Women in Italy'; Leneman, 'Sara Coppio Sullam'; and esp. Sulam, *Jewish Poet and Intellectual in Seventeenth-Century Venice*. As Don Harrán indicates in his introduction to the latter, 'Of the diverse spellings for Copia's name ... "Sarra Copia Sulam" appears as the signature of her two surviving letters' (p. 17).

[13] Cabezas Alguacil, 'Doña Isabel de Correa, traductora y poetisa sefardí'; López Estrada, 'Isabel Rebeca Correa: Defensa de la mujer escritora'.

[14] Galchinsky, *The Origin of the Modern Jewish Woman Writer*. Galchinsky dates the activity of this group of female Jewish writers to 1830–80.

above, she wrote her (unfinished) memoirs intermittently between 1823 and 1829; earlier in her life she had translated several works from English into German, though her name is not mentioned anywhere in the published texts and only the correspondence of Friedrich Schleiermacher, who acted as mediator between Herz and the publisher, bears witness to the fact that she was responsible for the translations.[15] Marianne Meyer, too, was active in some type of literary activity, but evidence to that effect is scarce.[16] A most prolific writer who deserves mention is Rebecca Salomon, who published under the pseudonym Regina Frohberg (having earlier taken the name Saaling, she is also known by that of the husband she later divorced, Friedländer); however, as she was born only in 1783, she lies beyond the chronological scope of this study (which is devoted to the generation of women born in the 1760s and 1770s).[17] Rather than presenting a literary and aesthetic analysis of the works of the four writers considered here, the focus will be placed—as far as the sources allow—on historical questions related to the act of writing itself, with brief descriptions of some of their works appended where necessary.

ESTHER GAD — BETWEEN IDEOLOGY AND PRACTICE

Among the German women who openly attacked contemporary attempts to restrict women's fields of action to the point of condemning their literary activity was Esther Gad,[18] perhaps 'the first German female author to be born as a Jew'.[19] A native of Breslau, daughter of Raphael Gad and Nissel Eybeschütz—herself a daughter of Rabbi Jonathan Eybeschütz, one of the best-known German rabbinical figures in the eighteenth century[20]—Gad

---

[15] The texts that Herz translated are: *Mungo Park's Reise in das Innere von Afrika in den Jahren 1795 und 1797* (Berlin, 1799) and *Isaac Weld's des Jüngern Reisen durch die Staaten von Nordamerika, und die Provinzien Ober- und Nieder-Canada, während den Jahren 1795, 1796 und 1797* (Berlin, 1800).

[16] See Hahn, *Unter falschem Namen*, 33 n. 35.

[17] Rebecca Salomon's literary work is discussed in Weissberg, 'Bodies in Pain'. The letters she received from Rahel Levin are printed in *Briefe an eine Freundin*, ed. Hertz.

[18] Besides Esther Gad, other German women in the last decade of the 18th century who publicly denounced the limitation imposed on women's fields of activity included Emilie Berlepsch and Marianne Ehrmann. See Dawson, '"And this shield is called—self-reliance"', esp. pp. 160 ff. These women were joined by numerous others who expressed their ideas anonymously, through channels including leading periodicals such as the *Berlinische Monatsschrift* and the *Berlinische Archiv der Zeit und ihres Geschmacks*.

[19] Brilling, 'Eibenschütziana', 270 n. 8. Gad was not only *born* as a Jew; as we will see now, she started to publish as a Jew, before her conversion to Christianity.

[20] In the list of the famous rabbi's descendants, Nissel figures as his eighth child: Brilling, 'Eibenschütziana', 268. Raphael Gad was a respected member of the local Jewish community and head of Breslau's traditional *ḥevrah kadisha* (burial society) in 1800 (Lewin, *Geschichte der Israelitischen Kranken-Verpflegungs-Anstalt zu Breslau*, 126 n. 55).

lived for some years in Berlin, in close contact with the other Jewish women discussed in this study. Gad was not merely very active as an author, as will soon become apparent; she also addressed theoretical issues related to women's involvement with intellectual endeavour. In 1798 she published in *Der Kosmopolit*, a short-lived German periodical, a subversive essay defending women's right and ability to engage in writing and learning.[21] This provocative text, which openly confronted one of the most influential pedagogical figures of the German Enlightenment, Joachim Heinrich Campe, was sufficient to prompt one of her contemporaries to refer to her as the 'German Wollstonecraft'.[22] Earlier in the same decade Mary Wollstonecraft, the English writer and early feminist thinker, had published a seminal treatise discussing the conditions of female existence and pleading for women to be granted equal rights and opportunities to men, which immediately gave rise to a wide public debate in England and other European countries.[23] In *A Vindication of the Rights of Woman* (1792), which would become a classic text in feminist thought, Wollstonecraft gave especial emphasis to the importance of women having equal opportunities in education, drawing on the claims made by enlightened thinkers and at the same time exposing conceptual contradictions in the gender order espoused by those same thinkers.[24] Like her English counterpart, Esther Gad also denounced—though employing the more modest format of an essay—the inconsistency of enlightened thought

---

[21] The essay is included in a collection of historical sources on women and education: see Gad, 'Einige Aeußerungen'. The original bibliographical reference is Esther Gad, 'Einige Aeußerungen über Hrn. Kampe'ns Behauptungen, die weibliche Gelehrsamkeit betreffend', in Christian Daniel Voß (ed.), *Der Kosmopolit. Eine Monathsschrift zur Beförderung wahrer und allgemeiner Humanität*, vol. iii (Halle, 1798), 577–90.

[22] This appellation, first granted her by her friend Johann Gottlieb Schummel in a book he edited in 1801 (*Schummels Breslauer Almanach für den Anfang des 19 Jahrhunderts*), was also used in the 1820s by Carl Wilhelm O. A. von Schindel in his book on German female authors of the 19th century. He described Gad as a 'second Wollstonecraft' in acknowledgement of her defence of 'the abilities and the vocation of her sex also to higher education of the mind' (Schindel, *Die deutschen Schriftstellerinnen*, i. 104). The appellation was revived in its original form—'German Wollstonecraft'—in a pioneering study on Esther Gad's literary activity in favour of women's and Jews' rights, published in 1988: Rudert, 'Die Wiederentdeckung einer deutschen "Wollstonecraft"'.

[23] Shortly after its publication in England, the book was translated into various languages. The German version, with certain corrections considered necessary by the editor in order to 'balance' the author's biased opinions in favour of her sex, was printed soon after the first English edition and enjoyed relative success: Maria Wollstonecraft, *Rettung der Rechte des Weibes mit Bemerkungen über politische und moralische Gegenstände. Mit einigen Anmerkungen und einer Vorrede von Christian Gotthilf Salzmann*, 2 vols. (Schnepfenthal, 1793–4). On Wollstonecraft's reception in Germany as reflected in the German press, see Weckel, 'Gleichheit auf dem Prüfstand', esp. p. 224 ff.

[24] Wollstonecraft was not without her own contradictions. Despite her ardent defence of women's rights and her iconic position in the history of feminism, she has been charged of endorsing misogynist views. Taylor, 'Misogyny and Feminism'.

on gender, using the arguments of the Enlightenment to criticize the gender order disseminated by contemporary thinkers.

The comparison between Gad and Wollstonecraft was not coincidental. The connection between the two women was suggested by Gad herself in a long footnote she appended at the beginning of her essay, where she situated her work in a wider cultural context. In this footnote, she presented her text as a contribution to the same gender discussion as that in which Wollstonecraft was participating, taking special care, however, to insist on the originality of her own thoughts. In order to assure her readers that, although she was joining the same public debate as this prominent author, she was by no means copying her ideas, she affirmed that she had deliberately refrained from reading Wollstonecraft's 'famous book', and that in fact it was only long after finishing her own essay—which, she claimed, 'had been sitting in my desk already for a number of years', that she had learned that Wollstonecraft's work had discussed the same issue. The fact that she was engaging with a topic that another woman had already dealt with constituted no problem at all: Gad doubted that Wollstonecraft had exhausted it completely, 'otherwise I would not have had my essay printed'. Indeed, she considered it beneficial that several people should contribute their points of view to public debate. Given the issues at stake—women's well-being, and indeed human happiness—it was justified and even advisable that the subject 'be considered from all sides' by whoever was able to contribute with his or her ideas, including herself.[25] Perceiving herself as an enlightened individual no less endowed with reason than men, she aspired, through this essay, to join the wide public debate taking place in journals and books regarding gender differences, taking on herself the responsibility of representing an entire section of the public; that is, speaking, as she explained to her audience, 'really not for myself, but for my sex'.[26] In publishing this essay, Gad was thus deliberately performing as a critical being, competent to examine the social, cultural, and political reality in which she lived and confident enough to share her insights with a large audience.

The immediate purpose of Gad's essay was to contradict central assertions and demands made by Campe in his influential *Väterlicher Rath für meine Töchter* regarding the gender division of roles.[27] This book, first

---

[25] Gad, 'Einige Aeußerungen', 56.   [26] Ibid. 57.

[27] The full title is: *Väterlicher Rath für meine Töchter. Ein Gegenstück zum Theophron. Der erwachsenern weiblichen Jugend gewidmet.* Campe occupies an interesting position in modern Jewish literature. Starting from the time of the German Haskalah, throughout the 19th century and as late as the beginning of the 20th, many of his children's books were repeatedly translated into Hebrew and Yiddish, and served as inspiration for original books written for a young Jewish audience. See Shavit,

published in 1789 and soon one of the most popular works on girls' education in German-speaking Europe,[28] advocated the bourgeois separation of spheres that confined women to household responsibilities and left the public realm as men's exclusive domain. Campe stressed women's domestic role as mothers, wives, and housekeepers, condemning women's pursuit of learning and women's writing as digressions from the female ideal he promoted and as posing a danger to the bourgeois family life he glorified. No learned conversation between husband and wife, no novel from a housewife's quill, he claimed, could exonerate a salty, burnt, or tasteless meal, a chaotic household, a wasteful domestic economy, neglected laundry, or pampered children—all of which he identified as direct consequences of the housewife's engagement with writing and learning.[29]

As a firm believer in women's mental capabilities and an aspiring author herself, Gad was sharply critical of these sweeping assertions. Campe, she complained in her essay, has a 'monstrous idea of learned women'; her aspiration, she said, was to eradicate such 'misguided ideas' from among both men *and* women.[30] Like others before her, notably the French Cartesian philosopher François Poulain de la Barre in the previous century,[31] she claimed that 'the mind has no sex' and that women, as human creatures, were endowed with reason in equal measure to men; therefore, she insisted, women could engage in intellectual pursuits, such as learning and writing, just as legitimately as men, and, moreover, they could do this without endangering the well-being of society. Significantly, in defending women's right and ability to take up the pen, Gad did not reject the gender order altogether. Perhaps aware of the adverse results of too revolutionary a feminist stance—writing as she did after the failed attempts to transform the gender order during and

---

'Literary Interference between German and Jewish-Hebrew Children's Literature'; ead., 'From Friedländer's Lesebuch to the Jewish Campe'. Interestingly, Campe's above-mentioned book for girls (*Fatherly Advice*) was apparently never translated into Hebrew or Yiddish, while a parallel work by Campe from 1783 directed at boys, *Theophron oder der erfahrene Rathgeber für die unerfahrene Jugend*, was published in a Hebrew translation by Hirsch Anapolsky, who adapted it for a Jewish audience (*Avi'ezer*, Odessa 1863); much earlier it served as a model for numerous books published in the German-speaking world, such as Herz Homberg's *Imrei shefer* (Vienna, 1808) and Heimann Schwabacher's *Keren tushiyah* (Fürth, 1817). See Shavit and Ewers, *Deutsch-jüdische Kinder- und Jugendliteratur*.

[28] According to Pia Schmid, 'without counting reprints and pirate editions, there were ten editions of the book until 1832 and it is the most popular contemporary book on girls' education' (Schmid, 'Weib oder Mensch', 331). See also Kersting, 'Prospekt fürs Eheleben', 371.

[29] Campe, *Väterlicher Rath für meine Töchter*, 46–72, esp. p. 53. For a discussion of Campe's text see Kersting, 'Prospekt fürs Eheleben'. [30] Gad, 'Einige Aeußerungen', 63.

[31] On Poulain de la Barre's defence of the equality of the sexes, see Stuurman, *François Poulain de la Barre*.

immediately after the French Revolution—she pitched her demands at a level less radical than those of her French and English counterparts, and also those of a contemporary German male proponent of female rights, Theodor Gottlieb von Hippel.[32] In fact, nowhere in her essay did Gad reject—at least, not explicitly—one basic assumption in Campe's argument, namely that responsibility for the domestic sphere lies primarily with the woman.[33] Nevertheless, she was in total opposition to Campe in her refusal to accept that this was women's sole mission and definitely that it precluded any female involvement in learning and writing. In Gad's eyes, a woman's performance in typically feminine fields was not necessarily harmed by her engagement with intellectual pursuits any more than men's activities in male occupations, for instance as state officials, preachers, and jurists, prohibited their involvement in scholarship.[34] Therefore, Gad concluded, 'erudition and motherhood should not be denounced as heterogeneous virtues, which necessarily exclude each other'.[35] For 'if female kindness may exist together with a lack of erudition and skills, so scientific knowledge in a woman must not ever rule out domestic and therefore more important attributes'.[36]

Gad's essay, though formulated as a private letter addressed to a 'dear friend'—apparently the editor of the journal in which it was published—as the beginning of a learned correspondence between the female initiator and the male addressee, was in fact a 'revolutionary pamphlet' in the full sense of the term.[37] This polemical text reflects the personal involvement of a concerned author alongside an uncompromising determination to defend principles which were for her, as a woman who devoted her life to expanding her knowledge and to writing, an existential issue. Her argument was not, certainly, that *all* women should write for publication; but, in her opinion, it

---

[32] See Ch. 6 below, around n. 8.

[33] Interestingly, another text written by Gad clearly shows that she did not accept the widespread view according to which household chores were in essence a female duty. In a book published several years after this essay, she presented the exchange of roles between husband and wife as a viable possibility, and in certain cases even a desirable one. During a trip from Berlin to London Gad met a couple who lived idyllically, despite their awkward situation: the husband, a carpenter who had lost his arm and therefore his ability to earn a living, was the one who performed the tasks usually assigned to women in married life (cooking, cleaning, and the daughters' education), while his wife, a talented seamstress, went out to work and was able to support the family. In the wife's words, quoted by Gad: 'It is a holy law of nature that the strongest must earn a living, and now I am it' (Bernard, *Briefe über England und Portugal*, i. 18 ff.; quotation here from p. 20).

[34] Gad, 'Einige Aeußerungen', 57. As Gad indicates there, most men of letters are engaged in these professions, and they are well able to leave their writing desks in order to take care of their duties. Why cannot writing women do the same, Gad wondered, when their domestic duties require their presence?   [35] Ibid. 58.   [36] Ibid. 63.

[37] Rudert, 'Die Wiederentdeckung einer deutschen "Wollstonecraft"', 229.

was desirable that those who were able to do so should do so, as dictated by enlightened ideals: 'If in the educated world it is recognized as a definite fact that the expansion of knowledge promotes also the dissemination of truth, and thus general happiness'—a principle to which she subscribed—'then I do not see why a woman's quill should not also do so, if she is capable.'[38] She herself acted according to this call to contribute to the common good. Her essay against Campe was neither the first nor the last she published, but just one in a long series of publications, both a theoretical reflection on her own literary performance and that of other female authors, and a fervent defence of women's right to take an active part in the diffusion of the Enlightenment through the printed word.

We know little about Esther Gad's life, but those details we do have relate mainly to the period of chief interest here, namely the last decade of the eighteenth century and first years of the nineteenth. When her essay against Campe was published, her life was in a stage of change. In 1796 she divorced her Jewish husband Samuel Bernard, whom she had married in 1791.[39] Some time after their separation Gad moved with her children from Breslau to Berlin, where she established contacts with a wide range of people including German intellectuals and state officials as well as other enlightened women like herself, Jews and non-Jews. Among the women she met in Berlin was Madame de Genlis, a French author with a strong feminist consciousness, who may have exercised a decisive influence on her own views about women's position and rights.[40] In 1801 Gad decided to leave Germany and join Wilhelm Friedrich Domeier, the personal physician to an English prince, whom she married after converting to Christianity and with whom she bore a child. Following a short stay in England, Domeier's work took the couple to Lisbon, where they spent a year. They also lived in Malta for some years before eventually returning to settle in London. It is likely that Esther Gad lived here until her death, which took place some time after the autumn of 1833.[41]

[38] Gad, 'Einige Aeußerungen', 62.

[39] This emerges from the records of Breslau's Jewish community, as presented in Brilling, 'Eibenschütziana', 270.

[40] On Madame de Genlis see Ch. 1 n. 111 above. During her stay in Berlin, Genlis established personal contact with Esther Gad, who 'liked her very much' (as Gad said in one of her letters: Hahn (ed.), '"Geliebtester Schriftsteller"', 29). Aware of this close relationship, when preparing for her trip to France Rahel Levin asked Gad for a letter of recommendation to Genlis in Paris, which would allow her to visit the French author during her stay there. Levin Varnhagen, *Briefwechsel mit Ludwig Robert*, 633 n. 117.

[41] The last trace we have of Gad is a letter she sent in October 1833 to Karl August Varnhagen, in which she states, among other things, that she has become blind. This letter is mentioned in Hahn (ed.), '"Geliebtester Schriftsteller"', 14. After conversion she took the name of Lucie, but her original name, Esther, continued to appear in some of her publications.

Despite the scarcity of biographical sources, enough traces remain to reconstruct a considerable amount of the literary activity in which Esther Gad was involved. Interestingly, her debut as an independent author was connected to an event related not to women but to another underprivileged group to which she belonged: the Jews. In March 1791 a modern Jewish school, the Königliche Wilhelmsschule (William Royal School), was established in Breslau, her native city. This institution, set up under the auspices of the Prussian government, was headed by Joel Loewe-Brill, a teacher and prominent member of the Haskalah. Its creation was unwelcome to a large proportion of the local Jewish community, who wanted their sons to receive a traditional Jewish education and rejected the reformist orientation evident in the curriculum of the new school.[42] Joining the modernist camp, Gad daringly affiliated herself with the minority who supported this institution by writing a poem for the new school's inauguration. Having just married Samuel Bernard and established a Jewish home, she welcomed this innovative project with optimism. About five years earlier, in an ostentatious event organized by the Breslau Jewish community in honour of the new Prussian king, Frederick William II, and attended by prominent representatives of the state and the Jewish community, the young Esther Gad had presented the king with a poem composed especially for that occasion, purportedly by the famous maskil Hartwig (Naphtali Herz) Wessely.[43] Now, in the inauguration ceremony of the school in 1791, which was also attended by leading figures of the government and the community, the young Jewish woman changed roles: this time it was she who wrote a German poem for the festive event and a Jewish boy who recited it in front of the audience.[44]

In her poem, Gad embraced ideas and ideals identified with the Haskalah. Her emphasis on broadening the horizons of Jewish education as a means to promote the integration of Jews into the state, and her positive

---

[42] On the Breslau school, see Eliav, *Jewish Education in Germany* (Heb.), 80–7. For a depiction of the struggle within the Jewish community between traditionalists and innovators over the new school, see Reincke, 'Zwischen Tradition, Aufklärung und Assimilation'. See also Freudenthal, 'Die ersten Emancipationsbestrebungen der Juden in Breslau'.

[43] Freudenthal, 'Die ersten Emancipationsbestrebungen der Juden in Breslau', 44–5.

[44] This information appears ibid. 341. Josel Pick of Reichenau, a contemporary of Gad who published a lengthy report on the inauguration of the school in *Hame'asef* (7/1 (1794), 68–77; 7/3 (1796), 229–51), makes no mention of Gad's name. He indicates that the ceremony started with a poem and ended with a poem, without any hint that a woman was involved. Gad's poem, however, was printed along with other speeches and greetings pronounced at the ceremony (as Esther Bernard, geb. Gad, 'Gedicht') in *Nachricht von dem unter dem Namen Wilhelmsschule zu Breslau errichteten Institut*, 85–8. This book is extremely rare, the only known copy being held in the British Library. Several stanzas of the poem were reproduced in Schummel, *Schummels Breslauer Almanach*, and were later reprinted in Rudert, 'Die Wiederentdeckung einer deutschen "Wollstonecraft"', 224.

attitude towards the state's intervention in this process, reflect a position indistinguishable from that of leading maskilim of her generation.⁴⁵ Gad praised the initiative of Count Carl Georg Heinrich von Hoym, governor of Silesia, a 'noble and wise man', who was sympathetic to the enlightened ideas proposed by the Prussian bureaucrat Christian Wilhelm von Dohm in his 1781 treatise on the emancipation of the Jews and saw the establishment of a modern school as a step that would help ameliorate the Jews' situation.⁴⁶ In her poem, Gad depicted the establishment of this state institution, in which Jewish children would receive an instruction that went far beyond that which they traditionally received, as an egalitarian act, which raised the Jews to the 'rank of the other sons of the Earth' and would help prepare them to serve the country as loyal citizens—one of the main aspirations of the maskilim at the end of the eighteenth century.⁴⁷

Gad's poem may not be a work of originality or great literary distinction; nevertheless, it was unique in the landscape of the Jewish Enlightenment and grants Gad an exceptional position in its history. For we know of no other poem or text, even one as modest as this, written before the nineteenth century through which a Jewish woman so unambiguously took a clear, self-conscious stand on an issue concerning the Jews' legal status, giving her opinion a public voice. As far as is known, then, this was the first public statement on the subject of the emancipation of the Jews and the position they could aspire to in German society formulated by a Jewish woman.⁴⁸ More than this, it was an unprecedented attempt by a Jewish woman in Germany to assume the role of a modern intellectual in the Jewish public sphere, addressing her

---

⁴⁵ See Hartwig Wessely's controversial pamphlet *Divrei shalom ve'emet* ('Words of Peace and Truth'), published in Berlin in 1782 in response to the 'Edict of Toleration' issued by the Emperor Joseph II. See also the case of Isaac Euchel, who in a letter of 1784 addressed the Danish king seeking to obtain his support for the plan to establish a modern Jewish school in Copenhagen. This missive was printed in Euchel, *Vom Nutzen der Aufklärung*, 45–58. See Feiner, 'Isaac Euchel' (Heb.), 445–8; Kennecke, *Isaac Abraham Euchel*, 109–10.

⁴⁶ On Count Hoym's attitude towards the Jewish issue see Freudenthal, 'Die ersten Emancipationsbestrebungen der Juden in Breslau', 47–8, and Eliav, *Jewish Education in Germany* (Heb.), 80–1. Cf. Reinke, 'Zwischen Tradition, Aufklärung und Assimilation', 197–8.

⁴⁷ Bernard, 'Gedicht', 86.

⁴⁸ The assertion that this poem makes Gad 'the first German female poet' to adopt a public stance on the 'Jewish question' appears in Rudert's essay on Esther Gad, 'Die Wiederentdeckung einer deutschen "Wollstonecraft"', 224. Rudert's interpretation of the poem—which relies on a partial reading of it, since only the stanzas published by Schummel were available to her—differs significantly from the one suggested here, based on the whole poem. Placing it in the tradition of the critical poetry of the German Enlightenment, and not in the context of the Haskalah, Rudert reads the poem primarily as a complaint at discrimination against the Jews. She detects an ironic tone in the poem and maintains that Gad's main purpose was not so much to praise Hoym for his steps in favour of Jewish emancipation as to criticize the inferior status of her co-religionists.

Jewish 'brethren' directly and urging them to act according to maskilic ideals by acknowledging the historical moment in which they were living and responding positively to the challenge presented by the government, taking full advantage of the opportunity that was being given to them to enhance their standing with the help of the new institution.

Gad's intervention in the Haskalah discourse was as short-lived as it was exceptional, for throughout her long subsequent career as an author she never again touched on maskilic issues. Her detachment from the Haskalah may have stemmed from her growing alienation from Jewish topics and from Judaism in general, which eventually led to her conversion to Christianity. She shared a preference for activity in the European literary field and for issues not specifically related to Jews with many male Jewish intellectuals in Germany at this time who, like Gad, were making a conspicuous entrance into the general public sphere. Another factor, specific to her gender, in her decision to distance herself from the Haskalah may have been that this movement failed to provide her with a suitable framework within which she could develop her intellectual ambitions as a woman of letters. The Haskalah—certainly at this point—was a male movement. All those involved in producing its texts and transmitting its ideas were Jewish men, as were most of its consumers. Lacking further opportunities to contribute actively to its efforts, she turned away from this movement to look for other fields of activity where she could participate, as a woman, in the advancement of reason and attempt to influence public opinion through the printed word.

It was indeed to this purpose that she devoted most of her literary efforts. Gad turned to various genres in her effort to assume the role of the modern intellectual and confidently express her personal views in the public sphere. After failed attempts to get an (unfinished) novel into print during the time she spent in Berlin, she succeeded in publishing, in 1802 and 1803, two volumes of a book written in a genre that was fashionable at the time, though not particularly among women writers—travel literature.[49] Her trip from Germany to England and Portugal provided suitable background material, enabling her to share with her readers not only the experiences of the

---

[49] The first volume was published as E. Bernard geb. Gad, *Briefe während meines Aufenthalts in England und Portugal an einen Freund*. The second volume was published a year later as Lucie Bernard geb. Gad, *Neue Reise durch England und Portugal. In Briefen an einen Freund*. A second edition including both volumes published in 1808 is available at http://gdz.sub.uni-goettingen.de; this is the text quoted here. For a more detailed discussion of the book and its author, see Naimark-Goldberg, '"The Mind Has No Sex"' (Heb.); Martin, *Moving Scenes*, 68–89. On women's travel literature in the 18th and 19th centuries and the breakaway from gender norms connected with it (first and foremost the departure from the 'normal' life of women at home), see Frederiksen, 'Der Blick in die Ferne'.

journey but notably also her personal opinions on a variety of subjects, including political regimes, cultural and social institutions, the popularization of the Enlightenment, Jewish religion, and, again, the situation of women.[50] Another book she wrote, which was printed first in English and then in her own German translation, was a critique of a famous work written in French by Madame de Staël, *De l'Allemagne* ('On Germany'). Staël's book, first published in France in 1810 but confiscated by Napoleon on account of the author's purportedly positive attitude towards German culture, appeared in England in 1813. It attracted numerous reviews, especially among German literary circles, from writers including several women intellectuals. One of the most notable responses written by a woman was that of Esther Gad, who thereby situated herself as a committed member of the public sphere where ideas and opinions were shaped.[51] In 1820 she published yet another travel book, *An Appendix to the Descriptions of Paris*, which she again ventured to write in English, excusing herself for the 'many imperfections with respect to the purity of the language, which neither my long residence in this country, nor the study of its classical authors, have yet enabled me altogether to rectify'.[52]

As well as these major works, from the 1790s until the last years of her life in the early 1830s Gad contributed reviews and articles to various journals which offered a platform for discussion of current affairs, new cultural products, and modern social institutions. In 1799, casting herself in the role of a correspondent from Dresden for the *Berlinisches Archiv der Zeit und ihres Geschmacks* ('Berlin Archive of the Age and its Taste') she wrote an enthusiastic article, 'Über das Museum in Dresden' ('On the Museum in Dresden'). In the article, which took the form of a letter addressed to 'Doctor Feßler', one

---

[50] Gad turns her attention to issues that relate specifically to women but, as she emphasizes, have wider implications for society as a whole. Reporting from England, for example, she describes two institutions which impressed her very much: one was a maternity hospital for poor women which opened its doors not only to married women but also to those giving birth out of wedlock; the other was an almshouse for former prostitutes that offered them a space for rehabilitation and even helped some of them become exemplary mothers and housewives. Bernard, *Briefe über England und Portugal*, i. 139–42; Naimark-Goldberg, '"The Mind Has No Sex"' (Heb.), 97–8. Other women writers using travel literature to discuss themes related specifically to women are examined in Frederiksen, 'Der Blick in die Ferne'.

[51] The titles of Gad's English and German books are: *A Critical Analysis of Several Striking and Incongrous Passages of Mme. de Staël's Work on Germany, with some historical accounts of that country, by a German* (London, 1814); *Kritische Auseinandersetzung mehrerer Stellen in dem Buche der Frau von Staël über Deutschland. Mit einer Zueignungsschrift an den Herrn Jean Paul Richter*, trans. from the original by the author (Hanover, 1814).

[52] Domeier, *An Appendix to the Descriptions of Paris*, p. iv (the author's name as stated on the title page is 'Madame Domeier').

Briefe
über
England und Portugal
an einen Freund
von
E. Bernard geb. Gad.

Neue Ausgabe

Erster Theil
mit einem Kupfer.

Hamburg, 1808.
bei August Campe.

PLATE 4. Title page of the second edition of Esther Gad's travelogue, first published 1802–3

of the editors of the periodical in which her review was published, she sought to acquaint the German public with an innovative institution recently established in Dresden, aimed at fostering the enlightened ideals of propagating knowledge and eradicating ignorance among the population at large.[53] A critical review of a production of Friedrich Schiller's play *Piccolomini* appeared the same year in *Denkwürdigkeiten und Tagesgeschichte der Mark Brandenburg* ('Memorabilia and Everyday History of the March of Brandenburg')—a publication which, incidentally, granted considerable space to Jewish contributors and to Jewish affairs.[54] The historical significance of Esther Gad's published contributions to these and other periodicals lies in the position that she sought to occupy in the cultural world of her time, as a critical observer who carefully studies the reality around her, not just presenting facts neutrally but rather expressing clearly her own opinions and judgements. This was a role that throughout her career Gad assumed openly, not hiding behind conventions such as anonymity or writing under the name of a man, or disguising her criticism in forms of expression considered more appropriate to females, but writing with an assertiveness and self-confidence rare among contemporary women writers.

The steps taken by Esther Gad to get her work published provide further evidence of how far she was from being inhibited by prevailing norms that encouraged modest and passive behaviour in women. Unafraid of engaging with the literary world on a commercial as well as an intellectual level, she promoted her career as a writer with active resolve, approaching editors and publishers on her own initiative.[55] A letter she sent in April 1799 to Friedrich Schiller, a figure of great stature on the German literary scene, is testimony to her self-confidence. In it, Gad exhorted the illustrious poet and playwright to publish two of her poems in the *Musenalmanach*, the periodical he edited that offered a platform for German poets. Contrary to what would have been expected at that time, her letter to Schiller is significantly devoid of any

[53] Bernard, 'Über das Museum in Dresden'.

[54] The positive attitude towards Jews of Johann Wilhelm Andreas Kosmann, the editor of *Denkwürdigkeiten und Tagesgeschichte der Mark Brandenburg und der Herzogthümer Mecklenburg und Pommern* (16 vols., 1796–1803), is stressed in Geiger, 'Mittheilungen aus Berliner Zeitungen, Zeitschriften und Brochüren', 297–8. Esther Gad's 'Etwas über Schiller's Piccolomini' was published in 1799, in the third volume of the periodical (pp. 383–9).

[55] Such conduct was more common than may be inferred from contemporary discourse and 20th-century assessments. An essay focused on the unpublished correspondence of female authors with German publishers at the end of the 18th century and the beginning of the 19th examines the strategies employed by women writers in order to evade limitations that derived from the prevailing gender ideology, and reveals how they manoeuvred their way into the literary marketplace and nurtured their commercial connections in order to get published (Fronius, 'Der reiche Mann und die arme Frau').

apologetic tone for daring to write to him without being invited to, and for taking the initiative in their communication—behaviour widely considered unsuitable in a woman. Instead of excuses, the letter contains statements aimed at proving her professional credentials—she mentions, for instance, her success in getting her critical review of a production of Schiller's own play in Berlin published earlier in the year. Having received no reply from the editor after two months Gad sent him yet another letter, kindly but firmly requesting him to let her know whether he intended to publish her poems or not.[56]

A businesslike letter she sent from London in October 1802 to the author and publisher Friedrich Justin Bertuch in Weimar is no less surprising for its boldness and disregard of the conduct expected of bourgeois women at the time.[57] From the letter it emerges that Bertuch, in writing to a mutual friend, a certain Mr König, had taken an interest in Gad's plans for the future, and was especially curious as to whether she was continuing with her literary activities. When Gad learned that Bertuch had enquired about her, she decided to ignore what she considered superfluous niceties and address him directly, speaking as an author: 'Since in my opinion I can answer your questions better than any other person', she wrote to him, 'I will defy all ceremony which one should sacrifice without qualms for opportunities in which our intellectual refinement is promoted rather than impaired.' Here again, by writing unsolicited, Gad ignored the convention that required passivity and self-effacement of women, even though she was well aware of it. In place of gender norms that discouraged women from taking any steps on their own initiative, Gad suggested a different point of departure for their communication—the idea that women could stand on equal terms with men as intellectuals by virtue of the mental capabilities that were common to members of both sexes: 'If indeed [the world] begins to believe that the soul has no sex, and if I may be allowed to surmise that I have shown some soul here and there, you will not necessarily be surprised to receive a letter from a woman to whom you have not written yet.'

Having stated her belief in the equal mental abilities of men and women, Gad made Bertuch an offer of commercial cooperation, describing a wide array of literary products she could supply, some ready for submission, others still projects waiting to be realized: 'For some years now I have been writing a novel, and the largest part of a women's almanac lies ready in my escritoire,

---

[56] Gad's efforts were futile. Schiller's periodical closed in 1800. Esther Gad's two letters to Schiller were published by Schulz, 'Jean Paul, Breslau und die Breslauer Schriftsteller', 349–50.

[57] The letter is cited ibid. 351–2. All the following quotations are taken from there.

and now I am much inclined to translate lectures for women on astronomy from the English, written by a certain Mrs Bryan.' Avoiding circumlocution, she straightforwardly asked: 'Which of these works do you wish to publish?' Gad requested information on the conditions that Bertuch could offer her as a publisher, an indication that she would not work with him at any price. The same assertive position can be seen in her expressions of appreciation for his work as publisher, as if she wished thereby to indicate that were she not convinced of his competence and position she would not seek this collaboration: 'Knowing all I do about you, I hold you in esteem not only as an author but also as a publisher, and it will therefore be a pleasure for me to get to know you more closely and to enter into negotiations with you.'

As an author, Esther Gad experienced bitter disappointments, such as the failure of her efforts to publish the novel she wrote, as well as successes, such as the popularity of her travelogue about England and Portugal that saw it go into a second edition. Although her name was not preserved in either the German or the Jewish collective memory, her position in the public sphere as a writer is unquestionable. The picture of Gad that emerges from the account of her literary activity is that of an ambitious writer who ventured into different genres, felt confident in her insights, and believed her ideas could attract the interest of the educated reading public. Without openly denying the basic role division between men and women generally asserted at the time, or directly objecting to the domestic responsibility thereby conferred on women, she employed enlightened thinking to impose a new interpretation on these bourgeois assumptions and thus justified—and even encouraged—women's activities in the fields of learning and writing.

DOROTHEA MENDELSSOHN'S LITERARY CAREER

In contrast to Esther Gad's trenchant defence of her position as a female public intellectual stands Dorothea Mendelssohn's more ambiguous attitude towards publication. Mendelssohn did not make open declarations promoting women's right to write and publish, and at times even expressed opinions that distanced her from so strongly feminist a position. Nevertheless, the reservations about female authorship evident in some of her comments were sometimes at variance with her actions or feelings about her own writing as expressed in the written testimony she left behind. Indeed, as the discussion below will illustrate, her apparently dismissive attitude towards her own literary activity, as if she engaged in it only out of necessity in order to earn a living, coexisted with a sense of mission and a search for personal fulfilment brought to fruition through writing. Dorothea Mendelssohn's case shows vividly how hard it is to speak in absolute terms when dealing with the discourse of gender consciousness developing among female authors at the end of the eighteenth century and the beginning of the nineteenth, and how misleading it can be to label the attitude of any particular individual either 'feminist' or 'conservative'.[58] As the discrepancies in Dorothea Mendelssohn's position indicate, a much more illuminating approach is to identify the many shades and variations in their attitude towards feminist positions and the conflicts in which they were involved, not only with the society around them but also within themselves.

The beginning of Dorothea Mendelssohn's formal career as a writer coincided with the end of an earlier career—that of a Jewish housewife. Evidence that she was devoting substantial time and energy to writing begin to emerge around the time of her separation from Simon Veit in December 1798[59]—a separation which led to her divorce early in the following year from the Berlin businessman to whom she had been married for about fifteen years, and who was the father of her children, Jonas and Philipp Veit.[60] Once the divorce had been made official with her receipt of the *get*, the rabbinic divorce document, her literary activity moved into high gear, and remained relatively intense for several years thereafter. The output of this period included original works, outstanding among them her unfinished novel *Florentin*,[61] the first part of which was published in 1801 with Friedrich Schlegel's name displayed on the title page as its 'editor'; critical essays in periodicals, especially those edited by Schlegel, such as *Athenaeum* and *Europa*; adaptations of ancient works, such as the story of Merlin, King Arthur's magician, and *Lothar und Maller*, a story of knightly chivalry written in the fifteenth century by the Duchess of Lorraine and translated by her

---

[58] This point is stressed by Ruth-Ellen B. Joeres in her discussion of Sophie von La Roche, one of the most prominent German female authors in the last decades of the 18th century (Joeres, '"That girl is an entirely different character!"').

[59] On 17 December 1798 Dorothea was already living in her own apartment, as testified in Friedrich Schlegel's letter to his friend Novalis (*Briefe von und an Friedrich und Dorothea Schlegel*, ed. Behler, xxiv. 215).

[60] Both children would become well-known painters. The Veits had two other children who died in infancy.

[61] Dorothea never finished the second part of *Florentin*. Perhaps this was owing to daily concerns, which kept her busy to the point of despair; perhaps she was unhappy with the reception of the first part of the novel, or was too self-critical, believing herself unable to create a finished work worth printing. Partial drafts of a sequel have survived, and these fragments have appeared in several publications; among them is Schlegel, *Florentin*, a 1993 edition of the novel which also includes historical sources related to the production of the book. Quotes from this novel itself are taken from the English translation: Mendelssohn Veit Schlegel, *Florentin. A Novel*.

daughter into a German dialect, then still in manuscript form;[62] translations, one of the most notable being a German rendition of *Corinne*, a celebrated novel penned by the French Madame de Staël;[63] and finally also simple technical work, especially as Schlegel's secretary and copyist.

Florentin, her most remarkable piece and the first known novel published by a Jewish woman, was written in the period of her life after her divorce. She had begun work on the project in November 1799,[64] and during 1800 she laboured on it diligently, despite circumstances and conditions not always conducive to creative endeavour. At the end of 1799 Dorothea Mendelssohn and Friedrich Schlegel, her new companion, moved to Jena, lodging at the house of August and Caroline Schlegel, Friedrich's brother and sister-in-law. From there Mendelssohn reported to her friend Rahel Levin on the practical difficulties she was facing. 'Our beautiful life has been disturbed by an evil demon!', she wrote in April 1800, referring to a sickness which had attacked Caroline six weeks earlier. 'This misfortune prevents anything good, even my work, because I must be with her a lot, and also because for that reason my room is not respected enough. You will surely understand how much especially this last fact, on which my whole existence depends, frightens me. If I cannot work, I should not want to live!' ('Kann ich nicht arbeiten, so darf ich nicht leben wollen!').[65]

This quotation hints at two different facets of Dorothea Mendelssohn's attitude towards her own writing. On the one hand, her last sentence reflects the immense spiritual satisfaction she derived from writing, and her feeling that writing gave meaning to her life. But her claim that her 'whole existence' depended on her writing may be interpreted as referring to a more practical imperative, as if she were explaining to her friend that she depended on writing for a living, and were it not for writing she would be destitute. This reading is reasonable in the light of Mendelssohn's poor economic circumstances

---

[62] *Geschichte des Zauberers Merlin* appeared as the first volume in a collection edited by Friedrich Schlegel (*Sammlung Romantischer Dichtungen des Mittelalters. Aus gedruckten und handschriftlichen Quellen*, 2 vols. (Leipzig, 1804)). The full title of the second book mentioned is *Lothar und Maller. Eine Rittergeschichte. Aus einer ungedruckten Handschrift bearbeitet und herausgegeben von Friedrich Schlegel* (Frankfurt am Main, 1805). Two additional books translated and adapted by Dorothea Mendelssohn, and dealing with female historical figures, also appeared under Schlegel's name: Friedrich Schlegel (ed.), *Geschichte der Jungfrau von Orléans. Aus altfranzösischen Quellen. Mit einem Anhange aus Hume's Geschichte von England* (Berlin, 1802), and Friedrich Schlegel (ed. and trans.), *Geschichte der Margareta von Valois, Gemahlin Heinrichs des Vierten. Von ihr selbst geschrieben. Nebst Zusätzen und Ergänzungen aus andern französischen Quellen* (Leipzig, 1803).

[63] The translation appeared barely two months after the publication of the original, as Friedrich Schlegel (ed. and trans.), *Corinna. Oder: Italien* (Berlin, 1807).

[64] See Dorothea Mendelssohn's letter to Schleiermacher of 15 Nov. 1799 in Schlegel, *Florentin*, 265.   [65] *Dorothea v. Schlegel und deren Söhne, Briefwechsel*, ed. Raich, i. [10–11].

PLATE 5. Dorothea Mendelssohn, later Veit, later Schlegel (1764–1839)
Pencil drawing, 1798: artist unknown
© bpk / SBB

following her separation from Simon Veit, which she had initiated.[66] The final divorce was granted only 'after many contestations, scenes, after much vacillation and doubting', as Dorothea Mendelssohn indicates, and she came out with few assets: 'a very small income—on which I can live only if I am extremely thrifty... my piano, and the beautiful desk that you gave me', as she wrote to her friend Karl Gustav von Brinckmann in February 1799, shortly after the divorce.[67] Although the financial agreement between the couple guaranteed Dorothea a monthly revenue, it was a modest one. 'All her assets are deposited and she receives only the interest', wrote Friedrich Schlegel in one of his letters from that period.[68] Even though Simon Veit later turned out to be the ideal ex-husband, generous and supportive— Dorothea herself admired him and praised the way he treated her[69]—immediately after the divorce and for a period of several years thereafter Dorothea Mendelssohn's financial position was dire, and it did not get any better after she settled down with her beloved Schlegel.[70]

There is no doubt that Friedrich Schlegel was keenly aware of the financial profit to be derived from Mendelssohn's writing: he hoped that Dorothea's novel, and her literary activity in general, would serve as a source of income for the couple and so relieve their hard-pressed economic situation. A letter he sent to Schleiermacher in January 1800 explicitly indicates his main interest in his partner's literary activity: 'U[nger] offered to pay for Florentin... an honorarium of two Louisd'or... since the first volume will be ready soon, there is a ray of hope regarding the finances.'[71] When the

[66] 'My wife Brendel [i.e. Dorothea] wants to divorce me', Veit wrote in his declaration at the rabbinical court in Berlin when granting the *get*. 'I have used all means to dissuade her from this intention, but she remains firm on it' (microfilm copy of this document at the Leo Baeck Institute in New York, Jacobson Collection, I-78).

[67] An English translation of this letter was published in Blackwell and Zantop (eds.), *Bitter Healing*, 339–41.

[68] Letter to Novalis of 17 Dec. 1798, in *Briefe von und an Friedrich und Dorothea Schlegel*, ed. Behler, xxiv. 215.

[69] In a letter sent by Dorothea Mendelssohn to Simon Veit in 1819, after having heard that he was very unwell, she noted how moved she had been by his forgiveness and his loyal friendship and expressed the hope that God would forgive her for her deeds, 'just like you did'. A copy of the letter was printed in Zondek, 'Dorothea Schlegel und Simon Veit', 303–4. On Dorothea's lack of hostility towards Simon Veit after their divorce, see Geiger, 'Dorothea Veit-Schlegel', 130 ff.

[70] For years the couple were dogged by financial problems. In a letter of 1803 from Paris (where they lived between 1802 and 1804) Dorothea appealed, on her own initiative and according to her without her husband's knowledge, to a German nobleman, hoping that with his help Friedrich could obtain a position and thus relieve their financial plight (*Briefe von und an Friedrich und Dorothea Schlegel*, ed. Körner, 48–51).

[71] Schlegel, *Florentin*, 266. Friederike Helene Unger was a German author, translator, and publisher.

negotiations with the publisher, Friederike Unger, proved unsuccessful—probably owing to the enmity between Unger and Mendelssohn[72]—the manuscript was sold to another publisher by the name of Bohn, who offered a deal no less favourable: 'I will not lose a thing from Unger's rejection [of the manuscript]', Dorothea wrote in a letter from May that year. 'Bohn voluntarily offered to give me two hundred Reichstaler by Michaelmas, and besides that he also gave us the most generous terms as to the format and the printing.'[73]

It is thus clear that not only Schlegel but Mendelssohn herself ascribed an economic purpose to her literary activity. She worked in order to support her household at a time of need, when the stable economic foundation provided by her husband during their years of marriage was no longer there. As she bound her destiny to a man who was creative but at that time had lapsed into idleness,[74] she took upon herself the financial burden of supporting them and considered writing an appropriate vocation to fulfil this material need. And yet Dorothea's literary activity cannot be reduced to a primarily practical affair, as many researchers over the years have suggested. About a century ago Franz Deibel, perhaps the first scholar to devote an academic study to Dorothea's literary work, opened his book on the subject with the explicit assertion that 'Dorothea Schlegel never had the ambition to be considered an author ... Her literary work was never a purpose in itself, but was entirely at the service of the man she loved blindly, and in whom she believed with unshakeable persistence.'[75] Coming at her subject from a totally different perspective, informed by feminist concerns, Barbara Becker-Cantarino reached a similar evaluation in a much more recent study dealing with the

---

[72] Because of the hostility between the two women (which belies the easy assumption of a common feeling of 'sisterhood' and mutual support among women), Dorothea and Friedrich submitted the manuscript anonymously and copied by a different hand, apparently in order to blur the identity of the author. However, when Friederike Unger rejected the novel, Dorothea had not the slightest doubt about the reason: 'The cat', she wrote, referring to Unger, 'may well have smelled from whence it came, and then she was really base enough to allow herself this whole, pathetic revenge' (Schlegel, *Florentin*, 267). In fact, Unger despised not only Dorothea but also other Jewish women who, according to her, aspired to 'climb the cultural ladder' but were characterized by lack of taste, mediocrity, and miseducation (*Verbildung*). Unger expressed this opinion in a book she published anonymously, *Über Berlin*, in 1798. Her words are quoted in Och, *Imago Judaica*, 262–3.

[73] Schlegel, *Florentin*, 267, letter of 15 May 1800.

[74] Dorothea complained to Schleiermacher more than once about Schlegel's idleness. Were he not so lazy, she wrote in one of her letters, 'he could still compose something out of his enormous stock of materials. What is the purpose of the heaps of paper he increases every hour?' Letter of 16 June 1800, ibid. 268.

[75] Deibel, *Dorothea Schlegel als Schriftstellerin*, 1. Some years later, Heinrich Finke too claimed that it was the necessities of life which had turned her into a writer, and that she would otherwise have written only letters. Finke, *Ueber Friedrich und Dorothea Schlegel*, 77.

literary activity of German women in the Romantic period. Critical of Dorothea Mendelssohn's submissiveness as a woman, she asked: 'Was she merely a "Brotschreiberin" [a 'writer for bread'], in order to earn money and promote Friedrich's literary plans?'[76] and answered the rhetorical question in the affirmative. In Becker-Cantarino's eyes, Dorothea Mendelssohn made a very bad deal when she

> exchanged her (relatively) privileged position in Jewish society with that of a (married) woman in the literary elite. Internalizing the Romantic female image of the beloved muse, she found herself in the (un)romantic real-life role of the poet's amanuensis and housekeeper. Confined to the privacy of the home in this patriarchal society, Dorothea placed also her literary activity at the service of her man and published her own thoughts in anonymous contributions to journals, adaptations, translations, and private letters—making no artistic claims for them.[77]

A similar conclusion was reached by Liliane Weissberg, who wrote that Dorothea Mendelssohn 'was not interested in the fame of authorship. Writing was a necessity. Dorothea Veit [i.e. Mendelssohn] wrote for money.'[78]

The argument advanced by Weissberg, Becker-Cantarino, and Deibel is far from unfounded: the sources left by Mendelssohn herself provide ample basis for it. She stated clearly in her notes that she wished 'to be able to earn so much by writing that Friedrich need not write for money any more'.[79] Elsewhere she depicted her role as that of an artisan who worked to support Schlegel's art. 'What I do lies in the following limits: to create quietly and to earn bread as an artisan, even modestly, until he [Schlegel] can.'[80] The fact that Dorothea's publications appeared not under her name but under Schlegel's (as editor) further reinforces the claim regarding her subordination to her partner and second husband.

Nevertheless, alongside the sources that depict a subservient Dorothea serving Friedrich's interests, a parallel set of quotations may be presented that support a different assessment of her attitude towards her literary activity. True, even these sources do not give us the image of a feminist fighter imbued with a spirit of mission and independence, as Esther Gad's do. And yet close attention to Dorothea Mendelssohn's voice reveals a more complex

---

[76] Becker-Cantarino, *Schriftstellerinnen der Romantik*, 120.   [77] Ibid. 122.

[78] Weissberg, 'Nachwort', 219. See also ead., 'The Master's Theme, and some Variations'.

[79] *Dorothea v. Schlegel und deren Söhne, Briefwechsel*, ed. Raich, i. 91 (translation in Mendelssohn Veit Schlegel, *Florentin. A Novel*, p. xxviii).

[80] Weissberg quotes these words from Dorothea Mendelssohn's private notes in her two articles on *Florentin*, stressing the distinction made by Dorothea between her almost mechanical labour as an 'artisan', and Schlegel's creative work as an 'artist' (Weissberg, 'The Master's Theme, and some Variations', 173; ead., 'Nachwort', 219).

stance towards her activity as a writer. Dorothea did speak about her devotion to her partner's activity; she also emphasized the economic goal of her 'labour'. It is important to note, though, that in stressing the instrumental purpose of her writing she was behaving no differently from most contemporary female authors: only a few women at that time dared to claim that they wrote in response to an internal need, or that they were creating art. Many of them felt the need to justify their literary activity by asserting its usefulness, usually by reference to two purposes: earning a living and/or instructing other women.[81] Nevertheless, Dorothea's literary activity clearly also satisfied inner needs of a more spiritual nature, as hinted at in the passage quoted above.[82]

First of all, the idea that Dorothea was moved to write by artistic inspiration, urged by an inner impulse, should not be dismissed. In her introduction to *Florentin*, entitled 'Dedication to the Editor' (not included in the first edition of 1801), Dorothea described in poetic language the beginning of the process of creation—a process much more indicative of the creative mind of the artist than of the workmanlike approach of the artisan:

With deep joy I still remember the dear, cheerful morning when I first recalled the little stories in this book. They lay slumbering in my soul as violets during the winter; a new spring, the returning sun had awakened them all. Glowing and joyfully impatient, I wrote down the first pages and then placed them so contentedly and naively on my writing desk, as if I had completed a whole oeuvre; for what I secretly dreamed and imagined adding to the couple of pages was as good as written on paper, as far as I, the ingenue, was concerned.[83]

It is also hard to overlook the enthusiasm that Mendelssohn felt for the products of her pen, especially when referring to the lyrical fragments she inserted in the novel, to which she devoted her best efforts.[84] 'I wrote a pretty song for my novel', she announced in the early stages of writing to her friend Schleiermacher, to whom she confided her thoughts and hesitations

---

[81] Zantop, 'Trivial Pursuits?', 31–2.   [82] See above at n. 65.

[83] Schlegel, *Florentin*, 193 (Eng. trans. from Blackwell and Zantop (eds.), *Bitter Healing*, 343. For a slightly different translation, see Mendelssohn Veit Schlegel, *Florentin. A Novel*, 152). Although Dorothea then goes on to regret having written at all, adding that she would not have done it had Friedrich not insisted ('You were the one who did not let me have peace until I had completed the work just as the world would have it, and I obeyed in humility; for it was not at all my will'), her hesitation has to do with the implications of writing itself and the problem of language—the gap that existed between thought and the written word: 'To me, in my own way, it was more complete when I was carrying it [the work] secretly within myself and quietly shaping and reshaping it' (Blackwell and Zantop (eds.), *Bitter Healing*, 344).

[84] Weissberg also asserts that Dorothea Mendelssohn felt 'a certain pride' in her novel 'which went beyond her financial considerations' (Weissberg, 'Nachwort', 220).

throughout the whole process of creation.⁸⁵ Some weeks later she asked his opinion about the verses she had composed, not attempting to hide how proud she felt that they were 'turning out so well'.⁸⁶ Because of the importance she ascribed to those poems and the hopes she invested in them as one of the climaxes of her artistic creation, she expressed deep disappointment when they were ignored by critics and friends: 'About the beautiful sonnets you wrote nothing, you wicked people, not even one word.'⁸⁷

To the poetical urge that drove her to create we must add the critical impulse which clearly stands behind much of Mendelssohn's work. Dorothea saw herself in the modern intellectual's role of the critic who carefully observes the world around her and offers a reasoned judgement on various issues of public interest. She sought to fulfil this role not only through the essays and reviews she published over the years, in which she discussed and evaluated artistic works, but also through her own most prominent work, *Florentin*, in which she addressed social, political, and religious issues. The critical attitude she assumed in *Florentin*, which reflects her connection with the German Enlightenment,⁸⁸ is itself ample evidence of interests other than financial in writing her book.

The novel tells the story of Florentin, a young nobleman who is on an adventurous journey from Italy through Germany on his way to America. At the beginning of the book Florentin is heartily welcomed by a noble family, after having saved the life of its head, Count Schwarzenberg. He is invited to stay at the Schwarzenbergs' castle and, despite his initial hesitation and his wandering spirit, decides to accept the offer. During the course of the narrative Florentin visits two principalities, which share a rather exceptional feature: both are governed by women. In the first, the female ruler's husband, Count Schwarzenberg, is present; but, as the latter explains to Florentin, the responsibility of government rests not on his but on his wife Eleonora's shoulders.⁸⁹ In the second, there is not even a male figurehead: Clementina, Count Schwarzenberg's sister, is the sole ruler. These two unusual environments that Florentin encounters give the author an opportunity to address current social and political issues and express her personal views.

The two female sovereigns, depicted in ideal terms, embody the values Dorothea Mendelssohn believed desirable in a ruler. It is no accident that they constitute the antithesis of the prince in Rheinsberg, whom Dorothea

---

⁸⁵ Schlegel, *Florentin*, 265.   ⁸⁶ Ibid.   ⁸⁷ Ibid. 271.
⁸⁸ Enlightened features, such as those that will be emphasized below, appear in the book side by side with certain Romantic elements (for instance, knightly and medieval motifs).
⁸⁹ Mendelssohn Veit Schlegel, *Florentin. A Novel*, 9–10.

had described in a letter to Rahel Levin in the most negative terms.[90] As noted in Chapter 1, in that letter of 1792 following a visit to Rheinsberg Dorothea expressed her shock and anger at the prince's spending fortunes on luxuries and worrying only about himself and his personal comfort, while his subjects lived in dreadful conditions. Dorothea compared '*his house, his garden*', which were 'lush and magnificent', with the 'scantiness and misery' that were to be found everywhere else, pointing out that only a short distance from the monarch's house one would find 'no roof intact, no clean street, no completely dressed child'.[91] For Clementina and Eleonora, on the contrary, their peoples' well-being is their chief concern. Strolling with Eleonora through the streets of the village at the foot of the hill on which her castle lies, Florentin perceives a reality opposed in every detail to Dorothea's description of Rheinsberg from several years before: 'They were respectfully greeted by the people who met them, without fear and without servile abasement. Health and joy radiated from each face; order and cleanliness glowed out of every house. Beautiful, happy children danced on the lawn in the glow of the setting sun.' The hero of her story, Florentin, feels 'as if he found here the golden age'.[92]

As he arrives in the town ruled by Clementina, Eleonora's sister-in-law, Florentin encounters a no less encouraging reality. Clementina's private estate covers a huge area, but she does not keep her garden to herself: she opens it to all the inhabitants, so that everyone can enjoy the vast grounds and the beauty they offer, walking freely around or sitting in the shade of tall trees. On seeing this unusual scene, indeed, Florentin is uncertain 'whether it was a public garden or belonged to the house'.[93] Here Clementina organizes cultural performances open not only to courtiers and friends, as was common among the nobility, but to the people as a whole—to the enormous astonishment of Florentin, who, like most of his contemporaries, has been accustomed to a wholly different type of relationship between a monarch and his or her subjects. One of the principles underlying Clementina's beneficent rule is a more equal division of property and natural resources. Among the first enterprises she has launched for the benefit of the population is a public bathing establishment serving sick poor people, depicted by a doctor who works with her as an act of social justice aimed at reducing both the gap between the living conditions of the poor and the rich, and the dependency of the former on the charity of the latter. The doctor's account gives a good

---

[90] See Ch. 1 above.   [91] *Briefe von und an Friedrich und Dorothea Schlegel*, ed. Behler, xxiii. 64.
[92] Mendelssohn Veit Schlegel, *Florentin. A Novel*, 9.   [93] Ibid. 119.

description of Clementina's world-view, which is clearly one that Dorothea herself endorsed:

> It was an extremely painful feeling for her compassionate heart, sensitive to every stranger's pain, to see a class of people who were at the bath on account of real, very severe infirmities suffering from every deprivation; meanwhile, others who were there only for pleasure and to pass away time had every convenience. At her own cost, she had every comfort erected for the poor, sick people and everything was so good, so clean and comfortable, that she availed herself of them as well. So the poor, the plagued, no longer have to beg miserably for the leftovers of the rich and wait for help for their pains until those who are often suffering less are satisfied.[94]

In describing the utopian regime led by Clementina, Dorothea Mendelssohn was clearly criticizing despotic forms of government and revealing a radical political and social stance concerning the organization of the state. Guided by a concern for the lower classes and a belief in social justice, this monarch has initiated a welfare policy aimed at caring for all the inhabitants of her domain, including the poor. Admittedly, the power of decision remains in her hands and not in those of a democratically elected government; but it is clear that Clementina stands on the side of the people and not on the side of the wealthy, and, prompted by an enlightened and egalitarian world-view, is even prepared to act against the interests and privileges of her own class. She espouses an ideal of social justice so fundamental that she sweeps away the barriers that traditionally separate the aristocracy from the common people (as, for instance, in opening up the bathing facilities to common use). Thus *Florentin* contains a harsh critique of tyrants who treat state resources as if they were their private property and expresses a radical repudiation of the enormous gaps between classes that gave rise to unjust and inhuman circumstances, as well as offering a depiction of a utopian alternative world.[95]

As well as political criticism, the book also articulates clear anticlerical views, which are much more in the spirit of the Enlightenment than that of Romanticism, the movement to which Dorothea Mendelssohn's name is usually attached and with which she did indeed have strong but not exclusive connections. Ironically, the anticlerical views she voiced in 1801 in *Florentin* criticize the religious denomination she would embrace several years later when choosing to exchange the Protestant Christianity to which she first converted for Catholicism. Through the hero of her novel Mendelssohn laid

---

[94] Mendelssohn Veit Schlegel, *Florentin. A Novel*, 126.
[95] Cf. a different evaluation of Dorothea Mendelssohn's political critique in *Florentin* in Roberts, 'The Perennial Search for Paradise'.

grave charges against the Catholic Church and its representatives;[96] she also castigated its adherents for surrendering their independent use of reason and decision-making capacity in subservience to selfish monks. During an excursion with the Schwarzenbergs' daughter and her fiancé, Florentin narrates the story of his life, in which religious fanaticism and unthinking obedience have played a central role. He was brought up by a good but weak woman who destined Florentin and his sister, whom she raised as her own children, to a religious life. She was led to this decision by her confessor, a domineering Benedictine prior who exercised total power over her after her husband had left her a young, wealthy widow. Florentin depicts in dark colours the childhood years spent under the yoke of Catholicism, secluded in a miserable room—a 'tomb' whose 'bare, gray walls were only decorated with the gloomy pictures of saints' and a 'large crucifix' which made him quiver every morning when he awoke[97]—his only company the priest who was in charge of his education and his preparation for life at a monastery. This authoritarian figure repressed the child's spirit and freedom, forcing him to devote all his time to agonizing over the study of religious texts and denying him any kind of recreation appropriate for a child. 'How I longed for the moment to free myself from the hard-hearted, foolish tyrants, not to have to fear them any more!'[98] Using his intelligence and determination, the young Florentin contrived to thwart the prior's plan to lock him away in a cloister, eventually escaping his clutches to attain independence. His sister, however, was unable to make the break: she was sent to a convent, and despite Florentin's desperate efforts to save her from the life of a nun, she refused to interfere with the prior's decisions by cooperating with her brother's plans to set her free. Blinded by the Catholic faith and the values she had imbibed from infancy, she surrendered to her fate and took the veil, to Florentin's overpowering disappointment.[99]

In the light of Mendelssohn's strong religious and political criticism, and her clear interest in spreading her personal views, as amply evidenced by *Florentin*, it is hard to maintain that she was motivated to write by material considerations alone. Any such assertion seems even less plausible when one considers her personal involvement with her creation, expressed in her mixed feelings towards the novel she wrote. She conceived of the birth of the protagonist, Florentin, as a personal and emotional experience, like the birth of a child: 'As long as he haunted my body as an idea I had to really and truly give

[96] As Karin Stuebben Thornton has argued, 'It is significant . . . that amidst a Romantic atmosphere and in a supposedly Romantic novel, Dorothea expressed a view that is diametrically opposed to the Romantic glorification of Catholicism' (Stuebben Thornton, 'Enlightenment and Romanticism in the Work of Dorothea Schlegel', 165).

[97] Mendelssohn Veit Schlegel, *Florentin. A Novel*, 37.   [98] Ibid. 39–40.   [99] Ibid. 50–5.

birth to him and bring him into the real reality.'[100] At times she cared for the book as one cares for a beloved creature, and treated it and its protagonist with fondness and affection, referring to the novel's hero as 'my good Florentin' or 'my stepson Florentin'.[101] In moments of anxiety and uncertainty regarding the reception of the book by the public, however, these terms of endearment were replaced by derogatory metaphors, and she saw the book as a 'weed' or a 'wild plant'.[102] Looking at the book when it had just been printed, she reacted with similar distaste: 'I quite laughed when I saw the silly book on vellum.'[103] She followed the process of production and distribution of the book with both excitement and apprehension. '*Florentin* is really being printed, to my great horror', she wrote to August Schlegel, Friedrich's brother.[104] She sent a copy of it to Schleiermacher 'with a pounding heart and a blushing face'[105]—signs of the anxiety at putting work into the public domain that characterized so many female authors in the past.

A glance at Dorothea Mendelssohn's list of publications might lead one to the mistaken conclusion that she started to write only around the year 1800, when financial constraints began to make themselves felt. In fact, her inclination towards both creative and critical writing preceded her public literary career by many years, until coming into the open following radical changes in her life, perhaps even as the crystallization of an old dream. 'How can you, my friend, be so astonished by my poetic progress?', she reproached Schleiermacher at the beginning of 1800, after he had praised her poetic talent. 'Haven't I always said, and prided myself, that I could become something if I were well?'[106] Dorothea had been writing for a long time before first getting into print in those decisive days at the turn of the century. Like many of her female contemporaries, she had employed the safety of private correspondence to develop her literary skills and to participate actively in the cultural life of her time.[107] Even in her private letters Mendelssohn habitually expressed her opinions and judgements on cultural events and literary works, and on social and political issues, using the same critical style she would later employ in the reviews she wrote for publication. One of her earliest letters, as

---

[100] Schlegel, *Florentin*, 274, in a letter to Schleiermacher of 16 Apr. 1801, in response to the reviews of the book. [101] Ibid. 265, 266.

[102] Ibid. 268. [103] Ibid. 271. [104] Ibid. 269. [105] Ibid.

[106] Ibid. 266. (Eng. trans. from Mendelssohn Veit Schlegel, *Florentin. A Novel*, p. xxix.)

[107] Much has been written about the role of the letter in the 18th century as a 'bridge' to literary, 'serious' writing among women. Scholars have stressed that in that period letters frequently served to circumvent gender norms that extolled female passivity, offering women a legitimate and accessible channel to express themselves in writing. See e.g. French, *German Women as Letter Writers*; Becker-Cantarino, *Schriftstellerinnen der Romantik*, 162–83; Nickisch, 'Briefkultur'; Nörtemann, 'Brieftheoretische Konzepte im 18. Jahrhundert'.

noted in a previous chapter, contained critical comments on a performance of the French opera she had attended at Rheinsberg.[108] Some years later, in a letter to an unidentified female friend in July 1798, she wrote a reasoned assessment of the qualities and shortcomings of another production, this time in Berlin, taking a personal position contrary to the prevailing view about the same performance.[109] Her numerous reviews of new books and other cultural events, which appeared in periodicals such as the *Athenaeum* and *Europa*, show a similar style and acute insight.

In the numerous letters she wrote while still married to Simon Veit, Dorothea Mendelssohn also cultivated her descriptive talents. A case in point is an early letter, from November 1788, sent to a scholar with whom she was acquainted, most probably the German aesthetician Friedrich von Blankenburg in Leipzig.[110] Most of the letter is taken up with everyday matters and written in a correspondingly unremarkable style; but one passage stands out as distinct in both content and form. Dorothea, herself recently returned to Berlin from a visit to Leipzig, wanted to persuade another friend, through Blankenburg, to bring his family on a reciprocal visit to Berlin as soon as possible, and not to postpone the projected trip until the spring. On this topic she slipped into a higher register than that she used in the rest of the letter, employing all her powers of description to persuade her friend of the city's attractions. The figurative language of this fragment gives it an aesthetic value that isolates it from the rest of the letter and highlights Dorothea's literary aspirations.

As a different part of this same letter shows, Dorothea Mendelssohn came into contact with the world of publishing long before she made her first efforts to get her novel or translations into print herself. When still only a young woman, as Moses Mendelssohn's daughter she met many prominent figures in the publishing field who visited her parents' home, and after her father's death she took a keen interest in her mother's efforts to get his works published. From the letter sent to Blankenburg it becomes clear that Dorothea had detailed knowledge of what was involved in this undertaking, from the necessary personal contacts to legal aspects such as copyright and the financial implications of the whole enterprise. Blankenburg had apparently requested that she send him a copy of one of her father's works. In

---

[108] See Ch. 1 above, around n. 107.

[109] Letter of 9 July 1798, *Briefe von und an Friedrich und Dorothea Schlegel*, ed. Behler, xxiv. 143–4.

[110] Although the recipient's name is not indicated, the editor of the letters assumes that the addressee was almost certainly Blankenburg. It is in any case certain that the recipient was a learned man, for in her letter Dorothea writes: 'I think a lot about you . . . all surrounded by books and erudition.' The letter, dated 18 Nov. 1788, was printed ibid. xxiii. 4–6 (quotation from p. 5).

reply she claimed—whether in truth or as an excuse it is impossible to know—that she was unable to fulfil his request because 'my mother holds on to the things with both hands, I cannot get from her even one small sheet'.[111] Dorothea then described in detail the steps that had been taken up to that point towards publishing her father's literary estate, in a tone critical of the way things had been handled. In the end, her mother's efforts to publish Moses Mendelssohn's works bore no fruit.[112] After Schlegel's death in 1829 Dorothea Mendelssohn found herself in a similar position to Fromet's, in possession of a large number of unpublished manuscripts by her prominent husband. However, unlike her mother, she was successful in getting her husband's works into print. It seems that Dorothea, better equipped than Fromet with appropriate knowledge and skills, played an important role in the publication of Schlegel's essays and lectures, including editing his book on the philosophy of language and organizing the numerous manuscripts he left behind.[113] Thus, once again, in a spirit of both admiration and independence, she combined her love for and appreciation of Schlegel with the expression of her intellectual skills.

PERSONAL LETTERS AS LITERATURE: RAHEL LEVIN'S UNIQUE OEUVRE

While Esther Gad's name is displayed on the title page of more than one book and Dorothea Mendelssohn is the acknowledged author or translator of a number of books and essays, Rahel Levin's credentials as an author are more ambiguous, and until recent decades were not uncontested. It seems uncontroversial that a basic requirement of authorship is the existence of a printed oeuvre, or at least a complete work in manuscript, and in Levin's case this condition was not obviously met. As opposed to many female writers, who at some point in their lives participated in established literary genres and wrote novels, stories, plays, poetry, or essays, Rahel was drawn to a kind of writing that lacked both defining rules and norms and any formal status in literature: the epistolary genre. As her biographer Heidi Thomann Tewarson points out, she deliberately 'made the letter her almost exclusive literary

---

[111] *Briefe von und an Friedrich und Dorothea Schlegel*, ed. Behler, xxiii. 4. This letter provides interesting testimony to her mother's attempts to intervene in the publication of Moses Mendelssohn's works.

[112] The first edition of Mendelssohn's collected works was printed only in the 1840s, on the initiative of his son Joseph and with the editorial assistance of his grandson, Joseph's eldest son, university professor Georg Benjamin Mendelssohn. See Altmann, '"Moses Mendelssohn's Gesammelte Schriften"'. [113] Blackwell and Zantop (eds.), *Bitter Healing*, 336.

means', using it to convey a wide range of content including poetic passages, literary and philosophical discussions, and reviews of cultural events.[114]

The numerous letters Levin crafted, though widely read and admired, were not automatically considered literary products. The fact that during her lifetime fragments from those letters and from her diaries were published in several journals could have contributed to establishing her status as an author. However, these texts, read only by a few, were quickly forgotten even among her contemporaries.[115] And while the extensive selections of her private letters published by her husband shortly after her death nurtured her reputation as a prominent personality in German cultural history, they did not establish her status as an author. They reinforced Rahel's central place not as a writer but as a *salonnière* and one of the most remarkable women in the *Goethezeit*—the 'age of Goethe', as the period encompassing the last decades of the eighteenth century and the first decades of the nineteenth in Germany is often designated—who as muses and spouses encouraged the work of prominent (mainly male) intellectuals.[116]

In the last few decades, however, Rahel Levin's position in literary history has changed. A scholarly discussion of her work became possible following a shift in literary theory, in great measure thanks to the influence of feminist thought, which objected to the canonization of genres no less than to that of individual authors or works. Literary scholars in recent years have explained that epistolary literature was excluded from the literary canon for so long as a direct result of its strong identification with women. They have claimed that the letter's classification as a typically female mode of writing, especially from the eighteenth century onwards, devalued it in the eyes of generations of scholars.[117] The expansion of the concept of 'literature' to include the epistolary as a recognized genre has made possible a renewed evaluation of Rahel

---

[114] Thomann Tewarson, *Rahel Levin Varnhagen*, 48.

[115] According to Barbara Hahn, texts that Rahel Levin published during her lifetime had a restricted and short-lived audience because they were hard to read and understand: Hahn, '*Antworten Sie mir!*', 20–1.

[116] Feilchenfeldt, 'Die Anfänge des Kults um Rahel Varnhagen', 214–16; Hahn and Isselstein, 'Vorwort', in eaed. (eds.), *Rahel Levin Varnhagen*, 7.

[117] French, *German Women as Letter Writers*, 29–47; Runge and Steinbrügge, 'Einleitung', in eaed. (eds.), *Die Frau im Dialog*, 9. The strong connection between women and letter-writing—in fact, the belief that women were 'predestined' to write letters (ibid.)—emerged from several factors, among them the characterization of the letter in 18th-century epistolary theory, especially after the publication of Gellert's book on letter-writing (see Ch. 1 after n. 38 above), as a natural, unceremonious form of expression, believed to correspond typically to women's nature; and, in addition, the fact that letters often dealt with issues of the private sphere believed to be women's domain. On the favourable and unfavourable implications of the connection posited between women and letter-writing for women's literary activity, see Nörtemann, 'Brieftheoretische Konzepte im 18. Jahrhundert', esp. pp. 221 ff.

Levin as one of the most prominent women writers in Germany in the late eighteenth and early nineteenth centuries. New editions of her texts, which began to appear in 1979, paved the way to the 'rediscovery' of Rahel Levin as an author.[118] Contrary to many previous editions, which presented an idealization of Rahel Levin, promoted her cult, and thus distorted her image and her historical role,[119] collections of her letters and writings published since the late 1970s portray her as a significant woman of letters as they reveal different aspects of her oeuvre. These editions set out to deal in a new way with the unique character of Levin's epistolary writing, emphasizing rather than downplaying its dialogic nature and the fact that a collection of letters is not a closed work, with a clearly defined beginning and end.

Rahel Levin's letters, along with her diaries and the many aphorisms she wrote, are thus seen today as the literary creations of a fully fledged author. However, a more relevant question for our discussion in this chapter is: did Rahel Levin see her writings as literary creation and herself as an author? Did she write only for her friends and relatives, as the predominance of personal letters in her oeuvre would seem to indicate, or did she also intend those letters to reach a wider audience? Rahel Levin, like many other women of her generation, had a complex attitude towards authorship. There is no doubt that even at a relatively early stage, long before she submitted her first contribution to a German periodical in 1812, by which time she had turned 40, Rahel Levin saw the potential readership of her letters as far wider than their direct addressees. In a letter she sent to David Veit in 1795 she expressed her wonder and even disappointment at learning that he had refused to show an earlier letter she had sent him to other people:

Why did you not want to show anyone a letter which I myself wrote? It would not have made a difference to me, nothing in it should shun to be seen. Do you, by any chance, want the truths that I tell you sometimes, or the way we are with each other, not to be seen? I do not understand this.... Why did you not want to show a letter which I myself wrote, but rather burn them all? I cannot figure out any reason.[120]

Such an expansive attitude towards private letters was common among Levin's contemporaries. It has already been noted that a letter sent to a friend or relative was generally intended (unless otherwise indicated) for a wide cir-

---

[118] Reflected in the title of the book edited by Hahn and Isselstein, *Rahel Levin Varnhagen. Die Wiederentdeckung einer Schriftstellerin* ('Rahel Levin Varnhagen: The Rediscovery of a Female Author'). As Vivian Liska has indicated, the reception of Rahel Levin among literary critics in the last decades of the 20th century oscillates between an attempt to integrate this 'marginal' figure into the mainstream and a celebration of her marginality as a privileged status. Liska, 'Mainstreaming the Margins'. [119] Feilchenfeldt, 'Die Anfänge des Kults um Rahel Varnhagen'.
[120] *Briefwechsel zwischen Rahel und David Veit*, ii. 135.

cle of family members and acquaintances.[121] The content of a letter would pass naturally into a general domain as its addressee read it aloud, either in its entirety or in part, or handed it to another person to read. Rahel Levin undoubtedly shared this attitude.[122] Of course, there were those who disapproved of the general sharing of the personal letter and zealously tried to preserve its private character. Henriette Mendelssohn, for instance, emphatically disagreed with the practice and protested against it. In a letter she sent from Paris to her friend Karl August Varnhagen she specifically asked him not to pass around a letter she had sent him and clarified her motives:

> I am not ashamed to turn to you with a request with which I wish to entrust you. Do not let anybody see my letters, none of them, without exception! You cannot misjudge this request, because I have never hidden my exclusive inclination towards you, but I cannot bear the thought of writing for any person other than the one I am thinking of.[123]

Thus, as Henriette claims here, it was not that she wished to keep secret her feelings towards her correspondent; rather, she disapproved of the widespread practice of inviting other people to observe and comment on a personal communication between two individuals.

Rahel Levin's approach was diametrically opposed to this. Not only did she not object to having her letters circulated among readers other than the addressees; she even envisioned their future publication. It is true that her husband, wishing to preserve the spontaneity of her writing in the eyes of later generations, affirmed that 'whatever she [Rahel] wrote was not written for the public. I alone have to answer for the fact that her words have reached it.'[124] Rahel Levin's first biographer took the same view: he claimed that 'Mrs Varnhagen did not like to see herself in print' and even insisted that she was

---

[121] See above, Ch. 1. See also Becker-Cantarino, *Schriftstellerinnen der Romantik*, 166–7.

[122] Two illustrative passages clearly indicate that Rahel Levin was aware that her letters were read by others and that she had no objection to that. In 1795 Fradchen Liebmann informed Rahel Levin as a matter of fact: 'I went yesterday to Mrs. Marchetti in order to read her your letter, but she was not at home. I left her the letter, she just sent it back to me' (Bosold, 'Friederike Liman', 7). On another occasion, in November 1800, Rahel received a letter from Jean Paul Richter in which he let her know that he had read some letters she had sent to a friend 'with indescribable interest; but with just as much pain. You treat life poetically and therefore life treats you the same' (Bruyn (ed.), *Rahels erste Liebe*, 304).   [123] Letter of 20 Sept. 1810, *Bankiers, Künstler und Gelehrte*, ed. Gilbert, 19.

[124] Varnhagen's words were written down in his diary towards the end of his life. This quotation, originally in Ludmilla Assing (ed.), *Aus dem Nachlaß Varnhagen's von Ense. Tagebücher von Karl August Varnhagen von Ense* (Hamburg, 1861–70), vol. i, p. iii, was cited by Isselstein, 'Rahels Schriften I', 23. The original German sentence is: 'Daß ihre Sachen zu dieser gelangt sind, habe nur ich zu verantworten.'

proud to remain a great unpublished author, rejecting the possibility that she might herself have encouraged the publication of her writings.[125] However, as Ursula Isselstein has shown, Levin in fact destined every word she wrote for print, sooner or later, and herself prepared the ground for the collection and publication of her letters.[126] At a time of despondency after her separation from Karl von Finckenstein following a strained love affair, before leaving for Paris in the summer of 1800 she entreated her friend Hitzel Bernhard to take upon herself the mission of collecting every trace of her correspondence when the time should come: 'When I die, try to collect *all* my letters . . . from *all* my friends and acquaintances . . . and organize them together with Brinckmann. It will be an original story, and poetic.'[127]

Rahel Levin also played a pivotal role in editing her work for publication. In the case of the few fragments that were printed during her lifetime, she made the selections from the copious quantities of letters, diaries, and aphorisms she had written on various subjects of public interest such as literature, music, and art, and prepared them for publication in various periodicals and magazines. The letters she exchanged with journal editors provide explicit evidence of her active involvement in this process. One example is a letter she sent in 1825 to Franz Elsholtz, the editor of the periodical *Eos*, containing her instructions for the publication of one of her essays along with a plea to protect her anonymity.[128] Another is a letter sent by the editor of a different journal in 1830 rejecting one of her submissions but suggesting she prepare a new essay in its stead: again it is clear that it was Levin herself who was negotiating with the publisher.[129] Perhaps more surprising is her active involvement in the editing of the collections of letters that were printed posthumously. In examining relevant sources and documents discovered in the boxes of the Varnhagen archive in Kraków, Isselstein found solid grounds for stating that the published form of Rahel's correspondence, and especially her first book

---

[125] This quote, taken from Eduard Schmidt-Weissenfels, *Rahel und ihre Zeit* (Leipzig, 1857), 239, is cited in Hahn, *'Antworten Sie mir!'*, 20. [126] Isselstein, 'Rahels Schriften I', 23.

[127] Letter from the beginning of July 1800, in Bruyn (ed.), *Rahels erste Liebe*, 302. Rahel's close friend Hitzel (Hedwig) Bernhard was also born in Berlin. She had been married to the Jewish doctor Isaac Beer Fließ but at that time used the name of Wilhelmine von Boye (at the time of her baptism she had taken the name Johanna Hedwig Wilhelmine), as the converted wife of a Swedish baron and military officer.

[128] This letter was printed for the first time by Ursula Isselstein, who considers the fact that it was not included by Varnhagen in the collections he edited to be proof of his tendency to maintain the fiction of Rahel as a naive writer, who did not intend her words for the eyes of the public (Isselstein, 'Rahels Schriften I', 24–5).

[129] Hahn, *'Antworten Sie mir!'*, 20–1 n. 14. On Rahel Levin's publications during her lifetime see ibid. 20–6, 223–4.

of letters, *Buch des Andenkens*, was a product of her editing no less than her husband's.[130]

All this indicates clearly that Rahel Levin did not in principle oppose the publication of her writings. But this does not mean that she unproblematically assumed the status of an author. The fact that she did not openly declare her aspirations as a writer by putting her name to those of her works that were published in her lifetime is certainly significant. Her wish to remain anonymous may be explained in part as evidence of the anxiety which prevented her at first from publishing at all, and then, when she gradually gained self-assurance and allowed some of her texts to be printed, from coming out of the shadows. Even when, after much hesitation, at the age of 41 she finally decided to publish fragments of her writings, her name did not appear on them, although she did not hide the fact that she had written them from her friends and relatives.[131] Her preference for anonymity may also have been attributable in part to her inclination towards avant-garde forms of writing: unidentified, she may have felt freer to experiment with unusual modes of expression, aware as she was that her fragmentary and associative texts constituted an innovative kind of writing.[132] Moreover, as Ursula Isselstein points out, her contradictory attitude towards publication may well reflect the paradox of her literary activity: writing in the knowledge that every single word she penned might be published, and yet writing as if she was oblivious to this possibility.[133]

Besides the anonymous publication of fragments from her own correspondence and diaries, Rahel Levin found another way to participate in the public literary sphere without disclosing her name: namely, by closely collaborating with her brother, Ludwig Robert. Without receiving or indeed wanting public recognition for her substantial contribution to his literary production, Rahel Levin played a central role in Robert's establishment as a writer, to an extent which justifies seeing her as co-author of some of his works. She performed three important functions regarding Robert's works: as an agent; as a critic and editor; and as an actual collaborator in his writing. As agent, she served more than once as mediator between Ludwig and journal publishers and editors, using her and her husband's connections to

---

[130] Isselstein, 'Rahels Schriften I'; ead., '"Dies ist die Beute!"'. As Isselstein indicates, new evidence found in the Varnhagen collection confirms previous assumptions according to which Rahel Levin took an active part in the planning of a collection of her letters (ibid. 90 n. 15).

[131] Thomann Tewarson, *Rahel Levin Varnhagen*, 201. According to Ursula Isselstein, Rahel wanted to act on the literary scene, but at the same time remain behind the curtains; she believed she would not be able to cope with the consequences of a public appearance (Isselstein, 'Rahels Schriften I', 25).

[132] Thomann Tewarson, *Rahel Levin Varnhagen*, 48. See the discussion of Rahel's 'strategies of writing and publishing', ibid. 200 ff.   [133] Isselstein, 'Rahels Schriften I', 26.

promote her brother's career.[134] As critic, she regularly examined manuscripts that Ludwig handed to her for comment, drawing on her wide knowledge and her familiarity with the contemporary literary field to suggest changes, sometimes major revisions, that would improve the final products.[135] Frequently, Ludwig gave his manuscripts first to Rahel, whom he viewed as his most reliable critic, sending them on to the editor of the journal in question only after her revisions had been made and she had approved the final version.[136]

Most significant, though, is Rahel's role as an actual literary partner of her brother. Consolina Vigliero, who edited and published the correspondence between the two, claims that 'in a sense, Rahel may also be considered Ludwig's "co-author"'.[137] Her assertion is based on a thorough examination of the original sources, which shows that Rahel Levin composed considerable parts of some of the essays published under her brother's name. Thus, for instance, in 1825 Robert asked his sister to formulate some ideas on the music of the Italian composer Gaspare Spontini, since 'I would like to write and have published a detailed essay on him'. Rahel replied with a letter devoted to this subject, which was published by Robert under his name, with only slight changes, in a journal that same year.[138]

This behind-the-scenes activity was of course intended to help promote the career of Rahel's younger brother, for whom she cared a great deal. However, this should not be taken as implying that she saw herself in the subordinate position of a helpmate, as if she were serving her brother's interests alone: for her, it was a collaboration between equal partners. The kind of cooperation she established with Robert was in line with her novel perception of authorship as a common enterprise—a perception also apparent in her epistolary activity, which was clearly the result of the input of more than one person, her own contribution inextricably involved with and dependent on that of her correspondents. In the same way, her joint literary activity with her brother provided an outlet for her literary impulses and enabled her creations to reach the public sphere, even though her part in this common creation remained openly unacknowledged.[139]

---

[134] In 1815, for instance, Rahel Levin asked Ludwig Robert to send her a manuscript—'You certainly have quite a lot of unprinted things lying around'—since she and Varnhagen had intervened on his behalf to get his work into print in the *Deutsche Blätter* (Levin Varnhagen, *Briefwechsel mit Ludwig Robert*, 128).   [135] For an example of this critical input, see ibid. 79.
[136] Vigliero, '"Mein lieber Schwester-Freund"', 50.   [137] Ibid. 51.   [138] Ibid. 51 n. 11.
[139] Consolina Vigliero considers Rahel Levin a 'selfless co-author' who had no interest in claiming recognition for her contribution to the texts published under her brother's name, and was content when her texts were reproduced word by word as she had formulated them. Vigliero, '"Mein lieber Schwester-Freund"', 51.

SARA MEYER—A FORGOTTEN FEMALE AUTHOR

Whereas Rahel Levin's attitude towards authorship was always ambivalent, her friend Sara Meyer reached a firm decision at a certain point in her life to pursue a career as a writer and took active steps to bring this about. Her success in gaining public recognition on her own account was limited, however: the world of literature knows Sara Meyer more as Goethe's friend, correspondent, and devoted reader than as an accomplished writer. Nevertheless, although relatively little is known about her literary output, there are enough traces to indicate that she wrote an appreciable amount and that she made serious efforts to get her work published. Reference to Meyer's literary activity is found in the papers left by Karl August Varnhagen who, as we have seen, took upon himself the task of documenting the period, taking a special interest in his wife Rahel Levin's friends. It is clear from his notes that Sara Meyer's literary activities covered a wide range of genres: he recorded, for example, that she 'had made attempts at stories, dramas, moral and even political essays in French and German'. Varnhagen's comments also suggest that her writing was received positively among her acquaintances, some of whom even urged her to publish.[140] Today, with the exception of a few texts preserved in the Varnhagen archive, including a story written in French entitled *Sophie ou la différence de l'Education* ('Sophie or the Difference of Education') and two German manuscripts—the essay 'Ansichten einer deutschen Frau' ('Opinions of a German Woman') and a play, *Die deutsche Erzieherin* ('The German Governess')—most of Sara Meyer's works appear to have been lost.[141] Even texts she apparently published during her lifetime are unavailable today, as they were already more than a century ago when the German Jewish historian and author Ludwig Geiger wrote a short biographical note about her.[142]

---

[140] Karl August Varnhagen, 'Frau von Grotthuß und Frau von Eybenberg', in id., *Gesammelte Schriften*, ed. Ludmilla Assing, vol. xviii (Leipzig, 1874), 80, as quoted in Hahn, *Unter falschem Namen*, 32–3.

[141] Hahn, *Unter falschem Namen*, 142; Hahn, 'Sophie von Grotthuss', in *Jewish Women Encyclopedia*. See also Stern (ed.), *Die Varnhagen von Ensesche Sammlung*, 295. This 1911 catalogue listing the contents of the Varnhagen archive includes, as well as a detailed list of the letters that Sara Meyer exchanged with more than a dozen correspondents that are to be found in the Varnhagen collection, lists of other 'poems and literary works' kept in this collection, among them the play and the essay mentioned here and a printed supplement—a cantata performed in 1824 at the Oranienburg Church—but not the French story mentioned above.

[142] In his notes to Sara Meyer's correspondence with Goethe, which he edited and printed in 1893, Geiger mentioned her literary activity. From his remarks it may be inferred that he had seen German

In the absence of a solid body of work from which to recover her status as an author, Sara Meyer's position in literary history is very different from that of Rahel Levin. As has been pointed out by Barbara Hahn—the first scholar to discuss Meyer's literary activity—her works are not included in any bibliography;[143] not surprisingly, her name is rarely if ever included among the authors of the period. Nevertheless, although most of her texts are missing, historical questions concerning her authorial work and her self-perception as a creative female intellectual may be addressed, using a personal source that proves helpful for this purpose: her correspondence with Goethe. Some of these letters reveal her self-awareness as an author and partially illuminate her efforts to publish her manuscripts and to obtain public recognition as a writer.

Although Sara Meyer had been writing for years, the first explicit trace of her intention to seek wider recognition of her work appears in a letter to Goethe in November 1814.[144] From that point in her correspondence she withdrew from her long-standing role as reader of Goethe's texts and admirer of this famous man of letters, and started to correspond with him from the position of an aspiring author trying to pave her own way as an independent writer. From Dresden, she informed Goethe that she was preparing a 'short essay' on a recent publication that had stirred up heated responses in the German intellectual world and had been a major subject of discussion in their mutual correspondence that year—Madame de Staël's *De l'Allemagne*. Meyer's essay 'Ansichten einer deutschen Frau', which remained unpublished, repudiated some of the assertions made against Staël's publication, specifically those levelled by a well-known German woman of letters, Caroline de la Motte Fouqué, who—like many of her compatriots—strongly disagreed with what she perceived as the distorted image of Germany that emerged from Staël's controversial text. In her letter, Meyer asked for Goethe's permission to quote in her rebuttal a passage from one of his letters to her, in which he had discussed this book.[145]

Taking up arms against Fouqué and the prevailing hostility towards Staël's work, Meyer dared to articulate a different, more favourable evaluation of the book. Thus, in picking her moment to step into public debate she

manuscripts of unpublished essays. On the other hand, 'her printed stories in French, including one which according to its title was probably part of her autobiography, are unavailable to me' (Geiger (ed.), 'Einundzwanzig Briefe', 100–1).

[143] Hahn, *Unter falschem Namen*, 32–5.

[144] For a discussion of the relationship between Sara Meyer and Goethe as reflected in this correspondence, see Anderson, 'Franco-German Conversations'.

[145] Geiger (ed.), 'Einundzwanzig Briefe', 59. Rahel Levin also discussed Staël's book in her letters, as did Esther Gad (see n. 51 above), who unlike Sara Meyer joined the numerous critics of the book. As indicated, Meyer's essay is preserved in manuscript in the Varnhagen collection.

PLATE 6. Germaine de Staël (1766–1817)
Coloured etching by Bartolomeo Pinelli (c. 1815)
© bpk / Dietmar Katz

not only chose an issue that was already the subject of controversy among men and women of letters, she also planned to put forward a viewpoint that was at odds with the general opinion in her own country and indeed the dominant patriotic discourse of the time.[146] She did not shrink from voicing a cosmopolitan and indeed relatively pro-French attitude when discussing *De l'Allemagne*, either in her private correspondence with Goethe or in the essay she intended to publish about the work.

This eagerness to defend a book that had aroused strong reactions in Germany, almost all of them negative, is of particular significance. Meyer dared to present an opinion that ran contrary to prevailing attitudes, and in doing so to continue defending Enlightenment ideals that had ceased to be popular in Germany. Prompted by a sense of mission that prevented her from keeping her dissenting opinion to herself or her circle of acquaintances, she felt impelled to try to get her argument printed and thereby to put her claims before a much wider audience—a goal that remained unrealized. She had put her hand to writing, so she claimed, mainly to mobilize public opinion—to promote what she considered helpful and beneficial ideas and to avoid the propagation of misjudgements, especially among women. Adopting a stance very similar to that of Esther Gad in respect of her self-appointed task as an author, she stressed her determination to reject error and defend truth.[147] Her emphasis on the general benefit as one of the main goals that motivated her to write could be interpreted as reflecting an attitude common among women writers, who excused their writing by reference to the need to educate their fellow women. But it could also indicate the much more self-assured attitude of a modern intellectual, confident of possessing important and useful ideas, and aspiring to influence and indeed significantly change public opinion—in her case, specifically female public opinion, for her own words imply that her essays were directed mainly towards women.

In the years after 1814, probably up to her death in 1828, Sara Meyer remained active in the literary sphere. Her correspondence with Goethe was interrupted for almost a decade, so that even this—almost the only correspondence of Sara Meyer's that has been preserved—fails to provide any hints of what she did in this area. Eventually, however, after a decade of silence, in 1824 she approached Goethe again, now as an accomplished writer seeking the help of an influential friend. In one of her letters from that year she expressed the hope that Goethe could help her in her publishing efforts by recommending her to one of the leading German publishers, Johann

---

[146] Anderson, 'Franco-German Conversation', 567.
[147] Geiger (ed.), 'Einundzwanzig Briefe', 59.

Friedrich Cotta. In the past she had interceded with Goethe—in his capacity as director of the Weimar court theatre—on behalf of another writer, Rahel Levin's brother Ludwig Robert, in the hope of getting a play he had written produced.[148] Now she turned to him hoping to advance her own personal interests as an author. By then she could boast the publication of several works, although, as she pointed out, these had brought her no financial reward: a story, *Sophie ou la différence de l'Education*, and numerous contributions to the *Athénée des Dames*, a French women's periodical of which only traces survive.[149] But her approach seems to have been fruitless.

Objectively, Sara Meyer's literary career could be summarized as rather unmemorable, her relatively modest achievements amounting to several forgotten publications and a handful of manuscripts that never reached the printing press. Indeed, we should not ignore the obscurity into which the literary activity of Sara Meyer and other women fell, the frustrating obstacles that limited their possibilities of publishing so that many of their works disappeared or were disregarded. But it is possible, nevertheless, to present their case from a different angle, stressing not the failures but the achievements. A different historical evaluation, valid for all the women discussed in this chapter, would stress their tireless activity as authors; their perseverance, expressed among other ways in their refusal to be deterred from seeking ways to publish their works; the sense of mission that motivated them, imbued with a belief that they were acting as rational creatures, capable of analysing cultural, social, or political events and situations, and that their insights could contribute to the common good; and their intense desire to disseminate their opinions, despite the anxiety expressed by some of them as to how their literary works would be received.

[148] Sara Meyer, as Goethe's friend, sent him the manuscript of Robert's play, *Die Tochter Jephthas* ('Jephthah's Daughter'), finished in 1810, in order to obtain his opinion and if possible to have it presented on stage. On the play and Sara Meyer's intervention, see Weissberg, 'Dramatic History'.

[149] Geiger (ed.), 'Einundzwanzig Briefe', 127. A periodical entitled the *Athénée des Dames* is known to have appeared in France in 1808. Judging by the two single issues remaining at the French National Library, this short-lived publication, edited exclusively by women and addressed to a female public, presented subversive ideas about women's place in state and society. On this periodical, see Sullerot, *Histoire de la presse féminine en France*, 115–23.

FOUR

SOCIABILITY AND ACCULTURATION IN GERMAN SPAS

THE MANY LETTERS left behind by Jewish women who lived in Berlin at the end of the eighteenth century and the beginning of the nineteenth constitute, as we have seen, an important historical source for research into Jewish acculturation in Germany at the beginning of the modern era. They contain a great deal of information about the far-reaching social and cultural changes that occurred in their lives and in the lives of the German Jewish urban bourgeoisie during those crucial years of Jewish modernization. They also contain information on hitherto unexamined aspects of the process by which these women became integrated into non-Jewish European culture and society. One of the phenomena addressed in these sources that has not yet received sufficient attention is the practice of visiting spas.

Their letters tell us that these women often chose to spend the summer months at one of the spa centres of central Europe. These inland watering places, based around springs of mineral water reputed to have therapeutic properties, gained in popularity during the eighteenth century, especially in the latter decades, and began to attract an increasingly diverse clientele among the population in German lands, notably within the educated and the property-owning classes. As we will see, the spas offered many advantages alongside their original function as places of healing and recuperation: the semi-urban way of life which developed in these resorts over the course of the eighteenth century offered visitors a wide array of pastimes and enjoyments such as musical and theatrical performances, parties, and walks along the main boulevards and in more rural surroundings. For Jewish women in particular, the unique, liberated atmosphere of the spas offered a space in which they could widen their circle of acquaintances, integrate themselves into non-Jewish society, and take an active part in discussions on cultural and other issues. Thus the annual visit to one or more spas, which became a notable feature of bourgeois life, constituted an important component in the acculturation of the modernizing Jewish women discussed in this book. Visits to the spas indicated the adoption of modern concepts and values, such as the setting aside of a certain period in the year as dedicated to vacation and recuperation, to a change in daily routine, and to the care of body and soul. Moreover, these visits constituted an integral part of these Jewish women's involvement in the general world of culture and their incorporation into the contemporary social fabric—a function that was especially significant in that, as women, they were often excluded from more institutionalized social and cultural frameworks.[1]

THE SPAS: PLACES OF CURE AND PLACES OF SOCIABILITY

One of the Jewish women who joined the swelling stream of visitors to the spas was Fradchen Liebmann, who spent a month at Freienwalde in the summer of 1795. From her home in Berlin she travelled to the fashionable resort, about 50 kilometres north-east of the Prussian capital, in the company of her friend Hitzel Bernhard. Upon arrival Liebmann went straight to the healing springs, immersed herself in their waters, and claimed to have felt their effect immediately. 'The water has a big impact on me, as it is causing me great pain', she wrote to Rahel Levin in the course of her vacation, 'but whether it will help me, God knows.'[2] As someone whose health overall was not good—in letters of June 1795, a short time before the vacation, she complained of a poor general disposition, a rash on her entire body, and a cough—she hoped that her visit to the spa would bring about an improvement in her physical condition. In accordance with contemporary medical understanding, she ascribed therapeutic powers to the springs and saw them as a remedy for many ailments, although her words betray an undertone of doubt regarding their effectiveness that was apparent in the words of many visitors to the spas.

Even though a spa visit entailed considerable expense and a long and difficult journey,[3] it was perceived by Fradchen Liebmann and many others as

---

[1] James van Horn Melton stresses the significance of spas and resorts as places which offered women with intellectual interests the opportunity to meet like-minded men and women: see *The Rise of the Public*, 153, 211–12.   [2] Bosold, 'Friederike Liman', 23.

[3] According to Hermann Sommer, 'The journey by mail carriage was not only arduous but also extremely expensive... When necessary, part of the distance was covered on foot, in the saddle, or by

a worthwhile investment in their physical and emotional health. Friends of Liebmann's among the Jewish women of Berlin wrote of returning from a spa visit with a sense of improvement in their general well-being and, as a consequence, also in their external appearance. Returning that same year of 1795 from a two-month stay at Carlsbad and Teplitz, Marianne Meyer was convinced of the positive effects of the summer vacation on her health and appearance: 'I returned from Teplitz feeling quite well. I will try at *any* expense to maintain this well-being. I am generally told that I look very well. If I do not fulfil my resolution, vanity will renew my strength.'[4] A few years later, in December 1800, Meyer explained in one of her letters from Vienna that 'my health demands another visit to Pyrmont', since 'it has saved me once before'.[5] The healing process was not always easy or enjoyable, and often tiresome: 'Seven hours a day was required for my treatment, twice bathing, twice drinking, and this exhausted me so', she lamented in December 1803; nevertheless, looking back to the summer months, she consoled herself with the fact that 'now I feel the beneficial results of my perseverance'.[6] Even when the results were not encouraging, there was always the hope that continuing or repeating the treatment would eventually yield benefits. Thus, even though a disappointing personal experience often left no room for anything but scepticism, Jewish women, like many other visitors to the spas, continued to go back in the hope of finding healing for their illnesses,[7] and while there were punctilious in observing the regimes prescribed by the specialist physicians who worked there, immersing themselves in the springs and drinking their waters as instructed.[8]

---

those who had the means, in their private carriages.' Only when the railways were established in the 19th century was the journey to these places made easier (Sommer, *Zur Kur nach Ems*, 30).

[4] Geiger (ed.), 'Einundzwanzig Briefe', 28.

[5] Sauer (ed.), *Goethe und Österreich*, 120.   [6] Ibid. 159.

[7] A combination of hope that the spring water might indeed have healing powers with a considerable measure of scepticism is noticeable in the words of the Jewish physician Marcus Herz, who travelled to the springs of Freienwalde in 1800 in search of therapy, but found no miracle cure in immersion: 'It has been two hours already since I bathed', he wrote with dry humour to his mother-in-law a short while after his arrival at the place, 'but I still cannot praise the divine miracle of the baths, I am just the same as I was the day before yesterday, and I have to wait patiently for twenty more immersions' (Landsberg (ed.), *Henriette Herz*, 158–9).

[8] Marianne Meyer described the circumstances of the extension of her stay at Teplitz in September 1808, after most of the visitors had left: 'I have not been feeling well for several days again, and my nerves are affected more than usual. This fact forces me to stay here longer, and even though I have remained almost entirely alone in Teplitz, I will stay until October 1, so that I will be able to immerse myself many times. The doctor claims that these pains will have beneficial effects in the future. I have been given such assurances many times, and the results were not as I expected. But I am childish enough to believe' (Sauer (ed.), *Goethe und Österreich*, 204).

However, the quest for improved health was not the only reason (indeed, in most cases it was probably not even the main reason) why these women visited the spas. An additional important attraction was the social intercourse that was part of the way of life there, offering opportunities to communicate with many people—including, notably, non-Jews—and thereby to broaden their circle of acquaintances. The second half of the eighteenth century offered prosperous and educated Jews in Germany, especially in Berlin, various environments for social and cultural interaction with non-Jews. The social and scholarly associations of the late Enlightenment opened their ranks, at least partially, to Jewish intellectuals;[9] business connections established by affluent Jews sometimes turned into friendly relations and brought members of the German nobility and middle class to their homes; the city boulevards and the theatres the Jews visited also served them as places of contact and sociability. To this list one can add the spas, as another context in which encounters across religious divisions were possible. As an informal public space, equally accessible to members of both sexes, this environment especially suited Jewish women who wished to make new acquaintances and cultivate social connections with non-Jews.

Evidence of the social connections that were formed in the course of a stay at a spa emerges from the letters that Fradchen Liebmann sent during her vacation at Freienwalde in 1795. Born some twenty-four years earlier as Fradchen Marcuse, the daughter of a wealthy banker, she had grown up as a member of Berlin's Jewish upper class. In 1786 she married Abraham Nathan Liebmann, the son of another banker and leading member of the city's Jewish community, Nathan Halberstadt Liebmann.[10] When the couple and their son converted to Christianity in 1809,[11] she adopted the name Auguste Friederike Liman. By the middle of the following decade, after a divorce and involvement in a court case over her father's estate, her financial situation had deteriorated to the point where she could no longer afford to visit the spas.[12] But at least during those years around 1795 Fradchen Liebmann lived a life of

---

[9] In addition to the known case of Moses Mendelssohn, who also was an honorary member of the prestigious Mittwochsgesellschaft, other Jews began to join mixed enlightened circles, such as the Gesellschaft der Freunde der Humanität and the Philomatische Gesellschaft. See Ch. 5 below.

[10] For basic information on these figures, see Jacobson, *Jüdische Trauungen in Berlin*.

[11] Some of their relatives were also baptized in the same year, e.g. Fradchen's brother-in-law Isaac Nathan Liebmann and her nephew Nathan (Ferdinand) Liman (ibid. 265, 354). Steven Lowenstein, in his book on the Berlin Jewish community, provides a genealogical table which shows the proliferation of cases of conversion among the descendants of Nathan Liepmann (i.e. Liebmann), a 'wealthy member of the burial society' (Lowenstein, *The Berlin Jewish Community*, 158–9).

[12] See Fradchen Liebmann's letter to Rahel Levin in 1816 (Bosold, 'Friederike Liman', 80).

relative ease, which enabled her to spend four weeks at the healing baths in relatively comfortable accommodation.

Shortly after her arrival at Freienwalde, Liebmann began to establish contacts with new acquaintances and old friends—Jewish and Christian guests of both sexes, who, like her, spent their vacations here and were happy to share their hours of leisure between treatments. These connections were important enough for Liebmann to list them in the letters she sent to her close friend Rahel Levin during her vacation, in which she described in detail how these contacts quickly expanded. Immediately after settling down with her friend Hitzel Bernhard in one of the guest houses in the town, she met some upper-class non-Jewish visitors who were staying in the same establishment. These included a certain Mrs von Ramin, who resided 'right above me'; a Miss von Retzow, from the entourage of the wife of the Prince of Prussia, 'with whom I am already in contact'; and Countess Haack, who 'comes and enters our hall' and 'by the way, the company [*Gesellschaft*] starts here'—that is to say, this is where social life begins. This group was joined by others, including Otto Friedrich Ludwig von Schack, a Prussian officer who was friendly with Fradchen Liebmann and Hitzel Bernhard in Berlin, and an unidentified man by the name of Rothenburg.[13]

Liebmann then continued with a description of what she and her friends did to give variety to their days. Among other things they played blind man's buff together and took excursions into the area round the town: the latter was a typical pursuit of spa visitors, who would frequently go out in groups to enjoy the pleasures of nature together. 'Jette [Henriette Mendelssohn] is here after all ... I am pleasantly surprised by her presence. Yesterday we and part of the society, in fact, the elite, took a trip to the Schlossberg [*eine partie nach den Schlosberg*], where we ... enjoyed ourselves.'[14] A few days later she asked Rahel to tell Sara and Marianne Meyer that she had invited 'a large party' to their family's estate in that area.[15] In both cases, Liebmann, Bernhard, and apparently also Henriette Mendelssohn, the youngest of Moses Mendelssohn's daughters, spent time with a group that included non-Jewish guests,

---

[13] Fradchen Liebmann's letter to Rahel Levin in 1795, 20–1.

[14] Ibid. 23. Schlossberg, a hill near Freienwalde with relics from the Middle Ages, is still a tourist site today. Here and elsewhere Liebmann uses the expression 'partie', which was common at this time and meant 'a group of people spending time together'. As Heikki Lempa explains, around 1800 this term was used frequently in the context of the spas, and it encompassed a variety of activities undertaken for leisure and pleasure, especially card games and excursions into nature (Lempa, 'The Spa', 62–3).

[15] Bosold, 'Friederike Liman', 25. According to Jacobson (*Jüdische Trauungen in Berlin*, 251), Sara's father, Aaron Meyer, was lessee of the alum factories in Freienwalde. Jacobson indicates that he died in the summer of 1795.

taking full part in their common activities. Liebmann clearly enjoyed telling her friend how she, as part of the high society among the visitors to the little town, participated in the splendid event of a royal reception. This came about when the daughters of the Prussian king arrived at Freienwalde, accompanied by their husbands, to visit their mother, Friederike Louise, queen of Prussia. To mark the occasion the queen gave a midday party (*déjeuner dansant*) by the springs, and Fradchen Liebmann was among those present. 'All were invited, and I was lucky enough to be introduced to the Queen.'[16]

Rahel Levin was herself spending the summer in Bohemia, enjoying similarly exclusive company at the famous spas there. Her letters to Fradchen Liebmann have not been preserved, but from Fradchen's answers and from other sources, such as Rahel's correspondence with her friend David Veit and reports by other visitors to the spas, we can learn a good deal about her experiences there and the impact this young Jewish woman made on her fellow guests, quite a few of whom were impressed by her personality and her wisdom. For example, in one of her letters Fradchen Liebmann told Rahel about an Austrian prince who was full of admiration for her: 'Mrs Wollf [Cäcilie Wulff] told Jettchen [presumably Henriette Mendelssohn] . . . that Prince Karl of Liechtenstein wrote to her that his brother Moritz had written to him about a woman named Levin, whom he met at Carlsbad, in such a fascinated tone that he must be in love with her.'[17] Other visitors, among them Goethe, also spoke with great appreciation about 'the little Levi'—a nickname that stuck to the diminutive Rahel.

Rahel Levin's journey to the more exclusive and distant spa sites in Bohemia was of a different character from Liebmann's visit to the relatively local Freienwalde: this was one of the long and protracted journeys to the baths which became common in the eighteenth century among the well-off. As was customary on journeys of this sort, the trip fanned out to incorporate several destinations. Before her departure, Rahel indicated that she planned to stay in Carlsbad for the first four weeks, and then go to Teplitz for three weeks.[18] Her vacation eventually included visits to other places as well, since the long journey to distant spas necessitated stops on the way. A curious traveller, Levin took advantage of the opportunity to see Dresden, which she longed to get to know, and took particular interest in the city's various cultural and social attractions, such as the theatre, the art galleries, and the parks.[19]

---

[16] Bosold, 'Friederike Liman', 26.
[17] Ibid. 26–7. On Cäcilie Wulff, née Itzig, who was then staying in Freienwalde, see Ch. 1 n. 93 above.   [18] *Briefwechsel zwischen Rahel und David Veit*, ii. 154.   [19] Ibid. 186.

Just before leaving on her vacation Rahel Levin complained of being in a fragile physical and emotional state—the perfect reason (or excuse) for visiting a spa. She remarked on her poor health in a letter of May 1795 to her friend David Veit, who was studying in Jena at the time, as she set out her plans for the approaching summer and the possibility of their meeting somewhere. A little later, at the beginning of June, she explained to him that her mother had encouraged her to travel to the spas, where she might convalesce: 'I was feeling indisposed, and mother herself suggested this trip to me', she wrote, already on her way to Carlsbad.[20] The absence of a suitable companion had almost torpedoed her plans—after all, in those days women did not usually travel without company, certainly not in Germany.[21] A plan to go on the journey with Hitzel Bernhard did not materialize, and only at the last moment did Levin join another friend, a renowned German actress named Friederike Unzelmann.[22] Together they travelled to Carlsbad and Teplitz for a vacation which was to last for over two months.

From the spas Rahel wrote enthusiastic letters full of accounts of her experiences; she longed for the visit not to end, and was delighted when her planned return trip was postponed, explaining the benefits of this decision in terms not only of health but also of leisure and sociability. The extension of her stay not only made it possible for her to complete the medical treatment which she had been forced to interrupt due to a decline in her health;[23] it also gave her the opportunity to continue cultivating the social contacts she had established at the resort, mainly with non-Jews, which she held so dear. From her references to these contacts it is abundantly clear how extensive were the opportunities the spas offered for visitors from different geographical areas and social circles to meet and cultivate personal relationships with one another. This young Jewish woman numbered among her acquaintance, for

---

[20] *Briefwechsel zwischen Rahel und David Veit*, ii. 154. How ill Levin and many other spa visitors actually were is a matter for debate. Concern for one's health was a widespread theme among contemporaries of their social class; hypochondria was a prevalent affliction in the 18th century, and it brought many visitors to the spas. Kuhnert, *Urbanität auf dem Lande*, 67.

[21] About a month before her departure, Rahel Levin wrote to David Veit from Berlin: 'I'm staying here, since there is no one who will come with me' (*Briefwechsel zwischen Rahel und David Veit*, ii. 115). The issue of a travelling companion recurs in a letter from Henriette Mendelssohn of April 1799, when making her way from Berlin to Vienna (*Briefe von und an Friedrich und Dorothea Schlegel*, ed. Behler, xxiv. 270–4). In contrast, Esther Gad (on whom see below in this chapter), writes that unlike in Germany, in England women would travel on their own without any anxiety, as she had learned on her travels there (Bernard, *Briefe über England und Portugal*, i. 154).

[22] Friederike Unzelmann, later Bethmann, a Berlin actress, had close connections with Jewish women including Rahel Levin and Fradchen Liebmann. For more on Unzelmann and her special relationship with Liebmann, see Ch. 6 below.

[23] *Briefwechsel zwischen Rahel und David Veit*, ii. 160, 163.

example, the Belgian Prince Charles Joseph de Ligne and his family, whose company she enjoyed and with whom she frequently spent time.[24] 'The prince ... is marvellous, and I like him better and better', she wrote; 'his children are charming already, too.'[25] Above all, she was pleased by the expectation of spending additional days in the company of Countess Josephine von Pachta, whom she had just met—'the kindest woman ... whom I'm afraid to devour with my eyes'. The extension of Rahel's stay at Teplitz prevented the two women having to part almost as soon as they had met: 'Today we expressed our regret that we found each other so late, and we agreed to meet every hour during the remainder of my stay, and we already arranged to meet next year. How happy she will be to see me this afternoon!'[26]

THE DEVELOPMENT OF THE SPAS AND THE RISE OF THE BOURGEOISIE

The places mentioned above—Carlsbad, Teplitz, and Freienwalde—are but three of the many spa towns that dotted the map of the German-speaking countries and other parts of Europe in the later eighteenth century. Along with the most famous such resorts—Bath in England, Spa in Belgium, Carlsbad in Bohemia, and Pyrmont in Lower Saxony—dozens of other towns and villages developed to serve the increasing clientele of invalids seeking healing and travellers looking for rest or simply a pleasant sociable holiday.

The history of the spas did not, of course, begin with this vigorous development at the beginning of the modern era. In antiquity, the Greeks and especially the Romans flocked to the baths, and these places earned an important position in classical culture both for reasons of hygiene as well as for the healing qualities that were ascribed to the spring water. The sophisticated and magnificent buildings around natural water sources built by the Romans for the well-being of the population also served as venues for all kinds of

---

[24] Following a military career, the Prince de Ligne, a native of Brussels, devoted himself to the social and cultural worlds. On his many visits to the cities and resort towns of Europe, he met the women discussed in this book. He has an unusual place in Jewish history as a result of a memorandum he wrote in 1797, in which he analysed the poor condition of the Jewish people (especially in eastern Europe), of which he had become aware while visiting Bohemia, Galicia, and Poland in 1780–95 during military campaigns, and sketched a solution in the form of the establishment of a Jewish state in the Land of Israel under the protection of Turkey. He presented his plan to Sara Meyer, after she had converted to Christianity, in the form of a 'Defence for your people'. On this episode, see Kobler (ed.), *Juden und Judentum in deutschen Briefen*, 169–71; Schulsinger, *Un précurseur du sionisme au XVIIIe siècle*; Gelber, *Vorgeschichte des Zionismus*, 33–8; Adler, *Restoring the Jews to their Homeland*, 124–6; Michaelis, 'The Ephraim Family and their Descendants', 232–5.

[25] *Briefwechsel zwischen Rahel und David Veit*, ii. 161–2.   [26] Ibid. 161.

activities connected to the cultivation of the body.[27] With the fall of the Roman empire, the healing baths also lost their prominence, and only in the late Middle Ages did they begin to develop anew. The revival of the principles of classical medicine in the early modern era restored the baths to fashion,[28] leading to the steady increase in their popularity which reached its peak in modern times.

It would be a mistake to take at face value the assertions of Renaissance thinkers that Europeans deserted the baths for a thousand years, for there are testimonies to their being enjoyed during the Middle Ages.[29] However, it is true that the Renaissance saw the beginnings of a systematic study of the use of springs, emphasizing anew the healing qualities of the waters and contributing to the rise in social status of the spas' clientele.[30] Throughout the early modern era scientists, especially physicians working at the spas, toiled to arrive at a precise analysis of the chemical composition of the spring waters in every place. Thus balneology—that is, the science of the medical use of healing baths—blossomed as a field of research. As particular healing qualities came to be ascribed to the different kinds of water, so it became possible to recommend them as means of treating specific illnesses, rather than for their general therapeutic advantages alone.[31] Accordingly, from the sixteenth century onwards, the use of natural springs gradually became less spontaneous and more a matter requiring the strict supervision of medical specialists.[32] Treatment at the spas became more professional, dispensed by local physicians considered expert in the field. The Jewish women with whom we are concerned here, among them Marianne Meyer, Rahel Levin, and Fradchen Liebmann, embraced this scientific discourse, hired the services of local physicians, and followed their instructions—though not always with absolute confidence in the medical advice they received.

---

[27] Bynum and Porter (eds.), *Companion Encyclopedia of the History of Medicine*, ii. 951–2. It is known that spas were built by the Romans in the Land of Israel in antiquity, for example at Hamat Gader and Tiberias. Jews visited these places in the days of the Second Temple, at the time of the Mishnah and the Talmud, and from rabbinic sources it is evident that these visitors included even the greatest among the sages (Dvorjetski, 'Medicinal Hot Springs in Erets Yisra'el in Antiquity' (Heb.)).

[28] According to Richard Palmer, Renaissance thinkers saw in the 'return' to the baths a kind of renewal or revival, after 'a long, dark age of neglect'. Balneology was one of the areas they wished to study anew, under the influence of Renaissance ideals and methods, including the rediscovery of forgotten texts and the publication in print of a wide range of medical literature from the ancient world (Palmer, 'Italian Baths in the Era of the Renaissance', 14–16). [29] Ibid. 15–16.

[30] On the role of the physicians and the new medical knowledge in turning spa visiting from a popular affair into an occupation of the nobility in 17th-century France, see Brockliss, 'The Development of the Spa in Seventeenth-Century France'.

[31] Bynum and Porter (eds.), *Companion Encyclopedia of the History of Medicine*, ii. 953.

[32] See Roy Porter's introduction to *The Medical History of Waters and Spas*, p. x.

As the renewed emphasis on the therapeutic advantages of spring water attracted more, and more discerning, visitors to the springs, the absence of adequate infrastructure to cope with the influx rapidly became apparent. The essayist Michel de Montaigne, travelling to the springs in Italy at the end of the sixteenth century, found himself in conditions far from those to which he was accustomed.[33] It was not long before architectural developments began with the aim of satisfying the needs of a new and more demanding clientele. The new facilities reflected a tendency which over time became a salient characteristic of spa towns, that is, a trend towards combining in one place the provision of medical care and of relaxation, recreation, and sociability. In the seventeenth century German rulers began to cultivate gardens and walkways alongside the bath-houses they built around the water sources. With the advent of the eighteenth century came a real building boom, in which the dual function of the baths as a place of health and a place of recreation and enjoyment was even more pronounced; indeed, the two became intertwined, with leisure conceived of as an integral part of the healing process. The architectural development of a town like Pyrmont testifies to the importance ascribed to leisure activities at the spas. The ballrooms and theatres built at this time symbolize the centrality of social and cultural recreation in the lifestyle of the spas in the eighteenth century.[34] Together with the coffee-houses and shops located along the main boulevard of the town near the bath-houses, these buildings constituted a lively urban space that made Pyrmont, like other top-ranking spas, part of the German public sphere.

Not only architectural changes but also transformations in the social make-up of the visiting community changed the face of the spas in the course of the eighteenth century. Members of the lower classes continued to visit, as they had done in the past;[35] and, as in the previous century, members of the nobility also continued to use the spas, giving an aristocratic touch to the

[33] Palmer, 'Italian Baths in the Era of the Renaissance', 19–21.

[34] Burkhard Fuhs, who examined the development of the spas in Germany, with particular attention to their architecture, goes so far as to claim that the central function of a place like Pyrmont in the 18th century was socio-cultural and not medical. He cites as evidence the fact that in the 1720s two ballrooms were built, while a plan to build a new bathhouse in 1723 was postponed by fifty years (Fuhs, *Mondäne Orte*, 63).

[35] Sommer emphasizes that although the presence of the ruling class at spas is noticeable in sources from the early modern era, people from other classes—farmers, craftsmen, merchants, clerks, and ministers—were also present at these places (Sommer, *Zur Kur nach Ems*, 19–20). As Reinhold Kuhnert explains in his book on the town of Pyrmont, the crowd of visitors included a significant number of people from the lower classes, such as farmers and members of the petty bourgeoisie; however, since most of them were illiterate, these guests did not leave behind any documentation, and the historical record of their visits is correspondingly deficient (Kuhnert, *Urbanität auf dem Lande*, 18, 130–1).

local way of life. But at the same time there was a significant increase in the number of middle-class visitors of both sexes, until eventually, and very conspicuously in the nineteenth century, the journey to the spas became a central component of their lifestyle. To what extent capitalism brought with it a new concept of vacant time, a new differentiation between work and leisure, and thus promoted the establishment of the modern practice of taking an annual holiday, is a controversial issue.[36] In any case, even though many scholars today reject the claim that the phenomenon of leisure is a clear product of the process of modernization, and contend that this concept pre-dated modern times, there is no doubt that the modern era in the Western world saw an increase in the popularity of the yearly vacation to the point where it became institutionalized; and one prominent form of this institutionalized annual holiday was the spa visit. During the eighteenth century, and especially in its last decades, the particular type of leisure activity associated with an annual visit to the spas gained ascendancy in Germany, significantly among the upper middle class. Members of the *haute bourgeoisie*, adopting this form of leisure once typical of the nobility, assumed the habit of spending an extended period of leisure time away from home, especially during the summer. For this prosperous but thrifty sector of society, a form of commercialized leisure such as the spa summer vacation was an ideal recreational activity. Being justified on health grounds, it provided an excellent rationale for spending money and time on leisure and consumption; furthermore, it helped transform economic success into status by providing a space where cultural consumption and display could take place.[37] Gradually, Jews also joined the ranks of the spa goers, and this practice of a visit to the watering towns began to occupy an important place in their lives.

THE JEWISH PRESENCE AT GERMAN SPAS IN THE LATE EIGHTEENTH CENTURY

The presence of Jews at the spas of central Europe was clearly evident in the eighteenth century, notably during the last three decades, with the development of the spas as middle-class resorts. Whereas in earlier centuries the Church and local authorities had striven to keep Jews away from the com-

---

[36] See Burke, 'The Invention of Leisure in Early Modern Europe'; Marfany and Burke, 'Debate: The Invention of Leisure in Early Modern Europe'; Borsay, *A History of Leisure*. For a discussion of the rise of the term *Freizeit* in the German context, see Nahrstedt, *Die Entstehung der Freizeit*.

[37] Borsay, *A History of Leisure*, 89–91.

pany of Christian bathers,[38] the greater tolerance and openness of the modern era were apparent in the (at least partial) removal of obstacles erected by Christians to the participation of Jews in the use of facilities at the spas. The question arises to what extent the visits of Fradchen Liebmann, Rahel Levin, Marianne Meyer, Henriette Mendelssohn, and Hitzel Bernhard represented a pioneering phenomenon. In fact, they had been preceded by Jews of both sexes and widely varying ages and economic backgrounds, from a number of different cities in Germany, who began to join the broadening circle of visitors to the spas—as English Jews had done from the first half of the eighteenth century onwards, visiting Bath for leisure and convalescence.[39] So, as various sources indicate, while the Jewish women from Berlin who travelled to the spas in the mid-1790s were part of a relatively new phenomenon, they were not the first in Jewish society to spend their summers this way.[40] Nor were their visits to the spas exceptional during their own time.

About twenty years earlier Moses Mendelssohn, accompanied by other representatives of the Jewish community of Berlin, had made two visits to Pyrmont, then one of the most famous spas in Germany. These visits are documented in several letters written by the philosopher himself and by his contemporaries. Pyrmont, a town in Lower Saxony quite near Hamelin, which itself is not far from Hanover, was at that time just at the beginning of a period of rising prosperity. In the years after the Seven Years War, especially the 1770s, it attracted increasing numbers of visitors, including some from more distant places and even from other countries, rather than the predominantly local clientele on whom it had previously relied. Advised by his physicians to bathe in the natural springs of Pyrmont and drink their waters, Mendelssohn did not follow their recommendation immediately: in a letter dated June 1772 to his friend Johann Georg Zimmermann, the court physician in Hanover, he explained that 'domestic circumstances' (probably his workload) prevented him from making the trip.[41] Eventually, however, in the summer of 1773 the journey to the spa did materialize, following an

---

[38] In 1267 the Synod of Vienna forbade Jews to visit Christian baths, and in 1440 Jews and Christians were forbidden to bathe together. According to Kuhnert, efforts were made to separate Christian and Jewish guests at mineral springs as well (Kuhnert, *Urbanität auf dem Lande*, 202). Also, a decree of Landgrave Ernst from the end of the 17th century ruled that Jews should remain at least fourteen steps away from the wells at Schwalbach, and were not allowed to draw the water by themselves (Genth, *Kulturgeschichte der Stadt Schwalbach*, 49).

[39] See testimony to this in Roth (ed.), *Anglo-Jewish Letters*, e.g. pp. 103–5, and in the correspondence of Abigaill Levy Franks, a Jewish woman from New York, with her son, who lived in England: Franks, *The Letters of Abigaill Levy Franks*.

[40] I am currently carrying out a study on the Jewish presence at central European spas in the first half of the 18th century.   [41] Altmann, *Moses Mendelssohn*, 277–8.

invitation from Zacharias Veitel Ephraim, the son of Veitel Heine Ephraim, a leading figure in the Berlin Jewish community, to accompany him on a planned trip to Pyrmont.[42] Mendelssohn travelled in the comfortable private carriage belonging to his friend and business associate and the two men spent a short period together in the resort.[43] A year later Mendelssohn visited Pyrmont again, once more in the company of a member of the Ephraim family—this time the family friend Rösel Meyer, Zacharias Veitel Ephraim's sister, who had married Aaron Meyer. Rösel's young daughter Sara Meyer also joined the party. The three stayed at Pyrmont for several weeks—including, incidentally, the traditional period of mourning at the beginning of the month of Av, considered by some religious authorities an inappropriate time to visit a watering place.[44]

Both of Mendelssohn's trips to Pyrmont were taken in search of a remedy for a prolonged and 'mysterious' nervous disease, for which the doctors had struggled to find a cure. Consequently, his time at the spa was much taken up with therapeutic treatment: 'I am immersing myself today for the fourth time', he wrote to his wife Fromet a few days after his arrival. 'Thank God the success has been good so far, and I am willing anyway to take a rest and immerse myself every day.'[45] Medical considerations also led to the extension of his second visit: the date of return was postponed, because 'according to the doctors' judgment, we still haven't immersed ourselves enough'. Mendelssohn expressed satisfaction at the improvement in his sense of well-being in a cheerful report to his wife in Berlin, corroborated by a letter from Rösel Meyer to Fromet Mendelssohn in which she promised: 'You will have a rather healthy husband when he comes home.'[46] Mendelssohn did not rule out the possibility of making a return visit one day from choice for preventative treatment: 'I already know what kind of treatment will be the most

---

[42] Altmann, *Moses Mendelssohn*, 279. On Zacharias Veitel Ephraim, see Michaelis, 'The Ephraim Family'.

[43] In a letter sent to Gotthold Ephraim Lessing from the city of Braunschweig on 16 July 1773, on his way to Pyrmont, Mendelssohn suggested that his learned friend travel with him to the spa. After all, 'I am travelling there with Mr Zacharias Veitel Ephraim . . . We have a very comfortable carriage with four seats at our disposal, and so there is room for two more people' (Mendelssohn, *Gesammelte Schriften. Jubiläumsausgabe*, xii, pt. 2, 37).

[44] The first of the surviving letters (apparently the second Mendelssohn sent from Pyrmont) is dated '3 Av 5534' (11 July 1774), and the last one, in which he announces that he will leave the place the next day, is dated '17 Av 5534' (25 July 1774). The 1715 Frankfurt communal ordinance, in its last clause, explicitly forbade local Jews to visit the spa of Schwalbach during the first nine days of Av, leading up to the fast of the Ninth of Av commemorating the destruction of the two Temples in Jerusalem. This ordinance was printed by Johann Jacob Schudt, with his own translation and remarks: *Neue Franckfurter Jüdische Kleider-Ordnung*.

[45] Mendelssohn, *Gesammelte Schriften. Jubiläumsausgabe*, xix. 193.   [46] Ibid. 196.

PLATE 7. View of the promenade at Pyrmont, *c.* 1780. Artist unknown
© Galerie Gerda Bassenge

pleasant to me, when I come to the healing springs just for the sake of enjoyment.'[47]

Nevertheless, even though Mendelssohn's trips to Pyrmont were prompted by health considerations (as indeed was Rösel Meyer's visit), they clearly had a social aspect as well. During his first days at the spa, time passed without incident: 'Here one day passes like another. We have no other diversion except drinking [from the spring waters] and bathing, bathing and drinking, seeing strangers arriving, strangers departing ... actually, we wouldn't know how to kill the time if bathing and drinking didn't take up part of it.'[48] After a few days of this, however, things began to look different. In a letter dating from a week later, a totally different tone can be heard regarding the social side of the visit—not from Mendelssohn himself, but from Rösel Meyer, who tells Fromet how some of those passers-by Mendelssohn had remarked on had turned into friends. Like many of the learned individuals who visited the spas, Mendelssohn, the enlightened philosopher, attracted the attention of other visitors. Noblemen staying at the spa saw the members of the educated middle class as worthy interlocutors, and expressed an interest in establishing contact with them.[49] 'Everybody wants to meet him', writes Rösel Meyer in her letter. 'The Count and Countess of Bückeburg especially enjoy his company very much. He was just taken to breakfast by the count's carriage and servants.'[50] An invitation to breakfast in this context was of more social than culinary significance, for breakfast was an activity that received great attention at the spas. It was highly recommended by spa physicians not to eat alone in one's room, but rather to take the meal in the company of others, surrounded by music and conversation, all of which was believed to be advantageous to the patient's health.[51] In Pyrmont, in the bathing season, a great communal breakfast was held every day under the trees of the central boulevard of the town, a social event which brought together 'good society' and served as a regular venue for the cultivation of personal relationships.[52] It is possible that this was the kind of event to which Mendelssohn was invited. Rösel Meyer continued her letter, 'Now, dear

---

[47] Mendelssohn, *Gesammelte Schriften. Jubiläumsausgabe*, xix. 193.
[48] Ibid.   [49] Kuhnert, *Urbanität auf dem Lande*, 158.
[50] Mendelssohn, *Gesammelte Schriften. Jubiläumsausgabe*, xix. 196. The person referred to here as 'the Count of Bückeburg' is identified by the editor of the letters as Count Wilhelm von Schaumburg-Lippe. According to him, the appellation used in the letter refers to his capital, Bückeburg.
[51] See e.g. Zwierlein, *Allgemeine Brunnenschrift für Brunnengäste und Aerzte*, 85.
[52] Kuhnert, *Urbanität auf dem Lande*, 158–9.

Fromet, you have no reason to be jealous of my daughter[53]—now be jealous of the Countess of Bückeburg', signing off as 'your sincere friend, Rösel'.[54]

It was not only Mendelssohn, a celebrated intellectual, who attracted attention and mingled with the non-Jewish company that visited the baths. In the book *Das Pyrmonter Brunnenarchiv von 1782* ('The Pyrmont Spring Archive of 1782'), which was printed in Berlin in 1782 and contains a survey of the prominent guests at Pyrmont from the middle of the eighteenth century until that year, the editor notes the presence of 'Demoiselle H., a Jewess from the city of H. This well-mannered, shapely and well-educated woman spent a few weeks in July 1779 at Pyrmont, together with her relatives. With her animated tone and her polished manners she attracted a large company to herself.' He adds:

During her visit the state secretary, Boie, had prepared the following poem:
> I think according to reason, which nobody will steal away from me,
> Not a pope, not an orthodox man, not a Turk, not an idolater:
> But facing the grace of the race of Israel,
> How was my faith shaken yesterday, my friend![55]

According to the editor's account, a man named Schink, who was also staying at Pyrmont and apparently knew this Jewish woman, responded to Boie's words with a poem of his own, emphasizing that acquaintance with the young Jewess did not have the same impact on him as on his friend. 'My faith may not be as firm as that of those men who died for their faith', Schink admitted in his short poem; however, he went on, 'it isn't as weak as yours', nor as easily shaken. In concluding his account of this episode, the editor of the book wrote: 'Would my readers like to know what the state of the editor's faith is with regard to this issue? He saw her and talked to her without his faith being endangered the slightest bit. In general, he is not so easily led astray from a faith once adopted.'[56]

It is worth noting that although there is no trace of religious hatred in the words of any of these three men, none of them forgot for a second the religious affiliation of the young woman they were talking about, which was at the centre of their portrayals and discussion of her. Furthermore, it is significant that the encounter with a modern Jewish woman of beautiful appearance

---

[53] In the notes accompanying the German transliteration of the letters (which were originally written in Hebrew characters), Rösel Meyer's daughter is identified, apparently erroneously, as 'Sara Bernhard, married since 1759 to Götting' (Mendelssohn, *Gesammelte Schriften. Jubiläumsausgabe*, vol. xx, pt. 2, 294). However, in an earlier letter, she is correctly identified as Sara Meyer, who was born around the year 1760 (ibid. 292). [54] Ibid. xix. 196.

[55] The quotation is taken from the new edition of the book: Düll (ed.), *Das Pyrmonter Brunnenarchiv von 1782*, 54. [56] Ibid. 55.

and exemplary demeanour, no different in her polite behaviour from non-Jewish upper-class women, was perceived as a threat by these German guests, all members of the educated class.[57] We do not know who the anonymous editor of the book was; but Boie was a known figure in the world of German culture, who in addition to being a publisher, translator, and adapter of literary texts served for a certain period as secretary of the general staff in Hanover and later as district governor in his native town;[58] and the man he names as Schink was probably the poet and playwright Johann Friedrich Schink.[59] It is significant for the study of the roots of modern antisemitism that these words were written at the time of the German Enlightenment, considered to be the age of tolerance; they reflect a mixture of acceptance of the Jews with a vestige of Christian apprehension of the 'threat against the faith', even when the faith in question is enlightened faith—the faith in human reason.

What is most significant in this passage with regard to the subject of the present study is not only the very fact of a visit by a young Jewish woman to the baths, but also the social contact that took place between her and some of the non-Jewish visitors. According to the *Pyrmonter Brunnenarchiv*, the woman in question was staying in the town on holiday with her family, a visit that lasted several weeks. During this time she met and socialized with members of non-Jewish society, including representatives of the educated class and government officials. As the editor of the text testified, Boie and Schink were not the only ones who came into contact with this young woman: many people were attracted to her and communicated with her.

Two other important points stand out from this testimony. First of all, the event described took place in 1782, a number of years before the visits of most of the women who are the focus of this study. While we have seen that Sara Meyer spent a vacation in Pyrmont a few years earlier than this, as a young girl, most of the documented visits are from the 1790s and later. The passage in the *Pyrmonter Brunnenarchiv* clearly indicates that Jewish women had begun to participate in the spa culture some time before the appearance

[57] On the motif of the 'beautiful Jewess' in German literature, see Krobb, *Die schöne Jüdin*.

[58] On Heinrich Christian Boie, see *Allgemeine Deutsche Biographie*, iii. 85. Among other things, he translated and adapted poetry from various languages into German, as well as founding a leading magazine called *Deutsches Museum*, together with none other than Christian Wilhelm von Dohm, the author of the famous 1781 treatise on the emancipation of the Jews, *Ueber die bürgerliche Verbesserung der Juden*. Boie had contacts with other Jews, including Moses Mendelssohn, whom he met when the latter visited Hanover in 1777 and with whom he discussed the publication of one of Mendelssohn's articles in the periodical he edited (Altmann, *Moses Mendelssohn*, 320).

[59] Johann Friedrich Schink was active in the *Leipziger und Göttinger Musenalmanach*. See *Allgemeine Deutsche Biographie*, xxxi. 297.

of the Jewish women who are our central concern here.⁶⁰ The second point is connected to the place of origin of the Jewish women who visited the spas: the *Pyrmonter Brunnenarchiv* states explicitly that the young woman in question came from the town of H. (perhaps Hanover or Hamelin, both of which were not far away, or even possibly Hamburg; perhaps none of these). This snippet of information makes it clear that visits to spas, and a significant level of social integration there, by Jewish women were not confined to those who came from Berlin, and that such characteristics of modernization and acculturation were also discernible among Jewish women from other towns in Germany.

The examples of Mendelssohn and the young woman H. may give the impression that Jewish participation in the spa culture was limited to the economic and intellectual elite; that interaction at the spas between Jews and non-Jews was limited to the highest stratum of society. This is not so. The few studies carried out to date on specific places show that less affluent and less well-known Jews were also involved in spa life in the eighteenth century, whether as innkeepers, as pedlars, or as regular visitors.⁶¹ However, as far as may be inferred from the few available sources, their experience and the character of their contact with their non-Jewish surroundings were different from those described above, reflecting a combination of a certain degree of integration and clearer segregation.

Once more, Pyrmont serves as an excellent example. In Reinhold Kuhnert's exhaustive work on this town an additional Jewish aspect appears, more 'folksy' than that described so far. A source from the period cited in Kuhnert's book refers to a Jewish presence at the spa and indicates that contemporary observers would often include the Jews in the category of the simple folk who visited Pyrmont, alongside servants, farmers, and soldiers.⁶² These Jews certainly did not enter into the same type of contact with non-Jews as did the upper-class Jews mentioned above. Other testimonies reveal that the establishments which offered their rooms to the many guests who visited the town during the summer bathing season included Jewish guesthouses. According to Kuhnert, a majority of the Jewish visitors in Pyrmont preferred to lodge in the houses of their co-religionists, the Jews Beermann

---

⁶⁰ Some testimonies regarding the integration of wealthy and/or enlightened Jewish men into the society of visitors in Pyrmont are to be found in Kuhnert, *Urbanität auf dem Lande*, 203–4.

⁶¹ Kuhnert finds in the lists of visitors in Pyrmont in the last third of the 18th century 'about two dozen Jews' mentioned by name, among them 'a number of rabbis, or their family members'. It is possible that Kuhnert drew the conclusion that some of the Jewish visitors were 'rabbis' on the basis of the appellation 'Reb', which is often added to the name of a Jew as an honorary title, with no connection to rabbinical ordination (ibid. 203). ⁶² Ibid. 128.

and Behrens.[63] But there was no strict division of accommodation according to religion. One can find Jews on the guest lists of Christian houses at all levels of cost and sophistication. Thus, for example, when Zacharias Veitel Ephraim and Moses Mendelssohn visited Pyrmont in 1773, they stayed at the house of a Christian merchant.[64] Similarly, non-Jews stayed in Jewish houses, which included middle-class visitors and even some members of the nobility among their clients. Thus, for example, in 1797 a widowed princess named Christine von Lippe-Detmold lodged with the Jew Herz Behrens, and another nobleman, Peter Friedrich Ludwig von Oldenburg, rented a room from the brothers Levi and Moses Behrens.[65] In fact, the choice of accommodation tended to be made more on financial than on social grounds.[66] The sources on Pyrmont also show us that some Jews came to the spas to pursue their occupations. Jewish merchants with permits to engage in trade sold their merchandise on the city's famous promenade,[67] where every day the upper-class visitors took their walks (the common people were prohibited from entering), and Jews also appear in Pyrmont as partners in gambling businesses, both as players and as moneylenders, and not always in a positive light.[68]

There is no reason to assume that these phenomena were exclusive to Pyrmont; it seems more reasonable to ascribe the quantity and range of information that has accumulated about Jews in this town largely to the considerable scholarly efforts that have been devoted to this resort. Studies from recent years, though mainly devoted to a later period—namely, the nineteenth and twentieth centuries—have revealed a Jewish presence at other spas in the eighteenth century. A Jewish inn is known to have been active in Bad Ems, a watering place near Koblenz, before 1800, catering to the needs of the Jewish clientele.[69] In Baden-Baden Jewish guests had their own facilities from the second half of the eighteenth century at least: an excellent testimony to this is the changing of the name of one of the springs in the town into 'Jews' Spring' (*Judenquelle*), 'because it supplies the water to the bathhouse which the Jews use', according to the words of a Christian physician from 1794.[70] In Wiesbaden, too, there were facilities catering for Jewish

[63] Kuhnert, *Urbanität auf dem Lande*, 117.   [64] Ibid.
[65] Ibid. 116.   [66] Ibid. 115.   [67] Ibid. 97, 117.
[68] Ibid. 188, 203. A study on the Jewish presence at the spa of Schwalbach in the 18th century that I am currently carrying out has revealed the existence of a *Spielhaus*, a gambling hall, owned by Jews as early as the 1730s.
[69] Sommer, *Zur Kur nach Ems*, 328. In contrast to Kuhnert's book, which deals mainly with the 18th century, Sommer's work refers to a later period, 1830–1914. Accordingly, the information he contributes on Jewish activity in the place is connected mainly to this period.
[70] Schindler, *Der verbrannte Traum*, 19.

guests in the second half of the eighteenth century, although there are indications that some of the Jewish visitors—including, for example, some members of the Ephraim family who visited in 1770—preferred to lodge at non-Jewish boarding houses rather than those of their co-religionists, which seem to have been less luxurious.[71] This would support the assertion made above in connection with Pyrmont that choosing a boarding house was often primarily a financial more than a social decision. There is no wide-ranging research which summarizes the extent of the Jewish presence at spas in the eighteenth century, from a social-historical or other perspective, in contrast with the growing interest in the presence of Jews at spas and holiday resorts in the last decades of the nineteenth century and the first decades of the twentieth, which focuses mainly on the topic of antisemitism at spas and resorts (*Bäderantisemitismus*).[72] Nevertheless, the evidence presented above suggests that this presence went beyond a few wealthy individual Jews in a limited number of places.[73]

The scattered data available suggest that, in the last third of the eighteenth century, characteristics not necessarily connected to religious affiliation played a central part in determining the position of various Jews at the

---

[71] Bembenek, 'Das jüdische Badhaus "Zum Rebhuhn" in Wiesbaden' (the Ephraim case is mentioned on pp. 110–11).

[72] The most important work on this subject is Bajohr, *'Unser Hotel ist judenfrei'*. Another aspect stressed in studies on Jews' visits to spas is the role of this practice in matchmaking (Kaplan, '*Unter uns*: Jews Socialising with Other Jews', 53–4). See also Brenner, 'Zwischen Marienbad und Norderney'. It may be the perception of holiday resorts as places for matchmaking, which was common among Jews in the 19th century, that gave rise to the tale told by Berthold Auerbach at this time about how Moses Mendelssohn and Fromet Gugenheim met. According to Auerbach, Mendelssohn made the acquaintance of Fromet's father, Abraham Gugenheim, in Pyrmont, and following this encounter was introduced to Fromet. As the pre-wedding correspondence between the couple proves, there is no basis for this story (Mendelssohn, *Brautbriefe*). Auerbach's story is related as an anecdote in Kohut, *Moses Mendelssohn und seine Familie*, 63–5. Sebastian Hensel, unlike Kohut, adopts Auerbach's version as a reliable account: Hensel, *The Mendelssohn Family*, i. 22–3. See the description of the meeting and courtship between the partners, emphasizing Fromet's perspective, in Goch, *Im Aufbruch*, 153–67.

[73] It should be emphasized that my intention is not to imply that the spa visit was a phenomenon which involved (at this period) a major part of Jewish society. Even an educated and wealthy man like Baruch Lindau, a maskil who lived in Berlin during the Enlightenment period and absorbed contemporary scientific concepts, still regarded the spas as an environment that had nothing to do with him, a concern of aristocrats. In a geographical survey which he presented to the readers of his book *Reshit limudim* ('Beginning of Learning') in the year 1789 he describes the town of Carlsbad as follows: 'Known and famous for its hot springs, to which will come every year at summertime kings, viceroys and ministers, to occupy themselves with medicine' (p. 128). On the other hand, from the early years of the 19th century prominent rabbis in central Europe were increasingly spending the summer months at the springs for (as they claimed) medicinal purposes, as is evident from the many halakhic responses that they sent from these places.

spas: there were important differences among the Jewish visitors in, for example, education, profession, economic situation, prior social and professional contacts (developed in their home towns and cities or elsewhere during periods of study), place of origin, fields of interest, and indeed way of life during the rest of the year. Most Jews probably lived at the spas much as they did at home, in circles separate from non-Jews; it is possible that these Jews preferred to lodge at the houses of their co-religionists, perhaps to make it easier to continue observing the Jewish commandments. However, as we shall shortly see, the Jewish women at the focus of this study (and other wealthy Jews) integrated well and with enthusiasm into a non-Jewish society which showed a degree of openness between religions and social classes. As educated women, and as members of Berlin's upper class with social contacts outside the Jewish community, they succeeded in entering a society with whose members they had—leaving aside their religious affiliation, already weakened—much in common.

SOCIABILITY AT THE SPAS

The presence of a Jewish woman from Berlin in company with a Belgian prince, an Austrian noblewoman, or a German actress, or with a young woman from the entourage of the wife of the prince of Prussia and a Prussian officer—as described in the letters of Rahel Levin and Fradchen Liebmann— was not a rare sight at the spas at the end of the eighteenth century. The towns built around the healing baths had turned into places where social contacts crossed the boundaries of class, nationality, religion, and sex. In the summer, the spas were 'places where many different worlds came together'.[74] To be sure, this was not an egalitarian society, and distinctions were preserved, especially between upper-class visitors and those from the lower strata of society, but also, to varying extents, between nobility and middle class, between Jews and Christians, and even between Catholics and Protestants of similar economic standing.[75] And yet, in spite of enduring tensions and sensitivities between the classes and between the religions, in the last

---

[74] Blackbourn, 'Fashionable Spa Towns in Nineteenth-Century Europe', 17.

[75] Examining inter-religious relations among visitors at Bad Ems in the 19th century, Hermann Sommer found a tendency among members of the dominant Protestant religion to recoil from the presence of members of 'other' religions, not only Jews but also Catholics (Sommer, *Zur Kur nach Ems*, 485 ff.). Reinhold Kuhnert claims that during a stay at the spas there was more opportunity to transgress the norms of one's social class than in everyday life, but insists that the barriers of social communication by no means completely disappeared, even in the more relaxed atmosphere of the baths. Kuhnert, *Urbanität auf dem Lande*, 146–7.

decades of the eighteenth century a culture of communication and sociability developed in these places which encouraged relationships with individuals from backgrounds different from one's own and attached particular value to social contacts across class and religious boundaries. Despite the ambivalent attitude towards Jews manifested by certain non-Jewish visitors, which may have been shared by some of those who mixed with the Jewish women discussed in this study, the spas were highly significant for these women, as spaces where they could mix with non-Jewish society—however limited or insincere their acceptance may have been. 'Respectable society' at the spas, which included both the nobility and the wealthy and/or educated middle class, was also open to Jews, at least those who were endowed with suitable qualifications.

Interestingly, it was precisely the remaining vestiges of the noble way of life at the spas that fostered relationships between the classes, the religions, and the sexes. Forms of recreation that had been common at the period when many of the spas in Germany were frequented mainly by the nobility —masked balls, banquets, concerts, and theatrical performances—were adopted in the course of the eighteenth century by the middle classes who began to visit these towns in increasing numbers. These forms of recreation encouraged interaction between members of different classes—as, for example, at the festive breakfast in Pyrmont, a daily event which brought together distinguished guests from the nobility and the middle class;[76] or at the balls, where members of the nobility could invite young middle-class girls to dance. From the letters of the Jewish women discussed here one can infer that they, too, participated in the various pastimes, not necessarily as Jews, but more as members of this newly confident middle class that was carving a path for itself in modern society. On their visits to the spas in the last decade of the eighteenth century, even before they converted, they participated in meals and parties, in parlour games and excursions, and simply in friendly conversation with other visitors.

Nevertheless, these visits to the spas had particular implications for these individuals not only as Jews but also as women. By offering female guests a welcome change in their daily routine, which was usually more restrictive than men's; by enabling women to strengthen existing friendships and create new ones; by providing an arena in which they could exchange ideas and express their own views—in all these ways, visits to the spas served as a

---

[76] Kuhnert, *Urbanität auf dem Lande*, 158–9. It is important to keep in mind that although members of the nobility and the middle class could attend some of the same social events, at times class distinctions continued to be maintained through separate seating areas. Ibid. 150.

means of female empowerment. Rahel Levin, Fradchen Liebmann, Marianne Meyer, and others were well aware of these advantages and exploited them to the utmost.

The fact that many of the Jewish women who visited the spas did so accompanied by female friends—even the married ones often travelled without their husbands—does not seem to have been coincidental. Fradchen Liebmann and Hitzel Bernhard, Rahel Levin and the (non-Jewish) actress Friederike Unzelmann, Esther Gad and 'Mselle Boye':[77] these companions are a representative example of the interesting phenomenon of women, married or single, who travelled together to the spas. Many of the Jewish women who arrived at the spas without a male companion were single, divorced, or in conflict with their husbands, but this was not always the case. Rebecca Ephraim, daughter of the wealthy Daniel Itzig,[78] who as far as we know lived peacefully with her Jewish husband, spent time in Freienwalde without him until she was called back to Berlin to take care of him after an accident.[79] About a century later, this tendency had even become stronger. Testimonies collected by Marion Kaplan in her research on the Jewish middle class in Germany during the Wilhelmine era show that many Jewish women would go on a convalescent trip accompanied by a female relative. Kaplan suggests that the practice had an empowering effect for women, who, she argues, found that staying with other women at a place of recuperation and sharing with them all the common experiences such places offered—using the spring water, taking festive meals, making excursions on foot which often ended by spending time at a coffee-house—strengthened networks of closeness and friendship between them and at the same time gave them a secure temporary refuge both from male domination and from the everyday worries and boredom that went with the bourgeois lifestyle at this period.[80] The phenomenon

---

[77] Esther Gad, in a letter she wrote before her journey to Freienwalde in the summer of 1800, mentioned that she intended to lodge with 'Mselle Boye'. See Hahn (ed.), '"Geliebtester Schriftsteller"', 31. 'Mselle Boye' is the same Hitzel Fließ née Bernhard who accompanied Fradchen Liebmann on her journey to Freienwalde in 1795; since then she had been divorced from her Jewish husband, the physician Isaac Beer Fließ, and married a Swedish nobleman and military officer, Gustav von Boye (see Rahel Levin's letter of 8 January 1799, in Bruyn (ed.), *Rahels erste Liebe*, 266, commenting on the groom). A third, later, husband was also a Swede, General von Sparre.

[78] Daniel Itzig was one of the wealthiest Jews in Berlin. He was among the leaders of the Jewish community in the city and a supporter of the Haskalah.

[79] In July 1795 Hitzel Bernhard announced to Rahel Levin: '[Rebecca] Ephraim has to take the earliest [postal carriage] to Berlin tomorrow, and apparently she will not return, because her husband, who fell off a horse, is lying there, very ill' (Bosold, 'Friederike Liman', 27).

[80] Kaplan, *The Making of the Jewish Middle Class*, 125. Kuhnert, too, sees the phenomenon of women travelling to the spas in the 18th century (especially in the last decades) without male accompaniment as an expression of emancipatory tendencies among some of the female visitors (Kuhnert,

was certainly not specifically a Jewish one, but was common right across middle-class society: statistical data show a rise throughout the nineteenth century in the number of women who travelled to the spas of Germany unaccompanied by their spouses or other male relatives. As one scholar has noted, 'in a German spa, the nuclear family was not necessarily the predominant form and agent of social interaction, and women, alone or accompanied by female friends, enjoyed a relative freedom to shape their own lives'.[81] Such statements regarding the nineteenth century are also valid for the end of the eighteenth.

Whatever the reason for her trip to the spa, and whether she travelled with a single companion (sometimes a servant who would not accompany her socially once the destination was reached) or a larger party, having arrived at the spa a woman was unlikely to remain isolated from wider company for long. The Jewish women discussed here met friends from their home towns or from previous trips; in addition, they made contact with new people during their stay, either through chance meetings or through introductions by mutual acquaintances. The atmosphere at the spas encouraged conversation and sociability and made it easier to enter into social contacts with people who had previously been strangers. We have already seen how quickly Fradchen Liebmann forged new friendships. Several decades earlier the English bluestocking Elizabeth Carter, writing to Elizabeth Montagu in 1759, described the atmosphere at the English resort of Bristol Hot-Well in terms that could just as well have been used of German spas towards the end of the century:

> It is to be doubted perhaps whether the acquaintance which one forms here might give one equal pleasure anywhere else. In a situation like this, conversation is carried on with much more ease and freedom than is usually consistent with the set forms of more regular life. One can talk upon subjects in the corner of a ball-room, in a saunter through the gardens, or in a window in the summer-house, which it would be mighty difficult to introduce into a downright visit.[82]

In this respect the spas played an important role in the lives of these Jewish women. While some of the new acquaintances they struck up at the spas may have been fleeting, superficial, and inconsequential, in many other cases the relationships formed in the course of these visits turned out to be

---

Urbanität auf dem Lande, 196). A similar assertion is made by Peter Borsay to explain the female profile of English resorts. See Borsay, 'Health and Leisure Resorts', 795–6.

[81] Lempa, 'The Spa', 52.

[82] This quotation, taken from *Letters from Mrs. Elizabeth Carter, to Mrs. Montagu, between the years of 1755 and 1800* (London, 1817), i. 55, appears in Hurley, 'A Conversation of their Own', 8.

crucial to their future lives. Among the many contacts made by Marianne and Sara Meyer on their vacations in the spas of Bohemia, the encounter with Goethe in Carlsbad was of particular relevance. This meeting between the Meyer sisters and Goethe in the summer of 1795 produced a friendship which lasted many years and was maintained both through correspondence and through repeated meetings at various spas in the years that followed. The time the two women spent with Goethe that first summer, the many conversations they had among themselves and with common friends in moments of rest in between treatments, all made a lasting impression on both sisters, as the letters written following the visit to Carlsbad testify.[83] The correspondence between the Meyer sisters and Goethe that followed this encounter played an important role in the lives of both sisters and even determined their entry into Jewish and German historiography, since it is doubtful whether in its absence so many details regarding their lives would have reached our hands.

An encounter at a spa also significantly influenced the life of Esther Gad. One of the several new relationships she forged in this way that left a deep mark on her life was that with the German writer Jean Paul Richter, whom she met in Franzensbad in the summer of 1797 and with whom she corresponded thereafter.[84] Gad was staying at the Bohemian spa in the company of a (male) friend after her divorce from her Jewish husband when she met Jean Paul, who was convalescing there. They had spent some time together, enjoying one another's company along with that of other friends, when the death of Jean Paul's mother compelled his sudden departure; when Esther learned this news in the middle of a ball, her disappointment was acute. In a letter sent at the end of July 1797 she implored him to return, in spite of the circumstances which had taken him away, and announced: 'If you can't [come], I can: I will come to Hof',[85] where he lived—and that is what she did. They met again in Berlin in 1800, after Esther had moved to the Prussian capital. There they moved in the same social circles, attending the theatre together; Esther also entertained Jean Paul in her house, often treating him to elaborate dishes which she had prepared herself, over which they could enjoy intellectual conversations about literature, philosophy, and science.

---

[83] Rahel Levin, too, met Goethe during that summer. However, in spite of the high esteem in which she held him, this encounter did not lead to a correspondence.

[84] When mentioning the connections of women such as Marianne and Sara Meyer and Esther Gad with famous writers, it is important to remember that there were contacts with less famous people going on at the same time, but that in most cases no evidence of these was left behind.

[85] Hahn (ed.), '"Geliebtester Schriftsteller"', 18. In this contribution to the *Jahrbuch der Jean-Paul-Gesellschaft* Hahn published Esther Gad's letters to Jean Paul for the first time. His letters to her had appeared in print earlier.

Perhaps inevitably, rumours spread of a romantic relationship between the two, encouraged by at least one friend, but Esther resolutely denied any such connection.[86]

The lasting impression left by Esther Gad's relationship with Jean Paul Richter is apparent in her literary works. The first book Gad published, *Briefe während meines Aufenthaltes in England und Portugal an einen Freund*, that is, a collection of letters written to a 'friend' during the author's stay in England and Portugal, refers by implication to Jean Paul: one of the first texts included in this book is a revised copy of a letter Gad had sent to Jean Paul as she was on her way to England. Another book, published in 1814, is explicitly dedicated to Jean Paul Richter, 'an admired friend, to whom I owe many a beautiful hour in my life'.[87]

The relationships forged during visits to spas had a significance that reached beyond the individuals directly involved. It is important not to underestimate the central role played by these resorts in widening the networks of communication among cultured people in Germany and beyond—networks in which the Jewish women discussed here were involved. It is clear from Esther Gad's correspondence that on her return to Breslau after fourteen months' absence her acquaintance with Jean Paul Richter in Franzensbad placed her in the position of mediator between him and writers and intellectuals in her home town.[88] Relationships which Gad forged in Franzensbad opened doors for her in Prague, which she visited as part of her vacation. Here, 'through a letter of recommendation from the poet [Karl Friedrich] Kretschmann', whom she had met in Franzensbad, she met August Gottlieb Meißner, a professor of aesthetics and classics as well as a writer.[89]

No less important than the friendships which developed at the spas between these Jewish women and prominent figures like Goethe and Richter were the relationships established between the Jewish women and other female visitors, and even among the Jewish women themselves. As noted above, some of the associations that developed at the spas developed into close and lasting, even lifelong, relationships. Rahel Levin laid the foundations for some of her closest friendships with other women during visits to the spas: Countess Josephine von Pachta, mentioned above, was one intimate friend made in this way. Levin's relationship with Esther Gad also developed

[86] See letter from Esther Gad to Jean Paul of June 1800 (ibid. 27).
[87] The reference is to the book *Kritische Auseinandersetzung mehrerer Stellen in dem Buche der Frau von Staël über Deutschland*, mentioned above in Ch. 3 n. 51 (Hahn (ed.), '"Geliebtester Schriftsteller"', 11).
[88] Schulz, 'Jean Paul, Breslau und die Breslauer Schriftsteller'.
[89] Hahn (ed.), '"Geliebtester Schriftsteller"', 22.

in the summer of 1796, when both of them stayed at Teplitz. The earliest hint of an acquaintance between the two—perhaps merely a mutual awareness at this stage—comes in a letter Levin sent to her brother in Breslau in 1787, in which she mentions 'die Gad' and sends her cordial greetings.[90] They certainly met in person and spent time together in 1794, when Levin visited Breslau.[91] In any case, their time at Teplitz two years later without a doubt solidified the relationship between the two women. Firm evidence for the basis of this firmer relationship is hard to come by, but it is reasonable to assume that the Jewish woman from Berlin and the Jewish woman from Breslau found they had many things in common, not least their strong gender awareness, and also that they exchanged ideas on subjects which were to be of critical importance in their lives. It is clear that Rahel Levin very much appreciated the wisdom of Esther Gad, whom she called 'the wise woman from Breslau'.[92] When Gad moved to Berlin about three years later, the friendship grew stronger, and was to endure over many years, even when the two were separated by a considerable distance. The seeds of another friendship of great significance for both women involved were sown in 1794 at Freienwalde. It was during Rahel Levin's visit to this spa that she met Pauline Wiesel, who was to become her bosom friend. Wiesel, the daughter of a mixed marriage— her mother came from a well-known Huguenot family in Berlin, her father was a Catholic government clerk and a native of the city—entered German history, to put it somewhat bluntly, as 'the lover of Louis Ferdinand, Prince of Prussia'.[93] Although it is known that Rahel Levin had already heard about Pauline César, as she then was, through common friends before they met in Freienwalde, it seems that it was only in the summer of 1794 that personal contact between the two was established. Notwithstanding the ups and downs in their relationship, Pauline Wiesel remained a faithful friend until Rahel Levin's death in 1833. With her Levin shared, both in person and through letters, the vicissitudes of her life, and with her she discussed the questions which preoccupied people, and especially women, at the time;

---

[90] This letter, written when she was 16 years old, was according to Rahel Levin's husband Karl August Varnhagen the earliest from Rahel that was preserved. See Levin Varnhagen, *Familienbriefe*, 10.

[91] See Rahel Levin's letters from her trip to Silesia in the summer of 1794: Levin Varnhagen, *Familienbriefe*, 16–43.

[92] In a letter she sent from Teplitz to her friend Karl Gustav von Brinckmann in summer 1796, Rahel Levin points out that she is in the company of Marianne Meyer and 'Mrs Bernard, the wise woman from Breslau'. The quote appears in Hahn (ed.), '"Geliebtester Schriftsteller"', 12 n.15.

[93] As in the name of the subtitle of the first book dedicated to her: Carl Atzenbeck, *Pauline Wiesel. Die Geliebte des Prinzen Louis Ferdinand von Preußen. Ein Charakterbild aus der Zeit der Romantiker in zeitgenössischen Dokumenten* (Leipzig, 1925). See Hahn, '"Ein Mann kann nicht denken wie Wir"', 722–3.

among other things, they touched upon their status as women who consciously chose unusual behaviour in a patriarchal and conservative society.[94]

It needs to be emphasized that not all the Jewish women who visited the spas wanted to spend their time at fashionable venues and in a constant social round—at least, not all the time—and that some of them preferred to spend their vacations in simpler surroundings, in more modest company, and in a less sociable fashion than others. Writing to her friend Ehrenfried von Willich on her return to Berlin in 1802 after a nine-week summer vacation with her husband, Henriette Herz[95] gave vent to her disappointment about her visit to Pyrmont: 'The accommodation was very poor, and likewise the weather, and I was hardly able to climb the beautiful hills surrounding Pyrmont. Every day I had to dress meticulously, for the society was elegant and numerous and partly noble. In short, I longed to be elsewhere, in spite of the great friendliness with which I was received.'[96] This stay of three weeks in the stylish resort town had been preceded by a visit in Nenndorf, a rural spa near Hanover with markedly fewer pretensions:

They had described Nenndorf to us in such a negative light everywhere that we went there with a heavy heart, and—we liked it, especially I, much more than expected. The environment is extraordinarily lovely and the atmosphere much less spa-like than in the large spas. I related to it as a stay in the country, I went for walks on my own through field and valley, and here and there I mingled with the unassuming society.[97]

It is apparent from Henriette Herz's words that she felt accepted by society in both places she visited, the spa of high fashion as well as the simpler, more rural one. At home in the upper echelons of Berlin Jewish society and famous for her social skills, she claimed to have been received with 'great friendliness' in the exclusive society of Pyrmont, and also to have mingled without difficulty among the simpler guests in Nenndorf.[98] But the society

[94] The interesting correspondence between Rahel Levin and Pauline Wiesel appeared only recently, in the framework of the project of publication of the Varnhagen collection. About the assumed meeting place of the two women, see ibid. 723.

[95] Henriette Herz got to know Ehrenfried von Willich, a student of theology and later a cleric, during her visit to Prenzlau, where her sister Johanna lived with her husband. Willich was a friend of her sister's family. Through Henriette Herz, Willich met Friedrich Schleiermacher, and a deep friendship developed between the two. After Willich's untimely death, his wife Henriette, née Mühlenfels, married Schleiermacher. See Boenigk (ed.), *Schleiermacher und seine Lieben*.

[96] Ibid. 38.   [97] Ibid.

[98] Henriette Herz's report of her ease in company here may be compared to another description of Nenndorf at the beginning of the 19th century, according to which the Jews living and visiting there were subject to insulting treatment and constraints on trade: Kaplan (ed.), *Jewish Daily Life in Germany*, 164, 375.

lady reportedly preferred to spend her vacations at the less glamorous place, which was so different from her home city, a place where she could enjoy nature and spend her time in thoughtful seclusion. Such pleasures were another side of the summer vacation, developing in parallel to the emphasis on sociability.[99]

VISITS TO THE SPAS AND WOMEN'S PARTICIPATION IN THE PUBLIC SPHERE

In seeking to understand the communication networks which made it possible to transmit ideas and opinions across Europe, cultural and social historians researching the beginning of the modern era focused on prominent means and places of communication, notably printing, coffee-houses, reading societies, and salons, among others. Until recently, the spas were hardly included in these discussions, even though they served as an important arena in the new public sphere. One of the first researchers who identified the role of the spas in the communication of ideas was Reinhold Kuhnert, who, as we have seen, thoroughly researched eighteenth-century Pyrmont. According to Kuhnert, the function of the spas as centres of communication was especially crucial in the German-speaking lands of central Europe, which, fragmented by political division, lacked the single centre provided by the capital cities of France and England, which attracted the most prominent thinkers and concentrated the country's cultural activity. The spas served as meeting places for intellectuals from different areas and made it possible for men of letters to meet and cultivate personal relationships.[100]

But it was not only thinkers of stature in German culture who enjoyed the possibilities of communication available at the spas. Kuhnert shows that the lifestyle in Pyrmont offered many opportunities for encounters and communication to the broad educated public. Through contact with other holiday-makers, either in the course of the various social gatherings or even on a shared walk along the central boulevard in the town, these visitors could learn about new ideas and share their own opinions and viewpoints. While Kuhnert's conclusions are based on only one case—the town of Pyrmont—similar circumstances seem to have existed during this period at other spas in

---

[99] Borsay, *A History of Leisure*, 188–91.

[100] Kuhnert goes so far as to say that in contrast to a place such as the English town of Bath, whose public was a sort of 'copy' of London society in the summer months, a German town like Pyrmont 'did not draw its public from the reservoir of the capital, but on the contrary, attracted people from the most varied places and areas, and thus fulfilled part of the tasks of the missing metropolis' (Kuhnert, *Urbanität auf dem Lande*, 41).

Germany, at least at the more prominent and popular among them. These spas provided a platform on which women such as those discussed here, who had adopted an enlightened attitude and insisted on the right and capability of individuals of either gender to express their opinions, could exchange ideas and disseminate their own views. This function of the spas as a significant space in the public sphere proved highly significant for female empowerment.

An event described by Marianne Meyer at the end of her visit to Pyrmont in 1797 encapsulates the combination of social and intellectual activity that was so characteristic of the spa environment and exemplifies the relevance of their communicative function to a woman in her position. In the course of her visit that summer Meyer spent time in the company of several noblemen, among them an English lord and a German prince. On one occasion a stormy discussion developed regarding the status and importance of German literature. Meyer was incensed by the derogatory opinions of the two noblemen, and had a hard time hiding her anger. Eventually she accepted the Englishman's prejudice: 'I have forgiven Lord Bristol for his doggedness against the Germans and their literature', she wrote to Goethe in September of the same year; after all, 'he expresses himself fundamentally against all other nations.' In the face of the same negative attitude on the part of the German nobleman, however, she was less willing to compromise. Entirely and deliberately ignoring the modesty and self-effacement which, according to her upbringing (and, one might add, prevailing gender norms), should have guided her behaviour, Meyer, in her own words, quite bluntly 'handed out truths' to the German prince, who dared to say that German literature was not even worth talking about. 'It hurt me', she wrote, 'that with his innate capacity for seeing things differently and judging differently, just out of a need to imitate, because Frederick II had seen it that way, he decided the same way. I could not keep myself from telling him that if one strives to become similar to this great man, one should not begin by adopting his prejudice, of all things.'[101]

In commenting on this letter, we could analyse the content of Meyer's words and discuss, for example, the extent to which the attitude latent in what she wrote to Goethe, which she presents as a quote from her reply to the German prince during their conversation, reflects an enlightened outlook. Her aversion to the blind acceptance of prejudices and her insistence on the rational power of the individual could certainly serve as a basis for evaluating

---

[101] Geiger (ed.), 'Einundzwanzig Briefe', 32–3. Frederick II (the Great) is known for having treated German literature with contempt and having preferred French culture.

the degree of her identification with ideas of the Enlightenment. Likewise, we could raise conjectures regarding the degree of Meyer's dependence on the opinions of others—in this case, Goethe—when she takes a stand regarding the quality of German literature; and we could reflect on the apparent discrepancy between this kind of reliance on a famous writer and her call to use one's own judgement. But all these lines of enquiry would take us far from the subject of this chapter. It will suffice here to note that, as Meyer herself points out, she does not find any fault with this kind of attitude, as long as one applies one's own judgement in forming a position on a given subject. More important in the present context are the circumstances in which the conversation took place: that is, the fact that the discussion on literature, patriotism, and the principles of the Enlightenment came about in the course of an encounter in the hours of leisure during a visit to Pyrmont. Three people from different places and classes—a German prince, an English nobleman, and a Jewish woman who had just converted to Christianity—met in a place where, alongside various leisure activities such as excursions into the natural world and indoor parlour games, they could also engage in serious conversation on topics of current public interest, and take the opportunity both to present their own opinions and to hear those of others.

While the letter from Meyer quoted above testifies only to one specific case, another source actually shows us the frequency and diversity of encounters at the spas in which Marianne Meyer was involved. Goethe's diaries include, among other things, notes from his stay at Carlsbad in the summer of 1808, when he spent time with many people (mostly women), among them 'Frau von Eybenberg'—that is, Marianne Meyer. It is apparent from these notes that Goethe met Marianne Meyer almost every day, after an early morning treatment in the springs and a spell of work at his writing. Goethe took pains to mention in his diary (albeit in telegraphic form) a detail or two about each meeting, and thus casts light on the lifestyle at these places. We learn that the two mostly met at Meyer's lodgings and talked, for example, 'about her stay in Italy, about Vienna, about Frau von Staël'—the French writer who had caused heated discussions following the publication of her scandalous book about Germany;[102] 'about Werner and Jean Paul';[103] about 'the present situation of politics and war';[104] 'about the Viennese, their attitude towards the theatre, literature and taste in general'.[105] Often Goethe and Meyer dedicated

---

[102] Entry of 17 June (*Goethes Werke*, 348).

[103] Werner is perhaps the author Friedrich Ludwig Zacharias Werner, with whom Goethe corresponded: entry of 21 June (ibid. 350).

[104] Entry of 26 June (ibid. 353).

[105] Entry of 8 July (ibid. 358–9).

their time to reading together. On one occasion they read a play by Goethe which had not yet been published, *Pandorens Wiederkunft* ('Pandora's Return'), and following the reading they talked about 'German literature in general';[106] another time they read Gentz's statement on the Russian manifesto against England after the Peace of Tilsit, sparking a conversation that lasted several days.[107] Sometimes other people joined these meetings. Thus, for example, during one of Goethe's visits to Meyer's lodgings a man named Methfessel arrived, 'who played the guitar very nicely'.[108] They also spent time together outside Meyer's lodgings. Goethe reports in his diary a walk during which he and Marianne talked about 'personages from Vienna', mainly about the French ambassador Andréossy and his adventures with Countess Palffy;[109] on another occasion he recorded that he went for a walk in the meadow accompanied by Meyer, Count Rasumofsky, and four noblewomen whom he had met the same day: 'the two daughters of the Duchess of Curland, the Princess of Hohenzollern, and the Duchess of Acerenza'.[110]

The exchange between Marianne Meyer and the two noblemen and Goethe's diary entries recording their meetings and conversations indicate the range of interaction that became possible in places like Pyrmont or Carlsbad, which brought together people from different places in Europe and offered an abundance of opportunities for communication. Goethe's diary notes also feature a cultural activity besides conversation that occupied many visitors—including Jewish women—during their vacations and served as another arena for the transfer of ideas: reading. In the many hours of leisure after the treatments in the spring water, especially on rainy days, when walking outdoors was not an attractive option, recourse was had to books. But in this context reading, today perceived as a private occupation, was not necessarily a solitary pastime, frequently being done in groups of two or more people. Thus it was simultaneously a social and a cultural activity, involving mutual listening and an exchange of ideas and interpretations. 'At the moment I am reading Tristram in English, together with Jettchen [Henriette Mendelssohn]', Fradchen Liebmann wrote to Rahel Levin in July 1795 from Freienwalde, referring to Laurence Sterne's book, *The Life and Opinions of Tristram Shandy, Gentleman*.[111] In Teplitz, Levin herself read *Iphigenia* and *Tasso* (that is, the plays *Iphigenia in Tauris* and *Torquato Tasso*) by Goethe,

---

[106] Entry of 26 June 26 (ibid. 353).
[107] Entries of 3, 5 July (ibid. 357).
[108] Two days later this musician gave a concert in the presence of Goethe: entries of 22, 24 June (ibid. 350, 351).
[109] Entry of 23 June (ibid. 351).
[110] Entry of 3 July (ibid. 356).
[111] Bosold, 'Friederike Liman', 25.

together with her friend Wilhelm von Burgsdorff,[112] apparently also in the company of Marianne Meyer.[113] Reading groups were by no means unique to the spas: Esther Gad, for example, participated in a similar activity in Prague in 1797, together with two noblewomen whom she had met on her journey there from Carlsbad.[114] Nevertheless, communal reading was an ideal activity for visitors to the spas who, with many hours of leisure in the course of the day and an appetite for both company and an interesting and useful occupation, found in it the answer to their needs.

Up to this point, in discussing the function of the spas in facilitating communication the main emphasis has been on the contacts that occurred between Jewish women and non-Jews. However, in discussing the spa as a place of conversation and sociability we should not ignore the contacts these women maintained and fostered with their co-religionists—not only with women friends of their own age, but also with other members of the Jewish community. Fradchen Liebmann informs us about an encounter of this kind during her visit to Freienwalde. In one of her letters to Rahel Levin, Liebmann describes an invitation 'to lunch at [Mrs] Bernhard's, who is leaving tomorrow, with Mr Friedländer, who was here, Herz, and the two Euchels'.[115] Even though it is impossible to determine with total certainty to whom all these names refer, it seems likely that these were members of the Jewish economic and intellectual elite of Berlin. '[Mrs] Bernhard' apparently was Fanny Bernhard née Fließ, mother of Hitzel Bernhard and at this point still a wealthy woman (she lost her assets a few years later, following the death of her husband). 'Mr Friedländer' can be identified as the wealthy scholar and radical maskil David Friedländer, 'Herz' as Marcus Herz, physician, Henriette's husband, and a leading figure of the Enlightenment, and the 'two Euchels' as Isaac Euchel, one of the founders of the Haskalah movement, and his brother Gottlieb. This passing mention of a social occasion reminds us that these modernizing Jewish women and the representatives of the Haskalah did not live in two separate worlds and that they had many opportunities for social contact and exchange of ideas (though unfortunately Liebmann does not volunteer the content of the conversation on this occasion)—in, among other places, the intimate atmosphere of the spas.

In conclusion, visits to the spas broadened the horizons of Jewish women and enriched their lives, offering them varied personal experience, a feeling

[112] Rahel Levin met Burgsdorff in Teplitz in the summer of 1795. A year later they met again in the same place. At the end of her visit to Teplitz, she travelled on with him to Prague and Dresden. See Bosold, 'Friederike Liman', 43 n. 230.   [113] *Briefwechsel zwischen Rahel und David Veit*, ii. 221, 223.
[114] See Esther Gad's letter from October 1797 (Hahn (ed.), '"Geliebtester Schriftsteller"', 21–2).
[115] Bosold, 'Friederike Liman', 21.

of health and rest, and enjoyment of the treasures of nature, as well as new social contacts and ideas and opinions which they were free to accept or reject in the course of conversations with a wide range of people. As a practice which enabled and encouraged communication, it is evident that the journey to the spas does not represent a new and extraordinary phenomenon in the lives of these women: indeed, this practice played a role similar to that ascribed to the salons of Berlin, as a meeting place for Jews (women and men alike), nobility, and members of the German middle class, along with intellectuals and government representatives from different countries. There was a difference in that unlike the social activity that occurred in their home towns and cities (to be discussed in the following chapter), which continued throughout the year, the encounters at the spas had defined limits (a stay generally lasted about a month or two, and would not necessarily be repeated every year); consequently, some contacts made there would also be limited. But the quality of the contacts did not necessarily suffer from this: indeed, the reverse could be true, the brevity of an acquaintance made in the course of a vacation often lending it intensity and often leading to its continuation through correspondence.

It is interesting that, even though this practice of visiting the spas fulfilled functions corresponding to those ascribed to the famous salons, until recently it did not attract attention from researchers. This may be attributable in part to the fact of watering places being less glamorous environments than the salons (as they are generally described), and in part also to the ambiguous status of the spa towns, in that visitors came to them mainly under the pretext of care for their health and not with a declared goal of social or intellectual activity. In fact, it was precisely their ambivalent character which turned them into an especially discreet and comfortable place for women to promote the values of sociability and dialogue, and in the specific case of the Jewish women, to pursue their integration into German culture and society.

FIVE

SOCIAL GATHERINGS IN PRIVATE HOMES

SOCIABILITY AND CONVERSATION were central features of eighteenth-century life among the educated classes and were closely connected with Enlightenment culture. Though not all forms of sociability practised in the eighteenth and early nineteenth centuries can be attributed to the Enlightenment or associated with enlightened goals—many, indeed, perpetuated and elaborated earlier practices—sociable communication both received a great boost from the Enlightenment and constituted one of its defining attributes.[1] The scientistic character traditionally ascribed to the Enlightenment, with its central image of the enlightened intellectual as a detached, solitary observer of the universe committed to the search for objective knowledge, has been replaced in research on this era by an image of the Enlightenment as a world of discourse and of enlightened men and women as sociable individuals engaged in conversational exchange.[2]

The importance accorded to interpersonal communication in the eighteenth century is reflected in the remarkable proliferation across Europe, including the German lands, of arenas in which people could socialize, enabling individuals of different ranks and backgrounds to intermingle. The array of discursive and cultural spaces that evolved during the Enlightenment to facilitate the circulation of ideas and opinions ranged from informal public places to institutionalized societies, encompassing coffee-houses, reading societies, learned academies, Masonic lodges, and—as discussed in the previous chapter—entire spa towns.[3]

---

[1] See Peter Albrecht, Hans Erich Bödeker, and Ernst Hinrichs' introduction to eid. (eds.), *Formen der Geselligkeit in Nordwestdeutschland*, 1–4; Klein, 'Enlightenment as Conversation'. As Dorinda Outram affirmed, 'Sociability was key to the Enlightenment' (Outram, *Panorama of the Enlightenment*, 62).

[2] Klein, 'Enlightenment as Conversation'.

[3] On Enlightenment societies in Germany, see Van Dülmen, *The Society of the Enlightenment*. See also a collection of essays on less institutionalized forms of sociability in north-west Germany,

Like many of their contemporaries, modernizing Jews in Germany endorsed the significance of sociability as a factor that could contribute to personal and social improvement, and sought to participate in a variety of social contexts. Sociability and conversational culture were integral to the lives of the Jewish women in Berlin at the heart of this study, and they assiduously employed the means of communication available to them—helping, indeed, to shape and transform some of them. Previous chapters have shown how these women participated in the circulation of ideas among a cultured European public through reading, writing, and publishing, and how they implemented ideals of sociability and communication by exchanging letters and visiting the spas. This chapter will focus on another practice that served the same ends—the gatherings that took place in private homes, providing a setting for social interaction and cultural exchange among themselves, with other members of the Jewish community, and, significantly, with non-Jews.

CHALLENGING GENDER HIERARCHY IN SOCIAL FRAMEWORKS

Receiving guests and visiting others' homes, a widespread practice among the middle and upper classes in German cities, was an activity of threefold significance in the life of enlightened Jewish women. It was important to them as members of the cultured strata of German society, in that it offered them the opportunity to engage in cultivated conversation, and by extension to inform themselves and develop their intellectual powers. It had a particular significance for them as Jews, in bringing them into contact not only with members of their own religious community but also with non-Jews, thus strengthening their connections to the German and European world. And it had a further implication for them as women, in offering them an accessible forum for discussion at a time when communication was valued as an important means to foster enlightenment and human progress but women were excluded from many of the formal structures created to facilitate it. This less institutionalized form of sociability thus joined the practices of visiting the spas and exchanging letters as a viable option for female participation in cultural and conversational activity.

Many social and intellectual frameworks excluded not only women but Jews of either sex.[4] However, in the second half of the eighteenth century and

including small, largely short-lived associations: Albrecht et al. (eds.), *Formen der Geselligkeit in Nordwestdeutschland*.

[4] The extent of Jewish integration in non-Jewish associations is discussed in the chapter 'The Semineutral Society' in Katz, *Out of the Ghetto*, 42–56.

especially towards its end, a certain number of intellectual clubs and scientific associations in German cities opened their doors to Jews as members, so that there were quite a few formal institutions which Jewish men seeking intelligent company and debate could join. Associational life in German cities, and notably in Berlin, offered a number of possibilities to male Jewish intellectuals. Moses Mendelssohn was accepted as an honorary member of the distinguished Berliner Mittwochsgesellschaft (Berlin Wednesday Society), an intellectual club of 'friends of the Enlightenment'[5] established in 1783—although his appointment to the exclusive Berlin Academy of Sciences was never ratified by the Prussian king; Marcus Bloch, a physician and famous ichthyologist, was affiliated to several leading German and European scientific societies;[6] Lazarus Bendavid, a radical maskil, was a member of the Gesellschaft der Freunde der Humanität (Society of the Friends of Humanity), as was Wolf Davidson, and indeed headed it for a decade from 1798; Bendavid was also a leading member of the Philomatische Gesellschaft (Philomathic Society), serving as its secretary from its foundation until at least 1806, when he wrote his autobiography;[7] and Rahel Levin's brother, the playwright Ludwig Robert, was one of several Jewish members of the writers' club known as the Nordstar Bund (North Star Club), along with his friend David Koreff and converted Jews such as Julius Eduard Hitzig, formerly Isaac Itzig.[8]

There were also specifically Jewish societies. As part of efforts to disseminate the ideas of the Haskalah, modern Jewish intellectuals had established separate Jewish associations that fostered the values of sociability and communication. Hevrat Doreshei Leshon Ever (the Society of Friends of the Hebrew Language), founded in Königsberg in 1782, and Hevrat Shoharei Hatov Vehatushiyah (the Society for the Promotion of Goodness and Justice), an association for maskilim in Königsberg and Berlin created in 1787, are two of the most prominent examples.[9] A somewhat different associ-

---

[5] This was what the members of the society called themselves: Schneiders (ed.), *Lexikon der Aufklärung*, 60. On Mendelssohn's participation in this society, see Altmann, *Moses Mendelssohn*, 654–6.

[6] Bloch's numerous affiliations appear on the title pages of many of his books. See e.g. the long list of affiliations on Bloch, *Naturgeschichte der ausländischen Fische*. Significantly, this book is dedicated by the author to Joseph Banks, president of the Royal Society in London.

[7] Bendavid, 'Selbstbiographie', 71. A lecture by Bendavid on the third anniversary of the Gesellschaft der Freunde der Humanität entitled 'Ueber den Nutzen literarischer Gesellschaften. Eine Rede am Stiftungstage der literarischen Gesellschaft der Freunde der Humanität' was published in a German journal, the *Neue Berlinische Monatsschrift* (1799), 369–83.

[8] Hertz, *How Jews Became Germans*, 62. For more on David Koreff, see Ch. 2 n. 82 above. Isaac Itzig is mentioned in Ch. 7 below.

[9] On these two associations see Feiner, *The Jewish Enlightenment*, 185–99, 251–7.

ation was the Gesellschaft der Freunde (Society of Friends), established in Berlin in 1792 by male contemporaries of the Jewish women discussed here. In addition to its purpose as a society for mutual social and financial support, this brotherhood established premises specifically to meet its members' need for a place to socialize.[10]

While enlightened Jewish men were thus relatively well catered for, their female counterparts had access to relatively few organized forms of sociability. As women, they were excluded from maskilic associations—the Gesellschaft der Freunde, for example, specifically stipulated in its statutes that 'persons of the female sex are not accepted'[11]—as they were from most formal German institutions, a notable and rare exception being the Feßlersche Mittwochsgesellschaft (Fessler Wednesday Society) established in 1795, which was open to female members.[12] To be sure, Jewish women in Germany had been setting up associations since the middle of the eighteenth century; but these were mutual aid and charitable voluntary societies devoted to benevolent purposes such as care for the sick and the performance of burial rites, not to the encouragement of learned conversation.[13] The paucity of formal contexts in which women could meet to discuss matters of cultural and intellectual interest certainly added to the significance for them of more informal settings. Along with the practices of reading, corresponding, and visiting spas mentioned in previous chapters—as well as others not specifically discussed in the present study, such as casual encounters on city promenades, at the theatre, or even en route while travelling—holding and taking part in social gatherings in private homes became an instrument for female empowerment, enabling women to participate in the public sphere in Germany and to intervene in public discussion, as well as helping them to develop their intellectual abilities and further their own education.

It is important to emphasize that the fulfilment of such goals was not a natural or inevitable result of participation in informal gatherings at private homes, as is clear from an examination of the gatherings that took place at the

---

[10] Ludwig Lesser, who summarized the history of this society on the occasion of its fiftieth anniversary, noted that in 1795 it was decided to rent special premises to satisfy the social needs of members. Here they could spend time pleasantly, 'partly engaged in friendly conversation, partly reading out new and interesting writings' (Lesser, *Chronik der Gesellschaft der Freunde*, 29).

[11] Ibid. 10.

[12] Among the members of this society were Henriette Herz and 'two daughters of Daniel Itzig', along with Jewish men such as Isaac Euchel, David Friedländer, and Marcus Herz, non-Jewish intellectuals including Friedrich Schlegel and Schleiermacher, the composer Carl Friedrich Zelter, and the theatre director August Wilhelm Iffland (Panwitz, 'Die Berliner Vereine', 21–4).

[13] On the voluntary associations of Jewish women in Germany in the late 18th and 19th centuries, see Baader, *Gender, Judaism, and Bourgeois Culture in Germany*, 161–83.

Herzes' home. Some of the women were involved in the intellectual circle that gathered around Marcus Herz. A few of them attended the lectures that Herz, respected as a physician and philosopher in late eighteenth-century Berlin, gave in his house on philosophy and natural sciences; however, the considerable public that came to hear these was mostly male. His wife Henriette, who was present on these occasions, left a written record of her experience, writing in her memoirs about her contacts with guests who came to the couple's house in order to hear her husband's lectures. She stressed the advantages she felt accrued to her from the conversation of these educated men:

> Herz became more and more known as a good physician and gave a course of philosophical lectures. As a result, many and distinguished people came to our house, who were also sometimes invited for evening meals, but mostly men only. Even as young and ignorant as I was, they still conversed a lot with me because they persuaded me and apparently also themselves that I was clever, since I was pretty; these conversations were not without their usefulness to me, for those who participated in them were for the most part intelligent people, and even if they could not always speak *with* me, they could nevertheless speak *to* me.[14]

In addition to the lectures, less formal gatherings also took place at the Herz home, and these were attended not only by Henriette but also by some of her female Jewish friends. With time, however, these women became dissatisfied with the way in which these meetings were conducted and the place in them allocated to women: they wished to take an active part in the exchange of ideas, to contribute to debates, and to expand their knowledge, all of which they found hard to do in the existing male-led frameworks. In view of these aspirations, it is not surprising that they strove to organize their own activities, where they could put the principles of sociability into practice for themselves and engage with other like-minded individuals on more favourable terms.

The disenchantment of Henriette Herz's female visitors with the established gatherings is evident in many of their letters. Writing to her friend David Veit in November 1794, Rahel Levin described her experience of conversation with two other guests who happened to be personally acquainted with him. 'Yesterday I visited the Herzes for the first time since returning to Berlin', she told him. 'Professor Meyer sat next to me, and Michaelis, the bookseller, opposite me.' The ensuing conversation between her and these

---

[14] Landsberg (ed.), *Henriette Herz*, 132 (emphasis in original). The English translation relies only partially on Blackwell and Zantop (eds.), *Bitter Healing*, 321–2, since the version there does not totally correspond to the German original.

two educated men was far from satisfactory from Levin's point of view.[15] After referring to the 'stupidity' (*Dummheit*) of Professor Meyer and to Michaelis' superfluous observations, which she was compelled to listen to politely, perhaps as it was expected from her as a woman, she summarized her general feeling about the gathering in a tone of revulsion: 'I am so mad; so *much rude* and stupid stuff I had to hear yesterday, and I am not used to it any more!'[16]

Similar dissatisfaction and discomfort were also experienced by Dorothea Mendelssohn, who several years earlier had expressed a wish to extricate herself from these occasions. 'The famous Friday evenings at H[erz] still continue', she reported to Karl Gustav von Brinckmann in December 1791, during his stay in Sweden, 'but they are getting so horrendously dull that I will seriously try to disengage from this club.'[17] On at least one occasion the following year she tried not only to evade an unpromising gathering being arranged by Marcus Herz, who had invited 'people who might cause boredom to all of us', but to do so by organizing an alternative gathering more to her liking.[18] Perhaps it was the subjects discussed in the gatherings organized by Marcus Herz that made them unpalatable to Dorothea; more likely, it was the attitude towards women evident on the part of the men who attended them. Women were forced to sit and listen to the conversations led by men, she complained, adding with heavy irony that 'we are forbidden to say a word, since we would be desecrating philosophy'.[19]

A sense of discomfort in a male atmosphere that belittled and inhibited women with intellectual aspirations is also evident in Rahel Levin's account of another discouraging evening she spent at the Herzes'. In June 1795 Levin found herself by mistake at one of the famous Friday events. 'Yesterday I was ... at the Herzes", she wrote to David Veit; 'the moment I arrived, I realized, to my greatest surprise and consternation, that it was Friday.'[20] Left with no choice she entered the house, once more meeting Michaelis. The Jewish

---

[15] Heinrich Salomo Michaelis was born in Hameln but lived at the time in Neustrelitz, where he established a court bookshop and a publishing house with the support of Duke Carl II of Mecklenburg-Strelitz, serving for some time as Schiller's publisher. Michaelis eventually became an author himself and obtained a position as professor of French and German in Tübingen. See 'Dr. Salomo Heinrich Karl August Michaelis'; Rüllmann, 'Adolf Freiherr Knigge und die Juden', 208–10. In a letter of December 1796, Ludwig Robert, then in Hamburg, wrote to his sister Rahel Levin about Michaelis' (unfulfilled) plan to marry Henriette Mendel, the sister of David Mendel, later known as the Church historian Johann August Wilhelm Neander (Levin Varnhagen, *Briefwechsel mit Ludwig Robert*, 14).   [16] *Briefwechsel zwischen Rahel und David Veit*, i. 265–6.
[17] *Briefe von und an Friedrich und Dorothea Schlegel*, ed. Behler, xxiii. 36.
[18] Letter of August 1792 (ibid. 60).   [19] Ibid. 36.
[20] *Briefwechsel zwischen Rahel und David Veit*, ii. 140.

bookseller had just returned from Jena, where he had met Veit; the latter had asked him to deliver to Rahel Levin a philosophical journal that Michaelis had just published, containing an essay that Veit had recommended to Levin in one of his letters.[21] The conversation between Levin and Michaelis about this commission began with the latter's addressing the young woman loudly: Rahel tried to make their exchange more discreet, fearing that its topic would reach the ears of the other men present. This situation would cause her great embarrassment, intimidated as she felt about exposing her intellectual aspirations among the scholars sitting there:

If this harangue had been noticed—for 'Mr Veit, journal, compliments, especially synonyms, reading, excuses, my journey' and so on appeared in it—my suffering would have come to an end yesterday. For I would not have survived to have made it clear to *all* professors, doctors, assessors, artists, officers and religions of *all* kinds, what, how, where, when and why was my business with Mr Veit regarding a journal for me or from me. *Asked?*—they *all* would have.[22]

Discouraged by this sort of gathering, which deterred women from participating actively in learned debate, stifled their aspirations, did not allow them to develop their intellectual and social abilities freely and confidently, and failed to grant them the position in cultured society that in their opinion they merited, enlightened Jewish women set out to arrange alternative encounters, adapting the existing forms of sociability to their needs and to the needs of other women. Their response did not manifest itself in a new mode of sociability: theirs were also sociable gatherings hosted in private homes, following widespread contemporary practice. The main difference was that the new frameworks were more supportive of female aspirations, for here the gender hierarchy, while not entirely obliterated, was at least blurred. In contrast to the established male-led social gatherings, these meetings offered the women a context in which they were not present merely to serve as ornaments or foils for the men,[23] but rather stood in the centre and played a major role.

---

[21] In a letter written by Veit a little earlier (20 May 1795), he had told Rahel Levin about the article; he later informed her that he had learned that Michaelis, the publisher of the journal in which the article was published, had arrived in the city, and expressed his intention of asking him to hand her a copy of the relevant issue (*Briefwechsel zwischen Rahel und David Veit*, ii. 120–3).   [22] Ibid. 140–1.

[23] In this context it is worth noting the function assigned to women in social gatherings of serving men's need to refine themselves, to develop moral virtues and proper social behaviour, as presented in *Igerot meshulam ben uriyah ha'eshtemo'i* ('Letters of Meshulam the son of Uriah the Eshtemoi'), a series of fictional letters published in the maskilic periodical *Hame'asef* in 1789–90 by Isaac Euchel, one of the leading maskilim living in Berlin at that time. On the advantages of mixed-sex sociability for the perfectibility of men as seen by this maskil, see Naimark-Goldberg, 'The (Questionable) Appraisal of Women in Euchel's *Haskala*'.

PLATE 8. Rahel Levin, later Varnhagen von Ense (1771–1833)
Pastel painting by Peter Friedel (*c.* 1800)
© bpk / SBB

THE CONCEPT OF THE SALON REVISED

The social activity of these women attracted quite a lot of attention among their contemporaries and also became the subject of study by later observers. The gatherings held by this generation of Jewish women in Berlin became known as the 'Jewish salons', and many historians, from the nineteenth century until this day, have devoted much time and effort to describing and analysing this intriguing phenomenon, conceived of as a distinctive episode, perhaps unique in German Jewish history, of peaceful coexistence between Jews and non-Jews. The word 'salon', which was first applied to this kind of event in the 1840s—the women themselves used terms such as 'society' (*Gesellschaft*) or 'circle' (*Kreiß*)[24]—is used to denote encounters that took place more or less regularly in private homes, in which the main activity was edifying conversation and intellectual exchange between educated individuals, through close social interaction. These gatherings, usually led by a woman, the so-called *salonnière*, were attended by a variety of individuals from different social and occupational backgrounds. Regular participants formed a circle of habitués who frequented one or more salons, and were joined by occasional guests who, although they did not require formal invitations to attend the open house, did require the services of a sponsor to introduce them to the hostess.[25]

Since the late 1980s the way in which salons are perceived and presented in research has changed significantly, and a new evaluation is emerging of the social life of these Jewish women and the context of their activities. Assumptions previously central to the description of the salon are being revised, among them the dominant interpretation of the salons as ideal places of emancipation for women and Jews. On the basis of historical descriptions emphasizing the mixed character of the Jewish salons in Berlin, these places were typically presented as 'miniature utopias',[26] bringing together elements

---

[24] Hahn, *The Jewess Pallas Athena*, 42. Speaking of the Parisian salons, Dena Goodman notes that 'the term "salon" was not used to refer to anything but a room in a house or apartment until the nineteenth century' (Goodman, 'Enlightenment Salons', 330 n. 2).

[25] Two of the most exhaustive discussions of the Jewish salons in Berlin are Hertz, *Jewish High Society*, and Wilhelmy, *Der Berliner Salon*. See also Bilski and Braun (eds.), *Jewish Women and their Salons*.

[26] This is the title of the chapter in Amos Elon's *The Pity of it All* in which he discusses the salons and the *salonnières* (pp. 65–100, see esp. p. 73). Elon draws on terminology used by Deborah Hertz, who had spoken of the Berlin salons as 'the fulfillment of the assimilationist dream in miniature' (Hertz, *Jewish High Society*, 13). It should be stressed, however, that Hertz significantly abstained from presenting too ideal a description of the relationships between the participants of the salon and pointed at the 'anti-semitic attitudes' of some of the guests. Hertz, *Jewish High Society*, 251–85 (quotation from p. 13).

of the population that did not usually meet socially on egalitarian terms: aristocrats and commoners, women and men, Christians and Jews. Special emphasis was given to the high social status attached to the salons, as evidenced by the prominence of certain individuals who attended: for example, the presence at Rahel Levin's home of the Prussian prince Louis Ferdinand, the nephew of King Frederick II, was always mentioned, along with a long list of other distinguished visitors.

This interpretation of the salons as sites of emancipation is now being exposed as a myth, or an idealization, and is being qualified.[27] Engaging in a closer and more critical study of the sources on which depictions of the Jewish salons have usually been based—first and foremost the laudatory descriptions contained in a small number of memoirs, anecdotes, and literary texts from the first half of the nineteenth century[28]—scholars leading this

---

[27] See the chapter entitled 'The Myth of the Salon' in Hahn, *The Jewess Pallas Athena*, 42–55—first published in German as 'Der Mythos vom Salon. "Rahels Dachstube" als historische Fiktion', in Schultz (ed.), *Salons der Romantik*; Weckel, 'A Lost Paradise of Female Culture?'.

[28] Reconstruction of the phenomenon relied almost exclusively on the following sources: Henriette Herz's memoirs in Fürst's 'revised' and expanded edition—a text of questionable validity as a historical source (see Ch. 2 n. 1 above; one of the important differences between the original version of Herz's memoirs and Fürst's rendering was precisely his addition of a great amount of information on the salons and Berlin social life, notably lacking in Herz's original version); the historical novel *Prinz Louis Ferdinand* by the German Jewish author Fanny Lewald which, although a fictional work written only in 1849, was used as a historical source; and above all Karl August Varnhagen's documentary enterprise. Two central texts that Varnhagen collected (or perhaps composed himself, or edited, as some scholars now suggest), describing two exemplary evenings in Rahel Levin's home ('Rahel Levin und ihre Gesellschaft. Gegen Ende des Jahres 1801 (Aus den Papieren des Grafen S****)' and 'Der Salon der Frau von Varnhagen. Berlin, im März 1830', in K. A. Varnhagen von Ense, *Vermischte Schriften*, vol. xix (Leipzig, 1876), 158–82, 183–210), along with other texts he wrote about the women and the social activity that took place in their houses, served as the main basis for describing the Jewish salons as places that attracted the most prominent representatives of German culture and society. As critics point out today, these are later texts, written or published by Varnhagen out of a clear wish to present a certain image of Rahel Levin and the social life that took place around her, and therefore his words should not be taken as a reliable and impartial description of the social reality at the end of the 18th century and the beginning of the 19th. Pointed criticism of the uncritical use of Varnhagen's works as historical sources has been expressed by Isselstein, 'Die Titel der Dinge sind das Fürchterlichste!' and Hahn, *The Jewess Pallas Athena*, 50–2. Of Varnhagen's two texts, Isselstein wrote: 'The authenticity of these . . . accounts remains at the very least doubtful; in any case, neither one of them is a chronicle committed to paper directly, but presumably both are stories based on old notes and reminiscences, certainly not freely invented, but nevertheless stylized. Only with this reservation can they be used as sources for [learning about] the actual social practice' (Isselstein, 'Die Titel der Dinge sind das Fürchterlichste!', 174). Isselstein herself chose explicitly not to use these sources when studying Rahel Levin's 'first salon', i.e. in the years around 1800, before she married Varnhagen. Deborah Hertz, writing before this critique was published, relied on this type of source: for instance, she based her description of Sara Levy's salon on the memoirs of her much younger relative Felix Eberty, a descendant of the famous Ephraim family, from 1878, and on later secondary sources; the description of Philippine Cohen's salon is based entirely on Varnhagen's report from

revisionism are examining the degree to which these institutions actually reflected ideas of tolerance and constituted a space that really did bring together individuals of different status, religion, and gender. The facts on which the emancipatory interpretation was built are being scrutinized,[29] giving rise to new claims that the presentation of the salons as the embodiment of an era of ethnic and class coexistence in a tolerant and pluralistic society was greatly exaggerated, the historical reality being significantly different. The idealized picture presented by some scholars, it has recently been argued, was a 'construction after the fact', deriving from the humanist dream of later generations more than reliable historical sources and adduced to support 'the idea that at least once German and Jew lived together harmoniously'.[30]

Another aspect of the revision has focused on the time frame of the Jewish salons. The history of the salons in Germany reaches from the second half of the eighteenth century to the beginning of the twentieth, but within this long interval historians have commonly distinguished the last two decades of the eighteenth century and the first years of the nineteenth as a period of outstanding Jewish prominence in these institutions, when the gatherings often took place in Jewish homes and many were headed by Jewish women. This period is said to have come to an end after 1806, with the rise of Prussian nationalism following the defeats at Jena and Auerstedt.[31] These military defeats, and in general the French occupation of German lands during Napoleonic times, led, so it was claimed, to increasing hostility towards the Jews and the alleged Francophile cosmopolitanism of the salons; the spirit of tolerance that had prevailed in previous years and was indispensable for the continuance of the Jewish salons was rejected, and the homes of, Jewish women no longer attracted German intellectuals as they had formerly

1843 in *Denkwürdigkeiten des eigenen Lebens*, with no documentary additions or critical reference to his words; the description of the social and intellectual activity of Dorothea Mendelssohn and Sara and Marianne Meyer relies almost completely on secondary sources, including Meyer Kayserling's book *Die jüdische Frauen in der Geschichte, Literatur und Kunst* (1879). Patently lacking are primary sources, especially any written by the women themselves.

[29] The emancipatory character of the salon, from both a Jewish and a female perspective, is emphasized by Petra Wilhelmy-Dollinger in 'Emanzipation durch Geselligkeit'.

[30] Quotations from Weckel, 'A Lost Paradise of Female Culture?', 313, and Hahn, *The Jewess Pallas Athena*, 45. Barbara Becker-Cantarino, a scholar of German literature and culture, claims that contrary to the perception of the salon as a site of social openness, the salon guests in fact included 'but few women and Jews, and no petits-bourgeois, craftsmen or merchants' (Becker-Cantarino, *Schriftstellerinnen der Romantik*, 194).

[31] In her famous biography of Rahel Levin, Hannah Arendt claimed: 'The salon which had brought together people of all classes, in which a person could participate without having any social status at all, which had offered a haven for those who fitted in nowhere socially, had fallen victim to the disaster of 1806' (Arendt, *Rahel Varnhagen*, 176).

done.³² Yet recent work has challenged the assumption that the Jewish salons ceased to exist in 1806. As Deborah Hertz indicates in the preface to the 2005 paperback edition of her *Jewish High Society in Old Regime Berlin* (originally published in 1988), her previous assertion that 'the era of the Jewish salon came to a close once the Napoleonic wars disrupted social life in Berlin' is ripe for revision and she now argues that Jewish salons continued well after 1806, albeit under changed conditions.³³

Both of these qualifications—by no means the only correctives to the historical narrative of the salons suggested by recent critics³⁴—are related to a more fundamental point that has been raised in scholarly debate and will be emphasized in this chapter. This is the claim that 'salon' is an inadequate term to encompass the at-homes hosted by the Jewish women discussed in this study, implying a narrower range of social interaction than was actually involved in these gatherings. As Ulrike Weckel suggested in a critical essay on the historiography of the Berlin Jewish salons, the social life of the so-called *salonnières* should be perceived not as a distinct and separate category but rather as part of a much broader phenomenon in German life, which encompassed a significant part of the educated public and expanded beyond the chronological limits of 1780–1806. Instead of equating the sociability of these Jewish women with the French institution of the salon, Weckel argued, it is more accurate to consider their hospitality within the context of 'the contemporary culture of visiting among educated people' that was a widespread and everyday occurrence in German cities.³⁵

---

³² Deborah Hertz's study specifically focuses on the years 1780–1806—but see below for her changed position in this regard. Petra Wilhelmy continues the story of the salons after 1806, but turns her attention away from the Jewish salons to the patriotic salons of Romanticism (Wilhelmy, *Der Berliner Salon*).

³³ See Hertz's preface to the paperback edition of *Jewish High Society*, p. xviii. Among the personal sources that clearly indicate that some Jewish women's houses continued to be a focus of social activity also after 1806—though not necessarily the dazzling settings implied by the term 'salon'—see Levin Varnhagen, *Briefwechsel mit Ludwig Robert*, 75, where Rahel Levin describes the social life she led after the French occupation. See also Ch. 7 below on the gatherings that took place at the house of Amalie Beer.

³⁴ Focusing on the circle that formed around Friedrich Schlegel and Dorothea Mendelssohn in Paris in the years 1802–4, Irina Hundt questions the leading role attributed to Berlin as the almost exclusive location of the German salons, showing that there was a 'German salon in Paris' (Hundt, 'Geselligkeit im Kreise von Dorothea und Friedrich Schlegel').

³⁵ Weckel, 'A Lost Paradise of Female Culture?' (quotation from p. 318). Specific cases of social visiting in Germany during this period are discussed in Albrecht et al. (eds.), *Formen der Geselligkeit in Nordwestdeutschland*; Spalding, *Elise Reimarus*, esp. ch. 6: 'Tea at Six: The Hamburg Tea Table', 177–98; and Habermas, *Frauen und Männer des Bürgertums*, 182 ff., which emphasizes the centrality of domestic sociability in the life of a bourgeois family in Nürnberg.

It is through this expanded phenomenon of sociability that the case of the enlightened Jewish women will be approached here. As the following discussion will show, the social lives of enlightened Jewish women were not restricted to semi-formal events in which a 'core group of habitués' gathered more or less regularly around a learned hostess;[36] they also included a more casual and frequently more intimate type of social visiting than that usually implied by use of the term 'salon'.[37] It is on the latter type of socializing that this chapter will focus. Especially significant for the study of Jewish history is the fact that this shift of focus brings into the picture other contemporary Jews who do not usually feature in accounts of the salons. Thus, as well as offering a better acquaintance with the way of life of the Jewish women themselves, this discussion throws light on the modernization not only of the restricted group of Jewish *salonnières* who usually attracted the attention of later generations but also of other Jewish women and men who were also involved in similar patterns of social interaction. This social interaction, it should be noted, was significant not only when it involved encounters across the religious divide but also when the encounters were between Jews, especially in view of the fact that Jews who went through a significant degree of acculturation served as agents of German culture no less than did non-Jewish Germans.

INTIMATE GATHERINGS IN PRIVATE HOMES

Interestingly, whereas contemporary sources and the personal testimonies left by enlightened Jewish women make only occasional references to semi-formal and well-attended salon-like events in private homes, they contain a significant amount of material on the more intimate and casual type of social interaction mentioned above. Numerous visits are mentioned in letters written by these women and by the men and women who were in contact with them, and reference is often made to the nature of these gatherings: thus we learn that they involved intellectual activities such as joint reading or studying, learned discussions, and debate about current issues—alongside, of course, the discussion of private subjects and just friendly conversation. Intimate gatherings of this type, which were common among educated people not exclusively in Berlin but in German cities in general, were at least as important to the social and intellectual life of the women involved as the salons that assembled larger groups: by taking part in the culture of visiting

---

[36] Bilski and Braun, 'The Power of Conversation: Jewish Women and their Salons', 2.

[37] The concept of 'intimate' gatherings refers here to encounters between just a few individuals—perhaps only two—as opposed to the salons, which usually involved a larger number of guests.

the women could actively exchange ideas and opinions with numerous individuals, influence the intellectual and cultural activity of other women and men, and absorb values current at the time.

Such a mixture of social and intellectual ingredients in a framework quite different from the more formal salons recurs in a number of sources that illuminate the social life of Henriette Mendelssohn, Moses Mendelssohn's youngest daughter, which until now have received little attention. At the end of the eighteenth century Henriette, a single woman in her early twenties, lived in the house of her elder sister Dorothea and her brother-in-law Simon Veit in Berlin, and took advantage of Dorothea's social life to establish new relationships, which she cultivated along with older friendships. A welcome guest to Dorothea's house whom Henriette met frequently during his 1798 visit to Berlin was the scholar and critic August Schlegel, Friedrich's brother. Henriette enjoyed talking with him and exchanging opinions on various subjects, such as music, literature, and theatre, and missed him acutely when he left for Jena, where he worked as a professor of philology. They kept in touch by letter, but for Henriette this type of communication was only partially successful in filling the void left by her friend's departure:

> Your letter and all you so kindly disclosed to me pleased me more than you yourself can imagine. It was the first real, genuine pleasure I have had since you left us. But that I now have to *write* you my thanks, and cannot expect a friendly morning visit to thank you, irritates and frightens me.[38]

Mendelssohn was certainly pleased that their correspondence offered her the chance to continue discussing both cultural events and private matters with Schlegel, as they did when they met in person. However, she considered correspondence a poor substitute for face-to-face conversation and kept hoping that they would meet again and resume their friendly conversations.

Social visits were also a prominent part of Henriette Mendelssohn's life in other cities. After leaving Berlin in 1799 she settled at first in Vienna, where she established and maintained social contacts with various acquaintances, including the physician and author Friedrich Ludwig Lindner, Rahel Levin's brother Ludwig Robert, Rahel's former fiancé Karl von Finckenstein and his cousin Wilhelm von Burgsdorff, Major von Möllendorf, and her friend and Berlin acquaintance Fanny von Arnstein.[39] But it was her meetings with Wilhelm Wiesel, who in 1799 was serving as a high-ranking official in the Prussian war ministry in the Habsburg capital, that gave her the greatest

---

[38] Henriette Mendelssohn's letter to August Schlegel, dated 16 Aug. 1798, was printed in Holtei (ed.), *Dreihundert Briefe*, 165–8 (quotation from p. 165).

[39] Peez, 'Henriette Mendelssohn', 104.

pleasure. 'I see Wiesel very frequently, every day and a lot', she wrote to Rahel Levin in April 1800, about a year after arriving in Vienna.[40] To be sure, Mendelssohn was also on friendly terms with Wiesel's wife Pauline César (one of Rahel Levin's closest friends) and her relatives: as she indicated in her letter to Levin, 'I do not spend as much time with anyone as I do with the César family and with Wiesel.'[41] Henriette was fond of Pauline: she 'is not really good or learned', she admitted, 'but she is charming and naïve'.[42] The deeper relationship, however, was the special bond between Henriette and Wilhelm Wiesel, which was based on mutual appreciation and spiritual sustenance. 'Wiesel does not let one day pass without seeing me. Since I demand so little and just derive pleasure from him, he sees me as the second half of his wife', she wrote with the lack of self-esteem that characterizes many of her letters from that period.[43]

Thus, although Henriette Mendelssohn had access to the most fashionable social setting in Vienna at the time, the house of Fanny von Arnstein, 'almost the only place where one can properly appreciate and enjoy Vienna', and although she felt at ease in this famous salon—'at her house, one spends time in good company, without any constraints, as comfortably as in one's own house'[44]—it was the more intimate meetings with Wiesel that gave her the greatest satisfaction. Unsurprisingly, when Wiesel left the city she was downcast, feeling she now had no real partner to engage in thought-provoking conversation: 'I may boldly state that since Wiesel left, I have not heard even one clever word', she noted sadly in a letter from August 1801.[45]

After settling in Paris a short time later, Henriette Mendelssohn began to attract friends to her house there—new acquaintances made in the French capital as well as familiar faces visiting from Berlin. Among the latter was Ludwig Robert, who during his stay in Paris in 1806–7 wrote to his sister Rahel Levin several times about the social and intellectual pleasures of moments spent with Henriette. 'Jette Mend[elssohn] I see frequently and gladly', he told Rahel in September 1806, shortly after arriving in the city, adding that it was possible to spend an enjoyable evening in her company and that of Madame Fould, a well-to-do Jewish woman in whose garden house

---

[40] Varnhagen von Ense (ed.), *Galerie von Bildnissen*, i. 68.
[41] Ibid. 71.   [42] Ibid.   [43] Ibid.
[44] Ibid. 73. Fanny von Arnstein was born to the wealthy and powerful Itzig family in Berlin, but after her marriage to the Viennese Jewish banker Nathan Adam von Arnstein she lived in the Austrian capital, where she led an extremely active social life. An exhaustive biography of this outstanding woman was published in German by Hilde Spiel and translated into English in 1991 (Spiel, *Fanny von Arnstein*).   [45] Varnhagen von Ense (ed.), *Galerie von Bildnissen*, i. 75.

Henriette Mendelssohn was living.[46] Conversations about literary themes were an integral part of these visits, and Robert, who was at that time trying to make his way as a playwright, was glad to find in her an appreciative listener: 'Jette was beside herself with my acrostics and the last poem to Bartholdy', he wrote proudly to his sister.[47]

Another visitor who enjoyed Henriette Mendelssohn's company in Paris was Karl August Varnhagen, whose memoirs contain reports on visits in 1810 and 1814. To be sure, his description of gatherings in her house is reminiscent of the traditional image of the salon, with a cosmopolitan crowd—which, if his account is accurate, was itself remarkable in this period of conflict between European nations. At Henriette Mendelssohn's, according to Varnhagen, a French politician, an Italian composer, authoresses from Germany and France, a wealthy Viennese Jew, and many other guests would typically engage in 'remarkable conversations' about literary subjects, at times even sliding into politics, 'when the ground was safe'.[48] But he reserved his main enthusiasm for the quiet hours he spent alone in the company of a woman he depicted as educated and clever, gifted with 'a quick intelligence, wide knowledge, clear judgment, the most refined courtesy, and the choicest tact'.[49] As he wrote reminiscently years later, 'In spite of the keen interest of such society [i.e. the salon-like gatherings at Henriette Mendelssohn's], I found a greater charm in quiet domestic evenings with Fräulein Mendelssohn alone, when German subjects were discussed in the German language.' They used to sit for hours in her drawing room, 'calling up the beloved images of our native country, our mutual friends and acquaintances, more of whom we constantly discovered to share our predilections in art and poetry; sometimes we discussed the highest and most sacred human interests'.[50]

Henriette Mendelssohn herself recorded intimate conversations in her house with various male and female visitors whom she knew personally or by

---

[46] Levin Varnhagen, *Briefwechsel mit Ludwig Robert*, 67.   [47] Ibid.

[48] Varnhagen von Ense, *Denkwürdigkeiten des eigenen Lebens*, iii. 137 (Eng. trans. in Hensel, *The Mendelssohn Family*, i. 44). Varnhagen's tendency to emphasize the presence of outstanding figures, as in his accounts of the gatherings at the Levin house, should be kept in mind. Interestingly, letters sent by Henriette Mendelssohn to August Schlegel throughout 1810 mention intimate visits to her home by numerous individuals, but do not make specific reference to salon-like events (Körner, *Krisenjahre der Frühromantik*, ii).

[49] Varnhagen von Ense, *Denkwürdigkeiten des eigenen Lebens*, iii. 136 (Eng. trans. in Hensel, *The Mendelssohn Family*, i. 43).

[50] Varnhagen von Ense, *Denkwürdigkeiten des eigenen Lebens*, iii. 137–8 (Eng. trans. in Hensel, *The Mendelssohn Family*, i. 44–5). See also Mendelssohn's own concise report on her meetings with Varnhagen, her 'evening companion' (*Abendsgesellschafter*) of those days (Körner, *Krisenjahre der Frühromantik*, ii. 152).

recommendation. Certainly, this was not invariably a pleasant experience. In 1810, for example, she referred to a disappointing visit from Karl Sieveking, a young student of jurisprudence from Hamburg who was visiting Paris. A future syndic and diplomat, Sieveking came from a family that had special ties with members of the Jewish community, including acquaintances and relatives of Henriette. His mother was the niece of Elise Reimarus, a leading figure of the Enlightenment in Hamburg, who had been in close contact with Moses Mendelssohn, Henriette's father, and had maintained lively connections with local Jews, who were welcome guests at her famous 'tea table'.[51] His Hamburg relatives were most probably acquainted with Henriette's brothers Joseph and Abraham, who lived in the city at that time, and may have given the young Sieveking his introduction to their sister. Karl Sieveking, however, belonged to a younger generation than Henriette and had a different outlook: as a result, the visit was not a success.[52] As Henriette herself recalled, he 'came one evening, I do not know how it happened, but we found more than ever that we had nothing to say to each other'; therefore 'he left after half an hour of rather uneasy conversation'.[53] Notwithstanding this and possibly other failures, it is clear from the case of Henriette Mendelssohn that intimate, informal gatherings were a common occurrence in the lives of modern Jewish women of her time.

Such visits, moreover, could be paid without invitation—indeed, impromptu calls were not a rare occurrence but constituted an essential part of daily social interaction. A person would send a slip of paper or 'billet' announcing his or her imminent arrival at a friend's house or seeking to coordinate the time for a visit, or even drop by without any advance notice. Some houses were open to visitors at all times of the day, so that unannounced visits could be made even in the mornings. In a letter to David Veit in April 1794 Rahel Levin described one morning in which an especially long list of visitors flocked to the Levin house, constantly interrupting her attempts to get down to her letter-writing: 'Just you try and write, as Mad. Lüdeken, two children

---

[51] See Spalding, *Elise Reimarus*, especially the chapter entitled 'Jewish Contacts in Hamburg's Enlightenment Circle: From Strangers to Friends' (pp. 259–79). On the relationship between Elise Reimarus and Moses Mendelssohn and her attitude towards the Jewish philosopher, see Badt-Strauß, 'Elise Reimarus und Moses Mendelssohn'.

[52] Almut Spalding notes Karl Sieveking's 'attempts to escape the Enlightenment tenor of his home, dominant among his elder family members, by embracing Romanticism' (Spalding, *Elise Reimarus*, 13 n. 7).

[53] *Bankiers, Künstler und Gelehrte*, ed. Gilbert, 19. Sieveking was also a close friend of David Mendel, mentioned above in n. 15, both having graduated from the Akademisches Gymnasium (Academic High School) in Hamburg (Mendel was in fact the first Jewish graduate of the institution). See *Allgemeine Deutsche Biographie*, xxxiv. 227–31; Spalding, *Elise Reimarus*.

from Hamburg, Scholz, Markus, Bing, Fließ, Peschier, Brinckmann, Mr Koch, Mrs Veit, Jettchen, Mrs Marchetti and who knows who else come to you one midmorning; Darbes also came to me in the morning.'[54]

These visits were distinguished from the Berlin Jewish salons as usually depicted not only by their more casual and informal nature and by the times of day at which they occurred, but also by the visitors themselves. While some of the names mentioned in the written records belong to known personalities, others are hard to identify: so by definition not all of them were famous or even well known. One name in the list cited by Rahel Levin in the letter quoted above, that of Bing, is especially interesting since it provides evidence of Rahel Levin's contacts with less well-known members of the local Jewish community and points at the fact that young Jewish men sought and valued the company of an intelligent and educated Jewish woman such as Rahel. From this and other letters it may be surmised that this visitor was Abraham Herz Bing, a physician from Berlin and an active member of the Jewish Gesellschaft der Freunde (Society of Friends) mentioned above (where Bing and Levin could not have met, since women were excluded from this association).[55] Bing, a friend of David Veit who supported the latter in his study of medicine—according to Veit, 'he is the *only* person who has *full confidence* in me'[56]—is mentioned in various letters between Levin and Veit. Yearning for witty conversation, Bing tried to get close to Rahel Levin and paid her several visits. On one occasion in 1794 he called in one Friday evening on his way back from the synagogue, and apparently spoke with her about things that happened during the prayers. As Levin informed Veit in a letter she was writing as the unexpected guest came in, Bing 'just came from *shul*, where out of thrift, a cantata by Zelter that was to be performed was transformed into a neatly rendered *mekabel shabbes* by Räseburg'.[57] Although it is hard to know for certain what exactly lies behind this comment, which

---

[54] *Briefwechsel zwischen Rahel und David Veit*, i. 220. For further testimony to unexpected visits in the morning hours, see Henriette Herz's memoirs: Landsberg (ed.), *Henriette Herz*, 142.

[55] For basic information on Bing, see Jacobson, *Jüdische Trauungen*, 440–1. On his affiliation to the society and his functions as a leading member, see Lesser, *Chronik der Gesellschaft der Freunde*, 14, 17, 23, 28 (where the text of an almost 'poetic' letter he wrote as 'first secretary' of the society is included), among others.

[56] Letter to Rahel Levin, Nov. 1793 (*Briefwechsel zwischen Rahel und David Veit*, i. 65).

[57] Ibid. 105. *Mekabel shabbes* actually applies to the person receiving the shabbat, and here refers probably to *Kabalas shabbes* or *Kabalat Shabbat*, which is the service at the beginning of the sabbath. 'Zelter' was most probably Carl Friedrich Zelter, a German composer, conductor, and music teacher. He indeed is known to have made a musical contribution to early Reform liturgy in Berlin—but apparently only some time later (in fact, 'modernized services . . . were held in Berlin beginning in 1815': Meyer, *Response to Modernity*, 45).

appears to allude to musical innovations in the Jewish liturgy, including the performance at sabbath services of compositions by non-Jewish composers, more than two decades before reformed services were conducted in Berlin, it is a significant fact that through visits such as this Rahel Levin could keep herself informed as to the most recent developments in the Jewish community and more precisely in Jewish ritual practices, in this case regarding Jewish prayers. As for Bing's relationship with Levin, eventually he sensed that he was more enthusiastic than his hostess, and after some time his visits ceased altogether.[58]

Along with Bing, Rahel Levin included in the list of visitors on that busy morning a well-known portrait painter by the name of Darbes and an Italian singer, Maria Marchetti, who was an intimate friend of hers. In addition to their acquaintanceships with orchestral directors and other leading artists, Levin and other Jewish women kept up close relationships with female singers and actresses, with almost daily contacts including visits at home. One of the many testimonies to this kind of relationship appears in a letter written by Fradchen Liebmann in June 1795, where she writes:

Tonight I will be at Mrs Eigensatz's for dinner . . . yesterday I was at the house of F [Freude Fränkel, née Meyer], who is in town now, with Mrs Marchetti; Mrs Marchetti was so courteous as to get tickets for the operetta in Charlottenburg for us, even for my brother. We will go to have lunch with her at Mrs Flies' [sic], and then we will drive out.[59]

The invitation to dinner (*souper*) at the home of Christel Eigensatz, a non-Jewish actress, is particularly noteworthy, indicating that not only did Jews open their homes to Christians, as is well known, but there were also Christians (though perhaps only a few) who were happy to host Jewish guests. Though isolated testimonies such as this do not justify the conclusion that Christian society in general was open towards Jews, it is worth remembering that such cases existed.[60] It should be emphasized, moreover, that when non-Jews received Jewish guests, the social interaction of the Jewish visitor was not restricted to the individual Christian friend or acquaintance alone but

---

[58] On one occasion, Rahel Levin told David Veit about Bing's impressions of his visits to her, as these became known to her through a female friend: 'Bing said he was getting stupid, that he had no one to talk to. Then she [the friend] asked, "Why don't you go to Miss Levin?"—"Oh well, she gets bored with me, I see it, no matter how well she hides it . . . I still see it, that's how it seems to me"' (*Briefwechsel zwischen Rahel und David Veit*, i. 173).   [59] Bosold, 'Friederike Liman', 12.

[60] This type of Christian hospitality took place in other German cities as well. According to one account, the Jewish merchant Moses Wessely was invited to join Elise Reimarus' table in Hamburg, where he ate 'ham with the cabbage', as a Christian visitor noted, ignoring Jewish dietary laws (Spalding, *Elise Reimarus*, 269).

frequently extended to embrace other members of his or her family. When Dorothea Mendelssohn visited Leipzig in 1788, for example, accompanied by Henriette Herz, both women visited the home of a local professor, where they were warmly received by all the members of his household. In a letter sent upon her return to Berlin, Mendelssohn expressed her gratitude to the whole family for their generous hospitality: 'Give my regards to Professor Oeser, his venerable wife, his two daughters, the grandchild, remind all these people of the two women from Berlin, who frequently remember the jolly hours and the friendly reception they enjoyed at their homes.'[61] How much of a family matter this socializing could be, for Jews and non-Jews alike, is further indicated by the fact that at the end of the letter, after sending greetings from her own husband, Simon Veit, Dorothea Mendelssohn invited the Leipzig scholars and their families to reciprocate with a visit to Berlin.[62]

A similar impression arises from Henriette Herz's well-known intimate relations with members of Schleiermacher's family—and Schleiermacher's own connection with Herz's close relatives. In the first years of their acquaintance, Herz and Schleiermacher, having established a close friendship, met mostly at her house. He became very close to members of Herz's family, especially her sisters, one of whom, Brenna de Lemos, he called in his letters 'my sister' and another, Sara, 'my little daughter'.[63] After she became a widow (in 1803) and he a married man (in 1809), Henriette became a frequent guest at the Schleiermachers', developing close relationships with the philosopher's wife, sister, and children and becoming almost a member of the family.

SOCIAL GATHERINGS AND WOMEN'S INFORMAL LEARNING

More than a decade before his marriage Schleiermacher became, as noted above, a close friend of Henriette Herz and a constant visitor to the house she shared with her husband.[64] A description included by Schleiermacher in a letter to his sister Charlotte in May 1798 gives us an insight as to what went on in his early visits to Henriette:

Most of the time I now spend with Mrs Herz. Over the summer, she dwells in a cute little house near Thiergarten, where she sees few people and I can therefore

---

[61] *Briefe von und an Friedrich und Dorothea Schlegel*, ed. Behler, xxiii. 5.

[62] Ibid. 6. This letter is also discussed in Ch. 3 above, around n. 110.

[63] See e.g. Schleiermacher's letter to his sister Charlotte in February 1801 (Schleiermacher, *Schleiermacher als Mensch*, i. 203).

[64] The platonic relationship between Henriette Herz and Friedrich Schleiermacher is discussed in Schirmer, 'Die große Jette', esp. p. 103.

entirely enjoy her company. I usually spend at least one whole day with her every week. I could do that with few people, but with a variety of pastimes and pleasures, this day with her passes very pleasantly. She has taught me Italian, or strictly speaking, she still does so, we read Shakespeare together, we occupy ourselves with physics, I pass on to her some of my knowledge of nature, we read this and that from a good German book, and in between we go for walks during the most beautiful hours and talk from the depths of our souls about the most important things.[65]

As Schleiermacher's succinct description of their routine indicates, the intimate gatherings in which enlightened Jewish women participated usually fulfilled more than one role, offering a combination of light-hearted pleasures and more serious activity. One that is emphasized here and was very important for these women was that of expanding their education.

It will have become abundantly clear by this point that the ideal of learning was of central importance for these enlightened Jewish women. Their ambition to learn, the importance they attributed to gaining knowledge as a source of power and satisfaction, the efforts they invested in developing their minds—all these have already emerged as prominent features in their lives. Learning filled a considerable part of their time as adults, although it did not proceed either along the lines drawn by most contemporary thinkers and pedagogues, who at best—strongly influenced by Jean-Jacques Rousseau—promoted women's education but restricted it to the requisites necessary to prepare them for their prescribed domestic roles, or within the kind of structured schedule followed by those who pursued a formal, institutionalized education. Rather, learning became integrated into their daily life, something which, one way or another, they were doing most of the time, and according to their own understanding.

Informal ways of learning—including social visits along with other practices such as reading, letter-writing, and even visits to the spas—had particular significance for women with intellectual aspirations, given the fact that most formal learning institutions and frameworks were closed to their sex. The institutional restrictions affecting women across Europe at this time

---

[65] Letter from Schleiermacher to his sister Charlotte, May 1798, in Schleiermacher, *Schleiermacher als Mensch*, i. 105. If in the summer of 1798 he tried to spend 'at least one whole day... every week' with Henriette Herz, at other times his visits were even more frequent. For example, he reports in a letter of 1801 to Ehrenfried von Willich, a mutual friend: 'With Jette [Henriette Herz] I usually spend every other day, from one to five; we eat together, read, chat, also sleep and go for walks' (*Bis nächstes Jahr auf Rügen*, ed. Schmitz, 15). As already noted, no romantic relationship existed between Henriette Herz and Schleiermacher, just a deep friendship. At the time he wrote that letter in 1801, Schleiermacher was desperately in love with another woman, and indeed the correspondence between the three friends—Herz, Willich, and Schleiermacher—partly revolved around this issue.

placed enlightened Jewish women in a very different situation from that of contemporary Jewish men who aspired to expand their knowledge in secular fields. By the end of the eighteenth century religious affiliation was gradually becoming less of an obstacle for Jewish boys and men who wished to attend formal educational institutions, although undoubtedly it remained a very significant factor. Leading high schools in various German cities were beginning to accept Jewish pupils, offering them suitable preparation for continuing their academic studies; German institutions of higher education had been opening their gates to Jewish men as early as the end of the seventeenth century,[66] and since then Jewish students had been attending the faculties of medicine at various universities in growing numbers.[67]

It is true that around 1800 many doors, including those of most university faculties, still remained closed to Jews. Furthermore, even those who completed their studies were barred from holding academic office,[68] and prominent institutions of learning, academies, and learned societies continued to exclude Jews throughout the nineteenth century. These restrictions notwithstanding, at least limited admission to some institutions was available to male Jewish students—as was not the case for their female co-religionists. In the second half of the eighteenth century, there were hardly any appropriate schools for girls of the well-to-do bourgeoisie, and they received whatever education they were granted mainly at home, through private tutors. European universities had been semi-clerical, male institutions since their establishment, and most had excluded women from the outset.[69] Discrimination against women on the part of higher education institutions continued up to the end of the nineteenth century, and only then were they allowed to

[66] According to Monika Richarz, Jewish students were accepted by a German university for the first time in 1678—the year Richarz chose to begin her account of Jewish entry into the academic world (Richarz, *Der Eintritt der Juden in die Akademischen Berufe*). In Italy Jews were accepted into medical faculties even earlier: see Carpi, *Between Renaissance and Ghetto* (Heb.), 96–130. On the far-reaching outcomes of the exposure of Jewish students, including those from German lands, to the world of science and secular culture at Italian universities, especially the University of Padua, see Ruderman, *Jewish Thought and Scientific Discovery*, esp. pp. 100–17.

[67] See the table in Richarz, *Der Eintritt der Juden in die Akademischen Berufe*, 46. Jewish students started to matriculate in faculties other than medicine, such as law and philosophy, towards the end of the 18th century, when efforts towards Jewish emancipation raised the prospect of wider professional opportunities, and structural changes in German universities allowed for a greater integration of students from different religious backgrounds (ibid. 56, 62, 91).

[68] Isaac Euchel was almost appointed to a teaching position at the university in Königsberg in 1786, but in the end his candidacy was rejected because of his Jewishness. See Feiner, 'Isaac Euchel' (Heb.), 437. Forty years later the jurist Eduard Gans, one of the founders of the Verein für Cultur und Wissenschaft der Juden (Society for the Culture and Science of the Jews), was forced to undergo baptism before being appointed professor at the law faculty in Berlin.

[69] Lundt, 'Zur Entstehung der Universität als Männerwelt'.

matriculate.⁷⁰ The increasing institutionalization of knowledge in the eighteenth century did not favour women who wished to educate themselves (as it did, to some extent, those Jewish men who wished to do so). On the contrary, indeed, it has been suggested that while in the early modern period women were able to participate in the world of science and discovery—since frequently this work took place in private homes—as science and other forms of learning became institutionalized they were taken out of the female ambit into official institutions that sought to dominate knowledge, including scientific academies; and these institutions excluded women.[71]

Thus, while Jewish men gradually gained partial admission into some universities, persisting gender limitations continued to exclude their female counterparts from the higher institutions of learning—first and foremost as women rather than as Jews. Lazarus Bendavid could attend lectures at the universities of Göttingen and Halle, even without being registered or studying for a formal degree; his female Jewish counterparts from Berlin certainly could not.[72] While David Veit developed his intellect in an institutional setting while studying medicine in Göttingen, Rahel Levin worked hard at her home in Berlin, coping almost on her own with complicated books and unfamiliar corpuses of knowledge.[73] Thus it was not their

---

[70] As Patricia Mazón indicates, following long public debate, from the late 1890s German universities began to accept women as auditors on a more regular basis than in previous years, and 'with special permission auditors could in fact earn doctorates . . . formal admission occurred on a state-by-state basis between 1900 and 1909'. Mazón, *Gender and the Modern Research University*, 10; see also Freidenreich, *Female, Jewish and Educated*. According to Beatrix Niemeyer, in the 18th century there was no explicit prohibition on women studying at universities, and there were even isolated cases of women who graduated from these institutions. But universities were typically male institutions, and the mere presence of a woman was considered intolerable, so that the few female students who did attend lectures sat behind a curtain or a slightly open door (Niemeyer, 'Ausschluss oder Ausgrenzung?').

[71] Schiebinger, *The Mind Has No Sex?*; ead., 'Wissenschaftlerinnen im Zeitalter der Aufklärung'. Thus, while the 18th century is usually seen as a time of progress in the educational field, when the experience of women is taken into account a very different picture emerges. This claim, presented by Elke Kleinau and Claudia Opitz in their introduction to a collection of essays on the history of women's education in Germany, draws on Joan Kelly's arguments in her famous essay 'Did Women Have a Renaissance?': Kleinau and Opitz, 'Vorwort', in eaed. (eds.), *Geschichte der Mädchen- und Frauenbildung*, 9–13. See also Kelly, 'The Social Relation of the Sexes', 2–4.

[72] Bendavid visited these universities as the companion of a young medical student. As well as the lectures he heard and the intellectuals he met, he especially enjoyed the treasures of the library that were made available to him during these visits, as he indicated in his autobiography: Bendavid, 'Selbstbiographie', 55–6.

[73] This emerges from their correspondence in 1793–4. It is interesting to compare the different environments in which their learning took place: David Veit sits in his room and enjoys relative silence and tranquillity, spending entire days plunged in his studies, while Rahel Levin is constantly distracted by daily matters, including the care of her heavily pregnant sister-in-law.

Jewishness but their femaleness that was the main obstacle barring the way of German Jewish women to systematic education and inhibiting their pursuit of knowledge.

Nevertheless, as is clear from the example of Rahel Levin just noted, women's exclusion from educational institutions did not necessarily lead to their alienation from learning. Enlightened Jewish women, like other women in Germany, were able to some extent to circumvent the prevailing gender limitations and achieve their educational goals. Equipped with personal initiative and self-discipline, many of them succeeded in finding non-formal ways to pursue their aspirations.[74] This frequently resulted in non-systematic, random learning, accompanied at times by a certain measure of frustration and dissatisfaction. The social and cultural activities discussed in previous chapters helped women with intellectual aspirations to cope with established norms that undervalued the intellectual capacity of women and denied them the need and the right to learn and develop their intellect; these activities also helped them to overcome the practical obstacles on their way to gaining knowledge. Social gatherings were another such activity that, along with their other functions, helped to facilitate the acquisition of knowledge.

In this respect, social gatherings of the more intimate kind discussed in the previous section may have been more helpful than larger and more illustrious ones. In the smaller and less formal setting, women often felt more comfortable about posing questions, for example asking for arguments to be clarified and concepts explained, without the constant fear of being mocked for finding it hard to grasp a certain point or merely ridiculed for wishing to understand matters supposed to lie beyond a woman's interest and capabilities. Indicative of this attitude among women is a case mentioned in one of the letters that Esther Gad sent to Jean Paul. While living in Berlin, the aspiring Jewish authoress and the accomplished German writer used to meet quite frequently, and her letters to him contain numerous invitations to intimate social events. On one occasion, for example, she asked him to visit her and have 'the best [coffee] that human hands can make'. In the same letter she

---

[74] In order to learn about women's education in the past, it is imperative to look beyond institutionalized education. As Shaul Stampfer has shown in the case of Jewish women in 19th-century eastern Europe, the identification of learning with schooling has led to mistaken conclusions about the extent of female literacy and education. Stampfer showed that despite the relatively limited number of girls and women who attended learning institutions, Jewish women acquired education in other ways, and therefore it may be said that focusing excessively on formal education distorts the historical picture (Stampfer, 'Gender Differentiation and Education of the Jewish Woman'). The significance of informal learning in the education of girls has also been stressed by Yemima Chovav in her study of Ashkenazi women in the early modern period (Chovav, *Maidens Love Thee* (Heb.), 406–45).

informed him of her intention to show him 'the letter of a *dying* woman, whose only solace is *Hesperus* [Jean Paul's famous novel]'.[75] Some days later, Gad invited Jean Paul to join her on a visit to the house of 'the banker Lipmann', where he could make the acquaintance of an 'angel' (probably Fradchen Liebmann), who was extremely eager to meet him.[76] She also urged him to pay a short visit to a blind woman, almost certainly Recha Itzig, perhaps the same 'dying woman' mentioned above. He could thus 'bring a ray of light to the life of Miss Itzig, because anyhow no ray of light can penetrate her eyes'.[77] In yet another letter she assured him that in her house he could always find 'tea, rum, a small, frugal meal and some cordiality'.[78] It is clear from the terms of these invitations that they have a social purpose; but it is also clear that Gad intended to use Jean Paul's visits to further her education. Writing in November 1800, she told him quite openly that she meant to take advantage of an imminent visit of his by asking him to explain to her 'a physics-related subject about which I heard yesterday at Herz's from Preacher Bocquet. I could not make sense of his schoolmasterly blather.'[79] There, at Herz's, she dared not call for such an explanation; but she felt quite comfortable requesting it from a friend, in a friendly and intimate setting.

It is worth pausing here to emphasize how the relations between enlightened women and intellectual men of that time, as presented here, differ from most historical descriptions. Usually, women are seen primarily as serving the needs of men in a male-dominated world, acting as the 'muses' who inspired German intellectuals. If the personal motivations of the women were considered at all, the assumption was that their sole concern was to elevate their position in society through their relationships with noble or famous men. Either way, men were assumed to occupy the central position in women's activity. Examining the relationships between men and women in the way suggested here, from the perspective of women, on the basis of their own writings, including the opinions and aspirations they expressed in their letters, presents an image almost diametrically opposed to the established interpretation—one in which it is the educated men who 'serve' the intellectual needs of the women.[80]

---

[75] Hahn (ed.), '"Geliebtester Schriftsteller"', 27.
[76] Ibid. 30.
[77] Ibid. 31.
[78] Ibid. 34.
[79] Ibid. 36.
[80] Dena Goodman makes a similar claim when explaining women's participation in the Paris salons in the 18th century. While according to common interpretation the enlightened *salonnières* in Paris established salons in order to 'gain fame and power through association with brilliant and powerful men', Goodman insists that 'the initial and primary purpose of Enlightenment salons was to satisfy the self-determined educational needs of the women who started them'. Contrary to widespread opinion, the *salonnières* did not act out of a wish to climb the social ladder (they were not 'social climbers', in

A remarkable case of a woman 'exploiting' social ties for the purpose of non-formal education appears in the frequent meetings between Marianne Meyer and Friedrich von Gentz in Vienna, where both lived at the beginning of the nineteenth century.[81] The relationship between Meyer, by this time a Christian convert and a widow, and her friend, a German political journalist, was perceived by contemporaries as based on romantic attachment. However, in her letters to Goethe Meyer presents their connection in a totally different light, to a large extent as an intellectual relationship based on conversation and cultural exchange. 'G[entz] visits me almost every day', Marianne told Goethe in 1803; 'he informs me about all that interests him, has confidence in me and reads to me.'[82] According to Marianne Meyer, the intellectual input she derived from her relationship with Friedrich von Gentz was one of the reasons why she appreciated their friendship: his conversation, she wrote, 'is endlessly interesting to me, it is instructive and pleasant; he corrects and organizes some of my ideas, and not seldom he has to fight for his point, which exercises our skills and forces him to be thorough'.[83] Unlike many other intelligent people she knew, she claimed, Gentz was gifted with a rare verbal ability that allowed him to transmit things that were hard to grasp in an easy and clear way. As a woman who wished to understand abstract thoughts and ideas from the fields of metaphysics and politics, with which she was not well acquainted, she clearly enjoyed talking to an intelligent man and appreciated the valuable knowledge she derived from her meetings with him.

She also appreciated, no less than his articulacy and conversational powers, an additional trait in his attitude towards her: 'It does not occur to him at all that I am a woman, and I have often been glad to see that he does not think about it at all, but rather treats me, talks to me and behaves towards me, as to a man.'[84] She may or may not have been right about Gentz's indifference towards her as a woman and his 'real' intentions.[85] The fact remains that this

---

Goodman's words), but rather as intelligent women who adopted and implemented the values of the Enlightenment 'Republic of Letters'. Using these values, they reshaped the traditional salon of the 17th century and adapted it to their social, intellectual, and educational needs (Goodman, *The Republic of Letters*, 53–89, esp. pp. 75–8: quotations from pp. 75–6). See also Introduction n. 85 above.

[81] Friedrich von Gentz was close to the circle of enlightened Jewish women from Berlin. His annotated translation of Edmund Burke's famous attack on the French Revolution (*Reflections on the Revolution in France*, 1790) gained him recognition as a writer. Having initially been an enthusiastic supporter of the French Revolution, he turned into its implacable enemy. On Gentz see *Allgemeine Deutsche Biographie*, viii. 577–93. See also Hertz, *Jewish High Society*, passim.

[82] Sauer (ed.), *Goethe und Österreich*, 167. [83] Ibid. 167–8. [84] Ibid. 167.

[85] A source left by Gentz indicates there was no romantic element in his relationship with Marianne Meyer. In 1803 he wrote in his diary that there was not so much as a shadow of truth in the rumour that was circulating of their impending marriage. Gentz's words are quoted ibid. 375.

is how she chose to present this relationship in her letter to Goethe, and how she most probably saw it. It is interesting that she presents Gentz's perceived indifference towards her as a woman as an advantage. Her words indicate an obstacle often encountered by women who became close to men who could contribute to their intellectual development, especially when the learning took place in the home, in the context of intimate meetings whose tone oscillated between the social and the educational. In such circumstances the possibility arose that the educational purpose of the meetings would be disturbed by an attempt to turn the relationship into a romantic liaison—especially in the case of an attractive, unmarried woman, as Marianne Meyer was at this time.[86] Indeed, Meyer complained to Goethe that many people around her, unable to imagine a relationship of an intellectual or even simply friendly nature between a man and a woman, assumed that there existed a love relationship between her and Gentz and even spread rumours that they were about to marry. 'Of course, few are able to grasp that he likes me, without supposing anything additional—what do they know about the nature of such a relationship . . . ? Here they are not interested in anything but the sensuous.'[87] That was not the case with Gentz, she argued: he was a good friend of hers, and so far as she was aware he had no romantic intentions towards her at all; on the contrary, she insisted, he ignored her sexual identity—a situation she considered ideal for realizing her intellectual aspirations.

It is clear from the instances discussed here that the social and cultural-intellectual aspects of these occasions were interwoven, and that social visits, including the more intimate ones, are to be seen among other things as practices that contributed to the acquisition of knowledge and served to further the women's intellectual development.

THE EXPANDED CIRCLE OF SOCIABILITY

The phenomenon of sociability, as indicated above, was not solely the domain of a narrow elite within Jewish society. Interestingly, when examining Jewish society using a concept of sociability that goes beyond the salons, it becomes clear that participation in informal social gatherings was becoming quite widespread among modernizing German Jews. There are reports of

---

[86] Henriette Herz, as a young married woman, was forced to interrupt her English lessons with a Scottish teacher after learning that he had fallen in love with her: Landsberg (ed.), *Henriette Herz*, 132–3. Many years later, as a widow in 1819, her private tutor Immanuel Bekker became so close to her that he proposed matrimony, an offer she rejected owing to the wide difference in their ages: Bekker, born in 1785, was more than twenty years her junior. See *Letters to Immanuel Bekker*, ed. Putzel, 25, 29–31.   [87] Sauer (ed.), *Goethe und Österreich*, 168.

friendly encounters in private homes in several cities in Germany, involving Jewish men and women participating in various types of gatherings at both Jewish and Christian homes. In Dessau, the Jewish teacher and maskilic author Wolf Dessau often paid visits to Christian Gotthilf Salzmann, a leading pedagogue at the city's famous Philanthropinum school, who had become a close friend and with whom he held intellectual conversations;[88] in Hamburg, Jews including among others the merchant and maskil Moses Wessely and his wife and the scholar Chaim Salomon Pappenheimer attended the famous 'tea table' at the Reimarus household as integral members of this enlightened circle;[89] in Breslau, Jews and non-Jews met at private homes and spent time together in conversation and social games, as is clearly indicated in the letters sent by Rahel Levin during her stay in that city in the summer of 1794.[90] Although these scattered cases certainly do not constitute the rule for Jewish society in general at the time, and do not prove the development of an idyllic relationship between Jews and non-Jews, they do indicate that the culture of visiting, and especially religiously mixed social gatherings, was a more pervasive phenomenon than has been assumed from an exclusive focus on the salons.

Even within the particular context of the enlightened Jewish women in Berlin, it was not only those women known as *salonnières* who were involved. Frequently other members of their families took an active part in hosting both Jewish and non-Jewish guests, in the conversations that took place in domestic settings, and in other social and cultural events. Even though the better-known women seem to have played a prominent, perhaps even dominant, role in these activities, they were far from being the only individuals who participated in the phenomenon of sociability. Thus, although research tends to stress the centrality of a few women who developed relationships with prominent figures in German and European culture, it should

---

[88] Dessau's friendly relationship with Salzmann is described by the latter's biographer, who also briefly reports on an intellectual exchange that took place in one of these visits. See Ausfeld, *Erinnerungen aus Christian Gotthilf Salzmanns Leben*, 67–9.

[89] See the chapter entitled 'Jewish Contacts in Hamburg's Enlightenment Circle: From Strangers to Friends' in Spalding, *Elise Reimarus*, 259–79. Pappenheimer was the son of Salomon Pappenheimer, who made significant contributions to Hebrew literature as a maskil, first and foremost his *Agadat arba kosot* ('Legend of Four Glasses', Berlin, 1790), in addition to several German works he published, mainly on philosophical and religious subjects. On Pappenheimer the son, see Ruiz, 'Auf dem Wege zur Emanzipation'. Cf. Arno Herzig's assertion that in Hamburg, in contrast to Berlin, there were hardly any social contacts between Jews and non-Jews, although they did have business connections. Herzig, 'Die Juden in Hamburg 1780–1860', 62.

[90] Rahel Levin's letters contain considerable evidence of interreligious gatherings in Breslau, among whose participants was her good friend Esther Gad, a native of that city, who at that time was still living there as a married woman. Levin Varnhagen, *Familienbriefe*, 40 and *passim*.

be recognized that such relationships also existed more widely within Jewish circles. Tracking this phenomenon is important in order to understand both the social environment in which these women acted and the modernization of certain sectors of Jewish society in Berlin.

The names of Henriette Herz's siblings, for instance, are hardly ever mentioned in historical accounts, despite the fact that at least some of them were active in the German social and cultural scene. Brenna de Lemos, an unknown figure in research, seems to have been an integral part of the social life in the Herz household. Brenna, who never married, was close to her eldest sister's circle of friends. Like Henriette and their common friend Dorothea Mendelssohn, Brenna de Lemos belonged to the Tugendbund, the 'League of Virtue' established in 1787 by these women and some of their non-Jewish friends, notably Wilhelm and Alexander von Humboldt, as a secret society whose purpose was to work together towards moral self-improvement.[91] The young Ludwig Börne was also well acquainted with Brenna de Lemos, having met her while living at the Herzes' home during his student days in the first years of the nineteenth century. In his letters to Henriette, Börne, still signing himself Louis and before changing his family name from Baruch to Börne, mentioned Brenna's name with affection, referring to her humorously as 'Brenna Raphaele' or 'Raphaele Brenna', because of her painting talents.[92] Other members of Henriette's family, as well as being close to her friends, also led their own social circles. Her sister Johanna, for example, was married to a doctor by the name of Simon Herz and lived in the city of Prenzlau, north of Berlin. The correspondence between Henriette Herz, Friedrich Schleiermacher, and Ehrenfried von Willich contains evidence of the lively social activity that took place in Johanna's house and of the close acquaintance between Henriette's friends and her younger sister—in fact, Henriette and Schleiermacher met Willich for the first time in Johanna's house.[93] Even the mother of the family, Esther de Lemos, is mentioned at least on one occasion as having participated with Henriette in a birthday celebration for one of her daughter's non-Jewish friends.

The participation of members of Rahel Levin's family in an active social life is even more conspicuous and has already been stressed by some scholars.

---

[91] Seibert, 'Der "Tugendbund"'. As member of this society, Brenna de Lemos was part of its correspondence network. See e.g. a reference to her epistolary exchange with Wilhelm von Humboldt: ibid. 59–60.

[92] See e.g. Geiger (ed.), *Briefwechsel des jungen Börne und der Henriette Herz*, 107, 118.

[93] *Bis nächstes Jahr auf Rügen*, ed. Schmitz. Among this sister's friends was a priest by the name of Wolf and his wife Julia. Henriette Herz met this priest at her sister's house, and it would be he who baptized her, years later in 1817.

Barbara Hahn insisted on this point when debunking as a myth the pervasive concept of 'Rahel's attic', showing that, far from having her gatherings in a separate attic room, Rahel Levin received visitors in the family salon, in the presence of her mother and siblings. Her mother, her brothers and sister, her sister-in-law, and even her nieces took an active part in these social gatherings.[94] Nor did the stream of visitors attracted to Chaie Levin's house cease when her daughter Rahel was absent. In the summer of 1795, while Rahel was away in Carlsbad, her mother offered a lunch on Saturday to which she invited, according to Rahel's sister Rose, a man by the name of Sarauton, perhaps a secretary at the finance ministry, together with his wife and his four children; Mrs Eigensatz, a friend of the Levins and the mother of Christel, a singer and actress; and—an interesting guest—Joseph Haltern, a maskil born in Altona in 1739.[95] Most remarkably, the following year Mrs Levin received Count Karl von Finckenstein, a non-Jewish man with whom Rahel had a romantic relationship. Rahel's being away at the Bohemian spas in the summer of 1796 did not prevent the count from visiting the Levin house. 'Yesterday I visited your mother at an early hour', Finckenstein informed Rahel Levin. Chaie Levin welcomed him warmly, either as a friend or the suitor of her daughter: 'she treated me to marrow cake [*Markstorte*][96] and expressly instructed me to write you about it'.[97]

If this friendliness from a Jewish woman of the older generation towards a Christian suitor of her daughter seems surprising, a similar attitude on the part of Rahel's relatives of her own generation is perhaps less so. In one of his letters to Rahel in Teplitz, Finckenstein tells her that he 'went out with Jettchen [Henriette] Mendelssohn to . . . the little sister-in-law'—most

[94] Hahn, *The Jewess Pallas Athena*, 42–55. Cf. Hannah Arendt's references to Rahel Levin's 'garret flat' or 'garret room', a social area which 'stood outside the conventions and customs of even the Jewish salons', which themselves were 'outside of society'. Arendt, *Rahel Varnhagen*, 126–7.

[95] Levin Varnhagen, *Familienbriefe*, 45. According to Varnhagen, as quoted in the notes to this edition of the letters, Haltern arrived in Berlin as a teacher and worked in a commercial office there, also translating poems from German into Hebrew for *Hame'asef*, including some by Mendelssohn. Moshe Pelli's annotated index to *Hame'asef* indicates that Joseph Haltern translated poems and fables by Albrecht von Haller, Carl Wilhelm Ramler, Christian Fürchtegott Gellert, and an anonymous author, all of which were published in 1784, in the first volume of this Hebrew journal: Pelli, *The Gate to Haskalah* (Heb.), 90, 95. Rahel Levin referred to Haltern scornfully—sometimes calling him 'beast'—in the letters she sent during her trip to Silesia, when he accompanied her, her mother, and her sister on the journey. Levin Varnhagen, *Familienbriefe*, 20 ff.

[96] This seems to have been a favourite dish in the Levin family: it is mentioned more than once in the sources, especially in the context of special occasions.

[97] Bruyn (ed.), *Rahels erste Liebe*, 89. Further testimony to Chaie Levin's participation in social life with non-Jews appears in a letter from Fradchen Liebmann, who in the summer of 1795 told Rahel Levin (then on vacation) that she had gone with her uncle and Rahel's sister and mother to a surprise party in honour of the actress Christel Eigensatz (Bosold, 'Friederike Liman', 17).

probably referring to Hendel Levin, later also known as Henriette, who was the sister of Fradchen Liebmann's husband and was married to Rahel's eldest brother Marcus Levin. 'We ate together, Jettchen Mendelssohn, the sister-in-law, your brother, and I'—four people, he added, who held Rahel very dear.[98] A few days later he visited Hendel Levin again and in her house met a mixed group of Jews and Christians that included both women—'Humboldt [most probably Caroline, Wilhelm von Humboldt's wife], Veit, Jettchen Mendelssohn, Fließ, Herz, Marchetti [the actress]'—and men: 'your two brothers, Prince Reuß and Burgsdorf [almost certainly Wilhelm von Burgsdorff]. As you can imagine, we were very merry.'[99]

The participation of Chaie Levin in social events involving both Jews and non-Jews, along with hints of similar behaviour on the part of other parents of Rahel's contemporaries, does not constitute sufficient basis for firm conclusions regarding the degree to which members of the older generation were involved in the process of rapprochement with Christian society. Nonetheless, these testimonies force us to reconsider whether the gap purportedly separating parents and children was in fact so deep as to justify referring to it as a 'generational conflict'.[100] There were undoubtedly crucial differences in attitude and behaviour between parents and children at this historical juncture; but it is important to remember the common points as well as the differences. Moreover, the prominent role in this exchange of Hendel Levin—a Jewish woman who has been accorded no place in the history of the salons but who led an active social life, as hostess as well as guest at Jewish and non-Jewish homes[101]—makes one wonder about the extent of the phenomenon of sociability and points at the many ramifications that remain concealed given the overwhelming focus in historical accounts on her sister-in-law Rahel Levin and a few other women like her.

The extent to which the social relationships of a woman like Rahel Levin were a family affair can be inferred from a letter of complaint she sent her mother on leaving the family home, in which she lamented her miserable situation as a single daughter. With unconcealed bitterness she poured out her heart in bemoaning the humiliating treatment she had received at the hands of her brothers and perhaps even her mother, despite her unconditional devotion to the well-being of the family. Conscious of the central role she played in the household as the one who assembled around her the lively social

---

[98] Bruyn (ed.), *Rachels erste Liebe*, 90. Marcus Levin and his younger brother Moritz would change their surname to Robert-Tornow.

[99] Ibid. 91.   [100] Lowenstein, *The Berlin Jewish Community*, 111–12.

[101] For further testimony to the social activity of Hendel Levin (dubbed Hans in some of the letters), see Bosold, 'Friederike Liman', 30, 50, 54.

and cultural life from which all her relatives benefited, she chastised her mother: 'Which of your two daughters has been helpful to the family up until now, eager to be useful, which one was turned to in need, asked for advice, every single person's friend; and which one succeeded in making life pleasant for your children through convivial joys—the married, protected, praised one, or the unhappy one?'[102] Rahel Levin was thus conscious of her special position as the centre of attraction and as connecting link between family and friends, but at the same time she identified her social activity to a large extent as an important contribution to a common family undertaking.

Not only the generational but also the gender gap appears to be less profound than is commonly assumed. The gender distinction widely believed to exist between Jewish women and their husbands, or in the respective participation of Jewish women and men in social and cultural life, does not always stand up in the face of the evidence, at least in the context of Berlin in the 1790s. Social and cultural integration with non-Jewish society was an enterprise shared by members of both sexes to an extent greater than is usually indicated in historical descriptions, which tend to isolate women's field of activity from that of men. The influential studies of Jacob Katz, for instance, stressed the gender difference in the social field, and claimed that this derived from the contrasting types of education given to Jewish boys and girls. Drawing on Wolf Davidson's assertion from 1792 that 'education is the reason why among the Jews the female sex is more beautiful and well-formed than the male, and beside the ugliest, dirtiest boys stands the daintiest, most beautiful girl', Katz explained that whereas boys and young men received an almost exclusively religious education, the secular instruction given to girls and young women made it easier for them to acquire the tools necessary for social integration.[103] Women, he said, were 'the first to learn the language of their neighbors, to acquire a familiarity with foreign languages and literature. They were also the ones to acquire the social graces that enabled them to move easily in a society not limited to Jews', whereas 'men found it more difficult' to do so. At the time of the literary salons, Katz explained, 'some of these men, whose wives were the life and soul of social gatherings, were too embarrassed to put in an appearance'.[104]

---

[102] Letter of 27 Feb, 1809 (Levin Varnhagen, *Familienbriefe*, 198).

[103] The quotation, taken from Davidson's booklet *Ein Wörtchen über Juden. Veranlasst durch die von Herrn Friedländer herausgegebenen Aktenstücke* (1792), appears (in German) in Katz, *Out of the Ghetto*, 236 n. 11.

[104] Katz, *Out of the Ghetto*, 84. An example frequently given in this context is Simon Veit, Dorothea Mendelssohn's purportedly unacculturated husband. Cf. Badt-Strauß, 'Moses Mendelssohns Tochter Dorothea'. Badt-Strauß rejects the image of Simon Veit as an uneducated, indifferent, average

However, this analysis is not borne out by the sources available. Beyond the obvious case of Marcus Herz mentioned above, Isaac Beer Fließ, for instance, is not included in the list of men involved in salon life in Berlin, although his wife is acknowledged as an active participant;[105] and yet in fact he was an acculturated physician, who participated vigorously in the social and cultural life of Berlin and gained public recognition as a talented composer and musician.[106] In 1798 the very Wolf Davidson quoted above on the effects of Jewish education, himself a physician and writer in Berlin, drew up a list of outstanding Jews in Prussia who contributed to German cultural life: on it was a 'Dr Flies the younger', who was none other than Isaac Beer Fließ. According to Davidson, this man had 'a great musical talent and has already delivered various works to the public'.[107] Some years before that, in the summer of 1795, Fradchen Liebmann reported on the arrival of 'Fließ' in Freienwalde, and from the information she gives it is clear that he was visiting the spa town as a musician: over the course of his two-day stay he performed one of his musical compositions for a noble family on vacation, who were very impressed by both content and rendition.[108]

Moreover, the home of Isaac and Hitzel Fließ, not mentioned as one of the 'Jewish salons of Berlin' in the relevant literature, features in the letters of the enlightened Jewish women as an open house and a frequent meeting place in the 1790s, and Isaac Beer Fließ is portrayed as a host no less than his wife. Fradchen Liebmann, a good friend of Hitzel, writes about gatherings of Jews and Christians at the Fließ home, before the couple divorced towards the end of the century. On one occasion in the summer of 1795, for instance, she notes that those present included, along with the hosting couple and

Jew, claiming rather that he clearly had philosophical interests. See also Renate Heuer's brief discussion in 'Mutter in Israel—Muse der Romantik', 40–1. According to testimonies cited by Heuer, Veit participated in Moses Mendelssohn's morning study hours, studied Maimonides' classic medieval philosophical work *Guide of the Perplexed*, and compared this work with its Latin translation, indicating that he possessed, or acquired, some knowledge of this language. He also visited prominent German intellectuals, as mentioned in Ch. 1 above.

[105] Deborah Hertz indicates that 'eight of the sixty-nine salon men were Jewish' (Hertz, *Jewish High Society*, 147 ff.), but does not include Fließ in this list. Fließ's wife, Hitzel, is mentioned by Hertz under different names as one of the *salonnières* (see e.g. ibid. 104, 206–7). A similar omission occurs in Petra Wilhelmy's *Der Berliner Salon*.

[106] Isaac Beer Fließ, a scion of one of the wealthiest and most famous families of the Berlin Jewish community, should not be confused with his uncle Joseph Fließ, who was also a physician. Isaac Beer Fließ converted to Christianity before 1802 and changed his name to Carl Eduard Fließ.

[107] Davidson, *Ueber die bürgerliche Verbesserung der Juden*, 108. Another work from the same year, attributed to Davidson, also mentions the 'musical talent' of Dr Fließ, indicating that he 'has now composed an operetta, supposedly quite excellent, which is what is to be expected after his previous works' ([Davidson,] *Briefe über Berlin*, 90).   [108] Bosold, 'Friederike Liman', 28.

Social Gatherings in Private Homes 213

Liebmann herself, the singer Maria Marchetti and a guest by the name of Wessely. This last was the Jewish musician Carl Bernhard Wessely, probably a nephew of the famous maskil Hartwig Wessely;[109] in his youth he had attended Moses Mendelssohn's *Morgenstunden* ('morning study hours'), along with the philosopher's son Joseph (Wessely's schoolmate) and his son-in-law Simon Veit, and at this time was serving as music director of the Berlin National Theatre.[110] Rahel Levin, too, hinted at the visit of a Christian guest to the Fließ house: with enormous excitement she told David Veit in January 1794 about the imminent arrival of a famous composer she admired, Johann Friedrich Reichardt, whom she saw on his way there as she was leaving the house of Mrs de Lemos (Henriette Herz's mother) together with Euchel.[111]

Isaac Beer Fließ not only received Jewish and Christian guests in his house; he also attended other social events in which some of the Jewish women took part along with non-Jews, as for example in the summer of 1795, when he participated in a festive dinner (*souper*) organized by Liebmann at Charlottenburg. He was accompanied that evening, among others, by Wessely and a man by the name of Schack, most probably Otto von Schack, the Prussian officer with whom Liebmann spent time in Freienwalde.[112] On the basis of even these few testimonies it may be deduced that Isaac Beer Fließ was not cut off from the social and cultural activity in which his wife and other Jewish women participated. At least in the case of this couple it is inap-

---

[109] The meeting at the Fließ home is reported ibid. 13. Wessely, a Jew who converted at the end of the 18th century, was among other things a leading figure in the Berlin Gesellschaft der Freunde. Wolf Davidson stressed his prominence in the contemporary world of music as follows: 'The merits of Director [*Capellmeister*] Wessely as a musician and composer are known, and although the late cantor Rolle claimed that from a mathematical point of view it is impossible that a Jew should be able to compose, Director Wessely proved the opposite. He converted, but still as a Jew he was music director [*Musikdirector*] and, after that, director [*Capellmeister*]' (Davidson, *Ueber die bürgerliche Verbesserung der Juden*, 108). Wessely was apparently the nephew of Hartwig Wessely. According to Alain Ruiz, he was educated, among other places, at the Philanthropinum school in Dessau. He was appointed by Prince Heinrich of Prussia as music director in Rheinsberg (Ruiz, 'Auf dem Wege zur Emanzipation', 199). Finscher (ed.), *Die Musik in Geschichte und Gegenwart*, 822, states that this musician was the son of Aaron Behrend Wessely, the owner of a velvet and silk factory, who was born around 1740. Cf. Spalding, *Elise Reimarus*, 273 n. 49, who affirms that this musician was the son of Hartwig Wessely and his wife Sara. Carl Bernhard Wessely is also mentioned as a friend in the correspondence between Rahel Levin and David Veit.

[110] Wessely's attendance at Mendelssohn's 'morning study hours' is mentioned in Mendelssohn, *Gesammelte Schriften*, i. 32. See also Heuer, 'Mutter in Israel—Muse der Romantik', 40. These study sessions that Moses Mendelssohn dedicated to instructing this small group of students gave their name to his last philosophical work, called *Morgenstunden, oder Vorlesungen über das Daseyn Gottes* ('Morning Hours, or Lectures about God's Existence'), first published in 1785, shortly before his death in January 1786.

[111] *Briefwechsel zwischen Rahel und David Veit*, i. 107–8.   [112] Bosold, 'Friederike Liman', 12–13.

propriate to speak of a clear gender difference according to which women were the agents of social assimilation, while their husbands 'were too busy with the economic side of the matter', as Hannah Arendt suggested.[113]

Other examples caution against underestimating the extent of social and cultural integration among Jewish men in comparison to that of Jewish women. Abraham Nathan Liebmann (later Carl August Liman), for instance, mixed with his wife Fradchen's friends. We hear that he went with her to visit the singer Maria Marchetti, and then the actress Friederike Unzelmann, 'of his own will'. He also 'came one evening when I was having tea there with Hans [Hendel Levin]. He spoke at length with Q[uast], who thinks highly of him.'[114] Fradchen's brother, too, accompanied her to some of her social visits and cultural entertainments. As she wrote in one of her letters to Rahel Levin: 'I already was at Charlottenburg, all alone with my brother, this week, in order to listen to the rehearsal. I had made an appointment with Mrs Marchetti to meet her there, because she already had plans with other company, and we indeed were together during the rehearsal.' Thus Fradchen Liebmann introduced her brother to her friend the singer and the latter's friends.[115] Joseph and Abraham Mendelssohn are known to have maintained close contact with German scientists and thinkers, who frequently visited their house.[116] And, as noted above, Rahel Levin's brothers, not only the author Ludwig Robert but also Marcus and the youngest, Moritz, mixed with the company that gathered around their sister.

In short, Jewish men's participation in social gatherings similar to those attended by women was perhaps more extensive than has hitherto been believed. To be sure, it should be kept in mind that, as mentioned at the beginning of this chapter, men had other institutionalized settings for social interaction and therefore the significance of social gatherings in private homes was different for them than for Jewish women, to whom these occasions were central as a means of empowerment and a way into cultural life. Some of the enlightened Jewish men mentioned in this chapter—Bing, Wessely, Fließ, and Abraham and Joseph Mendelssohn—were among the founders of the Society of Friends, an institutionalized grouping that offered

---

[113] Arendt, *Rahel Varnhagen*, 108. Arendt was referring to the case of Austria but also, by extension, to the Berlin salons. Deborah Hertz affirms that the 'new social universe' of contact with non-Jews and their culture, in which Jewish women from Berlin were involved, 'was closed to most Jewish men' (Hertz, 'Seductive Conversion in Berlin', 70).

[114] Bosold, 'Friederike Liman', 38. According to Bosold, Q. stands for Otto von Quast, a Prussian officer (*Rittmeister*).

[115] Ibid. 13.   [116] According to *Bankiers, Künstler und Gelehrte*, ed. Gilbert, pp. xxx–xxxii.

a setting for socializing but excluded women.[117] It is ironic that the same men sought also to maintain social interaction with enlightened Jewish women and with members of non-Jewish society, which they were able to do to a significant extent by participating in social events in the domestic context.

[117] All the names mentioned here appear in the first list of members of the Gesellschaft der Freunde (Lesser, *Chronik der Gesellschaft der Freunde*, 17–21). 'The Musical Director B. Wessely', for instance, was as an active figure in the institution's first years. He was appointed to the committee as adviser at the time it was founded (ibid. 12), and even gave a speech after the statutes of the society were ratified by its members, at the general assembly that took place in August 1792 (ibid. 16).

SIX

FEMALE EMANCIPATION

ONE OF THE BEST-KNOWN outcomes of the age of Enlightenment for Jews in central and western Europe was the public debate that developed on the issue of civil emancipation towards the end of the eighteenth century. Seemingly contradictory ideas about the Jews that had gained currency following the religious wars of the seventeenth century determined the framework in which their situation was analysed and in which the granting of civil rights was demanded. On the one hand, the principle of tolerance required that an effort be made to improve the Jews' civil status; on the other hand, the prevalent unfavourable image of the Jews as a purportedly morally defective nation required that this effort be matched by steps to bring about their moral regeneration. This approach was supported by the Prussian bureaucrat Christian Wilhelm von Dohm in his famous and influential book of 1781, *Über die bürgerliche Verbesserung der Juden*. This treatise prompted a public discussion on the question of Jewish emancipation in the German lands (and beyond), and shaped the debate on the subject over the next hundred years.[1]

Among those who joined the debate over the civil status of the Jews in the wake of Dohm's book were not only German intellectuals and bureaucrats but also the maskilim.[2] From the early 1780s, and especially after the death of Frederick the Great in 1786, when hopes of achieving civil rights intensified with the crowning of a new Prussian king, the maskilim drafted petitions and published reform proposals addressed on the one hand to fellow Jews and on the other hand to policy-makers. To their Jewish brethren they issued exhortations to prepare themselves for emancipation by abandoning what they perceived as misguided customs and prejudices and improving their moral

---

[1] Sorkin, *The Transformation of German Jewry*, 21–33; Liberles, 'Dohm's Treatise on the Jews'. The numerous responses collected in the second volume of Dohm's book, published in 1783, give evidence of the debate that ensued immediately after his proposal of 1781.

[2] Jewish intervention in the debate started before the publication of the treatise by Dohm, who in fact was drawn to this issue by his friend Moses Mendelssohn. See Heinrich, '"Juden müssen sich also gar nicht einmischen..."'.

character. From Christian rulers they asked for the exercise of the enlightened ideals of tolerance and equality in recognition of Jews as individuals worthy of the same rights and obligations as Christian citizens, and in redress of the historical injustice which had consigned the Jews to their current exclusion from civil and political society.

While enlightened Jewish men worked at formulating public calls for improvements in the Jews' legal status, a different kind of emancipatory activity was taking place among a group of Jewish women in Prussia. Their pursuits, less public in nature than those of Jewish men, concerned their situation as women more than their status as Jews. Certainly, as Jews, they were directly concerned in the efforts being made to achieve Jewish emancipation, and this issue engaged them to some extent. But their proximity to Enlightenment discourse led them to ponder with even more intensity their condition as members of another group equally deprived of rights and status, namely as women, and about the incongruence between the progressive ideas being voiced in the public discourse of the time and the actual living conditions of members of their sex.

As women, they could expect no significant improvement in their personal condition to result from the granting of rights to Jews. Reform proposals submitted to the government by the maskilim allegedly represented the Jews as a whole; in fact, they embodied first and foremost the interests of a specific group among the Jews, and more precisely among Jewish men. Plans for emancipation paid no regard to the interests of whole sectors of Jewry, such as Orthodox and poor Jews, many of whom disagreed with some of the central provisions in these proposals, such as the abolition of communal authority in religious matters and the revocation of collective responsibility for the payment of taxes imposed by the authorities on the Jews.[3] For another group—well-to-do Jewish women such as those discussed in this study—the stated goals of emancipation did not necessarily imply a worsening of their situation, as may have been the case for the groups just mentioned, but neither did they promise a significant improvement, for the demands expressed

---

[3] Lowenstein, *The Berlin Jewish Community*, 80–1. For a critical examination of Jewish emancipation, exposing not only the advantages but also the disadvantages involved in this process, see Baron, 'Newer Approaches to Jewish Emancipation'. The tension between Jews of different social classes and outlooks surrounding the campaign for emancipation is reflected in a letter of complaint sent by the rabbi and maskil Salomon Pappenheimer to the government official Friedrich Albert Zimmermann in Breslau in 1789 or 1790: speaking in the name of 'common Jews' (*gemeiner Juden*), Pappenheimer sought to defend the interests of this group in the efforts to achieve emancipation, rejecting the egoistic demands of 'proud Breslau and Berlin Jews', who had set their sights on becoming eligible for offices and prestigious positions (Freudenthal, 'Die ersten Emancipationsbestrebungen der Juden in Breslau', 423 n. 1).

clearly male interests and aspirations, with little direct relevance to the personal lives of these women. The removal of occupational restrictions, for instance—a central measure advocated by most proponents of Jewish emancipation, who perceived these impediments as a main obstacle preventing Jews from becoming integrated in the polity—would influence them indirectly by affecting their fathers, husbands, brothers, and sons, but would not bring about any direct change in the lives of Jewish women, who in any case would still be subject to most such restrictions not as Jews but as women. Little wonder, then, that the issue of their status and their situation as women occupied them in great measure, and in many cases much more than the issue of Jewish emancipation.

To speak of female emancipatory activity among these Jewish women is not to imply that they made demands similar to those voiced by supporters of Jewish emancipation, for instance that women be granted equal civil rights or made eligible for membership of state institutions. Just like most of their contemporaries who criticized the subordination of women in society and struggled to improve their status, enlightened Jewish women did not demand political rights for members of their sex. To be sure, the question of women's political emancipation was not absent from the public agenda in Europe at the end of the eighteenth century. It was certainly present in France, where it gained practical significance in the wake of the French Revolution. As early as 1790 the renowned French intellectual the Marquis de Condorcet published an essay, *Sur l'admission des femmes au droit de cité* ('On the Admission of Women to the Rights of Citizenship'), in which he condemned the exclusion of women from the rights of citizenship as an act of tyranny, and accused the enlightened philosophers and legislators who drafted the 1789 Declaration of the Rights of Man and of the Citizen of violating the principle of equality of rights by depriving half of humankind of their rights.[4] One of the most explicit demands for civil equality composed at the time was the *Déclaration des droits de la femme et de la citoyenne* ('Declaration of the Rights of Woman and the Female Citizen') published in 1791 by Olympe de Gouges,[5] a revolutionary author of plays and political pamphlets who paid with her life for publicly defying the political, social, and cultural norms of the day.[6] Basing her argument on the natural rights discourse, she protested against the exclusion

---

[4] Bock, *Women in European History*, 41–2; Clinton, 'Femme et Philosophe', 295–8.

[5] For an English translation of this pamphlet, see Kramnick (ed.), *The Portable Enlightenment Reader*, 609–18.

[6] Condemned as a counterrevolutionary and charged with treason, de Gouges was executed in 1793. On her political activity, see Scott, *Only Paradoxes to Offer*, 19–56. For a discussion of her writings, see Diamond, 'The Revolutionary Rhetoric of Olympe de Gouges'.

of the female sex from the 1789 Declaration of the Rights of Man and of the Citizen, a text which despite its universalist claims interpreted 'man' as 'male'. Aspiring to redefine 'man' as 'human' and thereby to include women as equally human beings, she stressed the important role of women—as mothers, daughters, and sisters—as representatives of the nation, and advocated their full civil and legal equality.

Women's emancipatory claims, fuelled by the French Revolution, were raised not only in France but around the continent. Voices expressing similar ideas could be heard in England as well (Mary Wollstonecraft's famous 1792 defence of women's rights has already been mentioned) and even in Germany, albeit less intensively than in France.[7] The most prominent German contribution to the subject—in fact, one of the few contemporary works in Germany to defend the granting of political rights to women—was *Über die bürgerliche Verbesserung der Weiber* (*On Improving the Status of Women*), written in 1792 by Theodor Gottlieb von Hippel, a high-ranking Prussian bureaucrat and a writer.[8] Claiming that the exclusion of women from public life was the result of a regrettable historical process, which had led human society far away from its natural state, where women had enjoyed the same rights as men, he insisted repeatedly that women should be allowed a voice in matters of state. True, he conceded, women might not become good citizens all at once: in France, he noted, women would 'throw themselves into the affairs of state ... without any preparation', leading to adverse results.[9] This could be avoided by ensuring that their entrance into public life was gradual and accompanied by proper instruction. Women, after all, he argued, did possess the traits necessary for good citizenry 'and it is but a matter of educating them to this role!'[10] Hippel recognized the existence of sexual differences, but denied that this justified women's subjection to men or their alienation from state matters, and therefore he pleaded for immediate changes.

Notwithstanding these notable examples, at the end of the eighteenth century and the beginning of the nineteenth the main efforts to challenge male hegemony and improve women's position in society were not channelled towards achieving political equality, considered a utopian goal especially in

---

[7] On the widespread repercussions of the controversy over women's rights during the French Revolution in other European lands, see Offen, *European Feminisms*, 68–76.

[8] An English translation of the book was published by Timothy F. Sellner in 1979: Hippel, *On Improving the Status of Women*. A clear parallel exists between Hippel's book on women and Dohm's treatise on the Jews, from the almost identical titles to a similar analysis of the situation of these two underprivileged groups. See Carlebach, 'The Forgotten Connection'; Frevert, 'Die Innenwelt der Außenwelt'; Volkov, *The Magic Circle* (Heb.), 130–40.

[9] Hippel, *On Improving the Status of Women*, 160.   [10] Ibid. 124.

the repressive climate of the counter-revolution.[11] Women with a feminist awareness chose to act in areas where more practical and immediate achievements could be envisaged, and this was the approach adopted by enlightened Jewish women. Like many other contemporary women with feminist concerns, they saw the broadening of their educational horizons in emancipatory terms, as a precondition for improving their overall position, and as we have seen they made determined attempts to extend their knowledge, at the same time as criticizing attempts to exclude them from intellectual life.[12] Another area in which these Jewish women struggled for emancipation, having experienced personally the full force of male privilege and domination, was their private life. As we shall see in this chapter, their efforts in this area make clear their aspiration to attain personal autonomy, freedom, and independence, and their wish to see implemented the right of every individual to live a life filled with happiness—a relatively new ideal. Equipped with the critical spirit of the Enlightenment, which subjected every aspect of society to thorough examination, they turned their gaze on the patriarchal institution of marriage as a prominent focus of inequality and grappled with questions related to marriage, divorce, and independence. In some of their letters they present marriage as practised in their day as an institution that limited their natural rights, amounting to a form of slavery which deprived them of liberty and was frequently forced upon them against their will. Some of the women made efforts to free themselves from this imprisoning framework, or to avoid altogether falling into its chains. Even if in the end they did not reject marriage out of hand, the fact that they pondered on and debated the nature of this institution—instead of complying unquestioningly with its established forms and imperatives—raised their consciousness of the possibility of undermining settled norms and of bringing about radical change.

---

[11] As Karen Offen argues, 'The backlash that developed in Europe against women's emancipation in the wake of the revolutionary repression was severe, and its consequences would endure for decades' (Offen, *European Feminisms*, 75).

[12] In the second half of the 19th century, the main efforts of the women's movement in Germany were still devoted to questions of education and occupation. As the leader of the feminist movement in Germany, Louise Otto-Peters, pointed out in 1876, the demand for political rights came at the bottom of the list (Frevert, 'Die Innenwelt der Außenwelt', 85). Even then, given the political situation in Germany, where the government was much less representative than in England and the United States, demands for female suffrage were far less likely to succeed, and feminists gave primacy to social and economic problems. Kaplan, *The Jewish Feminist Movement in Germany*, 63. Feminist texts written by maskilot in eastern Europe also focused their demands on education, occupational training, and economic independence for Jewish women. Cohen and Feiner (eds.), *Voice of a Hebrew Maiden* (Heb.), esp. pp. 84–92.

FROM 'SLAVERY' TO 'REDEMPTION': MARRIAGE, DIVORCE, INDEPENDENCE

As the historian Steven Lowenstein asserts in his comprehensive study *The Berlin Jewish Community: Enlightenment, Family, and Crisis, 1770–1830*, during the last decades of the eighteenth century and the first decades of the nineteenth the Berlin Jewish community experienced a severe crisis. The process of Jewish modernization, having started calmly, soon took a radical turn, leading to rapid changes that deeply affected various aspects of life, one of the most prominent of which was the institution of the family. Drawing on the impressive quantity of statistical data he compiled about Berlin Jewry, Lowenstein shows that the period between the late 1780s and 1806 witnessed a sharply rising number of divorces among Jewish couples, extra-marital births, and romantic liaisons between Jewish and Christian women and men. These increases, to levels unprecedented in previous times, were the result of the growing acculturation of the current generations of Jews, who went so far as to abandon traditional family values and adopt instead the more permissive sexual mores of the surrounding culture.[13]

The *get* or bill of divorce handed by Michael Joseph (aka Jechiel) Fränkel to his wife Freude, née Meyer, in 1796 after nine years of marriage seems to represent just one more case among all the data amassed by Lowenstein to demonstrate the increased rate of divorce during this period of crisis in Berlin Jewry. The case of the Fränkels would also seem to exemplify the divorce model which, according to another scholar, Deborah Hertz, characterized a certain group of Jewish women in Berlin at the turn of the eighteenth and nineteenth centuries. In her book *Jewish High Society in Old Regime Berlin* (and in other essays) Hertz pointed at the conspicuous connection between the decision of many of these women, whom she describes as the Berlin Jewish *salonnières*, to dissolve their marriages, and their religious conversion and marriage to non-Jews. Hertz explained the convergence of divorce, baptism, and marriage to non-Jews (usually members of the nobility) by reference to the aspiration of these women to climb the social ladder and to assimilate into Christian high society. To be sure, Hertz acknowledged the

---

[13] Lowenstein, *The Berlin Jewish Community*, esp. pp. 3–9, 111–19. It is interesting to note that in the second half of the 18th century the Sephardi Jewish community in Amsterdam also experienced a grave crisis in the institution of the family and a weakening of traditional sexual mores, as Yosef Kaplan has convincingly demonstrated in a study largely based on communal records: Kaplan, *An Alternative Path to Modernity*, 280–300.

element of protest against arranged marriages in divorce, but maintained that opportunistic considerations played the dominant role.[14]

The bare facts of the case of Freude Meyer do indeed conform to the pattern suggested by Hertz. Shortly after divorcing her Jewish husband, Meyer converted to Christianity and married an Austrian businessman, entering European high society with the honourable title of Frau von Pobeheim. Thus her divorce seems to have served as a prelude to her almost immediate marriage to a Christian nobleman, upon conversion.[15] However, a closer examination of the case, and especially of the events leading to the divorce, using personal sources that have survived to this day, enables us to offer a more nuanced interpretation of Freude Meyer's decision to separate from her Jewish husband and reveals it as more than a mere attempt to assimilate or a desperate act in the effort to climb the social ladder. References to the divorce of the Fränkels—as well as that of a more famous couple, Dorothea Mendelssohn and Simon Veit—in personal letters from the 1790s offer an inside view of the well-known phenomena of separation and divorce and cast the decisions of these women in a different light as part of a protracted process of liberation from what they perceived as the yoke of their spouses and other family members—as an act of independence in an effort to shape their own future.

Moreover, such personal testimonies also offer the opportunity to examine the quantitative data provided by social history in the light of individual cases. While no detailed information exists for most members of the community who feature in Lowenstein's collection of data, these extant sources provide a rare chance to look beyond the statistics and study the motivations and thoughts that propelled some individuals into action. Needless to say, no general conclusions may be reached on the basis of these isolated cases: it is clear that the numerous Berlin Jewish women involved in divorces in those decades came from various socio-cultural backgrounds, and their acts may have been prompted by any of a wide range of different motivations. Nevertheless, there remains a possibility that the thoughts and actions of the few women for whom we do possess more detailed information may illuminate the cultural background of at least some of the women at that period,

---

[14] Hertz, *Jewish High Society*. Hertz also published numerous essays on this subject. See Introduction n. 84 above.

[15] As Deborah Hertz indicates, actual intermarriages did not exist at the time. Until 1874 there was no civil marriage in Prussia, so that in order to marry both partners had to belong to the same religion. However, since contemporaries saw marriages with Jews who had converted to Christianity as intermarriages, they may justifiably be so labelled (Hertz, *Jewish High Society*, 208–9).

and it is therefore worth paying attention to the significance they attached to their own actions.[16]

One individual case depicted in some detail in the sources is, as noted above, that of Freude and Michael Joseph Fränkel, which moved numerous friends and relatives to comment. Freude Meyer was married in 1787 in her native city of Strelitz to a man her family had chosen for her: a wealthy jewellery merchant from Berlin, more than twenty years her senior, and more than twice her age at the time of their wedding.[17] If the couple enjoyed any happiness, it did not last long. From 1790, just three years after the wedding and six years before the couple's final divorce, hints start to emerge in the sources indicating the precarious state of their marriage and Freude's wish to escape from it. In a letter to Karl Gustav von Brinckmann in November that year, Dorothea Mendelssohn, both a friend and a relative of Freude's,[18] mentioned the 'uncomfortable domestic situation' in which both she and her friend found themselves. Dorothea even alluded to the resolution of both women to take steps to end their marriages.[19] As time went by the relationship between the Fränkels worsened, as is apparent from another letter from Dorothea to Brinckmann a year later: 'I am with Mrs. Fränkel very often; she is an amiable, sensitive creature! One must be Fränkel in order to have the audacity to mistreat this dear woman.'[20] It is hard to determine what precisely was meant by 'mistreat' (*mißhandeln*)—whether it was physical injury or emotional abuse at the hands of her husband. In any case, in 1793 Freude left her home in Berlin and moved back to her parents' house in Strelitz, intent upon separating from her husband for good.[21] In the summer of 1795, however, she was back in Berlin, having returned to Fränkel's house apparently not out of love or desire but lack of choice. Her return raised many eyebrows among her acquaintances, aware as they were of her distaste for her husband. They tried to find a logical explanation for her acts. Henriette Herz, who was

---

[16] On the issue of conversion, Deborah Hertz insists on a similar point: 'Because we know more about their lives than we do about the anonymous converts and those who married out, study of the salon women can give insight into the motivations of their more obscure contemporaries' (Hertz, 'Seductive Conversion in Berlin', 70).

[17] As noted above, Michael Joseph Fränkel was born in 1746 (Jacobson, *Jüdische Trauungen*, 305); Freude Meyer in 1767 (Bosold, 'Friederike Liman', 282). According to Jacobson, *Jüdische Trauungen*, 305, they were married in June 1787.

[18] Freude was the sister of Mendel Meyer, Recha Mendelssohn's husband, and of Henriette (Hinde), who would marry Joseph Mendelssohn in 1793. In other words, Freude was the sister-in-law of two of Dorothea's siblings.

[19] *Briefe von und an Friedrich und Dorothea Schlegel*, ed. Behler, xxiii. 9.   [20] Ibid. 36.

[21] On the basis of the (as yet unpublished) correspondence between Freude Meyer and Rahel Levin, Bosold points out that Freude left Berlin that year. Dorothea Mendelssohn reports the same in a letter from August 1793: ibid. 112.

involved in this affair as a friend of Freude's, attributed her return to financial constraints. As Fradchen Liebmann reported in June 1795 after meeting Herz in a social visit at the house of her sister-in-law, Esther Liebmann: 'She [Henriette Herz] claims that F[ränkel, i.e. Freude Meyer] certainly does it out of distress and of course has no money.'[22] In any event, the reconciliation did not last long and in 1796 the couple were divorced.

In the light of these details, Freude Meyer's decision to seek a divorce appears as the culmination of a process throughout which she tried to stand up for what she perceived as her right to a life of happiness and satisfaction. For years she had made tentative attempts to end her relationship with her Jewish husband, but these remained fruitless, in great part owing to lack of support. Her close relatives were utterly unable to comprehend her motivations for transgressing social norms. Rather than backing her up, for instance by offering her the financial support she needed to proceed with separation, they tried to deter her from the attempt by making her feel guilty. Unable to grasp what she 'lack[ed] in order to be happy', they saw her aspirations as no more than 'chimeras' put into her head by her non-Jewish friends.[23] As she swam against the tide, the sisterly solidarity shown by her close group of friends was crucial.[24] These female friends, especially the Jewish ones, identified with the distress she suffered in a forced marriage to an older man; they understood her aspiration to bring about a radical change in her life and supported her as much as possible.[25] Thus, while Freude Meyer's father claimed that his daughter only 'imagines now that she cannot live happily with her good, respectable husband', her friends, who shared with her a common world-view, grasped 'diverse things' in a way that 'shallow people'—that is, her own relatives—found it difficult to understand.[26]

Like Freude Meyer, Dorothea Mendelssohn was married for some years to the man her father had chosen for her, the Jewish merchant and banker Simon Veit. Like Meyer, Mendelssohn wished to put an end to an unwanted union and bring about a change in her life that would free her from the feel-

---

[22] Bosold, 'Friederike Liman', 8.

[23] These comments were made by Dorothea Mendelssohn to Karl Gustav von Brinkmann (*Briefe von und an Friedrich und Dorothea Schlegel*, ed. Behler, xxiii. 9).

[24] On the central function of female friendship in Germany at that time, as expressed in women's correspondence, and on the network of mutual support that grew out of this friendship, see the chapter dedicated to 'women's friendship in letters' in French, *German Women as Letter Writers*, 75–111.

[25] See e.g. Dorothea Mendelssohn's letter to Rahel Levin of 4 Aug. 1793, *Briefe von und an Friedrich und Dorothea Schlegel*, ed. Behler, xxiii. 112–14. In this letter, Dorothea criticizes another woman, 'Mrs. Ephraim', who not only failed to support Freude Fränkel née Meyer in the divorce process but even did her harm by making derogatory comments about her to her husband. Dorothea's words lament the disloyalty of a woman towards her sisters. [26] Ibid. 9–10.

ings of misery and suffocation that overwhelmed her in her marriage. Unlike Freude Meyer's divorce, however, the story of Dorothea attracted considerable attention in Jewish historiography, undoubtedly because she was the daughter of the famous Moses Mendelssohn.[27] Here again, sources from the decade preceding Dorothea Mendelssohn's acquaintance with Schlegel, who was to become her second husband, throw new light on the divorce of the Veits. As we shall see, the metaphors used by Dorothea Mendelssohn to describe her condition in that decade and her separation from Simon Veit indicate that the steps she took were prompted by a sense that her life had taken a course she did not want and were seen by her as an act of liberation. The acquaintance with Schlegel appears as a catalyst in a long process stretching over ten years at least, not as the factor which set the process in motion (as is often claimed).

Letters written throughout the last decade of the eighteenth century indicate that there was no direct link between Dorothea's acquaintance with Friedrich Schlegel and her fundamental decision to divorce Simon Veit. In fact, she began planning the separation as early as 1790, although she implemented it only in 1799, when she felt she had reached a decisive crossroads. A clear indication of the tensions in the couple's relationship almost a decade before their divorce may be gained from a letter of rebuke that Dorothea Mendelssohn sent to her friend Brinckmann in 1790, when en route to his native Sweden he stayed as a guest with Freude Meyer's and Dorothea Mendelssohn's relatives in Strelitz. This letter (the same one quoted above, in which Dorothea speaks of her and Freude's 'uncomfortable domestic situation') reveals that against her insistent pleading Brinckmann had spoken openly to Freude's father and Dorothea's sister Recha about the dissatisfaction of both women in Berlin with their married lives—a breach of confidence which, according to Dorothea Mendelssohn, could severely harm both women's position in the family and their plans for the future.[28] In principle, both women had by this point already resolved to end their marriages; but Dorothea believed a woman who sought a divorce had to think things out in advance, lest she emerge weakened from the battle. Over-hasty action, she explained to Rahel Levin in 1793, could be harmful. Thus she deplored the

---

[27] Discussing the case of Dorothea in his book on Moses Mendelssohn and his family, Adolph Kohut characterized as 'repulsive' the celerity with which 'a mother of four children [in fact, only two were alive], the daughter of the morally strict Moses Mendelssohn, the wife of one of the noblest men in Berlin', threw herself into the hands of the 'frivolous and immoral Friedrich Schlegel'. This step might be explained psychologically, he claimed, but could by no means be pardoned (Kohut, *Moses Mendelssohn und seine Familie*, 85).

[28] *Briefe von und an Friedrich und Dorothea Schlegel*, ed. Behler, xxiii. 9.

thoughtlessness exhibited by Freude Meyer in first leaving her husband's home without properly preparing the ground for her departure, thus taking a step which proved mistaken and prevented her at that stage from proceeding with the separation:

> She has been acting very carelessly of late and has thereby much complicated the step she now wants to take. I really thought she had by now prepared herself in the best way possible, but everything is in such disorder, as if the matter had very much surprised her. This disorder in everything she leaves behind not only damages her reputation, but, what is worse, it now causes her husband to put severe constraints on her, and that is quite disastrous for her.[29]

Evoking the main political event of the era, Dorothea Mendelssohn compared Freude Meyer's careless attitude and its unfavourable results with the thoughtlessness with which the French nation had proceeded with its revolution and its adverse outcome: 'She did it like the nation that, also out of recklessness, sacrificed to the graces at the expense of reason, and like it, she turned a very good thing into a very bad one.'[30]

As far as Dorothea's own circumstances were concerned, the propitious moment for separation arrived in the late 1790s, after she met Schlegel and entered into a romantic relationship with him.[31] Having postponed the crucial decision for years, Dorothea, now in her mid-thirties, felt that her last chance had arrived: 'had I not seized this last propitious moment and made use of it, it would then have been too late'.[32] Having just learned about her rights as a divorced woman ('up until now I was not really acquainted at all with my rights', she confessed), and convinced she would receive the support of her close friends (whereas in previous years she was afraid to 'have to stand all alone' if she decided to dissolve her marriage, now 'Schlegel, Schleiermacher and Mrs Herz have genuinely supported me'[33]), Dorothea Mendelssohn took what her sister Henriette described as her 'last great step towards happiness'.[34]

Dorothea Mendelssohn's separation from her well-to-do Jewish husband was, from her perspective, a bold move towards self-emancipation. Her use when discussing her marriage and intention to divorce of terms such as 'slavery', 'liberation', and 'freedom', characteristic of the contemporary discourse of revolution and emancipation that was adopted by many thinkers through-

---

[29] *Briefe von und an Friedrich und Dorothea Schlegel*, ed. Behler, xxiii. 112–13. [30] Ibid. 112.

[31] Schlegel arrived in Berlin in the summer of 1797, and established a relationship with Dorothea shortly thereafter. In a letter of November 1798 to his close friend Novalis, he said: 'About fourteen months ago I wrote to you about a friend. Since then, from step to step, she became my wife [*meine Frau*] and she will remain so forever' (ibid. xxiv. 196).

[32] Ibid. 224. [33] Ibid. 224–5. [34] Holtei (ed.), *Dreihundert Briefe*, 171.

out the eighteenth century to analyse women's situation in society,[35] is indicative of how she perceived her life and the choices she made. In a letter she sent to Brinckmann shortly after her divorce, summarizing her acts and motivations, Mendelssohn compared her married life with Veit to a 'long period of slavery', from which she succeeded in 'free[ing] herself' by an act that required 'all my alertness' and left her feeling like a 'freed woman, who only now can call something her own, since she herself belongs to herself'.[36] Like someone who 'for a long time carried a heavy load: he still imagines that he feels it, long after having rid himself of it', she found it difficult to perceive the full force of her liberation, even though the positive signs of her new situation did not escape her: 'Now I am what I should have been long ago, dear friend! Now I am happy.'[37]

Dorothea Mendelssohn was not alone among her Jewish female friends at experiencing her marriage as a heavy burden and its demise almost in terms of redemption. Sara Meyer expressed herself in a similar way when complaining to Goethe about her miserable life with her Jewish husband, Jacob Isaac Wulff, to whom she was married for a decade from 1778: 'I was married at fifteen, through Moses' [Mendelssohn's] force and my mother's coercion, to a miserable wretch, who for ten years turned my existence into infernal torture, took away all my physical attractiveness and prevented my continued intellectual development, until my beloved saviour appeared.'[38]

Divorce did not necessarily change Dorothea Mendelssohn's life for the better: the spiritual uplift she experienced immediately after the event would soon subside, as she faced financial difficulty and social ostracism. A further change came as her reliance on enlightened discourse gave place to an outlook more attuned to Romanticism. In the new framework she chose to live in, as Friedrich Schlegel's partner and a member of the Romantic circle, she

---

[35] According to Sylvana Tomaselli, in the 18th century 'the language of liberty and slavery provided the terms in which the relation between the sexes was spoken of'. The 'conceptualisation of the condition of women as one of slavery is so frequent as to be almost a common-place in the Enlightenment' (Tomaselli, 'The Enlightenment Debate on Women', 114, 112).

[36] Letter of 2 Feb. 1799 (*Briefe von und an Friedrich und Dorothea Schlegel*, ed. Behler, xxiv. 223–4).

[37] Ibid. 224.

[38] Geiger (ed.), 'Einundzwanzig Briefe', 53. According to the matrimonial records presented by Jacob Jacobson, Sara Meyer and Jacob Isaac Wulff divorced after a decade of marriage. However, Dolf Michaelis and Barbara Hahn maintain that after ten years Wulff died, leaving Sara a widow (Michaelis, 'The Ephraim Family and their Descendants', 226; Hahn, *The Jewess Pallas Athena*, 184 n. 20 (Sara's husband is here identified as Lipmann Wulff)). Only a decade or so after she separated (or became a widow), at the end of the 1790s, did Sara marry again, this time a Christian. According to Jacobson, Jacob Isaac Wulff married his second (Jewish) wife in 1789 (Jacobson, *Jüdische Trauungen*, 331). According to the data provided by Jacobson, this Wulff was the brother of Cäcilie Itzig's first husband, Benjamin Isaac Wulff (ibid. 245).

may have moved closer to the ideas of early Romanticism and its perception of women—on the one hand, as the incarnation of the highest ideal of humanity, but on the other hand, precisely as such, as devoted helpmates and muses to their husbands, especially if these were creative spirits such as Schlegel.[39] Nevertheless, when discussing Dorothea's accommodation to Romanticism, two points should be stressed: first, that even if Dorothea Mendelssohn was devoted to 'serving' Schlegel in this new phase of her life, it was *she* who chose whom to serve—that is, the decision was hers; and second, that to acknowledge the presence of Romantic traits in her later world-view is not to deny her espousal of enlightened ideas, especially in earlier stages of her life. The enlightened discourse, with its insistence on the quest for human happiness and natural rights, and its emphasis on the rational power of the individual, was clearly a major force that motivated Dorothea to examine critically the framework in which her life was conducted and, finding it defective, to launch a radical change.

TO MARRY OR NOT TO MARRY? QUESTIONING AN AGE-OLD INSTITUTION

Freude Meyer and Dorothea Mendelssohn were two of several Jewish women of their generation who in their youth had acquiesced in the customary arranged marriage, and over time had gained the courage to break the traditional pattern thus forced upon them. In the same circle of friends there were other women, though not many—we know of only two—who refused from the outset to bow to family and social pressure and overtly repudiated this custom. Not only did they decline to enter into a match planned by their parents, according to age-old tradition;[40] even more remarkably, they were

---

[39] Schlegel's conception of feminity and gender difference is discussed in Becker-Cantarino, *Schriftstellerinnen der Romantik*, 122–31. On the image of the female muse as a central motif in Romanticism, see Schmidt, 'From Early to Late Romanticism'. It should be emphasized that Dorothea did not embrace uncritically the ideas and opinions of the early Romantics, among whom she lived for a time while living in Jena. See e.g. a discussion of her political views as reflected in *Florentin* in Roberts, 'The Perennial Search for Paradise'.

[40] According to the traditional norms of matchmaking in Ashkenazi society, as described by Jacob Katz in his classic 1945 essay, 'Marriage and Marital Relationships at the End of the Middle Ages' (Heb.), and later in *Tradition and Crisis*, the marriage was arranged by the parents of both bride and groom. In this sense, the betrothal of women such as Freude Meyer or Henriette Herz to their Jewish husbands diverged from the traditional model: whereas the bride continued to be subjected to her parents' decisions, the groom, who was not a boy or a young lad as had been usual in the past but an independent man, 'represented' himself and chose a bride according to his own personal considerations. Deferral of marriage by men to a later age had occurred previously, but according to Katz was considered a digression from the norm. See also Shohet, *Beginnings of the Haskalah* (Heb.), 160. For a

sceptical about marriage itself and remained single for many years, criticizing the institution of matrimony and claiming for themselves the right to decide on the course of their future life. As we shall see, this position was not taken out of caprice or thoughtlessness, but rather derived from reflections on both theoretical and practical considerations arrived at through engagement in serious debate on the subject.

By adopting a hesitant position towards marriage, these women were distancing themselves from one of the most firmly established institutions in Jewish society. In fact, the conscious and deliberate preference of the single life over marriage was extremely rare in the Jewish world. In a society that lived according to Jewish law, the commandment to procreate and the laws of 'family purity' (*taharat hamishpahah*) led to the recognition of marriage as one of the central ideals and a binding norm for men as well as women.[41] Celibacy was never validated as a religious virtue by mainstream Judaism, and was adopted as an ideal only by certain sects within it at certain times.[42] The Sabbatian movement, which defended the doctrine of the holiness of sin, supported sexual promiscuity and the deliberate breaking of central commandments such as the prohibition on adultery, as well as the opposite phenomenon of bachelorhood and sexual abstinence.[43] Rabbinic Judaism severely condemned those—especially women—who voluntarily chose the single life. This hostility was clearly reflected, for instance, in the attempts

---

discussion of early marriage as practised in 19th-century east European Jewish society and the sharp criticism of this institution by the maskilim, who envisioned the implementation of a new bourgeois marital ideology in Jewish society, see the chapter entitled 'Eros and Enlightenment' in Biale, *Eros and the Jews*, 149–75.

[41] Katz, 'Marriage and Marital Relationships at the End of the Middle Ages' (Heb.); id., *Tradition and Crisis*, 115–16; Berger, *Sexualität, Ehe und Familienleben*. According to Adiel Schremer, the idea that the central purpose of marriage is to implement the command 'be fruitful and multiply' begins to emerge in Jewish sources from the end of the Second Temple period: Schremer, *Male and Female Created He Them* (Heb.), 304. With the popularization of kabbalah during the 16th century, marriage acquired an additional sacral connotation: the sexual union of man and wife was perceived as the symbolic union of God and the Shekhinah (the divine presence), of the masculine and feminine divine attributes, and was thus accorded mystical significance (Idel, *Kabbalah and Eros*; Von Rohden, 'Jüdische Ehe', 330; Scholem, *Major Trends in Jewish Mysticism*, 235).

[42] It is common to cite the celibacy of the Essenes during the Second Temple as an exceptional case in Jewish history. However, disagreement exists regarding the extent of ascetic tendencies even among this sect and the actual status of marriage in their community (Fraade, 'Ascetical Aspects of Ancient Judaism', 266–9).

[43] Because the Sabbatians—adherents of the messianic sect named after its leader Sabbatai Zevi (1626–76)—believed that they were living in the messianic age and consequently all commandments had been abolished, transgressions/sins, such as adultery, could be considered religious acts. The theoretical background to Sabbatian antinomianism is thoroughly discussed in Scholem, 'Redemption through Sin'.

to put an end to the unmarried status of Sabbatian women visionaries—attempts that must be understood, of course, as part of the harsh opposition to Sabbatianism.[44] A similar attempt to intervene was made in the well-known case of the 'Maiden of Ludmir', a hasidic woman born in early nineteenth-century Russia who was 'popularly known as the only woman in the history of Hasidism to function as a rebbe or charismatic leader in her own right'. Aware that 'for a Jewish woman, marriage and a life of piety and learning were incompatible', she chose not to wed but to devote herself instead to a spiritual life. Her abstention from marriage was considered as a deviation from her proper female role, and she was forced to retreat from her position and to marry—even though her betrothal was only a formality and, according to the oral traditions on which her story is based, she remained celibate.[45]

An interesting and unresolved question is to what extent the Jewish ideal of marriage actually matched reality in various historical contexts—that is, how far the widespread assertion of the centrality of married life for Jews was reflected in social practice. Sources from the Middle Ages do not indicate that remaining single was an accepted option in medieval Jewish society. It is telling that a comprehensive study such as Avraham Grossman's book on Jewish women in medieval Europe contains detailed discussions of married, divorced, and widowed women, but no section devoted to 'unmarried women'.[46] As for the early modern period, references to single men and women do appear in the sources, indicating that remaining single was, if not widely prevalent, at least acknowledged as an existing practice. Nevertheless, when analysing these sources historians such as Jacob Katz and Azriel Shohet presented singlehood as in most cases a transient phase in an individual's life, closely connected to an important change in Jewish society: the delaying of marriage. During this period various factors, including economic constraints, restrictions regarding the right to settle in certain communities, and limitations imposed by the authorities on the number of marriage permits

---

[44] Rapoport-Albert, 'On the Position of Women in Sabbatianism' (Heb.).

[45] After divorcing her first husband, the Maiden of Ludmir, Hannah Rochel Verbermacher, married a second time, but again separated from her husband without consummating the marriage, remaining a 'maiden' until her last day. For a thorough discussion of the issues of marriage and asceticism in the life of the Maiden of Ludmir, see Deutsch, *The Maiden of Ludmir*, esp. pp. 124–43 (quotations here from pp. 4, 130). See also Rapoport-Albert, 'On Women in Hasidism'.

[46] Even when discussing the Beguine movement in Christian society, a semi-monastic order of unmarried women devoted to a spiritual life, and its influence on the religious life of Jewish women, Grossman does not mention any parallel phenomenon of single women in the Jewish world (Grossman, *Pious and Rebellious*, 177 ff.).

that could be issued in a certain place, led to an overall rise in the age at which Jews got married, thus creating a stratum of adult single Jews that had previously not existed in Jewish society.[47] In spite of these changes, Katz—in line with his well-known argument that deep cultural transformations in Ashkenazi Jewry occurred only from the late eighteenth century[48]—denied that there was any change in the *ideal* of marriage throughout the early modern age. He admitted that 'despite the tremendous pressure to marry . . . there were obviously some who remained single' and that 'the same factors that often delayed marriage could also prevent it altogether', so that some people perforce remained single.[49] But he emphasized that 'there was no positive social value attached to remaining single; even someone who had lost more than one mate to divorce or death would try to marry yet again'.[50] The possibility that the ideal of marriage may have lost some of its moral force under secular influences over the course of the eighteenth century is a hypothesis which deserves further study.

In contrast to traditional Jewish society, Christianity, as is well known, offered practical and highly regarded options for leading a life of fulfilment without marriage, the most popular being joining a monastery or other religious community.[51] The perception of marriage and family life as a supreme value came to Christianity relatively late, in fact as an innovation. In its early days Christianity merely permitted marriage 'as a concession to the weakness of the flesh', whereas celibacy was regarded as 'a more Christian way of life'. Even after it was transformed into a sacrament in the eighth century, and even though the Church gradually developed a positive theory on marriage in the late Middle Ages, 'the concept of marriage as an inferior way of life to chastity did not disappear'.[52] It was only in the sixteenth century that Luther and the Reformation brought a fundamental change in the attitude towards marriage among large numbers of Christian believers. Priestly celibacy of both monks and nuns was abolished among Protestants, and the duty and

---

[47] On the impact of restrictive legislation on the increasing tendency to postpone the age of marriage among Ashkenazi Jewry in the 18th and 19th centuries, see Lowenstein, 'Ashkenazic Jewry and the European Marriage Pattern'. Lowenstein also emphasizes the decisive influence of surrounding culture, specifically the adoption by the Jews of the European practice of later marriage, which had been replacing the medieval pattern of early marriage since the 17th century.

[48] Katz, *Out of the Ghetto*. See also Ch. 7 n. 47 below.

[49] Cf. Azriel Shohet, who claimed that in Germany 'we do not hear about complete singlehood'. Shohet, *Beginnings of the Haskalah* (Heb.), 160.   [50] Katz, *Tradition and Crisis*, 123.

[51] Another group in medieval European society for which bachelorhood was a viable option—indeed, a necessary condition—was university scholars. See Shahar, *The Fourth Estate*, 73–7; Algazi, 'Abelard, Heloise, and Astrolabe' (Heb.).   [52] Shahar, *The Fourth Estate*, 65–6.

blessing of marriage was stressed.[53] Even this, however, did not make marriage a universally accepted option.[54]

Indeed, despite the new importance granted to marriage and family life in Reformation Europe, Protestant reformers as well as humanists were concerned by the low regard in which the estate of marriage was held, with many continuing to denigrate this form of life, though not necessarily on religious grounds. Parallel to the more famous *querelle des femmes*, the protracted literary debate about the attributes of women and their place in society which went on in various European lands throughout the early modern age, a *querelle du mariage*—a debate on marriage—prevailed among lay thinkers and writers, including female disputants, many of whom vehemently criticized men's tyranny towards women within marriage and condemned the institution on that basis.[55] Among those who intervened in the debate were the French *salonnières* of the seventeenth century, the so-called *précieuses*, some of whom considered marriage to be a plague and examined ways to curb men's power in it.[56] Another outstanding voice against marriage was that of Mary Astell, an English writer and thinker who herself remained single throughout her life. This intriguing female author, who combined progressive enlightened ideas with reactionary political views, depicted marriage as a hostile and harmful institution for women, aimed at serving men's interests in domination and the perpetuation of their name.[57] At the end of the eighteenth century the issue of marriage was still being debated as hotly as ever, with men and women alike advancing the full gamut of arguments for and against marriage.[58] At this point the discussion was joined by at least two enlightened

[53] On the reformers' attitude towards marriage and the changing image of this institution, see Bock, *Women in European History*, 19 ff.; Ozment, *When Fathers Ruled*, 1–49.

[54] For a concise discussion of the misogynist position adopted by a considerable number of thinkers in Europe in the early modern age and the connection between misogamy and misogyny, see Bock, *Women in European History*, 14–27.

[55] This is not to say that only women objected to female submission in marriage. See e.g. Voltaire's satirical piece 'Femmes, soyez soumises a vos maris'.

[56] Bock, *Women in European History*, 26.

[57] Perry, 'Mary Astell's Response to the Enlightenment'; Bock, *Women in European History*, 26. In a book of 1694, entitled *A Serious Proposal to the Ladies, for the Advancement of their True and Greatest Interest, &c*, Astell put forward an interesting initiative, which met no success: she urged wealthy single women to use their dowry funds to establish female 'colleges' to serve as an alternative framework for unmarried women where they could live together and devote themselves to intellectual work. See Perry, 'Mary Astell's Response to the Enlightenment', 17 ff. Astell also published another work on a similar subject: *Some Reflections upon Marriage* (London, 1700).

[58] Interestingly, men who chose a bachelor life maintained a position diametrically opposed to that held by women who denigrated marriage, namely, that the latter was a most unfavourable institution *for men*. There were of course those who favoured marriage and tried to promote a positive image of it. One contemporary example of this position is found in the article published in the *Berlinische*

Jewish women, who considered leading a single life a practical option for themselves.

A letter written by Rahel Levin to her friend Henriette Mendelssohn in March 1793, discovered in the Varnhagen collection and published by Barbara Hahn, illuminates the reservations of both young women about marriage.[59] Although this single letter does not suffice to prove that both women rejected marriage out of hand as an option for life—indeed, later sources and events hint at a more moderate attitude—it does tell us something about their hesitations at that time concerning the institution of marriage as an (un)necessary and (in)appropriate way of life. The significance of this document, and of the historical juncture it records, deserves to be emphasized: two young Jewish women in the late eighteenth century deliberate with the utmost seriousness whether it is worthwhile to marry or not.[60] It is important to note that the kind of criticism of marriage encountered here is quite distinct from that voiced by the maskilim—beginning at about the time when Rahel's letter was written with a little-known essay entitled 'Ueber die allzufrühen Ehen der jüdischen Nation; physisch, politisch und pädagogisch betrachtet' ('On the all too early marriages among the Jewish nation, considered from a physical, political and pedagogical perspective'), published in 1790 by a radical Jewish maskil from Breslau, Moses Hirschel, and continuing among nineteenth-century east European maskilim—against certain customary practices relating to marriage in traditional Jewish society, first and foremost adolescent marriage.[61] It was also distinct from the kind of criticism expressed by the Jewish women mentioned above of the way spouses were chosen. Rahel Levin and Henriette Mendelssohn do not refer—at least at this stage—to the need to adopt a new model for marriage, based on love and companionship, in place

---

Monatsschrift in 1796 by F. W. A. Schmidt entitled 'Glück der Ehe. An einen Hagestolzen' ('The Joy of Marriage: To a Confirmed Bachelor'). Another relevant example is that of the enlightened Jew Lazarus Bendavid (a lifelong bachelor), who published an essay in the same year and the same journal strongly condemning the submission of women in marriage. Bendavid, 'Und er soll dein Herr sein'.

[59] Hahn, '*Diese trostvolle, sanfte Verbindung*'. As Hahn indicates, the fact that the broader epistolary exchange between both women, as part of which this letter was written, was not preserved makes it difficult to infer the precise circumstances in which it was written and the events to which it refers. Nevertheless, the letter remains illuminating for the topic discussed in it.

[60] Other Western women from that period expressed similar scepticism about the accepted belief that marriage was the proper destiny of every woman, and consciously chose not to wed. For a discussion of the relatively widespread phenomenon of spinsterhood in the United States in the years 1780–1840, see Chambers-Schiller, *Liberty, A Better Husband*. According to Chambers-Schiller, the conscious rejection of marriage by women who sought to obtain personal autonomy and to widen their intellectual horizons constituted a new form of female independence, and thus 'enacted ideas and values of the European Enlightenment and American Revolution' (p. 1).

[61] Biale, *Eros and the Jews*, 149–75; Hirschel, 'Ueber die allzufrühen Ehen der jüdischen Nation'.

of the traditional system of arranged marriages based on economic interests and other rational considerations external to the personal needs and desires of the couple. What we have here is, rather, a reflection on and an assessment of the institution of marriage itself from a clear feminist perspective.

In the letter discussed here Rahel Levin, then in her early twenties, expressed her unusual attitude towards marriage in reply to a query raised by her 18-year-old friend Henriette Mendelssohn in a previous letter (now lost). As becomes clear from the letter, this was actually the continuation of a debate on marriage they had started the previous summer, when they had apparently met personally and discussed the pros and cons of the institution. The debate was renewed by correspondence some months later following a change in Mendelssohn's position on the subject, as is clear from Levin's words: 'This past summer you seemed to me so much inclined towards married life, and in your last letter to me so much the opposite—I think not for good reasons in either case.'[62]

In the letter she sent Mendelssohn in the spring of 1793, Levin took upon herself a difficult task: to encourage her friend to reconsider the negative position towards marriage she had developed since their earlier discussions. The difficulty arose in part from the fact that Rahel Levin herself harboured heretical feelings towards the institution of marriage, at least as it was practised among her contemporaries. From the letter it becomes apparent that she saw marriage as an institution that oppressed women and deprived them of their natural rights, while preserving the existing hierarchical relationship between the sexes. But although she herself did not believe in conjugal union and did not see it in any way as an ideal institution, she feared that her friend might be drawn to a similar position. For it was clear to her that the only alternative—lifelong spinsterhood—was probably even more difficult to bear than matrimony itself. With a clear-sighted practicality she understood that, under existing conditions, wedlock was a necessary compromise, at least for most women. Therefore in writing to Henriette Mendelssohn she tried to coax her out of her hesitations: 'In the given social situation, what can be better for a person healthy in body and mind than this comforting, gentle bond of marriage?'[63] Levin felt under an obligation to warn her friend against falling into the same state as herself, which she viewed as a source of deep sorrow: 'You are surprised to see me defending what I so much *opposed* last summer [i.e. marriage]. I am not applying all these beautiful reasons to

---

[62] Hahn, '*Diese trostvolle, sanfte Verbindung*', 358. [63] Ibid. 358–9.

myself—for *I* can no more—*I* am already spoiled. But precisely because of this I warn you. You should be afraid—it is a great misfortune.'[64]

On what grounds did these young women base their respective positions when discussing the institution of marriage? These attitudes were certainly not the product of mere whim or impulse: on the contrary, they were clearly informed by the contemporary discourse regarding the subject. Levin and Mendelssohn were both well acquainted with the arguments for and against marriage voiced by contemporary thinkers in numerous books and articles. Levin is sure that she need not remind Mendelssohn of the position taken by one of the most prominent *philosophes* on this subject: 'The best arguments against an unmarried life [*uneheliche Leben*] you surely learnt by heart from Diderot', she wrote.[65] In addition, their views had been formed by personal experience and the empirical knowledge gained by observing the surrounding world. '*One* experience'—possibly her own, or perhaps a particular case about which she had heard—had led Henriette Mendelssohn to retreat from the theoretical position she had previously held about marriage and to reject the institution. In Rahel's case, too, 'true but sad experiences have strengthened me in my way of thinking; only today I learnt there are unfaithful husbands, who nevertheless do not trust their wives' shadows'.[66] A case she had just heard about made it clear to her how a husband's suspicions could dishonour his wife and deprive her of the right to prove her innocence. Thus equipped with both theoretical and empirical knowledge, these two young Jewish women reached a considered critical stance towards one of the most ancient institutions in human society—an institution, moreover, adopted by the middle class to which they belonged as a central foundation of proper social life.

Henriette Mendelssohn, who at one point had viewed matrimony as a practical option, having previously—as Rahel Levin noted in her letter—

---

[64] Ibid. 359.

[65] Ibid. Diderot's position concerning marriage, expressed in many of his works, was in fact complex—as was Rahel Levin's—and it is perhaps no accident that she chose to quote him. On the one hand, he condemned the indissoluble character of marriage and the folly of eternal vows, which in his opinion were contrary to the natural inconstancy of the human heart, causing much unhappiness and turning many people into criminals. On the other hand, 'Diderot looked for a rational reconciliation of human nature and desires with the need for an ordered society' (Sokol, 'Jeremy Bentham on Love and Marriage', 17 n. 131), and did support marriage as a civilizing institution. Even though it was a 'stupid and troublesome state', marriage was necessary to maintain the family and property. See McLaughlin, 'Diderot and Women' (quotation here from p. 300). According to Katherine Clinton, Diderot, like other *philosophes*, advocated the bourgeois view of marriage and family life as opposed to that of the nobility, and he romanticized middle-class home life in plays that reflected a renewed emphasis on domesticity, as for instance in *Père de famille* (1758) (Clinton, 'Femme et philosophe', 294).

[66] Hahn, '*Diese trostvolle, sanfte Verbindung*', 359.

revealed an inclination towards married life, remained single to the end of her days. Rahel Levin, at this point so resolute in her rejection of marriage, eventually chose to wed—but not for another twenty years and more, when in 1814 she married Karl August Varnhagen, fourteen years her junior. No personal source revealing Henriette Mendelssohn's explicit stance towards the institution of marriage in later years has come down to us, and therefore it is hard to determine whether there was a direct connection between the early hesitations referred to in that single letter from 1793 and the path of her life as a mature woman. If we are to believe Karl August Varnhagen's report from 1835, when he set out to present a comprehensive picture of the childhood female friends of his late wife Rahel, Henriette Mendelssohn lacked no opportunities to cast in her lot with a man:

In Vienna . . . Eskeles wanted to marry her, but she rejected the wealthy match, considered a splendid stroke of luck, because although she admired him, she did not love him. In Paris it seemed as if Dr [David] Veit, who came to the city with her brother Abraham, was meant to be her husband. They loved each other very much, only the matter fell through, probably because the external conditions were not propitious.[67]

It is impossible to know what the 'external conditions' were that prevented the relationship between Henriette Mendelssohn and 'Dr Veit' from becoming established—if indeed the possibility ever existed.[68] However, the explanation given by Varnhagen for Mendelssohn's behaviour in the case of her previous suitor, Eskeles, throws some light on her reasons for remaining single: for it appears from Varnhagen's report that while her continued spinsterhood was largely a matter of choice, in this case she decided to reject her wealthy suitor not—according to Varnhagen—because of a principled opposition to marriage (the position she held in 1793) but rather because of an idealistic view of that institution. The motive given by Varnhagen—'she did not love him'—suggests that Mendelssohn had in the meantime embraced the ideal of romantic marriage, that is, 'the radical new idea that love should be the most fundamental reason for marriage and that young people should be free to choose their marriage partners on the basis of love'.[69] This relatively new and sharply different attitude towards marriage,

[67] Bosold, 'Friederike Liman', 149. The same Eskeles would later marry Cäcilie Wulff, née Itzig.

[68] An earlier hint at the possible relationship between Henriette Mendelssohn and David Veit appears in a letter Veit sent to Rahel Levin in 1795, in which he tells her that he has received 'a letter from Jettchen [i.e. Henriette], the answer. She assures me with much frankness that she deems me capable of love only in jest, not in truth.' Henriette Mendelssohn may have been replying to a declaration of love by David Veit (*Briefwechsel zwischen Rahel und David Veit*, ii. 128).

[69] Coontz, *Marriage, a History*, 5.

which became more widespread over the course of the eighteenth century, had in fact guided her own parents in their decision to wed,[70] and was taking hold of a growing number of Jews in different countries.[71]

As opposed to the paucity of evidence regarding Henriette Mendelssohn's attitude towards marriage, Rahel Levin's subsequent remarks amply testify that the hesitations she expressed in her letter of 1793 had not faded away years later, although they do not represent the same steadfast rejection of matrimony. The issue continued to preoccupy her, emerging from time to time in her correspondence with female and male friends. It recurred, for instance, in letters she wrote in 1799, when her years-long romantic relationship with the German Count Karl von Finckenstein was coming to an end. Along with the firm opposition of Finckenstein's conservative family to his liaison with a bourgeois Jewish woman, it is apparent from Levin's words that her own doubts about marriage contributed in no small measure to their final separation. 'Marry, you say', she wrote to Brinkmann, when the possibility of throwing in her lot with Finckenstein was still up for discussion, even though their relationship had become tense:

I cannot marry, because I cannot lie ... Otherwise I would do it now. I would make it my task and my mission in life to cause happiness to a man who loves me with all his might, whom my mere presence pleases. But I cannot bring myself to utter expressions of love for him: therefore it is impossible.[72]

Rahel Levin could not accept the unequal relationship in marriage between husband and wife, nor comply with the role designated for a married woman, almost as an object whose function it was to give satisfaction to her husband. The role of a woman who submits herself to her spouse, one who takes it upon herself to 'cause happiness to a man', even if this requires her to lie and 'utter expressions of love' just to bring him pleasure, was not a realistic option for her. Levin profoundly disagreed with placing women's satisfaction second to men's, and she was unable to bring herself to put her prospective husband's well-being above her own, at the price of her own right to be happy and at peace with herself.

[70] On the love-based marriage of Moses Mendelssohn and Fromet Gugenheim, see their pre-nuptial correspondence in Mendelssohn, *Brautbriefe*; also Goch, *Im Aufbruch*, 139–209. See also the discussion of the romantic pre-nuptial correspondence of a Bavarian Jewish couple from a lower class in the early 19th century in Kaplan, '"Based on love"'. On the connection between the idealization of marriage and the increasing numbers of those who chose to remain single in the 19th century see Berend, '"The Best or None!"', which discusses spinsterhood in 19th-century New England.

[71] A significant amount of evidence pointing at a shift from rational to romantic marriage in the Sephardi community in Amsterdam in the second half of the eighteenth century is discussed in Kaplan, *An Alternative Path to Modernity*, 280–300.

[72] Varnhagen, *Rahel Varnhagen. Briefwechsel*, iii. 98.

Well aware that the nonconformist behaviour of a woman who chose to remain single and did not succumb to the pressure upon her to fulfil her female role as wife and mother was likely to have unpalatable consequences for her, Levin refrained from trying to persuade other women to follow her lead. Instead, she preferred to give her female friends practical advice on how to cope with a compromise marriage. Having earlier accepted that in the prevailing condition of society marriage was the preferable option for women, at the turn of the century the pragmatic advice she gave women on how best to endure an unhappy marriage was to control themselves, behave wisely, and avoid unnecessary confrontations, which were likely to be futile given that men usually had the upper hand. The advice she gave a 'young female friend' (most probably Nanette Renaud Marcuse, a niece of Fradchen Liebmann, née Marcuse) in the autumn of 1799 was: 'If you marry without love, do not talk to your husband. Please him as much as you can stand; but do not reason, never prove that you are right, that he is wrong.'[73] Opting for silence and pretence was not, however, a solution she herself could implement: 'a stupid man must not force me to lie, to pretend as if I honoured him. I must be able to say whatever I like', she wrote earlier that year.[74]

Few women chose the path of personal integrity at all costs, as Levin did. One who did, sacrificing much in order to pursue the life she wanted for herself, was her intimate non-Jewish friend Pauline Wiesel. Wiesel broke more than one cardinal gender norm, and was severely criticized as a result. Not only did she have many lovers, among them Louis Ferdinand, the Prussian prince, and after 1806 more than one officer of the invading French army; she even gave birth to a child by one man while still married to another.[75] Levin shared with Wiesel her bitter feelings as a woman who chose, like her friend, to live truthfully in a world that recompensed hypocrites (and here we may interpret her words to include those who agreed to abide by society's dictates even if they opposed their own beliefs and understanding) and punished those who swam against the current:

We [Levin and Wiesel] are made to live the truth in this world. And by different routes we arrived at one and the same point. We exist at the margins of human society. For us there is no place, no office, no vain title! *All* lies have one. The eternal

---

[73] Bosold, 'Friederike Liman', 140. Nanette Renaud Marcuse had an illegitimate daughter with Wilhelm von Burgsdorff in 1802. Many years later, Burgsdorff, a friend of Rahel Levin and other Jewish women, and a cousin of Karl von Finckenstein, Rahel's lover, was believed by Nanette Marcuse to have claimed in society that Jews and Christians should remain apart and that Jewish and Christian blood should not mix (ibid. 75–6, esp. n. 405).

[74] Varnhagen, *Rahel Varnhagen. Briefwechsel*, iii. 99.

[75] Hahn, '"Ein Mann kann nicht denken wie Wir"', 722–8.

truth—true living and feeling . . . has *none*! And so we are shut out of society, you because you insulted it (I congratulate you on it! At least you had something— many days of pleasure!), I, because I can't sin and *tell lies* with it. I know fully your inner history. Every insult you heaped on society, even if it was justified for *you*, really wounded you yourself . . . You would gladly have been 'a homey little wife, caressing and kissing your husband', as Goethe says in his distich; but it didn't work.[76]

Women who behaved contrary to the gender role allocated to them, who did not play according to the rules of the game set by society and culture, who deviated too far from the prescribed path, often found themselves on the margins of society. Rahel Levin, like Pauline Wiesel, took the liberty of choosing her own path. It was not an easy one, but it was her conscious choice. This was her 'emancipation', and, as she was well aware, she paid a high price for it.

FEMALE INDEPENDENCE

As noted above, Henriette Mendelssohn remained single all her life; we have no way of knowing whether her reluctance to marry diminished as time went by, and whether at a certain point she would have liked to establish a family but was unable to do so. In any event, in 1799, about six years after corresponding with Rahel Levin on the issue of marriage and just a few months after witnessing her sister Dorothea's divorce, at the age of 24 she decided to take a step of independence and try to build her own future, embarking on a path that would indeed grant her a feeling of accomplishment, though not great happiness. The occupational choices available to a bourgeois woman who sought to support herself were very limited. One of the few accessible fields was education, and, using the many connections that she and her acquaintances had, Henriette obtained a position as a governess in Vienna.[77] In March 1799, shortly before travelling there, she wrote to her friend August

---

[76] The letter is dated 12 Mar. 1810, and is printed thus in Bruyn (ed.), *Rahels erste Liebe*, 312–14, as well as in Blackwell and Zantop (eds.), *Bitter Healing*, 411–14 (from where the English translation is taken, here at p. 412). However, on the basis of Wiesel's reply Barbara Hahn asserts that the letter was written only in 1811. See Hahn's note to the letter in Levin Varnhagen, *Briefwechsel mit Pauline Wiesel*, 537.

[77] She was apparently employed as governess in the house of a wealthy Jewish banker, 'whose name is unknown to us' (Peez, 'Henriette Mendelssohn', 103). The possibility raised by Jean-Jacques Anstett that Henriette Mendelssohn worked in Vienna as tutor to Fanny von Arnstein's daughter is no more than a conjecture, as he himself admits (Anstett, 'Henriette Mendelssohn', 85–6). It seems unlikely, since Arnstein's only daughter, Henriette, was then almost 19 years old (having been born in November 1780).

Schlegel, the brother of her sister's partner Friedrich, about her imminent change of domicile and her uncertain future:

I do not expect anything pleasant there [in Vienna], and I am unable to imagine any kind of happiness in my new profession. However, your wife quite correctly judged the reasons that nevertheless led me to this choice. This is a step designated to try my abilities and to extract myself from the dependence to which I am accustomed. I had to begin somewhere in order to expand the horizons of my future, to at least change my prospects.[78]

It is clear from the tone of this letter that Henriette Mendelssohn did not consider this an ideal step: that she would certainly have chosen a different path had one been open to her. Her choice represented a compromise, her best chance of escaping the state of dependency in which she lived, as did most middle-class single women of her period.

A year later, she felt no happier and her prospects for the future were far from promising: 'The past gives me no beautiful memories, the present gives me no pleasure, and on the future I don't set any hope.'[79] Finally, in 1801, she decided on a new departure and moved to Paris, which quite soon also became the temporary home of her sister Dorothea and Friedrich Schlegel, and also of her brother Abraham. In the French capital Henriette continued to earn her living as a governess, this time in the house of the Jewish banker Ber Leon Fould. After some time she moved on to managing an educational institution for girls set up on the Foulds' property, an occupation that she pursued with great diligence and from which she derived commensurate satisfaction.

A new period in her life started in the second decade of the nineteenth century with her employment as governess of the daughter of Horace François Sebastiani, a diplomat, a politician, and a general in Napoleon's army. This took her into the luxurious home of the Sebastianis, 'next door to the Emperor', where she had at her disposal 'a suite of four rooms, with a view of the Champs Elysées'.[80] Here she looked after Fanny, her pupil, as a daughter. In letters to her relatives in Berlin she spoke of her love and dedication to the girl:

---

[78] Letter from Henriette Mendelssohn to August Schlegel, March 1799, in Holtei (ed.), *Dreihundert Briefe*, 169–70. See also Dorothea Mendelssohn's letter to Brinkmann of February 1799, where she presents her sister's move to Vienna as an attempt to put to the test her independence—and her pedagogy. *Briefe von und an Friedrich und Dorothea Schlegel*, ed. Behler, xxiv. 225.

[79] Varnhagen von Ense (ed.), *Galerie von Bildnissen*, i. 67.

[80] Letter from Henriette Mendelssohn to her brother Abraham and his family, quoted in Hensel, *The Mendelssohn Family*, i. 46–7.

I spend my evenings quite by myself, and what is generally called pleasure must be out of the question, as I never leave the child and will not let her get into irregular habits. This retirement, however, appears gloomy only to others, and does not frighten me; I know nothing I would not do for this child, so inexpressibly lovely is she.[81]

Henriette Mendelssohn served as Fanny Sebastiani's governess until her charge married in 1824. Then the harsh facts of reality broke in on her, as she realized that her role as carer to the girl she had loved, and the way of life that went with it, were at an end, leaving her, at a relatively advanced age, without any clear direction in life.

The question of so-called sympathising friends, 'What do you intend to do?' is to me like a sharp-edged sword. That all the devotion I have lavished upon the girl these many years was really nothing but a *rôle*, and that now the curtain is to fall, and Fanny, to-morrow, to act in a new piece, with no part for me to play—I ought all along to have told myself this, and perhaps I did now and then: but how different is the reality![82]

These words, written by Mendelssohn some months before she was separated from her pupil, convey the pain of a woman who never gave birth to children of her own and had no stable social or family framework. Her distress as a woman with no offspring was shared by some of her friends, for instance Henriette Herz and Rahel Levin (both of whom, unlike Henriette Mendelssohn, were married at some point in their lives). These women too expressed on several occasions the pain they felt at being childless.[83]

Nevertheless, despite her trials and tribulations, and contrary to the widespread image of the 'old maid' as an embittered and dependent spinster, Henriette Mendelssohn was able to lead an active life of achievement, to develop an independent career, to establish herself on a firm economic footing, and to support herself comfortably in a respectable way.[84] Unlike Rahel Levin, who until her marriage in 1814 was for many years financially dependent on the goodwill of her brother, who controlled her inheritance, and her mother (until the latter's death in 1809),[85] Henriette Mendelssohn depended

[81] Ibid. 47. [82] Ibid. 54.
[83] Two other women who never had children—a phenomenon not at all exceptional among the women discussed in this book—were Sara and Marianne Meyer.
[84] The stereotype of the old maid who spends her time at home, in solitude, tormenting relatives and friends with her bad temper and being a burden on those around her has been challenged recently by studies of specific cases in various countries. These studies prove that, on the contrary, many women who remained single led lives of independence and achievement. See Chambers-Schiller, *Liberty, A Better Husband*; Berend, '"The Best or None!"'; Adams, 'A Choice Not to Wed?'.
[85] Although she received an inheritance from her father after his death, the family funds were managed by her brother Marcus (Thomann Tewarson, *Rahel Levin Varnhagen*, 22). This situation led to friction among the siblings as well as between Rahel Levin and her mother.

neither on her relatives' protection nor on their approval for the steps she took, although she did maintain strong ties with her brothers Joseph and Abraham and consulted them in making her decisions. Her economic independence granted her the power to direct the course of her own life to an extent quite unusual among women of her time and class.[86]

Not all the enlightened Jewish women shared the hesitations expressed by Rahel Levin and Henriette Mendelssohn in their reflections on the drawbacks of marriage for women. But even those who did not doubt that marriage was an indispensable institution could still disagree with certain conventions and values that had been attached to it. Henriette Herz, one of the few women in this group who did not divorce the Jewish husband she had married in her youth, took what appears at first to be a conservative approach towards marriage. More than once she expressed her faith in matrimony as a desirable state for women, indeed as their destiny. She described an unmarried female friend of hers, who lived with her brother and sister-in-law and witnessed the happiness of the married couple, as someone aware of having missed out in life in not having had the opportunity to marry: 'At certain moments she must feel, deeply and painfully, that she was destined by nature to enjoy the same happiness she could have enjoyed [in a similar relationship], if the world and its circumstances did not stand between her and her destiny.'[87] Although these words referred to Louise von Willich, according to Henriette Herz they applied also to her unmarried sister Brenna de Lemos, who spent much time in the Herz household and so had the chance to witness married life at close quarters.

Even though Herz had no doubts as to the benefits of the institution of marriage, closer examination of her words provides grounds for claiming that she held 'progressive' opinions, even with traces of feminism. She rejected the conventional view of marriage according to which a clear hierarchy should prevail, with husband ruling over wife. Proof of this attitude is found in her negative impression of the relationship between Nanny Schleiermacher (half-sister of the philosopher Friedrich Schleiermacher and Herz's friend) and her husband, Professor Arndt, after visiting their home in Bonn on her way back to Berlin after a trip to Italy. As she revealed in 1819 to her friend Immanuel Bekker: 'I whisper in your ear, that this is not my ideal of a happy marriage—A[rndt], this I have known for a long time, sees women in general

---

[86] According to one contemporary source, after the marriage of her pupil Fanny Sebastiani, Henriette Mendelsohn 'received a pension of nearly 3,000 francs for the rest of her life, which allowed her to return to live in her native Berlin' (Bodley (ed.), *Goethe and Zelter*, 533).

[87] Boenigk (ed.), *Schleiermacher und seine Lieben*, 108.

as light and flowery creatures, and with such as these, issues of depth cannot be shared or discussed, one can only dally, frolic and joke.'[88] Henriette Herz deplored the prevalent contemporary image of woman in marriage as a superficial creature devoid of reason, an object meant to serve as mere ornament for the pleasure of her husband. According to Herz, the ideal marriage should be based on a true appreciation of women's mental capacities and consequently be characterized by friendship, reciprocity, and a deep bond of affection between the spouses. The wife was not to be considered as inferior to man but rather as a true companion and a reliable adviser who should be treated with respect.[89]

Beyond Herz's principled support of women's improved status in the marital relationship, she also advocated the independence of women who did not live in this framework.[90] As a widow she aspired to realize this ideal, although she was aware of the difficulties involved, which she most probably encountered herself, and which she tried to understand in the context of both contemporary social practice and her own situation. 'Independence is taken from us women so early, through education or circumstances', she wrote to a friend at the end of 1803, after her husband's death, 'that if by fortune or misfortune we are left alone, without a supportive environment, we feel no stable ground underneath our feet, and we falter; looking for support, we frequently believe we have found it, and depending on it, we sink.'[91] In subsequent years she often expressed pride in the freedom and independence she had managed to gain, with great effort and despite the fact that she had not been appropriately prepared for that effort. This autonomy allowed her to lead her life as she saw fit—and, above all, spared her the necessity of relying on her nearest and dearest as a single, dependent woman. She was ready to manage on a small income, to live in a small and modest apartment, and even to work for a living, as long as she could keep her independence. Aware that her behaviour was untypical of most contemporary women, she felt great satisfaction in her

---

[88] *Letters to Immanuel Bekker*, ed. Putzel, 33.

[89] On the ideals of companionship and intimacy in matrimony, see Coontz, *Marriage, a History*, 145–60. Calls for improvements in women's position within marriage had been advanced by women in Germany with greater intensity since the French Revolution. One notable example is Emilie Berlepsch's 'Ueber einige zum Glück der Ehe nothwendige Eigenschaften und Grundsätze' ('On Some Characteristics and Principles Necessary for Happiness in Marriage'), published in the *Teutscher Merkur* in 1791, in which this author condemned the pervasiveness of misogyny and its destructive effect on marriage. Pondering 'the psychological cost of submissiveness to women and the cause in husbands of derogatory behavior towards wives', and utterly rejecting the androcentric view of women as supplementary to men, she suggested an innovative cure against these ills: educating women to self-reliance. Dawson, '"And this shield is called—self-reliance"' (quotation from p. 164).

[90] Cf. Davies, 'Portraits of a Lady'.   [91] Boenigk (ed.), *Schleiermacher und seine Lieben*, 63–4.

achievements and tried not to be deterred by the difficulties—economic and social—she faced, as her correspondence with the young Ludwig Börne testifies.

In March 1804, about a year after the death of Marcus Herz, Börne wrote excitedly in one of his many letters to Henriette about the rumours that had reached him in Halle, where he was studying at that time: 'Recently Mrs. Reil [in whose house Börne lived] told me that at a social gathering where people talked about you, they said that you live in Berlin in a palace, with a princess, a duchess, or even a queen; I don't know.'[92] Börne, who adored Henriette Herz, was thrilled by this picture; but the rumour contained no more than a grain of truth. Surprised to find that her private life was of any interest in Halle, Herz explained to her curious friend that what had given rise to this rumour was the fact that she was actually *employed* by a noble family, as part of her efforts to lead an independent life: 'I do not live in a palace, my dear Louis,[93] but in the small house you saw furnished—and I don't have special connections with any duchess beyond the fact that I teach English to the young princess of Curland, for which I get paid.' The rumours were perhaps fuelled by the privileged treatment she received at the noble residence, 'beyond all payment': as she said, 'the duchess herself as well as the princes and princesses who belong to her house and her family treat me with utmost respect'. They even gave her an exceptional honour by being willing to share a table with her, 'a commoner—a Jewish woman'.[94]

The terms in which Henriette Herz described in her letter to Börne how she had overcome the trials of her sudden widowhood are very telling: 'I know that most ordinary people would have been glad to see me endure the hard fate that befell me with less fortitude, and they would be pleased if I were unhappy with the present limitations of my life and if I had made myself dependent upon them.'[95] Against the expectations of society—*despite* the expectations of society—which in her opinion hoped to see her submissive, broken, and dependent following the unexpected change in her fortunes, Henriette Herz succeeded in her determination not to sink under the blow of widowhood or to rely on others for her subsistence, but to remain in command of herself and her circumstances, and thus to retain her autonomy and her freedom. This was not at all the obvious course of action for a woman of her position and background. A more conventional response to the loss of a

---

[92] Geiger (ed.), *Briefwechsel des jungen Börne und der Henriette Herz*, 105.

[93] 'Louis' is Ludwig Börne, who used that name when signing his letters to Henriette Herz and in his publications until 1818, the year he converted to Christianity, signing as Louis Baruch.

[94] Geiger (ed.), *Briefwechsel des jungen Börne und der Henriette Herz*, 110.   [95] Ibid.

husband and father was that of Moses Wessely's wife and daughters. Wessely, a merchant and a member of enlightened circles in Hamburg, brother of the famous maskil Hartwig Wessely, passed away in 1792, leaving his widow and daughters in poverty. Although the daughters were offered respectable work opportunities, they turned them down, preferring to depend on the help they could get from their father's friends.[96]

Henriette Herz's attitude remained unchanged even in harder times, which came sooner than expected. With the French occupation of Berlin in 1806, the payment of her pension and interest was suspended, and therefore Herz was forced to find a temporary position to see her through the time of crisis. Firm in her decision not to be a burden on anyone, and willing 'to be useful in exchange for what I am given', she declared herself willing to serve as governess or companion in exchange for board, lodging, and travel expenses.[97] From among the offers she received, including one from Paris and another one from Vienna (at the house of one of the Itzig daughters there),[98] she chose to work as a governess in Rügen, an island in the Baltic Sea, at the house of Charlotte von Kathen, not only because she had a personal connection with the family who opened their house to her,[99] but also because of the relative geographical proximity to Berlin and to Prenzlau, where her sick mother and sister would remain.[100] The decision to leave Berlin was not an easy one, especially as she considered that by taking up a job she was in fact relinquishing her freedom. Nevertheless, she found comfort in the thought that it was only a temporary expedient:

I am sure I will find something somewhere that suits me, and it will in any case only be for a short period—after the war I will regain my freedom. I think I can weather the separation from my relatives with courage and ease and calmly leave my home, whose mistress I was. However, I am afraid that when it all comes closer, it will cost

---

[96] Almut Spalding, *Elise Reimarus*, 276–7. Soon after their father's death the daughters converted to Christianity, and not long after that one of them, Esther, married a Christian physician.

[97] Boenigk (ed.), *Schleiermacher und seine Lieben*, 122. 'If in addition the people [who will hire me] will feel that they have to give me money for my services, I will accept it for the sake of calming them, not because I need it. For I still have enough left for clothing and for fulfilling my various obligations' (ibid. 120).

[98] This emerges from a letter of 2 Dec. 1807 (Boenigk (ed.), *Schleiermacher und seine Lieben*, 123–4).

[99] Henriette Herz was hired by Charlotte von Kathen, Schleiermacher's sister-in-law, to teach her children.

[100] Boenigk (ed.), *Schleiermacher und seine Lieben*, 124. Henriette Herz was a devoted daughter and sister, who took care of those close to her for many years. Her concern for the health of her unmarried sister Brenna and her mother is often expressed in her letters and, as indicated above, loomed large in her personal decisions.

me all my strength to remain upright. With some sacrifice I have so far retained my independence. It will not be easy to give up on it. My friends are still screaming because I wish to leave Berlin, but I shall do what I believe I must.[101]

Even though she was conscious that her behaviour contradicted gender conventions widespread at the time, Henriette Herz tried not to let the circumstances in which she found herself undermine her self-reliance.

Such resolute independence was likely to harm a woman's good name, but some of them were ready to cope with the predictable consequences. When facing the choice between following prevalent gender norms or pursuing an independent way of life which often attracted social censure, Marianne Meyer consciously chose the second option. 'I will never be able to prevent erroneous interpretations of my actions', she wrote with resignation in a letter to Goethe from Vienna in 1803, some years after her (non-Jewish) husband had passed away, sharing with the German author her experiences as a woman who chose to live independently. 'This lies in my situation; I live alone, I travel alone, I have full freedom to do as I wish.'[102] The conclusions reached by others did not surprise Marianne Meyer, for she well knew that according to the received wisdom of the time a woman, even a mature adult woman was a creature who had to be restrained by an authoritative figure—preferably a husband or a parent—lest she break the rules of morality: 'The majority think this way: there is nobody to control her. Why should she not do what she wishes, since she can[?]'[103] But censorious gossip did not make Marianne Meyer change her way of life. She knew that, as a woman living on her own, she would always attract critical comment, and therefore she did not even try to contradict the hostile rumours about her. As she said in her letter to Goethe, it was far more important to her that she obtain recognition for her intellect: 'it seems to me I have achieved enough for people to see themselves forced to show me respect; for nobody having the gall to take me for lightheaded', she confessed, 'is all I strove to achieve here'.[104] Therefore she invested great energy in developing her intellect and widening her knowledge. Despite the circumstances, Marianne Meyer zealously kept her independence: an account for her deeds, she wrote to Goethe, 'I no longer give to anyone other than my dearest friends'.[105]

ALTERNATIVE FRAMEWORKS

Some women who lived on their own, whether as widows or as divorcees, sought companionship outside the conventional familial structures of mar-

---

[101] Geiger (ed.), *Briefwechsel des jungen Börne und der Henriette Herz*, 184–5.
[102] Sauer (ed.), *Goethe und Österreich*, 168. [103] Ibid. [104] Ibid. 168–9. [105] Ibid. 168.

riage or life with close relatives, motivated in many cases by a wish for independence coupled with limited financial resources and perhaps a feeling of loneliness—especially in the cold winters, when harsh weather conditions, inadequate pavements, and early nightfall inhibited social visiting. One option—not always successful in practice—was sharing a household with other women in a similar situation. These arrangements usually did not last long, and in many cases perhaps were never intended to serve for more than a limited period. Their significance lies in the attempt to find alternatives to the patriarchal family framework as a source of social and economic security, and to devise creative solutions that would offer both independence and emotional comfort. Central to all these attempts is the strength of mutual support and friendship among women, a theme that has already recurred many times in this study.

One such attempt to establish an alternative framework appears in another, slightly earlier, letter sent by Marianne Meyer to Goethe, this one dating from 1800. Shortly after moving to Vienna as the widow of the Austrian Prince von Reuss, Meyer shared her home for some time with an exceptional woman whom she met in the Austrian capital, in what seems to have been a relationship among equals—very different from the hierarchical situation that prevailed in conventional marriage. She explained the many advantages of this female alliance:

An association with an extremely interesting woman, a Countess Salis who lives with me, alleviates much of what would be harder for me to bear and fight in solitude. Her cheerful spirit, her loving heart, her bright reason dispel many a dark cloud on my horizon. Her example of bearing the vicissitudes of life has an utterly beneficial effect on me, teaches me to smile at many things, to despise much and to use what offers itself . . . our togetherness makes us both much more independent, more self-reliant.[106]

This framework of female partnership, a clear digression from normative patriarchal frameworks of family life, is depicted by Meyer as a source of female empowerment. Not only did living with this female companion serve as an antidote against loneliness and as a source of comfort in the face of an uncertain future,[107] making it easier for her to bear 'much of what would be harder for me to bear and fight in solitude'; living together made both women

---

[106] Sauer (ed.), *Goethe und Österreich*, 117.

[107] Not only did Marianne Meyer have to stand up for her rights as Prince von Reuss's widow (see Ch. 1 above, around n. 72), she also stood on bad terms with her mother and was affected by the bankruptcy of her family after her father's death. The legal proceedings following his demise are mentioned in Geiger (ed.), 'Einundzwanzig Briefe', 97; Michaelis, 'The Ephraim Family', 228.

'much more independent' and gave them the strength to maintain their independence in a hostile environment.

A relationship of a very different character from that between Marianne Meyer and her friend the Countess Salis was the short-lived partnership between two other women, Recha Mendelssohn and her widowed friend Henriette Herz, in the early 1820s. Recha Mendelssohn, Moses Mendelssohn's second daughter, had divorced her husband Mendel Meyer years earlier and had never remarried. She had managed to bring up her only daughter, Betty, on her own, establishing a boarding school for young girls in Altona, 'with great vigour and much success', in Karl August Varnhagen's words.[108] At a relatively mature age, back in Berlin, she tried to share a household with Henriette Herz, perhaps with a view on both sides to avoiding loneliness and saving money, but the attempt was not a success. In 1823 Herz informed her friend and correspondent August Twesten calmly about the end of this partnership, citing differences between herself and Mendelssohn that precluded any close relationship:

My marriage [*Ehe*] with Mrs. Meyer [Recha Mendelssohn] will be dissolved from Michaelmas on. She is nearly always ailing and sometimes quite seriously ill, so that it is more comfortable for her and for Betty [her daughter] . . . to live together. Our relationship will remain what it used to be, a very friendly, sociable one. Given the disparity of our natures, our views, and our dispositions it could not go deeper. Moreover, the disparity of our ways of life and our connections hindered a closer cohabitation, and therefore the necessary and *entirely peaceable* separation is not as unpleasant to me as it would be under different circumstances.[109]

Although Henriette Herz does not mention specifically the issue of religion, the fact that she had converted to Christianity several years earlier, while Recha Mendelssohn and her daughter Betty remained Jewish, may well have significantly contributed to these differences of opinion and lifestyle.

Certainly the most unusual case of female partnership among the women studied here is to be found in Fradchen Liebmann's life story. Married in

---

[108] Varnhagen's words are quoted in Bosold, 'Friederike Liman', 149. See also Hensel, *The Mendelssohn Family*, i. 43. Other enlightened Jewish women who established schools were Recha Mendelssohn's younger sister Henriette in Paris (as mentioned in a letter to Varnhagen of 1810, in *Bankiers, Künstler und Gelehrte*, ed. Gilbert, 16–20; see also above in this chapter) and her elder sister Dorothea in the Schönhausen district in Berlin (*Dorothea v. Schlegel und deren Söhne, Briefwechsel*, ed. Raich, i. [8–9]). Sara Meyer and Henriette Herz may also have been involved in similar activity.

[109] Heinrici (ed.), *Briefe von Henriette Herz an August Twesten*, 344. Early in the second decade of the 19th century, while studying in Berlin, August Twesten served as Henriette's private tutor in classical languages and history, and a close friendship developed between the young scholar, who was more than twenty years her junior, and his pupil. When Twesten left Berlin after completing his studies, the two began a correspondence that lasted for many years.

PLATE 9. Recha Meyer, née Mendelssohn (1767–1831)
Pencil on cardboard by Wilhelm Hensel (1830)
© bpk / Kupferstichkabinett, SMB / Jörg P. Anders

1786, when she was only 15, to the Jewish banker Abraham Nathan Liebmann,[110] Fradchen never enjoyed close relations with her husband. The long letters she sent to Rahel Levin describe periods of separation attributable in part to his frequent business trips. Yet despite obvious difficulties in her marital life, Fradchen's surviving letters do not suggest that she wished to end her marriage, as did Dorothea Mendelssohn or Freude Meyer.[111] On the contrary, at times she hoped that their life together would continue and even improve. In August 1795, for example, she wrote: 'He [Abraham] has changed very much in his humours and moods, in short as I believe until now much to my advantage—he also has already bought a very neat house today . . . in which one can be very happy: I hope we will be so there.'[112] However, such hopes proved ill founded. In a letter from 1799 the relationship between the two appears as tense as before, and if it endured it was only because of the conscious restraint demonstrated by Fradchen towards her husband. As Rahel Levin wrote to a young friend—Fradchen's own niece—in giving advice on how best to cope with marriage, 'all her tranquillity and freedom she owes to her muteness'.[113] Fradchen's deliberate silence, which far from expressing passivity was a conscious act of restraint, constituted a practical solution for surviving in a miserable marriage, a tactic with the help of which she acquired freedom of action. In the end, the marriage was dissolved.[114] Although the exact date of divorce is unknown, Church protocols indicate that the separation took place some time between 1809, when the

---

[110] See Ch. 4 above, around n. 10. According to Varnhagen, Liebmann married at the age of 14 and became a mother at 15: Bosold, 'Friederike Liman', 144. Jacob Jacobson's list of Jewish weddings in Berlin indicates that Fradchen Marcuse married Abraham Nathan Liebmann (i.e. Carl August Liman) in December 1786. Although Jacobson does not give Liebmann's date of birth, he does note that her husband, who was certainly older than her, was born in 1767. According to the data presented by Jacobson, Liebmann was at that time an orphan: her mother had died in 1783, her father in February 1786. She had, however, at least two elder brothers who might have been left in charge of the family affairs—Koppel (Jacob) Marcuse, born in 1754, and Mordechai (Marcus Abraham) Marcuse, born in 1763—as well as two elder sisters, Gitel and Hanna (Jacobson, *Jüdische Trauungen*, 132, 221, 298, 311).

[111] It should be borne in mind that owing to the random selection of Fradchen Liebmann's correspondence in our hands many chapters of her life have remained in darkness. From the approximately fifty letters written by her which have survived until today, about twenty were written within a period of a few months in the summer of 1795. On the other hand, there is not even one letter from the period between February 1801 and February 1815, years during which Liebmann converted, got divorced, and changed her way of life.   [112] Bosold, 'Friederike Liman', 29–30.

[113] Ibid. 140. Rahel Levin's letter has been discussed earlier in this chapter, around n. 73 above.

[114] According to Birgit Anna Bosold's perceptive analysis of Liebmann's correspondence, the primary reason for their separation was the difference of opinion between the spouses regarding the main function of marriage: Abraham Nathan Liebmann considered it to be producing offspring, while Fradchen rejected this view. She had only one child (ibid. 220).

couple both converted to Christianity, and 1813, when Abraham Nathan Liebmann, by then known as Carl August Liman, married another woman.[115]

Up to this point the story of Fradchen Liebmann's life seems similar to that of many other Jewish women; but there was more to it. Unlike many of her Jewish friends who divorced their husbands, Liebmann did not marry a Christian aristocrat later on. In fact, she did not marry again at all. Nor did she choose to lead an independent life as a divorcee. Rather, Liebmann embraced a completely different lifestyle, finally free to express the emotional and passionate feelings for women that she had felt for quite some time.

Liebmann's attraction towards members of her own sex dated back to the period when she was still married. The first indication is in fact to be found at the beginning of the earliest letter of hers that has been preserved in the Varnhagen collection. In the spring of 1795, at the house of the Itzig family, she met Maria Josepha Sebottendorf, a converted Jew from Vienna and a close friend of Fanny von Arnstein, née Itzig, who aroused strong emotions in her.[116] 'You know', wrote Liebmann to Rahel Levin, in a letter to which she attached an English love poem,

that I have always been a bit in love with her, but yesterday, I believe, I was really enchanted with her. I have never seen her so graceful and interesting, with her hair combed out, in a black dress, and then this stature and her languishing character. In short, a white woman conquered me.[117] I was driven by my usual demon. I was unable to fall asleep, I thought all the time about this interesting woman and how she suspected nothing at all about me. Finally, I got up, lit a candle and immediately wrote these verses.[118]

Several months later, in July 1795, her passion for the same woman was revived. 'I am having another Sebottendorf epoch' (*eine Sebottendorf epoche*), she wrote to Rahel Levin from her vacation in Freienwalde, finding herself in a state of emotional turmoil. A French book that her friend Cäcilie Wulff (née Itzig) had lent her, Claude-Joseph Dorat's *Les Sacrifices de l'amour* ('The Sacrifices of Love', published in Paris in 1771), which Wulff in turn had

---

[115] Ibid. 157.

[116] On Fanny von Arnstein, see Ch. 5 n. 44 above. Maria Josepha Sebottendorff, née Königsberger, was according to Hilde Spiel 'the daughter of a court agent' who 'had turned away from Judaism when she married Freiherr, later Lieutenant-General, von Sebottendorf'. Spiel, *Fanny von Arnstein*, 52.

[117] As the editor of Liebmann's letters indicates, this phrase is a quote from Mozart's *The Magic Flute*.

[118] Liebmann wrote at the beginning of her letter to Rahel: 'I am attaching here a small poetic attempt that I wrote', which in her opinion showed that she had 'genius for love' (Bosold, 'Friederike Liman', 5).

received from Maria Josepha Sebottendorf, 'in which she had personally written something, reawakened my passion for her. I am always on the lookout for a chance of hearing something from Mrs Wolff [Wulff] about her [Sebottendorf's] amiability.'[119] Liebmann was glad to learn that in the winter Sebottendorf would visit Berlin accompanied by her husband, and she was resolved 'not [to] waste the opportunity to worship her then'.[120]

Upon returning to Berlin from her visit to Freienwalde, Liebmann found her attention drawn with the same intensity towards another woman, the actress Friederike Unzelmann, to whom she had felt attracted before and with whom she would develop a long, intimate relationship. 'She [Unzelmann] has entirely enchanted me again; she appears to me much more beautiful, much kinder, and what is certain, much wiser.' The passionate feelings she experienced for this other woman and the reactions her presence evoked caused Liebmann some confusion, and she had a hard time explaining her emotions to her friend:

Her absence had a much better effect on me than her presence. I looked well; after my arrival here [upon return from Freienwalde] everybody told me [and] I also thought so; I slept well and was calm. Since she is there I am as if turned upside down; I look pale, cannot sleep and I am restive even with *her*. What is this? I am certainly a fool, and in fact a very rare one; because I would not exchange this condition for anything in the world. But I am also happy, because now I am convinced that she likes me; and she also shows this to me, and I wanted nothing more.[121]

As historians have emphasized in recent decades, women who loved women have existed throughout human history, at all times and in all societies, including Europe around 1800;[122] but until the early twentieth century it was hard to find a model with which such women could easily identify. So Liebmann had good reason to feel perplexed about her own emotions, lacking perhaps the appropriate discursive means to interpret the puzzling physical impact that the presence of this woman had on her.[123] As Karl August Varnhagen stressed, writing about Liebmann: 'Regarding her own feeling she seems to have remained entirely in the dark for a long time, guess-

---

[119] Bosold, 'Friederike Liman', 24–5. On Cäcilie Wulff, daughter of the Berlin banker Daniel Itzig and sister of Fanny von Arnstein, see above, Ch. 1 n. 93 and Ch. 4 around n. 17.

[120] Bosold, 'Friederike Liman', 25.   [121] Ibid. 32.

[122] Despite their elusiveness, historians have documented numerous cases of intimate relationships between women in various lands at the turn of the 18th and 19th centuries. See e.g. Smith-Rosenberg, 'The Female World of Love and Ritual'; Clark, 'Anne Lister's Construction of Lesbian Identity'; Hansen, '"No Kisses is Like Youres"'; Vicinus, *Intimate Friends*. See also Schmölzer, *Frauenliebe*.

[123] For a succinct 'global history of love between women from the beginning of time to the present', see Rupp, *Sapphistries*.

ing neither its origin nor its outlets. She did not know what her condition was, what was going on inside her. She fought her way through the most passionate storms without having understanding or a name for them.'[124]

Giving a name to Liebmann's attraction to and relationships with other women was not only a challenge for Fradchen Liebmann herself (or for a contemporary such as Varnhagen); it is also a complex task for historians. This is not simply, or indeed primarily, because we know little about the nature of her connection with other women. For although Liebmann's letters do not indicate how her love for women manifested itself—whether her bond with other women was limited to a 'sensual romantic friendship', or perhaps involved physical intimacy[125]—they do unambiguously show that she felt passionate about other women. Even if we knew with certainty the nature of Liebmann's relationships, it would be problematic to characterize her inclinations employing today's labels. Current terms such as 'homosexual' or 'lesbian', used since the medicalization of homosexuality by sexologists and psychiatrists in the late nineteenth and early twentieth centuries, describe more than same-sex attraction or sexual orientation: they define to a great extent an individual's identity, implying an affiliation to a certain community or 'subculture'—a connotation which would hardly apply to Liebmann's case.[126] The problem of naming is exacerbated by the fact that in Liebmann's case, as in many other cases of same-sex attraction, her bond with women did not exclude other types of connection, first and foremost heterosexual relationships with men.

Liebmann's relationship with Unzelmann seems to fit the model of romantic friendship that flourished in the Western world in the late eighteenth and early nineteenth centuries. Such romantic friendships constituted one of several possibilities that existed in the period discussed here for women who loved women—an intimate type of relationship between women

---

[124] Varnhagen's words are quoted in Bosold, 'Friederike Liman', 145.

[125] Liebmann's letters do not hint at the second option, but we must bear in mind that even if there was physical intimacy with members of her own sex, it would have been unlikely to appear in writing.

[126] In *The History of Sexuality: An Introduction*, Michel Foucault depicts the construction of sexual identities as a modern phenomenon that came into being only in the late 19th century as a result of the increased discourse on sexuality which steadily proliferated in the Western world throughout the 18th and 19th centuries in fields including medicine, psychiatry, and the law. Homosexual relations, once perceived as discrete acts that an individual might perform from time to time, became in modern times a defining characteristic of a person, the core of his or her identity—his or her 'natural essence'. Foucault's chronology is now questioned and, as Anna Clark indicates, numerous scholars 'have extensively documented gay male subcultures that flourished in eighteenth- and nineteenth-century cities, long before sexologists and psychiatrists invented "the homosexual"' (Clark, 'Anne Lister's Construction of Lesbian Identity', 25). Lesbian subcultures may have existed in Liebmann's time, but there is no evidence that she was part of any such culture.

that was to a certain extent accepted by middle-class society and could, as in the case of Liebmann and Unzelmann, sometimes successfully coexist with heterosexual marriage.[127] It is clear that neither of these two women saw their partnership as incompatible with different kinds of relationship, for instance a romantic relationship with a man.[128] Unzelmann's intimate ties with various men over the years were no obstacle to her continuing special relationship with Liebmann. In 1800, several years before divorcing her husband, Fradchen informed Rahel Levin, who was then in Paris, with excitement and happiness that 'my U[nzelmann]' had given birth to a child.[129] Not even the actress's second marriage to Heinrich Eduard Bethmann, also an actor at the Berlin theatre, in any way displaced her deep bond with Liebmann, who continued to admire the actress and accompany her everywhere: 'The two women were now almost always seen together: they travelled together, they gave their lives as many common references as they could. Mrs Liman was the confidante of all the big and small adventures assailing Mrs Unzelmann.'[130] At some point Liebmann moved with the Bethmanns, and they all lived in 'the happiest cohabitation [*Zusammenleben*] . . . equally desirable and pleasant and useful for all involved'.[131]

Unzelmann's sudden death in 1815 dealt a hard blow to Fradchen Liebmann, whose immense pain at the loss of her beloved one may have been exacerbated by the loss of the sense of security she had derived from the unique familial framework in which she lived and the feeling of being useful and needed:

Oh! Dear R[ahel], what have I lost! It is so painful to me, especially at this age, for every day she needed me more, not an hour passed without her having something to tell me or ask me for advice. Now of all times, that she was so entirely in peace, in prosperity, so happy with her family as she had never been. After I helped her bear all the storms of life faithfully and honestly, now she is suddenly torn away from our harmonious, peaceful circle, without any preparation.[132]

---

[127] 'Because women were perceived as fundamentally different from men and because middle-class society tended to separate female and male social worlds, it seemed natural that women would find their soul mates among other women' (Rupp, *Sapphistries*, 127–8). The opinion that female romantic friendships were widely approved and valued in the 18th and 19th centuries was challenged by Lisa Moore in '"Something more tender still than friendship"'.

[128] As Martha Vicinus has indicated in her study on 'women who loved women' between 1778 and 1928, 'Women then, as now . . . could live long and emotionally complicated lives that changed over time. One woman, one kind of love, did not automatically exclude other lovers or kinds of love.' Many possible configurations existed, including women who flirted with both men and women, as well as married women who were involved in same-sex relationships (Vicinus, *Intimate Friends*, p. xix).

[129] Bosold, 'Friederike Liman', 44–5.   [130] According to Karl August Varnhagen (ibid. 145).
[131] As reported by Karl August Varnhagen (ibid.).   [132] Ibid. 71.

PLATE 10. Friederike Unzelmann-Bethmann (1760–1815) Lithograph (*c.* 1858) from *Album des Königlichen Schauschpiels und der Königlichen Oper zu Berlin* (1858)

© bpk / SBB

Liebmann continued to live with the Bethmanns after Friederike Unzelmann's death, in accordance with the actress's instructions to her husband.[133] Yet a year later she had embarked upon what would become an intimate friendship with another woman: the singer Anna Milder, to whom she would remain emotionally attached for many years to come.

*

In the light of the picture that emerges from the variety of cases presented throughout this chapter, it is hard to interpret the decisions made by these Jewish women on how to conduct their personal lives as driven merely by a desire to assimilate into the surrounding society, or to exchange a marriage relationship with a Jewish husband for one with a non-Jewish and preferably noble man. What we have seen here is a comprehensive undermining of the foundations of the existing gender order—an order that strove to perpetuate the domination of men (above all, fathers and husbands) over women. In a display of female consciousness perhaps unprecedented in Jewish history, strongly nourished by enlightened ideas, these women protested in word and deed against the situation of subordination forced upon them, insisting on their independence and their freedom, especially in matters related to how they led their personal lives. A close examination of their deeds has revealed the wide variety of ways in which these women acted in order to become autonomous beings and to direct their lives according to their own personal views.

[133] When in 1817 Bethmann sold the house in which he and Liebmann continued to live after Unzelmann's death, Liebmann found herself in a precarious economic situation. See her letter of 9 Feb. 1817 in Bosold, 'Friederike Liman', 88–90.

SEVEN

BETWEEN ACCULTURATION AND CONVERSION

DRESSED IN AN ELEGANT COSTUME and accompanied by her friends Esther Gad and Friederike Unzelmann, Fradchen Liebmann arrived at the Berlin opera house one evening in mid-February 1801 to attend a carnivalesque festivity which was taking place there.[1] It was not the first time that Liebmann had attended a *Redoute*, the city's by then traditional masquerade ball. The previous year she had attended this exclusive celebration accompanied by Rahel Levin—who was absent from the 1801 *Redoute* as she was away in Paris. With marked self-confidence Liebmann mingled with non-Jewish guests and established contact with some strangers, amazing new acquaintances with her knowledge of several languages, including Italian and English.[2] Her experience at the ball, she noted later, gave her great pleasure.[3]

Earlier that month, Liebmann had attended an event celebrated in a quite different social circle: the *Judenball*, a ball organized by members of the Jewish community. At that time Liebmann was leading an active social life and cultivating numerous acquaintanceships in mixed society, and her ties to Jewish circles were becoming looser. Indeed, her decision to attend the Jewish ball derived precisely from a wish to maintain her connections with the members of her family and her religion: she insisted on attending the Jewish celebration 'just so as not to exclude myself, since this winter there were so many picnics and dancing parties in *our* family in which I never participated, and at this ball I delivered these commitments *en masse*'. Somewhat to her surprise, she enjoyed the Jewish ball, even though her

---

[1] According to Liebmann's report, the three women arrived in bat costumes, a popular choice at the time (Bosold, 'Friederike Liman', 57).

[2] As Liebmann wrote in a letter she sent in February 1801 to Rahel Levin in Paris, a man whom she and her friends met that evening 'thought we were from Babylon since we spoke all languages' (ibid. 58). [3] Ibid. 57.

report on this event lacks the enthusiasm and cheerfulness that characterized the description of her experiences at the non-Jewish celebration.[4]

Beyond the conclusions that may be drawn from this short account about the lifestyle of well-to-do Berlin Jews, which clearly included recreational pastimes such as family outings and dances which would not be typically identified with a traditional lifestyle, it is interesting to note the ambivalent attitude of an acculturated woman such as Fradchen Liebmann towards Jewish society—even its modern wing, to which her relatives belonged.[5] On the one hand, as she indicated, she tended frequently to be absent, at least in that winter of 1800–1, from family social events in Jewish circles, while participating actively in non-Jewish cultural and social life, as her letters testify. On the other hand, she expressed the wish to maintain some kind of contact with her Jewish relatives and friends, even if this contact was rather tenuous.

Moreover, Liebmann's parallel participation in two spheres of activity—the Jewish and the Christian—which in the past had been mutually exclusive, shows that in Berlin at the beginning of the nineteenth century religious affiliation, for all the importance still accorded to it, was not decisive in determining an individual's field of activity. Thus, for a Jewish woman such as Liebmann, conversion was not indispensable in order to participate in German cultural and social life. In this sense her baptism some eight years later did not constitute a decisive turning point in her life: as a Jew she was already accepted in various social circles (though by no means *all* social circles) and able to take an active part in cultural events.

We have seen in previous chapters that Liebmann and other modernizing Jewish women entered the social and cultural world of their time even before converting to Christianity. When Fradchen Liebmann visited the spas and mingled with members of German high society—she was Jewish. When Sara and Marianne Meyer started to exchange ideas and opinions with Goethe through correspondence—they were Jewish. When Dorothea Mendelssohn published her novel *Florentin*; when Rahel Levin started to publish her letters on German literature; when Esther Gad published her opinions on the education and erudition of women—all were Jewish.[6] When Henriette

---

[4] Liebmann told Rahel Levin about her attendance at the Jewish ball in the same letter of February 1801 quoted in n. 2 above (Bosold, 'Friederike Liman', 54).

[5] On the intensive acculturation of the members of the Liebmann family as reflected in the multiple cases of religious conversion, see Lowenstein, *The Berlin Jewish Community*, 158–9.

[6] Gad's essay against Campe was printed in 1798; her conversion to Christianity took place in 1801 or possibly earlier. In 1790, some years before this essay appeared, Gad published the German translation of a short English text under the title 'Markus und Monimia', without concealing her Jewishness—indeed, in this first text that appeared in print under her name she highlighted this fact at the beginning

Mendelssohn hosted contemporary leading figures in culture, society, and politics at her home in Paris, while running a respected educational institution for girls—she did so as a Jew. When Henriette Herz educated the young princess of Curland and the children of Charlotte von Kathen, a German aristocrat—she was Jewish.

Despite the indisputable importance of religious conversion, in most cases the act itself did not mark a decisive point of departure in either the social life or the world-view of these women. Baptism was not a ceremony that sharply divided their lives into two clear chapters, before and after conversion. On the contrary, in fact, baptism blended into the way of life which most of them had already been leading for many years. The act of conversion, whether deriving from religious motivation, such as the belief in a particular version of Christianity, or from more immediate and pragmatic considerations, usually as a precondition to marriage with a member of the Christian faith, constituted not a sudden leap from one world to another so much as one more step in a continuing process of acculturation in German society and alienation from the Jewish world—a process throughout which a connection with certain parts of Jewish society and culture was kept, and which at times stretched over decades.

LONG ACCULTURATION, LATE CONVERSION

One of the most significant features of the act of conversion in the case of these Jewish women is the fact that for them it came in most cases at a relatively advanced age, despite the fact that their close involvement with German society and culture had started years before, in their teens or early twenties. The earliest cases of conversion among this group took place in the late twenties; however, most converted even later, after a long period in which they ruminated about the decision and its implications. Sara Meyer and her sister Marianne became Christians at the end of the 1790s, when Sara was about 35 and Marianne close to 30;[7] Esther Gad converted around 1800, at 33 or so; Dorothea Mendelssohn was baptized only in 1804, at the age of 40; Fradchen Liebmann converted together with her husband in 1809, when she was 38 years old; Henriette Mendelssohn became a Catholic in 1812, aged 37; Rahel Levin converted in 1814 at the age of 43; Henriette Herz did so as late as 1817, when she was 53.

of her translation: 'I am a Jewess', she wrote, 'and I must, *even in Prussian states*, thank God that I am tolerated' (quoted in Rudert, 'Die Wiederentdeckung einer deutschen "Wollstonecraft"', 223).

[7] It should be remembered, however, that the sisters' first attempt to convert took place about a decade earlier. On the story of their double conversion, see Ch. 1 above, around n. 71.

All these women, then, spent many years distancing themselves in practice from the traditional Jewish way of life, blurring the borders that separated the Jewish and Christian worlds. During those years they usually lived as non-observant Jews, who gradually abandoned Jewish practices but nevertheless remained affiliated (albeit sometimes weakly and even against their own inclinations) to the Jewish people. At that time quite a few Jews, not only in Berlin but also in other central European cities, saw the traditional Jewish way of life as an unnecessary burden which did not fit in with the way of life in the modern world.[8] Among them was this group of Jewish women, who over time ceased to observe the commandments and customs that determined the unique character of traditional Jewish society and distinguished its members from the rest of the population.

The protracted nature of this process can be seen in the story of Rahel Levin. In December 1793, aged 22, Levin told David Veit about a daring act of public desecration of the sabbath:

Imagine, yesterday, on the sabbath, in broad daylight, I rode with her [Maria Marchetti, a singer and close friend] in a royal carriage to the opera rehearsal at half past two; nobody saw me, and I would have denied it and would and will deny it to anyone—even to the one who helped me out of the carriage! Methinks this is what one can and must do in my situation.[9]

What is significant about this confession is not only Levin's rejection of a major commandment of the Jewish religion—the keeping of the sabbath[10]— but the fact that she tried to conceal it from her co-religionists. It shows that on this occasion she transgressed the Jewish law not on principle so much as out of a wish to take advantage of an opportunity to participate in the cultural life the city offered—in this specific case, to share the experiences of the

---

[8] See Feiner, *The Origins of Jewish Secularization*, a recent study on the conspicuous minority of freethinking Jews in central and western Europe.

[9] *Briefwechsel zwischen Rahel und David Veit*, i. 76. This episode is included in many accounts concerning Rahel Levin. See e.g. Arendt, *Rahel Varnhagen*, 91; Meyer, *The Origins of the Modern Jew*, 110; Hertz, *Jewish High Society*, 101.

[10] By that time, the sabbath does not seem to have been kept strictly at the Levin house, certainly not by Rahel. See e.g. her letter of 3–4 Jan. 1794, written on Friday evening and throughout Saturday. On Saturday morning she had time to write to David Veit because 'my English teacher did not arrive'. She also informs him of the arrival of Lehmann, the music teacher, at her house that morning, apparently for a music lesson (*Briefwechsel zwischen Rahel und David Veit*, i. 98–109). Cf. an earlier letter sent by Chaie Levin to her daughter Rahel in 1790 from Breslau, specifically indicating that she planned to make a stop for the sabbath on her way back to Berlin. Interestingly, in another letter that year Chaie Levin informed her daughter from Leipzig that she had purchased tickets to attend the balloon flight of the pioneering French balloonist Jean-Pierre Blanchard, planned for the upcoming sabbath (Levin Varnhagen, *Familienbriefe*, 11).

acclaimed Italian singer whose acquaintance she had recently made. Rahel Levin's concern for the opinion of her fellow Jews—a concern that would soon disappear—was utterly rejected by David Veit, who criticized her efforts to hide what she was doing: 'If you travel on the sabbath, you should not disavow it, otherwise I will believe that you do not want to contribute anything to the reformation of the Jews.'[11] Veit's words suggest that he and Levin had previously discussed between themselves the issue of the 'reformation of the Jews', and perhaps had agreed to join forces to champion this goal. In any case, more than twenty years went by between that Saturday afternoon when Rahel Levin rode in the royal carriage and her formal conversion.

In Henriette Herz's case, more than three decades separated what was perhaps one of her first steps in consciously distancing herself from Jewish tradition—her decision to give up covering her hair, as was customary for married women—and her baptism. The issue of the head-covering occupied her a lot as a young wife, and it recurs several times in her short memoirs. As she indicates there, her discomfort with the requirement to cover her hair began immediately after her wedding. In the morning after the ceremony, when she was getting ready for the nuptial celebration at her parents' home, 'I dressed—was not pleased with myself—fussed with my finery many times, but still was not any more pleased with myself—the reason was that, according to Jewish custom, as a married woman I had to cover my hair completely, and the headdress [*Kopfzeug*], decorated with pearls and flowers, did not suit me at all.'[12]

The issue of head-covering gave rise to confrontations with her mother, with whom she had a tense relationship in her youth. On that very first day as a married woman she had to bear sharp criticism from her mother, who 'rebuked me since here and there a little of my hair was visible from under the headdress'.[13] How alienated she was from this custom is clear from the feelings she recalled years later when drafting her memoirs: so deep was her revulsion at the obligation to cover her head that it caused her to neglect her personal care and to feel discontented with her whole appearance when appearing in society.[14] Later, she took advantage of a contemporary religious ruling in order to evade the custom which was so foreign and annoying to

---

[11] *Briefwechsel zwischen Rahel und David Veit*, i. 90.

[12] Landsberg (ed.), *Henriette Herz*, 129 (Eng. trans. in Blackwell and Zantop (eds.), *Bitter Healing*, 319).

[13] Landsberg (ed.), *Henriette Herz*, 130 (Eng. trans. in Blackwell and Zantop (eds.), *Bitter Healing*, 319).

[14] Landsberg (ed.), *Henriette Herz*, 139 (Eng. trans. in Blackwell and Zantop (eds.), *Bitter Healing*, 327).

her: 'Around that time Jewish women received permission to wear hairpieces, even though not their real hair, in public. Since my parents had nothing against this, a wig that suited me was made, and soon it too was put aside and was replaced with my own shiny, coal-black hair.'[15]

To sum up, then, at the beginning of her marriage Henriette Herz respected Jewish custom and wore a head-covering, but did so neither out of conviction nor out of respect for her husband, but merely to avoid her parents' censure. This compliance lasted only a short time. Feeling that the obligation to cover her hair conflicted too strongly with her outlook and the modern lifestyle she and her husband followed, and even caused her embarrassment and confusion when mixing in German circles, she took the personal decision to evade the observance of this old custom.[16]

Direct testimonies such as these describing explicit acts of disengagement from Jewish ritual and customs are not numerous in the surviving sources,[17] but it may be assumed that this process intensified as the years went by until the women had almost completely abandoned the traditional Jewish lifestyle.[18] As long as their parents were alive, the Jewish calendar was

---

[15] Landsberg (ed.), *Henriette Herz*, 140–1 (Eng. trans. in Blackwell and Zantop (eds.), *Bitter Healing*, 328). The use of wigs by observant Jewish women to cover their hair 'was at first denounced by rabbinic authorities, but eventually accepted by most rabbis'. Not only was this practice originally condemned as an 'inappropriate emulation of the "ways of the nations"'—for Jewish women were in fact imitating the French fashion of using wigs, in vogue since the 16th century; in the opinion of many rabbis the wig failed to fulfil the original purpose of women's hair-covering, i.e. to prevent unholy thoughts among men (Bronner, 'From Veil to Wig', 471, 472).

[16] Cf. the description of the removal of head-covering by Jewish women in 19th-century eastern Europe, as a protest against the traditional social order, in Parush, *Reading Jewish Women*, 164–5. See also Feiner, *The Origins of Jewish Secularization*, 151–60.

[17] A hint in a letter that Ludwig Börne sent to his sister in Frankfurt am Main in November 1802 seems to indicate that Jewish women in Berlin, perhaps even Henriette Herz herself or her sister Brenna, did not keep the dietary laws: 'I remember that once Miss Wezlar [apparently an acquaintance from his native city, Frankfurt] was in a quandary as to what German name to adopt. She could call herself Brenna, that is the name of Mrs Herz's sister. You Frankfurt girls who do not eat pork do not even have one Brenna to boast of' (Geiger (ed.), *Briefwechsel des jungen Börne und der Henriette Herz*, 41). Some twenty years earlier, in response to Dohm's treatise *Über die bürgerliche Verbesserung der Juden* ('On the Civil Improvement of the Jews'), the orientalist Johann David Michaelis expressed reservations about 'those who are Jews only in name or in origin and who do not believe in the Jewish religion'. Such a Jew eats pork 'in order no doubt to offend his religion', and therefore does not merit his trust. This response was published in the second part of Dohm's book, *Über die bürgerliche Verbesserung der Juden*, 31–71 (Eng. trans. in Mendes-Flohr and Reinharz, *The Jew in the Modern World*, 42).

[18] Lowenstein points to a turn he identified in the late 1780s among the Jews in Berlin, regarding the observance of the Jewish law and customs. 'In the 1780s we find the first evidence of considerable numbers of people who were no longer observing basic Jewish ritual laws. During Mendelssohn's lifetime such violations of Halacha seem to have been restricted to personal practice. It was not until after Mendelssohn's death [in 1786] that ideological advocacy of abandonment of the ceremonial law

observed to some extent, and the women participated at least in basic ceremonies, such as holiday meals. In 1794 Hendel Levin, née Liebmann, who was married to Rahel's brother Marcus, mentioned the festive meal at her mother-in-law Chaie Levin's house in honour of Simhat Torah.[19] Almost a decade later Chaie Levin was still observing Jewish holidays in the family circle: when her daughter Rahel heard about the delicacies that her mother was preparing in the kitchen—marrow cake[20] and anchovy salad—one day in February 1802, she assumed that these were preparations for the Purim feast, although she immediately realized that she was wrong, recalling that the holiday would take place 'only in two weeks'.[21]

The waning of the Jewish lifestyle was accompanied by a parallel development which intensified the women's alienation from their Jewish heritage: the gradual adoption of elements from German culture rooted in Christianity. Customs and practices that had Christian origins, even though they had to some extent lost their religious significance and had turned into part of the general culture of the bourgeoisie, spread among the Jewish women and their family circles even before they converted. A typical example was Christmas. The celebration of Christmas as a private event in the family home, with the brightly decorated tree at its centre, was a new custom spreading in non-Jewish society in Germany at this time, not coincidentally along with the rise of the bourgeoisie and the expansion of secularization. Less either a Christian religious holiday, the main focus of which was a special mass at church to commemorate the birth of Jesus, or a public winter carnival focused on food, alcohol, and games, Christmas in its modern form was largely perceived as a secular, private holiday, the celebration of the bourgeois family *par excellence*.[22] Jews throughout the nineteenth century who wished to integrate into the German middle class had no problem adopting it as such without feelings of guilt or remorse.[23]

An early testimony to this phenomenon is found in Rahel Levin's letters. While unequivocally indicating that Christmas was observed at the Levin home, Rahel's references to the holiday suggest that most members of her family did not see it as an occasion of religious significance or emphasize its Christian character. Rather, it was seen more than anything else as a celebration of love and fraternity, a holiday that offered the opportunity to display

was put into print. Thereafter the move away from tradition increased rapidly both in theoretical formulation and in practice' (Lowenstein, *The Berlin Jewish Community*, 53–4).

[19] Bosold, 'Friederike Liman', 41.　　　　　　　　　　[20] See Ch. 5 n. 96 above.
[21] Levin Varnhagen, *Familienbriefe*, 128.
[22] Eberspächer, 'Wie Weihnachten deutsch wurde'; Nissenbaum, *The Battle for Christmas*.
[23] Richarz, 'Der jüdische Weihnachtsbaum'; Eberspächer, 'Wie Weihnachten deutsch wurde'.

affection not only towards members of the family and friends, but also towards servants, who also took part in the celebration, if only as recipients of presents. In a letter of December 1808 Rahel Levin told Karl August Varnhagen how the holiday was celebrated at her maternal home, including the presents that she intended to shower on her relatives, friends, and servants. Two points deserve to be highlighted in her description: the education that was given from a very young age to her two nieces, who were born as Jews at the end of the eighteenth century but grew up engaged with German culture;[24] and the participation of the mother of the family, Chaie Levin, who belonged to the older generation of more traditional Jews, in the ceremony of exchanging Christmas gifts. 'Ever since Hanne and Fanny [Rahel's nieces] have had the power of reason', she wrote, the preparations for the holiday had been carried out meticulously: 'a table ready-laid, many candles, and as many sorts of presents as you could possibly get'. Thus they had celebrated the year before, she said, and thus they were planning to celebrate that year. 'Even for the domestics presents are set out, as well as cake, fruit, confitures. It always remains moving. Last year that is what it was like, and then at my place, where I gave presents to Robert, Pauline, Bribes, the cousin and Louis Liman[25] and Mama, and Pauline to me, Mama to the cousin and Robert, Robert to me.' To Varnhagen, who was away from Berlin, she sent a present in good time: 'To you, my favourite friend, I send the enclosed package which you will open no sooner, under penalty of death, than Christmas Eve at 6pm sharp.'[26]

Another Jewish woman who celebrated Christmas was Henriette Herz. Although in her case there is no indication that the festivity entered her mother's home, it certainly featured in Henriette's life before her conversion and while her mother was still alive: there is evidence that she spent Christmas Eve 1814 with the Schleiermachers, who were like a second family to her.[27] That same year Fanny von Arnstein put up a decorated Christmas tree in her mansion—home to one of the most glamorous salons in Vienna, where distinguished personalities met during the Napoleonic wars and the

---

[24] When Marcus Levin's first daughter was born in 1793, David Veit referred in a letter to Rahel Levin to the hesitations and thoughts of assimilating Jewish parents on the arrival of a child: 'Marcus is rightly happy with the increase of the fair sex, which at least can maintain religious neutrality for a time' (*Briefwechsel zwischen Rahel und David Veit*, i. 24). Clearly, the birth of a girl meant that the parents could postpone cardinal religious decisions. If a boy was born, they would have to decide immediately whether to circumcise him or not.   [25] Most likely Fradchen Liebmann and her son.

[26] Varnhagen, *Rahel Varnhagen. Briefwechsel*, ii. 69–70.

[27] Henriette Herz wrote to August Twesten in February 1815: 'Due to the scarlet fever I had not visited the Schleiermacher house for a long time . . . on Christmas eve I was able to go there for the first time again, and it was a double celebration to me' (Heinrici (ed.), 'Briefe von Henriette Herz an August Twesten', 310).

Congress of Vienna—thus becoming perhaps the first to introduce the custom, which she had brought from her native Berlin, to the Habsburg capital.[28] Joseph Mendelssohn and his wife Henriette, née Meyer, who never embraced Christianity, celebrated Christmas within the close family, apparently without granting the event a particularly religious significance.[29] Here, as in the Levin family, the festivity seems to have revolved mainly around the children and the custom of exchanging presents—two features which had indeed only recently become the main focus of the holiday.[30] At the end of December 1828 Henriette described how the holiday had been celebrated at the home of her son Alexander (among the last descendants of Moses Mendelssohn to die as a Jew) and his wife Marianne, née Seligmann: 'Here it looked very merry, which, by the way, is the case each evening, but, to be sure, especially on Christmas Eve. The children were absolutely charming. Their mother had laid out [the presents] for them in the sitting room, but they, too, had done the same in the study for their mother, their father and ourselves.'[31] Like many deeply acculturated Jews, they ascribed to Christmas a secular, universal message, devoid of religious attributes. So did Rahel Levin, who in the same letter quoted above shared with Varnhagen how she perceived the essence of this holiday: '[Christmas] is for me . . . the only feast of the year, because it is still alive, and really and truly relates to the life which we ourselves still live . . . The whole world wants to cause pleasure to the whole world, and so do I!'[32]

[28] Hilde Spiel, Fanny von Arnstein's biographer, claimed that hers was 'the first Christmas tree that Vienna had seen' (Spiel, *Fanny von Arnstein*, 292). Bruce David Forbes, emphasizing the leading role of the German nobility, which had only recently embraced Christmas trees, in the spread of this custom to other regions of the world, claimed however that 'in 1816 Princess Henrietta of Nassau-Weilburg introduced the Christmas tree to Vienna, and it spread throughout Austria' (Forbes, *Christmas: A Candid History*, 51). The concept of the family varied, so that it could at times include friends of the family, as in the case of the Arnsteins, or the servants, as in the case of the Levins. See Eberspächer, 'Wie Weihnachten deutsch wurde', 34.

[29] This is the opinion of H. G. Reissner in 'Henriette Mendelssohn, Unresolved Conflicts of Integration', 257–8. This Henriette Mendelssohn (not to be confused with Joseph's sister Henriette, or with the wife of the youngest brother Nathan, also Henriette (née Itzig)), a native of Strelitz, was the sister of Mendel Meyer, Recha Mendelssohn's former husband, and Freude Meyer.

[30] Nissenbaum, *The Battle for Christmas*, and Forbes, *Christmas: A Candid History*, discuss the (in their opinion excessive) commercialization of Christmas in the last two centuries or so, focusing mainly on the case of the United States.

[31] As quoted in Reissner, 'Henriette Mendelssohn, Unresolved Conflicts of Integration', 258. Reissner also notes that in 1813 Henriette Mendelssohn, née Meyer, attended a thanksgiving service in Berlin Cathedral following a Prussian military victory in the war against Napoleon, and was very impressed by the Christian ritual of Holy Communion (ibid. 252).

[32] Varnhagen, *Rahel Varnhagen. Briefwechsel*, ii. 69. A similar statement was made by Rahel Levin two years earlier in a letter addressed to Rebecca Salomon quoted in Richarz, 'Der jüdische Weihnachtsbaum', 69.

PLATE 11. Henriette Mendelssohn, née Meyer (1776–1862)
Undated: artist unknown
© bpk / SBB

While the new-style Christmas celebration as practised in the years around 1800 may be said to be a domestic festivity, celebrated 'within the secure confines of the family circle',[33] other cultural phenomena associated with Christianity with which Jewish women became involved were more clearly connected to the public world. One such was church music. The pleasure that acculturated Jewish women derived from this cultural form, which was very popular at the time and engaged the most highly regarded contemporary classical composers, often took them into churches, not in order to participate in Christian worship but as spectators attracted to an edifying and aesthetically pleasing event. Around 1781, the 17-year-old Henriette Herz arrived at the Nikolaikirche (St Nicholas' Church) in Berlin to attend a performance of the Passion oratorio *Der Tod Jesu* ('The Death of Jesus') at the invitation of her music instructor, the church's organist.[34] This devotional work, composed in 1755 by Carl Heinrich Graun to a libretto by Carl Wilhelm Ramler, enjoyed enormous popularity in Germany for over a century;[35] its annual performance at Easter attracted a large audience, including, as Herz's memoirs attest, acculturated Jews. More than two decades later, in 1803, Henriette Herz was to be found at another, similar event: Ludwig Börne, the Herzes' lodger in Berlin in his youth, arrived at the church in Berlin to attend a performance of the same oratorio and met 'Madam H[erz]' in the crowded hall.[36] This suggests that she may have continued to attend the annual performance of this popular work.

Another specific case shows that this enthusiasm for church music could encompass more than mere aesthetic appreciation as part of the audience: it could involve, in addition, actual participation in its performance, a remarkable fact given the strong Christian connections of this activity. Fradchen Liebmann, when still a Jew, joined the Sing-Akademie, a Berlin choral society founded in 1791 by Carl Friedrich Fasch, harpsichordist to the Prussian court, along with other Jews such as Sara Levy (née Itzig), Abraham Mendelssohn, and Lea Salomon, who was Sara Levy's niece and would become Abraham's wife. (Years later the couple's son Felix Mendelssohn-Bartholdy would also

---

[33] Nissenbaum, *The Battle for Christmas*, p. xi.

[34] Herz wrote in her memoirs: 'Every year, my teacher performed the *Tod Jesu* at St Nicholas' Church, and that year I went there, simply because he was my teacher' (Landsberg (ed.), *Henriette Herz*, 150 (the English translation of Herz's memoirs (Blackwell and Zantop (eds.), *Bitter Healing*) does not include this fragment)).

[35] See Howard Serwer's preface to Graun, *Der Tod Jesu*, pp. vii–xiv. According to Howard E. Smither, the *Tod Jesu* was the oratorio 'most often performed in Germany of the late eighteenth century' (Smither, *The Oratorio in the Nineteenth and Twentieth Century*, 7). See also id., *The Oratorio in the Classical Era*, 348–9.   [36] Geiger (ed.), *Briefwechsel des jungen Börne und der Henriette Herz*, 64.

join the Akademie.)[37] Fradchen Liebmann's membership of this bourgeois choral society, which 'began as a group of musically inclined individuals who met in the tradition of contemporaneous reading clubs and salons' and soon developed a public profile as a choir that gave concerts,[38] is significant in several ways. First, participation in this mixed-sex institution—perhaps one of the first mixed choral associations in the world—enabled Liebmann to perform a public role, opportunities for which were rare for women at this time. As Karen Ahlquist has noted, regarding the significance of women's participation in this type of society, choral singing 'allowed them to participate publicly in an artistic activity without claiming artistic or professional ambition. Eventually it offered many of them solo opportunities in public.'[39] Such was the case with another Jewish female member of the Sing-Akademie, Sara Levy. A lifelong Jew, Levy exhibited an extraordinary proficiency in music. A Bach enthusiast and close associate of the family of composers, she commissioned works from them which were then performed in the family circle.[40] The Akademie offered her a more public framework for her musical activities, especially after the death of her husband in 1806, when she 'became more engaged in the public concerts of the Sing-Akademie where she regularly appeared as a soloist with the orchestra'.[41]

Second, as a member of this bourgeois choral society Liebmann (and other Jews) took part in the performance of works of an explicitly Christian nature, appearing in public concerts in churches and cathedrals many years before being baptized. In 1800 Liebmann wrote to Rahel Levin about her participation in a Christian ceremony in memory of the recently deceased founder and director of the Sing-Akademie, in which Mozart's Requiem was performed: 'I am extraordinarily sorry that you will not hear Mozart's

---

[37] Wolff, 'A Bach Cult in Late-Eighteenth-Century Berlin'. Also, the contemporary Jewish doctor and writer Wolf Davidson attests that 'different Jews take part in the singing school of Fasch' (Davidson, *Ueber die bürgerliche Verbesserung der Juden*, 109). On Felix Mendelssohn-Bartholdy's complex relationship with the Sing-Akademie, see Little, 'Mendelssohn and the Berlin Singakademie'. The strong connection between the above-mentioned members of the Itzig and Mendelssohn families and the Sing-Akademie is also reflected in their significant contribution to its music archive: in later years, Abraham and Lea Mendelssohn donated to the Sing-Akademie the estate they had purchased from the Bach family, which included the complete works of C. P. E. Bach and a significant portion of the surviving works of J. S. Bach, while Sara Levy donated part of her large music collection to the library of this institution. See Wolff, 'A Bach Cult in Late-Eighteenth-Century Berlin'. See also the detailed list containing most musical works given by Sara Levy to the Sing-Akademie in Wollny, 'Sara Levy and the Making of Musical Taste in Berlin', 666–9.

[38] Ahlquist, 'Men and Women of the Chorus', 268.   [39] Ibid.

[40] Wollny, 'Sara Levy and the Making of Musical Taste in Berlin', 657–60.

[41] Wolff, 'A Bach Cult in Late-Eighteenth-Century Berlin', 29. See also Wollny, 'Sara Levy and the Making of Musical Taste in Berlin', 653.

Requiem, which we, that is the Sing-Akademie, will perform publicly the day after tomorrow at the Garnisonkirche [a church originally used by the military]. Our Fasch really died some weeks ago, and for his obsequies we are performing the Requiem.' Liebmann's passion for the works of prominent composers was strong, and it did not bother her at all that the musical compositions she admired most had deep Christian roots. 'There is no church music as divine as this [Mozart's Requiem]', she wrote to Rahel Levin, 'and in *my* opinion there *never* has been. Because even if Handel was *Handel*, he did not know Mozart. But Mozart did know Handel, and how he ennobled the old style with the new one and *blended* the two so sensitively.'[42]

Fradchen Liebmann's intensive involvement in the Sing-Akademie suggests that her Jewishness was no barrier to her active involvement in the contemporary musical world: not only did her religion not prevent her from participating in Christian ceremonies; the society itself seemed quite prepared to accept a Jewish woman performing as part of a Christian choir. In other words, in this case Liebmann's desire for social and cultural integration was matched by a reciprocal openness on the part of the wider society towards an acculturated Jewish woman like her.

Obviously, reality did not always match the expectations of assimilating Jewish women (or men), and they could not always count on a sympathetic reception.[43] There were undoubtedly cases in which women met hostility because of their Jewishness—a phenomenon which intensified in Germany with the spread of Romanticism and more reactionary political feeling. Nonetheless, there were also instances in which the fear of running up against such negative attitudes turned out to be unfounded. We have already seen that Henriette Herz was both pleased and surprised when a princess she knew ignored her Jewish—and bourgeois—origins and was willing to share her table with her.[44] Later, when looking for a place to stay during the French occupation of Berlin, she assumed that two obstacles would make it hard for her to find a position as governess or companion: her reputation and her religion. 'My very undeserved fame and my Jewishness stand in my way in Germany; because of the first, people fear my demands, because of the

---

[42] Bosold, 'Friederike Liman', 45–6. Another contemporary Jewish woman fascinated by Mozart was Fanny von Arnstein, Sara Levy's sister, who attended his concerts in Vienna. See Spiel, *Fanny von Arnstein*.

[43] 'For assimilation to proceed to its last stages, two mutually reinforcing factors must be present: the desire of the minority to become like and to join the majority and the receptivity of the majority to the participation of minority-group members in its midst' (Hyman, *Gender and Assimilation*, 13). See also Endelman, *Radical Assimilation in English Jewish History*, 1–8.

[44] See Ch. 6 above, around n. 94.

second, everybody shies away, so all that is left to me is to go abroad', she wrote in 1807.[45] As she revealed to her friend Henriette von Willich, she did not even dare to put herself forward for the post of governess at the house of her friends, afraid that her Jewishness would be a hindrance:

> Mrs [Charlotte] Kathen was looking for a governess for her children and asked me to search for one for her; now I wanted to suggest myself, but as someone else, and then come at the appointed time. But then it occurred to me that maybe a Jewess would not be right for the old Mrs Kathen [Christine Theodora], and that it would perhaps seem odd to Mrs Kathen [Charlotte] herself, so I did not dare to do it.[46]

In writing thus to Henriette von Willich, Charlotte von Kathen's sister, she may have hoped that if she was wrong and her fears were unfounded, her friend could intercede on her behalf. In the event she was indeed invited to the Kathen house as a governess, her religious affiliation notwithstanding.

A COMPARATIVE GLIMPSE AT RELIGIOUS CONVERSION

The acculturation depicted above entailed a distancing from the observance of Jewish law and Jewish customs and the adoption of habits from the dominant culture, along with a considerable degree of social integration, all without converting from one religion to another. Not long before this period, anyone wishing to join the majority society and its culture in such a comprehensive way would have been required to undergo religious conversion and to sever all ties with Jewish society. Both traditional Jewish society and Christian society had the power to prevent an individual from living outside either of the two religious frameworks. The Jewish community used its power as an institution that represented and controlled the life of the Jews under halakhic (traditional Jewish) law, including the tool of excommunication, to impose its authority on those who deviated from the norms of Jewish life, whereas Christian society locked its doors to Jews who did not take the step of apostasy. The walls that, according to Jacob Katz, separated the worlds of Jews and Christians in the early modern age were not in fact impenetrable,[47] and it is now clear that ideas and opinions travelled through them

---

[45] Boenigk (ed.), *Schleiermacher und seine Lieben*, 121.   [46] Ibid. 122.

[47] Jacob Katz insisted that during this period—to which he refers as the end of the Middle Ages—the 'social, environmental, and cultural barriers' that separated Jews and non-Jews were stronger than ever before (*Tradition and Crisis*, 19). The segregation in ghettoes and the attitude of estrangement that in his opinion characterized Ashkenazi Jewry until at least the 17th century began to lose their power only with the spread of Enlightenment and toleration, especially in the second half of the 18th century; and only then did the transition from separation to openness take place. Katz refused to

much more than was previously assumed;[48] nevertheless, until the beginning of the modern period the affiliation of an individual to one of two societies—the Jewish or the Christian—was clear-cut. 'Jews were Jews and Christians were Christians', as Todd Endelman has asserted.[49] A Jew who chose to live outside the world of Jewish law and in close contact with Christian society had, in effect, no choice but to convert; and this meant the severance of all ties with the Jewish environment.[50]

The situation changed in the modern period. Processes such as the propagation of the idea of tolerance, the gradual spreading of a secular outlook, and the disintegration of the feudal structure of German society, which in earlier times had prevented interaction between classes, all contributed to the blurring of the line between Jews and Christians during the second half of the eighteenth century, and especially in its last decades. The areas of contact between the members of the two religions expanded, especially in Berlin but also in other places, as may be gleaned from the hints that appear in the correspondence of the Jewish women discussed in this study as well as from many other sources. The social and intellectual ties between Jews and Christians in Berlin increased as daily contact became part of everyday life in the Prussian capital.[51] Conversion, as we have seen, was not a necessary precondition for this type of interaction.

ascribe historical significance to the frequent contacts between Jews and Christians in the early modern age, which he himself described, while granting decisive importance to the *ideals* which in his opinion dominated Jewish society in those days. 'Jewish social separateness', he claimed, 'did not imply total lack of contact between members of Jewish society and the non-Jewish world. The major importance of segregation lay in the fact that it expressed a theoretical value: It was in effect a declaration that absolute separation between Jew and gentile was desirable, were it only feasible' (ibid. 28–9). Therefore, despite the shifts that Katz himself found in traditional Jewish society between 1650 and 1750, he concluded that before the 'period of change'—i.e. the second half of the 18th century—'the structure of society as well as the systems of thought by which it was justified and supported, remained intact' (*Out of the Ghetto*, 41).

[48] Referring to Jewish society in German lands in the early modern period, Elisheva Carlebach claimed that 'the most common image of Jews in the early modern Ashkenazic communities, urban Jews segregated behind ghetto walls, held true for only a fraction of European Jews living in a handful of still extant, or newly created, urban ghettos . . . Even within these ghetto communities, the Christian world penetrated Jewish consciousness, invading every aspect of Jewish life' (Carlebach, *The Anti-Christian Element*, 6). See also Shohet, *Beginnings of the Haskalah* (Heb.).

[49] Endelman, 'Memories of Jewishness', 312.

[50] Carlebach, *Divided Souls* (2003), 7, mentions the 'sharp break from their families and religious and social communities of origin' among early modern Jewish converts to Christianity. Jewish converts were often in a problematic social situation, since they cut their ties with the Jewish world but were not necessarily accepted by Christian society. See Kedar, 'Continuity and Change in Jewish Conversion' (Heb.).

[51] Jersch-Wenzel, 'Die Juden im gesellschaftlichen Gefüge Berlins um 1800'.

Conversion to Christianity, then, was not the first step on the road to assimilation for these women but rather a later stage in a protracted and gradual process of acculturation. In this sense at least there exists a great similarity between the assimilation of the enlightened Jewish women in Berlin at the end of the eighteenth century and the beginning of the nineteenth, and the process of accelerated acculturation that took place in England throughout the eighteenth century. Todd Endelman, a historian of English Jewry and one of the most prominent scholars of Jewish apostasy in modern times, revealed in a comprehensive study on the assimilation of English Jews from the second half of the seventeenth century the extent to which assimilating English Jews became integrated into Christian culture and society before formally converting. Writing about the disengagement from Judaism of many of the wealthy Sephardi Jews in Georgian England, Endelman claimed that 'their abandonment of Judaism was the outcome of a prior process of partial integration into gentile society, rather than an initial attempt to gain access to new worlds or escape onerous restrictions'.[52] To be sure, Endelman emphasized the distinctiveness of the English experience as compared to that of central European Jewry—if only because of the much greater openness and flexibility of English non-Jewish society towards minorities within it. But it seems that clear parallels may be identified between English Jewry and the cases dealt with in the present study. As emphasized above, for the enlightened Jewish women in Berlin too, conversion was not an early step in their efforts to merge into non-Jewish society but the climax of a process of integration already under way. In earlier times, Endelman claimed, Jews who wished to convert

> exchanged one identity for another and one network of social relationships for another. Their break with Judaism was absolute (except perhaps in the psychological sphere, where early loyalties and prior sentiments are not so easily abandoned). The movement from one faith to another, whatever the motives, was a dramatic leap, not a gradual evolution or blurred transition, for there was little neutral ground between the two cultures.[53]

Like the assimilating Jews in England, the enlightened Jewish women in Berlin underwent a process totally different from that which had formerly characterized the transition from one religion to another. In the absence of

---

[52] One of the examples cited by Endelman is that of Sarah Salvador, a member of the Sephardi community in London, who 'did not become a Christian *in order to* live as an Englishwoman outside the framework of Jewish society. She was already well on the road to integration into gentile circles at the time of her baptism' (Endelman, *Radical Assimilation in English Jewish History*, 20–1 (emphasis added)).   [53] Ibid. 20.

that complete opposition or mutual exclusion between Judaism and Christianity that had been widespread for centuries, they too experienced a gradual transition from one culture to the other. The difference between this experience of drifting away from the Jewish environment and towards Christian society and that of converts at the beginning of the eighteenth century emerges from a comparison between the process of conversion and its social implications in the two periods.

In the first half of the eighteenth century, as Benjamin Kedar explained in an essay on Jewish conversion in Germany at that time,

from the moment when a Jew decided to convert until the moment when he was accepted into the Christian congregation, he had to go through a number of stages of defection and absorption . . . The first outcome of the decision of a Jew to convert was the severance of his or her ties with Jewish society. This break applied first and foremost to the family . . . In addition, many of those who wished to convert left their place of residence.[54]

In the years around 1800 things looked rather different. In many cases there was no break, certainly not a total rupture, between the converts and the members of the Jewish community. At times, certainly, rifts did open up between converts and their parents who, remaining faithful to Judaism, vigorously resented their children's decision and did everything in their power to prevent more such cases.[55] But even the strongest opposition tended to wane over time, and in many cases those remaining Jewish eventually accepted the outcome.[56] Such reconciliation was made easier by the very fact that in most cases there was no rupture between the apostate and other members of his or her family or the members of the Jewish community as a whole. According to Jacob Katz, towards the end of the eighteenth century the traditional pattern according to which baptism severed all ties between converts and their Jewish

---

[54] Kedar, 'Continuity and Change in Jewish Conversion' (Heb.), 165.

[55] One of the steps taken by parents who feared that their descendants might convert was to disinherit any who did so. The family trust established by the wealthy Berlin Jew Moses Isaac in the 1770s is a good example: Isaac stipulated in his will that any of his children or their descendants who left the Jewish religion would be excluded as beneficiaries of the trust. On the saga that ensued, see Cohn, 'The Moses Isaac Family Trust'. This case had repercussions in the German public sphere, and its legal aspects were discussed by the Prussian scholar Heinrich Friedrich Diez in 'Kann die von jüdischen Vätern verbotne Glaubensänderung ihrer Kinder den angedrohten Verlust des Erbtheils nach sich ziehen?', first published in *Berichte der allgemeinen Buchhandlung der Gelehrten vom Jahre 1783*, vii. 23–51, then separately in Dessau and Leipzig in 1783 and in Magdebug in 1787, and more recently in *Aschkenas*, 16/2 (2006), 494–508. Another type of parental intervention has already been mentioned: the Jewish parents of Sara and Marianne Meyer submitted a petition to the authorities and even to the Prussian king himself in order to annul the conversion of their daughters.

[56] This is what happened between Bella Salomon and her son Jacob Bartholdy. See below.

families 'no longer prevailed exclusively'. Also, in many cases contacts with other Jews continued, to the point where 'for baptized and unbaptized Jews to mingle freely became an accepted social phenomenon'.[57]

Reflecting this general pattern, the baptism of many of these enlightened Jewish women did not entail a severance of their ties with those who remained Jews. As noted in the previous chapter, the lifelong Jew Recha Mendelssohn and the convert Henriette Herz even shared a household for a short time. On the institutional level, too, conversion did not always bring about a cutting of ties. The Gesellschaft der Freunde, for example, established in 1792 by enlightened Jews in Berlin, allowed members who converted to remain affiliated and even to occupy senior positions in it.[58]

This picture of women (and men) who converted in Berlin at the end of the eighteenth century and the beginning of the nineteenth differs markedly from that which emerges from autobiographical narratives written by converts in Germany earlier in the second half of the eighteenth century. Having examined the life stories of converts between 1750 and 1800, Elisheva Carlebach concluded that they were destined for a life of social isolation, since baptism 'did not allow them to abandon their posture as solitary individualists battling a rigidly structured society. Rather than universal brotherhood, most converts entered a life of bitter loneliness.'[59] This conclusion does not apply to the women who converted in Berlin around the end of the century. Conversion did not necessarily consign them to the margins of Christian society, let alone to a life of 'bitter loneliness': as we have seen, not only were most of them able to retain their ties with Jewish family and friends, but Christian society opened its doors to them more readily than in previous years. Moreover, unlike the converts whose autobiographical accounts Carlebach studied these enlightened women did not take the step of conversion alone, apostasy being a relatively widespread phenomenon among their circle, including many of those closest to them, and so they could share their experiences with others in the same situation.

THE MOVE TOWARDS CHRISTIANITY

The processes of acculturation and integration into non-Jewish social circles that were widespread among affluent and/or enlightened German Jews in the last decades of the eighteenth century and the first decades of the nineteenth did not invariably lead to the ultimate step of conversion taken by many of the women discussed in this study. Following Todd Endelman in conceiving of

[57] Katz, *Out of the Ghetto*, 112–13. See also Lowenstein, *The Berlin Jewish Community*, 129–32.
[58] Lesser, *Chronik der Gesellschaft der Freunde*.   [59] Carlebach, *Divided Souls* (2003), 9–10.

Jewish acculturation in the modern period as a spectrum of responses to challenges faced by Jews in the modern world, the choice of baptism may be portrayed as a radical response to the same forces that in other Jews elicited more moderate forms of acculturation within the boundaries of the Jewish community.[60] Many Jewish men and women comprehensively embraced German culture and yet continued to lead their lives as Jews until their deaths.

This was the path taken by some of the modern Jewish women in Berlin, among them Recha Mendelssohn and Amalie Beer. Recha Mendelssohn, in contrast to her sisters and many female friends, died a Jew, despite the persistent pleas of her Catholic sisters to convert.[61] Recha's only daughter, Betty (Rebecca) Meyer, also remained faithful to the Jewish religion, unlike most of her cousins. She and her mother led their lives in a mixed society of Jews and non-Jews, their thorough immersion in the majority culture not at all inhibited by their religious affiliation. Amalie Beer and her husband Jacob Herz Beer, too—Betty Meyer's parents-in-law and among the richest Jews in Berlin[62]—did not feel the need to take the step from a life of involvement in German culture and society to radical assimilation through conversion. The Beers' home, where Amalie and Jacob hosted 'first-class cultural offerings', especially in musical performance, exerted a powerful attraction for members of both religions.[63] In bringing up their children, the couple sought to find a balance between their attachments to Judaism and to the European Enlightenment, ensuring they received both a modern Jewish education from maskilic teachers hired for the purpose along with a general education in varied secular fields such as music, history, German, French, and geography.[64] The philanthropic projects they established for the benefit of the local population, including charitable activities for wounded soldiers for which the Prussian king awarded Amalie the *Louisenorden*, the highest honour a female could receive in those days, reflect their commitment to the society in which they lived.[65] At the same time, their loyalty to the Jewish people was

---

[60] Endelman, *Radical Assimilation in English Jewish History*, 5–6. In order to emphasize that the phenomenon of conversion belongs to the study of *Jewish* history, Endelman affirmed (referring to English Jewry): 'conversion and intermarriage appear not as deviant or marginal forms of behavior, of little concern to serious students of the modern Jewish experience, but as radical responses to pressures and attractions to which all Jews were exposed' (ibid. 6).

[61] See below for Henriette Mendelssohn's words in her will in this respect.

[62] Meyer, *Response to Modernity*, 47; Bilski and Braun, 'The Power of Conversation', 38.

[63] Ibid. 38–44 (quotation from p. 41).

[64] Three of their children became well-known figures in German culture: Giacomo Meyerbeer as a composer, Wilhelm Beer as an astronomer, and Michael Beer as a poet and playwright.

[65] A special badge was prepared for Amalie Beer instead of the regular cruciform badge, which was considered unsuitable for a Jewish member of the Order. The story behind the decision to award this

never doubted. They supported the moderate reform of Judaism, and their mansion was soon providing a venue for the modernized services which, promoted by Israel Jacobson, started to take place in Berlin in 1815—outside the borders of the official community, so as to avoid rabbinical opposition. Given Amalie Beer's enduring attachment to Judaism, Michael Meyer, who has researched the history of the Reform movement, argued that 'it is not unlikely that she was an important influence behind the establishment of the temple in her home in 1815'.[66] Indeed, hers may have been 'the only residence that hosted a salon and a synagogue simultaneously'.[67]

What prompted other Jewish women to take the drastic step of complete assimilation through conversion? It is clear that in most cases pragmatic considerations played a decisive role in the decision to convert.[68] For many of the women who took this final step, the immediate incentive was their wish to marry a Christian: in the absence of any provision for civil marriage, in order to do this a Jewish woman needed to convert.[69] And indeed, in a considerable number of cases conversion was rapidly followed by marriage. Deborah Hertz rightly pointed to the connection between conversion and marriage to non-Jews. Steven Lowenstein's corrective refinement to Hertz's argument is nevertheless salutary: whereas Hertz claimed that one of the central reasons that led Jewish women in Berlin in the years around 1800 to convert was 'to seduce gentile men into marrying them', 'to make themselves more desirable wives for gentiles',[70] Lowenstein pointed out that women did not convert '*in*

recognition to a Jewish woman and the motivations for preparing a special badge are reviewed in Kuhrau, 'Amalie Beer, Salondame, Wohltäterin und Patriotin', 60–3.

[66] Meyer, *Response to Modernity*, 47. Modernized religious services in Berlin were held at first at Jacobson's own home, from the spring of 1815, but 'when attendance grew to over 400 on some Sabbaths, it was decided to transfer the gathering to roomier quarters in the home of Jacob Herz Beer' (ibid. 46). See also Kuhrau, 'Amalie Beer, Salondame, Wohltäterin und Patriotin'; Hertz, 'Ihr offenes Haus—Amalia Beer und die Berliner Reform'.

[67] Bilski and Braun, 'The Power of Conversation', 42.

[68] Todd Endelman takes the view that 'pragmatic considerations motivated most conversions [of Jews] in the modern period'. Baptism motivated by religious conviction was a much rarer phenomenon (Endelman's introduction to id. (ed.), *Jewish Apostasy in the Modern World*, 14).

[69] The same applies, of course, to Jewish men who wished to marry Christian women. Ludwig Robert, just like his sister Rahel Levin, converted on the eve of his marriage to Friederike Braun in 1819. See Miriam Sambursky's essay on Robert, in which she proves that, despite conflicting information on the date of his conversion to Christianity, it may be determined with certainty that his baptism did not precede that year and took place around the time of his marriage (Sambursky, 'Ludwig Roberts Lebensgang', esp. pp. 13–15).

[70] Hertz, *Jewish High Society*, 248. See also ead., 'Seductive Conversion in Berlin' and *How Jews Became Germans*. Similar arguments were advanced in the 19th century. In 1889 the historian Ludwig Geiger identified as one of the main reasons for conversion to Christianity among Jews in Berlin 'the desire of young women from the wealthier families to marry Christians, and thus occupy a social

PLATE 12. Amalie Beer (1767–1854)
Oil on canvas by Johann Karl Kretschmar (*c.* 1803)
© Hans-und-Luise-Richter-Stiftung/Stadtmuseum Berlin

order to make themselves more eligible for later intermarriage', since 'in many, perhaps most cases, the marriage was already planned at the time of the conversion'; rather, conversion was undergone to remove the last obstacle in the way of intermarriage.[71] Sara and Marianne Meyer (in their second conversion), Esther Gad, Freude Meyer, Rahel Levin, and even Dorothea Mendelssohn were all baptized soon before their wedding to non-Jews, following a previous decision to marry.

However, although the proximity of conversion and intermarriage suggests a direct connection between the two steps, apostasy on the part of the enlightened Jewish women in Berlin should not be understood solely as the removal of an obstacle on the way to marriage to a non-Jew. This motivation may indeed explain the timing of the conversion; but conversion would not have taken place at all in the absence of the appropriate mental attitude which had made this a feasible option. The decision to convert followed, as we have seen, a long process of acculturation, during which these enlightened Jewish women became strongly involved in German and European culture. In the course of this process, they adopted from the non-Jewish surrounding culture not only external characteristics in such matters as language, dress, and social behaviour,[72] but also many of its ideological elements, including modern perceptions about the Jewish and Christian religions—whether through the cultural products they consumed (such as books or plays), through their frequent contacts with non-Jewish society, or through their interaction with Jewish friends and relatives who were also undergoing a process of assimilation. These new perceptions of religion tended to devalue the Jewish heritage and traditional Judaism, and to weaken their bond to the religion of their ancestors.

One of the central ideas that these women absorbed was that Judaism was an anachronistic religion. The claim that Judaism was but a single stage in a larger process of development (of religion, of the human spirit), and the perception of its continuing existence as an atavistic remnant, was widespread in intellectual circles in the last decades of the eighteenth century and the first half of the nineteenth. It was held, in varying versions, by leading figures such

---

position corresponding to their education and their wealth' (Geiger, 'Vor hundert Jahren', 223). Even earlier, in 1870, Karl Hillebrand had stressed even more strongly conversion as a preparation for later intermarriage, when he wrote regarding Marianne Meyer: 'At the age of fifteen, without the knowledge of her parents, she converted to Christianity *to make easier her entrance* to the great aristocratic families, which she longed to penetrate' (Hillebrand, 'La Société de Berlin de 1789 à 1815', 454, emphasis added).

[71] Lowenstein, *The Berlin Jewish Community*, 166 (emphasis added).

[72] On these phenomena among the Jewish elite in Berlin, especially since the 1770s, see ibid. 43–54.

as Lessing, who in his last prose work, *Die Erziehung des Menschengeschlechts* (1780; *The Education of the Human Race*), insisted that in the universal history of religion and humanity Judaism constituted only an early stage of development, leading later to Christianity, which in theory could also be superseded by a higher religious truth, and decades later by G. W. F. Hegel, in whose thought Judaism constituted but 'a thrust in the dialectical progress of the World Spirit'.[73] These ideas resonated strongly among modernizing Jews in Germany, who nevertheless did not always reach the same conclusions as Christian intellectuals: while some of them—including many of the women discussed here—accepted the view that the independent existence of Judaism was anachronistic and favoured consigning it to the past, others, such as the Jewish reformers, 'sought to bring it into line with what they thought and felt were the essentials of religion for the modern human being'.[74]

This historical perception of Judaism, absorbed from Christian intellectuals and certain Jewish circles in Germany, made the enlightened Jewish women ponder the validity of the religion into which they had been born. The view of Judaism as an antiquated religion irrelevant to the modern world found clear expression in words written by Esther Gad around the time of her conversion. In *Briefe über England und Portugal an einen Freund* ('Letters to a Friend on England and Portugal'), first published in 1802–3, Gad presented Judaism as a religion that had ended its mission on earth and was bound to disappear. The description of Portugal gave her the opportunity to discuss the massive forced conversion of Portuguese Jews some 300 years before and the hostility of Portuguese Catholics towards the 'New Christians' in their midst.[75] She argued that, in comparison to this historical situation, there was no basis for a similar level of Christian hostility towards Jews in her own time, given the little 'that is now left of Judaism everywhere'.[76] 'Judaism is long since a dead religion', she wrote in one of her footnotes, 'and those who yet wear its livery are only sitting lamenting beside the imperishable mummy,

---

[73] Meyer, *Response to Modernity*, 17, 67 (quotation from p. 67).

[74] See ibid. 17. When discussing the influence of the idea of 'historical development' on David Friedländer, a proponent of Jewish reform who claimed to be Mendelssohn's successor, Michael Meyer states: 'Despite his Enlightenment philosophy Friedländer did not fail to appreciate the succession of ideas in world history, and in this respect he was more the disciple of Lessing than of Mendelssohn' (Meyer, *The Origins of the Modern Jew*, 71). On the manifestation of Hegelian thought in the perception of Judaism by the younger generation of Jewish intellectuals who established the Verein für Cultur und Wissenschaft der Juden (Society for the Culture and Science of the Jews) at the end of the second decade of the 19th century, especially Eduard Gans, see Schorsch, *From Text to Context*, 205–32, esp. pp. 216 ff.; Meyer, *The Origins of the Modern Jew*, 162 ff.

[75] Bernard, *Briefe über England und Portugal*, i. 420–4.   [76] Ibid. 423.

bewailing its sad neglect.'[77] As she noted, these words are quoted directly from the Protestant philosopher and theologian Friedrich Schleiermacher's work *Über die Religion. Reden an die Gebildeten unter ihren Verächtern* ('On Religion: Speeches to its Cultured Despisers'); but similar opinions were voiced in texts by acculturated Jews of her own generation. A prominent and well-known example occurs in a letter from Abraham Mendelssohn, Moses Mendelssohn's son, to his daughter Fanny on the occasion of her confirmation in the Church almost two decades later, in 1820. Explaining that the outward form of religion was 'historical, and changeable like all human ordinances', Abraham told his daughter that Judaism was a religion that belonged to the past ('Some thousands of years ago the Jewish form was the reigning one, then the heathen form, and now it is the Christian') and that in the Christian era Jews would do well if they adopted the creed of most civilized people.[78] Heidi Thomann Tewarson, in her biography of Rahel Levin, ascribes to her a similar view of Judaism, claiming that Levin 'firmly believed that Judaism, once the most advanced form of religious thinking, was now surpassed by Christianity'.[79]

Equipped with this modern belief in the truth and validity of Christianity, especially in its Protestant version, enlightened Jewish women were able to adopt the new religion without feeling remorse that they were acting against their beliefs. For most of them, this point was crucial: several voiced reservations about those Jews who converted to Christianity purely for selfish reasons, without having any knowledge of Christianity or faith in their new religion.[80] Even so, they were pragmatically aware that at times Jews, especially men who wished to improve their situation and obtain positions that were blocked to members of their religion, had no choice but to convert, even if they acted in a spirit of religious indifference. An explicit statement of the frustration generated by the gap between the aspiration to sincerity and the

---

[77] Bernard, *Briefe über England und Portugal*, i. 424. For the English translation I relied partly on Meyer, *The Origins of the Modern Jew*, 105, who quotes from Schleiermacher's text.

[78] Hensel, *The Mendelssohn Family*, i. 80. On Abraham Mendelssohn's religious views, see Meyer, *The Origins of the Modern Jew*, 88–9.   [79] Thomann Tewarson, *Rahel Levin Varnhagen*, 219.

[80] Such a concern led Henriette Herz, for instance, to take an interest in the considerations that prompted Benny (Georg Benjamin) Mendelssohn, Joseph's son, to undergo baptism. Writing to her friend August Twesten, who was close to Benjamin Mendelssohn and played a decisive role in his conversion, she enquired, 'Why did he get baptized?', intrigued whether he had taken this step 'for the right reasons' (Heinrici (ed.), 'Briefe von Henriette Herz an August Twesten', 344). Twesten guided Benjamin on religious matters, apparently diverting him from Catholicism to Protestantism. See ibid. 344 n. 3. Letters from the correspondence between Twesten and Benjamin Mendelssohn (in 1816 and 1821) were printed in *Bankiers, Künstler und Gelehrte*, ed. Gilbert, 238–42; and in vols. iii and vii of *Mendelssohn Studien*.

imperative of actual needs appears in a letter sent by Lea Salomon to Garlieb Merkel, the Christian man of letters with whom she corresponded in the late 1790s. Writing five years before she married Abraham Mendelssohn and more than twenty years before she herself converted, she considered the case of a Jewish relative (Isaac Itzig, like her a grandchild of the wealthy Daniel Itzig) who, having finished his study of the law in Wittenberg, had embraced Christianity and returned to Berlin.[81] 'Luther's birthplace[82] and the scene sanctified by his work have influenced him', she wrote. 'He could not resist the desire to be baptized under the image of this great man, and to be in some sort protected by him.' With open irony she added that 'by this step towards the salvation of his soul he has obtained the worldly advantage of soon getting a place in his profession'.[83] In other words, Lea Salomon regretted that members of her religion were forced to act out of hypocrisy and to convert out of entirely selfish considerations; but she understood that there was no escape: 'How I wish we could do without this hypocrisy', she noted, lamenting that, given the conditions in which Jews lived, any with aspirations to a life in the professions rather than commerce had little choice.[84]

It is important to stress, however, that for some individuals, including some of the women discussed in this study, deeper spiritual motives did play a role in the decision to convert. One of them, Henriette Herz, drew closer to the Christian faith as years went by; only after devoting long hours to the study of Christian texts did she take the decisive step of apostasy. Her quiet conversion, far away from the public gaze, took place in 1817, about a year after her mother passed away, in the town of Zossen, where a priest and friend named Wolf baptized her almost secretly.[85] In Dorothea Mendelssohn's case, too, a Christian religious fervour was apparent—but in this case it worked in a different way. Dorothea was first baptized a Protestant as a precondition to her marriage to Friedrich Schlegel; but it was only afterwards that a genuinely dramatic change took place in her religious feelings, to the point where, four years later, while living in Cologne, she decided to embrace Catholicism.[86] The precise circumstances of her sister Henriette's baptism

---

[81] After converting in 1799 and changing his name to Julius Eduard Hitzig, Isaac Itzig was accepted into the civil service and some years later became a high-ranking officer in the Prussian government. See Jacobson, 'Von Mendelssohn zu Mendelssohn-Bartholdy', 254; Lowenstein, 'Jewish Upper Crust', 196.

[82] Luther's birthplace was actually Eisleben. In Wittenberg he taught and served as a priest, and on the door of a church in this city he posted his famous theses.

[83] Hensel, *The Mendelssohn Family*, i. 67.   [84] Ibid. 68.

[85] See Schleiermacher's letter to Henriette Herz of July 1817, mentioning the rumours that were circulating in Berlin regarding her recent baptism: Landsberg (ed.), *Henriette Herz*, 416–17.

[86] A recent study that emphasizes the emotional dimension of Dorothea Mendelssohn's religious conversion is Hillman, 'The Conversions of Dorothea Mendelssohn'.

are uncertain. Nevertheless, whether she took this step out of deep religious conviction or whether her faith became stronger only after her conversion, she and her sister Dorothea differ from the other Jewish women discussed here not only in the enthusiasm with which they embraced their new religion but also in their choosing to join the Roman Catholic Church, a version of Christianity which for many contemporary Jews lay on the far side of a line they refused to cross.

For an illustration of the prevalent animosity against Catholicism even among converted Jews of this period we may turn to a letter written by the painter Wilhelm Hensel to his sister Louise in December 1823. At that time Hensel, born a Protestant, was involved in a serious romantic relationship with Fanny Mendelssohn-Bartholdy, whom he would later marry. In this letter he wrote of the outraged reaction of Fanny's parents, and especially her mother Lea, when they learned that he—a potential son-in-law—intended to convert to Catholicism. Lea, he said, having broached the subject of faith with him after a rumour had reached her regarding his religious inclinations and his wish to become a Catholic, 'declared that had she known about this, she would have never given her consent [to his relationship with Fanny], since it was not at all in accordance with her views to have a Catholic son-in-law, since Catholicism always leads to fanaticism and hypocrite devotion [*Kopfhängerei*]'.[87] Although Lea and her husband Abraham had baptized their children at a young age,[88] and a short time before the conversation reported in this letter had themselves converted (secretly, in order not to cause grief to Bella Salomon, Lea's mother[89]), they saw a huge gulf between the Protestant faith they chose as the new religion for their family and Catholicism. 'She [Fanny] is the daughter of parents who have only just converted to Christianity', explained Wilhelm Hensel to his sister; 'although she herself was baptized already as a child, she was raised very much in the Protestant

---

[87] *Bankiers, Künstler und Gelehrte*, ed. Gilbert, 59. *Kopfhängerei* is defined in Adelung's dictionary from this period, *Grammatisch-kritisches Wörterbuch der Hochdeutschen Mundart*, ii. 1714, as 'exaggerated and hypocritical avoidance of all pleasures and all cheerful disposition'. Lea Mendelssohn's resolute position may have resulted partly from the conversion of her sisters-in-law Dorothea and Henriette Mendelssohn to Catholicism, and what she viewed as their fanaticism.

[88] The couple's four children were baptized as Christians in 1816. Fanny was then 10 years old, Felix 7, Rebecca 5, and the youngest child, Paul, not yet 3. See Jacobson, *Jüdische Trauungen*, 472.

[89] Bella Salomon, Daniel Itzig's daughter, cut off contact with her son Jacob upon his conversion to Christianity in 1805, but was reconciled with him some years later. When she was required, like other Jews (following the 1812 Edict of Emancipation), to take a permanent family name, she chose Bartholdy, the name her son had taken on his conversion. See Jacobson, 'Von Mendelssohn zu Mendelssohn-Bartholdy', 256; *Bankiers, Künstler und Gelehrte*, ed. Gilbert, p. xxi; Jacobson, *Jüdische Trauungen*, 227. On the wave of conversion among Daniel Itzig's descendants, see Lowenstein, 'Jewish Upper Crust'.

PLATE 13. Lea Mendelssohn-Bartholdy, née Salomon (1777–1842)
Drawing by Wilhelm Hensel (1829)
© bpk / Kupferstichkabinett, SMB / Jörg P. Anders

spirit, had heard much talk against the [Catholic] Church and therefore must naturally have shared the customary prejudices against it.'[90]

Henriette Mendelssohn, too, seems at first to have shared this aversion to Catholicism and to the fanaticism that was commonly imputed to that form of Christianity, even though in the end she too joined the Catholic Church and devoted herself to it wholeheartedly. The testimony left by Karl August Varnhagen, who met her in Paris in the years 1810 and 1814, respectively before and after her conversion, suggests that she went through a dramatic change during those four years. Before her conversion, Henriette was described by Varnhagen as someone who 'followed the impulse of reason above all things, rejecting all other sources of knowledge'.[91] Dorothea's conversion to Catholicism, he said, astonished Henriette, who could not comprehend why she and her husband had taken this step: 'Her love for Frau von Schlegel had received a blow from her turning Roman Catholic with her husband; she [Henriette] had called her sister to account for so inconceivable a step'—but to no avail.[92] However, only few years afterwards Henriette followed Dorothea's footsteps and herself became a Catholic. Varnhagen hinted that the step was connected to her assuming the position of governess to Fanny Sebastiani, noting that, after meeting her in Paris in 1814, he had felt that 'a great change had come over her since she entered the Sebastiani family: she had become Roman Catholic, not yet in possession of a firm belief, but full of hope to acquire it'.[93] Judging by Varnhagen's account, it seems that her decision to convert stemmed from a combination of external circumstances (the requirement that she join the Catholic Church as a condition of her becoming governess to the daughter of a French general) combined with internal or personal motivations (sparks of Christian and/or Catholic faith).

A text left by Henriette Mendelssohn herself helps to put Varnhagen's account in context, revealing that as early as 1810 she had been troubled by thoughts about getting baptized. In October that year she put into words her religious position in a letter to her friend August Schlegel, her sister's brother-in-law. This revealing source, quoted here at length, hints at the long

---

[90] *Bankiers, Künstler und Gelehrte*, ed. Gilbert, 58.

[91] Varnhagen von Ense, *Denkwürdigkeiten des eigenen Lebens*, iii. 138 (Eng. trans. from Hensel, *The Mendelssohn Family*, i. 45). [92] Ibid.

[93] Ibid. Another source points at the same conclusion. Writing to Goethe in November 1831, the composer Carl Friedrich Zelter spoke of Henriette Mendelssohn immediately after her death, saying that 'her vocation as a governess in Paris had made her convert to Roman Catholicism' and that 'apart from her daily attendance at Mass, no appearance of positive religiosity was discernible' (Bodley (ed.), *Goethe and Zelter*, 533). Zelter knew Henriette personally; he was among other things the music teacher of her nephew, Felix Mendelssohn-Bartholdy. On Zelter, see Ch. 5 n. 57 above.

process of reflection and thought through which Henriette went on her way to conversion. The internal conflict expressed in her letter indicates that she came to the Church only following a prolonged and deep examination of the teachings and doctrines of the Christian religion.

I only want to confess to you that I fear and wish to avoid all external influence on my religious views. So far I have not followed any alien light, yes, I have closed my eyes, and yet, inside me came into being what I see as Christianity and the essence of Christ, submission, courage and faith, not in external things, but in a divine love and justice.—With the ceremonies of the church I cannot be reconciled, I do not like the mass, at least not here in France, yes, I even consider baptism as very inessential for passing into the bosom of the church. Tell me, dear friend, have you not entered more deeply into the essence of the Catholic religion than most of those who by education and outer appearances are part of it? Is there need for an intermediary other than faith in him who suffered for all?—I am ignorant, and bold with you, dear friend, I would never have the courage to talk about it with others, and knowing myself, I fear a true hardening of my heart, if somebody should try to force dogmas and superficial actions on me. In this I am far behind my sister, who with truly sublime self-denial can absorb foreign opinions!—From you I would much prefer to hear rather than from anybody else whether I am, or can be, a Christian in this, in my, sense.[94]

In this extract, ideas and attitudes redolent of the Enlightenment mingle with Romantic traits. The enlightened Henriette Mendelssohn seems to have grasped Christianity in universal moral terms, as a religion that emphasized belief in divine love and divine justice. She clearly recoiled from religious ceremonies and dogmas (even baptism as an entrance ticket to Christianity seemed to her 'inessential'); she shied away from external influences when forming her opinion and insisted on determining her religious position independently. No wonder she felt alienated from the submissive religious devotion exhibited at the time by her sister Dorothea. On the other hand, Romantic elements may also be seen at work here. The same rejection of outside influences led her to introspection as a way to discover the 'real faith'. By 'closing her eyes' and creating a barrier between herself and the world around her, Henriette expected to find within herself an authentic religious feeling.

Over the following years Henriette's hesitations gradually waned, to be replaced by a strong belief in Catholicism. Her last will shows that the reservations expressed in 1810 were only a stage on her religious quest: in it, she asked to be buried in a Catholic ceremony and, regretting that 'God has not

---

[94] Körner (ed.), *Krisenjahre der Frühromantik*, ii. 167. The text of the letter is also quoted in Rosenstrauch, 'Von der Peripherie ins Zentrum zur Peripherie', 122.

thought me worthy of the grace of converting my brothers and sisters to the true faith, the Roman Catholic', she prayed that Jesus may 'grant my prayers and inspire them all with the light of His grace!'[95]

The religious fervour of Henriette Mendelssohn and her sister Dorothea in their later decades was exceptional. The Christian religion adopted by most of their Jewish female friends was of a significantly milder hue—indeed, the religious enthusiasm of the Mendelssohn sisters was so alien to their friends and relatives that it elicited some critical remarks.[96] It is therefore hard to agree with the sweeping statements made by some scholars to the effect that a 'wave of emotion swept the hostesses of the famous Jewish salons towards Christianity', as if blind faith or an uncontrollable emotional impulse had led most of them to the doors of the Church.[97] On the contrary, it is remarkable that—leaving aside the words of the Mendelssohn sisters—it is hard to find, for instance, expressions of deep belief in Jesus. Many of the remarks on religious attitudes scattered in the women's writings reflect a universal belief in one God; Jesus, if mentioned at all, appears only as secondary to God himself and in clear distinction from him.[98] Henriette Herz, when

---

[95] Hensel, *The Mendelssohn Family*, i. 60. In a letter to Pauline Wiesel of June 1826, Rahel Levin describes the Henriette Mendelssohn of those days as a bigoted Catholic (Levin Varnhagen, *Briefwechsel mit Pauline Wiesel*, 364).

[96] Felix Gilbert, who edited the letters of the Mendelssohn family, emphasized in his introduction the hostility felt by some of the members of the family, including the composer Felix Mendelssohn-Bartholdy, Abraham's son, towards the fanatical Catholicism of Henriette and Dorothea and the latter's two sons: *Bankiers, Künstler und Gelehrte*, ed. Gilbert, pp. xvi–xxviii. Henriette Herz, who also disliked religious enthusiasm, felt obliged to stress in the letters she sent during her stay in Italy in Dorothea's company that she did not detect in her friend any sign of the fanaticism that was ascribed to her, and that not for a moment did she feel under religious pressure from her. See e.g. *Letters to Immanuel Bekker*, ed. Putzel, 19.

[97] Katz, *Out of the Ghetto*, 120. As noted above, even in Dorothea Mendelssohn's case the dramatic religious turn took place *after* her conversion to Protestantism. She originally took up Christianity out of pragmatic and cultural considerations more than out of deep religious conviction or a surge of religious emotion. According to her biographer Carola Stern, when she first converted in 1804 'basically, she was a Protestant as much or as little as she had been, according to her creed, Jewish. What was important was to be married to Friedrich [Schlegel] and to have severed her ties to Judaism also externally.' Only when she moved to Cologne with her new husband did religious feelings begin to awaken in Dorothea, and she then embraced the Catholic religion with extraordinary devotion (Stern, *'Ich möchte mir Flügel wünschen'*, 194–8, 221–45; quotation from p. 198). Cf. Hillman, 'The Conversions of Dorothea Mendelssohn'.

[98] It is interesting to note that the famous remark attributed to Rahel Levin regarding her belief in Jesus was not written by her in any of the thousands of papers she left, but was quoted by her husband, Karl August Varnhagen. According to Varnhagen, on her deathbed Levin meditated on her Jewish roots and said, among other things: 'I thought of Jesus and cried over his passion. I have felt, for the first time in my life, that he is my brother. And Mary, how she must have suffered! She witnessed the pain of her beloved son, and did not succumb, but kept standing at the cross! I could not have been able to do that; I would not have been strong enough. May God forgive me, I confess how weak I

already a Christian, felt uncomfortable with the central place often ascribed to Jesus, pushing God the Father to one side. Commenting on the faith of Lotte (Charlotte) Schleiermacher, Friedrich Schleiermacher's unmarried sister,[99] who in her youth had belonged to the Pietistic community of the Herrnhuters,[100] Herz wrote:

> Now that I know more about the whole thing I would hardly become a Herrnhuter—even if I would gladly live with them. The one who called himself the Son of Man stands higher among them than he who sent him to us as a Saviour—they pray almost exclusively to him, he no longer has the status of an intermediary but that of a God.[101]

Henriette Herz's critical attitude towards this cult was based on its focus on the 'son', to whom its members addressed their prayers rather than to God himself, forgetting that Jesus was in fact God's emissary, sent by him as a means to salvation. These are the words of a woman who took her new faith very seriously, who took the trouble to study Christian theology, and who insisted on the need for internal conviction as a condition for conversion.

ATTITUDES TOWARDS JEWS AND JUDAISM AFTER CONVERSION

The bonds of these enlightened Jewish women to Jews and Judaism after their baptism were preserved in part, as noted above, through the social connections that continued to exist between the two groups. They were also expressed in the attitude of at least some of the converts towards the nation they had left behind. Instead of playing down their previous affiliation with the Jewish people as much as possible and ceasing to take any interest in its fate, some of the women continued to identify themselves with the Jews, to variable extents and in different ways. This is not to say that there was a sudden awakening of feelings of sympathy or remorse on their part; indeed, at times such identification was accompanied by words of criticism against the Jews and/or Judaism. Nonetheless, it is significant that they acknowledged

---

am.' This translation is printed in Mendes-Flohr and Reinharz (eds.), *The Jew in the Modern World*, 261. For an additional reference by Rahel Levin to Jesus (and Mary), see Ch. 2 above, around n. 86.

[99] Lotte (Charlotte) Schleiermacher lived with her brother from 1813 and educated his children.

[100] This radical Pietistic sect was founded in the early 1720s in Saxony and later taken to the United States. Its members are also known as Moravians or members of the Moravian Church, since the founders of the movement were refugees who arrived from the region of Moravia. Friedrich Schleiermacher, like his sister Lotte, was also educated in the institutions of this church.

[101] From a letter to Immanuel Bekker in 1820 (*Letters to Immanuel Bekker*, ed. Putzel, 47).

their Jewish roots and displayed a certain closeness to their former co-religionists, especially in the latter's times of suffering.

The autobiographical account that Henriette Herz began to write in 1823, approximately six years after her conversion, is a typical example of the prominent place given to Jewish roots in texts written after apostasy.[102] At the very beginning Henriette chose to place those roots centre stage, thus: 'My father was a Portuguese Jew whose grandfather, along with many of his brothers in faith, was forced to flee Portugal to avoid falling into the hands of the Inquisition.'[103] Despite her loyalty to her new religion, Herz did not ignore her Jewish roots, nor did she try to efface them from public consciousness. It is significant that she chose to stress specifically her descent on her father's side from Sephardi Jews, who were generally held in greater respect than the Ashkenazim, thus implicitly distinguishing herself from the majority of the members of the Berlin Jewish community, who belonged to the latter group.[104] She stressed, for example, that her father's 'language was pure, since all Portuguese Jews lack the Jewish jargon and intonation'. Although he 'lived strictly according to the law of his religion', and 'the household was set up completely in accordance with Jewish laws and customs', all this was done with moderation, and he himself was 'tolerant with all those who acted against his faith'. Thus Henriette took pains to present her father's Judaism in a favourable light, downplaying the differences between the Jewish and the Christian religions and insisting that his general attitude was in fact Christian in essence, since he 'carried the gentleness and love of Christianity in his heart'.[105] Despite

---

[102] It is hard to see Herz's memoirs as belonging to the confessional autobiographical genre typical of many Jewish converts throughout most of the 18th century, whose purpose was to 'deliver their critique of Jewish society' through their personal life stories (Carlebach, *Divided Souls* (2003), 7). Herz's autobiography does contain some criticism of Jewish society and Jewish education, but this does not seem to be the main goal of her narrative.

[103] Landsberg (ed.), *Henriette Herz*, 101 (Eng. trans. in Blackwell and Zantop (eds.), *Bitter Healing*, 303).

[104] Interestingly, at the time she was writing her memoirs, the cultural and religious legacy of the Sephardim was being exalted by the members of the recently established Verein für Cultur und Wissenschaft der Juden, a society devoted to the scholarly study of Jewish literature and culture in Berlin. On the long-lasting veneration of Sephardi Judaism and its legacy among Ashkenazi scholars, accompanied by a criticism of the Ashkenazi heritage, starting in the 17th century and continuing through the time of the Haskalah into the 19th century, see Ismar Schorsch's 'The Myth of Sephardic Supremacy', in id., *From Text to Context*, 71–92. See also the collection of essays edited by Fontaine et al., *Sepharad in Aschkenaz*. The 'tendency to employ or exploit a positive valuation of Sephardi experience', in contrast to Ashkenazi 'failings and degeneracy', may also be traced in racial and racist German writings in the mid- to late nineteenth century. See Gelber, 'The Noble Sephardi and the Degenerate Ashkenazi'.

[105] Landsberg (ed.), *Henriette Herz*, 113 (Eng. trans. in Blackwell and Zantop (eds.), *Bitter Healing*, 310).

these qualifications of her father's Jewishness, Henriette Herz's original religion is not effaced but rather occupies a central place in her autobiography.

Furthermore, she showed instinctive empathy towards the members of the Jewish nation in response to the assaults they suffered towards the end of the second decade of the nineteenth century. 'What sort of times are we living in!', she wrote to Immanuel Bekker in August 1819. 'The Catholics vandalise the graves of the Protestants, the Christians stone the Jews . . . Ah, and the poor Jews! Should I not be forgiven for being in pain over their pain? . . . this I call to be outraged, when those who are accepted by the government are being stoned and expelled from town.'[106] Herz was referring here to the disparity that became acutely apparent in mid-1819 between the official acceptance of the Jews as part of the gradual process of legal emancipation begun in 1812 and the popular attacks on them, notably in the 'Hep Hep' riots which erupted at the beginning of August 1819 in southern Germany and quickly spread to other areas, causing much damage to Jewish property and undermining the Jews' sense of security.[107] She could not but lament the misery of the Jews (and of the Protestants in their own suffering), although when writing to her Protestant friend she deemed it necessary to justify her sympathy for the people from whom she had separated herself.

Herz's stance reinforces the point made by Elisheva Carlebach in discerning a shift in the attitude of converts towards Judaism and the Jews between the early modern age and the end of the eighteenth century, when, she asserts, 'the intense hostility to their former religion and community that characterized most earlier converts was lacking'.[108] Testimonies such as Herz's quoted above, together with more explicit manifestations of solidarity, indicate that hostility towards the Jews was indeed not the norm among this group of converts. Fradchen Liebmann, for example, seven years after her conversion, was not only still socializing with Jews but also praising the 'Jewish' spirit that in her opinion prevailed at the house of the Beer family. Writing in March 1816 to Rahel Levin, who at that time was living in Frankfurt am Main, she made a point of saying how much pleasure she derived from attending the famous gatherings at the Beers' house: 'Why do I

---

[106] Letter of 18 Aug. 1819, *Letters to Immanuel Bekker*, ed. Putzel, 34.

[107] For a description of the riots and the circumstances which led to their outbreak, see Katz, 'The Hep Hep Riots in Germany of 1819' (Heb.); Rohrbacher, 'The "Hep Hep" Riots of 1819'. Rohrbacher agrees with Jacob Katz that, rather than being an expression of social protest, as some scholars assumed, 'the riots were a genuine expression of Christian-Jewish conflict proper' (p. 31). Like Katz, he claims that it was resistance to the process of Jewish emancipation, and not extreme socio-economic crisis, which served as the immediate cause and the primary reason for the eruption of violence against the Jews in 1819. [108] Carlebach, *Divided Souls* (2001), 228.

like it best at the Beers[?] Because one is received totally unceremoniously and kindly there, where *Jewish* good-natured liberality of the highest degree rules, where one sees all classes of people, where everything is done together freely—playing, singing, reading.'[109]

Not only did both Liebmann and Levin continue socializing with Jews after their conversion; both explicitly repudiated the position of those converts who became estranged from Jews. When it was said of Rahel in Fradchen's presence that she avoided appearing in society with Jews, Liebmann responded fiercely: 'Whoever said that is an infamous liar—you could have said anything about R[ahel] and I would not have cared to contradict it, but precisely *this* is so *stupid* and so deviates from Rahel's principles that I cannot remain silent. At the same time it is also ridiculous for anyone who knows Rahle [*sic*].'[110] Liebmann's furious and unhesitating retort indicates that the issue was very dear both to her and to Levin, and that it was important to her to make it clear that conversion to Christianity by no means entailed—at least not in their case—a negative attitude towards Jews.

In trying to provide an explanation for these accusations made by Jews against converts, Liebmann suggested that they might have been provoked by an event that was causing alarm in the Jewish community at the time: the staging of the anti-Jewish comic play *Unser Verkehr* (translated as 'Our Crowd' or 'The Company We Keep'), published anonymously and ascribed to the physician Karl Boromäus Sessa. This farce, premiered in Breslau in 1813 and then successfully performed in Berlin in 1815, mocked what it presented as the ridiculous and hopeless attempts of Jews to adopt German language and culture.[111] The great popularity of a play which portrayed Jews in such a negative light at a time when Jewish emancipation seemed to be on its way appalled many Jews in Germany and made them particularly sensitive to any hint of anti-Jewish sentiment. As Liebmann commented, 'Since the *Verkehr* Jews have nothing in their heads but the *Risches* [maliciousness, especially against Jews] in *all* its forms, and in a way they may be right.'[112]

In her reply to Liebmann's report, Levin endorsed the rejection of the evil intentions ascribed to her, which utterly contradicted her real position:

---

[109] Bosold, 'Friederike Liman', 79.

[110] These words were written by Liebmann in a letter to Rahel Levin at the beginning of March 1816 (ibid. 81).

[111] The Jewish characters in the play make efforts to cast off their Jewishness, to no avail; their attributes reveal themselves as immutable. For a discussion of *Unser Verkehr*, see Lea, *Emancipation, Assimilation and Stereotype*, 78–86; Robertson, *The 'Jewish Question' in German Literature*, 206–8. On the identity of the author, see Geiger, 'Ueber den Verfasser der Posse: Unser Verkehr'.

[112] Bosold, 'Friederike Liman', 81–2.

'one is accused of *exactly* the opposite of what one does', she wrote to Liebmann, convinced that the person who defamed her was certainly 'someone who does not know me at all'. To corroborate her claims, she added: 'I was the first and only one to take along fifteen-year-old Adelheid Herz to the casino ball, out of my own incentive and in spite of the *Risches*. She was very beautiful and danced a lot among the dignitaries [*unter srores melukhe*]!'[113]

Like Henriette Herz, Rahel Levin also expressed her profound sympathy with the situation of Jews when the 'Hep Hep' riots broke out. Deeply moved, she voiced her pain in a letter of 29 August 1819 to her brother Ludwig Robert—with whom she maintained an ongoing dialogue on the subject of the Jews, Judaism, and baptism which continued after their conversion:[114] 'I am *boundlessly* sad, and in a way in which I have never been. Because of the Jews. *What* should this host of exiles do[?] They want to *keep* them, but only to torment and scorn them; to castigate them for their Jewish way of speaking [*mauscheln*]; for petty bargaining, to kick them and throw them down the stairs.'[115] Rahel's letter indicates that even after converting, and although she referred to the Jews in the third person, she followed with interest Jewish affairs and the general atmosphere that prevailed in her country regarding the integration of the Jews. This may be seen in her diagnosis of the situation that had arisen in that summer of 1819. She blamed the riots on German men of letters, who incited the populace—'For *three* years I have been saying that the Jews will be assailed. I have witnesses'—and went on to set out her evidence: 'The insinuations that for years have been making their way through all the papers. Professors Fr[ies] and Ri. [Rühs];[116] and whatever they are called. Arn[im,] Brent[ano],[117] *Unser Verkehr*, and other higher-ranking

---

[113] Ibid. 84–5.   [114] Thomann Tewarson, 'German-Jewish Identity'.

[115] Levin Varnhagen, *Briefwechsel mit Ludwig Robert*, 243.

[116] Jakob Friedrich Fries, a German professor of philosophy, and the historian Christian Friedrich Rühs were two German scholars who wrote polemical texts opposing the integration of Jews into Christian society that became very influential. On the role of the anti-Jewish literary campaign they set in motion on the outbreak of the 'Hep Hep' riots, see Katz, 'The Hep Hep Riots in Germany of 1819' (Heb.); Rohrbacher, 'The "Hep Hep" Riots of 1819'.

[117] Achim von Arnim and Clemens Brentano were two of the founders of the Christlich-deutsche Tischgesellschaft, a Christian German 'dining society' established in 1811. This social club, which included distinguished representatives of the Prussian intellectual and political elite, accepted only male members who were born Christians—i.e. no Jews or converted Jews and no women—and was famous for its anti-Jewish orientation. See Meyer, *The Origins of the Modern Jew*, 138; Brenner et al., *Emancipation and Acculturation*, 30–1. Rahel Levin and Clemens Brentano were personally acquainted (from 1804, according to Thomann Tewarson, *Rahel Levin Varnhagen*, 37, or 1809, according to Varnhagen, *Rahel Varnhagen. Briefwechsel*, iii. 415), and for some time there was even a friendship between them. The remaining letters of their short-lived correspondence are printed in Varnhagen, *Rahel Varnhagen. Briefwechsel*, iii. 331 ff.

prejudiced persons'—all these, in her opinion, bore responsibility for the outburst of violence. The populace, according to Rahel Levin, was totally innocent: the German nation, she believed, was the most civilized, good-natured, and peace-loving of all, and the most respectful of authority. However, it lacked confidence in its own judgement and allowed itself to be guided by bad influences:

> It does *not know* what it should request: only the well informed among the people may teach it to this nation: but among them, there are many uneducated ones, with coarse hearts, where there is also room for envy of a large number of such *Jews*, whom, due to the excesses of religion, it was permissible to hate, despise and persecute as inferior creatures.[118]

Of particular note in Rahel Levin's serious indictment against contemporary German intellectuals is her trenchant criticism of their adherence to obscure ideas identified with Romanticism, rather than to the lofty ideals fostered by the Enlightenment. The main responsibility for the gloomy atmosphere which prevailed in Germany, she claimed in the same letter to her brother, rested with an intellectual movement that was becoming more and more dominant and, as well as casting a particularly dark shadow over the Jews, also threatened the spirit of progress and optimism embraced by the former generation: 'The hypocritical new love for the Christian religion, may God forgive me my sin!, for the Middle Ages with its art, its poetry and its horrors, incites the people to the only horror to which, reminded by ancient permission, it will still be incited—attacking the Jews.'[119] According to her, people who espoused such ideas revived the old hatred of Jews, after a long period in which such 'mistakes' had 'perished' and an end had been put to the prejudice against Jews as inferior creatures, among other things thanks to 'some wise German rulers'. Reactionary views 'deeply grieved' Rahel Levin, almost to the point of 'heart-freezing'.[120] She stood unambiguously on the side of distinctively enlightened ideas, such as religious tolerance and human progress, utterly rejecting Romanticism's reactionary views and its dark spirit. Her words reveal a deep concern and even a certain fear of what seems to her a return to the world before the Enlightenment.

Rahel Levin's deep emotional involvement—five years after she converted to Christianity—in the fate of the Jews, and her great interest in the cultural, social, and political transformations that determined the attitude of

---

[118] Levin Varnhagen, *Briefwechsel mit Ludwig Robert*, 243.

[119] Ibid. On the Romantic atmosphere among young contemporary students and intellectuals, see Tal, 'Young German Intellectuals on Romanticism and Judaism'.

[120] Levin Varnhagen, *Briefwechsel mit Ludwig Robert*, 243.

the general population towards her former people, closely reflect the protracted and at times ambivalent character of the process by which most of the Jewish women discussed here distanced themselves from the Jewish religion and moved towards non-Jewish culture and society. As many of the selected cases presented in this chapter show, the long process that preceded conversion, which was bound up with radical assimilation, not only lasted for many years but did not always end with total separation. An enduring emotional connection to the Jewish people as well as social contacts with members of the Jewish community were not at all rare among those women who chose to convert. Conversion appears as just one phase in a sequence of processes which did not lead to alienation but left behind tangible remnants or traces of identity, perhaps for ever.

EIGHT

CONCLUSION

By listening attentively to female voices rather than focusing exclusively on male historical sources, it has been possible to show that the Jewish women discussed in this study were neither simple bystanders in the enlightened world of their time nor yet mere mediators who facilitated the cultural activity of men (the main role often attributed to the *salonnières*). The ample evidence presented clearly positions these women as both agents of culture and creators of culture: as intellectuals in their own right. Experiencing and expressing a nascent feminist consciousness, they actively opposed attempts to silence women, rejected demands for their self-abnegation, and contested the denial of independent female thought, striving instead to constitute themselves and other women as autonomous human beings. They joined the expanding public sphere that was developing in Europe, at times through formal literary activity, but also through less conspicuous practices such as conversation and letter-writing. They internalized ideas and values from the world of the Enlightenment, such as the acquisition of knowledge, the pursuit of happiness, the desire for self-improvement, and the critical stance, which in their case (as in that of other contemporary women) encouraged a feminist outlook. It is true that central currents of Enlightenment thought fostered anti-feminist ideas, helping to perpetuate women's subordinated position in society and culture by endorsing the age-old patriarchal tradition with modern claims; but there were other strands of Enlightenment thought that encouraged feminist positions and aspirations.[1]

---

[1] The opinion of some modern scholars that 'the Enlightenment was far from a great step' in women's history, and that 'the intellectual, economic, and spiritual options open to women of all classes decreased during the Enlightenment', contrasts with a more positive view of the Enlightenment's significance for women which emphasizes the improvement of their social condition and the greater intellectual opportunities that it offered them (Robertson, 'Women and Enlightenment', quotations here from pp. 692–3, taken from Phyllis Mack's review of four books on 18th-century English women published in the early 1980s under the title 'The History of Women

We have seen how these Jewish women turned their own critical eyes on the social, cultural, and at times political reality around them, and drew on basic principles of the Enlightenment to support their claim to the right to participate, as women, in the advancement of public reason. In this spirit they applied gender criticism to the dominant discourse, calling into question the social and cultural norms that constrained women's lives, scrutinizing even the patriarchal institution of marriage, in extreme cases to the point of undermining its foundations. Although, as noted in the Introduction, the Enlightenment was not the only influence on the cultural world of these women, it is revealed as a vital element in understanding their thought and actions.

In the light of this analysis, the label attached to them throughout this study, 'enlightened Jewish women', appears justified: for here we have a group of women, all of whom were born as Jews and for many years lived as Jews, who adopted basic ideas from the enlightened world and actively joined some of its frameworks. However, it is worth lingering a little longer on the meaning of this phrase, 'enlightened Jewish women', and considering its implications. To this end, a comparison between this group of women and the maskilim, and also with nineteenth-century maskilot and Jewish female intellectuals, usefully highlights both the clear similarities and the significant differences that exist between these groups, which in turn help to clarify the meaning of the word 'Jewish' in the phrase 'enlightened Jewish women'.

Perhaps one of the most important similarities was the critical attitude that these groups shared. The maskilim, imbued with a perception of themselves, typical of the Enlightenment, as autonomous and reasoning beings, believed they were qualified to analyse the conditions of Jewish existence, to propose ways to improve these conditions, and in fact to determine the proper manner in which modern Jews should live their lives.[2] As has been stressed throughout the various chapters of this study, the enlightened Jewish women exhibited a similar critical attitude. But there is a striking difference in the way they applied it: in contrast to the maskilim, these enlightened Jewish women did not occupy themselves with issues concerning Jewish society and culture; there was no serious attempt on their part to bring about internal change in the Jewish world, either to its culture or to its religion. These enlightened Jewish women did not suggest a new agenda for Jewish

in Early Modern Britain. A Review Article', *Comparative Studies in Society and History*, 28 (1986), 722). For a related discussion on the legacy of enlightened thought for modern feminism, see Scott, *Only Paradoxes to Offer*; Goodman, 'More than Paradoxes to Offer'; ead., 'Difference: An Enlightenment Concept'; Johnson, 'Feminism and Enlightenment'; Soper, 'Feminism and Enlightenment Legacies'; O'Brien, 'The Feminist Critique of Enlightenment'.

[2] Feiner, *The Jewish Enlightenment*.

society, they hardly ever participated in the internal Jewish discourse on the benefits and the advisable extent of modernization, and they certainly did not make any effort to enhance the modern Jewish republic of letters or to mobilize their Jewish co-religionists to implement a modern Jewish agenda. With the exception of one outstanding episode—that of Esther Gad's poem dedicated to the new modern Jewish school in Breslau—none of them contributed to the consolidation of the Jewish version of the European Enlightenment, the Haskalah. They did not even participate in the existing modern Jewish republic of letters as consumers of this literature.

In their indifference towards Jewish matters they differed greatly not only from the eighteenth-century maskilim, but also from many modernizing Jewish women in the nineteenth century, especially its latter half. During these years we encounter women taking part in the Haskalah, notably as consumers of its literature. The modernizing Jewish women in nineteenth-century eastern Europe depicted in Iris Parush's *Reading Jewish Women* joined the Haskalah, as readers of maskilic texts. The maskilot inhabiting Tova Cohen and Shmuel Feiner's anthology of Hebrew writings, *Voice of a Hebrew Maiden*, showed great interest in joining the modern Jewish public sphere as readers of secular Hebrew texts, as correspondents of maskilic authors and publishers, and in some cases as authors themselves. Of course, these women lived in conditions very different from those prevailing around 1800. For one thing, at the end of the eighteenth century there simply was no range of popular maskilic, secular literature of the kind that was available to female readers of later decades; most maskilic authors at the time hardly ever concerned themselves with writing for women.[3] Although some reverted to Yiddish to express social criticism (as in Aaron Wolfsohn-Halle's comedy *Silliness and Sanctimony*) or Jewish religious values (as in Joel Loewe-Brill's 1785 translation of the Pesach Haggadah, aimed primarily at women), most maskilic texts were written in Hebrew and therefore not accessible to female readers in Germany, who were not proficient in this language at the end of the eighteenth century. In fact, Hebrew literacy was uncommon among women even as late as the end of the nineteenth century; as Cohen and Feiner stressed, the exceptional instances of maskilot who read and wrote in Hebrew occurred only where the Haskalah prevailed for more than one generation—that is, among daughters of maskilim, who by definition did not exist in the first stage of the movement.[4]

---

[3] Feiner, 'The Modern Jewish Woman' (Heb.).

[4] Cohen and Feiner (eds.), *Voice of a Hebrew Maiden* (Heb.), 36–44; Cohen, 'Portrait of the *Maskilah* as a Young Woman'.

Jewish women in the nineteenth century differed from the enlightened Jewish women in the eighteenth century not only in their consumption of Jewish literature, but notably also in their role as female intellectuals. Like their predecessors, many Jewish women intellectuals, especially in the latter part of the nineteenth century, were informed by a feminist awareness and a concomitant opposition to male dominance in culture and society. A major difference between them and their earlier counterparts, however, was that a significant number of them focused their criticism and their suggestions for change specifically on Jewish culture and society. Moreover, they acted within the Jewish public sphere, using the Jewish cultural context to advance their claims: thus many of them interpreted Jewish canonical texts in an innovative way, giving them a feminist slant by means of their subversive reading.[5] Writing in Hebrew, Yiddish, or European languages, many of them decried the discrimination against women in the Jewish context. Refusing to be content with the marginal place traditionally granted to the members of their sex, some of them demanded educational opportunities, including the establishment of Hebrew schools for women and expanded opportunities for professional training. Unlike them, the enlightened Jewish women discussed in this study did not—indeed, did not see the need to—combine feminist criticism with calls for reform within Jewish society and culture.

One explanation for women's disengagement from the Haskalah and its goals might refer to the different cultural backgrounds of men and of women in the eighteenth century. It might be claimed that since women were excluded from Jewish high culture—the study of Torah—and from the high language of Jewish culture—Hebrew, embraced and glorified by the Haskalah—they lacked the means to act in the field of Jewish culture, and therefore found their interests elsewhere, outside the Jewish context. This could explain why a Jewish woman living in the years around 1800 might have preferred to make her way as an intellectual in European culture, which offered her more opportunities. This argument contains more than a grain of truth, but it requires qualification.

A gendered explanation of this kind would be valid if we were speaking of a generation earlier, before the decline of the Haskalah in Berlin, when most intellectual Jewish men who were inclined towards enlightened ideas pursued them through this movement. If Jewish women had at that point devoted all their energies to general culture, the argument outlined above could be

---

[5] In addition to the radical texts printed in Cohen and Feiner (eds.), *Voice of a Hebrew Maiden* (Heb.), see also Werses, 'Women's Voices in the Yiddish Weekly *Kol-mevaser*' (Heb.); also Loentz, *Let Me Continue to Speak the Truth*, which presents the famous case of Bertha Pappenheim.

advanced to explain why they chose this path, as opposed to most Jewish men, who addressed their efforts to amending Jewish society and promoting Jewish culture. Around 1800, however, there was not really a tremendous difference between the attitudes of enlightened Jewish men and women concerning their connection with Jewish culture and society—certainly not in Berlin. As described in this study, through a gradual process, which led eventually to radical assimilation, these women moved away from a traditional Jewish lifestyle, abandoned Jewish ideals and values, and became integrated into the surrounding culture, within which they pursued their main aspirations. But so, too, did many of their male co-religionists. In the period under discussion here—and especially in the last decade of the eighteenth century—in a city such as Berlin, ignorance of and indifference towards Jewish subjects, estrangement from Jewish ideals and values, and an inclination towards European culture were not unique to women but on the contrary were widespread among members of both sexes. These attitudes were part of a broader phenomenon that followed in the wake of the penetration of enlightened ideas and the rapid modernization experienced by the Jewish community in the last decades of the eighteenth century. In distancing herself from Jewish culture, a woman such as Rahel Levin was not all that different from her intellectual brother Ludwig Robert, who was also alienated both from traditional Jewish culture and from the goals and aspirations of the Haskalah. In the last years of the eighteenth century and the first years of the nineteenth it is possible to identify in Berlin and in other German cities a group of enlightened Jewish men, several of whom have featured in this book—such as Wolf Davidson, David Veit, Ludwig Robert, and David Koreff—who enthusiastically embraced Enlightenment culture and actively participated in it, notably through writing. The activities of this Jewish German intelligentsia represent the beginning of a massive entrance of Jews into the German and European public sphere in fields as varied as philosophy, medicine, belles-lettres, and music, among others, which would become highly conspicuous in modern times.

Interestingly, it was not only Jews alienated from the ideals of the Haskalah who turned to the non-Jewish cultural sphere: adherents of the Haskalah in Germany also did so in the years around 1800. A case in point is Joel Loewe-Brill, a contemporary of the enlightened Jewish women. Born, like them, in Berlin, he had played a central role in the Haskalah from the 1780s onwards—as one of the founders of leading maskilic societies, as the driving force behind some of the most popular publications of the Berlin Haskalah, as the first director of the modern Jewish school in Breslau, and as editor of the maskilic journal *Hame'asef* in the 1790s. However, at a certain point in his literary career, this hitherto typical maskil began to address many of his writings to a non-Jewish public, at the same time as continuing to work to extend the literature of the Haskalah. Deeply attracted by the non-Jewish literary sphere, he made significant efforts to carve out a role for himself in it, including publishing his own work and engaging in intellectual debates with leading figures in German culture.[6]

If enlightened Jewish women and men alike were attracted by non-Jewish culture, a close examination of the sources reveals that other significant gender distinctions commonly drawn when describing Jewish modernization in Berlin are also too sweeping and not necessarily well founded. Thus, for instance, this study has shown clearly (in Chapter 5 especially) that the fundamental gender distinction assumed by many historians, who placed Jewish men and women in separate spheres of activity—women in the domestic sphere and the salons, men in the economic, professional, and intellectual spheres—is not always valid. Nor is the complete distinction between the reading habits of men and women supported by the sources.

Nevertheless, along with the similarities and areas of contact between enlightened Jewish men and women there certainly were gender differences. Even though members of both groups were alienated from traditional Jewish culture and inclined towards acculturation, an important distinction was found in the extent to which men and women engaged with Judaism: to summarize somewhat simplistically, enlightened Jewish men tackled issues that had to do with Jews more than the women did, whereas the enlightened Jewish women, while not entirely uninterested in Jewish matters, were more preoccupied with subjects related to women and gender. This difference has its roots less in the intensity of their respective bonds with Judaism and more in the different function that the fact of being Jewish played in men's and women's lives.

With the propagation of the ideas of the Enlightenment and the public debate on the granting of equal rights to Jews, the aspirations of Jewish men to integrate into non-Jewish society and culture—and their opportunities to do so—increased. Even so, despite the discourse of toleration, at the end of the eighteenth century their Jewishness continued to stand as a barrier

---

[6] A notable example is his series of contributions to a journal devoted to the German language edited by Joachim Heinrich Campe, *Beiträge zur weitern Ausbildung der deutschen Sprache*. Loewe-Brill dedicated one of his essays to a critical discussion of the language used by Goethe in his *Iphigenia in Tauris*, a bold attempt that was received with contempt by the German author. See Naimark-Goldberg, 'Breslau's Maskilim'.

between them and the realization of their aspirations in the non-Jewish world. The situation was different for women: if many areas remained closed to them, this was primarily because of their sex, not their religion. Esther Gad, for instance, when trying to publish a novel, feared that her 'long skirt' would be an obstacle in her negotiations with a publisher.[7] That is, it was the fact that she was a woman, not the fact that she was Jewish, that constituted the main obstacle between her enlightened aspirations—in this case, her wish to take an active part in the public sphere—and the realization of her objectives. Such, in any event, was her belief, and we may assume it reflected her experience of the environment in which she lived. Many years later, her friend Henriette Herz expressed her frustration at the difficulties she encountered when trying to educate herself, complaining that her private Greek teacher, like many other tutors she had had, did not treat her seriously, and considered it 'unscientific' to discuss serious subjects with a 'superficial being' such as a woman was thought to be.[8] In her case, again, the path to fulfilment of her intellectual aspirations was blocked to a large extent not by her Jewishness but by her sex. Herz herself did not mention her religion as an obstacle, lamenting only and specifically the widespread reluctance of scholars to share with women the cherished knowledge they possessed.

Thus, while Esther Gad, Henriette Herz, and other Jewish women struggled to overcome the obstacles related to gender that stood in their way, and in doing so often cooperated with non-Jewish women, who obviously shared their concerns, Jewish men struggled to overcome the obstacles posed to their personal fulfilment by the fact of their Jewishness and their affiliation to Judaism. To take just one example: the physician Wolf Davidson, who held radical views concerning Judaism and its role in the modern world, felt it necessary to discuss Jewish issues in public and write a book on the emancipation of the Jews, which he hoped would improve his own chances, and those of other Jews like himself, of entering the German world. In general, then, it may be said that since men and women faced different obstacles to their integration into German culture and society, they experienced different fears and frustrations, and turned to different areas of activity and different tactics in attempting to overcome them.

This distinction also had implications concerning the choice to convert. If women did not hasten to change their faith (as we saw in Chapter 7, most did so relatively late), this was among other things because Judaism did not represent an insuperable obstacle to the pursuit of their intellectual and social

---

[7] Letter to Jean Paul of 26 Nov. 1800, Hahn (ed.), '"Geliebtester Schriftsteller"', 38.

[8] Heinrici (ed.), 'Briefe von Henriette Herz an August Twesten', 311.

aspirations. In fact, almost the only situation in which baptism was necessary for a woman was when she wished to marry a non-Jew.[9] Whereas many men converted in order to pursue professional careers and/or to make themselves eligible for official positions, baptism did not necessarily make it easier for women to progress in the fields of literature or learning; nor was it necessary to gain them entry to professional occupations—which, in any case, few of them sought (an exception being the case of Henriette Mendelssohn, who may have had to convert in order to assume her position as a governess in a French Catholic household). We have seen in detail throughout the preceding chapters that, despite the prejudice that no doubt existed against Jews in many circles of German society, women succeeded, as Jews, in entering this society and participating in cultural and social activities to a significant extent.

Given these circumstances, men and women made different use of Enlightenment ideas. While enlightened Jewish men struggled to achieve civil rights in order to gain a position in society equal to that of other (male) citizens, and engaged in learned debate based on typical enlightened ideas in pursuit of this goal, one of the most significant and singular results of Jewish women's engagement with enlightened ideas (which varied on matters concerning gender, as discussed for instance in Chapters 3 and 6 and above in this concluding section) was their growing recognition of the discrimination to which women were subject. They ceased to regard their inferior and dependent situation as a natural and inevitable fact or as a religious dictate and to accept their portrayal as immature creatures who needed a male authority figure possessed of greater reasoning power to control, guide, and defend them. The characteristic female attitude of submission to gender norms was now replaced by an active consciousness and the understanding that it was possible to intervene in social patterns and practices, that their position was not predestined, and that women had the right to seek a change in the attitude of society towards them and even to act to bring it about. Eventually, the desire for self-realization led them to effect a real transformation in their lives, as we have seen in detail in the various chapters, although not necessarily to the extent they could have wished.

It may be concluded, then, that the Haskalah was not the only form of Jewish Enlightenment, and that discussion of the Haskalah does not exhaust the encounter of Jews with the Enlightenment—not even in Berlin, the cradle of the Haskalah. On the contrary, and especially in Berlin, at the end of

---

[9] As discussed above, conversion was also undertaken in cases of religious conviction or as part of a 'family project', when several members of the same family were baptized simultaneously.

the eighteenth century and the beginning of the nineteenth there was *another* strand of enlightenment among Jews, different from that promoted by the maskilim. This strand of enlightenment—the one espoused by the Jewish women discussed in this study—was not Jewish in the sense that it did not offer solutions for Jewish society, nor did it contribute to Jewish culture per se; but it did offer solutions, albeit problematic ones, for Jews. It was Jewish in that it represented the choices of many Jews in the modern world. The critical attitude which characterized these women, and which would become part and parcel of the 'toolkit' of modern Jewish female intellectuals, would have to wait for another historical context in order to find direct expression in the Jewish world.

Bibliography

ADAMS, CHRISTINE, 'A Choice Not to Wed? Unmarried Women in Eighteenth-Century France', *Journal of Social History*, 29 (1996), 883–94.

ADELMAN, HOWARD E., 'The Educational and Literary Activities of Jewish Women in Italy during the Renaissance and the Catholic Restoration', in *Shlomo Simonsohn Jubilee Volume: Studies on the History of the Jews in the Middle Ages and Renaissance Period* (Tel Aviv, 1993), 9–23.

—— 'Finding Women's Voices in Italian Jewish Literature', in Judith R. Baskin (ed.), *Women of the Word: Jewish Women and Jewish Writing* (Detroit, 1994), 50–69.

ADELUNG, JOHANN CHRISTOPH, *Grammatisch-kritisches Wörterbuch der Hochdeutschen Mundart*, rev. edn., 4 vols. (Vienna, 1811).

ADLER, JOSEPH, *Restoring the Jews to their Homeland: Nineteen Centuries in the Quest for Zion* (Northvale, NJ, 1997).

AHLQUIST, KAREN, 'Men and Women of the Chorus: Music, Governance, and Social Models in Nineteenth-Century German-Speaking Europe', in ead. (ed.), *Chorus and Community* (Urbana, 2006), 265–92.

'AHR Forum: Revisiting "Gender: A Useful Category of Historical Analysis"', *American Historical Review*, 113/5 (2008), 1344–1430.

ALBRECHT, PETER, HANS ERICH BÖDEKER, and ERNST HINRICHS (eds.), *Formen der Geselligkeit in Nordwestdeutschland, 1750–1820* (Tübingen, 2003).

ALGAZI, GADI, 'Abelard, Heloise, and Astrolabe: A Note on Babies' Cries and Scholars' Peace of Mind' (Heb.), in Miriam Eliav-Feldon and Yitzhak Hen (eds.), *Women, Children and the Elderly: Essays in Honour of Shulamit Shahar* [Nashim, zekenim vetaf: kovets ma'amarim likhevodah shel shulamit shaḥar] (Jerusalem, 2001), 85–98.

Allgemeine Deutsche Biographie, 56 vols. (Leipzig, 1875–1912).

ALTMANN, ALEXANDER, *Moses Mendelssohn: A Biographical Study* (Alabama, 1973).

—— '"Moses Mendelssohn's Gesammelte Schriften". Neuerschlossene Briefe zur Geschichte ihrer Herausgabe', *Bulletin des Leo Baeck Instituts*, 11 (1968), 73–115.

ANDERSON, DONOVAN, 'Franco-German Conversations: Rahel Levin and Sophie von Grotthuß in Dialogue with Germaine de Staël', *German Studies Review*, 29/3 (2006), 559–77.

ANSTETT, JEAN-JACQUES, 'Henriette Mendelssohn', *Aspects de la civilisation germanique, Université de Saint-Etienne, Travaux*, 12 (1975), 73–122.

APTROOT, MARION, '"I know this book of mine will cause offence . . .": A Yiddish Adaptation of Boccaccio's *Decameron* (Amsterdam, 1710)', *Zutot*, 3 (2003), 152–9.

ARENDT, HANNAH, *Rahel Varnhagen: The Life of a Jewess*, ed. Liliane Weissberg (Baltimore, 1997).

AUSFELD, JOHANN WILHELM, *Erinnerungen aus Christian Gotthilf Salzmanns Leben* (n.p., 1813).

BAADER, BENJAMIN MARIA, *Gender, Judaism, and Bourgeois Culture in Germany, 1800–1870* (Bloomington, 2006).

—— 'When Judaism Turned Bourgeois: Gender in Jewish Associational Life and in the Synagogue, 1750–1850', *Leo Baeck Institute Yearbook*, 46 (2001), 113–23.

BADT-STRAUß, BERTHA, 'Elise Reimarus und Moses Mendelssohn (nach ungedruckten Quellen)', *Zeitschrift für die Geschichte der Juden in Deutschland*, 4 (1932), 173–89.

—— 'Moses Mendelssohns Tochter Dorothea', *Der Morgen*, 5/3 (1929), 244–8.

BAJOHR, FRANK, *'Unser Hotel ist judenfrei'. Bäder-Antisemitismus im 19. und 20. Jahrhundert* (Frankfurt am Main, 2003).

BALIN, CAROLE B., *To Reveal Our Hearts: Jewish Women Writers in Tsarist Russia* (Cincinnati, 2000).

Bankiers, Künstler und Gelehrte, Unveröffentlichte Briefe der Familie Mendelssohn aus dem 19. Jahrhundert, ed. Felix Gilbert (Tübingen, 1975).

BARON, SALO W., 'Newer Approaches to Jewish Emancipation', *Diogenes*, 8 (29) (1960), 56–81.

BARTSCH, CORNELIA, 'Lea Mendelssohn Bartholdy (1777–1842). "In voller geistiger Lebendigkeit"', in Irina Hundt (ed.), *Vom Salon zur Barrikade. Frauen der Heinezeit* (Stuttgart, 2002), 61–73.

BECKER-CANTARINO, BARBARA, *Schriftstellerinnen der Romantik. Epoche—Werke—Wirkung* (Munich, 2000).

BEHLER, ERNST, 'Le Premier Romantisme: Crise des Lumières', *Revue Germanique Internationale*, 3 [= *La Crise des Lumières*] (1995), 11–29.

BEINART, HAIM, 'A Fifteenth-Century Hebrew Formulary from Spain' (Heb.), *Sefunot*, 5 (1961), 75–134.

BEISER, FREDERICK C., *The Romantic Imperative: The Concept of Early German Romanticism* (Cambridge, Mass., 2003).

BEMBENEK, LOTHAR, 'Das jüdische Badhaus "Zum Rebhuhn" in Wiesbaden', *Menora*, 3 (1992), 99–120.

BENDAVID, LAZARUS, *Etwas zur Charackteristick der Juden* (Leipzig, 1793).

—— 'Selbstbiographie', in M. S. Lowe (ed.), *Bildnisse jetztlebender Berliner Gelehrten mit ihren Selbstbiographieen*, vol. ii (Berlin, 1806), 1–72.

—— 'Und er soll dein Herr sein. I Mose, III, 16', *Berlinische Monatsschrift*, 28 (1796), 354–67.

BEREND, ZSUZSA, '"The Best or None!": Spinsterhood in Nineteenth-Century New England', *Journal of Social History*, 33 (2000), 935–57.

BERGER, RUTH, *Sexualität, Ehe und Familienleben in der jüdischen Moralliteratur (900–1900)* (Wiesbaden, 2003).

BERGER, SHLOMO, *Yiddish and Jewish Modernization in the Eighteenth Century* [Yidish vehamodernizatsiyah hayehudit bame'ah hashemoneh-esreh] (Ramat Gan, 2006).

BERKOWITZ, JOEL, and JEREMY DAUBER (eds.), *Landmark Yiddish Plays: A Critical Anthology* (Albany, 2006).

BERLIN, ISAIAH, 'The Counter-Enlightenment', in id., *Against the Current: Essays in the History of Ideas* (New York, 1980), 1–24.
—— *The Roots of Romanticism* (Princeton, 2001).
BERLOVITZ, YAFFAH, 'Women's Literature in the Yishuv Period: Reorganization of an Excluded Culture' (Heb.), in Renée Levine Melammed (ed.), *'Lift Up Your Voice': Women's Voices and Feminist Interpretation in Jewish Studies* [Harimi beko'aḥ kolekh: al kolot neshiyim ufarshanut feministit belimudei yahadut] (Tel Aviv, 2001), 97–121.
BERNARD, ESTHER [née GAD], 'An Herrn D[oktor] F[eßler] in Berlin. Über das Museum in Dresden', *Berlinisches Archiv der Zeit und ihres Geschmacks*, 5/2 (1799), 445–51.
—— *Briefe über England und Portugal an einen Freund*, 2nd edn., 2 vols. (Hamburg, 1808).
—— 'Gedicht', in *Nachricht von dem unter dem Namen Wilhelmsschule zu Breslau errichteten Institut zu einer verbesserten Unterweisung der Kinder dasiger Juden-Gemeinde und der am 15. März 1791 erfolgten feyerlichen Einweihung desselben* (Breslau, 1791), 85–8.
See also GAD
BIALE, DAVID, *Eros and the Jews: From Biblical Israel to Contemporary America* (New York, 1992).
BILSKI, EMILY D., and EMILY BRAUN (eds.), *Jewish Women and their Salons: The Power of Conversation* (New York, 2005).
—— —— 'The Power of Conversation: Jewish Women and their Salons', in eaed. (eds.), *Jewish Women and their Salons*, 1–147.
BIRNBAUM, PIERRE, and IRA KATZNELSON, 'Emancipation and the Liberal Offer', in eid. (eds.), *Paths of Emancipation: Jews, States, and Citizenship* (Princeton, 1995), 3–36.
Bis nächstes Jahr auf Rügen. Briefe von Friedrich Daniel Ernst Schleiermacher und Henriette Herz an Ehrenfried von Willich, 1801 bis 1807, ed. Rainer Schmitz (Berlin, 1984).
BLACKBOURN, DAVID, 'Fashionable Spa Towns in Nineteenth-Century Europe', in Susan C. Anderson and Bruce H. Tabb (eds.), *Water, Leisure and Culture: European Historical Perspectives* (Oxford, 2002), 9–21.
BLACKWELL, JEANNINE, and SUSANNE ZANTOP (eds.), *Bitter Healing: German Women Writers from 1700 to 1830. An Anthology* (Lincoln, 1990).
BLOCH, MARCUS ELIESER, *Naturgeschichte der ausländischen Fische*, vol. i (Berlin, 1786).
BOCK, GISELA, 'Challenging Dichotomies: Perspectives on Women's History', in Karen Offen, Ruth Roach Pierson, and Jane Rendall (eds.), *Writing Women's History: International Perspectives* (London, 1991), 1–23.
—— *Women in European History*, trans. Allison Brown (Oxford, 2002).
—— 'Women's History and Gender History: Aspects of an International Debate', *Gender & History*, 1 (1989), 7–30.

BÖDEKER, HANS ERICH, 'Aufklärung als Kommunikationsprozeß', *Aufklärung*, 2/2 (1988), 89–111.
BODLEY, LORRAINE BYRNE, *Goethe and Zelter: Musical Dialogues* (Farnham, 2009).
BOENIGK, O. F. VON (ed.), *Schleiermacher und seine Lieben. Nach Originalbriefen der Henriette Herz* (Magdeburg, 1910).
BORSAY, PETER, 'Health and Leisure Resorts 1700–1840', in Peter Clark (ed.), *The Cambridge Urban History of Britain*, vol. ii: *1540–1840* (Cambridge, 2000), 775–803.
—— *A History of Leisure: The British Experience since 1500* (Basingstoke, 2006).
BOSOLD, BIRGIT ANNA, 'Friederike Liman. Briefwechsel mit Rahel Levin Varnhagen und Karl Gustav von Brinckmann sowie Aufzeichnungen von Rahel Levin Varnhagen und Karl August Varnhagen. Eine historisch-kritische Edition mit Nachwort', Ph.D. diss. (Hamburg, 1996).
BRANDES, HELGA, 'Die Entstehung eines weiblichen Lesepublikums im 18. Jahrhundert. Von den Frauenzimmerbibliotheken zu den literarischen Damengesellschaften', in Paul Goetsch (ed.), *Lesen und Schreiben im 17. und 18. Jahrhundert. Studien zu ihrer Bewertung in Deutschland, England, Frankreich* (Tübingen, 1994), 125–33.
BRENNER, MICHAEL, 'Zwischen Marienbad und Norderney: Der Kurort als "Jewish Space"', in *Jüdischer Almanach des Leo Baeck Instituts. Orte und Räume*, ed. Gisela Dachs (Frankfurt am Main, 2001), 119–37.
—— STEFI JERSCH-WENZEL, and MICHAEL A. MEYER, *Emancipation and Acculturation 1780–1871* (New York, 1997); vol. ii of Michael A. Meyer (ed.), *German-Jewish History in Modern Times*.
Briefe an eine Freundin. Rahel Varnhagen an Rebecca Friedländer, ed. Deborah Hertz (Cologne, 1988).
Briefe an Goethe. Gesamtausgabe in Regestform, ed. Karl-Heinz Hahn and Manfred Koltes, 7 vols. (Weimar, 1980–2004); <http://ora-web.weimar-klassik.de/swk-db/goeregest/index.html>.
Briefe von und an Friedrich und Dorothea Schlegel, ed. Ernst Behler, vols. xxiii and xxiv of *Kritische Friedrich-Schlegel-Ausgabe* (Paderborn, 1985–7).
Briefe von und an Friedrich und Dorothea Schlegel, ed. Joseph Körner (Berlin, 1926).
Briefwechsel zwischen Rahel und David Veit, 2 vols., ed. Ludmilla Assing (Leipzig, 1861).
BRILLING, BERNHARD, 'Eibenschütziana—Anhang: Die Nachkommen des RJE', *Hebrew Union College Annual*, 35 (1964), 255–73.
BROCKLISS, L. W. B., 'The Development of the Spa in Seventeenth-Century France', *Medical History*, no. 10 [= *The Medical History of Waters and Spas*, ed. Roy Porter] (1990), 23–47.
BRONNER, LEILA LEAH, 'From Veil to Wig: Jewish Women's Hair Covering', *Judaism*, 42/4 (1993), 465–77.
BRUYN, GÜNTER DE (ed.), *Rahels erste Liebe. Rahel Levin und Karl Graf von Finckenstein in ihren Briefen* (Berlin, 1998).

BURKE, PETER, 'The Invention of Leisure in Early Modern Europe', *Past & Present*, 146 (1995), 136–50.
—— 'Religion and Secularisation', in id. (ed.), *Cambridge Modern History*, vol. xiii (Cambridge, 1979), 293–317.
BYNUM, WILLIAM F., and ROY PORTER (eds.), *Companion Encyclopedia of the History of Medicine*, 2 vols. (London, 1993).
CABEZAS ALGUACIL, CONCEPCIÓN, 'Doña Isabel de Correa, traductora y poetisa sefardí', *Miscelánea de Estudios Arabes y Hebraicos*, 10 (1961), 111–29.
CAMPE, JOACHIM HEINRICH, *Väterlicher Rath für meine Tochter. Ein Gegenstück zum Theophron. Der erwachsenern weiblichen Jugend gewidmet von Joachim Heinrich Campe'n*, 5th edn. (Braunschweig, 1796).
CARLEBACH, ELISHEVA, *The Anti-Christian Element in Early Modern Yiddish Culture* (Ramat Gan, 2003).
—— *Divided Souls: The Convert Critique and the Culture of Ashkenaz, 1750–1800* (New York, 2003).
—— *Divided Souls: Converts from Judaism in Germany, 1500–1750* (New Haven, 2001).
—— 'Early Modern Ashkenaz in the Writings of Jacob Katz', in Jay M. Harris (ed.), *The Pride of Jacob: Essays on Jacob Katz and his Work* (Cambridge, Mass., 2002), 65–83.
CARLEBACH, JULIUS, 'The Forgotten Connection: Women and Jews in the Conflict between Enlightenment and Romanticism', *Leo Baeck Institute Yearbook*, 24 (1979), 107–38.
CARPI, DANIEL, *Between Renaissance and Ghetto: Essays on the History of the Jews in Italy in the Fourteenth and Seventeenth Centuries* [Betarbut harenesans uvein ḥomot hageto: meḥkarim betoledot hayehudim be'italiyah bame'ot ha'arba-esreh–hasheva-esreh] (Tel Aviv, 1989).
CAVALLO, GUGLIELMO, and ROGER CHARTIER (eds.), *A History of Reading in the West* (Amherst, 1999).
CHAMBERS-SCHILLER, LEE VIRGINIA, *Liberty, A Better Husband. Single Women in America: The Generations of 1780–1840* (New Haven, 1984).
CHARTIER, ROGER, *The Order of Books: Readers, Authors, and Libraries in Europe between the Fourteenth and Eighteenth Centuries* (Stanford, 1994).
CHOVAV, YEMIMA, *Maidens Love Thee: The Religious and Spiritual Life of Ashkenazi Women in the Early Modern Period* [Alamot ahevukha: ḥayei hadat veharu'aḥ shel nashim baḥevrah ha'ashkenazit bereshit ha'et haḥadashah] (Jerusalem, 2009).
CLARK, ANNA, 'Anne Lister's Construction of Lesbian Identity', *Journal of the History of Sexuality*, 7/1 (1996), 23–50.
CLINTON, KATHERINE B., 'Femme et Philosophe: Enlightenment Origins of Feminism', *Eighteenth-Century Studies*, 8 (1975), 283–99.
COHEN, TOVA, 'From the Private Sphere to the Public Sphere: The Writings of Hebrew Maskilot in the Nineteenth Century' (Heb.), in David Assaf et al. (eds.), *Studies in East European History and Culture in Honour of Professor Shmuel Werses*

[Mivilnah liyerushalayim: meḥkarim betoledoteihem uvetarbutam shel yehudei mizraḥ eiropah] (Jerusalem, 2002), 235–8.

COHEN, TOVA, 'Maskilot, Nineteenth Century', *Jewish Women: A Comprehensive Historical Encyclopedia*. 1 Mar. 2009. Jewish Women's Archive, 10 Oct. 2010; <http://jwa.org/encyclopedia/article/maskilot-nineteenth-century>.

—— *One Beloved, the Other Hated: Between Reality and Fiction in Depictions of Women in Haskalah Literature* [Ha'aḥat ahuvah veha'aḥat senu'ah: bein metsi'ut levidyon limetsi'ut beti'urei ha'ishah besifrut hahaskalah] (Jerusalem, 2002).

—— 'Portrait of the *Maskilah* as a Young Woman', *Nashim*, 15 (2008), 9–29.

—— and SHMUEL FEINER (eds.), *Voice of a Hebrew Maiden: Women's Writings of the Nineteenth-Century Haskalah Movement* [Kol almah ivriyah: kitvei nashim maskilot bame'ah hatesha-esreh] (Tel Aviv, 2006).

COHN, WARREN I., 'The Moses Isaac Family Trust, its History and Significance', *Leo Baeck Institute Yearbook*, 18 (1973), 267–79.

COONTZ, STEPHANIE, *Marriage, a History: How Love Conquered Marriage* (New York, 2005).

DARNTON, ROBERT, 'George Washington's False Teeth', *New York Review of Books*, 27 Mar. 1997, 34–8.

—— *The Kiss of Lamourette: Reflections in Cultural History* (New York, 1990).

—— 'Readers Respond to Rousseau: The Fabrication of Romantic Sensitivity', in *The Great Cat Massacre and Other Episodes in French Cultural History* (New York, 1984), 215–56.

[DAVIDSON, WOLF], *Briefe über Berlin. Erste Sammlung* (Landau, 1798).

DAVIDSON, WOLF, *Ueber die bürgerliche Verbesserung der Juden* (Berlin, 1798).

DAVIES, MARTIN L., *Identity or History? Marcus Herz and the End of the Enlightenment* (Detroit, 1995).

—— 'Portraits of a Lady: Variations on Henriette Herz (1764–1847)', in Margaret Ives (ed.), *Women Writers of the Age of Goethe*, Occasional Papers in German Studies 5 (Lancaster 1992), 45–75.

DAVIS, NATALIE Z., *Women on the Margins: Three Seventeenth-Century Lives* (Cambridge, Mass., 1995).

—— and ARLETTE FARGE, 'Women as Historical Actors', in eaed. (eds.), *A History of Women in the West*, iii: *Renaissance and Enlightenment Paradoxes* (Cambridge, Mass., 1993), 1–7.

DAWSON, RUTH P., '"And this shield is called—self-reliance": Emerging Feminist Consciousness in the Late Eighteenth Century', in Ruth-Ellen B. Joeres and Mary Jo Maynes (eds.), *German Women in the Eighteenth and Nineteenth Centuries: A Social and Literary History* (Bloomington, 1986), 157–74.

—— *The Contested Quill, Literature by Women in Germany 1770–1800* (Newark, 2001).

DEIBEL, FRANZ, *Dorothea Schlegel als Schriftstellerin im Zusammenhang mit der romantischen Schule* (Berlin, 1905).

DEUTSCH, NATHANIEL, *The Maiden of Ludmir: A Jewish Holy Woman and her World* (Berkeley and Los Angeles, 2003).

DIAMOND, MARIE JOSEPHINE, 'The Revolutionary Rhetoric of Olympe de Gouges', *Gender Issues*, 14/1 (1994), 3–23.

DICK, JUTTA, 'Freundinnen. Rahel de Castro, Ludmilla Assing, Ottilie Assing', *Menora*, 8 (1997), 181–98.

—— '"Wie Sie sicher durch Fräulein Rahel de Castro wissen..."', in Michael Studemund-Halévy (ed.), *Die Sefarden in Hamburg. Zur Geschichte einer Minderheit*, vol. i (Hamburg, 1994), 383–414.

DOMEIER [MADAME], *An Appendix to the Descriptions of Paris* (London, 1820).

DONOVAN, JOSEPHINE, 'The Silence is Broken', in Sally McConnell-Ginet, Ruth Borker, and Nelly Furman (eds.), *Women and Language in Literature and Society* (New York, 1980), 205–18.

Dorothea v. Schlegel geb. Mendelssohn und deren Söhne Johannes und Philipp Veit. Briefwechsel, ed. J. M. Raich, 2 vols. (Mainz, 1881).

'Dr. Salomo Heinrich Karl August Michaelis', *Neuer Nekrolog der Deutschen*, 22/1 (1844), 449–56.

DUBIN, LOIS C., *The Port Jews of Habsburg Trieste: Absolutist Politics and Enlightenment Culture* (Stanford, Calif., 1999).

DUBNOW, SIMON, *History of the Jews*, vol. iv, trans. Moshe Spiegel (South Brunswick, 1971).

DÜLL, SIEGRID (ed.), *Das Pyrmonter Brunnenarchiv von 1782. Nachdruck der Originalausgabe* (St Augustin, 1995).

DVORJETSKI, ESTÉE, 'Medicinal Hot Springs in Erets Yisra'el in Antiquity—Sacred Places or Popular Sites of Healing?' (Heb.), *Jerusalem Studies in Jewish Folklore* [Meḥkarei yerushalayim befolkelor yehudi], 16 (1994), 7–27.

EBERSPÄCHER, MARTINA, 'Wie Weihnachten deutsch wurde. Die Erfolgsgeschichte der modernen Weihnacht', in Cilly Kugelmann (ed.), *Weihnukka: Geschichten von Weihnachten und Chanukka* (Berlin, 2005), 33–9.

EISENSTEIN, ELIZABETH L., *The Printing Press as an Agent of Change: Communications and Cultural Transformations in Early Modern Europe*, 2 vols. (Cambridge, 1979).

ELEY, GEOFF, 'Nations, Publics, and Political Cultures: Placing Habermas in the Nineteenth Century', in Craig Calhoun (ed.), *Habermas and the Public Sphere* (Cambridge, 1994), 289–339.

ELIAV, MORDECHAI, *Jewish Education in Germany in the Period of Enlightenment and Emancipation* [Haḥinukh hayehudi begermaniyah biyemei hahaskalah veha'-emantsipatsiyah] (Jerusalem, 1960).

ELON, AMOS, *The Pity of it All: A Portrait of the German-Jewish Epoch 1743–1933* (New York, 2002).

ENDELMAN, TODD M. (ed.), *Jewish Apostasy in the Modern World* (New York, 1987).

—— *The Jews of Britain, 1656 to 2000* (Berkeley and Los Angeles, 2002).

—— *The Jews of Georgian England 1714–1830: Tradition and Change in a Liberal Society*, 2nd edn. (Ann Arbor, 1999).

ENDELMAN, TODD M., 'Memories of Jewishness: Jewish Converts and their Jewish Pasts', in Elisheva Carlebach, John M. Efron, and David N. Myers (eds.), *Jewish History and Jewish Memory: Essays in Honor of Yosef Haim Yerushalmi* (Hanover, NH, 1998), 311–29.

—— *Radical Assimilation in English Jewish History, 1656–1945* (Bloomington, 1990).

ENGELSING, ROLF, *Der Bürger als Leser. Lesergeschichte in Deutschland 1500–1800* (Stuttgart, 1974).

EUCHEL, ISAAC, 'Letters of Meshulam the Son of Uriah the Eshtemoi' (Heb.), in Yehuda Friedlander, *Studies in Hebrew Satire* [Perakim basatirah ha'ivrit], vol. i: *Hebrew Satire in Germany (1790–1797)* [Beshalhei hame'ah hashemoneh-esreh begermaniyah] (Tel Aviv, 1979), 41–61.

—— *Reb henoch, oder: woß tut me damit. Eine jüdische Komödie der Aufklärungszeit*, ed. Marion Aptroot and Roland Gruschka (Hamburg, 2004).

—— *Vom Nutzen der Aufklärung. Schriften zur Haskalah*, ed. Andreas Kennecke (Düsseldorf, 2001).

FEILCHENFELDT, KONRAD, 'Die Anfänge des Kults um Rahel Varnhagen und seine Kritiker', in Walter Grab and Julius H. Schoeps (eds.), *Juden im Vormärz und in der Revolution von 1848* (Stuttgart, 1983), 214–32.

FEINER, SHMUEL, *Haskalah and History: The Emergence of a Modern Jewish Historical Consciousness* (Oxford, 2002).

—— 'Isaac Euchel: "Entrepreneur" of the Haskalah Movement in Germany' (Heb.), *Zion*, 52 (1987), 427–69.

—— *The Jewish Enlightenment*, trans. Chaya Naor (Pennsylvania, 2003).

—— 'The Modern Jewish Woman: A Test Case in the Relationship between Haskalah and Modernity' (Heb.), in Israel Bartal and Isaiah Gafni (eds.), *Sexuality and the Family in History: Collected Essays* [Eros, eirusin ve'isurim: miniyut umishpahah bahistoriyah] (Jerusalem, 1998), 253–303.

—— *The Origins of Jewish Secularization in Eighteenth Century Europe*, trans. Chaya Naor (Philadelphia, 2010).

—— 'Out of Berlin: The Second Phase of the Haskalah Movement' (Heb.), in Ezra Fleischer, Gerald Blidstein, Carmi Horowitz, and Bernard Septimus (eds.), *Meah She'arim: Studies in Medieval Jewish Spiritual Life in Memory of Isadore Twersky* [Me'ah she'arim: iyunim be'olamam haruhani shel yisra'el biyemei habeinayim, sefer zikaron leyitshak tverski] (Jerusalem, 2001), 403–31.

—— 'The Pseudo-Enlightenment and the Question of Jewish Modernization', *Jewish Social Studies*, 3 (1996), 62–88.

—— and DAVID SORKIN (eds.), *New Perspectives on the Haskalah* (London, 2001).

FETTERLEY, JUDITH, *The Resisting Reader: A Feminist Approach to American Fiction* (Bloomington and London, 1978).

FINKE, FRIEDRICH, *Ueber Friedrich und Dorothea Schlegel* (Cologne, 1918).

FINSCHER, LUDWIG (ed.), *Die Musik in Geschichte und Gegenwart. Allgemeine Enzyklopädie der Musik*, 2nd, rev., edn., Personenteil, vol. xvii (Kassel, 2007).

FISHMAN, DAVID E., *Russia's First Modern Jews: The Jews of Shklov* (New York, 1995).

FONTAINE, RESIANNE, ANDREA SCHATZ, and IRENE ZWIEP (eds.), *Sepharad in Ashkenaz: Medieval Knowledge and Eighteenth-Century Enlightened Jewish Discourse* (Amsterdam, 2007).

FORBES, BRUCE DAVID, *Christmas: A Candid History* (Berkeley and Los Angeles, 2007).

FOUCAULT, MICHEL, *The History of Sexuality*, vol. i: *An Introduction*, trans. Robert Hurley (New York, 1978).

—— 'What Is Enlightenment?', in Paul Rabinow (ed.), *The Foucault Reader* (New York, 1984), 32–50.

FRAADE, STEVEN D., 'Ascetical Aspects of Ancient Judaism', in Arthur Green (ed.), *Jewish Spirituality: From the Bible through the Middle Ages*, vol. i (New York, 1986), 253–88.

FRAKES, JEROLD C. (ed.), *Early Yiddish Texts 1100–1750* (Oxford, 2004).

FRAM, EDWARD, *My Dear Daughter: Rabbi Benjamin Slonik and the Education of Jewish Women in Sixteenth-Century Poland* (Cincinnati, 2007).

FRANKEL, JONATHAN, 'Assimilation and the Jews in Nineteenth-Century Europe: Towards a New Historiography?', in Jonathan Frankel and Steven J. Zipperstein (eds.), *Assimilation and Community: The Jews in Nineteenth-Century Europe* (Cambridge, 1992), 1–37.

FRANKS, ABIGAILL LEVY, *The Letters of Abigaill Levy Franks 1733–1748*, ed. Edith B. Gelles (New Haven, 2004).

FREDERIKSEN, ELKE, 'Der Blick in die Ferne. Zur Reiseliteratur von Frauen', in Hiltrud Gnüg and Renate Möhrmann (eds.), *Frauen Literatur Geschichte. Schreibende Frauen vom Mittelalter bis zur Gegenwart* (Stuttgart and Weimar, 1999), 147–65.

FREIDENREICH, HARRIET PASS, *Female, Jewish and Educated: The Lives of Central European University Women* (Bloomington, 2002).

FRENCH, LORELY, *German Women as Letter Writers: 1750–1850* (Madison, 1996).

FREUDENTHAL, MAX, 'Die ersten Emancipationsbestrebungen der Juden in Breslau. Nach archivalischen und anderen Quellen dargestellt', *Monatschrift für Geschichte und Wissenschaft des Judentums*, 37 (1893), 41–8, 92–100, 188–97, 238–47, 331–41, 409–29, 467–83, 522–36, 565–79.

FREVERT, UTE, 'Die Innenwelt der Außenwelt. Modernitätserfahrungen von Frauen zwischen Gleichheit und Differenz', in Shulamit Volkov (ed.), *Deutsche Juden und die Moderne* (Munich, 1994), 75–94.

FRIEDLANDER, YEHUDA, *Studies in Hebrew Satire* [Perakim basatirah ha'ivrit], vol. i: *Hebrew Satire in Germany (1790–1797)* [Beshalhei hame'ah hashemoneh-esreh begermaniyah] (Tel Aviv, 1979).

FRONIUS, HELEN, 'Der reiche Mann und die arme Frau: German Women Writers and the Eighteenth-Century Literary Market-Place', *German Life and Letters*, 56/1 (2003), 1–19.

—— *Women and Literature in the Goethe Era 1770–1820* (Oxford, 2007).

FUHS, BURKHARD, *Mondäne Orte einer vornehmen Gesellschaft. Kultur und Geschichte der Kurstädte 1700–1900* (Hildesheim, 1992).

GAD, ESTHER, 'Einige Aeußerungen über Hrn. Kampe'ns Behauptungen, die weibliche Gelehrsamkeit betreffend', in Elke Kleinau and Christine Mayer (eds.), *Erziehung und Bildung des weiblichen Geschlechts. Eine kommentierte Quellensammlung zur Bildungs- und Berufsbildungsgeschichte von Mädchen und Frauen*, vol. i (Weinheim, 1996), 56–63.

See also BERNARD

GALCHINSKY, MICHAEL, *The Origin of the Modern Jewish Woman Writer: Romance and Reform in Victorian England* (Detroit, 1996).

GEIGER, LUDWIG (ed.), *Briefwechsel des jungen Börne und der Henriette Herz* (Oldenburg, 1905).

—— 'Dorothea Veit-Schlegel', *Deutsche Rundschau*, 160 (1914), 119–34.

—— (ed.) 'Einundzwanzig Briefe von Marianne von Eybenberg, acht von Sara von Grotthuß, zwanzig von Varnhagen von Ense an Goethe, zwei Briefe Goethes an Frau von Eybenberg', *Goethe-Jahrbuch*, 14 (1893), 27–142.

—— 'Die Juden und die deutsche Literatur', *Zeitschrift für die Geschichte der Juden in Deutschland*, 1 (1887), 321–65.

—— 'Mittheilungen aus Berliner Zeitungen, Zeitschriften und Brochüren (1741–1830)', *Zeitschrift für die Geschichte der Juden in Deutschland*, 4 (1890), 289–300.

—— 'Ueber den Verfasser der Posse: Unser Verkehr', *Allgemeine Zeitung des Judentums*, 67/7 (1903), 78–81.

—— 'Vor hundert Jahren. Mitteilungen aus der Geschichte der Juden Berlins', *Zeitschrift für die Geschichte der Juden in Deutschland*, 3 (1889), 185–233.

—— A. COHN, C. V. GORKI, M. HERTZ, L. HIRZEL, H. OLDENBERG, A. SAUER, and M. SEIDEL, 'Zweiunddreissig Briefe Goethes, nebst zwei Briefen an Goethe', *Goethe-Jahrbuch*, 7 (1886), 168–205.

GELBER, MARK H., 'The Noble Sephardi and the Degenerate Ashkenazi in German-Jewish and German-Anti-Semitic Consciousness: Heine, Langbehn, Chamberlain', in id. (ed.), *Confrontations/Accommodations: German-Jewish Literary and Cultural Relations from Heine to Wasserman* (Tübingen, 2004), 45–56.

GELBER, N. M., *Zur Vorgeschichte des Zionismus. Judenstaatsprojekte in den Jahren 1695–1845* (Vienna, 1927).

GELLES, EDITH B. (ed.), *First Thoughts: Life and Letters of Abigail Adams* (New York, 1998).

GENTH, ADOLPH, *Kulturgeschichte der Stadt Schwalbach* (Wiesbaden, 1858).

GILON, MEIR, *Mendelssohn's 'Kohelet musar' in its Historical Context* [Kohelet musar lemendelson al reka tekufato] (Jerusalem, 1979).

GINZBURG, CARLO, *The Cheese and the Worms: The Cosmos of a Sixteenth-Century Miller* (London, 1980).

GLIKL, *Memoirs, 1691–1719* [Zikhroynes, 1691–1719], ed. and trans. Chava Turniansky (Jerusalem, 2006).

GOCH, MARIANNE, *Im Aufbruch. Biographien deutscher Jüdinnen* (Frankfurt am Main, 2000).

GOETHE, JOHANN WOLFGANG VON, *Goethes Briefe*, ed. Karl Robert Mandelkow, 4 vols. (Hamburg, 1962–7).

—— *Goethes Werke. Weimarer Ausgabe*, pt. III, vol. iii. Digital version: <http://www.zeno.org/Literatur/M/Goethe,+Johann+Wolfgang/Tageb%C3%BCcher/180>.
GOITEIN, S. D. (ed.), *Letters of Medieval Jewish Traders* (Princeton, 1973).
GOODMAN, DENA, 'Difference: An Enlightenment Concept', in Keith Michael Baker and Peter Hanns Reill (eds.), *What's Left of Enlightenment? A Postmodern Question* (Stanford, 2001), 129–47.
—— 'Enlightenment Salons: The Convergence of Female and Philosophic Ambitions', *Eighteenth-Century Studies*, 22 (1989), 329–50.
—— 'More than Paradoxes to Offer: Feminist History as Critical Practice', *History and Theory*, 36/3 (1997), 392–405.
—— 'Public Sphere and Private Life: Toward a Synthesis of Current Historiographical Approaches to the Old Regime', *History and Theory*, 31 (1992), 1–20.
—— *The Republic of Letters: A Cultural History of the French Enlightenment* (Ithaca, NY, 1994).
GRAETZ, HEINRICH, *History of the Jews*, vol. v: *From the Chmielnicki Persecution of the Jews in Poland (1648 C.E.) to the Period of Emancipation in Central Europe (c.1870 C.E.)* (Philadelphia, 1895).
—— *History of the Jews* [Divrei yemei hayehudim], vol. ix (Jerusalem, 1972).
GRAUN, CARL HEINRICH, *Der Tod Jesu*, ed. Howard Serwer (Madison, 1975).
GRAUPE, HEINZ MOSCHE, *The Rise of Modern Judaism: An Intellectual History of German Jewry, 1650–1942*, trans. John Robinson (Huntington, NY, 1978).
GRIES, ZEEV, *The Book in the Jewish World, 1700–1900* (Oxford, 2010).
GRISWOLD, WENDY, 'The Fabrication of Meaning: Literary Interpretation in the United States, Great Britain, and the West Indies', *American Journal of Sociology*, 92/5 (1987), 1077–1117.
GROSSMAN, AVRAHAM, *Pious and Rebellious: Jewish Women in Medieval Europe*, trans. Jonathan Chipman (Hanover, NH, 2004).
HABERMAS, JÜRGEN, *The Structural Transformation of the Public Sphere*, trans. Thomas Burger (Cambridge, Mass., 1989).
HABERMAS, REBEKKA, *Frauen und Männer des Bürgertums. Eine Familiengeschichte (1750–1850)* (Göttingen, 2000).
HAHN, BARBARA, *'Antworten Sie mir!' Rahel Levin Varnhagens Briefwechsel* (Basel, 1990).
—— '"Apprenez l'européen!" Les Langues de l'acculturation vers 1800', *Revue Germanique Internationale*, 4: *Le Miroir allemand* (1995), 129–46.
—— 'Diese trostvolle, sanfte Verbindung. Rahel Levin schreibt an Henriette Mendelssohn', in *Ein solches Jahrhundert vergißt sich nicht mehr. Lieblingstexte aus dem 18. Jahrhundert*, selected and presented by authors of C. H. Beck Publishers (Munich, 2000), 356–60.
—— '"Ein Mann kann nicht denken wie Wir". Zum Briefwechsel von Pauline Wiesel und Rahel Levin Varnhagen', in Rahel Levin Varnhagen, *Briefwechsel mit Pauline Wiesel*, ed. Barbara Hahn, in co-operation with Birgit Bosold (Munich, 1997), 705–30.

HAHN, BARBARA, '"Geliebtester Schriftsteller". Esther Gads Korrespondenz mit Jean Paul', *Jahrbuch der Jean-Paul-Gesellschaft*, 25 (1990), 7–42.

—— *The Jewess Pallas Athena: This Too a Theory of Modernity*, trans. James McFarland (Princeton, NJ, 2005).

—— 'Der Mythos vom Salon. "Rahels Dachstube" als historische Fiktion', in Hartwig Schultz (ed.), *Salons der Romantik. Beiträge eines Wieperdorfer Kolloquiums zu Theorie und Geschichte des Salons* (Berlin, 1997), 213–34.

—— 'Rahels Schriften II. Überlegungen für eine künftige Edition', in Barbara Hahn and Ursula Isselstein (eds.), *Rahel Levin Varnhagen. Die Wiederentdeckung einer Schriftstellerin* (Göttingen, 1987), 37–46.

—— 'Sophie von Grotthuss', in *Jewish Women: A Comprehensive Historical Encyclopedia*. 1 Mar. 2009. Jewish Women's Archive. 12 Oct. 2012. <http://jwa.org/encyclopedia/article/grotthuss-sophie-von>.

—— *Unter falschem Namen. Von der schwierigen Autorschaft der Frauen* (Frankfurt am Main, 1991).

—— '"Weiber verstehen alles à la lettre". Briefkultur im beginnenden 19. Jahrhundert', in Gisela Brinker-Gabler (ed.), *Deutsche Literatur von Frauen*, vol. ii (Munich, 1988), 13–27.

—— and URSULA ISSELSTEIN (eds.), *Rahel Levin Varnhagen. Die Wiederentdeckung einer Schriftstellerin* (Göttingen, 1987).

Hame'asef [The Gatherer], 7 vols. (Königsberg, Berlin, and Breslau, 1783–97).

HANSEN, KAREN V., '"No Kisses Is Like Youres": An Erotic Friendship between Two African-American Women during the Mid-Nineteenth Century', *Gender & History*, 7/2 (1995), 153–82.

Hebrew Ethical Wills, ed. Israel Abrahams, 2 vols. (Philadelphia, 1926).

HECHT, LOUISE, *Ein jüdischer Aufklärer in Böhmen. Der Pädagoge und Reformer Peter Beer (1758–1838)* (Cologne, 2008).

HEINRICH, GERDA, '"Juden müssen sich also gar nicht einmischen . . .". Mendelssohn als Initiator und Mentor der Debatte um die "bürgerliche Verbesserung der Juden", 1781–1786', *Menora*, 12 (2001), 39–65.

HEINRICI, GEORG (ed.), 'Briefe von Henriette Herz an August Twesten (1814–1827)', *Zeitschrift für Bücherfreunde*, 5 (1914), 301–16, 333–47.

HENRY, SONDRA, and EMILY TAITZ, *Written out of History: Our Jewish Foremothers* (New York, 1990).

HENSEL, SEBASTIAN, *The Mendelssohn Family (1729–1847): From Letters and Journals*, 2 vols., 2nd, rev., edn. (New York, 1969).

Herrn I. A. Euchel und A. F. Wolff bey Ihrer Abreise gewidmet von einigen Freunden (Königsberg, 1787).

HERTZ, DEBORAH, 'Emancipation through Intermarriage? Wealthy Jewish Salon Women in Old Berlin', in Judith Baskin (ed.), *Jewish Women in Historical Perspective* (Detroit, 1998), 193–207.

—— *How Jews Became Germans: The History of Conversion and Assimilation in Berlin* (New Haven, 2007).

—— 'Ihr offenes Haus—Amalia Beer und die Berliner Reform', *Kalonymos*, 2/1 (1999), 1–4.
—— 'Intermarriage in the Berlin Salons', *Central European History*, 16 (1983), 303–46.
—— *Jewish High Society in Old Regime Berlin* (New Haven, 1988; paperback edn. 2005).
—— 'Seductive Conversion in Berlin, 1770–1809', in Todd M. Endelman (ed.), *Jewish Apostasy in the Modern World* (New York, 1987), 48–82.
—— 'The Varnhagen Collection is in Krakow', *The American Archivist*, 44/3 (1981), 223–8.
HERZ, HENRIETTE, 'Jugenderinnerungen von Henriette Herz', in *Mittheilungen aus dem Literaturarchive in Berlin*, vol. i (Berlin, 1897), 141–84.
HERZ, MARCUS, 'Freymüthiges Kaffegespräch zwoer jüdischen Zuschauerinnen über den Juden Pinkus oder über den Geschmack eines gewissen Parterrs' [republished by Gunnar Och], *Lessing Yearbook*, 20 (1988), 70–82.
HERZIG, ARNO, 'Die Juden in Hamburg 1780–1860', in id. (ed.), *Die Juden in Hamburg, 1590 bis 1990* (Hamburg, 1991), 61–75.
HESSE, CARLA, *The Other Enlightenment: How French Women Became Modern* (2001; Princeton, 2003).
HEUER, RENATE, 'Bücherschau—Zum Thema: Jüdinnen zwischen Tradition und Emanzipation', in Norbert Altenhofer and Renate Heuer (eds.), *Jüdinnen zwischen Tradition und Emanzipation* (Bad Soden, 1990), 156–91.
—— 'Mutter in Israel—Muse der Romantik. Brendel Mendelssohn Veit—Dorothea von Schlegel', in Norbert Altenhofer und Renate Heuer (eds.), *Jüdinnen zwischen Tradition und Emanzipation* (Bad Soden, 1990), 27–47.
HILLEBRAND, KARL, 'La Société de Berlin de 1789 à 1815', *Revue de deux mondes*, 86 (1870), 447–86.
HILLMAN, SUSANNE, 'The Conversions of Dorothea Mendelssohn: Conviction or Convenience', *German Studies Review*, 29/1 (2006), 127–44.
HINRICHS, ERNST, *Einführung in die Geschichte der Frühen Neuzeit* (Munich, 1980).
HIPPEL, THEODOR GOTTLIEB VON, *On Improving the Status of Women*, trans., ed., and introd. Timothy F. Sellner (Detroit, 1979).
HIRSCHEL, MOSES, 'Ueber die allzufrühen Ehen der jüdischen Nation; physisch, politisch und pädagogisch betrachtet', in Johann Joseph Kausch (ed.), *Freymüthige Unterhaltungen über die neuesten Vorfälle unsers Zeitalters, die Sitten und Handlungsarten der Menschen*, vol. i. (Leipzig, 1790), 60–94.
HOFFMANN, PAUL, *La Femme dans la pensée des Lumières* (Paris, 1977).
HOLTEI, KARL VON (ed.), *Dreihundert Briefe aus zwei Jahrhunderten*, vol. i, new edn. (Bern, 1971).
HUNDT, IRINA, 'Geselligkeit im Kreise von Dorothea und Friedrich Schlegel in Paris in den Jahren 1802–1804', in Hartwig Schultz (ed.), *Salons der Romantik. Beiträge eines Wiepersdorfer Kolloquiums zu Theorie und Geschichte des Salons* (Berlin, 1997), 83–133.

HURLEY, ALISON E., 'A Conversation of their Own: Watering-Place Correspondence among the Bluestockings', *Eighteenth-Century Studies*, 40/1 (2006), 1–21.

HYMAN, PAULA, *Gender and Assimilation in Modern Jewish History* (Seattle, 1995).

—— 'Two Models of Modernization: Jewish Women in the German and the Russian Empires', *Studies in Contemporary Jewry*, 16 (Oxford, 2001), 39–53.

IDEL, MOSHE, *Kabbalah and Eros* (New Haven, 2005).

ILAN, TAL, 'A Window onto the Public Realm: Jewish Women in the Second Temple Period' (Heb.), in Yael Azmon (ed.), *A Glimpse of the Lives of Women in Jewish Societies: Collected Essays* [Eshnav leḥayeihen shel nashim baḥavarot yehudiyot] (Jerusalem, 1995), 47–61.

ISRAEL, JONATHAN, *Radical Enlightenment: Philosophy and the Making of Modernity, 1650–1750* (Oxford, 2002).

ISSELSTEIN, URSULA, '"Dies ist die Beute!" Zu Rahel Levins Tagebüchern', in Barbara Hahn and Ursula Isselstein (eds.), *Rahel Levin Varnhagen. Die Wiederentdeckung einer Schriftstellerin* (Göttingen, 1987), 86–103.

—— 'Emanzipation wovon und wofür? Das Beispiel der Familie Levin aus Berlin', in Norbert Altenhofer and Renate Heuer (eds.), *Jüdinnen zwischen Tradition und Emanzipation* (Bad Soden, 1990), 80–113.

—— 'Rahels Schriften I. Karl August Varnhagens editorische Tätigkeit nach Dokumenten seines Archivs', in Barbara Hahn and Ursula Isselstein (eds.), *Rahel Levin Varnhagen. Die Wiederentdeckung einer Schriftstellerin* (Göttingen, 1987), 16–36.

—— *Der Text aus meinem beleidigten Herzen. Studien zu Rahel Levin Varnhagen* (Turin, 1993).

—— 'Die Titel der Dinge sind das Fürchterlichste! Rahel Levins "Erster Salon"', in Hartwig Schultz (ed.), *Salons der Romantik. Beiträge eines Wieperdorfer Kolloquiums zu Theorie und Geschichte des Salons* (Berlin, 1997) 171–212.

JACOBSON, JACOB, *Jüdische Trauungen in Berlin, 1759–1813* (Berlin, 1968).

—— 'Von Mendelssohn zu Mendelssohn-Bartholdy', *Leo Baeck Institute Yearbook*, 5 (1960), 251–61.

JERSCH-WENZEL, STEFI, 'Die Juden im gesellschaftlichen Gefüge Berlins um 1800', in Marianne Awerbuch and Stefi Jersch-Wenzel (eds.), *Bild und Selbstbild der Juden Berlins Zwischen Aufklärung und Romantik* (Berlin, 1992), 139–54.

JOERES, RUTH-ELLEN B., '"That girl is an entirely different character!" "Yes but is she a feminist?" Observations on Sophie von La Roche's *Geschichte des Fräuleins von Sternheim*', in Ruth-Ellen B. Joeres and Mary Jo Maynes (eds.), *German Women in the Eighteenth and Nineteenth Centuries: A Social and Literary History* (Bloomington, 1986), 137–56.

JOHNSON, PAULINE, 'Feminism and Enlightenment', *Radical Philosophy*, 63 (1993), 3–12.

—— 'The Quest for the Self: Feminism's Appropriation of Romanticism', *Thesis Eleven*, 41 (1995), 76–93.

KANT, IMMANUEL, 'An Answer to the Question: "What Is Enlightenment?"', in *Kant: Political Writings*, ed. Hans Reiss (Cambridge, 1991), 54–60.

KAPLAN, MARION A. (ed.), '"Based on love": The Courtship of Hendele and Jochanan, 1803–1804', in Marion Kaplan and Beate Meyer (eds.), *Jüdische Welten. Juden in Deutschland vom 18. Jahrhundert bis in die Gegenwart* (Göttingen, 2005), 86–107.

—— *The Jewish Feminist Movement in Germany: The Campaigns of the Jüdischer Frauenbund, 1904–1938* (Westport, Conn., 1979).

—— *The Making of the Jewish Middle Class: Women, Family and Identity in Imperial Germany* (New York, 1991).

—— '*Unter uns*: Jews Socialising with Other Jews in Imperial Germany', *Leo Baeck Institute Yearbook*, 48 (2003), 41–65.

—— 'Women and the Shaping of Modern Jewish Identity in Imperial Germany', in Shulamit Volkov (ed.), *Deutsche Juden und die Moderne* (Munich, 1994), 57–74.

—— (ed.), *Jewish Daily Life in Germany, 1618–1945* (Oxford, 2005).

KAPLAN, YOSEF, *An Alternative Path to Modernity: The Sephardi Diaspora in Western Europe* (Leiden, 2000).

KATZ, JACOB (ed.), 'German Culture and the Jews', in Jehuda Reinharz and Walter Schatzberg (eds.), *The Jewish Response to German Culture: From the Enlightenment to the Second World War* (Hanover, 1985), 85–99.

—— 'The Hep Hep Riots in Germany of 1819: The Historical Background' (Heb.), *Zion*, 38 (1973), 62–115.

—— 'Marriage and Marital Relationships at the End of the Middle Ages' (Heb.), *Zion*, 10 (1945), 21–54.

—— *Out of the Ghetto: The Social Background of Jewish Emancipation* (Cambridge, Mass. 1973).

—— *Toward Modernity: The European Jewish Model* (New Brunswick, NJ, 1987).

—— *Tradition and Crisis: Jewish Society at the End of the Middle Ages*, trans. Bernard Dov Cooperman (New York, 1993).

KAYSERLING, MEYER, *Die jüdischen Frauen in der Geschichte, Literatur und Kunst* (Leipzig, 1879; repr. Hildesheim, 1991).

KEDAR, BENJAMIN Z., 'Continuity and Change in Jewish Conversion in Eighteenth-Century Germany' (Heb.), in Immanuel Etkes and Yosef Salmon (eds.), *Studies in the History of Jewish Society in the Middle Ages and in the Modern Period* [Perakim betoledot haḥevrah hayehudit biyemei habeinayim uva'et haḥadashah] (Jerusalem, 1980), 154–70.

KELLY, JOAN, 'Did Women Have a Renaissance?', in ead., *Women, History and Theory: The Essays of Joan Kelly* (Chicago, 1984), 19–50.

—— 'The Social Relation of the Sexes, Methodological Implications of Women's History', in ead., *Women, History and Theory*, 1–18.

KENNECKE, ANDREAS, *Isaac Abraham Euchel. Architekt der Haskalah* (Göttingen, 2007).

KERSTING, CHRISTA, 'Prospekt fürs Eheleben. Joachim Heinrich Campe: Väterlicher Rath für meine Tochter', in Viktoria Schmidt-Linsenhoff (ed.),

Sklavin oder Bürgerin? Französische Revolution und neue Weiblichkeit 1760–1830 (Frankfurt, 1989), 371–90.

KLEIN, LAWRENCE E., 'Enlightenment as Conversation', in Keith Michael Baker and Peter Hanns Reill (eds.), *What's Left of Enlightenment? A Postmodern Question* (Stanford, 2001), 148–66.

—— 'Gender and the Public/Private Distinction in the Eighteenth Century: Some Questions about Evidence and Analytic Procedure', *Eighteenth-Century Studies*, 29/1 (1995), 97–109.

KLEINAU, ELKE, and CLAUDIA OPITZ (eds.), *Geschichte der Mädchen- und Frauenbildung*, vol. i: *Vom Mittelalter bis zur Aufklärung* (Frankfurt am Main, 1996).

KNOTT, SARAH, and BARBARA TAYLOR (eds.), *Women, Gender and Enlightenment* (Basingstoke, 2005).

KOBLER, FRANZ (ed.), *Juden und Judentum in deutschen Briefen aus drei Jahrhunderten* (Vienna, 1935).

KOGMAN, TAL, 'The Creation of Images of Knowledge in Texts for Children and Young Adults Published during the Haskalah Period' [Yetsirat dimuyei hayeda betekstim liyeladim yehudim be'aratsot doverot hagermanit bitekufat hahaskalah], Ph.D. dissertation, Tel Aviv University, 2000.

—— 'The Temptation is Great, and the Woman's Heart is so Weak': Tradition, Education and Modernization in the Reading Culture of the German-Jewish Girls in the Nineteenth Century ['Hapitui az, velibah shel ha'ishah koh ḥalash': masoret, ḥinukh vemodernizatsiyah ba'aron hasefarim shel habanot hagermaniyot-yehudiyot bame'ah hatesha-esreh] (Jerusalem, 2004).

KOHUT, ADOLPH, *Moses Mendelssohn und seine Familie* (Dresden, 1886).

KÖRNER, JOSEF (ed.), *Krisenjahre der Frühromantik. Briefe aus dem Schlegelkreis*, 2nd edn., 3 vols. (Bern and Munich, 1969).

KRAEMER, JOEL L., 'Women's Letters from the Cairo Genizah: A Preliminary Study' (Heb.), in Yael Azmon (ed.), *A Glimpse of the Lives of Women in Jewish Societies: Collected Essays* [Eshnav leḥayeihen shel nashim baḥavarot yehudiyot] (Jerusalem, 1995), 161–81.

KRAMNICK, ISAAC (ed.), *The Portable Enlightenment Reader* (New York, 1995).

KREMER, DETLEF, 'David Ferdinand Koreff', in Andreas B. Kilcher (ed.), *Metzler Lexikon der deutsch-jüdischen Literatur. Jüdische Autorinnen und Autoren deutscher Sprache von der Aufklärung bis zur Gegenwart* (Stuttgart, 2000), 332–4.

KROBB, FLORIAN, *Die schöne Jüdin. Jüdische Frauengestalten in der deutschsprachigen Erzählliteratur vom 17. Jahrhundert bis zum Ersten Weltkrieg* (Tübingen, 1993).

KRONICK, DAVID A., 'The Commerce of Letters: Networks and "Invisible Colleges" in Seventeenth- and Eighteenth-Century Europe', *Library Quarterly*, 71/1 (2001), 28–43.

KÜHNE, F. GUSTAV (ed.), 'Ein Brief von Frau von Grotthuis an Goethe. (Über Goethe's Leben, Mendelssohn und Lessing)', *Europa. Chronik der gebildeten Welt*, 27 (1850), 209–11.

KUHNERT, REINHOLD F., *Urbanität auf dem Lande. Badereisen nach Pyrmont im 18. Jahrhundert* (Göttingen, 1984).

KUHRAU, SVEN, 'Amalie Beer, Salondame, Wohltäterin und Patriotin: Das Programm einer individuellen Akkulturation', in Sven Kuhrau und Kurt Winkler with Alice Uebe (eds.), *Juden Bürger Berliner. Das Gedächtnis der Familie Beer-Meyerbeer-Richter* (Berlin, 2004), 49–66.

LANDAU, ALFRED, and BERNHARD WACHSTEIN, *Jüdische Privatbriefe aus dem Jahre 1619* (Vienna, 1911).

LANDES, JOAN B., *Women and the Public Sphere in the Age of the French Revolution* (Ithaca, NY, 1988).

LANDSBERG, HANS (ed.), *Henriette Herz. Ihr Leben und ihre Zeit* (Weimar, 1913).

LEA, CHARLENE A., *Emancipation, Assimilation and Stereotype: The Image of the Jew in German and Austrian Drama (1800–1850)* (Bonn, 1978).

LEMPA, HEIKKI, 'The Spa: Emotional Economy and Social Classes in Nineteenth-Century Pyrmont', *Central European History*, 35 (2002), 37–73.

LENEMAN, HELEN, 'Sara Coppio Sullam: Seventeenth-Century Jewish Poet in the Ghetto of Venice', *Response*, 15/3 (1987), 13–22.

Leopold and Adelheid Zunz: An Account in Letters, 1815–1885, ed. Nahum N. Glatzer (London, 1958).

LESSER, LUDWIG, *Chronik der Gesellschaft der Freunde in Berlin, zur Feier ihres fünfzigjährigen Jubiläums* (Berlin, 1842).

Letters to Immanuel Bekker from Henriette Herz, S. Pobeheim and Anna Horkel, ed. Max J. Putzel (Bern, 1972).

LEVIN VARNHAGEN, RAHEL, *Briefwechsel mit Ludwig Robert*, ed. Consolina Vigliero (Munich, 2001).

—— *Briefwechsel mit Pauline Wiesel*, ed. Barbara Hahn, in co-operation with Birgit Bosold (Munich, 1997).

—— *Familienbriefe*, ed. Renata Buzzo Màrgari Barovero (Munich, 2009).

See also VARNHAGEN

LEWIN, LOUIS, *Geschichte der Israelitischen Kranken-Verpflegungs-Anstalt und Beerdigungs-Gesellschaft zu Breslau Chevrah Kadishah 1726–1926* (Breslau, 1926).

LIBERLES, ROBERT, 'Dohm's Treatise on the Jews: A Defense of the Enlightenment', *Leo Baeck Institute Yearbook*, 33 (1988), 29–42.

LINDAU, BARUCH, *Beginning of Learning* [Reshit limudim] (Berlin, 1788).

LISKA, VIVIAN, 'Mainstreaming the Margins: Rahel Varnhagen at the End of the Twentieth Century', in Mark H. Gelber (ed.), *Confrontations/Accommodations: German-Jewish Literary and Cultural Relations from Heine to Wasserman* (Tübingen, 2004), 123–47.

LITTLE, WM. A., 'Mendelssohn and the Berlin Singakademie: The Composer at the Crossroads', in R. Larry Todd (ed.), *Mendelssohn and his World* (Princeton, 1991), 65–85.

LLOYD, GENEVIEVE, 'The Man of Reason', in Ann Garry and Marilyn Pearsall (eds.), *Women, Knowledge, and Reality* (New York, 1996), 149–65.

LOENTZ, ELIZABETH, *Let Me Continue to Speak the Truth: Bertha Pappenheim as Author and Activist* (Cincinnati, 2007).

LOHMANN, UTA, '"Sustenance for the Learned Soul": The History of the Oriental Printing Press at the Publishing House of the Jewish Free School in Berlin', *Leo Baeck Institute Yearbook*, 51 (2006), 11–40.

LÓPEZ ESTRADA, FRANCISCO, 'Isabel Rebeca Correa: Defensa de la mujer escritora en el Amsterdam sefardí del siglo XVII', in Fernando Díaz Esteban (ed.), *Los judaizantes en Europa y la literatura castellana del Siglo de Oro* (Madrid, 1994), 261–72.

LOWENSTEIN, STEVEN M., 'Ashkenazic Jewry and the European Marriage Pattern: A Preliminary Survey of Jewish Marriage Age', *Jewish History*, 8 (1994), 155–75.

—— *The Berlin Jewish Community: Enlightenment, Family, and Crisis, 1770–1830* (New York, 1994).

—— 'Jewish Upper Crust and Berlin Jewish Enlightenment: The Family of Daniel Itzig', in Frances Malino and David Sorkin (eds.), *From East and West: Jews in a Changing Europe, 1750–1870* (Oxford, 1990), 182–201.

—— 'The Pace of Modernisation of German Jewry in the Nineteenth Century', *Leo Baeck Institute Yearbook*, 21 (1976), 41–56.

LUBIN, ORLY, 'Women Reading Women' (Heb.), *Theory and Criticism*, 3 (1993), 65–78.

LUNDT, BEA, 'Zur Entstehung der Universität als Männerwelt', in Elke Kleinau and Claudia Opitz (eds.), *Geschichte der Mädchen- und Frauenbildung*, vol. i: *Vom Mittelalter bis zur Aufklärung* (Frankfurt am Main, 1996), 103–18.

LYOTARD, JEAN-FRANÇOIS, *The Post-Modern Condition: A Report on Knowledge*, trans. Geoff Bennington and Brian Massumi (Minneapolis, 1984).

MCLAUGHLIN, BLANDINE L., 'Diderot and Women', in Samia I. Spencer (ed.), *French Women and the Age of Enlightenment* (Bloomington, 1984), 296–308.

MAGNUS, SHULAMIT, '"Out of the Ghetto": Integrating the Study of Jewish Women into the Study of "The Jews"', *Judaism*, 30 (1990), 28–36.

MARFANY, JOAN-LLUIS, and PETER BURKE, 'Debate: The Invention of Leisure in Early Modern Europe', *Past & Present*, 156 (1997), 174–91.

MARTIN, ALISON E., *Moving Scenes: The Aesthetics of German Travel Writing on England 1783–1830* (London, 2008).

MAZÓN, PATRICIA M., *Gender and the Modern Research University: The Admission of Women to German Higher Education, 1865–1914* (Stanford, 2003).

MEISL, JOSEF, *Protocols of the Berlin Jewish Community 1723–1854* [Pinkas kehilat berlin 1723–1854], ed. Shaul Esh (Jerusalem, 1962).

MELTON, JAMES VAN HORN, *The Rise of the Public in Enlightenment Europe* (Cambridge, 2001).

MENDELSOHN, EZRA, 'Should We Take Notice of Berthe Weill? Reflections on the Domain of Jewish History', *Jewish Social Studies*, NS 1 (1994), 22–39.

MENDELSSOHN, DOROTHEA, 'Gespräch über die neuesten Romane der Französinnen', *Europa*, 1/2 (1803), 88–106.

MENDELSSOHN, MOSES, *Brautbriefe* (Berlin, 1936).

—— *Gesammelte Schriften*, ed. G. B. Mendelssohn, 7 vols. (Leipzig, 1843–5).

—— *Gesammelte Schriften. Jubiläumsausgabe*, 24 vols. (Stuttgart, 1971–98).

MENDELSSOHN VEIT SCHLEGEL, DOROTHEA, *Florentin. A Novel*, trans., annotated, and introd. Edwina Lawler and Ruth Richardson (Lewiston, NY, 1988).
See also MENDELSSOHN; SCHLEGEL

MENDES-FLOHR, PAUL and JEHUDA REINHARZ (eds.), *The Jew in the Modern World: A Documentary History*, 2nd edn. (Oxford, 1995).

MEYER, MICHAEL A., *The Origins of the Modern Jew: Jewish Identity and European Culture in Germany, 1749–1824* (Detroit, 1967).

—— 'Reflections on Jewish Modernization', in Elisheva Carlebach, John M. Efron, and David N. Myers (eds.), *Jewish History and Jewish Memory: Essays in Honor of Yosef Haim Yerushalmi* (Hanover, 1998), 369–77.

—— *Response to Modernity: A History of the Reform Movement in Judaism* (New York, 1988).

—— 'Where Does the Modern Period of Jewish History Begin?', *Judaism*, 24 (1975), 329–38.

MICHAELIS, DOLF, 'The Ephraim Family', *Leo Baeck Institute Yearbook*, 21 (1976), 201–28.

—— 'The Ephraim Family and their Descendants (II)', *Leo Baeck Institute Yearbook*, 24 (1979), 225–46.

MOORE, LISA, '"Something more tender still than friendship": Romantic Friendship in Early-Nineteenth-Century England', in Martha Vicinus (ed.), *Lesbian Subjects: A Feminist Studies Reader* (Bloomington, 1996), 21–40.

MOSELEY, MARCUS, *Being for Myself Alone: Origins of Jewish Autobiography* (Stanford, Calif., 2006).

MÜLLER, WINFRIED, *Die Aufklärung* (Munich, 2002).

MUNCK, THOMAS, *The Enlightenment, A Comparative Social History, 1721–1794* (London, 2000).

Nachricht von dem unter dem Namen Wilhelms-Schule zu Breslau errichteten Institut zu einer verbesserten Unterweisung der Kinder dasiger Juden-Gemeinde und der am 15. März 1791 erfolgten feyerlichen Einweihung desselben [Breslau, 1791].

NAHRSTEDT, WOLFGANG, *Die Entstehung der Freizeit. Dargestellt am Beispiel Hamburg* (Göttingen, 1972).

NAIMARK-GOLDBERG, NATALIE, 'Breslau's Maskilim in the Jewish and the German Republic of Letters' (Heb., forthcoming).

—— '"The Mind Has No Sex": Esther Gad and the Enlightenment' (Heb.), *Historia*, 22 (2008), 75–104.

—— 'The (Questionable) Appraisal of Women in Euchel's *Haskala*', in Marion Aptroot, Andreas Kennecke, and Christoph Schulte (eds.), *Isaac Euchel. Der Kulturrevolutionär der jüdischen Aufklärung* (Hanover, 2010), 261–75.

NAVEH, HANNAH, 'Life Outside the Canon' (Heb.), in Dafna N. Izraeli et al. (eds.), *Sex Gender Politics: Women in Israel* [Min migdar politikah] (Tel Aviv, 1999), 49–106.

Neue Franckfurter Jüdische Kleider-Ordnung ... Aus dem Hebräischen ins Hochteutsche übersetzt, ed. and trans. Johann Jacob Schudt (Frankfurt am Main, 1716).

NICKISCH, REINHARD M. G., 'Briefkultur. Entwicklung und sozialgeschichtliche Bedeutung des Frauenbriefs im 18. Jahrhundert', in Gisela Brinker-Gabler (ed.), *Deutsche Literatur von Frauen*, vol. i (Munich, 1988), 389–409.

NIEMEYER, BEATRIX, 'Ausschluss oder Ausgrenzung? Frauen im Umkreis der Universitäten im 18. Jahrhundert', in Elke Kleinau and Claudia Opitz (eds.), *Geschichte der Mädchen- und Frauenbildung*, vol. i: *Vom Mittelalter bis zur Aufklärung* (Frankfurt am Main, 1996), 275–94.

—— 'Der Brief als weibliches Bildungsmedium im 18. Jahrhundert', in Elke Kleinau and Claudia Opitz (eds.), *Geschichte der Mädchen- und Frauenbildung*, vol. i: *Vom Mittelalter bis zur Aufklärung* (Frankfurt am Main, 1996), 440–52.

NIGER, SHMUEL, 'Yiddish Literature and the Female Reader', trans. and abridged Sheva Zucker, in Judith R. Baskin (ed.), *Women of the Word: Jewish Women and Jewish Writing* (Detroit, 1994), 70–90.

NISSENBAUM, STEPHEN, *The Battle for Christmas* (New York, 1996).

NÖRTEMANN, REGINA, 'Brieftheoretische Konzepte im 18. Jahrhundert und ihre Genese', in Angelika Ebrecht, Regina Nörtemann, and Herta Schwartz (eds.), *Brieftheorie des 18. Jahrhunderts. Texte, Kommentare, Essays* (Stuttgart, 1990), 211–24.

O'BRIEN, KAREN, 'The Feminist Critique of Enlightenment', in Martin Fitzpatrick, Peter Jones, Christa Knellwolf, and Iain McCalm (eds.), *The Enlightenment World* (London, 2007), 621–34.

OCH, GUNNAR, *Imago Judaica. Juden und Judentum im Spiegel der deutschen Literatur 1750–1812* (Würzburg, 1995).

—— 'Jüdische Leser und jüdisches Lesepublikum im 18. Jahrhundert. Ein Beitrag zur Akkulturationsgeschichte des deutschen Judentums', *Menora*, 2 (1991), 298–336.

OFFEN, KAREN, *European Feminisms 1700–1950: A Political History* (Stanford, Calif., 2000).

—— RUTH ROACH PIERSON, and JANE RENDALL (eds.), *Writing Women's History: International Perspectives* (London, 1991).

OPITZ, CLAUDIA, ULRIKE WECKEL, et al. (eds.), *Ordnung, Politik und Geselligkeit der Geschlechter im 18. Jahrhundert* (Göttingen, 1998).

—— —— and ELKE KLEINAU (eds.), *Tugend, Vernunft und Gefühl. Geschlechterdiskurse der Aufklärung und weibliche Lebenswelten* (Münster, 2000).

OUTRAM, DORINDA, *The Enlightenment* (Cambridge, 1995).

—— *Panorama of the Enlightenment* (London, 2006).

OZMENT, STEVEN, *When Fathers Ruled: Family Life in Reformation Europe* (Cambridge, Mass., 1983).

OZ-SALZBERGER, FANIA, 'From Desperate Lover to Political Economist: The Eighteenth Century's Invention of Sentiment' (Heb.), *Zemanim*, 60 (1997), 38–46.

PALMER, RICHARD, '"In this our lightye and learned tyme": Italian Baths in the Era of the Renaissance', *Medical History*, no. 10 [= *The Medical History of Waters and Spas*, ed. Roy Porter] (1990), 14–22.

PANWITZ, SEBASTIAN, 'Die Berliner Vereine 1786–1815', in *Berliner Klassik. Eine Großstadtkultur um 1800/Online-Dokumente* (Berlin-Brandenburgische Akademie der Wissenschaften, 2001); <http://www.berliner-klassik.de/berliner_ klassik/projekte/forschung/werkvertraege/panwitz_vereine/vereine. html>.

PARUSH, IRIS, 'Readers in Cameo: Women Readers in Jewish Society of Nineteenth-Century Eastern Europe', *Prooftexts*, 14 (1994), 1–23.

—— *Reading Jewish Women: Marginality and Modernization in Nineteenth-Century Eastern European Jewish Society* (Waltham, Mass., 2004).

PAUL, ARNO, 'Die Formierung des jüdischen Theaterpublikums in Berlin im späten 18. Jahrhundert. Eine quellenkritische Skizze', in Hans-Peter Bayerdörfer (ed.), *Theatralia Judaica, Emanzipation und Antisemitismus als Momente der Theatergeschichte. Von der Lessing-Zeit bis zur Shoah* (Tübingen, 1992), 64–84.

PEEZ, M., 'Henriette Mendelssohn', in *Frankfurter zeitgemäße Broschüren*, NS 9/4 (1888), 96–128.

PELLI, MOSHE, 'The Beginning of the Epistolary Genre in Hebrew Enlightenment Literature in Germany: The Alleged Affinity Between Lettres Persanes and Igrot Meshulam', *Leo Baeck Institute Yearbook*, 24 (1979), 83–103.

—— *The Gate to Haskalah: An Annotated Index to Hame'asef, the First Hebrew Journal* [Sha'ar lahaskalah: mafte'aḥ mu'ar lehame'asef, ketav ha'et ha'ivri harishon] (Jerusalem, 2000).

PERRY, RUTH, 'Mary Astell's Response to the Enlightenment', in Margaret Hunt et al. (eds.), *Women and the Enlightenment* (New York, 1984), 13–40.

PHILLIPS STANTON, JUDITH, 'Statistical Profile of Women Writing in English from 1660 to 1800', in Frederick M. Keener and Susan E. Lorsch (eds.), *Eighteenth-Century Women and the Arts* (New York, 1988), 247–54.

The Poet's Friend: The Letters of Miriam Markel-Mosessohn to Judah Leib Gordon [Yedidato shel hameshorer: igerot miryam markel-mozeszon el yehudah leib gordon], ed. Shmuel Werses (Jerusalem, 2004).

PORTER, ROY, *The Enlightenment*, 2nd edn. (London, 2001).

—— (ed.), *The Medical History of Waters and Spas* [= *Medical History*, no. 10 (1990)].

—— and MIKULAS TEICH (eds.), *The Enlightenment in National Context* (Cambridge, 1981).

RABIEN, ILSE, 'Die Mendelssohns in Bad Reinerz. Zur Familie Nathan Mendelssohns', *Mendelssohn Studien. Beiträge zur neueren deutschen Kultur- und Wirtschaftsgeschichte*, vol. vii, ed. Cäcile Lowenthal-Hensel and Rudolf Elvers (Berlin, 1990), 153–70.

RAPOPORT-ALBERT, ADA, 'On the Position of Women in Sabbatianism' (Heb.), in Rachel Elior (ed.), *The Dream and its Interpretation: The Sabbatian Movement and its Aftermath: Messianism, Sabbatianism and Frankism* [Haḥalom veshivro: hatenu'ah hashabeta'it usheluḥoteiha: meshiḥiyut, shabeta'ut ufrankizm], vol. i (Jerusalem, 2001), 143–327.

RAPOPORT-ALBERT, ADA, 'On Women in Hasidism, S. A. Horodecky and the Maid of Ludmir Tradition', in Ada Rapoport-Albert and Steven Zipperstein (eds.), *Jewish History: Essays in Honour of Chimen Abramsky* (London, 1988), 495–525.

REICH, NANCY B., 'The Power of Class: Fanny Hensel', in R. Larry Todd (ed.), *Mendelssohn and his World* (Princeton, 1991), 86–99.

REINKE, ANDREAS, 'Zwischen Tradition, Aufklärung und Assimilation. Die Königliche Wilhelmsschule in Breslau 1791–1848', *Zeitschrift für Religions- und Geistesgeschichte*, 43 (1991), 193–214.

REISSNER, H. G., 'Henriette Mendelssohn, Unresolved Conflicts of Integration', *Leo Baeck Institute Yearbook*, 21 (1976), 247–58.

RICHARZ, MONIKA, *Der Eintritt der Juden in die Akademischen Berufe. Jüdische Studenten und Akademiker in Deutschland 1678–1848* (Tübingen, 1974).

—— 'Der jüdische Weihnachtsbaum. Familie und Säkularisierung im deutschen Judentum des 19. Jahrhunderts', in Miriam Gillis-Carlebach and Barbara Vogel (eds.), '. . . *und so zogen sie aus: ein jeder bei seiner Familie und seinen Vaterhaus*' *(4. Moses 2, 34). Die Vierte Joseph-Karlebach-Konferenz. Familie im Spannungsfeld zwischen Tradition und Moderne* (Hamburg, 2000), 63–78.

RIES, ROTRAUD, and J. FRIEDRICH BATTENBERG (eds.), *Hofjuden—Ökonomie und Interkulturalität. Die jüdische Wirtschaftselite im 18. Jahrhundert* (Hamburg, 2002).

ROBERTS, F. COREY, 'The Perennial Search for Paradise: Garden Design and Political Critique in Dorothea Schlegel's *Florentin*', *German Quarterly*, 75/3 (2002), 247–64.

ROBERTSON, JOHN, 'Women and Enlightenment: A Historiographical Conclusion', in Sarah Knott and Barbara Taylor (eds.), *Women, Gender and Enlightenment* (Basingstoke, 2005), 692–704.

ROBERTSON, RITCHIE, *The 'Jewish Question' in German Literature, 1749–1939: Emancipation and its Discontents* (Oxford, 1999).

ROHRBACHER, STEFAN, 'The "Hep Hep" Riots of 1819: Anti-Jewish Ideology, Agitation, and Violence', in Christhard Hoffmann, Werner Bergmann, and Helmut Walser Smith (eds.), *Exclusionary Violence: Antisemitic Riots in Modern German History* (Ann Arbor, 2002), 23–42.

ROSE, SONYA O., et al., 'Gender History/Women's History: Is Feminist Scholarship Losing its Critical Edge?', *Journal of Women's History*, 5/1 (1993), 89–128.

ROSENSTRAUCH, HAZEL, 'Von der Peripherie ins Zentrum zur Peripherie. Dorothea Schlegel und Henriette Mendelssohn', in Katharina Raabe (ed.), *Deutsche Schwestern. Vierzehn biographische Porträts* (Berlin, 1997), 89–127.

ROSMAN, MOSHE, 'Being a Jewish Woman in Poland–Lithuania at the Beginning of the Modern Age' (Heb.), in Israel Bartal and Israel Gutman (eds.), *The Broken Chain: Polish Jewry through the Ages* [Kiyum vashever: yehudei polin ledoroteihem] (Jerusalem, 2001), vol. ii, 415–34.

—— 'The History of Jewish Women in Early Modern Poland: An Assessment', *Polin*, 18 (2005), 25–56.

—— *How Jewish Is Jewish History?* (Oxford, 2007).
ROTH, CECIL (ed.), *Anglo-Jewish Letters (1158–1917)* (London, 1938).
RUDERMAN, DAVID B., *Early Modern Jewry: A New Cultural History* (Princeton, 2010).
—— *Jewish Enlightenment in an English Key: Anglo-Jewry's Construction of Modern Jewish Thought* (Princeton, 2000).
—— *Jewish Thought and Scientific Discovery in Early Modern Europe* (New Haven, 1995).
—— 'Was There a "Haskalah" in England? Reconsidering an Old Question', in Shmuel Feiner and David Sorkin (eds.), *New Perspectives on the Haskalah* (London, 2001), 64–85.
RUDERT, KARIN, 'Die Wiederentdeckung einer "deutschen Wollstonecraft". Esther Gad Bernard Domeier für Gleichberechtigung der Frauen und Juden', *Quaderni*, 10 (1988), 213–61.
RUIZ, ALAIN, 'Auf dem Wege zur Emanzipation. Der ideologische Werdegang des aufgeklärten "Gelehrten jüdischer Nation" H. S. Pappenheimer (1769–1832) bis zur französischen Revolution', *Jahrbuch des Instituts für deutsche Geschichte*, 3 [= *Deutsche Aufklärung und Judenemanzipation*, ed. Walter Grab] (Tel Aviv, 1980), 183–222.
RÜLLMANN, ALMUT, 'Adolf Freiherr Knigge und die Juden', in Horst Gronke, Thomas Meyer, and Barbara Neißer (eds.), *Antisemitismus bei Kant und anderen Denkern der Aufklärung* (Würzburg, 2001), 153–242.
RUNGE, ANITA, and LIESELOTTE STEINBRÜGGE (eds.), *Die Frau im Dialog. Studien zu Theorie und Geschichte des Briefes* (Stuttgart, 1991).
RUPP, LEILA J., *Sapphistries: A Global History of Love between Women* (New York, 2009).
SAMBURSKY, MIRIAM, 'Ludwig Roberts Lebensgang', *Bulletin des Leo Baeck Instituts*, 15 (1976), 1–48.
SAUER, AUGUST (ed.), *Goethe und Österreich. Briefe mit Erläuterungen*, vol. ii (Weimar, 1904).
SCHIEBINGER, LONDA, *The Mind Has No Sex? Women in the Origins of Modern Science* (Cambridge, Mass., 1989).
—— 'Wissenschaftlerinnen im Zeitalter der Aufklärung', in Elke Kleinau and Claudia Opitz (eds.), *Geschichte der Mädchen- und Frauenbildung*, vol. i: *Vom Mittelalter bis zur Aufklärung* (Frankfurt am Main, 1996), 295–308.
SCHINDEL, CARL WILHELM O. A. VON, *Die deutschen Schriftstellerinnen des neunzehnten Jahrhunderts*, 3 vols. (Leipzig, 1823–5; repr. Hildesheim, 1978).
SCHINDLER, ANGELIKA, *Der verbrannte Traum. Jüdische Bürger und Gäste in Baden-Baden* (Bühl, 1992).
SCHIRMER, WALTER F., 'Die große Jette. Henriette Herz und ihr Freundekreis', *Der Bär von Berlin, Jahrbuch des Vereins für die Geschichte Berlins*, 24 (1975), 92–115.
SCHLEGEL, DOROTHEA, *Florentin. Ein Roman*, ed. Wolfgang Nehring (Stuttgart, 1993).
See also MENDELSSOHN VEIT SCHLEGEL

SCHLEIERMACHER, FRIEDRICH, *Schleiermacher als Mensch, Sein Werden und Wirken. Familien- und Freundesbriefe*, ed. Heinrich Meisner, 2 vols. (Gotha, 1922, 1923).

SCHLICHTMANN, SILKE, 'Did Women Really Read Differently? A Historical-Empirical Contribution to Gender-Oriented Reading Research', *Women in German Yearbook*, 20 (2004), 198–214.

SCHMID, PIA, 'Weib oder Mensch, Wesen oder Wissen? Bürgerliche Theorien zur weiblichen Bildung um 1800', in Elke Kleinau and Claudia Opitz (eds.), *Geschichte der Mädchen- und Frauenbildung*, vol. i: *Vom Mittelalter bis zur Aufklärung* (Frankfurt am Main, 1996), 327–45.

SCHMIDT, F. W. A., 'Glück der Ehe. An einen Hagestolzen. 1795', *Berlinische Monatsschrift* (1796), 473–6.

SCHMIDT, RICARDA, 'From Early to Late Romanticism', in Nicholas Saul (ed.), *The Cambridge Companion to German Romanticism* (Cambridge, 2009), 21–39.

SCHMÖLZER, HILDE, *Frauenliebe. Berühmte weibliche Liebespaare der Geschichte* (Vienna, 2009).

SCHNEIDERS, WERNER (ed.), *Lexikon der Aufklärung* (Munich, 2001).

SCHOLEM, GERSHOM, *Major Trends in Jewish Mysticism* (1941; New York, 1995).

—— 'Redemption through Sin', in id., *The Messianic Idea in Judaism and Other Essays on Jewish Spirituality* (1971; New York, 1995), 78–141.

SCHORSCH, ISMAR, *From Text to Context: The Turn to History in Modern Judaism* (Hanover, NH, 1994).

SCHREMER, ADIEL, *Male and Female Created He Them: Jewish Marriage in the Late Second Temple, Mishnah and Talmud Periods* [Zakhar unekevah bera'am: hanisuyim beshalhei yemei habayit hasheni uvitekufat hamishnah vehatalmud] (Jerusalem, 2003).

SCHULSINGER, JOSEPH, *Un précurseur du sionisme au XVIIIe siècle: Le Prince de Ligne* (Paris, 1936).

SCHULZ, GÜNTHER, 'Jean Paul, Breslau und die Breslauer Schriftsteller', *Jahrbuch der Schlesischen Friedrich-Wilhelms-Universität zu Breslau*, 15 (1970), 329–54.

SCHUMMEL, JOHANN GOTTLIEB, *Schummels Breslauer Almanach für den Anfang des 19. Jahrhunderts*, vol. i (Breslau, 1801).

SCHWARZ, HERTA, '"Brieftheorie" in der Romantik', in Angelika Ebrecht, Regina Nörtemann, and Herta Schwarz (eds.), *Brieftheorie des 18. Jahrhunderts. Texte, Kommentare, Essays* (Stuttgart, 1990), 225–38.

SCOTT, JOAN W., 'Gender: A Useful Category of Historical Analysis', in ead., *Gender and the Politics of History* (New York, 1988) 28–50.

—— *Only Paradoxes to Offer: French Feminists and the Rights of Man* (Cambridge, Mass., 1996).

—— 'Women's History', in ead., *Gender and the Politics of History* (New York, 1988), 15–27.

SEIBERT, PETER, 'Der "Tugendbund". Ein soziales Experiment des späten 18. Jahrhundert', in Norbert Altenhofer und Renate Heuer (eds.), *Jüdinnen zwischen Tradition und Emanzipation* (Bad Soden, 1990), 48–66.

SHAHAR, SHULAMIT, *The Fourth Estate: A History of Women in the Middle Ages* (London, 1983).

SHAVIT, ZOHAR, 'From Friedländer's Lesebuch to the Jewish Campe: The Beginning of Hebrew Children's Literature in Germany', *Leo Baeck Institute Yearbook*, 33 (1988), 385–415.

—— 'Literary Interference between German and Jewish-Hebrew Children's Literature during the Enlightenment: The Case of Campe', *Poetics Today*, 13/1 (1992), 41–61.

—— and HANS-HEINO EWERS (with ANNEGRET VÖLPEL, RAN HACOHEN, and DIETER RICHTER), *Deutsch-jüdische Kinder- und Jugendliteratur von der Haskala bis 1945. Die deutsch- und hebräischsprachigen Schriften des deutschsprachigen Raums. Ein bibliographisches Handbuch*, 2 vols. (Stuttgart, 1996).

SHECHTER, TAMAR, *The Portrait of a Maskilic Woman in Galicia* [Deyokanah shel ishah maskilit begalitsiyah], MA thesis, Bar Ilan University, Ramat Gan, 1996.

SHMERUK, CHONE, *Chapters in the History of Yiddish Literature* [Sifrut yidish: perakim letoledoteiha] (Tel Aviv, 1978).

—— 'The East European Versions of the *Tsene-rene* (1786–1850)' [Di mizrekh eyropeishe nuskhoes fun der tsene-rene (1786–1850)], in *For Max Weinreich on his Seventieth Birthday* (The Hague, 1964), 320–36.

SHOHAT, AZRIEL, *Beginnings of the Haskalah among German Jewry* [Im ḥilufei tekufot: reshit hahaskalah beyahadut germaniyah] (Jerusalem, 1960).

SHOWALTER, ELAINE, 'Introduction: The Feminist Critical Revolution', in ead. (ed.), *The New Feminist Criticism: Essays on Women, Literature and Theory* (New York, 1985), 3–17.

SINKOFF, NANCY, *Out of the Shtetl: Making Jews Modern in the Polish Borderlands* (Providence, RI, 2004).

SMITHER, HOWARD E., *The Oratorio in the Classical Era* (Chapel Hill, 1987); vol. iii of *A History of the Oratorio*.

—— *The Oratorio in the Nineteenth and Twentieth Century* (Chapel Hill, 2000); vol. iv of *A History of the Oratorio*.

SMITH-ROSENBERG, CARROLL, 'The Female World of Love and Ritual: Relations between Women in Nineteenth-Century America', *Signs*, 1/1 (1975), 1–29.

SOBEL, DAVA, *Galileo's Daughter: A Historical Memoir of Science, Faith and Love* (New York, 1999).

SOHNI, HANS, 'Koreff, David Ferdinand', in *Neue Deutsche Biographie*, vol. xii (Berlin, 1980), 582–3.

SOKOL, MARY, 'Jeremy Bentham on Love and Marriage: A Utilitarian Proposal for Short-Term Marriage', *Journal of Legal History*, 30/1 (2009), 1–21.

SOMMER, HERMANN, *Zur Kur nach Ems. Ein Beitrag zur Geschichte der Badereise von 1830 bis 1914* (Stuttgart, 1999).

SOPER, KATE, 'Feminism and Enlightenment Legacies', in Sarah Knott and Barbara Taylor (eds.), *Women, Gender and Enlightenment* (Basingstoke, 2005), 705–15.

SORKIN, DAVID, 'The Berlin Haskalah: A Comparative Perspective' (Heb.), in Shmuel Feiner and Israel Bartal (eds.), *The Varieties of Haskalah* [Hahaskalah legivuneiha] (Jerusalem, 2005), 3–11.

—— *The Transformation of German Jewry, 1780–1840* (New York, 1987).

SPALDING, ALMUT, *Elise Reimarus (1735–1805), The Muse of Hamburg: A Woman of the German Enlightenment* (Würzburg, 2003).

SPIEL, HILDE, *Fanny von Arnstein: A Daughter of the Enlightenment 1758–1818*, trans. Christine Shuttleworth (New York, 1991).

STAMPFER, SHAUL, 'Gender Differentiation and Education of the Jewish Woman in Nineteenth-Century Eastern Europe', *Polin*, 7 (1992), 63–87.

—— 'Jewish Women Revisited' (review of Iris Parush, *Reading Jewish Women*), *Jews in Russia and Eastern Europe*, 1 (52) (2004), 244–8.

STERN, CAROLA, *'Ich möchte mir Flügel wünschen'. Das Leben der Dorothea Schlegel* (Reinbek bei Hamburg, 1993).

STERN, LUDWIG (ed.), *Die Varnhagen von Ensesche Sammlung in der Koeniglichen Bibliothek zu Berlin* (Berlin, 1911).

STERN, SELMA, *The Court Jew: A Contribution to the History of Absolutism in Europe*, trans. Ralph Weiman, with a new introduction by Egon Mayer (New Brunswick, 1985).

STUEBBEN THORNTON, KARIN, 'Enlightenment and Romanticism in the Work of Dorothea Schlegel', *The German Quarterly*, 39 (1966), 162–72.

STUURMAN, SIEP, *François Poulain de la Barre and the Invention of Modern Equality* (Cambridge, Mass., 2004).

SULAM, SARRA COPIA, *Jewish Poet and Intellectual in Seventeenth-Century Venice: The Works of Sarra Copia Sulam in Verse and Prose, Along with Writings of Her Contemporaries in Her Praise, Condemnation, or Defense*, ed. and trans. Don Harrán (Chicago and London, 2009).

SULLEROT, EVELYNE, *Histoire de la presse féminine en France, des origines à 1848* (Paris, 1966).

SUSMAN, MARGARETE, *Frauen der Romantik* (1929; Frankfurt am Main, 1996).

TAL, URIEL, 'Young German Intellectuals on Romanticism and Judaism—Spiritual Turbulence in the Early 19th Century', in *Salo Wittmayer Baron, Jubilee Volume, on the Occasion of his 80th Birthday*, vol. ii (New York, 1974), 919–38.

TAYLOR, BARBARA, 'Misogyny and Feminism: The Case of Mary Wollstonecraft', in Colin Jones and Dror Wahrman (eds.), *The Age of Cultural Revolutions: Britain and France, 1750–1820* (Berkeley, Calif., 2002), 203–17.

TAYLOR, CHARLES, *A Secular Age* (Cambridge, Mass., 2007).

THOMANN TEWARSON, HEIDI, 'German-Jewish Identity in the Correspondence Between Rahel Levin Varnhagen and her Brother, Ludwig Robert—Hopes and Realities of Emancipation 1780–1830', *Leo Baeck Institute Yearbook*, 39 (1994), 3–29.

—— 'Jüdinsein um 1800. Bemerkungen zum Selbstverständnis der ersten Generation assimilierter Berliner Jüdinnen', in Jutta Dick and Barbara Hahn (eds.), *Von einer Welt in die andere. Jüdinnen im 19. und 20. Jahrhundert* (Vienna, 1993), 47–70.

—— *Rahel Levin Varnhagen: The Life and Work of a German Jewish Intellectual* (Lincoln, 1998).

TIKTINER, RIVKAH [REBECCA] BAT MEIR, *Meneket Rivkah: A Manual of Wisdom and Piety for Jewish Women*, ed., with an introduction and commentary, Frauke von Rohden (Philadelphia, 2009).

TOMASELLI, SYLVANA, 'The Enlightenment Debate on Women', *History Workshop Journal*, 20 (1985), 101–24.

TSAMRIYON, TSEMAH, *Hame'asef: The First Modern Periodical in Hebrew* [Hame'asef: ketav ha'et hamoderni harishon be'ivrit] (Tel Aviv, 1988).

TURNIANSKY, CHAVA, 'A Correspondence in Yiddish from Jerusalem, Dating from the 1560s' (Heb.), *Shalem: Studies in the History of the Jews in Erets-Yisra'el* [Shalem: meḥkarim betoledot erets yisra'el veyishuvah], 4 (1984), 149–210.

—— 'The Maskilic Versions of *Tsene-Rene*' (Heb.), in David Assaf and Ada Rapoport-Albert (eds.), *Let the Old Make Way for the New: Studies in the Social and Cultural History of Eastern European Jewry. Presented to Immanuel Etkes* [Yashan mipnei ḥadash: meḥkarim betoledot yehudei mizraḥ eiropa uvetarbutah, shay le'emanuel etkes] (Jerusalem, 2009), vol. ii., 313–44.

—— 'The Stories in Glikl Hamel's Work and their Sources' (Heb.), *Jerusalem Studies on Jewish Folklore* [Meḥkarei yerushalayim befolkelor yehudi], 16 (1994), 41–65.

UECKERT, CHARLOTTE, 'Über Margarete Susman: Annäherung an ein "Zentrum ohne Peripherie"', in Arno Herzig (ed.), *Die Juden in Hamburg, 1590 bis 1990* (Hamburg, 1991), 263–74.

VALLER, SHULAMIT, *Women in Jewish Society in the Talmudic Period* [Nashim baḥevrah hayehudit bitekufat hamishnah vehatalmud] (Tel Aviv, 2000).

VAN DÜLMEN, RICHARD, *The Society of the Enlightenment: The Rise of the Middle Class and Enlightenment Culture in Germany* (New York, 1992).

VARNHAGEN, RAHEL, *Briefwechsel*, ed. Friedhelm Kemp, 4 vols. (Munich, 1979).

See also LEVIN VARNHAGEN

VARNHAGEN VON ENSE, KARL AUGUST, *Denkwürdigkeiten des eigenen Lebens*, 3rd edn., vol. iii (Leipzig, 1871).

—— (ed.), *Galerie von Bildnissen aus Rahel's Umgang und Briefwechsel*, 2 vols. (Leipzig, 1836).

VICINUS, MARTHA, *Intimate Friends: Women Who Loved Women, 1778–1928* (Chicago, 2004).

VICKERY, AMANDA, 'Golden Age to Separate Spheres? A Review of the Categories and Chronology of English Women's History', *The Historical Journal*, 36/2 (1993), 383–414.

VIERHAUS, RUDOLF, 'Aufklärung als Prozeß—der Prozeß der Aufklärung', *Aufklärung*, 2/2 (1988), 3–7.

VIGLIERO, CONSOLINA, '"Mein lieber Schwester-Freund". Rahel und Ludwig Robert in ihren Briefen', in Barbara Hahn and Ursula Isselstein (eds.), *Rahel*

Levin Varnhagen. Die Wiederentdeckung einer Schriftstellerin (Göttingen, 1987), 47–55.

VOLKOV, SHULAMIT, *The Magic Circle: Germans, Jews and Antisemites* [Bama'agal hamekhushaf: yehudim, antishemiyim vegermanim aḥerim] (Tel Aviv, 2002).

VOLTAIRE, 'Femmes, soyez soumises a vos maris', in *Œuvres complète*s, ed. Louis Moland (Paris, 1879; repr. 1976), vol. xxvi, 563–6.

VON ROHDEN, FRAUKE, 'Jüdische Ehe Zwischen Religiöser Norm und Alltagswahrnehmung im 16. Jahrhundert', in Andreas Holzem and Ines Weber (eds.), *Ehe—Familie—Verwandtschaft. Vergesellschaftung in Religion und sozialer Lebenswelt* (Padeborn, 2008), 329–44.

WECKEL, ULRIKE, 'Der Fieberfrost des Freiherrn. Zur Polemik gegen weibliche Gelehrsamkeit und ihren Folgen für die Geselligkeit der Geschlechter', in Elke Kleinau and Claudia Opitz (eds.), *Geschichte der Mädchen- und Frauenbildung*, vol. i: *Vom Mittelalter bis zur Aufklärung* (Frankfurt am Main, 1996), 360–72.

—— 'Gleichheit auf dem Prüfstand. Zur zeitgenössischen Rezeption der Streitschriften von Theodor Gottlieb von Hippel und Mary Wollstonecraft in Deutschland', in Claudia Opitz, Ulrike Weckel, and Elke Kleinau (eds.), *Tugend, Vernunft und Gefühl, Geschlechterdiskurse der Aufklärung und weibliche Lebenswelten* (Münster, 2000), 209–47.

—— 'A Lost Paradise of Female Culture? Some Critical Questions Regarding the Scholarship on Late Eighteenth- and Early Nineteenth-Century German Salons', *German History*, 18/3 (2000), 310–36.

—— *Zwischen Häuslichkeit und Öffentlichkeit. Die ersten deutschen Frauenzeitschriften im späten 18. Jahrhundert und ihr Publikum* (Tübingen, 1998).

WEINREB, RUTH PLAUT, 'Emilie or *Emile*? Madame d'Epinay and the Education of Girls in Eighteenth-Century France', in Frederick M. Keener and Susan E. Lorsch (eds.), *Eighteenth-Century Women and the Arts* (New York, 1988), 57–66.

WEINRYB, BERNARD, 'Historisches und Kulturhistorisches aus Wagenseils hebräischem Briefwechsel', *Monatsschrift für Geschichte und Wissenschaft des Judentums*, 83 (47 NS) (1939), 325–341.

WEISSBERG, LILIANE, 'Bodies in Pain: Reflections on the Berlin Jewish Salons', in Klaus L. Berghahn (ed.), *The German-Jewish Dialogue Reconsidered: A Symposium in Honor of George L. Mosse* (New York, 1996), 59–79.

—— 'Dramatic History: Reflections on a Biblical Play by Ludwig Robert', *Studies in Contemporary Jewry*, 12 (1996), 3–20.

—— *Life as a Goddess: Henriette Herz Writes her Autobiography* (Ramat Gan, 2001).

—— 'The Master's Theme, and Some Variations: Dorothea Schlegel's *Florentin* as Bildungsroman', *Michigan Germanic Studies*, 12/2 (1987), 169–81.

—— 'Nachwort', in Dorothea Schlegel, *Florentin. Roman, Fragmente, Varianten*, ed. Liliane Weissberg (Frankfurt am Main, 1986), 205–38.

WEISSLER, CHAVA, *Voices of the Matriarchs: Listening to the Prayers of Early Modern Jewish Women* (Boston, 1998).

WERSES, SHMUEL, 'Women's Voices in the Yiddish Weekly *Kol-mevaser*' (Heb.), in id., *'Awake, My People': Hebrew Literature in the Age of Modernization* [Hakitsah ami: sifrut hahaskalah be'idan hamodernizatsiyah] (Jerusalem, 2001), 321–50.

WESSELY, HARTWIG, *Words of Peace and Truth* [Divrei shalom ve'emet] (Berlin, 1782).

WETZLAR, ISAAC, *The 'Libes briv' of Isaac Wetzlar*, ed. and trans. Morris M. Faierstein (Atlanta, 1996).

WIECKENBERG, ERNST-PETER, 'Juden als Autoren des *Magazins zur Erfahrungsseelenkunde*. Ein Beitrag zum Thema "Juden und Aufklärung in Berlin"', in Barbara Hahn and Ursula Isselstein (eds.), *Rahel Levin Varnhagen. Die Wiederentdeckung einer Schriftstellerin* (Göttingen, 1987), 128–40.

WIESNER, MERRY E., *Women and Gender in Early Modern Europe*, 2nd edn. (Cambridge, 2000).

WIESNER-HANKS, MERRY E., *Gender in History* (Malden, Mass., 2001).

WILHELMY, PETRA, *Der Berliner Salon im 19. Jahrhundert (1780–1914)* (Berlin, 1989).

WILHELMY-DOLLINGER, PETRA, 'Emanzipation durch Geselligkeit. Die Salons jüdischer Frauen in Berlin zwischen 1780 und 1830', in Marianne Awerbuch and Stefi Jersch-Wenzel (eds.), *Bild und Selbstbild der Juden Berlins Zwischen Aufklärung und Romantik* (Berlin, 1992), 121–38.

WITTMANN, REINHARD, *Geschichte des deutschen Buchhandels*, 2nd edn. (Munich, 1999).

—— 'Das Jahrhundert des Briefes', in Ernst-Peter Wieckenberg (ed.), *Einladung ins 18. Jahrhundert. Ein Almanach aus dem Verlag C. H. Beck* (Munich, 1988), 151–5.

—— 'Was There a Reading Revolution at the End of the Eighteenth Century?', in Guglielmo Cavallo and Roger Chartier (eds.), *A History of Reading in the West* (Amherst, 1999), 284–312.

WOLFF, CHRISTOPH, 'A Bach Cult in Late-Eighteenth-Century Berlin: Sara Levy's Musical Salon', *Bulletin of the American Academy*, 58/3 (Spring 2005), 26–30.

WOLFSOHN-HALLE, AARON, *Silliness and Sanctimony* [Leikhtsin un fremelei] (*c*.1794).

WOLLNY, PETER, 'Sara Levy and the Making of Musical Taste in Berlin', *Musical Quarterly*, 77/4 (1993), 651–88.

WOOLF, VIRGINIA, *A Room of One's Own* (1928; London, 2000).

ZALKIN, MORDECHAI, 'Iris Parush, *Reading Women* [Heb.]: The Benefit of Marginality in Nineteenth-Century Eastern European Jewish Society' (Heb.), *Gal-ed*, 19 (2004), 78–87.

ZANTOP, SUSANNE, 'Trivial Pursuits? An Introduction to German Women's Writing from the Middle Ages to 1830', in Jeannine Blackwell and Susanne Zantop (eds.), *Bitter Healing: German Women Writers from 1700 to 1830. An Anthology* (Lincoln, 1990), 9–50.

ZFATMAN, SARA, 'The *Mayse-bukh*: An Old Yiddish Literary Genre' (Heb.), *Hasifrut*, 28 (1979), 126–52.

ZINBERG, ISRAEL, *Old Yiddish Literature from its Origins to the Haskalah Period*, vol. vii of *A History of Jewish Literature* (New York, 1975).
ZONDEK, THEODOR, 'Dorothea Schlegel und Simon Veit', *Bulletin des Leo Baeck Instituts*, 5 (1962), 302–5.
—— 'Dr. Med. David Veit (1771–1814). Eine Gestalt aus der Emanzipationszeit', *Bulletin des Leo Baeck Instituts*, 15 (1976), 49–77.
ZWIERLEIN, KONRAD ANTON, *Allgemeine Brunnenschrift für Brunnengäste und Aerzte* (Weißenfels and Leipzig, 1793).

Index

Dates of birth and death have been added for those figures for which this information is available

A

acculturation of Jews 1–4, 13 n. 41, 26, 147, 211
  and conversion to Christianity 1, 259–70, 274, 278
  in England 2 n. 4, 272, 275 n. 60
  gender differences 211, 299
  maskilim's criticism of 14
  non-Jews mock 290
Amsterdam, Jewish community:
  transformation of marriage as an institution 221 n. 13, 237 n. 71
anti-Jewish hostility 173 n. 98, 190–1, 269, 279, 290, 291
  among converts 289
Arnim, Achim von (1781–1831) 291
Arnstein, Fanny von (1758–1818) (née Itzig) 12 n. 35, 239 n. 77, 251, 252 n. 119
  Christmas celebrated by 264–5
  Mozart enthusiast 269 n. 42
  sociability of 193, 194
Ascarelli, Devora 106
assimilation of Jews 269 n. 43, 272, 275–6, 293, 298
  in historical narrative 6, 24–6, 188 n. 26, 214, 221–2
  see also acculturation of Jews
Assing, Ludmilla (1821–80) 35, 36
Assing, Ottilie (1819–84) 36
Astell, Mary (1666–1731) 232

B

Baader, Benjamin Maria 6
Bad Ems 164, 166 n. 75
Baden-Baden 164
Bartholdy, Jacob (1779–1825) 273 n. 56, 282 n. 89
Bath 153, 157, 174 n. 100
Becker-Cantarino, Barbara 125–6
Beer, Amalie (1767–1854) 191 n. 33
  Jewish allegiance of 275–6
  Louisenorden awarded to 275

Beer, Jacob Herz (1769–1825) 275–6
Beer, Michael (1800–33) 275 n. 64
Beer, Peter (1758–1838) 96
Beer, Wilhelm (1797–1850) 275 n. 64
Bekker, Immanuel (1785–1871), and Henriette Herz:
  correspondence with 37, 86–7, 100, 242–3, 287 n. 101, 289
  marriage proposal to 206 n. 86
Bendavid, Lazarus (1762–1832) 84 n. 72, 202, 233 n. 58
  associational affiliations 182
  'false Enlightenment' condemned by 14–15 n. 46
  reading habits of 82
Berlepsch, Emilie von (1755–1830) 107 n. 18, 243 n. 89
Berlin:
  family values decline among Jews 221–3
  French occupation of 88 n. 90, 98, 190–1, 245, 269
  gatherings at Jewish homes in 192–3, 196–7
  Haskalah in 12–13, 15, 21 n. 71, 40, 297, 301
  Jewish elite in 1–2, 49–50, 178, 258
  Jewish salons in 24–5, 27–8, 188–90, 191 n. 34
  Jews' interaction with non-Jews in 149, 182, 198, 199–200, 207–15, 244, 257–9
  reformed religious services in 197–8, 276
Berlin Wednesday Society (Berliner Mittwochsgesellschaft) 149 n. 9, 182
Berlinische Monatsschrift 7, 85, 97, 107 n. 18, 182 n. 7, 232–3 n. 58
Bernard, Esther, *see* Gad, Esther
Bernard, Samuel 112, 113
Bernhard, Fanny, née Fließ (1749–1825) 178
Bernhard, Hitzel (1772–1839) (later Hedwig Fließ, later Wilhelmine von Boye, later von Sparre) 138, 152, 178

Bernhard, Hitzel (*cont.*):
  hospitality at her Jewish home 212–13
  marriages of 138 n. 127, 168 n. 77
  visits spas 147, 150–1, 157, 168
Bertuch, Friedrich Justin (1747–1822)
  119–20
Bethmann, Friederike, *see* Unzelmann, Friederike
Bethmann, Heinrich Eduard (1774–1857)
  254, 256
Bing, Abraham Herz (1769–1835) 197–8, 214–15
Blankenburg, Friedrich von (1744–96)
  133–4
Bloch, Marcus (1723–99) 182
Boie, Heinrich Christian (1744–1806)
  161–2
Boye, Wilhelmine von, *see* Bernhard, Hitzel
Brentano, Clemens (1778–1842) 291
Breslau 40 n. 41, 98, 112, 172, 217 n. 3, 260 n. 10, 290
  acculturated Jews native of 31 n. 2, 61, 86 n. 82, 107, 233
  contacts between Jews and non-Jews in 171, 207
  modern Jewish school (Königliche Wilhelmsschule) in 113–15, 296, 298
Brinckmann, Karl Gustav von (1764–1847)
  35 n. 21, 138, 197
  correspondence with Jewish women 124, 172 n. 92, 185, 223, 225, 227
  private library 84
Burgsdorff, Wilhelm von (1772–1822) 178, 193, 210
  illegitimate daughter with Jewish woman 238 n. 73

C

Campe, Joachim Heinrich (1746–1818)
  108, 112, 299 n. 6
  in modern Jewish literature 109–10 n. 27
  Väterlicher Rath für meine Töchter 97, 109–11
Carlsbad 153, 165 n. 73
  Jewish women meet Goethe 50, 51 n. 73, 55, 90, 151, 170, 176–7
  Jewish women visit 99, 148, 151–2, 178, 209
Carter, Elizabeth (1717–1806) 169
Castro, Rahel de (1792–1871) 36, 48 n. 66
Catholicism/Catholics 100, 166, 275, 279, 280 n. 80, 289

Jewish converts' attitudes to, pre- and post-conversion 130–1, 282–4, 286
Jewish women's conversion to 130, 259, 281–2, 284–6, 301
see also conversion to Christianity
Cohen, Tova 16, 41–2, 296
Cologne 281, 286 n. 97
Condorcet, Marquis de (1743–94) 218
conversion to Christianity 1, 25–6, 28 n. 89, 50, 130, 223 n. 16
  age at 4, 259
  contacts with Jews after 248, 271, 273–4, 282 n. 89, 289–91
  gender differences in 300–1
  and integration in German society 201 n. 68, 258–9, 268–70, 272–3, 291 n. 117, 301
  motivations for, ideological 278–80
  motivations for, pragmatic 59, 221–2, 276–8, 280–1, 284, 301
  and religious conviction 276 n. 68, 281–2, 284–7
Copia Sulam, Sarra (1600/1?–41) 106
Correa, Isabel de 106

D

Davidson, Wolf (1772–1800) 182, 298, 300
  on Prussian Jewry 54–5, 211, 212, 213 n. 109, 268 n. 37
Deibel, Franz 125–6
Dessau 84, 207, 213 n. 109
Dessau, Wolf (1751–84) 207
Diderot, Denis (1713–84) 97, 235
divorce 26, 124
  and marriage to non-Jews 221–2, 225
  and women's emancipation 221–8
Dohm, Christian Wilhelm von (1751–1820)
  114, 162 n. 58, 216, 219 n. 8, 262 n. 17
Domeier, Lucie, *see* Gad, Esther
Domeier, Wilhelm Friedrich (1763–1815)
  112
Dresden 116–18, 142, 151, 178 n. 112
Dubnow, Simon 18, 19

E

Eberty, Felix (1812–84) 189 n. 28
education, Jewish 66 n. 7
  among 19th-century women 42 n. 49, 203 n. 74
  gender differences in 2, 12, 211, 297
  maskilim on 14–15 n. 46, 72–3, 113–14
  modern Jewish schools 12, 113–14, 297

education of women:
  contemporary views on   109–11, 200
  and emancipation   108, 220, 243 n. 89
  gender obstacles in   300, 301; exclusion from higher learning   48 n. 64, 200–3
  informal learning   25 n. 85, 200, 203; through letter-writing   47–8, 56; through reading   76, 81, 85 n. 77, 93, 96; through social gatherings in private homes   183, 199–200, 203–6
  Jewish female authors promote   108–11, 120, 144
Eigensatz, Christel (1781–1850)   198, 209
emancipation of the Jews   14 n. 46, 113–15, 188–90, 201 n. 67, 216–17, 289–90
  Edict of Emancipation   57, 282 n. 89
  gender perspective   217–18, 299–300, 301
emancipation of women   7 n. 17, 168–9 n. 80, 188–90, 220, 239
  struggle for civil rights   218–20
Endelman, Todd   271, 272, 274–5
Enlightenment:
  critical ethos of   7–8
  Jewish, image, revised   11–15, 301–2
  periodization   21–2
  and Romanticism, dichotomy   21–3, 91 n. 105
  secularism and   8, 93
  sociability and   180
Enlightenment, and women:
  feminist positions encouraged by   7, 217, 233 n. 60, 256, 301
  Jewish women adopt critical ethos of   7–8, 78, 109, 128, 130, 175–6, 220
  Jewish women embrace discourse of   20–1, 112, 144, 228, 285, 292
  women's inclusion in narrative of   8–11
  women's self-assertion promoted by   103 n. 2, 105
Ephraim, Rebecca, *see* Itzig, Rebecca
Ephraim, Zacharias Veitel (1736–79)   158, 164
Épinay, Louise [Madame] d' (1726–83)   18 n. 55
Eskeles, Bernhard (1753–1839)   55 n. 93, 236
Eskeles, Cäcilie, *see* Itzig, Cäcilie
Eskeles, Eleonore (1752–1812) (later Fließ)   55
Euchel, Isaac (1756–1804)   17 n. 53, 73 n. 34, 96, 114 n. 45, 201 n. 68
  enlightened Jewish women, contacts with   85–6 n. 81, 178, 183 n. 12, 213

Igerot meshulam ben uriyah ha'eshtemo'i   41, 186 n. 23
Reb henoch oder woss tut me' damit   14 n. 44
visits spa   178
European languages:
  Jewish women's efforts to learn   76, 100–11
  Jewish women's knowledge of   73, 79–80, 88, 200, 211, 257; criticized   14, 72
  publications of Jewish women in   105–6, 297
Eybenberg, Marianne von, *see* Meyer, Marianne
Eybeschütz, Rabbi Jonathan (1690–1764)   107

F

Fasch, Carl Friedrich (1736–1800)   267–8, 269
Feiner, Shmuel   13, 16, 296
female authors:
  and anonymity   107 n. 18, 118, 125 n. 72, 126, 138–9
  expansion in number of, in 18th century   102–3
  feminist literary criticism and 'rediscovery' of   103–4, 135–6
  in Jewish historical context   102, 105–7
  negative image of   104, 110
  publishing efforts of   118–20, 138–9, 141, 144–5
Fessler Wednesday Society (Feßlersche Mittwochsgesellschaft)   183
Fichte, Johann Gottlieb (1762–1814)   18, 19
Finckenstein, Count Karl von (1772–1811)   97–8, 138, 193, 209–10, 237, 238 n. 73
Fließ, Carl Eduard, *see* Fließ, Isaac Beer
Fließ, Eleonore, *see* Eskeles, Eleonore
Fließ, Hedwig, *see* Bernhard, Hitzel
Fließ, Isaac Beer (1770–1829) (later Carl Eduard Fließ)   138 n. 127, 168 n. 77, 212–15
Fließ, Joseph (1745–1822)   212 n. 106
Fould, Ber Leon (1767–1855)   240
Fouqué, Caroline de la Motte (1775–1831)   142
Fränkel, Freude, *see* Meyer, Freude
Fränkel, Michael Joseph (1746–1813) (Jechiel)   221–4
Franks, Abigaill (1696–1756) (née Levy)   67 n. 8, 157 n. 39
Franzensbad   55 n. 93, 170–1

Frederick II (the Great) (1712–86) 50, 60 n. 108, 175, 189, 216
Frederick William II (1744–97) 50, 113
Freienwalde 99, 148 n. 7, 153, 212
  Jewish women visit 147, 149–51, 168, 172, 177, 178, 213, 251–2
French Revolution 8, 21–2, 205 n. 81
  discourse of, employed by enlightened Jewish women 60–1, 226
  and struggle for women's emancipation 110–11, 218–20, 243 n. 89
  turning point in women's lives, perceived as 102 n. 1, 103 n. 2, 104 n. 7
Friedländer, David (1750–1834) 73 n. 34, 279 n. 74
  enlightened Jewish women, contacts with 178, 183 n. 12
friendship, female 1, 224, 247–8
  letter-writing, fostered by 43, 48 n. 65, 59
  romantic 253–6
  spa visits contribute towards 168, 171–3
Fries, Jakob Friedrich (1773–1843) 291

G

Gad, Esther (c.1767–1833?) (later Bernard, later Lucie Domeier) 1, 126, 152 n. 21, 207 n. 90, 257
  Campe, criticism of 108, 109–12, 258 n. 6
  converts to Christianity 107 n. 19, 112, 115, 258
  Haskalah, contribution to 113–15
  and Jean Paul Richter 89, 98–9, 170–1, 203–4
  on Judaism 115, 258–9 n. 6, 259, 278, 279–80
  literary activity of 98, 106, 107–20, 134, 142 n. 145, 144; publishing efforts 118–20; translates French literature 61; travel literature written by 115–16, 120, 171, 279
  Madame de Genlis, contact with 61 n. 111, 112
  Mary Wollstonecraft, likened to 108–9
  reading habits of 97, 98–9, 178
  visits spas 168, 170–2
  women's intellectual activity defended by 108, 110–12, 118, 119, 120
Gans, Eduard (1797–1839) 201 n. 68, 279 n. 74
Gaon of Vilna (Rabbi Elijah) (1720–97), and his daughters' reading 74, 75

Geiger, Ludwig 141
Genlis, Stéphanie-Félicité [Madame] de (1746–1830) 61–2, 112
Gentz, Friedrich von (1764–1832) 84, 85, 177, 205–6
Gesellschaft der Freunde, see Society of Friends
Gesellschaft der Freunde der Humanität, see Society of the Friends of Humanity
Glikl [Glückel] of Hameln (1645–1724)
  reading habits 67–8, 76, 87, 89
Goethe, Johann Wolfgang von (1749–1832) 18–19, 39, 62, 135, 176–7, 284 n. 93
  correspondence with: Cäcilie Itzig 55 n. 93; Eleonore Eskeles 55 n. 93; Marianne Meyer 30 n. 95, 37, 49–57, 59, 148, 170, 175–6, 205–6, 246–8, 258; Sara Meyer 30 n. 95, 37, 52 n. 83, 55–6, 90–2, 94, 141, 142–5, 170, 227, 258
  David Veit meets 31
  Iphigenia in Tauris, Joel Loewe-Brill's critique 299 n. 6
  Rahel Levin admired by 151
  readership 75 n. 41; Jewish female 55, 82–3, 92, 95, 239; Jewish male 82–3, 88, 95–6
  Sorrows of Young Werther 94, 95 n. 115, 96
Gomperz, Leon 96
Gouges, Olympe de (1748–93) 218–19
Graetz, Heinrich 18–19
Graun, Carl Heinrich (1704–59) 267
Grossman, Avraham 230
Grotthuß, Sophie von, see Meyer, Sara
Gugenheim, Fromet (1737–1812) (later Mendelssohn) 100–1 n. 142, 134, 158–61, 165 n. 72
  pre-nuptial correspondence 38, 76, 237 n. 70
  reading habits 76, 83 n. 66

H

Habermas, Jürgen 10
Hahn, Barbara 28, 142, 209, 233
Haltern, Joseph 209
Hamburg 48 n. 66, 67, 94, 101 n. 144, 163, 197
  contacts between Jews and non-Jews in 36, 196, 198 n. 60, 207, 245
  Fromet Gugenheim's home town 38 n. 32, 76

Ludwig Robert visits 185 n. 15
Hame'asef 12, 40, 113 n. 44, 186 n. 23, 209 n. 95, 299
Haskalah 21 n. 71, 86
  and the epistolary medium 40–2
  historiographical revision of 11–16
  Jewish women's alienation from 115, 297–8
  Jewish women's participation in 15–16, 41–2, 113–15, 296
  as a male movement 12, 115, 183
  societies 182–3
head-covering, by married Jewish women: practice abandoned 261–2
  use of wigs 262
Hebrew 6, 34–5 n. 12, 71, 81 n. 61
  Jewish women and: ignorance of 69, 72–3, 101, 296–7; knowledge of 34 n. 14, 67 nn. 10 & 11, 101 n. 143, 106, 296; literary creativity in 16, 41–2, 91 n. 104, 104 n. 7, 105, 296–7
  maskilim and: efforts at revival of 12; literary creativity in 40, 72, 109–10 n. 27, 207 n. 89, 209 n. 95, 296
Hegel, Georg Wilhelm Friedrich (1770–1831) 279
Heinrich of Prussia, Prince (1726–1802) 60 n. 108, 213 n. 109
Hensel, Fanny, *see* Mendelssohn-Bartholdy, Fanny
Hensel, Wilhelm (1794–1861) 282–4
'Hep Hep' riots 289, 291–2
Herder, Johann Gottfried von (1744–1803) 31–2, 96, 98–9
Hertz, Deborah 25–6, 27–8, 191, 221–2, 276–8
Herz, Henriette (1764–1847) (née de Lemos) 1, 18, 24, 223–4, 226, 274, 280 n. 80
  childlessness 241
  Christmas celebrated by 264
  church music, penchant for 267
  converts to Christianity 208 n. 93, 259, 261, 281, 286–9, 291
  correspondence of 30 n. 95, 36, 37–8
  education of 184, 199–200, 248 n. 109, 300; tutors' romantic proposals to 206 n. 86
  employment as teacher/governess 243–6, 259, 269–70
  Hebrew, command of 101
  Jewish customs neglected by 261–2
  literary activity of 106–7
  marriage of 80–1, 228 n. 40

  on marriage and marital relationship 242–3
  memoirs of 28 n. 89, 64–5, 189 n. 28, 288–9
  reading habits of 64–5, 75, 79–83, 86–7, 92–3, 95, 98, 99–100
  sociability of 183–4, 197 n. 54, 199–200, 208, 210
  visits spas 173–4
  as widow 83, 243–6, 248
Herz, Johanna, *see* Lemos, Johanna de
Herz, Marcus (1747–1803) 84 n. 72, 95, 183 n. 12, 183–6, 212, 244
  cultured women, views on 82
  Henriette Herz's reading habits criticized by 80–1, 82–3
  lectures at home 101 n. 145, 184
  visits spas 148 n. 7, 178
Hevrat Doreshei Leshon Ever, *see* Society of Friends of the Hebrew Language
Hevrat Shoharei Hatov Vehatushiyah, *see* Society for the Promotion of Goodness and Justice
Hippel, Theodor Gottlieb von (1741–96) 111, 219
Hirschel, Moses (1754–c.1823) 233
Hitzig, Julius Eduard, *see* Itzig, Isaac
Horowitz, Leah 105
Hoym, Carl Georg Heinrich von (1739–1807) 114
Humboldt, Alexander von (1769–1859) 101 n. 145, 208
Humboldt, Caroline von (1766–1829) 100, 210
Humboldt, Wilhelm von (1767–1835) 100 n. 140, 101, 208
Hyman, Paula 6

I
Iffland, August Wilhelm (1759–1814) 42, 54, 58, 183 n. 12
Isselstein, Ursula 28, 138–9
Itzig, Bella (1749–1824) (later Salomon) 57, 273 n. 56, 282
Itzig, Cäcilie (Zipora) (1760–1836) (later Wulff, later Eskeles) 55, 151, 227 n. 38, 236 n. 67, 251–2
Itzig, Daniel (1723–99) 57, 168, 183 n. 12, 252 n. 119, 281, 282 n. 89
Itzig, Isaac (1780–1849) (later Julius Eduard Hitzig) 182, 281
Itzig, Rebecca (1763–1847) (later Ephraim) 168

Itzig, Recha (1766–1841) 204
Itzig, Sara, *see* Levy, Sara

J
Jacobson, Israel 276
Jena 190, 193
  David Veit studies in 32, 152, 186
  Dorothea Mendelssohn moves to 61–2, 122, 228 n. 39
Jenisch, Daniel (pen-name Gottschalk Necker) (1762–1804) 54–5, 97 n. 126

K
Kant, Immanuel (1724–1804) 81, 96
  Enlightenment, definition of 7–8, 10 n. 27
  Jewish female audience of 84, 97; ridiculed 55 n. 90, 97
Kaplan, Marion 5–6, 168
Königsberg 96, 98, 201 n. 68
  maskilic activities in 40, 182
Koreff, David (1783–1851) 86, 88, 182, 298
Kretschmann, Karl Friedrich (1738–1809) 171
Kuhnert, Reinhold 163–4, 174–5

L
La Roche, Sophie von (1730–1807) 98, 121 n. 58
Lefin, Mendel, of Satanow (1749–1826) 13
Leipzig 83 n. 68
  Jewish women visit 133, 199, 260 n. 10
Lemos, Benjamin de (1711–89) 79–80
Lemos, Brenna de 199, 208, 242, 245, 262 n. 17
Lemos, Esther de (d. 1817) 85–6 n. 81, 208, 213
Lemos, Henriette de, *see* Herz, Henriette
Lemos, Johanna de (later Herz) 173 n. 95, 208
Lemos, Sara de 199
lending libraries 65, 75, 79–80
lesbianism 251–6
Lessing, Gotthold Ephraim (1729–81) 41, 158 n. 43, 279
  Jewish readership 84–5, 88 n. 89, 95, 96
letters:
  as historical sources 9, 27–30, 38–9, 76, 86, 146
  preservation of 33–8, 57–8 n. 101, 138; burning of 36–7; gender as determining factor in 34, 37–8, 49
  letter-writing 39–40

Jewish women and 26, 42–3, 67 n. 8, 196–7; cultural role of letter-writing for 33, 41–2, 44–9, 52–63, 181, 200, 294; as literary activity 46, 47, 132–3, 134–9
Levin, Chaie (1742–1809) 31, 209–11, 260 n. 10, 263–4
Levin, Hendel (1772–1822) (née Liebmann, later Henriette Robert-Tornow) 209–10, 214, 263
Levin, Marcus (1772–1826) (later Robert-Tornow) 210, 214, 241, 263, 264
Levin, Moritz (1785–1846) (later Robert-Tornow) 210 n. 98, 214
Levin, Rahel (1771–1833) (later Robert, later Varnhagen) 1, 24, 88, 112 n. 40, 286 n. 95
  as author 98, 106, 134–42, 258
  Christmas celebrated by 263–4, 265
  converts to Christianity 259, 276 n. 69, 278, 286–7 n. 98
  correspondence 29, 31–3, 44, 59–62, 134–9, 223 n. 21; from David Veit 96; from Dorothea Mendelssohn 122, 129, 224 n. 25, 225–6; from Fradchen Liebmann 99, 147, 149 n. 12, 150, 251, 254, 268–9, 289; from Henriette Mendelssohn 42 n. 50, 194; with Rebecca Salomon 28, 107 n. 17, 265 n. 32
  economic dependence of 241
  Hebrew alphabet used by 101
  historical image of 17 n. 54, 18, 20, 23 n. 80, 135–6
  Judaism and Jews, attitude towards 260–1, 280, 290–3, 298
  marriage, views on 233–9, 242, 250
  pursuit of knowledge by 202–3
  reading habits 83–6, 87, 89, 92–3 n. 108, 97, 177–8
  sociability of 184–6, 191 n. 33, 207, 213, 257; family members' involvement in 208–11, 214; visits at her house 189, 190 n. 31, 196–8, 209
  and the Varnhagen collection 34–7, 138–9
  visits spas 154, 157, 168; social contacts during spa visits 151–3, 166, 170 n. 83, 171–3, 177–8
Levy, Sara (1761–1854) (née Itzig) 189 n. 28, 269 n. 42
  as Bach enthusiast 268
  Sing-Akademie, affiliation to 267–8

Index

Liebmann, Abraham Nathan (1767–1837) (later Carl August Liman) 149, 214, 250–1
  marriage, view of 250 n. 114
Liebmann, Fradchen (1771–1844) (formerly Fradchen Marcuse, later Friederike Liman) 1, 137 n. 122, 210, 224, 238
  Christmas celebrated by 264
  converts to Christianity 149, 250–1, 259
  correspondence of 29, 36
  marital relationship of 250–1
  reading habits of 87–8, 99, 177
  sexual inclinations of 152 n. 22, 248–56
  Sing-Akademie, affiliation to 267–9
  sociability of 198, 204, 209 n. 97, 212–14, 257–8; social contacts with Jews after conversion 289–91
  visits spas 87–8, 99, 157, 168, 177; health concerns 147–8, 154; social contacts 149–51, 166, 169, 178
Ligne, Charles Joseph de (1735–1814) 153
Liman Carl August, see Liebmann, Abraham Nathan
Liman, Friederike, see Liebmann, Fradchen
Lindau, Baruch (1759–1849) 165 n. 73
literacy, women's 64
  among Ashkenazim 16, 66–74, 80 n. 54, 203 n. 74, 296
  in Germany 66
Loewe-Brill, Joel (1762–1802) 73 n. 34, 113, 296, 298–9
Louis Ferdinand, Prince (1772–1806) 172, 189, 238
Lowenstein, Steven 221–2, 276–8

M

'Maiden of Ludmir' (Hannah Rochel Verbermacher) (1806–88) 230
Maimon, Salomon (1753–1800) 31 n. 1, 84
Marchetti, Maria 137 n. 122, 197–8, 210, 213, 214, 260
Marcuse, Fradchen, see Liebmann, Fradchen
Marcuse, Nanette Renaud (1776–1821) 238
Markel-Mosessohn, Miriam (1839–1920) 16
marriage:
  arranged 222, 223–4, 227, 233–4
  Christian view of 231–2
  of female Jewish converts with Christian men 1, 24–6, 221–2, 259, 275 n. 60, 276–8
  institution criticized 97, 220, 228–9, 231–9, 242–3, 295
  love-based 233–4, 236–7, 243
  traditional Jewish ideal of 228–31
  see also divorce
maskilim 29, 30, 82, 295–6
  European literary sphere, participate in 298–9
  'false enlighteners' criticized by 14–15
  Jewish emancipation, efforts towards 113–14, 216–18
  Jewish women's intellectual needs ignored by 72–3
  Jewish women's reading habits criticized by 14, 71–2, 79, 80 n. 54
  on marriage 228–9 n. 40, 233
  religious authority defied by 78, 113
  Sturm und Drang and Romanticism, attitude towards 94–6
Meißner, August Gottlieb (1753–1807) 171
Mendel, David (1789–1850) (later Johann August Wilhelm Neander) 185 n. 15, 196 n. 53
Mendelssohn, Abraham (1776–1835) (later Mendelssohn-Bartholdy) 57, 236, 240, 242, 281
  religious views of 280, 282–4, 286 n. 96
  Sing-Akademie, affiliation to 267–8
  sociability of 196, 214–15
Mendelssohn, Dorothea (1764–1839) (née Brendel Mendelssohn, later Veit, later Schlegel) 1, 32, 88–9, 190 n. 28, 211 n. 104, 240
  authorship, attitude towards 120–1, 122, 125–33
  converts to Christianity 130, 259, 278, 281–2, 284–6
  correspondence of 38, 48 n. 67, 59–62, 132–3; burned 36–7
  critical attitudes of 128–31
  divorce of 121, 124, 222–8, 239, 250
  educational institution established by 248 n. 108
  enlightened outlook of 128, 130, 228
  financial problems of 122–6, 227
  Florentin 61, 121–2, 124–5, 127–32, 228 n. 39, 258
  literary activity of 61–2, 98, 106, 120–34
  reading habits of 85, 87
  Romanticism, connection to 17–20, 126, 128 n. 88, 130–1, 227–8
  sociability of 185, 191 n. 34, 193, 199, 208
  Yiddish, use of 101

Mendelssohn, Fromet, *see* Gugenheim, Fromet
Mendelssohn, Georg Benjamin (Benny) (1794–1874)   134 n. 112, 280 n. 80
Mendelssohn, Henriette (1775–1831)   1, 152 n. 21, 226, 248 n. 108, 258–9
  childlessness   241
  converts to Christianity   259, 281–2, 284–5, 301
  economic independence of   239–42
  letter-writing, attitude towards   42, 137
  marriage, views on   233–7, 242
  reading habits of   88, 97, 98, 177
  religious views of   275 n. 61, 282 n. 87, 284–6
  sociability of   193–6, 209–10
  visits spas   150–1, 157, 177
Mendelssohn, Henriette (Hinde), *see* Meyer, Henriette
Mendelssohn, Joseph (1770–1848)   101, 196, 214–15, 223 n. 18, 242
  Christmas celebrated by   265
  Moses Mendelssohn's collected works, initiates publishing of   134 n. 112
  Moses Mendelssohn's 'Morgenstunden', participates in   213
Mendelssohn, Lea, *see* Salomon, Lea
Mendelssohn, Moses (1729–86)   41, 84 n. 72, 99, 162 n. 58, 212 n. 104, 213
  Enlightenment associations, affiliation to   182, 149 n. 9
  Jewish descendants of   265
  Jewish emancipation debate, intervention in   216 n. 2
  posthumous publication of his works, wife's efforts towards   133–4
  pre-nuptial correspondence of   38, 76, 83 n. 66, 100–1 n. 142, 237 n. 70
  Sara Meyer's attitude towards   94, 227
  Sturm und Drang, attitude towards   94–5
  visits Pyrmont   157–61, 164, 165 n. 72
Mendelssohn, Nathan (1782–1852)   88, 98, 265 n. 29
Mendelssohn, Recha (1767–1831) (later Meyer)   30 n. 95, 223 n. 18, 225, 265 n. 29, 274
  as educator   248
  Henriette Herz, shares home with   248
  Jewish allegiance of   248, 275
  Yiddish, use of   101
Mendelssohn-Bartholdy, Fanny (1805–47) (later Hensel)   58, 280, 282–4

Mendelssohn-Bartholdy, Felix (1809–47)   57, 58, 284 n. 93, 286 n. 96
  baptism as child   282 n. 88
  Sing-Akademie, affiliation with   267–8
Mendelssohn-Bartholdy, Lea, *see* Salomon, Lea
Merkel, Garlieb (1769–1850)   57–9, 281
Meyer, Betty (Rebecca) (1793–1850)   30 n. 95, 248, 275
Meyer, Freude (1767–1857) (later Fränkel, later Sophie von Pobeheim)   198, 250, 265 n. 29
  converts to Christianity   278
  divorce of   221–6, 228
Meyer, Henriette (Hinde) (1776–1862) (later Mendelssohn)   223 n. 18
  Christmas celebrated by   265
Meyer, Marianne (1770–1812) (later von Eybenberg)   1, 97, 150, 190 n. 28, 258
  childlessness   241 n. 83
  converts to Christianity   50, 259, 273 n. 55, 278
  correspondence of   29, 30, 37, 49–57, 59, 170
  and female independence   246, 247–8
  intellectual aspirations of   56, 205–6
  literary activity of   107
  marriage of   50
  self-perception as cultured woman   54, 58, 175–6
  and sociability   205–6
  spa visits   50, 157, 168; health motivations   148, 154; social contacts during   170, 172 n. 22, 175–7, 178
Meyer, Michael   19, 276
Meyer, Recha, *see* Mendelssohn, Recha
Meyer, Rösel (*c.*1738–1803) (née Ephraim)   38, 49, 158–61
Meyer, Sara (1763–1828) (later Wulff, later Sophie von Grotthuß)   1, 49, 150, 153 n. 24, 190 n. 28, 258
  childlessness   241 n. 83
  converts to Christianity   50, 259, 273 n. 55, 278
  correspondence of   29, 30, 37, 144, 170
  as educator   248 n. 108
  literary activity of   55 n. 91, 98, 106, 141–5
  marriages   50, 227
  mental breakdown   51, 90
  and Moses Mendelssohn   94–5, 161, 227
  reading experience of   90–2, 93, 94–5, 97

visits spas 50, 158, 161, 162, 170
Meyerbeer, Giacomo (1791–1864)
  275 n. 64
Michaelis, Heinrich Salomo (1768–1844)
  184–6
Michaelis, Johann David (1717–91)
  262 n. 17
Milder, Anna (1785–1838) 256
Mittwochsgesellschaft, Berliner, *see* Berlin
  Wednesday Society
Mittwochsgesellschaft, Feßlersche, *see*
  Fessler Wednesday Society
modernization, Jewish 1–7, 12–13, 146,
  192, 221, 298
  gender perspective 5–7, 26–7, 29–30,
    94–5, 299
  Yiddish, role of 71 n. 26
Möllendorf, Major von (1724–1816)
  193
Montagu, Elizabeth (1718 or 1720–1800)
  169
Montaigne, Michel de (1533–92) 155
Moritz, Karl Philipp (1756–93) 31, 84
Morpurgo, Rahel, née Luzzatto (1790–1871)
  16 n. 49, 41 n. 46
music 260
  church music, Jewish women's enthusiasm
    for 267–9
  Jewish composers and performers of
    212–13, 215 n. 117, 298
  Jewish women discuss 58, 60–1, 133,
    138, 140, 193
  Mozart, Jewish women's fascination with
    251 n. 117, 268–9
  recitals at Jewish homes 48 n. 66, 275
  at spas 146, 160, 177, 212
  synagogue services, musical innovations in
    197–8

N
Napoleonic wars 8, 21 n. 71, 88, 264
  and Jewish salons' purported decline
    190–1
Nenndorf 173–4
Niger, Shmuel 69
North Star Club (Nordstar Bund) 182
Novalis (Friedrich Leopold von Hardenberg)
  (1772–1801) 23, 121 n. 59, 124 n. 68,
  226 n. 31
novels 39, 110, 134
  Jewish women read 65, 76, 79–80, 90–1,
    92–3 n. 108, 99, 204

Jewish women write 61, 115, 119–20,
  121–2, 300
women's alleged connection to 14,
  74 n. 37, 94–7, 103 n. 2
  see also Mendelssohn, Dorothea: *Florentin*

P
Pachta, Countess Josephine von (1771–1833)
  153, 171
Pappenheim, Bertha 297 n. 5
Pappenheimer, Chaim Salomon (1769–1832)
  207
Pappenheimer, Salomon 207 n. 89, 217 n. 3
Paris 99, 116, 245
  Dorothea Mendelssohn in 61, 124 n. 70,
    191 n. 34
  Henriette Mendelssohn in 88, 98, 137,
    194–6, 236, 240–1, 248 n. 108, 259, 284
  Ludwig Robert in 86, 194–5
  Rahel Levin visits 112 n. 40, 138, 254, 257
  salons in 188 n. 24, 204–5 n. 80
Parush, Iris 16, 296
periodicals/journals 10, 47, 75, 107 n. 18
  Jewish 12, 40, 41 n. 46, 42, 186 n. 23,
    209 n. 95
  Jewish women read 62, 85, 95, 97–8, 186
  non-Jewish, Jewish men write for
    84 n. 72, 139–40, 182 n. 7, 233 n. 58,
    299 n. 6
  non-Jewish, Jewish women write for:
    Dorothea Mendelssohn 62, 121, 126,
    133; Esther Gad 108, 11, 116–19;
    Rahel Levin 135, 136, 138; Sara Meyer
    145
  women's 45, 98, 104 n. 7, 145
Philomathic Society (Philomatische
  Gesellschaft) 149 n. 9, 182
Pobeheim, Sophie von, *see* Meyer, Freude
Portuguese Jews 36, 279, 288
Poulain de la Barre, François (1747–1823)
  110
Prague 34 n. 12, 105, 171, 178
Prenzlau 173 n. 95, 208, 245
Pyrmont 153, 155, 165, 167, 174
  Jews visit 148, 157–64, 165 n. 72, 173,
    175–6

R
Ramler, Carl Wilhelm (1725–98) 209 n. 95,
  267
reading habits:
  gender differences in 45, 52 n. 82, 299

reading habits (*cont.*):
  of Jewish women in historical context   16,
    65–75, 76–8, 296–7
  reading 'mania'   64–5, 73–5
  shifts in the modern period   75, 91 n. 103
  as social activity   93, 177–8, 200, 205, 290
Reimarus, Elise (1735–1805)   196, 198 n. 60,
  207
religious observance / laxity   2, 13 n. 41, 79
    n. 53, 260–3, 270
  brith milah, significance of   264 n. 24
  modernized Jewish services   197–8,
    276
  sabbath kept/desecrated   260–1
Rheinsberg   60–1, 128–9, 133, 213 n. 109
Richter, Jean Paul (1763–1825)   137 n. 122,
    176
  Esther Gad, contacts with   89, 98–9, 171,
    203–4
Riemer, Friedrich Wilhelm (1774–1845)   55
Robert, Ludwig (1778–1832)   29, 145,
    185 n. 15, 193, 214, 264
  converts to Christianity   276 n. 69, 291
  marriage to non-Jew   276 n. 69
  non-Jewish writers' club, affiliation to
    182
  in Paris   86, 88, 194–5
  Rahel Levin, literary cooperation with
    139–40
Robert, Rahel, *see* Levin, Rahel
Robert-Tornow, Marcus, *see* Levin, Marcus
Robert-Tornow, Moritz, *see* Levin, Moritz
Romanticism   91 n. 105, 100, 191 n. 32,
    196 n. 52
  Dorothea Mendelssohn's connection to
    62, 126, 128 n. 88, 130–1, 227–8
  early vs. late   20–3
  and hostility towards Jews   269, 292
  Jewish women's connection to   17–24,
    94, 285, 292
Rosman, Moshe   69–70
Roth, Cecil   33
Rousseau, Jean-Jacques (1712–78)   18 n. 55,
    39, 75 n. 41, 91, 99
  and women's education   200
Rühs, Christian Friedrich (1781–1820)   291

S
Salomon, Bella, *see* Itzig, Bella
Salomon, Lea (1777–1842) (later
    Mendelssohn-Bartholdy):
  Catholicism, animosity towards   282–4

  converts to Christianity   281, 282
  correspondence of   57–9, 281
  Madame de Genlis, contact with
    61 n. 111
  Sing-Akademie, affiliation to   267–8
Salomon, Rebecca (1783–1850)   28, 107,
    265 n. 32
salons   174, 268
  French   46 n. 61, 188 n. 24
  salonnières   25 n. 85, 232, 204–5 n. 80
salons, Jewish:
  in Berlin   1, 95, 179, 197, 276
  historiographical revision of   24–8,
    188–93, 206–15, 299
  in Paris   195
  salonnières   18, 135, 221, 223 n. 16, 286,
    294
  in Vienna   194, 264–5
Salvador, Sarah (d. 1763)   272 n. 52
Salzmann, Christian Gotthilf (1744–1811)
    108 n. 23, 207
Sarah bas Tovim   105
Schack, Otto Friedrich Ludwig von
    (1763–1815)   150, 213
Schaumburg-Lippe, Count Wilhelm von
    (1724–77)   160 n. 50
Schiller, Friedrich   52, 97, 185 n. 15
  Esther Gad's correspondence with
    118–19
  female writers, view of   104
  Jewish women discuss works by   58, 118
Schink, Johann Friedrich (1755–1835)
    161–2
Schlegel, August (1767–1845)   23, 62
  Dorothea Mendelssohn, contact with
    122, 132, 193
  Henriette Mendelssohn's correspondence
    with   193, 195 n. 48, 239–40, 284–5
Schlegel, Dorothea, *see* Mendelssohn,
    Dorothea
Schlegel, Friedrich (1772–1829)   23,
    50 n. 72, 62, 183 n. 112
  and Dorothea Mendelssohn:
    correspondence with   36–7, 38;
    marriage to   281, 286 n. 97; in Paris
    191 n. 34, 240; posthumous publication
    of his works by   134; relationship with
    18–19, 48 n. 67, 61, 122–7, 225–8; F as
    'editor' of D's publications   121–2
Schleiermacher, Friedrich Daniel Ernst
    (1768–1834)   18–19, 173 n. 95,
    183 n. 12

and Dorothea Mendelssohn:
  correspondence with 122 n. 64, 124–5,
  127–8, 132; supports 226
and Henriette Herz 30 n. 95, 38, 107,
  281 n. 85; social contacts 100,
  199–200, 208, 264
Judaism, perception of 280
Schleiermacher, Henriette, *see* Willich,
  Henriette von
Schleiermacher, Lotte (Charlotte)
  (1765–1831) 199–200, 287
Schwalbach 157 n. 38, 158 n. 44, 164 n. 68
Sebastiani, Fanny (1807–47) 240–1,
  242 n. 86, 284
Sebastiani, Horace François (1772–1851)
  240
Sebottendorf, Maria Josepha (née
  Königsberger) 251–2
secularization 263, 265, 271
secularization among Jews 1–2, 4, 8, 27,
  29
  and Haskalah 13, 14 n. 45
  learning practices affected by 2, 201, 211,
    275
  marriage practices affected by 231
  reading practices affected by 70–1, 78,
    83, 86–9, 93, 101, 296
sentiment, culture of 19
  and the Enlightenment 22 n. 75, 91
Sephardi Jews 5 n. 9, 106, 221 n. 13,
  237 n. 71, 272
  venerated 288
Sessa, Karl Boromäus (1786–1813) 290
  Unser Verkehr 290, 291
Sévigné, Madame de (1626–96) 40 n. 37
Shaftesbury, Anthony Ashley Cooper, 3rd
  earl of (1671–1713) 76
Shmeruk, Chone 69, 71
Shohet, Azriel 230–1
Showalter, Elaine 103–4
Sieveking, Karl (1787–1847) 196
sociability 180–1
  and the Enlightenment 2, 180
  Jewish frameworks for 182–3
  at spas 149, 155, 167, 169, 178, 179
  women's exclusion from frameworks for
    181, 183
social gatherings in private homes 181,
  183–6, 191–2
  'intimate' gatherings 192–200, 203–7
  Jewish men seek Jewish women's
    hospitality 197–8, 215

Jews visit Christian homes 198–9, 207
men's attitude towards women at 184–6
women's (informal) learning at 183–4,
  199–200, 203–6
see also salons
Society of Friends (Gesellschaft der Freunde)
  183, 197, 213 n. 109, 214–15, 274
Society of Friends of the Hebrew Language
  (Hevrat Doreshei Leshon Ever) 12,
  182
Society of the Friends of Humanity
  (Gesellschaft der Freunde der
  Humanität) 149 n. 9, 182
Society for the Promotion of Goodness and
  Justice (Hevrat Shoharei Hatov
  Vehatushiyah) 12, 182
Sparre, Wilhelmine von, *see* Bernhard, Hitzel
spas:
  antisemitism at (*Bäderantisemitismus*) 165
  development of modern 153–6
  and female empowerment 146–7, 167–9
  matchmaking at 165 n. 72
  visits to, medical motivations 147–8, 154,
    156, 158
spas, Jewish visitors to:
  attitudes towards 160–7, 173–4
  in historical context 156–66
  Jewish women's contacts at 50, 146–7,
    149–53, 161–2, 169–73, 175–9, 258
Staël, Germaine de (1766–1817) 61–2, 122,
  176
  De l'Allemagne 116, 142–4, 171 n. 87
Strelitz/Neustrelitz 60, 185 n. 15, 223, 225,
  265 n. 29
Sturm und Drang 94–5, 96
Susman, Margarete 19–20

T

Teplitz 51, 148, 151–3, 172, 177–8,
  209
theatre and performing arts:
  discussions of 176, 193; in Jewish
    women's letters 33, 47, 52–4, 58, 60–1,
    133
  Jewish women attend 14, 151, 170, 183,
    260, 269 n. 42
  Jews attend 2, 149, 214, 267
  portrayal of Jewish women attending
    54–5, 82 n. 65
  at spas 146, 155, 167
Thomann Tewarson, Heidi 28, 134–5, 280
Tiktiner, Rebecca (d. 1605) 105

tkhines 68, 105
travelling, gender limitations 32, 48, 115 n. 49, 152
Tsenerene 68, 72
Tugendbund 43 n. 53, 208
Twesten, August (1789–1876) 30 n. 95, 248, 264 n. 27, 280 n. 80

U
Unger, Friederike Helene (1751–1813) 124–5
universities:
    bachelorhood of scholars at 231 n. 51
    Jewish men admitted to 32, 84, 201–2
    women excluded from 47–8, 83, 201–3
Unzelmann, Friederike (1766–1815) (née Flittner, later Bethmann) 152, 168, 214, 252–6, 257

V
Varnhagen collection 28, 35–6
    Jewish women's texts preserved in 36, 141, 142 n. 145, 233, 251
    publication of 29 n. 93, 35–6, 138–9, 173 n. 94
Varnhagen, Rahel, *see* Levin, Rahel
Varnhagen (von Ense), Karl August (1785–1858) 35–7, 112 n. 41, 172 n. 90, 209 n. 95, 236
    on Fradchen Liebmann 250 n. 110, 252–3, 254
    on Henriette Mendelssohn 195, 236, 248 n. 108, 284; correspondence with 137
    intervenes on behalf of Ludwig Robert 140 n. 134
    on Jewish salons 189–90 n. 28, 195
    and Rahel Levin: correspondence with 87, 264, 265; on her attitude towards authorship 137–8; on her attitude to religion 286–7 n. 98
    on Recha Mendelssohn 248
    on Sara Meyer's literary activity 141
Veit, David (1771–1814) 202, 298
    Henriette Mendelssohn courted by 236
    Rahel Levin, correspondence with 31–3, 44, 88, 136, 151–3, 213; on reading 83–5, 92–3 n. 108, 96; on religious laxity 260–1, 264 n. 2; on social visits 184–6, 196–8
Veit, Dorothea, *see* Mendelssohn, Dorothea
Veit, Jonas (1790–1854) 121
Veit, Philipp (1793–1877) 121

Veit, Simon 133, 193, 199
    Dorothea Mendelssohn, divorce from 61, 121, 124, 222, 224–7
    intellectual interests of 31–2, 211–12 n. 104, 213
Vienna 34 n. 12, 55 n. 93, 157 n. 38, 245, 251
    Fanny von Arnstein in 264–5, 269 n. 42
    Henriette Mendelssohn in 152 n. 2, 193–4, 236, 239–40
    Marianne Meyer in 51, 52–4, 148, 176–7, 205, 246–8
Vigliero, Consolina 29, 140

W
Weckel, Ulrike 45–6, 95, 191
Weinreich, Max 70
Weissberg, Liliane 126
Wessely, Carl Bernhard (1768–1826) 213, 214–15
Wessely, Hartwig (Naphtali Herz) (1725–1805) 113, 114 n. 45, 213, 245
Wessely, Moses (1737–92) 198 n. 60, 207, 245
Wetzlar, Isaac (d. 1751) 71–3
Wieland, Christoph Martin (1733–1813) 31–2, 96, 99
Wiesbaden 164–5
Wiesel, Pauline (1778–1848) (née César) 172–3, 194, 238–9, 286 n. 96
Wiesel, Wilhelm (1771–1826) 193–4
Willich, Ehrenfried von (1777–1807) 173, 200 n. 65, 208
Willich, Henriette von (née Mühlenfels, later Schleiermacher) (1788–1840) 173 n. 95, 270
Wolfsohn-Halle, Aaron 79 n. 49, 84 n. 72
Wollstonecraft, Mary (1759–97) 108–9, 219
Woolf, Virginia 103
Wulff, Cäcilie, *see* Itzig, Cäcilie

Y
Yiddish language:
    neglected 2
    Jewish women's use of 42, 88–9, 101, 297
Yiddish literature 109–10 n. 27, 296
    and female readership 67–74, 87, 101
    women as authors of 105

Z
Zelter, Carl Friedrich (1758–1832) 183 n. 12, 197, 284 n. 93
Zinberg, Israel 69, 71